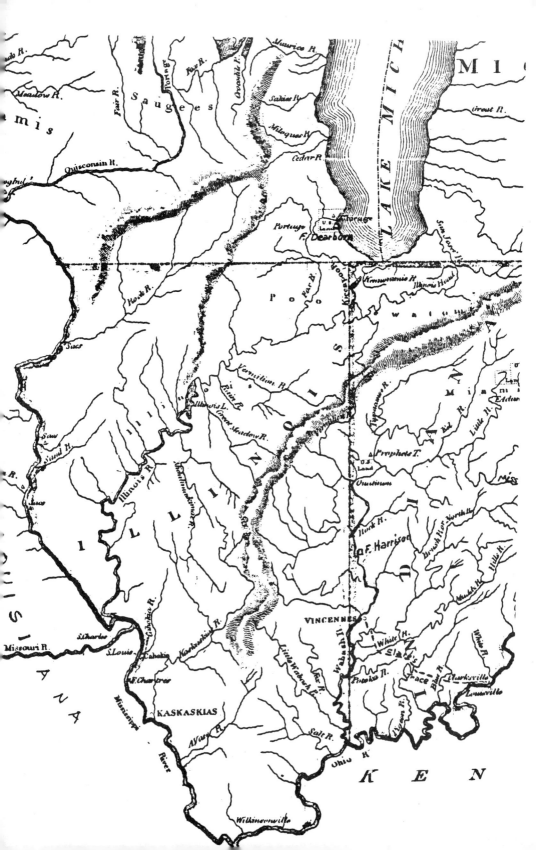

COUNTERPOINT

COUNTERPOINT

TECUMSEH vs. WILLIAM HENRY HARRISON

—— A NOVEL BY ——

JAMES HUSTON

THIRD PRINTING, January 1989

Library of Congress Cataloging in Publication Data

Huston, James A. (James Alvin)
  Counterpoint.

  1. Tecumseh, Shawnee Chief, 1768-1813—Fiction.
2. Harrison, William Henry, 1773-1841—Fiction
3. Shawnee Indians—Fiction. 4. Tippecanoe,
Battle of, 1811—Fiction. 5. Thames, Battle of,
1813—Fiction. 6. Indians of North America—Wars—
1750-1815—Fiction. I. Title.
PS3558.U81206   1987   813'.54   87-13466
ISBN 1-556-18024-1
ISBN 1-556-18025-X (pbk.)

First Original Edition

Published in the United States of America

by

Brunswick Publishing Company
RT. 1, BOX 1A1
LAWRENCEVILLE, VIRGINIA 23868

To
Anne
Sine qua non

The great tragedies of history occur
not when right confronts wrong but when
two rights confront each other.

— Henry A. Kissinger

Introductory Note

While presenting COUNTERPOINT in the form of a novel, I have attempted to retain historical accuracy. The characters, with the exception of a few minor characters such as those engaged in the tavern brawl, were true historical persons. I have tried to keep them at the right places at the correct times. Most of the major speeches and letters are from historical transcripts; quotations from *The Western Sun* of Vincennes are actual.

Historical accounts frequently are in contradiction, and where that has been the case here, I have chosen that which seems to fit best. I have relied on imagination to fill gaps in the historical record and to supply the private incidents and conversations that lie outside that record.

I hope that the result may be to contribute a little to a better understanding of, and appreciation for, a significant chapter in American history.

For assistance in gathering information and putting it together, I am indebted to Malcom Jamieson of Berkeley Plantation in Virginia; Loreatha Hamke, curator of Grouseland, the Harrison mansion in Vincennes, Indiana; Janice Fouts, director of the Tippecanoe Battleground Museum; to members of the staffs of the Ross County Historical Society in Chillicothe, Ohio, the Purdue University Library, the Indiana University Library, the Indiana State Library, and the Library of Congress, and to Mary C. Scudder, librarian, Carol J. Pollock, public services librarian, and other members of the staff of the Knight-Capron Library at

Lynchburg College, and to Kipp Teague, Wendell Russell, Gail Troy, Gregory Bailey, and Paul Johnson of the Lynchburg College Computer Center.

Special thanks are due the publishers, Marianne S. Raymond and Walter J. Raymond for their understanding and special care in all aspects of the publication.

Above all I am indebted to my wife, Anne Marshall Huston, for her incalculable assistance in preparing the manuscript for publication, and her helping in so many ways throughout the research and writing.

The quotation from Henry Kissinger is reprinted with permission from the August 1985 Reader's Digest.

The map inside the front cover is adapted from maps in the Library of Congress. The maps inside the back cover are from R. C. Buley, *The Old Northwest, Pioneer Period 1815-1840*, used with permission of the Indiana University Press.

The jacket/cover design is by Melissa Garrett, Nancy Blackwell, and John Roark.

J.H.

CONTENTS

Chapter		Page
I.	Shawnee and Virginian	1
II.	Growing Up	18
III.	Advanced Education	35
IV.	Love, Unrequited	52
V.	Baptisms of Fire	73
VI.	Vows of Peace and Marriage	113
VII.	Rising Stars	136
VIII.	Busy Beavers	161
IX.	Dreams of Empire	167
X.	Religious Ferment	209
XI.	Continuing Education	231
XII.	Schools of Romance, Literature and Politics	263
XIII.	Tales of Two Cities: Spring and Summer	290
XIV.	Missionary Journeys	333
XV.	Tales of Two Cities: Fall and Winter	356
XVI.	Equal Justice	383
XVII.	Worlds in Collision	393
XVIII.	Meeting Engagements	419
XIX.	Peaceful Pursuits	443
XX.	The Battle of Tippecanoe	466
XXI.	Paths of War	501
XXII.	Lake Erie	546
XXIII.	The End of the Trail	579
XXIV.	Epilogue	611

COUNTERPOINT

CHAPTER I

Shawnee and Virginian

1a

A shooting star of unusual brilliance and duration streaked across the southern sky, and disappeared beyond the west bank of the Little Miami River of Ohio. Pucksinwah, chief of the Kispokotha division of the Shawnee nation, watched in awe and amazement as he stood outside a makeshift shelter awaiting the birth of his third son. True, he had two daughters he adored, but it did not even occur to him that this would not be a boy. His first son, Chiksika, and daughter, Tecumapease, together with three other women of his clan waited beside the glowing embers of a small fire in front of the shelter. Three older women were inside to attend to his wife, Methotaska, and to assist with the birth.

The night was crisp and cool, though not unusually cold for early March. It was March 9, 1768. Without competition either from the moon or from large fires, bright stars filled the heavens. The only sounds came from a small rivulet of spring water nearby, and from occasional groans from within the shelter. Following their usual practice in this kind of situation, Pucksinwah and his helpers had set up this little maternity camp a quarter of a mile or so from the family wigwam which was in their tribal village of "old" Piqua, twelve miles north of "old" Chillicothe.

Now as he waited Pucksinwah felt the added excitement of what he was sure was an *unsoma*, an unusual event which would be a good omen for his new son. Ordinarily parents expected to wait ten or twelve days before experiencing the kind of *unsoma* thought to be necessary to guide the naming of their child. But not this time. It was in the stars. Clearly this child must be named for the shooting star — Tecumseh, which also meant Panther-Passing-Across.

Presently there was a strong cry inside the shelter, and a few minutes later the women called Pucksinwah. He was told that indeed he did have a new son. He went inside and smiled with delight as he saw by the oil light the mother and babe lying comfortably on the bed of cedar boughs covered with a heavy buffalo hide, with soft deerskin for coverlet. The baby, truly a Redskin, shone with the bear oil which the women had rubbed on him.

The chief knelt beside the bed, and told Methotaska about the shooting star. She at once knew that this was the child's *unsoma*. She agreed that there could be no other name than the one for Shooting Star and Panther-Passing-Across. He would have to be called Tecumseh.

Although Pucksinwah and Methotaska already had agreed firmly on what their new son's name should be, they went through the ceremony that in Christian societies was known as christening when friends acting as name-givers supplied the "appropriate" name. At dawn on the appointed day, ten days after the birth, relatives and the name-givers came down to the little matērnity hut for the ceremony, bringing with them food for breakfast. Methotaska bathed the baby privately, and then bathed him again in lukewarm water in the presence of the name-givers, two respected men of the village. Then, while the family remained seated, the name-givers each in turn arose to propose a name. By prearrangement, the second proposed "Tecumseh," and the parents chose that as being more suitable. Methotaska then handed her baby to the name-giver, and Pucksinwah handed him a string of white beads. After a speech in which he stressed the appropriateness of the name selected, the name-giver prayed to the Master of Life and returned the baby to his mother. The name-giver went on speaking, expressing hopes for a bright future for the child. Holding out the beads, he repeated four times, "Everyone will call him Tecumseh," and then he tied the string of beads around the little one's neck. The beads would remain there until the string broke. Then all the group shared breakfast, and Methotaska gave the little Tecumseh a taste of each kind of food by touching her fingertip to each dish and then letting the baby suck her finger.

Now, when the parents returned to their regular wigwam, the infant was ready for daily baths in cold water to enable him to grow strong, and now he had a cradle board in which he was secured most of the time. His head was fastened to a head board for safety and to encourage the growth of a head that would have the characteristic Shawnee flatness in the back. With the cradle board Methotaska would carry him on her back wherever she went, and when she was working outside she would hang him on the limb of a tree, and inside, she would hang him on a peg in one of the poles. With this care and attention, Tecumseh did indeed grow strong and straight.

1b

Benjamin Harrison V looked at his huge silver pocket watch and returned it to his waistcoat pocket without even seeing the time, as he gazed out of the second-story hall window of his Berkeley manor house toward the James River of Virginia. He looked at the watch again and walked back to look out the opposite window. Nothing really registered. He was awaiting the birth of his seventh child and third son on the ninth day of February in 1773. It was no easier this time than it had been on the six previous occasions, but at least he could reassure himself with the recollection that all had gone well in those cases.

His wife, the former Elizabeth Bassett, was being attended by a physician from Williamsburg and several black servant women who were skilled in midwifery. After a seemingly interminable delay, the doctor was about to resort to quilling — blowing a whiff of dry snuff through a goose quill over the wife's nostrils to induce sneezing, which sometimes was effective in expediting childbirth — but that turned out to be unnecessary. At last the new arrival entered the world with appropriate screams. While the attending women cleaned him up and applied a thin coat of lard, the physician went out to announce to Benjamin Harrison that he did indeed have a new healthy son. Benjamin hurried into the bedroom and broke into smiles of joy as he saw his wife and baby lying comfortably in the high bed on a feather mattress covered with linen and with eider down pillows and comforter. He leaned over and gently caressed Elizabeth and the baby.

"And who is this?" he asked in false wonder.

"This, sir, is William Henry," she replied softly with a smile, as they already had agreed to name it if a boy. "This is William Henry Harrison."

When little William Henry was six weeks old his parents took him to the Westover Church, at a Sunday morning service, for his christening in the ritual of baptism. The church house, an attractive brick building about thirty years old, was on Herring Creek, about a mile and a half north of the Byrds' Westover mansion. A friend and neighbor of the family, William Byrd, and the little one's uncle, Peyton Randolph, accompanied them as Godfathers. Mrs. Randolph, the boy's aunt, participated as Godmother.

After the Second Lesson in the order of service, the group went forward and stood at the font for the baptism. The priest stood in front of them and asked, opening *The Book of Common Prayer,* "Hath this Child been already baptized, or no?"

The three Godparents answered together, "No."

Then the priest read an introductory statement, followed by a prayer. Then he read a selection from the Gospel of St. Mark, a verse opening:

They brought young children to Christ that he might touch them....

Then a selection from St. John which concluded:

Except a man be born of water and of the Spirit, he cannot enter into the kingdom of God....The wind bloweth where it listeth, and thou hearest the sound thereof, but canst not tell whence it cometh, and whither it goeth: so is every one that is born of spirit.

And a selection from St. Matthew; concluding:

...lo, I am with you always, even unto the end of the world.

And then, after a prayer of thanksgiving and introductory statement, the priest said, "Dost thou, therefore, in the name of this child, renounce the devil and all his works, the vain pomp and glory of the world, with all covetous desires of the same, and the sinful desires of the flesh, so that thou wilt not follow, nor be led by them?"

The Godparents answered, "I renounce them all; and, by God's help, will endeavour not to follow, nor be led by them." Similarly, the Godparents promised belief in all the articles of Christian Faith, as contained in the "Apostle's Creed," and obedience to

God's Commandments, and their desire for baptism.

Then the priest said, "Having now, in the name of this child, made these promises, wilt thou on thy part take heed that this child learn the Creed, the Lord's Prayer, and the Ten Commandments, and all other things which a Christian ought to know and believe to his soul's health?"

The Godparents answered, "I will, with God's help."

After another series of prayers and a statement, the priest finally took the baby William Henry in his arms and said to the Godparents, "Name this child."

"William Henry," they responded.

Then naming him, "William Henry," the priest dipped him into the water of the font as he said, "I baptize thee in the name of the Father, and of the Son, and of the Holy Ghost. Amen."

The priest said, "We receive this child into the congregation of Christ's flock." And, making a cross on little William Henry's forehead, the priest continued, "And so sign him with the sign of the cross, in token that hereafter he shall not be ashamed to confess the faith of Christ crucified, and manfully to fight under his banner, against sin, the world, and the devil; and to continue Christ's faithful soldier and servant unto his life's end. Amen."

2a

Methotaska was glad to be back in the family wigwam, though frequent moves of her people and the custom of going out to smaller villages for hunting in winter left her without the deep attachment to place felt by other peoples less accustomed to moving about. Yet the home here was more permanent than usual. Their wigwam, made of bark stretched on poles, was about twenty feet long and fourteen feet wide. It was about six feet high at the apex of its pitched roof with vertical walls about four feet high. A screen of skins across the middle divided it into two rooms. It was one of about two hundred similar houses that made up the town of Piqua.

The town occupied a picturesque site overlooking a big bend of the river. Near its center, perhaps twenty feet above the river level, was a crude log fort surrounded by pickets and enclosing a big council house also made of bark and poles, but reinforced with logs. To the south the ground sloped gently over several hundred acres of grassland and over two hundred acres of plots cultivated in summer in corn, beans, pumpkins, and squash. To the north and northeast, fairly high bluffs dominated the town, while level woodlands extended westward to the river. Across the river more grasslands ran to the wooded hills beyond.

During the winter hunt, the town was sparsely occupied, but in summer it was full of activity.

2b

Berkeley was a great American house and a great plantation. The land, designated Berkeley Hundred, had come into possession of the Harrison family through purchase from Giles Bland and his brothers by Benjamin Harrison II. His eldest son, Benjamin III, had established his home there in the early 1690's. Benjamin Harrison IV, grandfather of young William Henry, built the great mansion in 1726.

With finely finished brick walls three feet thick, the house rose three stories to a sloping pedament roof pierced by three dormers on either side. It sat on a low knoll, and from the south front, lawns, gardens, and woods sloped in five carefully formed terraces toward the riverbank a quarter of a mile away. Entry doors, both on north and south, opened on either end of the central hall. On the east side of the hall were two large rooms separated by a massive fireplace, but with connecting doors on each side. Both rooms were finished in exquisite wood paneling. The Harrisons referred to these parlors as "The Great Room — South" and "The Great Room — North." Across the hall, on the side facing the river, was the formal dining room. In the other corner of the first floor, the northwest, was the family room-study which also had a spare bed. The master bedroom (at the southeast corner overlooking the river), and the nursery, and bedrooms for children and guests were on the second floor, with five additional bedrooms on the third. A full basement, with brick walls, provided space for the wine cellar and for storage.

A group of brick outbuildings arranged in a hollow rectangle to the north formed, with the main house, a central court. These buildings included kitchen, smoke house, ice house, laundry, children's playhouse and school room, and servants' quarters. A little farther away, connected by a "privacy arbor," was the "necessary" — a well-built brick outhouse with windows, a fireplace, and four seats. At a distance, to spare the family from odors and flies, were the stables and coach house, together with quarters for hostlers and coachmen. In support of its commercial activities, the plantation had its own grist mill, saw mill, blacksmith shop, and "merchant mills." Berkeley was a prosperous plantation which, with adjoining properties, comprised 20,000 acres. From its own produce and shops, from its own wharves along its three-mile river front, and even at times in its own ships (one was named *Charming Anne* for William Henry's grandmother) it shipped out cargoes of pork, beef, peas, corn, flour, lard, barrel staves, and other items, together with as much tobacco as could be gotten through British shipping restrictions.

3a

At the time of his birth, Tecumseh had two older brothers and two older sisters. The eldest was Chiksika, then about twelve years old, who would become head of the family. Next was the sister who was everyone's favorite, Tecumapease, who was ten. The other brother, Sauwauseekau, was less than two years younger than Tecumapease. The second sister was only about four. Two years later, a third sister was born. Then five years after that came a very special event for the family — the birth of triplets, seven years younger than Tecumseh. These were three boys. The first suffered from a birth defect and died in infancy. The other two, Laulewasika and Kumskaukau lived to make significant contributions. Laulewasika one day would become known as Tenskwatawa and The Prophet. About three years after Tecumseh's birth, Pucksinwah presided over the adoption of a seventeen-year-old white youth into the tribe. He was Marmaduke Van Swearingen who thereafter would be known as Blue Jacket. (He had been captured while out hunting with his younger brother. His consent to adoption was necessary for his brother to be freed and to spare both their lives. He always had been sympathetic toward the Indians, had admired their way of life, and actually had welcomed the opportunity for adoption.)

Tecumseh's parents had met and married during the long sojourn of their peoples in the South, in the Alabama-Florida area. Methotaska had lived so long among the Creeks that many thought her a member of that tribe, but she belonged to the Turtle clan of the Shawnee. Indeed, her name meant "Turtle Laying Its Eggs in the Sand." There were stories that her husband was the son of a white woman and Creek Indian, and that the white woman was the daughter of an English governor of South Carolina. Actually, Pucksinwah was all Shawnee too.

After seven or eight years in the South, Pucksinwah, with his family, had rejoined his own people in the Scioto valley of the Ohio country about 1761. He soon gained prominence as a warrior, and then, as chief of the Kispokotha division, became known among all the Shawnee and neighboring tribes as an able and respected battle leader. He worried about White encroachment. He saw no way to stop it except by determined fighting to protect the Indian villages and their hunting grounds. While the great Cornstalk, chief of all the Shawnees, counseled restraint and peace, Pucksinwah urged resistance and war.

Frustrated by what he saw as a failure to face reality in his own tribe, Pucksinwah took it upon himself to solicit the support of one of the most respected Indian leaders in the country — Talgayeeta, known better by Indians as well as Whites as Logan — the Mingo chief of the Cayugas. Remaining steadfastly neutral in the French and Indian War of the 1750's, and having nothing to do with Pontiac's conspiracy in 1763 nor the ensuing warfare, Logan had won the confidence and respect of the Whites while still being able to maintain his position of trust among the Indians. Now Pucksinwah was hopeful that Logan had seen things go far enough to give up his peaceful attitude toward the Whites and to rally many tribes in mutual defense, but again he was frustrated.

At last the Kispokotha leader had the grim satisfaction of seeing a change in attitude on the part of both Logan and Cornstalk. Logan was persuaded to take up the tomahawk by a brutal massacre of several members of his family near their camp at the juncture of the Yellow Creek with the Ohio River. Among the victims was his pregnant sister whom the White tormentors had shot, and while she still lived, had suspended her on a pole, torn away her clothing, and slashed open her belly. Cornstalk was persuaded partly by the treatment of him and of his brother and his Amazon-like sister when they had gone on a peace mission to Pittsburgh. Responding to a request from Colonel George Croghan, Indian agent at Fort Pitt, which had been delivered by a messenger under a flag of truce, they had made the trip to Pittsburgh, but, even as they were making their way to the inner headquarters of Croghan, a mob of frontiersmen pounced upon them and engaged in a melee which lasted until Croghan arrived on the scene firing his pistol in the air to emphasize his orders to stop. Apologies were not enough to persuade the Indians to remain.

Later when word came that Lord Dunmore, British governor of Virginia, was moving toward the Ohio with a force of nearly 1,900 British regulars plus an additional force of about 1,100 militia under Colonel Andrew Lewis, Cornstalk was reluctant to try to make a stand with a force of Shawnee warriors, together with a few Mingo, Delaware, and Wyandot brothers, which was half the size. But now the tribal war council was firm. If Cornstalk would not lead them in making battle, then Puckinswah would do so.

With good reports from his spies, Cornstalk managed it so that he could fall upon the smaller militia force while Dunmore's larger force was still far away. The place was Point Pleasant, an angle of ground formed by the entry of the Great Kanawha River into the Ohio. In canoes which they had brought up for the purpose, the Indians crossed the big river under cover of darkness and attacked about dawn. A furious battle raged on this October 1, 1774. About noon, Pucksinwah, his son Chiksika fighting by his side, received a bullet directly in his chest. As he fell, Chiksika rushed to him. It was apparent that the chief's life was ebbing. With his last breath he told his son that he would now be head of the family, and he must look after it. Above all he must teach his six-year-old brother, Tecumseh, and the other boys, the skills of war and the courage and honor of Shawnee warriors. The battle was a virtual draw. The Indians had inflicted more casualties than they had received, but that evening they returned across the Ohio and then to their Scioto villages. There they would await the possible pursuit of Lord Dunmore.

The forces of Lewis and Dunmore did follow toward the villages, but they accepted Cornstalk's protestations of desire for peace without further attack.

3b

When William Henry Harrison was born, his father at forty-seven, the fifth Benjamin Harrison, was a leading Virginia planter and a long-time and leading member of the House of Burgesses. A massive man whose weight hovered at 250 pounds and whose height was over six feet, he still bore himself in posture, attire, and manner like a royal prince. He was a member of the Committee of Correspondence, a link in a kind of underground news network which operated throughout most of the colonies to keep alive grievances and suspicions against the British. That summer he was chosen a member of Virginia's delegation to the First Continental Congress in Philadelphia.

Benjamin Harrison's wife, William Henry's mother, was Elizabeth Bassett, known throughout the Tidewater for her charm and beauty. Her brother was married to the sister of Martha Washington. Her father was Colonel William Bassett of Eltham, and her mother the former Elizabeth Churchill who was related to the Armisteads, the Wormleys, the Carters, the Carys, the Pages, and the "other" Harrisons of Brandon, the home of Nathaniel Harrison, across the James River from Berkeley. Numerous family ties of kinship and marriage bound the Harrisons as well to the Carters, the Byrds, and the Randolphs.

In his earlier years, Benjamin Harrison was an attractive figure in Williamsburg as well as on the plantation. He was a student eighteen years of age at the College of William and Mary when his father was killed by a bolt of lightning. At twenty-three he was elected to the House of Burgesses. He was elected again three years later, and then served continuously from 1752 to 1775. In 1765 he was a member of the Committee to oppose the Stamp Act. As a delegate to the First and Second Continental Congresses, he was active on the key committees — Committee on Foreign Commerce, Committee on Treaties, and the Board of War.

In June 1776, after Richard Henry Lee introduced Virginia's resolution for independence, Benjamin Harrison presided over the committee of the whole that debated it. When a committee was appointed to draft a statement to accompany the Declaration, Harrison and his friends maneuvered to keep Lee, as well as George Mason, off of it. This opened the way for Thomas Jefferson to become the drafter. It fell to Harrison then to read the Declaration to the Congress. The primary resolution was adopted on July 2 and the explanatory Declaration on the 4th. It was not until August that most of the members signed the parchment copy of the document. These included "Benj Harrison"; thereafter referred to as "The Signer," to distinguish him from the others in the long line of Benjamin Harrisons.

Virginia already had adopted its own resolution of independence and then adopted an unprecedented written constitution.

This instrument replaced the House of Burgesses with a House of Delegates, and replaced the Governor's Council with a Senate, which together would form the new General Assembly. In 1778, Benjamin Harrison defeated Thomas Jefferson for the speakership of the new House. A rival for his seat from Charles City County was his neighbor, John Tyler of Greenway. Three years later, Harrison was elected to the first of three one-year terms as Governor of Virginia.

William Henry was three years old when his father signed the Declaration of Independence. His oldest brother, Benjamin, Jr. (VI), then in his twenties, served as paymaster in the Southern army during the Revolutionary War. The other brother, Carter Bassett, in his early teens, and the four sisters — Anne, Sarah, Lucy, and Elizabeth — aged five to twelve, all were at home.

4a

The Shawnee Indians spoke an Algonquian language with a "southern accent." Actually in the language Shawnee meant "southerner." Linguistically they were related to many tribes of North America. The central Algonquian tribes with whom the Shawnees were most closely related included the Miami, the Kickapoo, the Wea, the Illiniwek, the Potawatomi, the Delaware, the Sac and Fox, and others. In the centuries before the coming of the White Man, Shawnee bands wandered through much of the eastern part of North America. Beginning in the area of the Canadian Shield, they moved to the Great Lakes, then to the New York area, and southward as far as Alabama and north Florida. When the French were coming into the Mississippi valley and the English were settling Virginia, groups of Shawnees were living in the region of the Delaware River (then referred to as the "South" River), and western New York, in the region south of Lake Erie, and in the Ohio valley. By about the 1680's their principal locations were in the Cumberland Valley of Kentucky and Tennessee and along the Savannah River in South Carolina, though some had moved northward toward Lake Michigan and to the Illinois country. They gave their name to the Suwannee River of Alabama and Florida and to the Sewanee area on the Cumberland Plateau. At the beginning of the eighteenth century, many of these Shawnees were converging on Pennsylvania from South Carolina, the Cumberland region, and Illinois. One group established several villages in the Valley of Virginia where some remained for twenty-five years. Under pressure from the Iroquois and to escape domination from White settlers, the Pennsylvania Shawnee began to migrate westward about 1730. About 1734, they built a town on the Ohio at the mouth of the Scioto River. A flood in 1753 drove them to higher ground, and five years later the inhabitants of that area moved to the upper Scioto and the Little Miami Rivers. On the Scioto, they established the first of five villages that would go by the name, "Chillicothe." After Henry Bouquet's expedition into the Ohio country and his treaty with several of the groups, they moved farther west. On the Little Miami they built the town that would be known as "Old Chillicothe." About twelve miles north of that they built Piqua, the birthplace of Tecumseh.

The Shawnee Nation comprised five divisions or subtribes: Chillicothe, Piqua, Kispokotha, Thawegila, and Maykujay. Something like the tribes of ancient Israel or the castes of ancient Persia and Hindustan, but without the social immobility of those systems, each of these divisions had a special role or responsibility in the Shawnee Nation. Like the Levis or the Brahmans, the Piquas provided religious leadership and had the main responsibility for maintaining tribal rituals. The Chillicothes and Thawegilas, sometimes in competition with each other, generally provided the political leadership for the tribe, while the Kispokothas were supposed to be the most adept at warfare, and they generally supplied the war chiefs. Maykujays specialized in health and medicine, and they often supplied the medicine men. Shawnee villages often took their names from whichever of these divisions had the greatest number of inhabitants.

Within these major divisions, the Shawnee people were further subdivided into a dozen patrilineal clans each named for its animal totem, such as Panther, Eagle, Bear, Racoon, Deer, Turtle, and so on. Members of one clan were given to teasing members of other clans as displaying the less desirable attributes of their totem, as the clumsy Bears, the timid Deer, or the slow Turtles. Lines of the clans were strictly observed, mainly to prevent inner marriage among close relatives but also as extensions of close family bonds. Individuals were not allowed to change their totems, and a man was forbidden to marry a woman whose totem was the same as his own.

Marriages generally were arranged by agreement between the respective families under the leadership of the bride's maternal uncle, but no one was directed into a marriage without his or her own consent. Divorce was easy but infrequent and adultery, especially on the part of the wife, was subject to severe punishment. Sometimes a man might take more than one wife, but this was rare. While the nuclear family was the household unit, and each dwelt in its own wigwam, the close family ties extended beyond. A Shawnee referred to all of his uncles and aunts as "father" and "mother," and at least his first cousins were "brothers" and "sisters." His nephews and nieces were "sons" and "daughters." Close family relation extended to grandparents as well, and the association of children with their grandparents had a very close and special meaning. When a warrior died, his brother was obliged to take the widow as his own squaw even though this might mean a second wife. Upon the death of a spouse the surviving partner went into a period of mourning for a year during which time he or she would neither wash nor change clothing. The mourning period ended when the family provided a feast and new clothing.

The Shawnees were an open and honest people who followed moralistic religious teachings and attempted to live in harmony with each other. Crime within the tribe was uncommon. When an offense did occur, it generally was a matter to be settled within the clan or between the clans concerned. Reparation was sought by the clan of the injured person. The family of the criminal would express sorrow for the crime and offer presents to the relatives of the victim. This usually settled the matter. A murder called for the death penalty, and the nearest male relative of the deceased served as executioner, but that was the end of it. The clans did not become involved in blood feuds.

The subtribes or divisions and the villages provided the bases for local government among the Shawnees. Each division had its own peace chief, or sachem, and might also have a war chief. The former were hereditary positions, though if no worthy successor appeared in a particular case, the leaders would turn to another family. The war chief was chosen altogether on merit, after demonstrating his skill and leadership in battle. The departure from Ohio of a number of the people from the other divisions in the 1770's left the Chillicothes and the Maykujays in a dominant position, and this led to some dissension. With divisional lines becoming less significant, the villages became more important as the local units. Now each village had its own peace chief and war chief, and a village council made up of older warriors who were recognized for their wisdom and experience. They had no specific authority but wielded a great deal of influence. In addition, the leading women of the village composed a group which supervised certain rituals, set the time for planting and harvesting, and even had strong influence on matters of war. A woman peace chief might intercede with the war chief not to go on the war path. In war these women might save prisoners from execution.

The overall tribal chief, now coming generally from the Chillicothes, was head of the tribe, but his authority did not extend to internal matters within the villages. When the tribe was together in the same area, a tribal council made up of chiefs and elders from all the divisions and villages served as an advisory body.

Bear skin, dressed and tanned, was the favored material for Shawnee clothing. In winter both men and women wore moccasins and full-length leggings, breech-cloths and girdles, the men a loose shirt and the women a longer overblouse. Both wore a hat of leather or fur, or a turban. Shirts and blouses had fringed borders and were decorated with dyed porcupine quills, brightly colored feathers, beads, and paints. In summer the men wore only a breach cloth and the women a loose blouse. Sometimes a headband and eagle feather would adorn the head, though many preferred turbans with feathers, or often no head dress at all. Men often would wear rings or other decorations in their noses and ear lobes.

The role of the men was to be the hunters and warriors. They made extended trips into the woods for hunting. They sought fish from the abundant sources in all the streams, and they trapped for fur-bearing animals in the winter. It was up to them to provide meat and hides and to protect the village from enemies. It was left to the women to provide most of the service for the family. They prepared the food, planted and harvested the crops of corn, pumpkins, beans, and other vegetables, dressed and tanned the hides, made the clothing and the bed clothing, kept the wigwam in repair, gathered the firewood, and looked after the children. Older folks were relieved from most of those duties. Older men might hunt and fish close by, and they would serve on the village council. The older women could enjoy their grandchildren and give advice to family and village. Younger members of the family saw to it that they had food and shelter.

The Shawnee subscribed to a theistic religion centered in one supreme being, or God, *Manitou*, the Master of Life. Subordinate to Manitou was *Wishemenetoo,* the Great Spirit, sometimes referred to as "Grandmother," and who especially looked over the Indians. Another subordinate deity, grandson of the Great Spirit, looked over the White people. In addition there was an evil Spirit, *Motsheemenetoo* who, while less powerful than the Great Spirit, was the source of all kinds of mischief. Moreover, the Shawnee maintained a belief in witches, and persons suspected of practicing witchcraft were put to death. *Manitou* was the source of all the sacred laws and direction in the proper way to live. He had made the Indians and furnished all the animals and plants that they needed. If all went well, when they died they would enter a pleasant hunting ground abounding in game, fish, and great fields of corn.

When a Shawnee died, the body was covered and left to rest in the wigwam for half a day, and then friends from a different clan prepared it for burial. This included painting it and dressing it in new clothing. They chose a funeral leader and handlers also from a different clan. Funeral ceremonies lasted for four days. The body was put into a grave about four feet deep, head toward the setting sun. The grave was lined with stone slabs or bark. The body was wrapped in skins or bark. Poles were placed over it to be covered with bark, and then this covered with earth. Then family and friends would assemble for a feast, after which the members of the immediate family would go into a twelve-day period of mourning during which they refrained from most work and other activities.

4b

The Virginians of the eighteenth century were predominantly of English stock, with significant numbers of Scotch-Irish in the West, and a number of Germans who had spilled over from central Pennsylvania and western Maryland in the North. Supported by taxes in Virginia, the Anglican or Church of England was the established church, and remained so even after the Revolution (as the Episcopal Church) until 1786 when the legislature approved Jefferson's Act for Religious Freedom. The Scotch-Irish brought their Presbyterianism with them, and the Germans were mainly of the Lutheran or the Mennonite persuasions. By the end of the third quarter of the century, the dissenters — Baptists as well as Presbyterians and Methodists (though the latter still considered themselves a part of the Mother Church) probably outnumbered the Anglicans. There was a good deal of controversy among the religious sects, though all professed belief in the same God, the·the Supreme Being; in his Son, the Saviour and Light of the World; and in the Holy Spirit, and most believed in an Evil One, known variously as Satan, Lucifer, and the Devil.

The economy of Virginia was based on agriculture and river commerce, both coastwise and overseas. Tobacco was the principal money crop, but there were also large exports of meat, grain and flour, vegetables, and timber products. At the top of the economic and social ladder were the great planters and a few great mercantilists. The plantation owners operated great holdings of thousands of acres, mainly in the tidewater area, worked by Negro slaves, indentured servants, and hired artisans. The aristocracy, made up of the landed gentry, great merchants, high professional men and, during colonial times, British officials, provided the political and social leadership. They set the standards in manners, patronized the arts, and cultivated personal alliances. For public events, the men dressed in brightly colored suits of silk coats, waistcoats, breeches with silver buckles, and ruffled linen shirts. The women dressed in extravagant silk gowns with full skirts and large pleats held out by hoops or panniers. After about 1780, the women's dresses had full-gathered skirts held out in the back by a bustle. Both men and women might wear powdered hair on special occasions.

Between the aristocracy and the indentured servants and slaves was a large middle class. This was made up mainly of yeoman farmers who tilled their own small farms around the fringes of the great estates or in the Piedmont and in the Shenandoah Valley. They were content to wear buckskin breeches or homespun pantaloons. Other elements of the middle class were the small merchants and shopkeepers and skilled artisans in the cities and towns. Below them on the scale were the hired hands and manual workers. In the mountains beyond the Shenandoah were the frontier farmers and hunters, trappers, and Indian traders. Although class distinctions seemed sharp, it was quite possible for anyone, except slaves, to move upward from one level to another.

Virginia operated as a royal province, directly under the authority of the British crown. The King appointed the Governor and Council, but concurrent legislative authority was in the

House of Burgesses whose members were elected by the land-owners. With independence, a House of Delegates replaced the Burgesses, and a Senate replaced the Council. Going back to earlier practice, the two houses elected the Governor, but his powers were strictly defined. The counties became the units of local government and representation. Williamsburg was the capital city until 1780 when the capital was moved to Richmond under the urging of Jefferson.

By this time the Virginia aristocrats were speaking the English language of the educated Londoner with what was becoming a distinctive "southern accent." It was not the heavy drawl which was developing in the lower South, but a soft, fluid speech with a certain slur characterized by dropping final r's, sometimes the insertion of a "y" sound after initial consonants, and sometimes by the compression of words and syllables, especially in proper names, so that Randolph became "Randuff," and Taliaferro became "Toliver." A distinctive peculiarity in pronunciation appeared on the Eastern Shore and lower Shenandoah Valley under Scottish influence in giving the "oo" sound as in boot rather than the "ow" for "ou" so that "house" and "about" became "hoose" and "aboot."

Perhaps an unjustified number of Virginians took pride in a supposed aristocratic connection through the Cavaliers who had taken refuge in the colony from Cromwell's "Roundheads" during the English Civil War in the mid-17th Century. It seemed that all Virginians took pride in their land and in each other. All shared the pride of association with the ladies and gentlemen of their own landed, political, and intellectual aristocracy.

CHAPTER II

Growing Up

1

One warm afternoon in the spring of 1779, in the Shawnee village of Piqua, Tecumseh, now eleven, sat on the ground with his young brothers listening as their mother spoke to them. Here and there a woman could be seen at work, but it was generally quiet. Light blue smoke curled upward lazily from an occasional fire. Flocks of blackbirds flew over the nearby woods, alighting now and then, and then resuming their flight. In spite of the tranquility of the scene, Methotaska betrayed a certain feeling of apprehension as she spoke earnestly to her sons about their proud race and about the dangers which had come:

"The Master of Life made the Shawnee before any other of the human race, and they sprang from his brain. He gave them all the knowledge he himself possessed, and placed them upon the great island, and all the other Red people are descended from the Shawnees. After he made the Shawnees, he made the French and English out of his breast, the Dutch out of his feet, and the Long Knives out of his hands. All of these inferior men he made White and placed them beyond the stinking lake."

The little ones were allowing themselves to be distracted by any other sound or sight that came in the range of their hearing or seeing, but Tecumseh listened intently. He had heard much of this before, but he concentrated on each word as if to discover new meaning. Methotaska paused to reunify the attention of her listeners and then continued:

"For many moons the Shawnees used the knowledge which they had received from the Master of Life in such a manner as to be pleasing to him, and they continued to be masters of the great island. But in a great length of time they departed from those good ways, and the Master of Life told them that he would take away from them the knowledge which they possessed and give it to the White people, to be restored when they would deserve it by a return to strong and good ways. Many moons later they saw something white approaching their shores. At first they took it for a great bird, but they soon found it to be a monstrous canoe filled with the very people who had got the knowledge which belonged to the Shawnee. After these white people came, they were not content with having the knowledge which belonged to the Shawnee, but they took their lands also. These things must one day have an end. The Master of Life is about to restore to the Shawnee both the knowledge and their rights, and he will trample the Long Knives under his feet."

While the younger ones ran off to follow their own more immediate interests, Methotaske turned to Tecumseh and said, "You must have the soul of a warrior to avenge the death of your father, killed by the Long Knives. Your soul will be as fearless as the rushing water, your arm as strong as a thunderbolt, your feet as swift as forked lightning."

The big event for the family that spring was the marriage of Tecumapease to Wasegoboah (Stand Firm), a warrior of the Chillicothe division. All were pleased that Tecumapease had such a fine man for her husband, but Tecumseh was especially saddened at the departure of his older sister from the family wigwam. He always felt especially attached to her, and she always had been considerate and helpful to him. For her part, Tecumapease had accepted additional cause for worry as the continuing rounds of warfare called her husband to danger.

One day in May word came that Long Knives were coming toward Chillicothe. Spies had seen them coming up the river valley. They would be there in two days. Tecumseh's older brothers responded at once. Chiksika and Sauwauseekau mounted horses and joined the other warriors of Piqua to hurry to the aid of their brothers in Chillicothe twelve miles away.

After four days of dreadful waiting by the old men and the women and children, the return of the warriors relieved the nervous tension. Chiksika and his brother tied their horses at the edge of the woods and quickly went to their wigwam where their family anxiously awaited them. Before they could speak, Tecumapease who had come to wait with their mother, inquired about her husband. "Wasegoboah? What about Wasegoboah? Is he all right?"

"Yes, yes, he is all right," Chiksika reassured her. Then turning to their mother he explained, "The Long Knives burned the Chillicothe village and then burned the fields of corn, but our warriors fought bravely and drove them back."

Cheers were going up in other parts of the village as the news reached those quarters. Chiksika continued, "The pale faces took all the food and implements they could carry, but then we arrived, and they ran away. There is no danger now to our village. But I am afraid more Long Knives will be coming."

When the family group broke up, Tecumseh went directly to Chiksika. "Why do the Long Knives attack our villages, and why do you say more will be coming?"

"They will keep coming," Chikisika responded gravely, "until we leave and they take our lands."

"What are we to do?" the boy asked.

"We must flee or fight."

"Which do you think we should do?"

Without hesitation Chiksika said firmly, "We must fight."

"But are there too many Long Knives? Can we stop them?"

"We must find a way."

"But why are the Long Knives attacking our villages just now?"

Patiently, Chiksika explained that each side was trying to punish the other.

"Why?"

"Two summers ago our great Chief Cornstalk, who always urged peace, went with son and three warriors to meet Americans at Fort Randolph at the place where our father died, where the Great Kanawha meets the Ohio. He went to help American chiefs make maps of the country. While he was in the fort some other pale faces entered and murdered him and his son and the three warriors."

"Why did they do that?"

"They said Cornstalk had killed White Man, but it was not true. Cornstalk was in fort the whole time."

"Then did Shawnee punish White Men?"

"Yes. Shawnee cannot let White Men kill our people without paying. When White Men kill Chief all Shawnee say many White Men must pay. One spring ago, thirteen moons, our warriors went on warpath and burned White Men's houses along the Great Kanawah. Four moons later Chief Blackfish led Shawnee warriors to attack White Men's village they call Boonesboro."

Tecumseh thrilled at the accounts of those bold exploits. "But does that not make White Men stop attacks?" he demanded.

"No, now White Men say they must attack our villages to punish Shawnee."

"Then we must punish them again. How can it ever end?"

"There will be no end unless Shawnee and their brothers can become strong enough that White Men cannot become their masters."

Later that summer Methotaska returned from a meeting with the women's council of the village with startling news. She called all the family together, including Tecumapease. "My children, things have been very difficult since the loss of your father," she began, "and now the Long Knives give us no peace. They attack our villages and our people. When our warriors stop them, they find more and come again . . . . Now many of our people have decided to move. They will walk many days toward the setting sun until they cross the Big River (the Mississippi), far away from the White Men. I must go with them."

It was as though a thunder bolt had struck the group.

"But my Mother," Chiksika protested, "we must not run away. We cannot hide from the White Men."

"My son, you must decide for yourself what you will do. I do not wish to leave my family, but I must go."

This was the greatest crisis the family had faced since the death of the father. Shawnee family bonds were so close that it was most unusual for a family to be permanently divided. But Methotaska was determined. She also was firm in allowing the others to decide for themselves. Tecumapease of course would remain with her husband. The real question was the position of Chiksika who, though only twenty-three, was the recognized head of the family.

Chiksika agonized only for a moment. "My Mother, I must remain here. I am sad that you will not be here, but I must remain."

"I will follow Chiksika," Tecumseh spoke up before anyone even asked him.

"What about the young ones?" asked Chiksika.

Tecumapease volunteered to look after the young boys as well as Tecumseh. Although her husband was of the Chillicothe division, they would continue to live in Piqua. The boys could share their wigwam. These words gladdened Tecumseh's heart. Already he was rather looking forward to the new arrangement.

"They will remain," said Chiksika.

The other son, Sauwauseekau, also would stay, but the remaining daughter, Nehaseemo, would go with her mother. Methotaska and her daughter would be joining nearly one thousand Shawnees, about one-third of the tribe, for the great migration to the west.

In spite of the loss of his mother, Tecumseh found the following year one of the greatest of his life. He was at the age to learn the most from his brother, to appreciate his sister, to enjoy games and contests with his fellows in the village, and to thrill to the unfolding secrets of the woods, the streams, and the stars. All through the year, running, jumping, swimming, and climbing were almost daily exercises, and in games of "follow the leader" the young Tecumseh always bested any of his companions who dared challenge him. Under the guidance of Chiksika he learned to make bows and arrows and to be an expert marksman. A favorite game was to make a hoop from a wild grape vine and cover it with bark to form a rolling target at which competing sides would shoot their arrows. Tecumseh's side always seemed to win. And he delighted in mobilizing all the boys of the village to engage in sham battles over the surrounding fields and woods.

From Chiksika he learned the art of tracking and stalking game, of building traps and snares for fur-bearing animals, and of angling, seining, and spearing for fish. He learned the names, characteristics, and usefulness of animals and birds. He learned the trees and plants of forest, marsh, and prairie, which to seek for food, which to avoid as poison, and which to use for wounds. He learned to strip bark for canoes or houses and to make tools for war and peace. Instruction followed in the arts of war — the use of tomahawk and knife, and musket and rifle as weapons, the skills of horsemanship, and how to make use of trees and boulders and ground furrows for cover, and bushes, grass, and soil for concealment. He learned to read the signs of broken twigs, crushed leaves, and scratched trees to follow a man through the forest while leaving no such signs of his own. He learned to detect the presence of White Men by the sites of their fires and to conceal signs of his own fires so that they could not be found. He learned to find directions by the moss on trees, the length of shadows, the flow of streams, the wind-bent trees, and the positions of stars, and to foretell weather by the clouds in the sky, the direction of the wind, and the dew on the ground.

Chiksika insisted on daily swims as an exercise in discipline and invigoration for the lad. Tecumseh was required to continue this throughout the year, including cold winter days when it was necessary to break the ice in the ponds in order to enter the water. He learned to conceal himself in streams by lying on his back, head upstream, with his hands grasping weeds, and to submerge until only his nostrils remained above water. He could remain hidden in this way for hours. For shorter and more perilous times, he could use a hollow reed for breathing while he submerged more deeply in the water.

But Tecumseh's early education and training went beyond the practical matters related to gaining a livelihood and making war. Chiksika also insisted that he know well the traditions of the tribe as their father had passed them on, while he taught him to bear pain without flinching, to suffer defeat without despairing, to face danger without fear, to accept triumph without pride, and to approach all things with self-discipline. His sister, lavishing more attention on him than on anyone else, impressed upon him the value of Shawnee honor which rested on an expectation of honesty as well as on courage, sympathy for the weak and unfortunate, and sensitivity to the welfare of others. Contrary to some of the others of her tribe, she taught that cruelty for its own sake, the infliction of unnecessary suffering, whether upon human beings or animals, was degrading to the one who had resorted to it.

At the same time Chief Black Fish, who had been acting as a foster father, provided spiritual guidance for the lad. After a regime of physical endurance, including a continuation of daily plunges in a cold stream, the Chief told him that now he should dive to the bottom of the creek to see whether or not he could find his *opawaka*, his religious token that would grant direct access to Manitou, the Master of Life. In his dive, Tecumseh came up with a white quartz stone. When he ran to show it to Black Fish, the Chief pronounced it good and bade the boy to tie a leather thong to it and wear it suspended from his neck so that he might seek the favor of Manitou.

One day early in the following summer, Chiksika called to the twelve-year-old Tecumseh. "My Brother, you have learned well the ways of the Shawnee in the woods and in the streams and in becoming a strong warrior. Now it is time for you to make your vision quest."

"I have heard others speak of it, but I am not sure what it is. Tell me, my Brother."

"You must go into the woods alone and remain without eating until you see a vision of great truth and meet your guardian spirit. Your guardian spirit will be in the form of an animal or a bird. It will bring you messages of great truths from our Grandmother, the Great Spirit. You must bring evidence such as a feather from this bird or hair from this animal."

"Oh, Brother, how will I know when I have met my guardian spirit?"

"There will be no doubt. If you are not certain, then you have not met your special spirit."

"What was your guardian spirit, my Brother?"

"A white snow bird."

"How long will it take to find my vision and my guardian spirit?"

"Sometimes only the time between the noon sun and the setting sun. Sometimes many days and nights. Sometimes the young people fail and must try again on another day. You will go tomorrow at the noon sun."

"Yes, my Brother."

At the appointed time Chiksika came to the wigwam of Tecumapease and led Tecumseh away. He covered the lad's face with charcoal, explaining that in this way all the people would know that he was on his vision quest, and they would not disturb him, would not call him away from his mission, and would not offer him any food. This would be a time of fasting and contemplation in complete solitude.

The young Tecumseh took this charge seriously. Off he went into the woods until he was far beyond any sounds of his village. Only occasional chirpings of birds and squirrels, the hum of a bee, and the rustle of leaves and grass in the light wind could be heard.

For a while he sat on the warm ground and watched intently as his thoughts wandered aimlessly. He thought of his own contentment, of his devotion to Chiksika and Tecumapease, of his regard for his other brothers, and of how he missed his father and mother. He thought of his people and wondered if they would be able to live in peace in this country.

Late in the afternoon he heard the whistle of a quail and wondered if this might be his spirit. Then the loud call of a crow sounded, and he wondered again, but in the fact of wondering he knew that this must not be it. As night fell he heard the loud and persistent call of a whip-poor-will. This continued so long and so loudly that he thought this must be it. But he was aware of no vision or special truth, and he dismissed it.

Darkness brought upon him a special self-consciousness. He never had spent a night in the woods completely alone. The question did enter his mind whether or not he should give up and try to find his way home. The hooting of an owl seemed at first to emphasize the wisdom of this course, but then it seemed more to be ridiculing the whole idea. Tecumseh determined that he would entertain no thought of doubt nor any feeling of fear. Coming upon a slight clearing in the dense undergrowth and trees, he lay on the ground to sleep. With some effort he relaxed and looked at the sky. He saw a shooting star and took this, "tecumseh," as a sign for reassurance, and he fell asleep.

In the bright sun of the next morning Tecumseh stirred himself to walk farther into the woods, taking care to notice marks to guide him on his return. About noon he sat to rest and think some more. To pass the time he began little tests of his own strength. He broke a twig from a tree, and then broke it again between his hands. Then he took several twigs and bound them together. He found that he could not break them. He grasped a wild grape vine and broke it easily. Then he twisted several strands together, and he could not break them. He took a broad leaf from a maple tree and easily tore it. He took two or three leaves and tore them just as easily. But when he pressed a hundred leaves together he could not tear them.

He walked farther. The sound of water attracted him. He continued until he came upon a little brook of white water rushing down the slope. He tossed a pebble into the stream and watched the water wash it away. He tossed several more stones into the water and saw the water sweep them aside as it continued its flow without interruption. He noticed a narrow spot in the stream. Here the water ran even more swiftly, but it also might be more easily constricted. Gathering a double handful of stones, Tecumseh put them all into this narrow place at the same time. Now the water delayed just a little and more slowly swept the stones away. Intrigued, Tecumseh gathered a whole supply of stones and stacked them beside the narrow place. Then he dug up a supply of mud. Working very quickly he put all the stones and mud into place at once. He brought up other stones, and now he was able to replace them more quickly than they could be washed away until he found that he had built an effective dam. Many stones, held together by a common bond, had stopped the white water.

As the water backed up, small pools began to form upstream. Then, strangely, he felt a presence. For a moment he felt as though his father were there. He turned and looked upstream. He could see the shadow of what he thought was a deer drinking from one of the pools formed by his dam. Carefully, he crept toward the animal, stalking, stalking. Now close to the spot, he very quietly parted the bushes just enough to allow him to see. He saw that it was a buffalo — a *white* buffalo.

Previously he had seen buffalo only in large herds or small groups. In recent years they were becoming scarce. But here was a lone white buffalo! Its being white meant that it must be the chief of all buffaloes. He had never seen a white one, though he knew that a white squirrel was chief of the squirrels and a white wolf chief of the wolves.

Tecumseh crept even closer. The animal looked up but did not flee. It had strange blue eyes, with eyelids tinged with pink. Those strange blue eyes looked straight into the eyes of Tecumseh. He knew at once that this was his guardian spirit! Cautiously, he crept closer until he could reach out and touch the buffalo's nose. The animal licked his hand. Carefully, skillfully, Tecumseh drew his hunting knife and deftly cut a tuft of hair from the buffalo's chin. The animal bounded away, and Tecumseh felt the exhilaration of discovery. He had found his quest; he had found his guardian spirit!

Tecumseh ran most of the way home to report his experience to Chiksika.

"What did you find?" asked his brother.

"A white buffalo! A *white* buffalo!"

"Oh, that is good, very good. But what wisdom did you discover?"

"I found that I could easily break one twig or one grape vine, but if I bound many together I could not break them. If I took one leaf, or two or three, in hand, I could tear them easily, but if I pressed together a hundred I could not tear them."

"Yes, yes, what is great about that? Anything else?"

"Yes, if I threw one stone at a time into the rushing brook the white water swept them away. But when I put many stones together, held together by a common bond of mud, they stopped the white water. That is when the white buffalo came and drank from a pool formed by my dam. Look, here is a tuft of hair from his beard!"

"And what great wisdom do you find in that?"

"Don't you see, my Brother, like the stones in the brook, when one or a few Red Men stand against the White Men, they are swept away. But if many Red Men, from all the tribes, can be held together by the mud of Manitou, they can stop the flow of the White Men"

"My young brother speaks wisely. He has found his guardian spirit; he has discovered his great vision!"

Tecumseh remained silent for a while. He was in deep, troubled thought.

"After the discovery of this wisdom, after you have found your guardian spirit, why are you troubled, my Brother?" asked Chiksika.

"If Manitou, the Master of Life, loves us, why does he allow the White Men to destroy our villages and kill our people? Why does he let them kill our father? Why does our Grandmother, The Great Spirit, lead our mother to a far-off land?"

"Because, my Brother, he wants us to be men, not chickens. Manitou has provided the forests and the animals and the corn that we need for our food and our shelter, but we must hunt and plant and build with our own hands. He has given us wisdom and the way to become strong. But with these we must make ourselves strong. We must become wise enough to find ways to protect our people and villages from the White Men. Perhaps he has shown you the way in your vision."

On the afternoon of August 7, 1780, Tecumseh was at play with his friends at the edge of the village when they looked up to see a large number of people approaching up the river valley. All of them ran to their wigwams to report what they had seen. Tecumseh heard from his sister that some of the warriors already had come in to report that the great tribal chief, Black Hoof, was coming with all of the warriors and people from Chillicothe. The Long Knives had come to their town. The Indians had hidden their implements and household goods and the silver which they had saved from their mining in the Little Miami gorge over many years. They had burned their village and departed before the Long Knives could get to them. Now they were joining their brothers at Piqua to fight the attacking army.

On his arrival Black Hoof called a council of all the leaders. Tecumseh, standing in awe, listened. The Chief, a solidly built, stocky man of fifty-four, but five feet eight inches tall, commanded immediate attention. He was a veteran of wars against the Whites since the defeat of Braddock near Fort Duquesne in 1755, and always had been an advocate of resistance against White encroachment. Now, he told the assembled leaders that it was not possible to defend Chillicothe with their small number of warriors against the Long Knives who numbered a thousand and were mounted on horses. And all his people had come to Piqua to join together in fighting the attackers. All the women and children and old people must be taken at once to hide in the deep woods while the warriors prepared for the battle. The Long Knives might attack this night or surely not later than the next morning.

Nervous with excitement, Tecumseh ran back to the wigwam. He was hoping that he might be allowed to take part in the battle, but Chiksika told him that he must wait for a more important day. Now, Tecumseh must help look after his sister and little brothers. Chiksika left to join most of the other warriors in a short version of their war dance.

Led by six selected warriors, Tecumseh, with Tecumapease and the younger brothers, joined the other women and children in the unbroken woods to make their camp. All night they waited, shivering in anticipation rather than coldness, but they heard nothing. Dawn appeared under a light haze. Still nothing. Then, about mid-morning, they could hear the sound of musket fire a distance to the south of their village. This continued for nearly two hours and then abated. After an interval of an hour, amidst a chorus of war whoops, the musket fire started again, now louder, now closer and more intense. Then they could hear the loud explosions of a cannon. Several times it fired. Then more musket firing, the distant sound of horse hooves, and then quiet. All through another night the Indian women and children of Piqua, with their Chillicothe comrades, waited in the woods — waited for word that it was safe to return to their homes.

At last the dawn came, bright and clear, and the world seemed completely peaceful again. Hopefully the Shawnee families collected together and walked back toward their village. As they approached it, hope gave way to despair, and the bright sun seemed covered by dark shrouds. The returning women and children were horrified to find the huts burned to the ground, the cornfields destroyed, and the bodies of scores of their brave defenders lying where they had fallen, many of them scalped.

Tecumseh and his younger brothers were deeply impressed with a terrible scene that they never would forget. They walked slowly and silently with Tecumapease back to the ashes of their wigwam. Without saying anything each sensed the sharing of a fear about what had happened to their older brothers and to the husband of Tecumapease.

After waiting aimlessly and hopelessly for some time, they were overjoyed when all three came up. All were exhausted, and Chiksika had a superficial wound on his arm, but otherwise they were all right. But they were bitter.

After giving assurances that the enemy had gone away, Chiksika said solemnly, "This was the work of the big chief Long Knife himself, the one they call George Rogers Clark. They have gone away because they believe that when they have destroyed our villages we will leave and go with the others beyond the great river. They forget that we build new villages every year. We have lost many brave warriors, but no more than they have, and most of our people are still safe."

Tecumseh wanted more details of the battle itself. Chiksika explained only that the Long Knives had attacked quickly on horses, that then the Shawnee warriors, forming a new line in front of the village, had very bravely run out toward the Long Knives and destroyed many of them. Later they ran back to the fort in the village, but the Long Knives had a big cannon which destroyed its walls. Then he mentioned that a young White man who had lived in the village with them for three years, the one called John Rogers, was a kinsman of the Long Knife Clark. When Rogers had run out to meet his kinsman, he was shot by his own people who thought he was a Shawnee.

Chiksika paused as he walked about looking over the scene. "Yes, the Long Knives have gone away because they think that when they have destroyed our villages they have destroyed us. But they are wrong. We will build our villages again. But then the Long Knives will come again and again unless we are strong enough to stop them."

"How can we do that?" asked Tecumseh.

"Today the people of two villages fought together and saved most of our people. One day many villages will fight together to stop the Long Knives."

2

William Henry Harrison's early years on Berkeley Plantation were on the whole joyful ones. He liked to roam over the acres of the great estate, and he found good swimming and fishing in nearby Kimadges Creek, as well as along the near shore of the James River. When he could find no other company he was likely to find a band of slaves' children and lead them on a merry chase through the thickets. At an early age he was riding horses and soon learned to shoot.

William Henry joined his brothers and sisters for school in the small brick building northeast of the Berkeley Mansion, called the Bachelor's House, which served as playhouse and sometimes as guest house. There, under the instruction of a tutor, he learned the alphabet and the rudiments of spelling and reading, letters and the rudiments of writing, and he learned numbers and the rudiments of ciphering.

His father had little time at the plantation during these years, but, when he could, he was careful to instill the values of courage and patriotism in the young lad. His mother gave more attention to him, and instructed him in social manners, in personal conduct, and in the virtues of honesty and benevolence. His rules of etiquette were essentially the same as those which young George Washington had noted as a schoolboy, including such points of consideration as, "Every action done in company ought to be done with some sign of respect to those present.... Sing not to yourself with a humming noise, or drum with your fingers or feet .... If anyone comes to speak to you while you are sitting, stand up though he be your inferior .... Persons of low degree ought not to use many ceremonies to lords and others of high degree, but respect and highly honor them, and those of high degree ought to treat those of low degree with affability and courtesy, without arrogance...." The boy was taught not to take advantage of those in inferior positions, and to be calm and considerate toward the servants, and even to the poorest slave.

William Henry listened in excitement and amazement as he heard his older brothers talk of the exploits of Colonel George Rogers Clark of Caroline County who had led an expedition of Virginians to the Ohio and all the way through the Illinois country to the Mississippi River, and then, in the dead of winter in

February 1779, had led a force across the flooded plains of Illinois to capture Vincennes, on the Wabash River, from the British.

In December 1780 came the frightening news that the traitorous Benedict Arnold had landed near the mouth of the James River with a force of British regulars and American Tories. Governor Thomas Jefferson had done little to organize an effective militia in Virginia, and near panic was setting in. Desperately, the legislature in Richmond asked Benjamin Harrison to hurry to Philadelphia to see if he could get some help from the Continental Congress. Before leaving he took the precaution of gathering up his wife and daughters and young son, William Henry, together with some household servants, and moved them to the houses of relatives in less exposed areas. William Henry went with his mother to Eltham, the home of her father, across the peninsula near West Point, where the Mattaponi and Pamunkey rivers joined to form the York River.

On January 4, 1781, Arnold sailed up the river and disembarked at the Byrds' plantation, Westover. He sent a company of the Queen's Rangers under Lieutenant Colonel Simcoe to disperse an ineffective band of militia which had gathered at Charles City Courthouse, while, with his main force, he followed the path across to the Berkeley Plantation. Here he drove off a third of the slaves, and he allowed the soldiers to use the cattle for target practice. He spared the buildings, perhaps in the hope of using them later for quarters, but he did resort to what amounted to an act of childish vindictiveness against a signer of the Declaration of Independence. He ordered all the Harrison family portraits and all other works of art taken from the mansion walls and thrown on a big fire out in front. This accomplished, he marched on, again with little or no opposition, to Richmond where the government now resided but had since fled. He burned several warehouses and other buildings there, though he missed the wooden frame building which was serving as temporary capitol. Then he sailed away to take up positions near Norfolk as a more or less continuing menace.

It was months before the Harrisons and their neighbors could return to their family homes. The summer brought another flurry of excitement. One day in July, William Henry could see clouds of dust rising from the road which passed a mile or so to the north of the house. He could hear sounds of men and horses. He ran through the fields until he could see the column of soldiers. Some were wearing blue coats; others were in green, and still others in butternut linens. Then he caught a glimpse of the general in blue coat and buff breeches. After the column had passed, he learned that it was Major General "Mad Anthony" Wayne with a force under the general direction of the Frenchman, Lafayette, who were going after the British general, Lord Cornwallis. Later that evening young Harrison could hear musket fire in the distance. It was coming from Green Spring Farm where indeed Anthony Wayne was going after Cornwallis. Later the force came back down the road and spent the night around Malvern Hill.

This was only the prelude. In the ensuing weeks other forces were arriving in the Williamsburg area. In September there were reports that Washington himself had arrived and with him, the great French general, Rochambeau. They had brought their armies all the way from New York. On September 28 the allied armies moved out from their camps in the Williamsburg area to challenge Cornwallis who had moved to Yorktown. The siege began on October 6, and on the 19th Cornwallis surrendered. Virginia was safe, and Benjamin Harrison would be able to spend more time with his family.

William Henry continued his schooling, including a short time at the school near Brandon Plantation across the James River, where he received an introduction to Latin. When he reached the age of twelve, it was time for his confirmation in the Anglican (Episcopal) Church. Studying the thirty-nine Articles of Religion, based upon those dating from Queen Elizabeth, and memorizing the catechism were unwelcome diversions from more pleasant activities such as roaming through the woods and fields, though no more of a chore than his regular school assignments. After many days of study and practice, he was able to give all the required answers to the catechist:

Question. What dost thou chiefly learn in these Articles of thy Belief?
Answer. First, I learn to believe in God the Father, who hath made me, and all the world.
Secondly, in God the Son, who hath redeemed me, and all mankind.
Thirdly, in God the Holy Ghost, who sanctifieth me, and all the people of God.

Then came a recitation of the Ten Commandments, and a little later an exchange about the Sacraments:

Question. How many Sacraments hath Christ ordained in his Church?
Answer. Two only, as generally necessary to salvation; that is to say, Baptism, and the Supper of the Lord.
Question. What meanest thou by this word Sacrament?

Answer. I mean an outward and visible sign of an inward and spiritual grace given unto us; ordained by Christ himself, as a means whereby we receive the same, and a pledge to assure us thereof.

And so, on through another dozen questions and answers about the doctrines of the church.

This done, the boy was ready for formal confirmation. There being no Anglican bishop in America, it fell to the Bishop's Commissary to preside over these exercises. On the appointed day, Mr. and Mrs. Benjamin Harrison drove their son by carriage to the Westover Church. There they met the boy's surviving Godparents, Mrs. Randolph and Mr. Byrd.

At the proper time in the service William Henry, together with four other candidates, stood in front of the Commissary, and then all the congregation stood as the priest said, "Reverend Father in God, I present unto you these persons to receive the Laying on of Hands." Then the Commissary read from the Book of Common Prayer a selection from the *Acts of the Apostles,* and then went on:

Do ye here, in the presence of God, and of this congregation, renew the solemn promise and vow that ye made, or that was made in your name, at your Baptism; ratifying and confirming the same; and acknowledging yourselves bound to believe and to do all those things which ye then undertook, or your Sponsors then undertook for you?

I do.

Do ye promise to follow Jesus Christ as your Lord and Saviour?

I do.

Commissary. Our help is in the Name of the Lord;

Answer. Who hath made heaven and earth.

Commissary. Blessed be the Name of the Lord;

Answer. Henceforth, world without end.

Commissary. Lord, hear our prayer.

Answer. And let our cry come unto thee.

Commissary. Let us pray.

Almighty and everliving God, who hast vouchsafed to regenerate these thy servants by Water and the Holy Ghost; and hast given unto them forgiveness of all their sins; Strengthen them, we beseech thee, O Lord, with the Holy Ghost, the Comforter, and daily increase in them thy manifold gifts of grace: the spirit of wisdom and understanding, the spirit of counsel and ghostly strength, the spirit of knowledge and true godliness; and fill them, O Lord, with the spirit of thy holy fear, now and for ever. Amen.

Then all of them in order kneeling before the Commissary, he laid his hand upon the head of every one severally, saying,

Defend, O Lord, this Child with thy heavenly grace; that he may continue thine for ever; and daily increase in thy Holy Spirit more and more, until he come unto thy everlasting kingdom. Amen.

Commissary. The Lord be with you.
Answer. And with thy spirit.

After the congregation had repeated the Lord's Prayer, and the Commissary read two more prayers from the Prayer Book, he concluded: "The Blessing of God Almighty, the Father, the Son, and the Holy Ghost, be upon you, and remain with you for ever. Amen." Then the newly confirmed partook of the Lord's Supper in their first communion.

CHAPTER III

Advanced Education

1

Tecumseh's more advanced education began in travels with his brother, Chiksika. His first lesson, introduction to warfare, provided an inauspicious beginning. Again in 1782 George Rogers Clark, together with Benjamin Logan, came up the Great Miami Valley on a punitive expedition. Again the Shawnees were not strong enough to offer effective resistance against the burning of their villages and their crops. Again they determined to save their people and abandon their villages, but first a party would go down to meet the point of the advancing Long Knives on the Mad River. This time Tecumseh, though still very young, was allowed to accompany his older brother. Their small party awaited the approach of the White Men. As the first ones came within range, the Indians opened fire. But a violent eruption of fire came right back at them. Tecumseh felt a new thrill as he discharged his musket, with what effect he knew not. But now the bullets cracked closely overhead. One caught Chiksika in the arm. As Tecumseh saw this, and bullets continued to crack close to his own head, his excitement of battle gave way first to fear and then to sudden panic. He threw down his musket and ran as fast as he could, back through the woods. Then out of range, he sat down and almost wept at the thought of what he had done. Humiliation

swept over him. The others of the party broke off the engagement and retreated in a more orderly fashion. Tecumseh was
relieved to see that his brother's wound was not serious, and
with his courage returning, he pleaded for another chance.
Chiksika reassured him that a young man such as he could be
forgiven for such behavior in his very first battle, but in the
future everyone would expect him to be a brave warrior worthy
of the Shawnee Nation.

Tecumseh grew a great deal in the following year, and when
the next opportunity came in April 1783, he, now fifteen years
old, was fully ready. This was an expedition to disrupt the White
Men's river traffic on the Ohio. For a time they were content to
harass the boats with long-range fire from the heights, in the
hope that this would discourage boatmen from continuing their
trips down the river. But this was not very effective. Moving
down to the river bank, the Indians lay in wait as a party of
thirteen White Men in a boat came ashore to make camp for the
evening. With determination the Red Men attacked. This time
Tecumseh was a model of bravery and skill. Defiant of close calls
of near death, he moved more speedily and more effectively than
any of the others in his party. When it was over, they had killed all
the White Men except one whom they held prisoner.

Chiksika commended Tecumseh for his action, and several of
the older warriors joined in. But now they moved to celebrate
their victory with a human sacrifice of the lone prisoner whom
they held. The young Tecumseh, remaining outside the circle,
felt a surge of misgivings as he sensed what was happening. He
watched in silence as the warriors went about their grim
business. While two or three warriors trimmed a young, sturdy
tree to form a pole, others piled wood in a circle all around, but
some distance from, the pole. When this was ready, three other
warriors carried out the unfortunate Pale Face, stripped him
naked, and with strong leather thongs and green vines tied him
securely to the stake. Deaf to his pleas for mercy, they then lit
the fire and watched with satisfaction as the flames grew higher.
Then, with long poles, they gradually pushed the fire closer and
closer to the prisoner until the flames licked at his feet. He let out
a blood-curdling scream as the skin on his feet blistered and
burst open and then turned black. Accompanied by even more
hideous screams, the flames worked up his legs. At last he fell
into the fire, and the warriors tossed up burning embers to cover
him. Now weakness diminished the volume of the outcries but

not the quality of their anguish and terror. At last the victim fell silent as the flesh continued to burn.

By now, Tecumseh was feeling a deep revulsion of what he saw. The stench of burning flesh made him sick. When the celebration finally quieted down a bit, the boy suddenly leaped to his feet. He stepped to the center of the group, raised his hand for silence, and then cried out in a voice which startled them all.

"Why? Why? Why do you do this?" The older men looked up in amazement.

The young Tecumseh went on, "Why do you do this? You think this is the way of brave warriors? It is the way of cowards! Our beloved Chief Black Fish advised against burning prisoners at the stake. I did not know that of which he spoke." He fingered his white quartz opawaka as he continued, "Now I know. And I know that this is not the way of our Master of Life, Manitou. I am young. I have not seen as many battles as you, but I know that it is not good to do this. This makes us lower than the White Men. Even when animals kill their prey they do not make them suffer. Are we lower than animals? Are we lower than the White Men? It makes me sick and ashamed. It does not honor our great Shawnee Nation. It does not honor our fathers. It does not honor Red Men. It is the way of the Evil Spirit, *Motchemenetoo*. It is not the way of *Wishemenetoo*. It is *not* the way of Manitou. Torture is degrading to the one who does it. Degrading, degrading! It is the way of the coward, not of the brave. It leads to weakness, not to strength. If we are to stop the White Man we must use the gifts of Manitou and become strong. Never, never again will I watch torture like this of a man or an animal. And I will never consider my friend any man who takes part in such torture. I will consider him a helper of *Motchemenetoo*, not worthy of being a true Shawnee warrior."

The warriors sat in stunned silence. They remained motionless for several minutes. Never had a young warrior ever dared to speak in such a way to his elders. But never had they heard anyone speak with such sincere and persuasive eloquence.

At last Chiksika arose and stood by his brother's side. In deliberate, measured words, spoken softly but loud enough in the quiet of all others to be heard, he said, "My little brother has spoken the truth. Who has not felt a certain shame after participating in a deed such as this? But who has had the courage to speak against it? Today no one fought more bravely or more effectively than Tecumseh. Now he speaks bravely for the way of

Manitou, for bravery in treating our enemies as well as in fighting them. We must be strong to fight the White Man and save our people and our hunting grounds. We must not degrade ourselves this way, because we become weak and cowardly. I am twelve years older than Tecumseh, but now I can learn wisdom from him. He speaks true. I accept his truth, and I vow that never again will I be a part of torture like this. Will others join me in this vow before Manitou?"

"I will." spoke up Frog Hunter, one of the older men. "Tecumseh speaks with wisdom. Some day he will be war chief."

One by one the others spoke up, "I will, I will," until all had made the vow.

That day Tecumseh became a man.

In the following years, while the Long Knives still harassed the villages, and it was necessary for the people to move repeatedly, building one new village after another burned one, Tecumseh remained close to Chiksika in hunting and fishing whenever possible, and in an occasional foray against White settlements. In June 1784, Chiksika, with Tecumseh at his side, led a strong band of Shawnees against Simon Kenton's Settlement on Limestone Creek, on the Kentucky side of the Ohio River. There they attacked the blockhouse, known locally as Hinkson's Fort. After only a brief fire fight, the defenders fled before there were serious casualties on either side, and then the Indians burned the blockhouse to the ground. Again Tecumseh was conspicuous in his bravery and accomplishment.

Three years later Chiksika and Tecumseh organized a sizable band of warriors from their Kispokotha division of the Shawnee for a long hunting expedition to the West. They moved out on horseback and went as far as the Mississinewa River where they paused for several months. Then they moved on across the Wabash and across the Illinois country to the Mississippi opposite the mouth of Apple Creek where they camped for another eight months. In the early spring during the Hunger Moon, they moved southward toward the Cherokee country. As they passed a point opposite Fort Massac on the Mississippi, they went off on a buffalo chase. Tecumseh was riding hard, ahead of the others, when his horse came so close to a buffalo that the shoulders bumped. The horse lost stride and lurched, throwing Tecumseh. In the fall he suffered a break in his right thigh. Chiksika presided over the setting of the break, but the mending required a delay of two months. Then all were ready to move southward again.

They stopped to visit with friendly Cherokees in Tennessee. Here they were told that the Cherokees were on the war path against White Men in the area, and they accepted an invitation to help their Red Brothers.

A few days later as the Indian party approached a small White settlement and fort in east-central Tennessee called Buchanan's Station, Chiksika said to his brother. "My young Brother, tomorrow we attack the White fort, and in the battle I will die. Last night I had a dream. The Master of Life came to me and said that I would join our father."

Dumbfounded, Tecumseh protested that it was not true.

"Yes, it is true," Chiksika insisted. "You know how many times when I have a premonition from Manitou it is true."

"My beloved Brother," pleaded Tecumseh. "I need you. Our people need you. If you think that you are sure to be killed, turn back. This is not the great battle for our people. Turn back!"

"No, my brother, I cannot turn back. We cannot escape our fate. Now you must lead our people. You will be their leader for the great battle."

The next day, at the call of the Cherokee chief, the attack began. It was a sharp engagement. The Whites stood firm, and the Indians persisted in their attack. Then about noon the battle quieted down. Chiksika crept up to the crest of the small hill where they were lying. A single shot rang out. He dropped, a bullet through his forehead. Tecumseh rushed to his side.

"My Brother, my Brother!" he cried. He took his fallen brother in his arms.

Chiksika looked up into the eyes of Tecumseh and managed a faint smile. "My Brother," he gasped in a low whisper, "you will be our leader. It is better that I die in battle than in a wigwam like an old squaw. My Brother, do not bury me. Let me lie here where the fowls of the air can pick my bones. I go to join our father."

Tecumseh lay there in deep sadness, unmindful that all the others were pulling back, unmindful of occasional bullets which still cracked overhead. Slowly, almost unconsciously he arose and began walking back, leaving his brother behind. He felt an overwhelming sense of loneliness. The sun which had seemed so bright only minutes before now was darkened, though there were no clouds. Sad of spirit, lonely of heart, he wondered if this must be the way of his whole life.

2

One morning during William Henry Harrison's fifteenth year, his father called him into his study in the Berkeley mansion. "Son," he said, "it is time for us to be thinking about college for you."

"Yes, sir," William Henry acknowledged with a note of excitement, "I hope I may go this year."

"Yes, the College of William and Mary, I suppose. That's where all of us have always gone."

"Father, I have been wondering. There's a new college called Hampden-Sydney over in Prince Edward County, and I was wondering if I might go there."

"Hampden-Sydney, yes I know of it. Nathaniel Venable has taken a great interest in it. It was empty during the war, but I understand it is operating again now."

"Yes, sir, and I should think it would be possible to study the same things there as at the College of William and Mary."

"I suppose so. Perhaps more. I have been thinking that it might not be a bad idea for you to study medicine. What would you think of being a doctor?"

"Oh, I don't know about that. Anyway, would it not be well for me to go to college first?"

"Yes, of course. But I understand that there is a professor at Hampden-Sydney who can help a boy get a good start toward studying medicine."

"Yes, sir."

"And anyway, I think the College of William and Mary probably is still full of Tories. They never did have much sympathy toward the Revolution and Independence over there. All right. Hampden-Sydney it will be."

"Thank you, Father."

That fall his mother worked to get his things organized, and the house servants packed his things in a trunk and bade a joyful goodbye to "Massa Billy" as his brother drove him over to meet the stage coach. It was an eighty-five mile trip on the stage coach and required most of two days. He stopped overnight at a wayside inn where he was able to get a hot supper and a featherbed with clean sheets for four shillings.

On his arrival at the college he was impressed by the big brick building, referred to locally as the "Red House," which, together with a few small outbuildings that housed the caretakers and provided space for the kitchen, comprised the facilities of the college. As soon as he was settled and properly introduced, and had paid his fees of sixteen pounds for a year's room and board and five pounds for tuition, young Harrison joined for the entrance examinations the other boys who were just beginning as students. Here he was required to show his acquaintance with "the English Grammar, Caesar's Commentaries, Saulust, Vergil, and the Roman Antiquities." This accomplished, he set about to make new friends and to learn more about the place.

He knew that Hampden-Sydney was supposed to be Presbyterian, but he found just as many Episcopalians. Everyone was fervently devoted to the Revolution and the new Republic. The course of study was based on that at Princeton which was not unlike the classical course at most of the colleges of the time. It emphasized "The cultivation of the English language, Geography, Mathematics, and Philosophy" which included natural science, and "a very accurate acquaintance with the Latin and Greek languages." Some study of French would be added later.

William Henry plunged into his studies as well as extracurricular activities with enthusiasm. He enjoyed his participation in the Union Society, a debating club, though he was a little disturbed by the religious fervor which gripped the campus. During his first year as a resident, an evangelical revival stirred the whole college. Visiting divines reported the students to be "very viscious and profane boys who treat religion and religious persons with great contempt and ridicule." But the president of the college, the Reverend John Blair Smith, delivered long sermons in which he was able to persuade some of his fourteen-and fifteen-year-old charges of the evil of their ways and to seek salvation through the doctrines of the new religion. Harrison's reports of these activities to his parents aroused little enthusiasm with these traditional Episcopalians. They shared the sentiments of Thomas Jefferson who wrote to a friend, "Hampden-Sydney . . . is going to nothing owing to the religious phrensy they have inspired into the boys . . . and which their parents have no taste for."

But these distractions aside, William Henry devoted himself to his studies. He developed a real passion for history, especially military history. He struggled without complaint to read Vergil and Tacitus and Thucydides in the original languages. And the reading of Charles Rollin's *Ancient History,* a work by the "Late Principal of the University of Paris," translated from the French and printed in eight volumes of small type, was like opening new vistas. Before he had reached the age of seventeen, he had read the whole thing three times. He was impressed with the opening of Book V:

> Of all the ancient nations, scarce have any been so highly celebrated, or furnished history with so many valuable monuments and illustrious examples, as Greece. In what light ever she is considered, whether for the glory of her arms, the wisdom of her laws, or the study and improvement of arts and sciences, all these she carried to the utmost perfection; and it may be truly said, that in all respects she has in some measure been the school of mankind.
>
> It is impossible not to be very much affected with the history of such a nation; especially when we consider that it has been transmitted to us by writers of extraordinary merit, many of whom distinguished themselves as much by their swords as by their pens; and were as great commanders and able statesmen as excellent historians.

And he read and thought about the Persian Wars, and the great battles at Marathon and Thermopylae and Salamis, and the great events of the Peloponnesian War, and the wars of Alexander the Great and his successors.

But after a couple of years, his father's doubts continued to grow. "Why not," he said, "come to Richmond and begin medical studies at once?"

William Henry was not really sure that he wanted to be a physician, and he did enjoy his studies. The religious revivalism disturbed him less than it did his father. He returned to Hampden-Sydney for the beginning of his third year but, acceding to his father's wishes, left in the middle of the year. He reported to his father that he was satisfied that he had developed a proficiency in "Belle lettres information and particularly in History," and that he was familiar with all the conflicts described by ancient authors "from Homer to Julius Caesar."

But now in his father's view, he should turn to more practical matters. He went to Richmond to begin his studies of medicine in the office of the most prominent physician of the city, Dr. Andrew Leiper, a graduate of the medical school of Edinburgh. Harrison read the physician's medical books and watched as he treated patients.

But the boy had leaped from the fire of religious damnation at Hampden-Sydney into the frying pan of abolitionism in Richmond. There, a Quaker by the name of Robert Pleasants with a following of Quakers and Methodists, had formed a "Humane Society" to agitate for gradual emancipation of slaves in Virginia. This appealed to young William Henry Harrison's natural humanitarian sympathies. He joined the "Humane Society" with a youthful fervor dampened somewhat by his hearing the denunciation of his own father by the leader of the Society. Pleasants denounced the elder Harrison's opposition to every bill for the abolition of slavery that had been introduced into the Virginia House of Delegates, and gave it as his opinion that Benedict Arnold's confiscation of forty slaves from the Berkeley plantation was a fitting and just punishment for one so committed to human bondage. All this was too much for Benjamin Harrison, and once more he sought a change of venue for his young son.

Still bent on a medical career for his son, Benjamin Harrison thought about his next move. Where should he go? Obviously to Philadelphia. There, at the University of Pennsylvania, was the seat of the only medical school in the country. There too was Dr. Benjamin Rush, probably the most renowned physician in America, who was an esteemed colleague in the Continental Congress and a fellow-signer of the Declaration of Independence. There, too, was his old friend, Senator Robert Morris, noted as the "financier of the Revolution." Harrison's second son, Carter Bassett, already was there trying to get a start in the mercantile business.

For this trip, William Henry boarded a sailing vessel at Jamestown. As he approached by the Delaware River on a Saturday afternoon, he was impressed by the city which spread out along its banks. On landing, he found a livery to take his trunk and walked up through the city. The streets were much broader than he had been used to, and the red brick buildings and houses were neater and cleaner. With a population of 40,000, the city was one of the two largest in America. Ships crowded its wharves, and goods crowded its warehouses. Harrison felt a certain thrill in walking through the streets of the capital city, noting the State House where his father had sat with the Continental Congress and had signed the Declaration of Independence. He was inspired by the sight of Christ Church whose 200-foot steeple tower and spire dominated the whole skyline. All these buildings were the largest he ever had seen anywhere. He felt a sense of busy activity and a feeling of being at the center of things as he watched the heavy traffic of horses and carriages and wagons and pedestrians.

He found his way to the house of Robert Morris where his father had arranged for a room. He was a little amazed to find this a very large brick house on High Street. It was next door to the Executive Mansion, the home of President and Mrs. Washington.

Robert Morris and his wife extended a cordial welcome to the new arrival from Virginia. The Senator read with interest a letter which Harrison had brought from his father and then called a servant to show the lad to his room and to help him get settled. Mrs. Morris invited him to join the family for dinner that evening though it was understood that ordinarily he would take his meals in his room or in the city.

Harrison's room was in the large rear wing of the house, a wing just as large as the front, which gave to the house the shape of a block T. His was a small room furnished with a single bed, a small table and straight chair, a wash stand with white bowl and water pitcher, and, most intriguing of all, a "Pennsylvania fireplace," sometimes referred to as a Franklin stove, which obviously would be far more efficient in heating the room than a conventional fireplace would be.

At dinner Morris took some pleasure in acquainting William Henry with Philadelphia and with the medical school. He invited the lad to accompany the family to church the next morning and then for a drive in the afternoon to see the city. All of this was most agreeable to William Henry.

The church was five blocks away, and they went by horse and carriage. Harrison was even more impressed than before with the magnitude and magnificence of Christ Church as he walked toward it with the others. He noted the tall spire at the west end with the golden mitre atop it, the mitre having thirteen stars for the thirteen states. He was impressed again by the very magnitude of the brick building with its two stories of round arched windows, and he found the high arches of the interior no less impressive. A few minutes after he had taken his place with the Morrises, he sensed something of a stir as President and Mrs. Washington entered and went to their pew, a specially decorated one at the front and center.

After the service Harrison had a chance to meet many of the parishioners. After most had gone, he and his hosts walked slowly through the churchyard.

"My boy," said Morris, "this is where the convention sat last year to organize the Protestant Episcopal Church in America. You might say this is where the constitutional convention for the Episcopal Church met just two years after the Federal constitutional convention met in the State House."

"Yes, sir, you know most Virginians are Anglican or Episcopalian."

"Of course. Now here in the convention they adopted the same prayer book that the Church of England had with very few changes. There are no changes in doctrine, just separate structure from England now. And they approved the feast days and so on—and they added a special American holiday, Thanksgiving, as well; England has one like it, but I guess this takes after the example of the Pilgrims in Plymouth."

"Mr. Morris, they had the first Thanksgiving at Berkeley, in Virginia before the Pilgrims even left England."

"Oh, oh, that so? Anyway it's official now in the Episcopal Church."

That afternoon Robert Morris alone took Harrison for a drive to see the city. Turning south into Sixth Street, they passed in the next block on the left the quarters of the State Department where Thomas Jefferson, the Secretary of State, had his office. Then they drove all the way around the State House yard.

Nodding toward the State House, Morris said, "There is where your father and I served in the Continental Congress and signed the Declaration of Independence, and where the new constitution was drawn. And that is where the Congress met for a while after the war, and then at various places until it ended up in New York. Even though the old Congress had very little power, still it did a few important things. I suspect one of the most important was the Northwest Ordinance just three years ago: the Northwest Ordinance of 1787, based on the proposed Ordinance of 1784."

"What's that?" Harrison wanted to know.

"Well that was for the organization of the territory northwest of the Ohio River. It provides a kind of bill of rights, prohibits slavery, requires just treatment of the Indians, provides for schools, and, maybe most important of all, it says that when there are enough people, new states—up to five of them—may be organized out of that territory and admitted into the Union on a basis of complete equality with the original states."

"That does sound important. Sounds as if they think the United States are going to grow."

"No doubt about it, my boy. That's one of the reasons I've been interested in western lands. There's bound to be a great future in the West."

Morris pointed to the building on the corner, west of the State House. "There is where the Congress will meet now. That was supposed to be the new County Court House, but when the Federal Government moved the capital here this year, that became the Congress Hall, with Senate on the second floor, and House of Representatives on the first floor. And on the other corner there, on the east side of the State House, is the new City Hall, but now that becomes the U.S. Supreme Court Building. And that large building just behind it is the American Philosophical Society. All three of those buildings were built just last year, and across the street on the corner is another new building which should be of special interest to you. That is the Library —The Library Company of Philadelphia—the first public circulating library, founded by Benjamin Franklin like so many other things around here."

"How does one become a member?"

"When it started it was 50 shillings to join and then 10 shillings a year. But you don't have to be a member to use it."

"You don't?"

"No, it's open to everyone. You can read there whenever it's open. If you want to take a book home you make a deposit equal to its value and pay a small fee; then return the book, get your deposit back and borrow another book."

Rounding the square, they turned east into Chestnut Street and then south again in Hudson's Alley. "We're going over Dock Creek now, the one the Indians called Cooconocon. It was all covered over five or six years ago. Now, there on your right is Carpenter's Hall where your father and I sat with the First Continental Congress back in '74. And now we swing around the corner here to Third Street and there on the corner of Walnut Street is Dr. Rush's house. I guess you'll be getting acquainted with him this week."

"Yes, sir. My father says he is a great physician."

"Maybe the best in the country, he and Dr. Shippens."

A turn back up to Chestnut Street took them past Clarke's Hall where Alexander Hamilton, Secretary of the Treasury, had his office, and then they went on leisurely down Second Street past William Penn's "Slate House," and then out West Pine Street for a distant view of the great Pennsylvania Hospital.

They returned northward via Seventh Street back to High Street where Morris pointed out John Graff's house where Thomas Jefferson had his lodging and wrote the Declaration of Independence in 1776. At the next principal street, Holmes Street, they proceeded eastward. At Fourth Street, Morris indicated the Old College building, site of the College of Philadelphia and now the University of Pennsylvania. He explained that the College of Philadelphia and the University of the State of Pennsylvania had just merged to form the University of Pennsylvania. He explained too that the medical school was in Armstrong Hall in the same vicinity.

As they drove along Holmes Street all the way to the waterfront, and then back on High Street, Harrison could almost feel his eyes popping. Williamsburg was nice, but it was nothing like this city, and Richmond, of course, could not be compared to either. He remarked on the broad streets, smoothly paved with pebbles, lined with brick sidewalks and with many street lamps and trees.

"Yes," Morris said, "these streets are twice as wide as the streets of London."

Hardly less remarkable were the shop windows. Harrison had never seen windows so decorated—cloth from India and England, draped over pottery in great swirls, the clocks and watches, the furniture, the hand tools, the clothing, and the bakeries and food shops. And the houses, some of which were as big as the plantation houses of Virginia. Even the small ones were neat and clean. He was also impressed by the orderliness that the city's plan itself emphasized. The streets were laid in a pattern perpendicular to each other so that the whole town was divided into small squares or rectangles, though large areas had been set aside for public buildings and squares. Streets running in a north-south direction, generally parallel to the river, were numbered east to west. Those running east-west—except for High Street in the middle—were named for trees. Within each block, houses were numbered according to a logical and uniform system.

Returning to Morris's home they passed directly in front of the Executive Mansion. This also was owned by Morris, and he and his family had lived there until he made it available to the President when the Government agreed to move from New York just this year. Morris also mentioned that the British General Howe had lived there during the British occupation in 1777, while

Washington and his men were freezing at Valley Forge, twenty miles away. Benedict Arnold had lived there the next two years.

Harrison wondered what Washington thought of that. But he was sure he was going to like Philadelphia. He was not altogether sure about the medical studies, but he thought that at least the city was going to be all right.

The next day he went out to find Dr. Rush and to get enrolled for his instruction. He found a very impressive-looking man who looked rather older than his forty-five years. Again Harrison learned that mention of his father was "Open Sesame." Rush was also a signer of the Declaration of Independence, and he retained a high regard for Benjamin Harrison even though he openly disagreed with him on the slavery question.

Young Harrison learned that the good doctor had been appointed Professor of Chemistry in the College of Philadelphia at the age of twenty-four. In 1789, he had become Professor of the Theory and Practice of Medicine, and now, with the merger into the University of Pennsylvania, he had been made Professor of the Theory and Practice of Medicine and the Institutes of Medicine and Clinical Practice. He was a pioneer in psychology. Although he had a multitude of duties at the university, at the hospital and in his office, he visited with young Harrison at length and indicated that he would be happy to be his sponsor for the apprenticeship, three years of which, in addition to the lecture courses, were required for a medical degree. Harrison expressed his gratitude for that.

Rush's comments broadened to add some of his own observations about Philadelphia, and then he mentioned one of his most notable patients, Benjamin Franklin. "When Doctor Franklin died last spring, this city and this state, and yes, the country lost one of its greatest men."

"Yes, sir, but I didn't know he was a doctor," said Harrison.

"No, he wasn't a medical doctor, but he received an honorary doctor of laws from St. Andrews, and in professional circles has been known as 'Doctor Franklin' ever since. Actually one of the students at St. Andrews, a Lord Cardross, sought his medical advice and later credited him with saving his life! He already had honorary master's degrees from Harvard, Yale, and the College of William and Mary. But just look at the things he has done —a leading printer and publisher and author, a founder of the Academy which became the College of Philadelphia, president of the board of trustees of the newly organized University of Pennsylvania, organizer of the state's militia, a scientist noted for his experiments with electricity, inventor of the Franklin stove, the lightning rod, and the stereotype; and God knows what else. He was active in the Continental Congress and the Constitutional Convention, and was a great diplomat in France, a negotiator of the peace treaty, a founder of the Pennsylvania Hospital, the Library Company, the Fire Company, and the Philosophical Society. He was also a great benefactor for education and President of the Commonwealth of Pennsylvania. On and on I could go."

"I must say that is very impressive indeed!"

"His funeral last April was the biggest I have ever seen. There were at least 20,000 people in attendance, the largest crowd seen in Philadelphia for anything." Then pausing, Rush inquired, "Tell me young man, how did you develop an interest in medicine?

"Frankly, sir, my father thought it would be a good idea."

"What do you think?"

"I'm not altogether sure, but I am sure that an opportunity to study with you would be a great one."

"Tell me, what are your chief academic interests outside of medicine?"

"History always has been my favorite subject," replied Harrison without hesitation.

"You know, Franklin was a moralist, and he thought that history was the most useful of the moral studies."

"Now I think him a greater man than ever."

"He had lots of interesting comments during these last three years when I was visiting him fairly frequently on account of his illness. For one thing, he never had used tobacco in any form during his eighty-four years. Do you smoke?"

"No, not really. I have tried it a time or two but never found it particularly attractive."

"And you from Virginia?"

"Yes, sir, and our plantation depends on a whole lot of other people's smoking and chewing."

"Franklin said that it seemed to him that the greatest part of the world's trade is carried on for luxuries most of which are injurious to health or society—tobacco, rum, tea, sugar, and Negro slaves. He also said that 'Quacks are the greatest liars in the world, except for their patients.'"

Harrison laughed at this.

"And something else he told me," Dr. Rush went on, "was that Dr. Pringle in England once told him that ninety-two fevers out of every hundred cure themselves, four are cured by art, and four prove fatal. I'm afraid he may be right about that. And once in a while he would offer an opinion for no particular reason. But he told me that he wrote a French friend after our Consitutional Convention to advise that they ought to call a similar convention in Europe to form a federal union of all the European states, as their good King Henry IV had proposed. And then he made another statement which rather bothers me as we look to our future in the West. He put it about in these words: 'During the course of a long life in which I have made observations of public affairs, it has appeared to me that almost every war between the Indians and the Whites has been occasioned by some injustice of the latter towards the former.'"

The medical course consisted of two series of lectures of sixteen weeks each. Harrison attended the first series in Anatomy Hall, a square brick building on Fifth Street. Dr. Rush explained that his favorite treatment for most inflammatory fevers, inflammation of the lungs, bladder, kidneys, throat and eyes, and for coughs, headaches, rheumatism, apoplexy, and epilepsy was calomel and bleeding—calomel as a cathartic, and the bleeding to relieve accumulations of blood resulting from a weakened heart, to bring out poisons, and to relieve pressure. As to the amount of blood that should be taken, Dr. Rush suggested ten to twelve ounces, but then he advised, "Bleed to syncope," that was,until the patient felt faint. In demonstrating the instruments for blood-letting, he recommended the recently developed spring lancet or lancet cup. This was a little brass box in which were mounted twelve pointed knives, half angled in a direction opposite the other six. These were held in place by a spring and released by a trigger as the physician held it tightly to a patient's side or arm. Then he applied a suction cup, activated by burning a piece of cotton saturated in alcohol to drive the air out, and then held it over the incisions to draw out the blood. When the spring lancet was not available, a more primitive lancet, made like a pocket knife, might be used, or leeches might be applied to suck the blood. Harrison also learned that it was advisable to cauterize wounds with an iron rod heated to a gray heat in order to prevent infection and stop excessive bleeding.

Although there was as yet no germ theory of disease, Dr. Rush had become convinced of the dangers of overcrowding and poor ventilation in hospitals from his experience as Surgeon General, and later Physician General of the hospitals of the Middle Department during the Revolutionary War. "During the war the hospitals claimed more American lives than the enemy did," he declared. He explained with approval how Dr. James Tilton had designed the hospital for the winter encampment at Jockey Hollow, New Jersey, in 1779-80. This consisted of a series of separate huts, where wards of five or six patients were separated from each other, and where wide windows and vents on the roof of each of the H-shaped log buildings provided good ventilation.

One further matter which he mentioned was inoculation for smallpox. This was a subject of great controversy, but in 1777 Washington had ordered that all the men under his command and local citizens as well at Morristown, New Jersey, should be inoculated. This was done by introducing smallpox matter into a person's arm or leg in order to induce a "mild" case of smallpox as a defense against a more serious case. Persons so treated were hospitilized or kept under close supervision in private homes during the time of the disease. The main advantage from the military standpoint was to infect the men at a time of inaction, and then to have immune troops ready when it was necessary to take them into active campaigns.

The more Harrison heard about all this, the less enchanted he was about a medical career. He did find it interesting, and perhaps useful, but he simply did not see himself in the role of a blood-letter.

CHAPTER IV

Love, Unrequited

1

On the death of his brother, Tecumseh automatically, without any question or any discussion, became the leader of the band of Shawnee warriors as they continued on their long trip to the South and Southeast until they reached southwest Georgia. Here was the site of a former Shawnee town. Here the mother and father of Tecumseh had lived for some years and, wherever he went, Tecumseh found friends among the Creeks.

But he remained restless. With his brother gone, and leadership of the group devolving upon him almost out of honor to his brother, Tecumseh felt a deep need to prove himself. He had to prove himself as a warrior simply for his own satisfaction, and he had to prove himself in the eyes of his comrades so that his leadership would have a firm basis in something more substantial than the honor of a brother. Beyond this, he wanted to gain the respect of the Creeks.

He welcomed any opportunity to lead a force against White settlers. With unusual skill as well as courage he excelled at the attack. Now as he went from one village to another, he was welcomed truly as a warrior rather than simply as the son of Pucksinwah and Methotaska. This accomplished, he was willing to settle for a time in the principal Creek village not far from the old Shawneetown.

Now nearly six feet tall, three or four inches taller than most of his comrades, with sturdy build and physique, he attracted attention wherever he went. His face was rather of an oval shape, and his dark eyes could sparkle in amusement or flash in anger. His black hair, cut somewhat shorter than shoulder length, provided a dark frame for his picturesque countenance. He usually wore a small ring in his nose, and a single feather rose from the back of his open turban, as much to distract gnats as for decoration.

Whenever he walked through the village with that distinctive gait, a walk of straightness in supreme confidence, punctuated by a slight limp which remained even after the mending of his broken leg, the eyes of every maiden turned upon him. The old men looked up to him with solicitation, while the younger regarded him with some apprehension and even jealousy.

The village chief, who had been a good friend of his father's, took a special interest in him. He told the young warrior that it was time for him to take a wife; he needed a squaw to look after him. Tecumseh's reaction was generally negative. He walked through the woods alone, circling about for miles, thinking, thinking. He was sure that his place was back with his people north of the Ohio. He must return one day. He was sure too that he would be involved in many battles. Should he take a wife? Of course most of his comrades did. But he had misgivings. When his thoughts should be upon how to deal with the White Man and how to lead warriors in battle, he might be thinking about his wife and might even worry too much about his own safety. Then he no longer would be a good warrior.

One afternoon when he returned from one of his "thinking walks" he saw the old friend of his father coming toward him with a young Indian woman. He stopped short. Indeed this was the most beautiful woman he ever had seen in all his travels.

"Tecumseh, my son, this is Mineshelana. She will be your squaw."

If he ever was to have a squaw, Tecumseh was sure that this would be the one. But he held in check any reaction of enthusiasm.

"My Father, you do many good things for me, and this must be the best. But I must return one day to my own people. I must be ready for war to help them against the Long Knives. I must not take a squaw."

The Indian maiden dropped her eyes as though in disappointment and bowed her head in the sadness of rejection. Then she lifted her head and with sparkling eyes caught Tecumseh's. In the meeting of her eyes, Tecumseh could sense a leap of electricity which went all through him. He allowed himself a trace of a smile, which in turn brought a broad smile to her lips.

"My dear Mineshelana," he finally said, "you are a good woman, but I cannot take you for my squaw. I must leave one day to return to my people."

"I will go and be one of your people," she said softly.

"No, I have much work to do. I must go away many times and for many moons."

"Yes, Tecumseh must go one day. But when he is here I will be his woman. If he is doing his work, he needs a woman to make ready his food, to sew his shirts, to make his wigwam a place to rest so that he will be strong. When he is here I am his woman."

The old chief smiled with a twinkle in his eye, nodded his approval, and turned away.

Without further words, Tecumseh reached out his hand to take the hand of Mineshelana and walked with her to his wigwam.

With complete understanding and full acceptance of the situation, Mineshelana fell to work to serve Tecumseh. She brought in new skins and new benches and table to make the wigwam comfortable. She ground corn, baked bread, roasted meat, and performed all the other chores to provide an attractive home base. Her skill in sewing made the handsome Shawnee more handsome than ever. She sewed for him a shirt and leggings of the finest, softest doeskin, and a neat, carefully measured and shaped knee-length tunic of the same material. Hems and seams were sewn in regular stitches, and she cut fringes all along the outer seams and lower hems of all the garments. For his feet he had soft inner moccasins of buckskin, and outer moccasins—or more nearly boots—of heavy buffalo hide. On his head he wore his favorite kind of turban with the usual single eagle feather. He carried in his belt a sharp, nine-inch knife, and his favorite weapon, a war club made of a smooth, oval-shaped stone the size of a double fist, fitted with a sturdy hickory handle, the whole, warhead and handle, covered with thick, tightly fitting rawhide.

Tecumseh was pleased with all the help Mineshelana gave. He greeted her more with gratitude than with passion, though as time went on he could not help feeling a real friendship and a growing affection for her. As the time approached when he decided he must go, he found it more difficult to anticipate the separation, but he held to his determination. Mineshelana plainly dreaded the thought of his departure, but she made no protest.

"My dear Mineshelana, soon I must go," he said. "And," he repeated his affirmation, "when I go, I must go alone."

"It is well," she replied sadly but bravely. "It is as you say. I help you when you are here. When you go, I stay. I understand."

"You are a good woman, a very good woman. For many women it is difficult for them to understand their man's work. They want him to stay in wigwam when he must be out to protect the village. They want him to stay in village when he must go far away to make war to help protect all his people. Some want him to be a little dog instead of a brave warrior. But a good woman helps a man to be a good man. A good woman can help a good man be a great warrior. You are a good woman. Always, I will remember Mineshelana." Tecumseh grasped her bare hands in affection.

2

After several Sundays, during which William Henry Harrison sometimes accompanied the Morrises to services at Christ Church, and sometimes did not, he decided one Sunday to go off on his own to St. Paul's. It was a cool, sunny day. Harrison walked briskly down Third Street toward Willing's Alley and the church. For daily wear he now favored pantaloons, but on Sundays and special occasions he wore breeches and silk stockings, protected by a dark great coat and a cocked hat on his head. Not yet eighteen years old, Harrison had attained a full height of six feet two inches. His slender build and almost frail appearance masked a constitution of vigor and vitality. His slender, handsome face showed a kind of tender firmness. His nose was almost Roman, and a shallow cleft lent a special character to his chin. Large, dark eyes, accented by dark eyebrows, were his most immediately noticeable feature. He always remained clean shaven, with only sideburns descending from his hair just as far as his ear lobes. His brown hair was cut short and clipped close on the neck. He brushed it forward with an angle toward his right eyebrow, the forelock brushed off his forehead to the right without any perceptible part.

Arriving at the church early, he took a turn around the yard and then entered. He found an empty pew. Arising from his prayer and taking his seat, he casually looked about the sanctuary. This was smaller and less elaborate than Christ Church, but with white pews and woodwork, white walls and gold trim, and round arched windows, it was, in its way, almost as beautiful. His eyes, dropping down from the decoration of the church, fell upon two young ladies seated apparently with their parents, across the aisle and two pews to the front. From then on, his eyes kept drifting in their direction. He found himself looking more at them than at the priest. He did notice on the other side an old friend of his father's, Thomas Willing, but the recognition of an old acquaintance held less fascination for him than the making of a new one.

At the conclusion of the service as people greeted each other outside the door, Harrison made himself known to the Willings, and then maneuvered an introduction to the young ladies who had caught his eye. One, a slender blonde with blue eyes and a dimpled smile, was named Jane Connelly. Her friend, somewhat taller with a rather more buxom build, with chestnut brown hair and brown eyes, was Sarah Cutler. Their fathers were business associates—merchants—and the families lived in the same block of West Spruce Street.

Harrison accepted a dinner invitation with the Willings and had a pleasant afternoon in exchanging family news, but he could not get his mind off Jane Connelly.

On Monday he sent off a note to her to invite her to attend the theatre on Saturday evening, but received one in return saying that she would be away the next weekend. On Wednesday he sent a note inviting her to accompany him to a musicale the following week, but after some delay, he received a note saying that she would have to help her mother with some entertaining that day.

On the following Sunday he returned to St. Paul's. Jane Conelly was not there, but Sarah Cutler was, and she was nice enough to visit with him for a few minutes after the service.

On Monday he wrote another note to Jane Connelly asking about possibilities for the week. On Wednesday he was in the library and happened to notice Sarah Cutler in the adjacent room. They went out to the parlor and this time had a longer visit. On Thursday he had a note from Jane to the effect that she would be so very busy all the week that she saw no possibility, but she was grateful for his inquiry and hoped there might be another occasion when circumstances would be more favorable.

Young Harrison's church attendance, previously sporadic, now became regular. On the following Sunday he arrived early and occupied a pew alone. The church began to fill, and soon all the pews were occupied. To his pleasant surprise, Sarah Cutler came in and sat beside him. He looked around quickly to see if Jane were with her. Seeing that she was not, he contented himself with the situation as it was.

On Monday he sent a note to Jane Connelly to invite her to an afternoon musicale on the next Sunday. On Wednesday afternoon he chanced to meet Sarah Cutler at the library, and this time he spent more time in the parlor with her than he did with the books that he had intended to read. As she took her leave she invited him to come to her house on Sunday afternoon to have tea with her and her mother. Spontaneously he accepted with pleasure. And then remembered to pray that Jane Connelly would not accept his invitation for the same afternoon. A note from Jane the following day reassured him on that point.

The next Sunday morning he waited around for Sarah to arrive for church, and then they found a pew together. After the service he walked home with her while the rest of her family went by carriage. He said this would be a good chance to learn how to reach her house so that he could find his way easily that afternoon —though in Philadelphia, with its rectangular pattern of streets and regular numbering system, it was easy to find any address.

The afternoon dragged on as young Harrison waited for tea time. As it was, he set out so early that he had to walk twice around the block to let sufficient time pass for a proper entry.

The tea was all that he expected, and more. Sarah actually was looking beautiful in a dark blue and yellow dress, somewhat shorter than the general style, and with only a small bustle rather than the more extensive hoops seen on more formal occasions. Her mother too was charming. The father was away on a business trip to New York. Younger brothers and sisters remained upstairs. Heat from a Franklin stove made the room comfortable though Harrison thought that somehow this lacked the warm hospitality of an open fireplace.

As they sipped their tea and ate small cakes, they talked at length about family and friends. Harrison could see that the ladies were favorably impressed when he told them that he was living at the home of an old friend of his father's, Robert Morris. They were impressed again when he mentioned that Thomas Willing, a leading banker of the city, also was an old friend of his father's, and again when he said that he was studying medicine under Dr. Benjamin Rush. They were intrigued by his description of his family home at Berkeley, and they expressed great sympathy with Virginia.

When they had finished their tea, Mrs. Cutler called for a servant to take out the tea cart, and then she went upstairs to leave the two young people alone. Harrison found himself no less impressed by Sarah's conversation. He did discover that she was a year and a half older than he—at which point he became vague about his own age while he found it all the more intriguing to become acquainted with a woman of such vast experience and obvious charm.

Harrison really had never paid much attention to girls before. Of course as a child he had shared school with his sisters and friends, and he had known the neighbor children. Vaguely he had rather assumed that when the time came he probably would marry a Carter or a Byrd, or a Randolph, though he never really had thought much about it. Now he was discovering that a young lady could be delightful company.

On Monday he did not write a note to Jane Connelly. On Wednesday he met Sarah Cutler at the library, this time by design rather than by chance, at least on his part. In their conversation, she affected a deep interest in history; she showed a keen interest in history, but even her questions betrayed her complete lack of knowledge of the subject. Yet he did not mind that at all. He was always glad for any chance to talk about history, and he welcomed an opportunity to instruct such a willing pupil.

On Saturday evening Harrison took Sarah Cutler to the theatre. He hired a carriage and driver and arrived in good style and in good time at six o'clock. Sarah looked more beautiful than ever as they walked into the lobby of the Southwark, on the south side, west of Fourth Street. They found their box and settled for a performance of *King Richard III*. They had good seats, assured by arranging for one of Mr. Morris's servants to come down at five o'clock and hold them. They were high enough to be over the convulsive pit, close enough to see well, and outside the dripping of the candles from the chandeliers. Presently the musicians in front began playing. Except for a few apple cores and orange peelings that went sailing toward the stage, all became calm as the big green curtain rose for the first act.

Harrison showed more interest in the play than he felt. He suspected Sarah of doing the same thing. At intermission they went below for a cup of coffee in the coffee house where ladies were especially welcome.

"You certainly are bold to be bringing me here," she said in mock dismay.

"What, to the coffee house?"

"No, to the play."

"To the play? What do you mean?"

"Don't you know that until just last year it was illegal to put on a play in Philadelphia?"

"Illegal? I don't understand."

"Why do you think this theatre is way down here on the south side? It's out of the city limits just so plays could be performed."

"I just don't understand," said Harrison in surprise. "In Williamsburg we've been having plays performed off and on since 1716. Even the students at the College of William and Mary were putting on plays over fifty years ago. Surely no one will dispute that Shakespeare's plays are the greatest literature in the English language—maybe in any language."

"Of course, but up in Boston that's all it is supposed to be, and here too until just recently. It was all right to read Shakespeare's plays but not to perform them."

"That doesn't make any sense. Shakespeare's plays are for performing, not just reading."

"Of course. Of course they are. They do perform them now, even in Boston, but to do it they have to be billed as 'moral lectures.' My uncle Monnaseh, the one who is a clergyman in Ipswich, says they must call *Richard III* 'The Fate of Tyranny,' and *Hamlet* 'Filial Piety.'"

"Amazing!"

"But I guess President and Mrs. Washington are making some changes around here. They were regular theatre goers in New York, and they come here fairly frequently. But, probably thanks to their influence, we shall be having a big new theatre soon. They are going to start building it next year, up on Chestnut Street."

"Good. There. I think I hear the manager's whistle. Time to get back to our seats."

Harrison found his interest picking up in the later acts, though he was more interested in the lady beside him. He nudged her gently as he recognized some favorite lines:

True hope is swift, and flies with swallow's wings; kings it makes gods, and meaner creatures kings.

And then he clapped his knee at his favorite line of all:

A horse! a horse! my kingdom for a horse!

And then he quoted the psalmist, "'The horse is a vain hope for deliverance, for all its strength it cannot save.'"

"Shh!" Sarah whispered.

On Wednesday afternoon they met again at the library. At sunset they went out and, finding it warm for that time of year, decided to go for a walk. Actually they were wanting more privacy than a coffee house or library parlor provided. Twilight brought privacy where none had been before. Presently they found themselves walking through the yard of Christ Church. They looked up at the tall steeple, silhouetted against the darkening blue sky. They walked on to the burial grounds and paused briefly at the grave of Benjamin Franklin.

"There was a great man," remarked Harrison. "Maybe the greatest in America—at least outside of Virginia."

"Virginia, indeed." she laughed. "Yes, he made this city what it is in many ways, and he surely was the greatest influence on the whole Commonwealth since William Penn himself."

"And look at his influence on the whole country."

They strolled on, quietly, until they came to a bench where they sat.

Sarah looked up to see the first star of the evening. "The first star that comes to sight, I'll have the wish I wish tonight," she said.

"What did you wish?"

"You know I can't tell, or it wouldn't come true."

"Do you believe that?"

"Course I do."

"Look again; see if you can find another."

As she looked, he stole a kiss. The reception being agreeable, he offered another. "I already got my wish," he whispered.

"So did I," she confessed even more softly.

"As Shakespeare wrote, if we dare quote Shakespeare in Philadelphia, *That full star that ushers in the even.* That is the evening star tonight. See how bright? It is Venus. And John Milton wrote, *The evening star, Love's harbinger.*"

Sarah smiled audibly and then said, "I must be going."

William Henry thrilled anew at each breath of her perfume, the touch of her hair, the rustle of her dress. They walked through the streets, hand in hand. The lights of the many street lamps now competed with the appearance of new stars. They arrived at her house all too quickly for him. At the front gate she offered another kiss before going in to greet her mother.

Taking his leave, Harrison walked back toward his own place. This distance was all too short for him to review the evening in his mind as many times as he wanted, too short for him to sort out his thoughts and his feelings.

Daily he returned to the library, hoping that Sarah might be there. As he read his medical books, he could not concentrate. He even turned back to the reading of ancient history in an effort to find some relief from Sarah's omnipresence. But even there, it seemed that on every page there was some reference to serve as a new reminder—tales of Helen of Troy, or Aphrodite, and Eros, or Cleopatra, and all the rest. He was besieged by a joyful torment altogether new to him. And in his growing infatuation for Sarah Cutler, he forgot that he had even met a Jane Connelly.

Once when he was with his brother, William Henry sought advice on these serious matters. "Carter, how can you tell if it's the real thing?"

"Oh, Billy, my boy, you can tell all right. If you have to ask, then you know it is not. At least that's what Ben always said, though I'm not really sure about that. Sometimes I have felt sure about someone one day and sure about someone else the next."

"Well, I guess I would be sure about just one at a time. But then what if she says she isn't sure?"

"Then I guess you've had it."

Through the winter William Henry seized every opportunity to be with Sarah. One Sunday afternoon they went to a musicale. On another they went to a public lecture, a boring lecture made so only because they wanted to get away, to be together. They made the rounds of respectable coffee houses and drank tea and chocolate. On another Saturday evening they went to another play, *She Stoops to Conquer* (advertised in Boston as "Immoral Education"), and were agreeably surprised to see General and Mrs. Washington in the presidential box. They even took in on occasion what Dolly Madison called the "chief social channel" —the "assemblies" at Oeller's Tavern on Chestnut where Harrison was careful to observe the dress code: "No gentleman admittible in boots, colored stockings, or undress."

Christmas was time for special festivities this year. William Henry enjoyed dinner on Christmas Eve with the Cutlers. At noon on Christmas Day, he and his brother had dinner with the Willings, and on Christmas night they had dinner with the Morrises. Each outdid the other in their servings of roast goose, ham, beef, dressings, potatoes, beans and peas, fruits and English plum pudding.

On New Year's Day they joined what appeared to be most of the city in going to the Executive Mansion for the traditional reception. The President and Mrs. Washington greeted each guest cordially with a bow and a word of welcome, but without shaking hands. Harrison learned that Sarah had been to one of Mrs. Washington's "drawing rooms" on Friday afternoon recently when Mrs. Morris, seated beside Mrs. Washington, was being referred to as the "second lady." Standing in line at the reception was tiring, but they thought how much more tiring it must have been for the Washingtons.

With the coming of spring, William Henry and Sarah's activities took more to the out-of-doors. One Saturday they went for a picnic. William Henry arranged for a boat on the Schuykill, and they rowed slowly up the river to Fairmount. There they tied the boat, took their ground cloth and picnic basket and walked up the open, grass-covered hill. Butterflies and bees were out. Birds flitted in the shrubs, and only an occasional cloud drifted overhead. They ate their delicious lunch of fried chicken, cabbage, sugar cookies, and white wine. This finished, they just rested a while, looking at the sky. They imagined what figures the clouds made. She would see the shape of a gown, or of a building, or some person; he would see the shape of a continent, or a horse, or a ship.

He stole a kiss. "You stole that." she protested. "You must give it right back."

And he did.

"This has been such a wonderful day," he said, "that it makes all the previous days wonderful too. May I have a souvenir to remember it by?"

"What kind of souvenir?"

He hesitated and then said, "A lock of hair?"

"I have no scissors."

"I have my knife. Look, you see there is a little curl there out of place."

"Take it."

And he did.

Well ahead of the cool of the evening, they gathered their things and walked haphazardly back to the boat. With less effort, they floated back to their starting place.

As they walked back to her house, William Henry dared make one further request for a souvenir. "Do you have a portrait, a miniature, that I might have?"

She didn't say anything, but when they arrived at her home she told him to wait. She ran into the house and returned shortly with a small box which she pressed into his hand. He opened it. It was a miniature, a beautifully done likeness of her. He pressed it to his heart, thanked her, and bounded away.

A few weeks later, weeks interspersed with other meetings and activities—sometimes to the neglect of his medical studies—Harrison suggested that they go up to Trenton on the following Saturday.

"That would be too far and too long for too little reason, wouldn't it?" she objected. "That's nearly thirty-five miles. It would take all day, and I don't know anything special about Trenton."

"I don't know anything about it either except that George Washington crossed the Delaware and surprised the Hessians there. But it's not Trenton we want to see, it's the ride."

"The ride? How are you going, horseback or carriage? I can't imagine anybody wanting to go seventy miles by either means just for the ride."

"But this is neither by horseback nor by carriage, though we might take the stage back."

"Don't tell me you're going to row a boat up there. I couldn't find enough chicken to last that distance."

"No, but you're getting close. We're going by steamboat."

"Steamboat! Have you lost your senses or something?"

"Haven't you heard of John Fitch's steamboat?"

"Oh, yes, I've heard Father say that Fitch had built some kind of contraption where he hooked long oars to a steam engine to make it go through the water."

"Oh, he has a better one now. He has one where the steam engine is hooked up to a paddle wheel on the stern, and he is taking passengers as far as Trenton. He says someday he'll be taking them up all the big rivers, and someday even across the ocean."

"Well, I doubt that. But if you're sure his boat won't explode, or won't catch fire, I'll go."

"Good, good."

The steamboat ride was a great adventure. The steamer did lots of puffing and stalling, but once under way it made a smooth voyage at about eight knots. Harrison was excited about the future for this thing. They made the trip in four hours and had good views all along the way. At Trenton there was little time to see anything, just time to catch the stage back to Philadelphia.

On his return to his room, Harrison found his brother there waiting for him. He could see by the sad expression on his brother's face that something was wrong.

"What is it?" William Henry asked.

"It's Father. He's dead."

William Henry gasped and then held to his brother's shoulder. "Have you told Mr. Morris?"

"Yes."

"Are you going home?"

"I don't think I can. The funeral is probably already over by now, and I am awaiting the arrival of a ship for some goods I have been expecting."

"Carter, I think I may try to go back for just a few days."

"All right, if you can arrange it that would be a good thing."

William Henry felt a dreadful need to be at home. He had not been very close to his father until just the last few years, but he did have great respect for him, and he felt a sense of deep family loss. He especially felt the loss that this would mean for his mother. He felt an urge to go home at once. But in another way he did not want to return. To be there would only confirm the loss which at a distance could seem only a temporary separation. In a way this would make his loss all the more painful. But he was always very close to his mother, and he wanted to be with her just now. He went in and talked it over with Robert Morris who gave his approval. The next morning he went to the livery and hired a horse and saddle. He went around to tell Dr. Rush that he would be away a few days. Then he rode over to Spruce Street to tell Sarah. Shortly thereafter he was on his way southward.

It took him five days to reach Berkeley. His appearance at the family home brought forth a new outburst of tears from his mother, but her delight in seeing him made the whole trip worthwhile. He visited the fresh grave of his father in a field not far from the house. He visited with his oldest brother, Benjamin, with his sisters, and with friends and relatives from the area. After three days he returned to Philadelphia.

Not long after his return he received a letter from his brother, Benjamin. William Henry learned that he had received the several hundred acres of Sherwood Forest estate from his father's will, but this could not be counted on to yield any substantial cash, and many debts remained to be paid. Benjamin stated that the financial means were not there to allow continuation of a sufficient allowance to enable William Henry to continue in his medical studies.

William Henry's first reaction was one of disappointment and a feeling of let-down. But as he thought about it, he realized that his main disappointment was not at discontinuing his medical studies, but rather at the thought of leaving Philadelphia. He already had more medical education than most of the doctors in the country even if he did not have a degree. But he was not at all certain he wanted to go into the practice of medicine.

He went around to see Sarah and told her of his plight. She obviously shared his disappointment. He was more anxious than ever to see her but knew that curtailing his financial security would curtail the theatre, the balls, and other such activities for him. Yet he could still look forward to meeting in the library, going to the coffee houses, and evening strolls. But he sensed a subtle change in Sarah's attitude. Meetings became less frequent, church attendance less regular, times together with less sparkle.

Several days passed without his seeing her at all. He tried to study but couldn't. Then one afternoon a note came. It was in her hand:

Dear William:

When I first started keeping company with you I had some confidence in a possible future for us together. Now I realize that your plans for the future diverge from mine, and I think it best for us to bring to an end, not our friendship, but our expectation of anything beyond that.

You are a fine person, and I have enjoyed knowing you. I have benefitted from your intelligence and your knowledge. But it would be unfair to continue in a way which could lead only to disappointment.

Therefore I must bid a very fond farewell.

Harrison was thunderstruck. His world was tumbling down. The sun stood dark in a cloudless sky. The signs of spring retreated under a cold wind on a warm day. With a sensation of numbness he went out into the street and began walking. He scarcely noticed the passing horses and carriages. The steeple of Christ Church no longer carried any inspiration. He walked until he had come to his brother's place.

Carter was sympathetic, but he failed to share William Henry's sense of tragedy. "Come on, let's go down and have a glass of ale," he said.

They walked up the street and encountered Charles Darby, a young business associate of Carter's, also known to William Henry, and he joined them.

"Where to my lads?" asked Carter. "How about the Indian Queen? Any objections? Then the Indian Queen it is."

They walked up High Street to Fourth. In front of the tavern they met another mutual friend, Cedric Robertson. They all went in and found a round table in a side room where they were the only patrons. They lit the candle on the table and had a glass of ale all around, and then another. Carter Bassett lifted his glass.

"Here's to the memory of Sarah," he said.

"To Sarah," said Darby, "whoever the hell she is. What is it, Carter, one of your company's ships go down?"

"She is one of the belles of the city that Billy had an eye for, but now he's thought better of it."

"Bravo!" called Robertson as he joined the others in raised glasses, "to the memory of Sarah, sweet Sarah."

"Billy, have you got a likeness of her?" demanded Darby.

William Henry slowly withdrew the miniature from his pocket and handed it to Darby.

She is a comely lass," the latter admitted, "but plainly she's not for you, not for you." He held it up for the others to see, and then lay it near the center of the table.

Robertson held up his hand for silence and then slowly recited: "My lads, do you remember the *Amphion Anglicus?*:

> *Sabina has a thousand charms*
> *To captivate my heart;*
> *Her lovely eyes are Cupid's arms,*
> *And every look a dart.*
> *But when the beauteous idiot speaks,*
> *She cures me of my pain;*
> *Her tongue the servile fetters breaks*
> *And frees her slave again.*

"Bravo! bravo!" came in general response.

William Henry took out the "Dear William" letter and folded and twisted it lengthwise, then lit the end of it by the candle on the table. As he got up and walked across the room with it, Charles Darby called out, "Look, look! Billy is still carrying the torch for Sarah!"

"It's the torch of liberty," he responded as he ambled deliberately over to the fireplace where he threw in the burning paper.

Robertson disappeared into the other room and returned with a handful of cigars. "How about a cigar, everyone," he said and started passing them around.

At first William Henry protested feebly. "No, thank you, I don't smoke," he said.

"Come on, this is a celebration. How are your Virginia plantations going to prosper if you don't smoke tobacco? Here, have a good Connecticut cigar!"

William Henry laughed and took one. Each in turn lighted his cigar from the candle.

Robertson said, "Ben Franklin's *Poor Richard* says *Love, cough, and smoke, can't well be hid,* but maybe we can hide the first with the other two. William gave an involuntary cough as he took his first draft. Everybody laughed and blew billows of smoke into the air.

Looking at the miniature portrait on the table, Darby said, "Let's darken those pretty brown eyes, just a bit," and he blew a puff of smoke over the portrait. The others followed suit.

"And I don't much like the way she does her hair," said Robertson. Again, puffs of smoke all around.

Carter Bassett added a line: "And again as *Poor Richard* says, *Love and tooth-ache have many cures, but none infallible, except possession and dispossession,* and he also says, *Three things are men most liable to be cheated in, a Horse, a Wig, and a Wife.* Remember that, all of you."

Soon the smoke was so thick that one could not see the table top. Only the candle retained visibility, standing there like a light-house in a dense fog.

"There, blown to obscurity," said Darby.

"Aye," said Robertson, "lost in a fog. She'll run aground and break up at any moment."

Robertson added this advice: "My daddy always said don't get hooked by the very first woman you meet. You've got to look around a little, make some comparisons."

"Sure," said Darby, there's lots more fish in the sea. She's not the only one."

"Nor the only tree in the forest, nor the only pebble on the beach," Carter Bassett added.

After the smoke had cleared in silence, William Henry turned to his brother and said, "Carter, I think I'll join the Army."

"My God, Billy, things aren't that bad!"

"Well, I've been thinking about it. I can't go on with the medical course, and I have to do something."

"Would you cast your lot with those cut-throats and ruffians for two dollars a month?"

"Oh, I would go for a commission."

"How are you going to do that?"

"By requesting it—through the right people."

"Through whom, for instance?"

"George Washington, for instance."

"Well, there's nothing like going to the top. But even if you had a commission, what future would there be for you—off to the wild frontier, fighting Indians? You'd disappear into a world more obscure than this table covered with smoke. And they don't have any lighthouses out there. Why don't you look for something around here first?"

During the next few days William Henry made the rounds of the mercantile houses, looking for a position as a clerk. He met a lack of success corresponding to the half-hearted effort he put into it. There were a few opportunities, but none aroused enthusiasm. With each desultory inquiry he became more certain that the Army was the place for him. And certainly it was not out of tradition for one with English antecedents. Many of the officers of the British Army and Navy came from younger sons of the gentry.

He knew he must clear his plans with Robert Morris, for one of his father's last requests had been for Morris to serve as his guardian.

Young Harrison approached the Senator one afternoon in his study and revealed his hopes of getting a commission in the Army.

"Never!" was Morris' immediate response. "I would be doing your father a great disservice, a great disservice indeed, to approve of anything so rash."

William Henry was crestfallen as he saw clearly Morris' negative reaction. He thanked the Senator for his concern and his help.

Morris went on, "We'll see if we can't figure a way to keep you in medical school. Perhaps we can arrange with Mr. Willing for a loan."

"Sir, I do not want to start a career in debt. Anyway, I just don't think I'm meant to be a physician."

"Well, let's see what we can figure. By the way, another old friend of your father's is in the city this week—Governor Henry Lee."

"Light Horse Harry," thought Harrison, "He may be able to help."

The next day Harrison sought out the Virginia governor at his City Tavern lodging. Lee was immediately sympathetic with Harrison's idea of going into the Army. "It's a great thing to give service to the country," he said. "And I'm sure you have the ability to do well. Billy, I'll speak to Washington about it myself, see if we can't get you that commission."

Harrison let a few days pass and then decided he would try to see Washington personally. Harrison was not overawed by Washington. After all, the General had been a visitor at Berkeley on a number of occasions, and he was known as a good friend of his father's. Harrison did hesitate to impinge on the time of the Great Man, but his determination to look to his own career overcame any doubts he might have entertained. He went around to the Executive Mansion and inquired of a secretary. He returned the first of the week and to his delight found that the President would see him on Thursday morning.

At the appointed time a young man serving as secretary ushered Harrison in. Washington greeted him with a warm smile and a handshake.

"Come in, Mr. Harrison," the President said. "I was very sorry to hear of the passing of your father. He was a fine man. Did a great service in the Continental Congress."

"Yes, sir, he always was interested in the government of Virginia and in the Continental Congress."

"And of course he was one of the signers of the Declaration. It has been fifteen years since then. I guess you were not very old then."

"No, Sir."

"There was only one point on which your father and I had a major disagreement—and that was a major one."

"What was that, Sir?"

"His opposition to our Federal Constitution. It always seemed a little strange to me that men like him and Patrick Henry, leaders in the Cause for the Revolution, then opposed having a strong central government to make our independence real."

"Yes, Sir, I guess they were concerned above all else for Virginia, and they were afraid of substituting a strong central government here for the government of the King and Parliament of England in dominating Virginia, and possibly interfering with her rights just as much. And I guess Father feared Northern domination of the South. He thought that giving the Congress the power to impose tariff duties on our imports could lead to serious trade restrictions. In fact he feared that under the Constitution the states to the south of the Potomac might become little more than appendages to those to the north."

Washington smiled indulgently and then said, "But I think some of our other fellow Virginians have seen to the question of interfering with rights—Mr. Madison, in guiding through the compromise for a balancing of powers, and Mr. Mason, who put together a "Bill of Rights" which I think will satisfy most of those who had reservations. In fact those Amendments are before the Virginia legislature this year, and, if they ratify it will put them into effect."

"Yes, Sir, that is very promising."

"Can you imagine what chance thirteen separate states would have on a continent dominated by France, Great Britain, and Spain? Always remember, my boy, in unity there is strength. Remember Aesop's fable about the *Bundle of Sticks?* There he said, as the moral of the story, "Union gives strength.""

"Yes, Sir, I remember that."

"But, my son, there is one thing for which I shall always hold your father in highest esteem. He was a strong opponent of ratification of the Constitution in Virginia, but once the vote was taken, even though it was close, he accepted it. I cannot say as much of some of the others. Henry and some of his associates resolved to try to overturn the result. They began holding secret meetings, planning in effect to plot revolution. Your father heard about a big meeting that was planned for late one night to discuss the question of how to proceed. He appeared at the meeting and took the floor. He spoke very earnestly without any of the humor he was famous for. He told the group that he shared their misgivings about the Constitution, but he urged them to accept the result, and if it appeared that any changes were needed, to seek these by the regular process of amendment which had been provided. The group agreed to his position. He may have saved the Union right there."

Harrison smiled. "Yes, Sir. Now I hope I can have a chance to take the oath to defend that Constitution."

"Yes, yes, I understand from General Lee that you are interested in a commission in the Army."

"Yes, Sir."

"Why do you want to do that?"

"Well, Sir, maybe it comes from the old English custom of younger sons going into the Army."

"Surely you don't feel bound by that."

"No, Sir, but I think I could do well in the Army, and I think that would be the best way I could serve my country. My father was in the Continental Congress; my oldest brother was in the Army during the Revolution."

"Yes, that is commendable, and I certainly would not be one to discourage a young man from serving his country or from seeking a career in the Army. Commendable, highly commendable. But what of your qualifications? Usually a period of apprenticeship is necessary," Washington inquired.

"Yes, Sir. I think I have a good education from Hampden-Sydney College and with nearly a year of medical education—although I'm sure now I do not wish to be a physician, I think I learned a lot in those studies. And on the plantation I learned to ride and shoot well."

"And you speak well. But you know, William, the Army's main duty these days is to fight the savages in the West."

"Yes, Sir, but Caesar led his armies against barbarians."

"Do you see yourself as a Caesar?" The President smiled broadly.

"Oh, no, Sir, I just meant that great armies often have been called upon to fight barbarians."

"But you have no experience upon the frontier."

"No, but I can ride and I can shoot, and I can give directions as well as follow them. And, Sir, two or three years on active service in the West should overcome my present inexperience."

"Yes, I dare say. Well, let me think it over, and I'll let you know very soon. You know, son, I have to be very careful of everything I do in this position. No one has ever done it before. I have no precedents to guide me, but everything I do becomes a precedent for my successors."

It was summer now, and the heat was beginning to show signs of the oppressiveness of which it was capable. One afternoon Mrs. Morris invited Harrison to have lemonade out on the courtyard behind the house. He was glad for the refreshment. Hettie, the Morris' daughter, was there, looking cool in a light dress. Harrison had spoken to her a few times, had seen her now and then, but had never paid her much attention. Somehow, at seventeen, she had seemed rather immature, especially when compared with someone like Sarah Cutler. But now he noticed that the slender, blue-eyed, brown-haired girl had a certain beauty of her own, and her reserve was in refreshing contrast to his previous encounter.

In the weeks that followed, Harrison overcame his impatience in waiting for word from the Government by seeing Hettie Morris from time to time. She had a quality for growth and expanding interests which intrigued him. He wondered why he had not noticed this before.

At last, one day about August 20, a message came for him to come to the War Office. On his arrival, he was handed his commission by Henry Knox, the Secretary of War himself. When Harrison saw Knox who weighed nearly three hundred pounds, he was reminded of his own father. He looked at the parchment. It was decorated with impressive art work—an eagle at the top, ornamental flags at the bottom, and decorative representations of cannon, muskets, drums, bayonets, powder horns, swords, and tomahawk. It was signed by President Washington and Secretary of War Knox and was dated August 16, 1791. Now he was an ensign in the United States Army. His assignment was to the lst Infantry Regiment. He was to join the regiment at Fort Washington, out on the Ohio. This was it! But first he was to remain in Philadelphia as a recruiting officer for a few weeks and then to lead a body of recruits to the West.

He ran to show his commission to Hettie Morris. She had not even known that he had applied. She was surprised but voiced no note of disapproval. With greater hesitation he brought himself to go up and show the commission to Senator Morris. The Senator had to control himself to keep from exploding, and finally, wishing a luke-warm "good luck" turned as though to wash his hands of the whole matter.

Harrison reported to the local barracks down near the Delaware and took up his duties as recruiting officer. Sometimes he would lead out a little detail of fife and drum to attract attention to the glamour and opportunities of the Army. During other hours he learned the basics of military drill from an old Revolutionary War sergeant.

During the afternoons and evenings of the few weeks yet remaining, he took his last opportunities for rounds of conversation, dinners, drives, and dances, sometimes with a friend of a friend, sometimes with his brother and other friends, as often as he could, with Hettie Morris. A subtly growing infatuation for Hettie Morris almost made him forget all about Sarah Cutler.

CHAPTER V

Baptisms of Fire

1a

After nearly two years in the Creek country of Georgia-Alabama, Tecumseh determined that it was time to rejoin his people north of the Ohio. In September, 1790, he collected eight of the faithful Kispokotha Shawnee warriors who had been with him throughout this sojourn and set out on horseback. Allowing themselves side excursions in pursuit of game and pausing frequently for fishing and swimming, they passed through eastern Tennessee and western Virginia at a leisurely pace until they approached the Ohio valley.

Here one night as they lay on their buffalo skins in a circle around a camp fire, sleeping after a long day's journey, Tecumseh sensed the approach of danger. Ever so faintly came the sounds of feet moving slowly through the leaves and brush. He sensed that they were surrounded by Long Knives and about to be attacked. Very deliberately, he arose and stretched and yawned. As he picked up a small stick and threw it on the fire, he spoke in a low, conversational tone, "Long Knives have made a ring around us. Keep eyes closed. Get tomahawks ready. When I give cry, all rush in direction of smoke through White Man's ring. Then follow me through woods." Just as deliberately he took another stick of wood and went to the other side of the fire to toss it on as he repeated his instructions.

Then he returned to his buffalo skin and just as deliberately lifted it and shook it gently as though straightening his bed to resume his sleep. Suddenly and quickly he whipped the buffalo skin into the air, whirled about and threw it over the fire. This brought instant darkness as he gave a loud war-whoop and, with lifted tomahawk, rushed in the direction of the smoke. As one man all the others leaped to their feet and rushed after him, spreading out on either side of him. Five White Men fell as the Indians broke through the ring. Tecumseh continued running through the woods for a distance of perhaps fifty yards as the others followed in single file. Then he led them in a wide semicircle around to the opposite side of the camp where, at his call, all turned, and in a broad line with loud shouts they rushed the other side of their assailants' circle. Seven more of the Long Knives fell to the tomahawk. Now it was the White Men who thought themselves surrounded, and the eighteen survivors of the party of thirty fled in panic. No Red Man had been injured.

Without further incident Tecumseh's party continued the next day to the Ohio River and crossed opposite the mouth of the Scioto. A few days later they were visiting the villages near the headwaters of the Mad River, and then they continued northwestward to the village of Wapakoneta on the Auglaize where Tecumseh was greeted with a warm welcome by the Shawnee Chief, Black Hoof.

Here he heard with satisfaction how Shawnee, Miami, and other warriors, under the leadership of Blue Jacket and Little Turtle, had routed a detachment of General Josiah Harmar on the St. Joseph River just a few days earlier and had sent Harmar and his whole army in headlong retreat back to Fort Washington on the Ohio. After suffering the forays of George Rogers Clark, Bowman, and others time after time, and to see their villages burned and crops destroyed, now, at last, they had turned the Long Knives back in defeat.

But as always, when one attack by the Long Knives had been turned back, another could be expected. Pending some word to that effect, Tecumseh contented himself with visiting with his brothers and sisters, calling upon the elders of the villages, giving them a hand in daily chores from time to time, renewing friendships with boyhood friends, and hunting and fishing. He was glad to see Charles Ruddell, a White captive who was still living with the Kispokotha people and who had been a good friend as a young lad. Tecumseh could see that Ruddell was torn by the continuing strife between White Men and Red Men. Often he expressed a wish that a way could be found to live in peace, but he had little hope.

"We do not wish to fight the White Man just for sport," Tecumseh maintained, "We want to live in peace. Anyone can have peace if he is willing to give up everything to the demands of his attackers. No, no, Little Turtle and Blue Jacket have found the only way to have peace. We must be strong enough and wise enough to drive the Long Knives away from our hunting grounds and our villages."

"That will never be, my friend," was Ruddell's response. "If you destroy five hundred of their warriors, they will return with a thousand."

Soon they learned that the Governor of the Territory, the White Chief himself, was preparing to return with three thousand warriors.

A steady stream of spies and informers brought reports on the movements of Maj. Gen. Arthur St. Clair and his lieutenants as they prepared what obviously was to be another invasion of the Red Men's country. Plans for Indian resistance received the encouragement of British agents. Although the British had ceded to the new United States all the territory south of the Great Lakes by the Treaty of Paris in 1783, the British continued to occupy posts at Detroit and other places along the lakes indisputably in U.S. territory. They did this on the pretext of trying to enforce payment of debts agreed to by the United States in the treaty but never met. These served as centers for Indian trade— including weapons and ammunition as well as other goods in return for furs and hides—and, with the support of the Indians, provided a buffer against American incursions into Canada.

On July 1, the British agent, Alexander McKee, met with a council of chiefs and elders from many tribes at the Miami Rapids. Here, after considerable delays, leaders had gathered from the Shawnee, Delaware, Wyandot, Ottawa, and Potawatomi tribes, and even some representatives from the Six Nations of the Iroquois. The British agent, while counseling peace, did not exactly discourage war.

"You should make peace with the United States." he said. "But you should do so only on terms consistent with your honor and interest. Whatever you decide to do, tell me what you need." He then presented large quantities of goods for the tribes—cattle, corn, tobacco, and gun powder and musket balls.

Tecumseh, at twenty-three, was not yet in a position of leadership with his tribe, but he listened eagerly and with excitement to these goings-on. In his mind the decision should be war, with all the Indian brothers helping.

In mid-September the greatest council of all met at the juncture of the Auglaize and the Maumee. Here the overwhelming sentiment was for war. The Long Knives must be stopped! After considerable discussion all agreed that they should stay with the leadership that had served so well in the previous year against the force of Harmar—Little Turtle of the Miamis as the chief commander, with Blue Jacket of the Shawnees as second-in-command. Crane, chief of the Wyandots would be next in line, and then Pipe, chief of the Delawares, and White Loon who would lead the Weas and Mohawks. Other tribal units who would participate included the Ottawas and Mingoes, Potawatomis, Kickapoos, Piankeshaws, Kaskaskias, and Eel River Miamis. Tecumseh was thrilled at this display of unity among the tribes, and he was delighted when Blue Jacket asked him to lead a party of lookouts to spy upon the invading army.

Within a few days Tecumseh could report that the American General had made his headquarters at Fort Hamilton, about twenty-five miles north of Cincinnati and Fort Washington. At the end of the month the Indian scout could see that about 1,500 men had assembled there—about half the number they had feared—some with horses, and with three or four small cannon. He could see the army start to move on October 4, footsoldiers, horsemen, pack animals, cattle, and even some women following. After ten days of marching, it halted for ten days to build another fort. One night Tecumseh and his band crept up to the fort and stole twenty horses tethered to its very walls. Tecumseh could also see that some of the men were turning back. He learned that some of them, for some reason, had been executed by hanging.

Near the end of October as the Long Knives came within fifty miles of the Miami towns, Little Turtle led his force of one thousand Indian allies out to meet them. Early in the afternoon of November 3, Tecumseh found that the enemy's army had made camp along the eastern fork of the Wabash River where that stream, not far from its headwaters, was no more than a creek thirty or forty feet wide. The soldiers were crowded on a narrow rise with swampy land on two sides and woods all around, and with some of their men on the other side of the creek. With these reports, Little Turtle and Blue Jacket went up to have a look for themselves. On their return they called a council of the leaders. Little Turtle explained that now was the time to attack before the Long Knives could reach the villages and when they were camping in such a small place. During the night the warriors would move around both sides of the camp, and careful to be unseen, they would surprise the Long Knives with an attack at sunrise. All on both sides huddled around fires during the night for there were flurries of snow and thin layers of ice coated the water pools.

Shortly after sunrise just as the Americans were leaving their reveille formations, bands of Indians, wildly painted and wildly shouting, attacked the outer line. Quickly they chased those Long Knives back across the creek and then surrounded the main camp. From concealed positions behind logs and trees the Indians poured deadly volleys of musket fire into the ranks of the White soldiers who remained in the open, in close formation, firing helplessly toward an unseen enemy. Little Turtle had instructed his warriors to pay special attention to the Long Knives' officers, which they did with devastating effect. All the officers and most of the men of the artillery were picked off before they could get their guns into effective action. Repeatedly the White soldiers would form and make a bayonet charge, but the Indians would flee into the woods too rapidly to be caught, and then as soon as their pursuers stopped would turn about, open fire again, and become the pursuers. By noon it had become a complete rout. Tecumseh, continuing to observe and report, was able to see much of the battle, though he remained on the periphery of the fighting.

The Indians pursued for four miles and then turned their attention back to scalping the dead, tomahawking the wounded, and gathering booty. They found more than 600 dead White Men, and they knew that many of those fleeing had been wounded. Less than fifty Indian warriors had been killed. In supplies the Indians gained horses, tents, guns, powder, axes, clothing, and blankets. And in warfare they gained confidence.

1b

Eager to get away from Philadelphia only a few weeks previously, William Henry Harrison, on discovering a new attraction in the city, now was searching for ways to remain. But he could delay his departure no longer. With the company of eighty recruits he had helped enlist, he set out for his foot-march across Pennsylvania on September 20.

"The goose honks high!" shouted the young ensign, full of anticipation. He called for all to join in singing, "The Girl I Left Behind Me" and "Yankee Doodle," and whatever improvisations anyone could develop. That enthusiasm lasted about a day.

The weather was even and temperate; the road was rough and irregular; the autumn foliage in the Alleghenies was delightful; the infrequent inns were sombre. But it was good to be walking across the country. Harrison's mind wandered; here he was an eighteen-year-old ensign, and already he was leading a military force on a march which would rival some of those of Caesar or Xenophan with his Ten Thousand Greeks. As he moved farther west he came upon birds and trees not previously known to him, and he kept a lookout for hostile Indians though he did not really expect to encounter any. They followed the road that General Forbes had "improved" on his march with British and Colonial troops to Fort Duquesne in 1758, via Lancaster, Carlisle, Shippensburg, Fort Loudoun, Raystown, and Loyal Hannon.

The thrill of adventure wore off in another two days. After four it was boring. Harrison could feel the protest of muscles unused to such exertion. But he kept up a good front and held to his determination not to be outdone by any of these recruits. Each mile represented a new conquest but gave ever more grim warning of the miles yet ahead. The road was dusty, muddy, rocky, never smooth; it was up hill or down hill, seldom level. Now with each mile the young ensign felt less like Xenophon leading his Ten Thousand and more like Phidippides in the last hour of his run from Marathon.

Harrison's interest picked up as he approached Pittsburgh at the forks of the Ohio. There he would have a few days to rest and to make arrangements to get his men on a boat for the voyage down the great river to their destination, Fort Washington, just beyond Cincinnati.

Pittsburgh was not a large town—it had something like 130 houses—but it had busy shops and stores filled with merchandise. It was the port of embarkation for the West. On the waterfront Harrison saw all kinds of river boats, coming, going, unloading, loading, and under construction. These included "Pirogues"—large, flat-bottom boats with oars and poles for moving upstream; "flatboats"—about 20 feet long and 10 feet wide, with a hull rising three to five feet above the water, and a house in the middle, and guided down stream by sweep or long oar at the stern (often a family would go down stream on a flatboat with livestock and furniture and then use the boat for lumber for building at the destination); scows—large flatboats, sometimes referred to as "arks"; "broadhorns"—like scows, but with sweeps both on the bow and the stern for steering down stream; barges—from 30 to 70 feet long and seven to twelve feet wide, equipped with mast, sails, and rudder, and with passenger cabin at the stern and a "fort" in the center, with loopholes for firing weapons; "Ohio packet boats"—larger barges, sometimes twice as large, and "keel boats"—built with heavy timber keels down the center and used mainly for freight. Most of the larger boats also towed a "skiff"—a small, flat-bottom boat which could be used for taking small parties or small quantities of goods ashore.

Harrison found Major Issac Craig, deputy quartermaster and storekeeper, and arranged through him for supplies and transportation down the river. Hoping for a barge, Harrison was assigned to a broadhorn, and that seemed attractive enough after the days of walking. Here the men found plentiful food, mainly fish from the rivers and game from the banks, but with good supplies of vegetables and fruits as well. A three-man crew guided the boat and looked after the passengers. It was a delightful voyage. Just drifting with the current, the boat gave no sounds other than the light lapping of water against its sides. The maples and oaks and elms and nut trees on the hills were coming into full fall color. An occasional clearing in the forest revealed a farm or village. It took eight days to reach Marietta, the town on the Ohio shore named for Queen Marie Antoinette. Here the boat stopped for several days to take on more food supplies and await the arrival of additional freight being sent downstream. This gave the military party a chance to do a little hunting and fishing as well as to become acquainted with some of the local taverns. Here Harrison also learned about the fabulous farmland where, it was reported, a tract of seven acres gave a yield of 700 bushels of corn. He also heard about the massacre of all the settlers at Big Bottom, just a few miles from here, by Indians on the preceding January 2.

The voyage resumed. It took another two days to reach Point Pleasant where the Great Kanawha entered the Ohio and nine days more to reach Limestone. By now "October's bright blue weather" was fading into gray November. By day no clearings, no smoke from settlers' cabins were to be seen, by night no light from cabin windows or campfires.

At last, on the morning of a bleak, cool November day, they approached their destination. The boatmen were eager to explain the area to the newcomers. One pointed over to the north bank and to a stream flowing into the Ohio. "That there is the Little Miami River," he said, "and just a few miles on down, the Great Miami comes in. This country is known as the 'Miami slaughter-house' from all the Indian killin's that used to go on around here. That little village there by the Little Miami is Columbia. They first settled it three years ago just about now."

"And that must be Cincinnati," said Harrison as another village came into view.

"Yep, that's it, settled 'bout the same time as the other, but it was called Losantville until General St. Clair changed it to Cincinnati last year. They say he named it for the Society of the Cincinnati, whatever that is."

Now Harrison could offer some explanation. "The Society of the Cincinnati is an organization of the former officers of the Army who served in the Revolution, headed by General Washington himself, and the honor of membership is passed on to future generations through the eldest sons. Of course, General St. Clair is a proud member. The Society takes its name from Cincinnatus, the famous Roman farmer and leader who was called from his plough on several occasions to lead the Roman army in the successful defense of Rome."

On a hill just beyond the village and overlooking the river was Fort Washington. Its walls gleaming white, with a big flag, the Stars and Stripes, floating over it, presented a striking sight. Harrison felt a little thrill of anticipation as he saw it.

"Yep, that's Fort Washington, all right," the river man went on. "Now young fella, how do ya reckon it got its name?" Harrison laughed, and the man continued, "Just a ways on down, near the mouth of the Great Miami, is Judge Symmes' settlement which he calls North Bend."

By now the boat was headed for the shore and soon was tied up. Harrison led his men off through little streets to the fort. The village consisted of a general store, some taverns and shops, and not more than forty or fifty houses—all log—and a population of not over 300. The greater number of cabins were in rows along the hillside and along the water front, with half a dozen others along Deer Creek and a few back in the woods. Fort Washington stood on an adjacent hill, its main gate toward the river. Proximity robbed it of some of its glamour, but it was attractive and sturdy enough. It was in the form of a square formed by two-story barracks, built of hewn logs. Each side of the square was 180 to 200 feet long. The barracks were connected at the corners by high pickets and blockhouses, also of hewn logs. These corner blockhouses extended ten feet beyond the barrack walls so that guns emplaced within them could rake the walls. On the north side of the fort were artificers' shops connected to a blockhouse by high palisades. On the south side in front of the main gate was a fine esplanade, about eighty feet wide and extending all the way across the front. A low paling separated it from the open ground which sloped to the river. On the east side of the fort were the officers' gardens. These obviously were very attractive and productive in season, and neat summer houses were in their vicinity. All sides of the fort itself were white-washed, so that it escaped the appearance of its true ruggedness.

As Harrison and his party walked quickly through the streets to the fort, they sensed an air of consternation. People with grim faces were scurrying about in disorder and disarray. On report-ing to his 1st Infantry Regiment in the fort, he soon found why. Streams of refugees were pouring in from a disastrous expedition that General St. Clair had led against the Indians to the north. From small clusters of officers he learned what had happened. His own regiment had been spared because the General had sent these regulars back to bring up the supply trains and to arrest deserters, so the militia had had to bear the brunt of the battle. There were more than 600 killed, and 280 wounded, and some-what to his surprise, Harrison learned that 56 women had been killed—over one-fourth of the 200 who had gone along as com-pany laundry women, wives, unofficial cooks, or just plain camp followers.

From a couple of pack horsemen who had survived, Benjamin Van Cleve and Thomas Irwin, Harrison learned more details. "They say that Red-headed Nance, her red hair flowin' behind her, led the flight through the woods and brush to get away," Van Cleve related. "But when I caught up with her she was walkin' at a painful gait and cryin' over the loss of her baby. She was walkin' beside a corporal who was cryin' because his wife had been killed, and the only survivin' officer of the artillery who was just in a plain daze. We all made it to Fort Jefferson a little after sundown."

"Oh, God, that artillery was the worst thing I ever did see," Irwin interjected. "I guess they just stood there, and time and again the Indians came back to pick them off; their guns never did do no good. When I got up there, their dead was all over the place. God! And they all had been scalped, for God's sake. I tell you all them skinned heads all over the place, it looked like punkins in a December corn field!"

Van Cleve resumed, "I don't know why the General let himself get caught like that, but one thing I'll say, he wasn't any coward. Two or three horses were shot right out from under him, and his coat was full of bullet holes. But he kept tryin' to turn them back. Finally he decided the only thing to do was retreat. The only horse he could find was one of our pack horses, and he got on that. Colonel Drake finally forced the Indians back from the road a little, and this made an opening where as many of the men as could poured through like a drove of bullocks. But then the Indians came back and attacked the rear. Major Clark tried to get what was left of his battalion to cover the retreat, but then he was killed."

Irwin interposed to continue his version, "After that things went wild. The men took after Red-headed Nance as fast as they could. It looked like their only choice was to run fast or get shot or tomahawked, and they turned into a real buffalo stampede as they tore through the woods. They threw away their muskets or anything else that might hinder them. Horses, men, women, all were mixed together, and I was running as best I could right with them—my pack horse was too slow for me!"

"My uncle and a good friend, a lad named Bonham, were with me in the pack groups." Van Cleve resumed. "My uncle got shot in the wrist, and the ball went all the way up to his shoulder, but he got away. Bonham got shot through both hips, so he couldn't walk at all. I found him a pack horse and got him up on it. He couldn't bear for the horse to do anything but walk, and he told me to run on ahead. I ran on ahead and looked back to see that the Indians were still coming. They were closin' in on Bonham. He saw the danger and tried to make the horse run, but the horse lurched, and Bonham fell off. The Indians had him with a tomahawk almost as soon as he hit the ground. I ran on for another two miles, I guess, when I came upon a boy who was about to fall from exhaustion and was cryin' for help. I grabbed him and pulled him along for another two miles. By then we both were ready to drop. Most of the horses had passed us, but I saw a couple comin' with three men on one of them and two men on the other. I stopped the second one long enough to get the boy on, and he got away with them. I saw some poor wretch on the ground, suffering from a shot in the knee. I tied my handkerchief around the wound, but I 'spect the Indians got him. Now I was gettin' a little afraid that I wasn't goin' to be able to make it. My upper legs were crampin' so that I couldn't hardly walk. Most of the others had passed me now, and I was gettin' close to the rear, which was no place to be, 'cause I could hear the Indians still comin' with their tomahawks. Then I pulled my shoes off, and the feel of the cool ground on my feet kind of revived me, and I set out again at a trot, wonderin' how long it would be before it came my turn. Pretty soon I was back up in the middle. The Indians stopped chasin' and that is when I caught up with Red-headed Nance, and we all walked the rest of the way."

"But couldn't the 1st Infantry help in that situation?" Harrison asked.

"Oh, they were comin' all right, but too late. Much too late. We met them before we got back to Jefferson. But by then there was nothin' they could do."

"Isn't it likely that their approach is what made the Indians stop their pursuit?"

"No, I don't think the Indians knew they were comin'. I think it was just that the Indians stopped to pick up loot. They always love loot. If it hadn't been for that, I don't think any of us would have gotten out alive, and they might've come all the way to here."

In the next two days Harrison familiarized himself with the area. The returning soldiers were seeking escape in drinking and brawling in the village taverns. Harrison saw more drunken men in those two days than he had seen in all his life before. "What kind of an army is this?" he wondered. "What am I getting into?"

The "old timers" among the young officers at the fort would not let the new ensign rest before filling his head with Indian stories. The chief narrator was a "veteran" lieutenant, while the others stood around to accompany him like a Greek chorus.

"Those Shawnees are wild, really wild," he began. "Heard about the massacre up near the mouth of the Scioto last spring?"

Harrison shook his head.

"They got forty-nine men, women, and children. First was Elijah Strong and a party of seventeen discharged soldiers who were walking along the north bank of the Ohio in that vicinity. They were all shot and scalped, and then butchered with tomahawks. About the same time the others had come along in boats and had been lured ashore by two White prisoners who were claiming they needed help. Then about the same thing happened to John May and his party of fifteen others. But they saved the worst for Jacob Greathouse and his party. They took him and his wife and their twelve children and two other young men and a girl who were with them. They took the young ones, including all the kids, and then lashed them to trees. They stripped them naked and then beat them to death with hickory sticks, built fires around their feet, and scalped them. But for Greathouse and his wife, they had a special treatment. For each one they stripped a sapling, and they tethered one of them by the neck to one of the trees and the other to the other tree. Then they stripped off their clothes. They slit open their bellies and tied the end of their guts to the trunk of the tree. Then they beat them and dragged them round and round the tree so their insides would be wrapped around the trunks. Then they scalped them and set fire to them.

"But why, why would they do that?" Harrison asked, incredulously.

"Well, they say it was 'cause Greathouse had killed Chief Logan's pregnant sister seventeen years ago. Do you want to hear more?"

"Yes, yes, go on," said one of the bystanders in the "chorus". "Tell him about Colonel Crawford, Colonel William Crawford."

"Yes, Crawford," the lieutenant said, "ever hear of him?"

"Yes, I have heard of him, but I never heard what really happened to him," answered Harrison.

"Let me tell you. That was nine or ten years ago, I guess. Anyway, Crawford was leading a force of militia volunteers against the Wyandot villages when he was attacked by a larger force of Wyandots and Shawnees and Delawares, led in fact by British rangers from Detroit. The militia fled, and a good many were killed or captured. Crawford himself, together with a man by the name of Knight, was captured by Delawares. Those captured by the Wyandots were simply tomahawked, and their heads stuck up on poles. But the Shawnees and Delawares wanted more entertainment. About a hundred Delawares, with a few Wyandot onlookers, gathered around. The renegade White, Simon Girty, was another spectator. While Knight watched so that he might see what his own fate would be, the Delawares stripped Crawford naked and tied his hands behind him. Then with a rope about six feet long, they secured him to a high stake. They built a fire several yards away, just big enough to scorch him. Then they threw red embers under his feet, and as he leaped back and forth around the stake, they shot powder into him which would ignite as it reached his skin, and they poked burning fagots against him. He stood the torment for nearly two hours, constantly praying to the Almighty for mercy. Finally he fell down. Then they scalped him and poured burning coals on his bare skull. Even then he was able to get up and walk around the post another time or two before he died. All the while the Indians, including the Wyandots, were laughing and clapping their sides. And so was that damned renegade, Girty."

Harrison involuntarily ran his hand over his scalp as though to make sure that it was still there. "And I suppose they did the same thing to Knight after he had watched all that?"

"No, actually they decided to send Knight up to the Shawnee villages to be burned, but on the way he escaped."

"Was there any special reason why they would want to torture Crawford?"

"Just Indians' delight, it seems to me, although they apparently thought he was responsible for the massacre of the Moravians some time before, but he really wasn't."

"What was that?"

"Oh there was supposed to be a bunch of Indians who had been converted by the Moravian missionaries, and they had been taught that they had nothing to fear from their White Christian brethren. Then some of the White men thought they had something to do with the murder of some White settlers near Pittsburgh, so they raised some militia to go after them. They got about two-thirds of these Moravian Indians rounded up into two houses, all the men in one house and the women and children in the other, and then the militiamen took a vote on what to do with them. They decided to do away with them, so they entered the houses and dispatched every one of them, ninety-six of them all together. That's been nine or ten years ago, but nobody has forgotten it."

"There seems to be no end to this sort of thing," Harrison observed. "Do the Indians always kill their prisoners?"

"No, sometimes one will escape, and sometimes there are young ones who just stay. Now you take this fella Slover who was another of Crawford's party who was captured. He had been captured by Indians over by the Kanawha when he was only eight years old. His father was killed. He had two little sisters who died on the way to the Indian villages, and his mother was later ransomed. For twelve years he lived with the Miamis and the Shawnees. He adopted their way of life and made no attempt to escape. Then one day he happened to be at Fort Pitt where he ran into some relatives who finally persuaded him to return to his own people. He later became a good Presbyterian, and he served in the Continental Army during the Revolution. Now after he was captured this time, he was taken around to various villages to witness the torture of his comrades. And then it came his turn. They tied him to a stake and built a fire under him. And then would you believe it, a heavy rain suddenly came up and doused the fire. They postponed it until the next day. During the night he was kept tied, without clothes, in a wigwam where three savages guarded him and chided him about what was in store for him. About dawn they fell asleep, and he was able to make his escape. Still naked, he caught a horse, grabbed a piece of old rug for a saddle, and galloped off with only the halter to control the horse. He kept the horse running for about seventy-five miles until late that afternoon when it fell dead. Then Slover got up and ran on foot. He tried to lie down for a little rest but jumped again when he heard pursuers in the distance. He could not stop for long at night on account of the mosquitoes. For six days he kept up his flight, living on berries and a couple of crawdads which he caught until he reached Fort Fincastle, what they now call Wheeling. He knew the Indian languages, and he reported that he heard them say at one of their councils that they would take no more American prisoners but would kill them all, and some British agents from Detroit appeared to approve that resolution."

"But I must mention another captive. That's Blue Jacket. He was captured by the Shawnees when he was seventeen. He was adopted into the tribe and now is one of their chiefs. In fact, I understand that he was one of the leaders in that attack against St. Clair—Blue Jacket, a White man!"

"Well, I'll be damned!"

"And you've heard of Simon Kenton?"

"I guess everyone has heard of Simon Kenton and Daniel Boone."

"You know, he saved Boone's life once, shot the Indian just as he was about to let ole Dan'l have the tomahawk. The Indians have captured him too, but they can't keep him. They can't kill him and they can't keep him. One time some years ago they captured him, and they took him all around their villages. They made him run the gauntlet eight times, and they tied him to the stake three times. Finally they gave up and ransomed him."

"Run the gauntlet? How do the Indians do that?"

"Well the first time was at one of the villages they call Chillicothe. They had dragged him to that place all bruised and bleeding, and told him that now he would have a chance to run the gauntlet. The men and the women and the boys, each carryin' a tomahawk or a war club or a stick, formed a line a quarter of a mile long. At the far end was a man with a drum and beyond him the council house. If Kenton made it to the council house he would be protected, at least until they could decide what to do with him next. At the sound of the drum he sprang forward and then suddenly took a sharp turn to the side, the whole mob flying after him. He darted around, escaped all but one or two blows and reached the council house. Later he was taken on tour of all the villages. At each one he either was tied to the stake to be beaten and switched by the women and boys, or he was forced to run the gauntlet, sometimes with sand thrown into his eyes, and sometimes having muskets loaded with powder only fired to singe his body. But, as you know, he survived it all."

"Which shows it can be done."

"But there are not many Simon Kentons."

In the next several days Harrison found a rather cooler reception than he had expected. Some of his fellow officers were openly disdainful. The senior captain in the regiment had a special grudge, for Harrison had obtained his commission as ensign by favors at the top rather than by going through the normal apprenticeship as a cadet, and he had done so at the expense of the captain's son who supposedly was next in line for appointment. Others thought that this somewhat urbane, rather frail-looking Virginian would not make it in the rugged West. He did find a friend in a young captain whom he had met once at Berkeley. But even the friend advised him to go home. He pointed to the lack of any healthy amusements to break up the monotony of the garrison life, and he pointed to the high mortality of young officers to alcohol and duelling. Harrison had seen enough of these to hold to a determination to have little to do with alcohol, and nothing with duelling even though that gruesome activity seemed to be a favorite pastime even for some of those who doubtless would hide at the approach of an Indian.

Actually there was less drilling and training than Harrison had anticipated and rather more so-called leisure time. He spent a good deal of time in the fort getting acquainted with the privates and noncommissioned officers as well as the officers. For diversion he was content to pull out his copy of *Cicero* or Blair's *Lectures* at any time, and he was glad to be left alone in his cabin to read and to think. Later he was able to borrow other books on military science. For military instruction he dwelt mainly on the works of Thomas Simes, including his four-volume *Portable Military Library,* his *Military Science* and *Military Guide* as well as his *Military Guide for Young Officers,* the *Military Medley,* and *A New Military Historical and Explanatory Dictionary,* though Harrison enjoyed more Marshall Saxe's *Memoirs Upon the Art of War.* At times he also turned to Steuben's *Regulations,* prepared during the Revolution. But the hardship of campaign held no dread for him.

He was always anxious to talk with the officers about their experiences, to learn as much from them as he could. He was especially taken by his regimental commander, Major John F. Hamtranck. The major, he learned, had been commandant at Vincennes, the old French town on the Wabash, before coming to Fort Washington, and less than a year ago he had led a successful expedition against the Indian villages on the Wabash.

"Yes, Vincennes was a pretty tricky place," the major said in a conversation one evening. "Those Wabash Indians seem all the time to be up to some kind of plunder or murder. Small detachments always had to be on the lookout for ambush. One of the main problems was that some of these Indians were friendly, especially toward the French, but you couldn't be sure who was who. The thieves and murderers would come into town and mingle with the friendlies, strolling around town and around the fort. They would give the word to their tribesmen when a party was going out, and then they might waylay them."

"Did you have much trouble when you went up against their villages?"

"Actually, they gave us no resistance. We burned the villages and came back. That slows them down for a while, but that won't stop them. They are used to building and rebuilding villages. They rebuild, and then there we are, right back where we started. Back in '88 George Rogers Clark came up with a band of Kentucky militia, but they didn't get anywhere. Clark was not the same as he used to be. In fact the militia refused to go beyond Vincennes itself. A couple of years before that the town got a real scare. In mid-July a force of several hundred Indians, flying red and white flags, came sailing down the river in forty-seven canoes. They sent word that they would not attack the French if they remained neutral. The French sent envoys out to try to talk them out of it. But they came right on. They came right through the town and up to the fort. But, finding the fort defended and unable to penetrate it, they gave up and withdrew. But I'll tell you, they had all the people mighty worried for a while."

Harrison was glad for the sturdy structure and the 1st Regiment at Fort Washington. "But if we persist in burning their villages, should we not expect them to try to burn ours?"

"Well, that's what we're afraid of. I doubt that burning villages does any good. Last May, I went with Wilkinson when he accompanied General Scott of Kentucky up the Wabash. I understand Washington himself ordered that strike. We took a force of 800 mounted Kentuckians against Ouiatenon and the other Wea villages. We were completely successful in destroying the villages, but I don't think that did any good either. In fact it may have provoked further Indian attacks up north. It does no good just to burn villages. You have got to annihilate the enemy's forces."

"Does that mean annihilation of a whole people?"

"Not necessarily, though I doubt there is going to be any solution short of driving them west of the river."

"West of what river, the Wabash?"

"No, the Mississippi."

"The Mississippi? You mean drive them all over into Spanish territory? How could you do that? You might as well try to drive them all north into British territory. They're the ones who seem to be behind a lot of their actions, aren't they?"

"Yes, I guess you're right. The British are their great defenders, but I'll bet the British won't offer them land in their territory."

If there were few amusements to relieve the winter months of garrison duty, there were winter marches to provide some diversion. Ensign Harrison got his first assignment for one of these only two weeks after his arrival. During the fall campaign St. Clair had built two outposts to provide links in his supply line. The first was Fort Hamilton, twenty-five miles to the north, and the other was Fort Jefferson, another forty-five miles beyond. Harrison was to take supplies up to Hamilton. On a cold, wet morning, the young ensign set out with a party of twenty men and a pack-horse train on his first real military expedition. After a climb over the hills above Cincinnati, the detachment moved down through the woods to a creek which it had to ford and then continued northward through the woods. Harrison and his men found shelter for the night in a deserted cabin which had been occupied by a settler who had been killed by Indians. Without any hostile interference, the detachment arrived at Fort Hamilton in good time and returned directly to Fort Washington where Harrison received a public commendation from the General.

In January, General St. Clair had to go to Philadelphia to report to the President and the Secretary of War and answer to Congress for his humiliating defeat. Brig. Gen. James Wilkinson who had been been second in command took over the command. He disliked inactivity, and he scheduled an expedition to go up to the scene of St. Clair's defeat and recover lost weapons and equipment, if the Indians had left any, and then to go on up and destroy the Indian village in the vicinity. On this occasion Harrison went along with his regular infantry regiment which preceded by a day a company of mounted militia. The force marched out in a soft, deep snow that blanketed the whole area. Then freezing rain glazed this with ice. Infantrymen struggled to break through the crust only to have the ice jab under their leggings. At night they slept beside big fires, though these offered only partial protection from the cold. One of the horsemen complained that while sleeping his head slipped off the saddle he was using for a pillow, and his long queue of hair froze fast to the ground. On the march, cold winds nipped exposed fingers and ears. Feet became numb. It took nearly a week to reach Fort Jefferson. Wilkinson, noting that the supplies would not hold up for the prolonged period it would take to reach the ultimate destination, and considering that fighting capabilities of men so long exposed to the bitter cold would be questionable at best, decided to give up the attack against the Indian town. He sent the regular infantrymen back to Fort Washington, but he had the militia ride on up to see if they could police St. Clair's battlefield. Ten days later the militiamen returned with further tales of horror of that battlefield. They had done what they could to bury hundreds of torn and mutilated bodies which remained and had picked up only a few items of equipment.

Harrison was glad for the opportunity to participate in one special gala occasion that winter—February 22 at Fort Washington, the celebration of George Washington's birthday. The wives of the officers, together with a dozen ladies from Cincinnati and Columbia joined the officers at the fort for the festivities. The firing of cannon and rockets opened the activities of riding, games, and informal visiting, followed by refreshment and dancing. Although Harrison had no "special" lady, he did enjoy visiting with several of those from the community. He had seen nothing like this since leaving Philadelphia.

Early in March, General Wilkinson decided to build another fort midway between Hamilton and Fort Jefferson. Harrison went along with a detachment of 200 regulars and militiamen assigned to the task. Again it was a march through cold, wintry weather. His own assignment was to guard duty. For three weeks he had command of the guard on alternate nights. While many of the others, generally thought to be much stronger, came down with pneumonia and pleurisy, the young ensign came through it all in good health and good spirits. By the end of this ordeal, everybody seemed willing to accept him.

When they got back to Fort Washington, the soldiers began to run wild again. Drinking and gambling and dueling were the order of the day. On at least three occasions village tavern keepers complained to the commandant about the riots and brawls the soldiers were getting into. This was an embarrassment to Wilkinson, and he resolved to do something about it. He appointed Ensign William Henry Harrison to take a patrol through the town at irregular hours and to punish any private found drunk outside the walls of the fort. Punishment was to be in the form of fifty lashes on the spot. Harrison did not much care for police duty, but he had no sympathy for drunken brawls, and he was determined to carry out his orders strictly. On one such foray he netted a couple of artificers from the fort. These men were not actually privates, but supposedly skilled artisans under army hire. Harrison drew no such fine distinctions and promptly ordered fifty lashes for one who obviously was very drunk and ten for his companion when he tried to interfere. The next day the artificers found lawyers who obtained a warrant for Harrison's arrest. Wilkinson issued an order to exempt artificers from punishment, but he also forbade the warrant to be served within the walls of the fort. However, Judge William Goforth, the local magistrate, gave instructions to arrest the ensign wherever he could be found. When a deputy sheriff undertook the task and held out the warrant to the ensign, Harrison promptly felled the deputy with a blow to his chin. Then he apologized and agreed to go along. He was severely scolded and locked up in McHenry's tavern for twenty-four hours which he spent in celebration with several of his companions, for no one was more grateful for his strict actions than Mr. McHenry.

Harrison knew the kind of men he had recruited in Philadelphia. He knew that they were not the best qualified soldiers in the country, but he hardly expected to get that at two dollars a month. They had behaved well enough on the long trip west, and he was confident that a good period of training would make tolerable soldiers out of them. But he was not prepared for the quality of the troops that he found at Fort Washington. The officers had little confidence in them, said they were the dregs of society, refugees from prisons, and ne'er-do-wells who preferred the imagined security of the Army to honest work. Major Hamtranck himself said, "The economic allowance of one hundred lashes allowed by the government does not appear a sufficient inducement for a rascal to act the part of an honest man."

Judge Symmes of North Bend, anxious for adequate military protection for his settlement and for his land holdings, had written a bitter letter in January 1792 in which he said that the men sent out here were a wretched set of men, weak and feeble. Many of them mere boys, and the others were rotten with drink and debauchery. He said, "These men who are to be purchased from the prisons, wheel-barrows, and brothels of the nation at foolishly low wages, will never do to fight the Indians." He went on to say that against the terrible enemies in the woods, first-class, specially trained troops were needed instead of trying to use "a set of men who enlisted because they could no longer live unhung any other way."

All this troubled Harrison. Yet, he thought, even the dregs of society are men, and if they are given good training, good weapons, and good leaders, even they can be made into soldiers.

Certainly different men have different special talents than others. Certainly some have the natural abilities to make better soldiers than others, but surely most men possess a basic quality, some capacity which will enable them to develop into at least acceptable soldiers. The militiamen, drawn from the frontiersmen, were better marksmen and better woodsmen than the regulars, but they were almost totally lacking in military discipline and in military maneuvers.

Spring restored a fragrant beauty to the Ohio valley. Harrison learned with enthusiasm that Congress had reorganized the Army, and General "Mad Anthony" Wayne had been selected to command it. St. Clair would continue as governor of the Territory but not as general. Wayne himself would be coming west. Then with added delight, Harrison got an opportunity to return to Philadelphia. He was to escort Mrs. Wilkinson and their two little boys when they returned to the capital city for the children to go to school. At least he would go with them on the boat as far as Pittsburgh.

On June 13 they departed from Cincinnati for the trip up the river together with other boats carrying troops. This was in sharp contrast with Harrison's voyage downstream. This time it was a barge. Now the accommodations were almost luxurious. The food was prepared exquisitely and served elegantly, and a crew of about twenty-five men worked at the sails, the oars, the poles, and the rudder. Several ladies and gentlemen were on board and all were well-dressed. The boys watched eagerly from one bend to the next, seeing real wolves and bears at times, and sometimes some Indians—mostly imaginary. It took about three weeks to reach Pittsburgh.

There Harrison met General Anthony Wayne for the first time, though he recalled having seen him pass Berkeley plantation when he was after Cornwallis eleven years earlier. Wayne had established a new base outside Pittsburgh where he was collecting and staging his army preparatory to taking it on to Fort Washington some months later. Now he told Harrison that he was to continue with General Wilkins' family to Philadelphia. He sent him a written order, dated 3 July:

> You will please proceed with the Lady and family of General Wilkinson to Philadelphia and return again to this place on or before the 1st day of next month. Upon your arrival in Philadelphia you will immediately wait upon the Secretary of War and inform him you are ready to take charge of any dispatches or commands he may have for me.

General Wayne went further. He had arranged for a coach from a Colonel O'Hara—one said to belong to Mrs. O'Hara—and had provided a team of his own horses, together with a reliable driver who was familiar with the road. In a special demonstration of thoughtfulness, he arranged for three saddle horses, one for Mrs. Wilkinson, one for the two boys, and one for Harrison, so that at times they might ride the horses to ease some of the fatigue of long hours in the coach. The party set out on the 4th of July, and as appropriate for the occasion, General Wayne and some of his officers, together with a detachment of dragoons, rode out with them the first seven miles in what appeared to be something of a patriotic parade. Again, Harrison could not help but note the difference in this trip over this road from the walk by which he had come over it the previous year. This was a delightful journey all the way, made the more delightful by the anticipation of seeing Philadelphia again. Even the inns along the way seemed much improved. It took about a week to cover the distance across Pennsylvania.

Although he had been away less than a year, Harrison felt a certain tug of nostalgia in seeing the familiar places again. After dropping off the Wilkinsons at their destination, he went directly to call on Robert Morris, but mostly to see Hettie. There he was offered accommodations, and the Senator greeted him with the same cordiality as before, even though he had been upset by Harrison's decision to go into the Army. Hettie was even more cordial, and Harrison almost forgot for a moment the other part of his mission which was "immediately" to wait upon the Secretary of War. He did that the first thing the next morning.

Surely as important to him as any dispatches for General Wayne was the news that he had been promoted to lieutenant, effective June 1.

At noon he dropped into the London Coffee House for lunch and celebration of his promotion and saw several old friends. In conversation here he heard that Washington really had exploded when he received the report of St. Clair's defeat.

"If you think the General hasn't got a temper, you've got another thing a coming," his friend Charles Bonsol said. "The story is that St. Clair's aide, a lieutenant by the name of Denny, arrived in Philadelphia with the report on December 19 and went straight to the Secretary of War. General Knox saw that this was something that the President should see at once, so he sent it over to the Executive Mansion. Washington was at dinner with some guests. He was called from the table to receive the news. He heard it very calmly and returned to his guests as though nothing had happened. He returned to his table conversation with no hint of anything extraordinary. Then, as soon as his guests had departed, he exploded like a volcano. He walked up and down the room and fairly shouted, 'He went off from here with my solemn warning that above all he must avoid ambush, he must not be taken by surprise, and yet to suffer that army to be cut to pieces, hacked, tomahawked, by a surprise, the very thing I guarded him against! Oh, God! Oh, God! He's worse than a murderer! How can he answer to his country?'"

"Zounds! Did he really say all that?" Harrison asked almost dumbfounded.

"Well, I heard that Washington's secretary reported as much to a secretary of General Knox, and actually I have heard other examples of his temper."

"I hope I never catch the brunt of it," responded Harrison. St. Clair, who had faced a court martial before, accused of treachery, cowardice, and incompetence in abandoning Ticonderoga and Mount Independence to Burgoyne without a fight during the Revolution, had faced another investigation after this defeat. As on the previous occasion, he was exonerated. Harrison heard the news with satisfaction—not that he had any particular sympathy for St. Clair, nor any full comprehension of the facts of the case. He just hated to see the Army held up to any kind of disrepute.

In the next two or three days Harrison paid his respects to Dr. Rush, visited with some other friends, and even spent two half days at reading in the library. Finally he persuaded Hettie Morris to have dinner with him.

Now with a coach at his disposal, he drove her in style to the City Tavern. Over a dinner of roast beef and Yorkshire pudding, with Madeira wine, they reviewed recent public and family events and exchanged thoughts and ideas.

"This is a completely different world," Harrison said, as he looked around to admire the decor, noticed the dress of the people and the quality of the food.

Hettie looked up to inquire, "What do you mean?"

"Oh, the food, the dress of the people, the decor of this place, sitting here with you—all completely different from being out west, especially from being in a fort or out in the wilderness."

"Not a different world, just different aspects of the same world," she suggested. "Aren't there bright moments and dull moments, bits of beauty and bits of ugliness in all of life, wherever you may be?"

"Yes, I suppose you're right, but sometimes it's a little difficult to adjust quickly from one aspect to the other."

"But don't those who can adjust from one to the other get a lot more out of the whole?"

"Of course they do, and as I think about it, that is what being a good soldier means."

"What do you mean by that?"

"Being able to adjust quickly from one situation to another. A soldier is always up against changing situations, and he must always be on his guard against surprise. General St.Clair found that out, all right."

"Sometimes it can be fun to be surprised."

"Not by a bunch of Indians."

"No, I suppose not. But do you think the Indians are really savages?"

"Depends on what you mean by savages, I guess."

"I mean like wild animals, not at all like civilized people."

"From some of the things I've heard they're worse than wild animals in some ways. Do wild animals torture others of their own kind just for amusement?"

"Do they do that?"

"Some of them do."

"But they must have families, and feelings of sympathy and tenderness, and hopes and ambitions for their little ones."

"Yes, I suppose they must. I really haven't met any yet. But I have seen some of the results of their activities."

"What about the activities of the White settlers against them and on their land?"

"Yes, I'm afraid there's some of that too." Harrison paused as the waiters brought in the dessert of baked custards. He ordered glasses of his favorite Virginia wine, Scuppernong.

"Hettie, I'm glad to see you," he said. "I am, you know. I wish I were not going to be so far away so that I might have a chance to see you more often."

"Oh, I thought you only had eyes for Sarah Cutler," she said with a smirk.

Harrison fought back a blush with two sips of Scuppernong. "Well," he said, "I can see much better now."

"Oh, have you got yourself a pair of Ben Franklin's eyeglasses?"

"No, but if I thought they would help me see you even better, I would go for a pair immediately. No, I guess I mean that the farther away I am, the more clearly I can see."

"Maybe you can go to France, or even Turkey, and then think how clearly you might see."

"Actually, I think Fort Washington is farther away than Paris in the sense of enabling one to see things in better perspective. When you're in the middle of a big forest it's difficult to see or recognize the finest trees from the more common ones. I never fully recognized the fineness of you until I was out of the forest of Philadelphia. Now when I am in the real forest, I find my thoughts turning toward you time and again."

"You had better keep your thoughts on what you are doing if you expect to escape the Indian's tomahawk."

"Yes, you're quite right, but it is difficult to suppress more pleasant thoughts of fancy when you're out in the wilderness. But it's not just that. It's not just a question of daydreaming to escape harsh realities. It's a matter of discovery and of seeing things more clearly, in perspective. I'm sure I would be thinking of you just as much if I were in Paris or in the middle of the Sahara."

"I think I'll stick to Philadelphia. I'm sure I can think better here than with Indians after me."

Harrison affected a laugh and noted that it was time to go.

2a

On returning to Pittsburgh, Lieutenant Harrison was pleased to learn that General Wayne had decided to retain him there, even though, or perhaps in part because, General Wilkinson was requesting his return to Fort Washington.

Wayne's new army had been designated the "Legion of the United States" with an authorized strength of 5,414. It was to comprise four "sublegions," each to include infantry, cavalry, and artillery. The Secretary of War even had designated distinguishing hat marks for the sublegions—white banding with white plume for the 1st Sublegion, red banding with red plume for the 2nd, yellow banding and plume for the 3rd, and black plume only for the 4th.

"The Legion of the United States"—Harrison liked that. He thought of himself as a member of a legion, even as the Romans under Caesar, which would be marching to protect the frontier against the barbarians. His own initial assignment was to Captain Ballard Smith's company of the 1st Sublegion. The 1st Regiment now would make up the major element of that organization. He found temporary quarters at Mr. Tannehill's tavern on Water Street and joined his company for drill at nearby Fort Fayette. Thrown in close association with newly arriving officers in this effort, Harrison quickly made many friends, such as Lieutenant John Whistler in his own sublegion, Lieutenant Solomon Van Rensselaer of the Dragoons, Lieutenant William Clark, Captain Montgomery Zebulon Pike, and, perhaps closest of all, the surgeon of the 2nd Sublegion, Dr. John M. Scott. In September Captain Smith was temporarily relieved of command on account of his part in a drunken riot which grew out of an incident involving him and the wife of his sergeant. Harrison was given command of the company.

The recruits that came in that summer, described as "a nondescript lot of beggars, criminals, and other cast-offs of the eastern cities" promised no improvement over those who had served under St. Clair. Indeed these suffered the further disadvantage of being unnerved by the horror stories from St. Clair's survivors. At one point when someone sounded a false alarm that Indians were coming, fully a third of the sentinels on duty fled their posts.

With ranks fairly swollen by these men of whatever caliber, in late autumn Wayne moved the whole body about twenty-five miles down the Ohio from Pittsburgh and set up a new camp which everyone came to refer to as "Legionville." Here began a regime of concentrated drilling and training the like of which no one in this army ever had seen before. For eight and ten hours a day, day after day, week after week, in foul weather or fair, all through the winter, the drilling went on. All troops were required to learn the "school of the soldier" and close-order drill. They had to learn the manual of arms and the precise drill for loading, priming, cocking, and firing the muzzle-loading muskets in fourteen movements. But they had to go beyond that. They had to learn to reload their muskets quickly, while on the run. They had to learn to handle the bayonet and to surge forward in furious bayonet charges, shouting at the top of their voices. They even learned to use the tomahawk and scalping knife. Harrison was sure this was what had been lacking in the previous commanders. Gone was much of the drunken idleness. By spring the results were showing. Clearly even these "dregs of society" could be whipped into a disciplined and effective force.

In April they were ready to move on to Fort Washington. Over two thousand strong, they did so in an impressive flotilla of barges and flatboats, all standing guards and with small arms and cannon ready to fire in case of attack. During any stop, infantry scouts fanned out for half a mile to provide security. On April 29 the Legion landed at Cincinnati. Finding Fort Washington much too small for this force, Wayne set up camp in open fields to the west of it. On the top of a sixty-foot high Indian mound in the midst of it, he had a platform built for a permanent lookout. He dubbed the new camp, "Hobson's Choice."

Reinforcements continued to arrive, and for them the same drilling had to start all over again while it continued for those who had now become veterans. They participated in small unit exercises and large-scale sham battles. Four companies of cavalry, divided according to the color of their horses—gray, bay, chestnut, and sorrel—were sent across the river for special training in the woods. All the soldiers practiced marksmanship and participated in contests in "shooting at marks"—generally an X drawn on a board.

Just about the time that the excitement of all this was about to succumb to new triumphs of tedium for William Henry Harrison, the young lieutenant received word that he was being called to the personal staff of the commanding general. He was to be aide-de-camp to General Wayne. He was especially pleased at the thought of the approval and recognition in the eyes of the General that this meant, but he also was not unaware that it carried with it a significant increase in pay. As a regular lieutenant he was receiving $26 a month, four dollars more than his pay as an ensign, but now the new appointment meant another $24, or a total of $50 a month. The General himself only received $166 a month, so proportionately he was doing very well.

The new appointment also brought special attention from his fellow officers. Some were jealous of the "youngster," but all were civil enough to see him as a source of good information straight from the General. Harrison never betrayed confidences, but he liked to discuss open information.

Everyone wanted to know how soon they would be moving out against the Indians. As the summer wore into the fall, Harrison too became curious about the delay. At one point he asked the General himself, and the only response he got was, "Son, I say it takes a soldier three years to learn to live on his rations and take care of his clothes." The Aide learned a good deal more just by keeping his ears open.

When not on watch, Harrison frequently would join other junior officers to while away the long evenings in games of cards and pints of spruce beer.

"Bring out the Devil's tickets," someone would shout, and as soon as they could find the cards, play would begin. Faro was the favorite, possibly because a month's pay could be won or lost so quickly at it. Another game, about as popular, was Farmer, and the newer versions of it that some, from the New Orleans influence, called "Vingt et Un," and others called "Black Jack."

Harrison much preferred Whist, a four-handed, partners game of less chance and more skill. He and Scott were the acknowledged champions. They would take on all comers. Everyone not involved in a game would stand around closely as kibitzers. Clark liked to play as well as anyone, but he felt frustrated at seldom being able to win.

One evening between hands of Whist, when the conversation turned to the inevitable question, Harrison was able to give a more complete report. "In the first place," he said, "the General told Philadelphia when they asked him to take command that he would do so only with the understanding that he would not be expected to move out with an expedition until the men were well-trained and he had adequate supplies and means for bringing up more supplies. That's something lots of people just seem to forget about. They think an army just appears out of nowhere, fights its battle, and then just goes back whence it came, just like that. Too many of them don't even think about the supplies which are needed to make an army effective."

"But for God's sake, how long does it take to get a force ready?" asked Captain Pike. "Haven't we trained enough by now?"

"Maybe we have," Harrison said. "And I guess I agree with my father who was always quoting Edward Young, 'Procrastination is the thief of time,' but now they have tied the General's hands for a while. They've told him he should make no hostile moves until they give the word."

"Well, then what are *they* waiting for?" asked Pike.

"Peace negotiations," answered Harrison.

"Peace negotiations!" Lieutenant William Clark cried out. "What kind of peace negotiations? I've learned from my big brother George not to put much faith in Indian peace negotiations."

Harrison explained, "Well, our Captain Alex Trauman of the 1st Regiment, that is the 1st Sublegion, is supposed to go up to the Miami villages, and a high-powered commission—Benjamin Lincoln, Timothy Pickering, and Beverly Randolph—are supposed to go to Detroit, and I think somebody is supposed to go to Vincennes."

"Vincennes, where the hell is that?" interrupted John Whistler.

"On the damn Wabash River," Clark put in, impatiently. "I was out there in '89 on an expedition under John Hardin, and again in '91 under Wilkinson on General Scott's expedition. That's where my brother caught the damned British Hamilton and his garrison back in February of '79."

"Yes, Major Hamtranck was stationed at Vincennes for awhile," Harrison recalled. "And he also went with Wilkinson on that expedition with Scott."

"Yes," Clark said.

Harrison went on, "He says it's mighty tricky out there. They burned the Wea villages all right, but apparently that did no good."

"No good at all," Clark confirmed. "We have got to push them all out of there. And there are lots of Frenchies at Vincennes. I'm never sure whose side they're on, but if you ask me, the damned English are still trying to get back in there, though I must say, it's such a God-forsaken place I don't know what they want with it."

"To get back to the immediate subject, what are these emissaries supposed to tell the Indians?" asked Doctor Scott.

"That we don't want war, that we want to live in peace with them, that we want to find a reasonable basis for a lasting peace."

"In a pig's eye," the doctor retorted. "Sure, sure we want peace. We'll grant them any reasonable demand. We'll give up anything—except our designs on their land, which is the only thing that matters."

Clark came back, "My God, Scotty, would you just let a whole continent stand empty except for a few Indians and racoons when it could be supporting a population of millions? Yes, millions. You know this land is richer than back east and could support five times the population of that eastern land."

"But we are supposed to pay them a reasonable price," Harrison added.

"How much is that?" Scott wanted to know. "About a penny an acre?"

"Probably."

"Well, our historian Billy, what did the Romans do about this kind of situation?"

Harrison replied at once, "Well, the Romans conquered the barbarians and then made good Romans out of them."

"Why can't we do that?" asked Whistler.

"And then later, the barbarians conquered the Romans," Harrison went on.

"And made barbarians of them?" Clark rejoined.

"No, actually, the Romans made Romans out of them again." Harrison paused and thought for a moment. "Think of that," he went on. "The Romans conquered the barbarians and made Romans out of them, and later other barbarians came down and conquered the Romans, but the Romans made Romans out of them too."

"My God," gasped Scott. "It really doesn't make any difference, does it? Does it? Maybe the superior civilization triumphs in the end no matter!"

"Come on, Doc, didn't you ever hear of the Dark Ages?" protested Clark.

Pike chimed in, "Maybe it won't make a big difference over several centuries, but it sure as hell will make a hell of lot of difference to the people involved at the time—like his scalp or mine!"

"Well, Gentlemen," said Scott, "maybe we should check all this out with the General before he decides to move at all."

Clark came back, "I say check it out with Washington and Henry Knox and Tom Jefferson, or whoever's doing it, and persuade them to call off the damned peace missions."

Several weeks later virtually the same group was together when Harrison reported the results of the peace efforts. "Well, I guess you've probably heard by now," he began, " that Alex Trauman was murdered by the Miamis."

"Damn, damn, damn!" exclaimed Clark. "I told you. I told you that you can't trust those bastards. Damn! Poor old Alex."

Harrison went on, "And the mission to Detroit never got to Detroit. Can you imagine that? The British would not let us in our own damned town!"

"There should be our objective," Clark came back. "By damn, I say let's take Detroit. Ole George Rogers tried and tried to get them to let him take it, but they never did. The damned British acknowledge that it's ours in the treaty, and now they just sit there and won't let us in."

"But our people finally did get to talk to the Lakes Indians," Harrison continued.

"Well, what happened?" Scott wanted to know.

"Oh, they are willing to grant peace. They say they don't want war with the White men, they just want to live in peace."

"Yeh? On what terms?"

"They said all we have to do is pull all the White men back south of the Ohio River, out of their territory, and there will be peace."

"There you are," said Scott. "There you are. Look at it from their point of view. Is that really an unreasonable demand?"

"To do that you would have to turn the whole Army on our own people," Clark came back. "And even if we did that, next they would want us to move out of Kentucky, and then there would be hell to pay."

"You sound just like the Indians," said Scott. "They say that if they clear out of the Miami region, then we'll demand that they go beyond the Wabash, and after that all the way to the Mississippi."

"Which wouldn't be a bad idea," Clark retorted. "Billy, what about Vincennes?"

"Oh, we had great success there. General Rufus Putnam went over there. Took a Moravian missionary along with him. He signed a treaty and left all of the Indians there happy."

Pike inquired, "How in hell did he do that?"

"Promised them we would protect their lands along the Wabash!"

"There you are!" exclaimed Scott.

"There's just one catch," Harrison added.

"What's that?"

"They say the Senate is not going to ratify it."

"Ha, that's the way to negotiate," said Clark. "Promise them anything, get out of there with your ass and your scalp intact, and then have the Senate reject it!"

"That's a hell of a note," the doctor protested. "How the hell are you going to explain that to the Indians?"

Wayne turned his attention to getting his supply situation in order. During the fall he sent out a detachment to cut a road through the fifty miles to Fort Jefferson. Finding this small fort altogether inadequate for his needs he built a new one five miles beyond. This he called "Fort Greeneville," in honor of his old Revolutionary War comrade, Nathanael Greene. In October he assembled his entire force of 2,600 officers and men and moved from Fort Washington to Fort Greeneville, where they went into winter quarters. They continued their drilling while Wayne sought more supplies. He was trying to get government contractors to store 270,000 rations at Fort Greeneville before the end of the year. But they delayed. He suspected that they were counting on a drop in food prices and had purchased only enough food to meet current needs, and when the General called for immediate delivery they had neither the foodstuffs nor the transportation to comply. Although the contractors lost seventy horses when Indians attacked their convoy, Wayne was not satisfied with their reason for nondelivery. Harrison gained a suspicion that General Wilkinson, again serving as second in command, might have had a hand in the delay in reassuring the contractors and de-emphasizing the need for the build-up of rations.

Wayne took more drastic action. He ordered his quartermaster to buy 250 pack horses and 40 pair of oxen or 60 wagon horses and charge them to the contractors, and he threatened to do much more. Meanwhile he sent out a detachment to build a new fort on the site of St. Clair's defeat, an area still bearing the gruesome marks of that disaster, and he called that fort, "Fort Recovery." Then he ordered the contractors to move up 50,000 rations from Fort St. Clair to the new fort, but they could not even do that. After two years of preparation, Wayne still found it impossible to launch his attack in the spring of 1794. Like St. Clair he faced the dangerous prospect of a fall campaign.

In June, a force of about 1,500 Indians attacked Fort Greeneville, but were beaten off with practically no loss to the defenders. This boosted the confidence of everyone in the Legion.

A few days later more troops arrived—1,400 mounted militia from Kentucky. Although they were "only militia" the Kentuckians quickly won the respect of the regulars. Invariably the militiamen outshot them in any contest of marksmanship. The real secret of their success was the Kentucky rifle. While all the regulars were armed with smooth-bore muskets, the militiamen carried rifles. These weapons differed from the muskets in that they were "rifled," with lands and grooves in the bore imparting a spin to the bullet which gave it a uniform flight pattern. Balls from muskets were apt to curve in any direction, but the spinning ball fired from a rifle would curve uniformly so that correct aim could be taken. The use of rifling in a muzzle loader was made feasible by some unknown genius who some years past had come up with the greased patch. Running the greased patch down the barrel made it possible to ram the cartridge down, and still keep the tight fit needed to prevent the gases from escaping around the ball when the piece was fired.

At last Wayne decided to move on July 27. He had the largest and the best trained army that had ever faced the Indians in the West. He never lost consciousness of St. Clair's surprise, and he always took precautions against ambush. He kept strong advance guards out in front, and flank guards and rear guards as well.

Beyond Fort Recovery, as they headed toward the Maumee River and the Miami villages, he sent wide-ranging patrols out to the front and flanks to flush out any Indians who might be lying in wait. On one occasion, Harrison led one of these patrols far out to the flank. Moving through the woods on foot, he took the precaution of organizing his ten-man patrol with a point out in front and flank and rear guards. Though his normal place was near the center, he actually moved with the point most of the time.

It was rough going, through the unbroken forest, up and down hills on a hot August day. At one point, in descending a hill, the lieutenant lost his footing. A pair of young saplings stayed his plunge down the steep slope, but only temporarily. At the bottom he collected his hat and his dignity and resumed his rightful position. Through areas thin of cover the sun burned down upon them. In the thickets the air was stifling. Presently, crossing a slight clearing they came upon a clear brook of fresh water whose series of pools invited their drinking. The careless ones dropped their muskets, ran to the edge of a pool, and threw themselves on the ground for long draughts of the cool, cool water. The more careful ones approached the pools more deliberately. Keeping their muskets close by, they scooped up the water in closed double hands from which they sipped while yet maintaining a sharp lookout. It was fortunate that they did. On the high ground ahead, a couple of Indians peered over the brow of a rise and took aim. But quick fire from two muskets chased them away. None other was seen in this vicinity the whole day.

On his return to the main body for the night encampment, Harrison came across several soldiers who were complaining of fever and nausea. He had seen several of those during the preceding days, but he had thought these the usual cases of summer ague. Now he noticed that red blotches were appearing on the faces of some of them. He sought out John Scott.

"What is it, Doc, is it what I think?"

"If you think it's smallpox it is."

"Oh God, what do we do now? Do we start bleeding them?"

"Hell no, the Indians probably will be bleeding them enough. Anyway, I'm not sure that bleeding is worth a damn, especially in an army. No, tell the General that this can be serious. We had better get them back to the fort if we can —mainly to keep them away from everybody else. Somehow this thing spreads from one person to another, and we have got to keep them separated."

Earlier, Harrison had taken part in repelling an assault against Fort Recovery. It seemed safe enough now, and the sick were taken back. Before it was over nearly a fourth of the command was affected, but Wayne pressed on.

2b

Tecumseh watched the approach of Wayne's army with apprehension. He now had won sufficient acclaim as a warrior to gain a following as a war chief, but he was not yet in any position of major responsibility. He had gone along with a band of Shawnees, Delawares, Potawatomis, Ottawas, and Chippewas under the leadership of Blue Jacket to attack a column of horses departing from Fort Recovery, mainly to acquire the animals. The raid had been a big success, but then the Potawatomi, Ottawa, and Chippewa warriors had foolishly assaulted the fort. In this way, they had succeeded only in losing a large share of their warriors. Disillusioned, about three hundred of them had left the Shawnee villages and returned to their villages near Lake Michigan. This was a serious blow to the strength of an Indian force which now faced the biggest and strongest army of Long Knives that any of them had ever seen.

This time Little Turtle, leader of the victorious forces against Harmar's detachment and leader of the great victory over St. Clair, counseled caution. This came as a shock to Tecumseh and other young leaders.

In a council of the leaders Little Turtle warned, "The Long Knives are now led by a chief who never sleeps. The night and the day are alike to him. During all the time he has been marching toward our villages, in spite of the watchfulness of our young warriors, we have never been able to surprise him. Something whispers to me that we should listen to his offers of peace."

Tecumseh and the other young leaders agreed that Little Turtle had grown too old, lost his spark. The old leader agreed that he would accept the will of the leaders and would help in the battle, but he would not be the chief leader. Unanimously they turned to the one who had been alongside Chief Little Turtle in the great victories—Blue Jacket.

Blue Jacket knew that he was seriously outnumbered, and he sent messengers to try to induce the recalcitrant allies to return to the effort. But even without them, he was confident that the Shawnees, Miamis, and Delawares could again drive back the Long Knives. Again they would abandon the villages if necessary and choose their best ground for their kind of fighting. They sent the women and children away to a camp in the north.

On August 8th Wayne's forces reached what had been the center of the Miami villages at the confluence of the Auglaize and the Maumee. All had been abandoned. For several days the troops remained in the vicinity to build yet another fort—Fort Defiance —and to harvest corn and other vegetables from the hundreds of acres that had been left standing. Wayne then proceeded along the left bank of the Maumee toward the British stronghold, Fort Miami, not far from where the Maumee flowed into Lake Erie.

Blue Jacket and his allies were able to assemble a force of about 1,500 warriors. They decided to make their stand in an area where a severe windstorm had uprooted trees and left trunks and branches strewn all over the place in all directions. The tree trunks would provide good cover for firing and obstacles for the enemy horsemen. Tecumseh was in charge of the advance guard.

His brothers, Sauwauseekau and Lalawethika, were beside him. Early on the morning of August 20, Tecumseh saw the approach of the American force. A battalion of horsemen led the way. When they came within range, Tecumseh gave the signal to fire by firing his own musket. It was a deadly fire that sent the horsemen reeling back. But soon infantrymen appeared in their place, infantrymen charging with bayonets.

Anthony Wayne had accepted the challenge. The night before, expecting the battle, he had a small fortification built which he called "Fort Deposit," and he had the troops drop all their packs and other baggage there. On this morning, suffering from such a severe case of gout that he had to be lifted into his saddle, he rode up to the attack. As they approached the firing up front Harrison called to his chief, "General, I'm afraid you may get involved in the fighting yourself and forget to give me the orders for the units!"

"Yes, that's right," Wayne called back. "Just remember, the standing order of the day is, 'Charge the damned rascals with bayonets!' and, Lieutenant, get on up there and tell the infantry to close the gap in front, and go after 'em with the bayonet. Tell Van Renssalaer to bring his dragoons up on the left flank to cut them off!"

Harrison dashed off to deliver the instructions. As he rode across the front he caught sight of a band of Indians out in front putting up a great fight under the direction of a very striking young leader—that was Tecumseh.

From his position up in front, Tecumseh looked out to see a young officer dashing to and fro on a horse. That was William Henry Harrison.

Tecumseh stood his ground until the trigger on his musket broke. Then he pulled back only until he found a fowling piece, which he picked up, and went back into action. But he could see that dragoons were threatening to cut him off, and infantrymen were charging from the front. His older brother fell dead beside him. He led his party on a wild flight to get away. Coming upon an American squad with horses and cannon, they chased the men away with war clubs and tomahawks, grabbed the horses, and rode them to the rear. But by now the whole Indian line was in flight.

Finding himself on a slow horse, with his pursuers closing rapidly as they approached a creek, Tecumseh leaped off the horse and into the stream. He ran downstream, through the water, to a slight bend. Quickly he cut a reed from the bank and plunged into the water. He turned over on his back and inserted the reed in his mouth. He swallowed the water that got into his mouth and, grasping weeds with his ri_ht hand to keep himselt fully submerged, he steadied the reed with his left and began to breathe. In just a few minutes he sensed turbulence in the water which he took to come from the crossing of enemy horsemen. He waited quietly. At first the water seemed refreshing, but then it felt very cold. Still he waited quietly. He remained beneath the surface of the water for another twenty minutes without sensing any other outside movement. When he came up all was quiet, and he made good his escape.

The whole battle lasted only forty minutes. Wayne's losses were thirty-three killed and one hundred wounded, of whom eleven died later. The Indians' losses were three times as great, but more important, the rout was complete. Although the British had helped instigate the Indians' defense, they kept the doors of Fort Miami closed to them as they ran back for protection. Wayne pursued all the way to the shadow of the fort though he did not attack it. Then at a more leisurely pace he went back up the Maumee, burning villages and crops as he went. On returning to Fort Defiance, he sent the 1st Sublegion under Colonel Hamtranck to the place where the St. Joseph and St. Mary's Rivers joined to form the Maumee, there to build another fort. This they named, in honor of their leader, Fort Wayne. The task completed, the Legion returned to Fort Greeneville for winter quarters.

One evening in the officers' barracks, several weeks after the return to hard training at Fort Greeneville, Lieutenant Harrison strode into the room obviously bursting with some kind of news. Clark, Pike, Scott, Whistler, and a few others, gathered around.

"Have you heard?" Harrison gasped. "There's an army of 15,000 men converging on Pittsburgh."

"On Pittsburgh!" cried Whistler.

"What kind of army?" Pike wanted to know. "You mean the British have come all the way down from Canada?"

"No," Harrison explained, "I mean an American army—really two armies, one coming from Carlisle and the other from Cumberland, Maryland, and converging on Pittsburgh, under Washington himself, and Alexander Hamilton."

"My God," William Clark fairly shouted. "That must be serious. That's the biggest American force since Saratoga, almost as big as all the forces at Yorktown, even counting the French. What is it? Are the Iroquois on the warpath? Every Indian in the country must be threatening Pennsylvania. I thought we had them cornered up here. Or is it the British? Are we in another war with them?"

"No, no," Harrison responded. "It's some kind of uprising of the farmers of western Pennsylvania who oppose the Federal tax on whiskey, and they've called out militia from all over to form these armies to put them down. They say that the farmers tarred and feathered two or three Federal revenue agents, and they burnt down the inspector's house."

"Bravo," called out Whistler. "Bravo! I'm for the farmers and cheap whiskey! Where could they find 15,000 men to march against that?"

"Hear, hear," chimed in Pike.

Harrison said, "My father never did agree to the new Constitution, said the new government could become just as tyrannical and repressive as the British ever had been. Right now he would be saying what's the difference between a stamp tax imposed from London, and a whiskey tax imposed from Philadelphia?"

"Much worse, if you ask me," said Whistler. "How much is the tax?"

Dr. Scott said that he thought it might be as much as twenty-five cents on the dollar.

"No wonder our whiskey costs so much!" several chimed in.

"You know where they first developed that American corn whiskey, made with Indian corn and a little rye?" Harrison asked.

"The Kentucky boys talk like they invented it," said Whistler.

Harrison came back quickly, "No, no, certainly not. It was first made on my home place, Berkeley, in Virginia, long before there even was a Kentucky or any White people living in that whole area. It was first made by a missionary from the Church of England, way back in 1621, man by the name of George Thorpe."

"Well, I'd say he did a mighty fine job," said Whistler. "Here's to Reverend Thorpe!"

"Hear, Hear!"

"But I still don't understand what all the big fuss is about," said Clark.

"It's really very simple," Doc Scott volunteered. "They've got no roads to speak of in the western Pennsylvania country, or western anything else, for that matter, and the farmers are hard pressed to get out any kind of cash crop if they're not on a river. If they try to send corn out, the cost of transportation and the time involved eats up all the profit. The only way to make any money is to take their corn out in the form of a liquid concentrate."

"I wonder if we'll be moving out for Pittsburgh too?" asked Whistler.

"Surely not, somebody has to watch the Indians," said Clark.

A few weeks later several of the group were together again early one evening for rounds of beer and Faro when Harrison came in with a newly arrived young ensign.

"Meet Meriwether Lewis," Harrison called out. "He's joining us here after participating in the western Pennsylvania expedition. Clark, he's being assigned to your company"

Everyone shook hands as Clark said, "Glad to have you, Lewis. And by the way, how's your game of Whist? We were just waiting for Lieutenant Harrison here to begin a round."

"Oh, I like it if I can find a good partner."

"You have just found one," responded Clark. "Now Harrison and Scott will have Lewis and Clark to contend with."

Scott spoke up, "I don't see that it will make a whole hell of a lot of difference if he can't play a lot better than Clark, do you, Billy?"

"No, not at all," answered Harrison with a grin as he sat down to the table opposite Scott. "Bring them on."

The Whist went about as usual, at first, though soon Lewis and Clark began winning.

During a lull between hands, Clark asked Harrison, "What is the news of that Berkeley whiskey war?"

"We would have to call it a great victory, I guess," responded Harrison, "but Ensign Lewis here is your authority on that."

"Yes, yes," Clark acknowledged. "Tell us, Lewis, what happened?"

"Nothing much, I'm afraid," the newcomer answered.

Harrison turned toward him and said, "But you found the experience fascinating enough to come over from the militia to the regular army."

"Oh, yes," said Lewis, "but I was looking more for a future in the West. That always has had a fascination for me. But the Pennsylvania thing didn't amount to much. Mostly show."

"How bad were the casualties?" asked Clark.

"Casualties?" Lewis laughed softly. "They were terrible all right." He paused, and then explained, "I understand one or two farmers were killed; two were captured, but Washington pardoned both of them, said one of them was insane and the other a simpleton."

This brought roars of laughter and calls for refills of beer to drink to the great victory.

"My, God!" exclaimed Clark. "It took 15,000 men to do that? That was worse than sending a twelve-pounder cannon to kill a mosquito. Think of that, they send 15,000 men to catch a couple of moonshiners and only 4,000 to pacify all the Indians in the Northwest!"

CHAPTER VI

Vows of Peace and Marriage

1a

"My Sister, I have seen a beautiful princess in the village."

Tecumapease raised her head from her corn grinding and smiled at her brother, Tecumseh. "You mean Monetohse? She is no princess. Her family has just come to the village a few days ago."

"My Sister, is it not time for me to take a squaw? Will you arrange it with her brother?"

"They say she has a reputation for avoiding work by her beauty and her sweet disposition. Is that what you want?"

"I am sure I can get along."

Unquestionably, Monetohse was the most beautiful maiden in this or any of the neighboring villages, but she had few positive attributes to accompany that special attraction other than an outwardly pleasant disposition.

Tecumseh's courtship extended only far enough to assure himself that she would be agreeable to an arrangement for marriage. One evening, carrying a highly ornamented, lighted calumet in his hand, he went to her wigwam when she was there alone. He entered the wigwam and offered her his lighted pipe. She began examining the pipe, admiring its beauty, and with an impish smile held it as though she was about to return it to him lighted. Then very quickly she extinguished the fire. That was her sign of acceptance.

Before the passage of another moon, Tecumapease prepared some presents—beadwork, leatherwork, some corn flour—and took them to the family of Monetohse. On her return, she could report to Tecumseh that the presents had been accepted, and that Monetohse's family would prepare a wedding feast in three days.

It was a clear, cool, fresh spring day when families and friends gathered at the wigwam of Tecumapease for the feast. Tecumseh's younger brothers were on their best behavior. When Monetohse arrived with her father and mother, and brother, she was looking more beautiful than ever. Tecumseh rose to greet the family and then grasped Monetohse's hands. A dozen friends of the bride and groom arrived to join in the festivities. The outdoor feast, with great quantities of fish, partridge, squirrel, corn cakes, and fruit went on for three hours. At sunset the friends and then the family members departed.

Tecumapease quietly came up to Tecumseh, alone, and said in a low voice, "Brother, do you wish me to accompany you into the wigwam?"

He smiled and said, "That will not be necessary, my Sister."

A year later a son was born. Tecumseh was thrilled. Monetohse seemed glad to get the ordeal over but shared little of Tecumseh's obvious enthusiasm. At the naming ceremony, Tecumseh preferred the name Peshewa (the wildcat or lynx), but according to the custom when there were such differences he acquiesced in Monetohse's choice of the milder Pachetha (cat).

In the months ahead, Tecumseh was worried about his family. He was coming to the conclusion that Monetohse's beauty was indeed only skin deep. Far from encouraging him in his determination to unite the Indians against the encroachments of the White Man, she complained about his long absences. Instead of praising his skill as a hunter and his unselfishness in distributing much of his kills to the elderly, she resented his devoting time and energy to such tasks. And she even expected him to do much of the work around the wigwam such as gathering wood, making repairs to the lodge, and grinding corn. Above all, he worried about the welfare of their son, for she sometimes neglected him—omitting some of his cold baths, leaving him unattended in the wigwam when she went out instead of carrying him on her back, and neglecting to tie his head securely in the cradle board.

Monetohse was sweet enough and suppliant to a fault. Her response to any request of Tecumseh always was, "Yes, Master; yes, Master," and then to do nothing about it.

Returning to the wigwam one afternoon, Tecumseh, seeing their son nowhere, demanded of his wife, "Where is Pachetha? Where is our son?"

"I think he is playing with Grandmother."

"He is not there. I just saw her." Raising his voice in a way not usual for him he said, "You neglect our son! He has no mother!" And he slapped her fully on the jaw.

Eyes flashing, the sweet little squaw turned into a wild tiger. "He has no father—you are always away, always far away with other people. He has no father to teach him the ways of the woods and warfare."

She grabbed his hair and pulled with a severe jerk. As the great chief raised his hands to relieve himself of that torture, she resorted to another—the ultimate weapon in the hands of a Shawnee wife. She grasped his testicles and pulled, twisted, and squeezed with all her might. His long training and practice in not wincing at pain was not enough to overcome this. With a loud cry he bent double. He staggered to the doorway and then outside. There he paused until he was able to stand up, partially, and then made his way to the wigwam of Tecumapease.

His sister had to hide an involuntary laugh when he told her what had happened. Recovering a more serious expression, she said, "I think Monetohse is not good for you."

"No, for me it does not matter," said Tecumseh. "No, I do not mind. But she is not good for my son. She must go."

"Yes, I think it better for her to go."

"She must return to her people."

"Bring your son to me. I will take care of him as I took care of his father."

Tecumseh grasped his sister's hands in thanks.

The next day Monetohse returned in disgrace to her people.

1b

In one respect William Henry Harrison felt a special sense of isolation in his military assignments. Ever since he had left Philadelphia after escorting Mrs. Wilkinson, he had hoped for some opportunity to return. It was not that he minded life on the frontier. He had maintained a flexibility which allowed him to adapt to circumstances whatever they might be. He was equally at home whether walking through an unbroken forest or dancing in a gala ballroom, whether eating salt pork and boiled beans beside a wilderness campfire or dining on broiled beef and grouse at a Chippendale table in a manor house, whether sleeping on a bed of pine boughs under the stars or under a satin comforter in a four-posted bed. Still, he felt a sense of loneliness, a loneliness exacerbated by the news a few months ago of the death of his mother.

What Harrison really missed about Philadelphia was Hettie Morris. In this case absence really had made the heart grow fonder, until his feeling for her completely eclipsed any feeling he might have had for Sarah Cutler or anyone else.

Some weeks after the Battle of Fallen Timbers, William Henry wrote a letter to his brother, Carter Bassett, who was in Philadelphia now as a member of Congress. Instead of recounting the details of the great victory over the Indians, he opened his heart:

> I shall make my address to Miss M.... If I should not succeed, I will not be vexed or mortified, for I have been long enough a Soldier, to have learned that there is no Disgrace in a *Well Meant Well Concluded* enterprise, even if it should fail....My Sword is almost my only patrimony—but while I wear that Sword the livery of my Country, I will not disgrace them by owning myself inferior to any person....
>
> There is but one way of making me decline my Purpose, ...that is to be convinced that there was some other person who could make her happier and love her more than I do — I love her so ardently I would forego my own happiness forever to contribute to hers.

Six months later Harrison received a letter from his brother, sent from Philadelphia, with which was enclosed a small newspaper clipping which read:

> In a ceremony performed at Christ Church on Sunday last (April 19, 1795), Miss Hestor Morris, daughter of Senator and Mrs. Robert Morris of this city, was wed to Mr. James Markham Marshall, son of Colonel and Mrs. Thomas Marshall of Kentucky.

2a

Harrison had no time to ponder this latest intelligence from Philadelphia before he was on his way to Lexington, Kentucky. There being no printing press in the Cincinnati area at the time, General Wayne sent his young aide to Lexington to obtain printed copies of his peace proclamation for use in negotiations with the Indians.

This gave Harrison an opportunity to visit an old friend of the family from Virginia, Major Peyton Short, who recently had married and was living in Lexington. On arrival at his friend's home, Harrison found that other visitors already were there, the stepmother and sister of Short's wife, Maria. Maria introduced Harrison to them, her stepmother, Mrs. Symmes, wife of Judge Symmes of North Bend; and her younger sister, Anna, who had just recently arrived with their father and stepmother from New York. They were staying with the Shorts until the completion of their new house at North Bend.

Harrison greeted them almost casually, but as the afternoon wore on, he began looking at Anna with greater interest. Age twenty, she was two years younger than Harrison and obviously younger than her sister, and was slighter of stature. A fair complexion added emphasis to her nearly black hair and dark eyes which fairly sparkled and which often gave away her thoughts and feelings before she expressed them. A dimple in her chin was rather more pronounced than Harrison's. She was one more likely to be described as "pretty" than "beautiful," but she was very pretty, and Harrison found himself recalling the sage advice of his friends that there were "more fish in the sea," and "more pebbles on the beach." He knew now that there was more than one pretty girl. He found her an intelligent and interesting dinner conversationalist, and, after the early dinner, he asked her if she would like to go for a walk. He was pleased, and a little surprised, at the promptness of her assent.

They took an exploratory stroll around the town. Turning up the main street they found a well-paved street eighty feet wide, with sidewalks on either side. A fairly heavy traffic was moving on the streets—about as many four-wheeled carriages as two-wheeled gigs, and a number of saddle horses as well. Clerks and shopkeepers, hurrying home from their work, passed strolling couples and families on the sidewalks.

Lieutenant Harrison and Miss Anna Symmes walked past several attractive houses of two or three stories and then past stores well-filled with merchandise of all kinds, and on past the market place and public library.

"Some of the local inhabitants call Lexington 'the Philadelphia of Kentucky,' " Anna remarked.

Harrison responded, "It has a way to go before it can equal Philadelphia. But I can see some justification for the comparison —the broad, neat streets, crossing at right angles; the brick houses as well as painted wooden ones; the library; a street that runs over a water stream; and the shops and the manufactories. I guess it *is* the biggest city in the West, bigger than Pittsburgh, even if it's not a big river port."

"Yes, and the schools," Anna added. "There is Transylvania University, and there are two or three boarding schools for girls."

"Yes, I have heard Peyton and another friend of mine from Frankfort, John Scott, speak of Transylvania."

"How old is it?"

"About fifteen years, I guess."

"It isn't very big is it?"

"No. They have three or four professors besides the president. It should grow. I understand it has the lowest tuition in the country, but it has some good financial support."

"How's that?"

"The state of Virginia gave it a grant of eight thousand acres of good land, five thousand of which are in the area and the other three thousand near Louisville, and now Kentucky has granted it another six thousand acres south of the Green river."

By now they had come to a fairly new coffee house, Terasse's Coffee House. They ventured in. Harrison was delighted to find a room with files of nearly forty newspapers from all parts of the United States. Attracted by the sound of music, they walked through a hall, past a game room where Harrison was tempted to stop for a game of billiards or chess or backgammon, but thinking better of it continued on with Anna to an attractive public garden in the back. It was called "Vauxhall." Taking seats in a little summer house formed of grape vines, they ordered glasses of wine and relaxed to the entertainment of two violinists.

"We are lucky this is Wednesday," Anna said. "That is the only day they have music."

"Very nice," Harrison acknowledged. "Beautiful music, beautiful flowers, good wine, and you."

Anna smiled as a slight blush tinted her face.

The owner of the place walked by and greeted them in passing.

When the owner had gone, Harrison turned to Anna and asked, "Where did Mr. Terasse come from?"

"From the West Indies, St. Bartholomew I think. He was moving to New York, but lost a lot of his property en route and decided to come out here."

"How did he choose Lexington?"

"He came out to teach French at the University. But he probably would have starved at that if he had not taught dancing as well."

Harrison chuckled. "Ha, yes, I guess dancing teachers are better compensated than are professors of anything."

"Yes, and then apparently he became discouraged about his future at the University, as they like to call it, and he decided to open this business."

"I'm glad he did," Harrison said.

Anna smiled again and agreed, "And so am I."

It took little coaxing to persuade them to join another couple on the small wooden platform in the center of the garden for a quadrille. By now flickering oil lamps were assisting the dimming sunset in providing an enchanting illumination for the garden.

"We're lucky it's Wednesday and they have music," Anna repeated.

"It's my lucky day," Harrison said with a broad smile as he turned his head to the music.

At the conclusion of the series they returned to their places for another glass of wine.

Anna half closed her eyes as she took in the light summer breeze that carried the fragrance of roses and wine across her face. After a few moments of quiet relaxation she suddenly sat up at attention and said, "And by the way, Lieutenant Harrison, what is your given name?"

"William Henry."

"Which?"

"Both."

"Well, what do your friends call you?"

"My brothers and sisters and friends in Virginia used to call me 'Billy'."

"I'll call you 'Henry.'"

"Does that mean you're not my friend?"

"Maybe it means I'll be your special friend."

"I hope so. And you are Anne? I like that. My grandmother's name was Anne."

"Mine is Anna, for my mother."

"What do your friends call you?"

"My father calls me 'Nancy'."

"I'll call you 'Anna'. Do you mind?"

"Course not. That's my name. Just so long as you call me something," she smiled.

"So your father is Judge Symmes."

"Yes. Do you know him?"

"No, not personally, but everyone around Fort Washington has heard of Judge Symmes. And you live at North Bend, a dozen miles from the fort, and I have to come all the way to Lexington to meet you."

"Well, that's where my home will be, but I haven't been living there yet. My stepmother and I will be going there as soon as the house is finished."

"Where have you been living before?"

"Oh, I've been going to school."

"That's obvious. Where have you been at school?"

"First to the female seminary at East Hampton on Long Island, New York, and then at Mrs. Graham's school in New York City."

"Are you from New York?"

"I feel that I am, though our original home, and my father's residence, was in Morristown, New Jersey, but I went to live with my grandparents on Long Island when I was only four years old."

"How was that?"

"My mother died shortly after my birth. My father was a colonel in the Continental Army, so he had to be away most of the time and, when New Jersey became the site of a lot of fighting, he thought I would be safer with my grandparents on Long Island."

"When was that?"

"I guess it was 1778 or 1779."

"But I thought the British were in control of New York and Long Island all that time."

"They were."

"Wasn't he afraid of what they might do to you?"

"No, after Washington withdrew from New York after the engagements at Brooklyn Heights, Harlem Heights, and Fort Washington, there was no more fighting in that area."

"But if Washington's army had withdrawn, and the British were in complete control, how did you get there?"

"You won't believe it, but Papa dressed up in a British uniform, wrapped me up in a blanket and, holding me in one arm, mounted his horse and rode right up through the British lines, crossed the rivers on ferries, and got me to my grandfather Tuthill's house at Southold. Then he got back safely to the American Army in New Jersey."

"Zounds! If he had been caught he would have been shot, and maybe you, too!"

"Maybe, but here I am."

"I'm glad."

"So am I. But what about you? I understand you are from Virginia, but what else? Were you in the Revolution?"

"Well, Benedict Arnold came through our place, Berkeley, on the James River, and once I saw General Wayne when he was after Lord Cornwallis."

"Sounds exciting. You might have been shot, too. Was your father in the war?"

"He was in the Continental Congress, signed the Declaration of Independence."

"Oh, I'm impressed. My father was in the Continental Congress, too, but after the war."

"And I had a brother in the Continental Army, but he was in the South."

"But what else?"

"About what?"

"What else did you do besides watch Benedict Arnold and General Wayne? Go to college?"

"Oh, I went to Hampden-Sydney College in Virginia for a while. Studied medicine for a while in Richmond and again in Philadelphia."

"Oh, you were going to be a doctor? How did you end up out here in the Army?"

"I never really had a great interest in medical studies. I have never been really convinced that doctors do much good. I always have had an interest in the Army. Probably comes from my long interest in military history."

"I like to read history, too."

"Good. I used to read a lot in the Philadelphia library. When my father died I decided to quit medical studies and try to get a commission. That was successful, and I was assigned to the 1st Infantry Regiment out here at Fort Washington."

"How did you get here?"

"Walked all the way from Philadelphia to Pittsburgh with a company of eighty recruits and then took boats down the river to the fort."

"I guess we had better go back in. The others will be wondering what has happened to us."

"I'll bet they haven't even missed us. Do you get along well with your stepmother? How long has she been in your family?"

"Oh, yes, she is very nice. My father came to New York and married her just in the last year. Judge Livingston of New York is her brother. Actually, she is my second stepmother."

"You mean your father's third wife?"

"Yes, my first stepmother died just a few years after they were married."

"I know he has been through some sad times."

"And lonely. He was not at all enthusiastic when Maria married and left home."

Over the next three days Anna and William Henry had an opportunity to deepen their acquaintance.

"When do you have to go back to the forest?" she wanted to know.

"As soon as the printing is done. Ordinarily I am very impatient to get things like this done, but now I have been rather hoping for delays."

Anna's eyes told him before she said anything that she hoped so too.

"How long before you and your stepmother return to North Bend?" he asked.

"It will be a few weeks yet before the house is ready."

One day Harrison visited his cousin, Carter Henry Harrison of Clifton, who recently had moved to Lexington. Then after a final evening with the Shorts, and with Anna, he was off early the next day to return to the fort.

4a

In watching Anthony Wayne follow up his victory at Fallen Timbers, William Henry Harrison had an object lesson on the object of war and in negotiations with Indians. Wayne was confident now that, after a generation of almost continuous warfare, the Indian wars in the Northwest were at an end. But to make it so he would have to get a treaty—one that was clear to everyone and agreed to by everyone concerned. The object of a war is not in military victory itself but in the political settlement which the military victory makes possible. Indian villages had been burned many times before, but that was all. The Indians had not been overpowered, and they had not agreed to any significant concessions. Now Wayne set about his task of getting a treaty. He set about it with a deliberateness and a thoroughness that was a marvel to young Harrison.

From early January 1795, Wayne had begun his negotiations. He was aiming for a general conference in mid-summer, but preparatory to that, he visited many of the tribes for preliminary discussions and encouraged them to hold councils of their own to discuss the wisdom of accepting a peaceful settlement. Further, he improved roads and trails leading to Fort Greeneville to which he invited all the tribes to send leaders and warriors for the conference. Harrison accompanied the commander at several of these preliminary conferences, and the young aide gained a respect for his chief as a negotiator to match that which he already had formed for him as a military commander.

Wayne had set the middle of June as the time for the conference, but only the Delawares arrived by the appointed time. Wayne patiently waited for the others, until by the end of July there was a formidable array of war chiefs, sachems, and warriors numbering all together 1,130 men from twelve tribes. Sensing what lay in store for the Indians, Tecumseh refused to attend, but Blue Jacket, Black Hoof, and Black Snake were there to represent the Shawnees. Little Turtle came with seventy-three Miamis. The Potawatomis had 240 there under New Corn, Asimette, and Sun. The Delawares had the largest contingent of all, 381, under Teteboxti, Peketelemund, and Buckangehela.

On his side Wayne had, in addition to Harrison, other members of his personal staff, the sublegion commanders, some of his most trusted scouts, including Simon Kenton and Isaac Zane, and a couple of representatives from the War Department.

White wampum belts, sometimes as long as six feet and three to four inches wide, and made of beads cut from mussel shells or obtained from White traders, were exchanged to signify peace. Council fires were kindled, and long orations began as Wayne took up, point by point, the terms of his proposed treaty. At the outset he explained that this treaty would be based partly on a treaty which had been signed in January 1785. Now new lines were to be drawn, but Indians could continue to hunt and fish peaceably even in the area to be ceded, so long as they did not interfere with White settlements.

In the discussions the Indians addressed Wayne as "Elder Brother," and he, in turn, spoke of them as "Younger Brothers." At the opening of the formal conference on August 3, Wayne read a letter from the Friends' (Quakers) Yearly Meeting of Philadelphia and delivered some accompanying presents. In explaining it the General said, "Younger Brothers—I have received a letter from your friends, the people called Quakers, with a message to all the people here assembled. The Quakers are a good people whom I much love and esteem for their goodness of heart and sincere love of peace with all nations. Listen then to their voices, and let them sink deep to your hearts. Their present, you see, is small, but being designed with the benevolent view of promoting the happiness and peace of mankind, it becomes of important value. They wish it to be considered merely as a token of regard for you and a testimony of their brotherly affection and kind remembrance of you."

The treaty itself was expressed in these terms:

A treaty of peace between the United States of America and the tribes of Indians called Wyandots, Delawares, Shawnees, Ottawas, Chippewas, Pottawatomies, Miamis, Eel rivers, *Weas, Kickapoos, Piankeshaws, and Kaskaskias,* to put an end to a destructive war, to settle controversies, and to restore harmony and friendly intercourse between the said United States and Indian tribes, Anthony Wayne, major-general, commanding the army of the United States, and sole commissioner for the good purposes above-mentioned, and the said tribes of Indians, by their sachems, chiefs, and warriors met together at Greenville, the head-quarters of said army, have agreed on the following articles, which, when ratified by the President, with the advice and consent of the Senate of the United States, shall be binding on them and the said Indian tribes.

Article 1. Henceforth all hostilities shall cease; peace is hereby established, and shall be perpetual, and a friendly intercourse shall take place between the said United States and Indian tribes.

Art. 2. All prisoners shall, on both sides, be restored. The Indian prisoners to the United States shall be immediately set at liberty. The people of the United States, still remaining prisoners among the Indians, shall be delivered up in ninety days from the date hereof, to the general or commanding officer at Greenville, Fort Wayne, or Fort Defiance; and ten chiefs of the said tribes shall remain at Greenville as hostages, until the delivery of the prisoners shall be effected.

Art. 3. The general boundary line between the lands of the United States and the lands of the said Indian tribes, shall begin at the mouth of the Cuyahoga river, and run thence up the same to the portage between that and the Tuscarawa's branch of the Muskingum; and thence down that branch to the crossing-place above Fort Lawrence; thence westerly to a fork of that branch of the Great Miami river running into the Ohio, at or near which fork stood Laramie's store, and where commences the portage between the Miami of the Ohio and St. Mary's river, which is a branch of the Miami which runs into Lake Erie; thence a westerly course to Fort Recovery, which stands on a branch of the Wabash; thence southwesterly in a direct line to the Ohio, so as to intersect that river opposite the Kentucky, or Cuttawa, river. And, in consideration of the peace now established, of the goods formerly received from the United States, of those now to be delivered, and of the yearly delivery of goods now stipulated to be made hereafter, and to indemnify the United States for injuries and expenses sustained during the war, the said Indian tribes do, hereby, cede and relinquish forever all their claims to the lands lying eastwardly and southwardly of the general boundary line now described, and these lands, or any part of them, shall never hereafter be made a cause or pretense, on the part of the said tribes, or any of them, of war or injury to the United States, or any of the people thereof.

In other words, the Indians were to cede what amounted to about the southern five-eighths of what would become Ohio, plus the northeastern corner, i.e., the lands of the east of Cleveland, and the southeastern corner of what would become Indiana. In addition they were to cede sixteen plots, mostly about six miles square each, at strategic points in the area beyond the noted boundary. These included such places as "Laramie's store," Fort Wayne, Ouiatenon on the Wabash River, the British fort on the Miami near Lake Erie, the mouth of the Chicago River on Lake Michigan, the mouth of the Illinois on the Mississippi, and the area around Detroit. Beyond all this the Indians were to acknowledge that their title had been "previously extinguished" for several other areas including George Rogers Clark's grant of 150,000 acres in southern Indiana near the rapids of the Ohio River, various French settlements, and the area around Vincennes on the Wabash.

The Indian chiefs protested at various points, but then went along. Two considerations persuaded them to do so. The first was expressed by a Chippewa chief when he said, "Elder Brother, you asked who were the true owners of the land now ceded to the United States. In answer I tell you, if any nations should call themselves the owners of it they would be guilty of falsehood; our claim to it is equal. Our Elder Brother has conquered it."

The other persuasive factor was that contained in the fourth article of the treaty:

And for the same considerations, and with the same views above-mentioned, the United States now deliver to the said Indian tribes, a quantity of goods to the value of twenty thousand dollars, the receipt whereof they do hereby acknowledge; and henceforward, every year, forever, the United States will deliver, at some convenient place northward of the Ohio river, like useful goods, suited to the circumstances of the Indians of the value of nine thousand five hundred dollars; reckoning that value at the first cost of the goods in the city or place in the United States, where they shall be procured.

The tribes to which those goods are to be delivered annually, and the proportions in which they are to be delivered, are as follows:

1. To the Wyandots, the amount of one thousand dollars.
2. To the Delawares, the amount of one thousand dollars.
3. To the Shawnees, the amount of one thousand dollars.
4. To the Miamis, the amount of one thousand dollars.
5. To the Ottawas, the amount of one thousand dollars.
6. To the Chippewas, the amount of one thousand dollars.
7. To the Pottawatomies, the amount of one thousand dollars.
8. And to the Kickapoo, Weas, Eel River, Piankeshaws, and Kaskaskias tribes, the amount of five hundred dollars each.

Provided, That if either of the said tribes shall hereafter, at the annual delivery of their share of the goods aforesaid, desire that a part of their annuity should be furnished in domestic animals, implements of husbandry and other utensils convenient for them, and in compensation to useful artificers who may reside with or near them, and be employed for their benefit, the same shall, at the subsequent annual deliveries, be furnished accordingly.

At the conclusion, Blue Jacket rose and made this statement: "Elder Brother, and you, my brothers, present: you see me now present myself as a war chief to lay down that commission, and place myself in the rear of my village chiefs, who for the future will command me. Remember, brothers, you have all buried your war hatchet. Your brothers, the Shawnees, now do the same good act. We must think of war no more."

"Elder Brother: you see now all the chiefs and warriors around you, have joined in the good work of peace, which is now accomplished. We now request you to inform our elder brother, General Washington, of it, and of the cheerful unanimity which has marked their determination. We wish you to inquire of him if it would be agreeable that two chiefs from each nation should pay him a visit, and take him by the hand, for your younger brothers have a strong desire to see that great man and to enjoy the pleasure of conversing with him."

In the end, all the tribal representatives accepted, and all the chiefs present made their marks on the treaty document. All together, ninety-two chiefs and twenty-seven White men signed, including Lieutenant Harrison.

This done, Wayne delivered a final address to the whole gathering, in which he said, "I now fervently pray to the Great Spirit that the peace now established may be permanent and that it now holds us together in the bonds of friendship until time shall be no more. I also pray that the Great Spirit above may enlighten your minds and open your eyes to your true happiness, that your children may learn to cultivate the earth and enjoy the fruits of peace and industry."

William Henry Harrison thought it an absolute marvel. He thought it was fair in guaranteeing Indian rights in the territory north and west of the treaty line. He thought it gave good promise for restoring peace, and he was sure that now, with the Ohio River at last safe for navigation and with vast areas now guaranteed for settlement, there would be an influx of settlers who through their farming and trade would bring prosperity to the whole region.

Tecumseh was sure that the Treaty of Greeneville was a total disaster even before he had heard its terms. Whatever the terms, he knew there would be concessions, and whatever they might be, they would be bad for the Indian. And even if there were many representatives who signed the treaty, they had no right to give up lands that belonged to all the Indians. And even if the Long Knives gave their assurances that they would guarantee the remaining Indian lands, he was sure that such guarantees would be worth no more than all the guarantees that had been given previously.

Blue Jacket was sufficiently concerned about Tecumseh's attitude and the attitude of many of his followers, that he made a special trip up to Deer Creek to explain to Tecumseh the terms of the treaty. Blue Jacket pointed out the advantages of ending the long season of wars, of the guarantees for Indian rights in the vast territory which remained to them, and the promise of annual payments which could be of great help to all their people.

Tecumseh was no more favorably impressed than before he had heard the terms. He again said firmly and bitterly that the White Man's guarantees were worth nothing, that when it suited him he would cross the treaty line and would always be demanding new cessions of territory until it all was gone. Even the annual payments could be a disadvantage. They would make the Red Men dependent on the good will of the Long Knives, and the Indians would become weak as they lost their incentive to hunt and to grow corn. Tecumseh let it be known that he was disappointed in seeing his old friend and great war chief, Blue Jacket, be blinded by the White Men, to be a party to such a treaty.

In conclusion Tecumseh said, "My heart is a stone: heavy with sadness for my people; cold with the knowledge that no treaty will keep Whites out of our lands; hard with the determination to resist as long as I live and breathe. Now we are weak and many of our people are afraid. But hear me; a single twig breaks, but the bundle of twigs is strong. Someday I will embrace our brother tribes and draw them into a bundle and together we will win our country back from the Whites."

4a

Several weeks had passed during which Harrison often thought of Anna but had no news from her. Then the commander of the fort called him in one day to say that he had a special mission for him. He wanted Harrison to lead a pack horse train over to North Bend. Harrison jumped at the chance. Judge Symmes already had arranged that the escorting officer should be his guest for lodging in his house.

The twelve or thirteen miles seemed twice the distance as Harrison rode over the rough trail with his detachment of guards and supply trains. When the supplies had been delivered, he called at the house of the Judge. It was a big, impressive house. On close examination, Harrison could see that it was built of logs, but these were covered with boards and painted white. The Judge welcomed him warmly and took him in to meet the ladies.

Harrison recognized them immediately. "Mrs. Symmes," he said as he bowed toward the new lady of the house, and "Miss Symmes," as he grasped Anna's offered hand.

"Oh, I see that you already have met," said the Judge.

"Yes," his wife explained. "We had the pleasure while we were visiting Maria and Peyton, and the Lieutenant came to Lexington on a mission for the General."

Harrison added, "Yes. The Shorts were old friends of our family in Virginia, and I make it a habit of visiting Peyton whenever I go to Lexington."

That evening Harrison enjoyed a dinner which rivaled those he had known at Berkeley. Afterward they all joined in general conversation. The Judge's main interest was in bringing settlers in to buy parcels of the large tract of land which he had purchased in the area. His special concern was for sufficient security against Indian attacks to assure the settlers of their safety. Otherwise there would be no settlers, and for him, no sales.

Harrison reassured him that the Greeneville Treaty, just signed, obtained all the lands of the southern two-thirds of Ohio for settlement, and one of his principal duties now was to keep a close watch to see that the Indians observed the terms of that treaty. The Judge agreed that that would be helpful, but they could not put their trust in any paper document so far as the Indians were concerned.

It took a good deal of hinting and coaxing on the part of Mrs. Symmes, but at last she persuaded the Judge to retire to their bed chamber and leave the parlor to the young people.

As soon as the coast was clear, Harrison exclaimed, "Anna, I am so glad to see you!"

"Henry!" was all she could say before he took her in his arms and kissed her. It seemed so natural that it did not even occur to him that this was the first time, and her response suggested the same attitude on her part.

From then on, Harrison took advantage of every opportunity to go to North Bend whether on official business or on leave.

Frequently the Judge was away, and Harrison was thankful for that because lately he had detected a coolness on the Judge's part.

One such evening in mid-September after dinner, Harrison walked with Anna out to the slope where a bright afterglow of the sunset reflected on the wide river. A rising moon, full and golden, competed with it from the east.

"Anna," said Harrison. He felt a dryness in his throat and a tenseness in his voice. In spite of the closeness he had come to feel for Anna, and even though he thought he knew her very well, he felt a strange nervousness. He never had been afraid of women. Maybe his tenseness now was the result of rebuffs he had had when he had reached the point of being willing to make a firm commitment. Maybe it was the fear of failure. Maybe it was the risk he sensed, for if he got a negative response that would not only defeat his big hope for the moment, but doubtless would also mean the end of what for him was truly a beautiful friendship.

"Anna, what a beautiful night it is," he said in a stall for more time.

"Isn't it," she responded.

"Anna."

"Yes?"

"Anna." His first breath fell short, and he paused to recapture it. Then summoning his full powers, he blurted out in a deep, strong voice that came out high and feeble, "Anna, I love you very much, and I wonder if I might speak to your father!"

"Oh, yes, yes, yes!" she cried as she threw her arms around him.

After several minutes of mutual exultation, she paused to caution him, "It may not be easy."

"No. I suppose not."

"No. I mean you had best be prepared for a negative response."

"Oh, what if it is? Then what?"

"That will be up to you."

An opportunity came on Harrison's next visit to North Bend. It was a Saturday afternoon, and Harrison found Judge Symmes out examining some fruit trees.

"Judge," he called as he approached.

"Good afternoon, Lieutenant, what can I do for you?"

"Judge, Miss Anna and I love each other, and I would like to ask your permission for her hand in marriage."

Judge Symmes did not take his eyes off the tree branch he was inspecting. After a prolonged silence, still looking at the tree, he responded, "I'm afraid that is out of the question, young man, altogether out of the question."

"But, Sir, we love each other."

"That is quite beside the point. What do you have to offer? Do you propose to carry her off to some wilderness outpost to be taken by the Indians?"

"But, Sir—"

"And if it has come to this, I think it advisable that you not see my daughter anymore."

Harrison spun about, and without even looking up at the house he strode through the yard, mounted his horse, and took off at an immediate gallop.

Within a week Harrison was back at North Bend. This time he took an orderly along with him. Stopping at a safe distance from the house, he sent the orderly up to the house with a note to be delivered to Miss Anna in person, and no one else. A few minutes later Anna came out to meet him. She was overjoyed to see him.

"After Papa told me what he had said to you, I was afraid I never would see you again."

"I couldn't stand that," said Harrison. "What else did he say?"

"Do you really want to know?"

"Of course."

"He said that you could neither bleed, plead, nor preach, but if you could even plow he might be satisfied. He said your best prospect probably is in the Army. He admitted that you had talents, and he said if you could dodge Indian bullets well enough for a few years you might very well become conspicuous."

"Well, that's not such a bad assessment, is it?" responded Harrison with a laugh. "I guess I can ride and shoot, and as a matter of fact I guess I can plow pretty well, too. As for the Army, that's all right for now, but I'm not sure I want to make a lifelong career out of it."

"Then what?"

"Who knows. I have always liked farming, and maybe even politics."

"But you know something? I don't think that it's really you that Father objects to. I think it's my getting married at all. You know many fathers are reluctant to give up their daughters to some strange man, and Father has been lonely, and he rejects the notion of having both Maria and me far away."

They walked over to a grove, well out of sight of the house or other buildings or the trail.

"Now what do we do?" asked Harrison.

"I said it would be up to you."

"Anna, I do love you, and I want you to be my wife. Will you marry me?"

"Henry, I love you, and I would be honored to be your wife. I shall be happy to marry you."

"Oh, my Darling, thank you, thank you," he whispered as he embraced her. Then he fairly shouted, "The goose honks high!" And after a few minutes of closeness in each other's arms, he said, "I must return to the fort now, but can I see you on Wednesday afternoon?"

"Yes, I'll ride down to meet you where we can be together, away from everyone. I like to ride."

"Good. I'll meet you on this side of where the trail crosses the creek."

"I'll be there."

Harrison did not have to wait long at the creek crossing for Anna to appear. They rode for a distance along the creek and coming to a grassy clearing, dismounted.

"Well, what's your plan, General?"

"We elope!"

"Elope? Oh, I don't know whether that would be such a good idea. I have always dreamed of a nice church wedding."

"You know your father said it was out of the question. If you are going to leave it up to me, we elope."

"How do we do that?"

"First we'll set the date. Then during the preceding week I'll send some pack horses up to pick up your things."

"To take them where?"

"Back to Fort Washington. I can arrange for quarters in one of the blockhouses there. Then on the day we choose—our wedding day, I'll come up close to your house with two horses. You'll come out and get on one of them, and we shall fly away to Cincinnati where we will go to our new home in the fort."

"Sounds exciting. What shall we set as the date?"

"Well, October has about ended already. Let's say next month, November."

"When in November?"

"That, my Darling, is for you to say."

"Let's see about the arrangements and meet again in a week to settle it."

Anna brought a picnic lunch for their next secret rendezvous. They enjoyed the fried chicken and muffins, enjoyed the scenery and the wild life, and then went on discussing their plans.

"Oh, I very carefully approached my stepmother, and she will help us."

"Wonderful. I have made arrangements for our apartment in a blockhouse of the fort. When is the great day?"

"How about November 25?"

"What day would that be?"

"Wednesday, wedding day!"

"Good. Now can you have all your things packed in bags and put them out in that shed beside the stable? I'll have some men come up on Saturday. I'll tell the sergeant to come up and ask for some water. If your father is here, tell him when to come back. If your father is away, show him where your bags are."

"I think we can do it! Isn't it exciting?"

"Hey, you know what Ben Franklin's Poor Richard's Almanac said about marriage?"

"No, what?"

"He said 'a man without a wife is but half a man.' If he was talking about me and you, I know it is true."

"And that works both ways, I think."

On Saturday the 21st, Harrison sent the pack horses up to North Bend. To his great delight, they returned in good time with Anna's bags. Harrison carried them into the blockhouse quarters which had been assigned. During the next days he used his spare time to make the quarters as attractive as he could—curtains for the windows, fresh linens and comforter for the bed, rag rugs for the floor, utensils for the kitchen fireplace, and robes for the chairs.

Early on the morning of the 25th, Harrison, in the company of his orderly and with an extra horse, set out through a heavy fog for North Bend. In a way he welcomed the fog for this clandestine enterprise. By mid-morning the fog had lifted to reveal a clear, cool day which he welcomed even more. Shortly after eleven o'clock, he arrived at the rendezvous. Promptly at eleven-thirty Anna came out, but instead of mounting the extra horse and flying away with him, she commanded him to tie the horses and follow her.

"Is something wrong?" he asked with growing concern. "Why the delay?"

"Just follow me. Trust me."

She led him directly up to the front door, the one facing the river, and into the parlor. To his astonishment the room was filled with people—Anna's stepmother, her sister, Maria, from Lexington, and Maria's husband, Peyton Short, and about all her neighbors from North Bend. Taking his hand, Anna led Harrison around to an anteroom.

"Father is away for the whole day, on business in Cincinnati," she whispered. "We certainly don't want to go to Cincinnati for our wedding, so we are going to have it right here. Now you just wait here until I am ready. Peyton is going to be your best man, and he'll let you know. Maria will stand up with me. We'll try to make it at high noon."

"I think I'm going to faint," Harrison said with a grin. "I'm afraid this will have to serve as my dress uniform."

"See you in a few minutes. This is your last chance to duck out!"

Harrison occupied himself with polishing his boots and brushing his hair. At high noon Peyton Short came into the anteroom and escorted Lieutenant Harrison to one end of the long parlor. A gentleman in formal dress, knickers, silk stockings, ruffled shirt, dark coat with velvet collar and cuff trims, was standing at the place to officiate. Harrison recognized him as Dr. Stephen Wood, a highly respected neighbor of North Bend who was a physician, treasurer of the Territory, owner of a general store, and a local magistrate or justice of the peace.

Presently, to the music of a black fiddler, Maria came down the aisle created in the center of the room. She carried a bouquet of fall flowers. Then came the bride. Everyone issued a sincere gasp at her beauty. She was wearing a dress of India silk, off-white, with purple sash, cut in the latest fashion without hoops or bustle, and falling just to the tops of the ankles. She carried blue and gold flowers. Harrison beamed involuntarily as she approached.

Dr. Wood made the ceremony simple, short, and dignified. Afterward everyone joined in the festivities. Fresh doughnuts served as the wedding cake, and jugs of whiskey and cider filled the sideboard. Everyone joined in dancing as the fiddler struck up the plantation jigs, "The Pigeon-wing," and the "Balance All."

At the height of all this, Anna went upstairs and changed clothes, and then the bride and groom slipped out the back door and mounted their horses. When they arrived at Fort Washington, the whole garrison was waiting for them. They fired a salute, toasted the bride and groom, and then the couple went in to a feast of fish, fowl, beef, vegetables, hot biscuits, and again, cider and whiskey, and now some beer and wine, too.

Harrison showed Anna to their rooms and then returned for a litte further celebration with his fellow officers. They tried in every way to get him drunk, but he resisted until he was able to slip away unnoticed.

Two weeks later General Wilkinson gave a farewell dinner at the fort for General Wayne. Judge Symmes and all the officials of the Territory were invited as special guests. Harrison dreaded this encounter worse than a meeting with Blue Jacket and Little Turtle. Arriving at the last minute and taking his place with his company officers, he avoided eye contact with Judge Symmes throughout the meal, the toasts, and the speeches. But he was determined to face the music. At adjournment, he immediately sought out Judge Symmes.

The Judge did not extend his hand but greeted him formally and coolly, and then said, "Young man, I understand you went ahead and married my daughter after all."

"Yes, Sir, I did."

"Tell me, young man, just how do you propose to support her in a proper way?"

The lieutenant took a step back, slapped his scabbard with his right hand, and then raised his hand as he replied, "By my sword and my own right hand."

The Judge was taken aback for a moment by the very audacity of the reply. Then, recovering his composure, he broke into a smile and extended his hand in an attitude of forgiveness.

That winter Lieutenant Harrison was given command of Fort Washington with its small garrison of eighty men.

Cincinnati now had grown from the village of twenty or thirty log cabins which Harrison had found there in 1791 to a population of about 400, and there was a steady stream of rivermen and immigrants at the local taverns.

In the next summer, 1796, still at Fort Washington, Harrison and his wife thrilled at the birth of their first child —a daughter whom they named Betsy Bassett for Harrison's mother, Elizabeth Bassett.

4b

Disappointed in his previous encounter with marriage, for a while Tecumseh resisted pressure from his family and his friends to take another wife. Further, he wanted nothing to detract from his central purpose. Marriage might interfere with his work of trying to unite his people. He knew that the French holy men did not take wives because they were bound to devote their full attention to their church. In a way he felt that the marriage of the tribes was his highest calling. Still, he recognized the importance of a good squaw for a good leader, and he recognized the desirability of setting a good example for the young men of the tribes.

Now he thought of Mineshelana, the Creek. She was a good woman. He knew that she was true and dependable as well as beautiful. He wished for her now. But he knew it was too late. She now was the faithful squaw of a Creek chief.

Then about mid-1795 he decided to take another wife. Although he could have had any maiden he wanted, he chose a woman somewhat older than himself but one known to be especially good with children. She was Mamate. Toward her, he felt more a respect and friendship than passionate love, but he was confident that she would do well in looking after his son, Pachetha, and he could hope for more sons—and daughters.

In October 1796, the time approached for the birth of his second son. He, with the help of several of the women of the village, built a maternity lodge at some distance from their wigwam. When the time came for her to be delivered, the women went in to assist while Tecumseh waited outside. He expected this sort of thing at night, but this time it was a clear October afternoon. It seemed an unusually cheerful day. He looked for a good omen.

He waited and waited for a good omen.

He waited and waited for the birth of his child.

In vain he waited for the reassuring scream of the new born. An old woman came out of the lodge to give sad news. His new son was dead. And his wife was very sick.

A few days later Mamate, too, died.

Sadly, Tecumseh looked up to the sky. Cheerfulness had abandoned the bright blue weather of October. "Must this be the fate of my people?" he cried out. "Must they die with no one to carry on? Or must they be born without a future? And what is the difference?"

CHAPTER VII

Rising Stars

1

T hat Blue Jacket should make a special effort to seek out Tecumseh was testimony in itself to the respect and support that the latter already had won among the Shawnees.

From early youth, Tecumseh had been recognized as a natural leader. His fighting ability and leadership during his trip to the South had added to his prestige, and his action in the Battle of Fallen Timbers had brought influence beyond his own village and even beyond his own division. Now, at twenty-seven, he had grown into impressive physical strength and moral courage. His defiance of the Treaty of Greeneville brought him additional following among dissident warriors of his and other tribes.

Tribal leadership was being perverted in a sense from the old system. In some cases the positions of the traditional sachems and long-established war chiefs had been undermined by those who came to be known as "Government Chiefs"—those who owed their position largely to the support of the United States Government, and whose influence over their tribesmen depended upon their control of the annuity payments from the U.S. Government. But this also opened the way for a man like Tecumseh to appeal to all those who shared his view that they should preserve their own way of life and should continue to defend their hunting grounds from the encroachments of White Men.

Already recognized as a war chief in his own village and clan, and then his division, Tecumseh in the next seven years or so rose to the position of *de facto* war chief of all Shawnees, and even as war chief of various groups of Miami, Wyandot, Delaware, Kickapoo, Potawatomi, and others as well. Tecumseh's star was rising, rising rapidly, though he was not without opposition. He was in a measure undermining the authority of the signers of the Treaty of Greeneville. In his appeals for support he went directly to the warriors. In by-passing the traditional chiefs he aroused their opposition. But his appeal was becoming overpowering.

Tecumseh was persuaded that the only way to preserve the Indian life was in unity of all the tribes in resisting White encroachments. This, in fact, had been a theme of the Shawnees for years. In 1786, two thousand warriors from several tribes had gathered at the Shawnee towns and agreed to take up the hatchet against the Americans, but efforts at forming a permanent union of some kind fell apart in the face of tribal jealousies and the failure of leadership.

Tecumseh was aware of this failure but no less sure of the necessity. He pondered earlier efforts and failures of united resistance. He knew how Metacom, who came to be known by the Whites as "King Philip," sachem of the Wampanoags, and warriors from a number of tribes had come close to expelling the White Men from parts of New England more than a century before. Metacom had failed because he had failed to unite all the tribes, and one of them, the Mohawks, proved to be his undoing when their attack against him weakened his forces. Tecumseh recalled how the great Chief Pontiac had brought many tribes together to resist the White Men, but he too had failed.

Tecumseh's view was that earlier attempts had failed because of a lack of firm unity among Indian tribes. Now he was beginning to conceive of a great confederation of all Indian tribes, north and south. This would not be a temporary war alliance. This would be no loose league of chiefs. This would be a permanent union of Indian peoples. Only in such unity could be found the strength for successful resistance against the White Americans.

He spoke eloquently to assemblies of followers and skeptical onlookers—"Where today are the Pequot? Where the Narraganset, the Mohican, the Pokanoket, and many other once powerful tribes of our people? They have vanished before the avarice and oppression of the White Man, as snow before a summer sun."

Tecumseh had ambition for power, but this was not the

ambition of a Napoleon, nor a Caesar, nor an Alexander. His attraction to power and his exercise of leadership were characterized by a selflessness and a humility altogether foreign to a Napoleon or even a Cromwell, though like Cromwell he held to a firm religious belief and saw himself as an agent of the Master of Life in defending the interests of his peoples. While others were paralyzed by doubt and by concerns for their own self-preservation, his vision was clear, his determination firm.

2

About the time of the Treaty of Greeneville and just in time to bring some additional income needed for the support of a wife, Harrison received his promotion to the rank of captain. He had impressed favorably all the officers under whom he had served, and he had won commendation from Wayne for his action at Fallen Timbers. The promotion almost was delayed through an error by which his name on the list which Wayne forwarded early in 1795 was below that of a man whom he was supposed to precede. As it turned out, the other officer became involved in some kind of affair out of which he was charged with violating regulations, and he accepted Wayne's offer of resignation rather than stand court martial. In any event this restored Harrison to the intended place on the list.

Although Harrison's military career now was well launched, and he did harbor a certain liking for military activity, he began to consider political possibilities. He hoped to avoid some of the separation from his family that military service entailed, but he also thought that there might be opportunities for greater service than he could expect to perform as an army officer, at least for some years to come.

He saw a special opportunity when the Secretary of the Northwest Territory, Winthrop Sargent, was appointed Governor of the Southwest Territory in the Mississippi area. He knew almost no one in the Government at Philadelphia, and the only members of Congress he knew were his brother, Carter Bassett, and an old friend, Robert Goodloe Harper, now a Federalist representative from South Carolina and chairman of the House Committee on Ways and Means. To the latter he turned for help. In a letter written at Fort Washington in late May 1798, he wrote to Harper:

I am by no means certain of the propriety of the request which I am going to make to you—but I think I have formed a very just opinion of the liberality of your Heart. I am sure, be it proper or otherwise, that it will meet with a candid and generous reception. I shall therefore waive all further apology and proceed immediately to the subject of my request. Intelligence has just reached us of the appointment of Colo. Sargent to the Government of the Territory on the Mississippi... which will of course make a vacancy in the Secretaryship of the Territory—to obtain this is the object of my wishes—I am convinced that your influence would ensure me success....

I have been so long in these woods that I have had no opportunity of making myself known to the officers of Government—I have never seen either the President or any of his Secretarys—indeed yourself and my brother excepted I do not know three members of either house—so that all my Hopes rest on you—for I know that you deservedly possess the Confidence of the President.

If General Washington still filled the Presidential chair I believe my success would be more certain, for that great man has on more than one occasion done me the Honor to express his approbation of my services.... From the manner in which I have heard my father speak of the President I am induced to think that there was an intimacy between them—the circumstance together with the knowledge which the President possesses of his services and sacrifices of property during the Revolution will, I should suppose, make in my favor.

One afternoon in July, Harrison rushed into their home at Fort Washington to tell Anna the news. "The appointment has come through," he said. He read from a paper in his hand, "On the 28th of June, 1798, the President of the United States was pleased to appoint, by and with the advice and consent of the Senate, William Henry Harrison to be Secretary of the Territory of the United States Northwest of the River Ohio."

"Wonderful!" Anna exclaimed. "Does this mean we can continue to live here?"

"Oh yes, since Cincinnati has become the functioning capital of the Territory."

"But what will be your responsibilities—will you be one of the Governor's private secretaries?"

"No, no. Secretary of the Territory is like Secretary of State in one of the states. He has custody of official documents and the official seal. He keeps the official records of the laws, of land surveys, decisions on land claims, and activities of the Governor."

"I have never heard of any legislature here. Where do the laws come from?"

"Our basic Constitution is in effect in the Northwest Ordinance which the Continental Congress approved in 1787, and which the new Congress reapproved in 1789. The Governor and the three judges can adopt any laws of any of the states, and then these become the laws of the Territory. As soon as the population reaches 5,000 free White male inhabitants, which is about now, we can advance to the second stage of territorial government and have an elected legislature and even a delegate in Congress."

"Is that all the Secretary has to do?"

"Isn't that enough? He also is *ex officio* the lieutenant governor of the territory. If the Governor is away or becomes incapacitated, he acts as governor."

"Well that all sounds pretty good for a young man of twenty-five, or whatever it is. What will the older men think about that?"

"Probably not much," Harrison said and then added, "At least I hope they don't think about it too much. Anyway, this should be good experience for the future."

"What kind of future?"

"Almost any kind of government service. This should be good experience for almost anything."

Harrison rather enjoyed the paper work of his new office, and he rather welcomed the change from Army life, though he had no intention of making a career in the secretaryship, but, truly, it did prove to be a school for politics and government on the frontier.

Now as a civilian, Harrison took up residence at North Bend. It pleased Anna to be near her father and stepmother. Harrison bought 180 acres of land there and built a modest house of logs covered with white clapboards.

Wherever he happened to be, whether for a short time or long, Harrison had a way of putting down roots and making it feel like home. He took an interest in local activities as well as in the broader territorial affairs. He helped organize an Episcopal Church—Christ Church—in Cincinnati and served on its first vestry. And whenever he could he worked in his garden.

A census in 1798 showed enough population for advancement to the second stage of territorial government, and the following year the Governor, though he was not sympathetic to a curtailment of his own authority, called for the election of a General Assembly, made up of a House of Representatives elected by the freeholders, and a Legislative Council appointed by the President from a list of men nominated by the lower house. Legislators arrived from as far away as Detroit and the Illinois country for the first meeting of the new General Assembly. One of them was a good friend of Harrison, Colonel Thomas Worthington of Chillicothe. The Harrisons invited the Colonel and Mrs. Worthington to be their house guests at North Bend during the legislative session.

Partly at the suggestion of Worthington, the Harrisons invited
two other representatives: Nathaniel Massie and Edward Tiffin,
and their ladies, from the Chillicothe area to join them for dinner
one evening during the week when the legislature was organizing.
After a delicious dinner of fish, quail, ham, green beans, green
corn, and stewed apples, the ladies withdrew, and the gentlemen
turned to politics.

Worthington began, "William Henry, you know one of the first
tasks of the new legislature, after electing a speaker, will be to
elect a delegate to represent the Territory in Congress."

"Yes, I know that," responded Harrison.

"It seems to us that here may be a chance for us to have some
influence in getting a change in the land laws," Nathaniel Massie
suggested.

"Yes," Worthington went on. "With all the new land which is
opening up as a result of the Greeneville Treaty we should get an
influx of settlers, and they are going to be looking for land that
they can afford."

Dr. Edward Tiffin, who had been following the conversation
closely, joined in. "The problem is to keep the land out of the hands
of the big eastern speculators and make it available on terms
which will be realistic for the settlers."

Harrison smiled knowingly and lowering his voice he said,
"This quarter section which I have right here, I bought from the
partner of my father-in-law, and it still cost me 50 percent more
than he paid the government for it."

"Exactly," Tiffin went on. "What we need is a change in the law
which will allow the farmer to buy land in smaller parcels. The
present system of selling in parcels of not less than thousands of
acres means that the land will not be sold at all for a long time, or it
will be bought by wealthy speculators who will sell it to the
farmers at a much advanced price."

"Oh, I'm all for changing that system," Harrison declared.

Worthington spoke up, "William Henry, if you really are
committed to that and would do all you could to bring it about, we
think you ought to be our delegate in Congress."

Harrison, surprised but pleased, protested only feebly. "Well, I
don't know, Gentlemen."

"Is anyone else being put forward?" asked Massie.

Harrison answered, "The only one I know is the Governor's
son."

"Arthur, Jr.?" asked Massie.

"Yes," Harrison said. "The present attorney-general."

"That only makes it more important that you make yourself available," Worthington urged.

"Yes, yes!" the others echoed.

"Do you think you have the votes?" asked Harrison.

"We think all the Republicans will vote with us. Now we know that parties are not as important here as they are back in Virginia. We are not even sure what your politics are, and we are not going to ask. Our main concern is for a new land act," said Worthington.

"What is Judge Symmes' position?" asked Massie.

Harrison responded, "I'm not sure how Republican he is, but I do know he has been quarreling with Governor St. Clair about the section of land in his grant that was supposed to be set aside for school purposes."

After a pause, Harrison finally said, "Well, I'll be glad to try."

"Good, good," all the others said.

Worthington went on, "We are all set to make Doc Tiffin here the Speaker of the House. Then I think we can make you delegate to Congress."

Harrison did not mention this development to St. Clair, or to anyone else other than Anna who, as always, gave her support and urged him to try for it. Just a few days after the dinner meeting, Harrison received a note from the Governor asking that he oversee the distribution of annuity goods for the Indians at Fort Wayne in October. To this Harrison responded frankly in a note:

> Having been solicited... to offer himself as a candidate for territorial delegate to Congress, having made... his intention of serving if elected the time fixed on for the delivery of the Goods being so late as to make it impossible for him to attend to this business in the event of a successful election, he must request the Governor to appoint some other person.

He went on to say that he would be willing to undertake the mission to Fort Wayne if he lost in the election.

The legislature agreed unanimously on Dr. Tiffin as Speaker, but the balloting for delegate to Congress could not have been closer. The vote was, William Henry Harrison, 11; Arthur St. Clair, Jr., 10.

In the fall of 1799, a few weeks after the election, William Henry Harrison was on his way back to Philadelphia. This time he was in the company of his own family—his wife, Anna, their three-year-old daughter, Betsy Bassett, and their infant son, one-year-old John Cleves Symmes. It was a pleasant journey in fine weather up the Ohio by barge to Pittsburgh, then by coach over the road which had become familiar to William Henry by his long march in 1791 and by horse and coach with the family of General Wilkinson. The road was familiar enough, that is, until they reached Lancaster. There Harrison was pleased to find a big change. The road had been completely rebuilt from Lancaster to Philadelphia, the Lancaster Turnpike. It had less severe gradients, had a firm foundation with gravel surface, and drainage ditches along either side. It had been built for sixty-two miles at an unheard-of cost of $465,000.

On arrival in the capital city, the Harrisons found lodgings at the City Tavern on Second Street at Logan's alley, just above Walnut, still reputed to be the "finest tavern in America." There they met William Henry's brother, Carter Bassett, still a member of Congress from Virginia, and his family, and Robert Goodloe Harper, the member of Congress from South Carolina who would serve as Harrison's sponsor when the new members were presented at the opening of the new session, yet several days away.

Over dinner Harrison was able to catch up on the news of Philadelphia. Most startling was the news that his former guardian and great family friend, Mr. Morris, was in debtor's prison right there in Philadelphia.

"That's incredible!" he exclaimed on hearing about it from his brother. "How in the world could that happen? I thought he was one of the richest men in the country. What happened?"

"I grant it is difficult to explain," said Carter. "Apparently his speculation in land got away from him. He had gradually sold out his mercantile and banking interests and put everything in land. He owned nearly all of the western half of New York state, and he had about two million acres in Georgia and a million acres in Virginia and another million in South Carolina—besides his million acres in Pennsylvania."

"Good heavens, all that land at only the government rate of $2.00 an acre would make him a millionaire many times over," commented William Henry.

"Yes, but that land was mostly undeveloped, and he could not get his money out of it. He had fairly large investments in a London bank which failed, and they say one of his partners, a John Greenleaf of New York, I think, made off with some of the funds. And surely you have heard of 'Morris's Folly.' "

"Morris' Folly? What is that?"

"His marble palace."

"You mean the house on High Street?"

"No, no. He was not content with the two mansions on High Street—the one where the President lived and—"

"The one where I lived," William Henry put in.

"Yes," Carter went on. "Well, he decided he should have a marble palace. He got some plots of ground between Chestnut and Walnut Streets and between Seventh and Eighth. He retained some renowned French architect, a Major l'Enfant, who told him this great mansion could be built for $60,000. Well, it took all of that just to build the three-story basement. He went out and raised enough more money to build the outside walls two stories up and put on a slate roof. But that was as far as he could go. In the meantime, he had imported all kinds of fine furniture, classic statuary and so forth to put in it, but he could go no further."

"What happened to it? Is it still there?" William Henry asked.

"Well, when he ran out of funds and could not pay his debts it was sold by the sheriff."

"Who got it?"

"A rich Quaker by the name of William Sansom bought the property, and Thomas Billington bought the materials. Just a few months ago they took it down to salvage the materials. The marble decorations are now scattered among different buildings all over the city. Some fine *alto relievo* tablets were placed over the windows in the wings of the new Chestnut Street Theatre."

"Zounds!" was all William Henry could say.

"Anyway, it came to the point where Mr. Morris could not raise the cash to meet loans which were due, or to pay his bills, and they put him in jail right over on Locust Street."

"Can nothing be done? How can they let the man who practically financed the Revolution sit in prison? Is there no way out? How long has he been there?"

"He went into the prison last year, and they say there is nothing to be done, that his financial ruin was of his own doing—an example of a rich man trying to get richer too swiftly without prudence about the risks he was taking."

"I don't see how it's going to help either him or his debtors for him to be sitting in prison."

More frightening was the news of the yellow fever epidemics.

"I heard about the epidemic in '93," William Henry said. "But I could not imagine how extensive it was."

"I tell you, people were dying here like flies on the coast of Guiana. They were burying from ten to eighty a day all through

August to November. I guess it carried away four to five thousand people all together."

"My God! I had no idea it was that bad. It's a lot safer out in the wilderness fighting Indians than it is in Philadelphia at a time like that!"

Anna Harrison already was regretting that she had brought the children to this place.

"Do they have any idea what caused it?"

"Dr. Rush thought it came from a pile of putrefied coffee down on the wharf, and that the air carried the poisons all over. Others thought it was transmitted by personal contact with a bunch of refugees who came in from Santo Domingo."

"And the doctors could do nothing?"

"Oh, they worked hard, all right, but obviously not with much effect. Of course I was not here—about everybody took flight —but I heard that Dr. Rush resorted to his old methods, only more so."

"You mean calomel and bleeding?"

"You guessed it, but he doubled his efforts. He found that somebody in Virginia back in 1741 had said that in this kind of fever the patient's abdomen becomes filled with blood, and this must be drained."

"Just shows you what too much study can do."

"Dr. Rush prescribed ten grains of calomel, and ten of jalap, and then increased the jalap to fifteen."

"That alone would be enough to lay a strong man low."

"But that was not all. He said that twenty ounces of blood should be drawn away."

"Twenty ounces! My God! How much blood does a man have? If a soldier suffered a gunshot wound and lost that much blood, he would be dead. Dead!"

"That's what some other folks thought, too," Carter went on. "You know John Fenno?"

"He's an anti-Jeffersonian pamphleteer, isn't he?"

"He was. In his newspaper, the *Gazette of the United States,* he called Rush a 'murderer' for his yellow fever treatment. Last year, in September, his wife died of the fever, and he suspended publication. Just a few days later he also died."

"My God!"

"And his great rival, Benjamin Franklin Bache who edited *The Aurora and General Advertiser* died about the same time. Now Fenno's son and Bache's widow have revived both papers. And haven't you heard about Benjamin Rush's libel suit against William Corbett for the same thing?"

"No, what do you mean?"

"You know Corbett was that Englishman who published *Porcupine's Gazette*. In there he also accused Rush of being a murderer, and old Ben sued him for libel. You don't know how much of this is medicine and how much is politics, Republican against Federalist, especially in view of the sharp divisions about the troubles with France."

"I can see how politics would be involved, but I think I would have grave doubts myself about Rush's treatment as you described it. How did it all come out? Has there been a decision?"

"It went to the Pennsylvania Supreme Court, and just this week the jury found in favor of Rush in the amount of $5,000 damages."

"That's an unheard of amount, especially when it is given to uphold such a questionable practice as drawing all that blood. Zounds! I'm glad I got out of medicine when I did."

"Maybe you would not have been so set in your ways in insisting on the old remedies."

"I can see why the people would flee Philadelphia—not just to avoid the poison air, or whatever it is, but to get away from the doctors!"

"But fortunately for some of them, there were some refugee French doctors who used a different approach, and a Dr. Stevens from the West Indies used a mild 'West Indies treatment' on his boyhood friend, Alexander Hamilton and Mrs. Hamilton, and they both recovered. One of the Frenchmen, a Dr. Nassy, over on Second Street, treated 117 fever victims and only 19 died, and of these 19, eleven of them had been treated by the Rush method before he got to them. Another Frenchman, Dr. Deveze, did a lot of good for patients taken to the quarantine center which the city established up on Bush Hill. They wouldn't even let fever victims in the Pennsylvania Hospital. Another Frenchman, Stephen Girard, was responsible for organizing the Bush Hill effort, and there Dr. Deveze simply prescribed cool liquids, cool baths, and mild medicines. A good many of his patients recovered, too."

"Remarkable! But I understand there have been other outbreaks since then."

"Indeed. Yes, in fact, it has returned every summer since '93 except for '95, though never nearly so bad. Last year was another fairly bad one, and government offices, banks, and businesses all moved out. They say the population in the city in October was only about 7,000. Thank God, we have escaped this year."

"Well, with all the bright news, there must be more."

"Oh, yes, we'll have to bring you up-to-date on the political questions, but Anna may be more interested in the new theatre on Chestnut Street, and Abigail Adams' 'drawing rooms' at the Executive Mansion, and the congressional balls and dinners. And of course you should know that the new Bank of the United States is in operation in its new building on Third Street under the presidency of our friend Thomas Willing, and the new U.S. Mint is in operation over on First Street, or what used to be Front Street."

During the next several days the Harrisons renewed old acquaintances and made new friends among the members of Congress who were assembling for the session.

Harrison's own political alignment was not sharply defined. Though he was aware of Federalist control of the Administration and of Congress, he wanted to be careful not to alienate the Jeffersonian Republicans. Theodore Sedgwick, a Federalist leader from Massachusetts, had given up a seat in the Senate in favor of election to the House of Representatives, and now he was slated to be Speaker. Harrison was glad to be greeted by two fellow Virginians who also were entering Congress for the first time, John Randolph of Roanoke and John Marshall, and by another newcomer from Delaware, James Bayard. Charles Pinckney had just arrived from South Carolina to serve in the Senate, and his cousin, Thomas Pinckney, continued as an influential Federalist member of the House.

From his brother, Harrison learned of the great Federalist banquet at Oeller's Hotel for John Marshall on his return from his post as Commissioner to France in June, a year ago. That was where some unknown enthusiast had offered the immortal toast, "Millions for defense, but not one cent for tribute!"

William Henry and Anna Harrison enjoyed the social whirl of Philadelphia that winter. Nothing could have been in sharper contrast with North Bend and Cincinnati.

Harrison was especially glad for the opportunity to meet personally President John Adams, Thomas Jefferson who now was Vice President, Secretary of State Timothy Pickering, Secretary of War James McHenry, Secretary of the Treasury Oliver Welcott, Secretary of the Navy Benjamin Stoddert, and an old acquaintance from Virginia, Charles Lee who was Attorney General. Stoddert was the first Secretary of the Navy, and he had been especially prominent in the undeclared naval war with France during 1798. All the other cabinet members had served in Washington's second administration and were continuing under Adams.

The Harrisons enjoyed the congressional dinners at the Executive Mansion. Anna attended several of Abigail Adams' "drawing rooms." They found Oeller's Hotel, next to Rickett's Circus on Chestnut Street, between Fifth and Sixth, especially attractive. It had just been opened this year in the building which previously had housed the Episcopal Academy. Its great Assembly Room was by far the most attractive ballroom in the city. It was fully sixty-feet square (as compared to the long room at the City Tavern which was about fifty by thirty feet) papered in the French style with pantheon figures, flowered designs to give the impression of festoons, and groups of antique drawings. There was an elegant music gallery at one end. Here the Harrisons learned to dance the new German waltz, and they looked forward to the great balls planned for later in the winter.

Another exciting event to which they looked forward was what was billed as a "spectacular pantomime," *Don Juan*, including a scene representing "the Infernal Region with a view of the mouth of Hell," to be presented at Rickett's Circus. But during the dress rehearsal on December 17, a fire broke out in the circus which also spread to Oeller's Hotel and burned both buildings to the ground. That put an end to ballroom events as well as circus acts at those sites.

Both Harrisons attended Mrs. Adams' Drawing Room on a Friday afternoon near the end of December. It was the most crowded of the year. Over a hundred ladies and nearly as many gentlemen attended, all in mourning for the death of George Washington. The ladies were all in white dresses, with black epaulets and black ribbons or two yards of black cloth in pleats, while all the gentlemen wore black coats and breeches.

The New Year's reception was larger than the one Harrison had attended when the Washingtons were in residence. The crowd consumed thirty to forty gallons of punch, nearly as much wine, and relative quantities of cakes.

One of the highlights of the year for the Harrisons was seeing the renowned Ann Merry as Juliet at the magnificent new theatre on Chestnut Street, just across the street from the site of Oeller's Hotel and Rickett's Circus. They were struck by the grandeur of the building at first glance. Set back from the street, it extended for ninety feet along Chestnut Street, including a wing of fifteen feet on each side in each of which was a green room. Pavilions extended from the wings out to the line of the street, and these were connected by a colonnade of ten Corinthian columns. In the center of the building was a great Venetian window.

The Harrisons found their way to their boxes by a flight of marble stairs in front to a lobby from which corridors led to the boxes. Their box was in the front, opposite the stage, where boxes were arranged in the form of an amphitheatre. There were three tiers of boxes which could accommodate, all together, nine hundred people. The pit and gallery had another 1,000 seats, for a total capacity of about two thousand. The theatre had a total depth, they found upon inquiry, of 134 feet, and the stage had a depth of seventy-one feet and a front of thirty-six feet between the boxes. The curtain was colorfully embellished in contrast to the more common green baize. Over the proscenium arch was an emblematic representation of "America Encouraging the Drama," with the motto, "The Eagle Suffers Little Birds to Sing."

The east stage box was specially fitted and decorated as the Presidential Box with the coat of arms of the United States on the front, and with red draperies around the interior, and cushioned seats, front and back. But it remained empty this evening. John Adams never was the theatre enthusiast that Washington was. In addition, the prominent and raucous Federalist-Republican political rivalries discouraged presidential appearances at such pubic places as this.

"I understand the Adamses seldom attend the theatre," observed Anna Harrison.

"No," responded her husband. "I don't think they are great enthusiasts for drama. Anyway, you know what Boston always thought about this sort of thing."

"Indeed. But I heard that Abigail Adams came here last year one time, *incognito*."

"Really? What was the occasion?"

"It was the introduction of that new patriotic song, 'Hail Columbia'."

"Oh, yes, I heard about the song. They say the whole audience joined in the singing and then went out into the streets, still singing it. More patriotic fervor at the expense of the French, I guess, and political fervor for the Federalists. So Mrs. Adams was here for that, was she?"

"So they say."

The Harrisons were not disappointed in the play. The scenery was attractively done. The lighting, done in the French way with oil lamps that could be raised or lowered to make the light bright or dim to suit the scene or the mood, was very effective, and the performance of Ann Merry was especially sensitive.

At Juliet's line, "O Romeo, Romeo, wherefore art thou Romeo," Harrison whispered to Anna, "Why art thou a Symmes?"

She giggled and whispered back, "I am a Harrison."

"How about *your* father?"

"A rose by any other name would smell as sweet."

Harrison laughed audibly, and she signaled him to be quiet.

And as Ann Merry spoke the words:

> Thou know'st the mask of night is on my face, Else would a maiden blush bepaint my cheek For that which thou hast heard me speak tonight.
> Fain would I dwell on form—fain, fain deny What I have spoke. But farewell compliment, Dost thou love me? . . . .

"Ay," whispered Harrison to his Anna. "I do, you know." He grasped her left hand in his left hand as they turned their attention back to the play with a new sense of delight.

Later in the year they returned for a new play by a young playwright who had arrived from Ireland only a few years previously, John Daly Burk. It was called *Female Patriotism* or *The Death of Joan of Arc*. It presented Joan as an honest, clearheaded, attractive character, and both the Harrisons were very favorably impressed.

For variety, and to become better acquainted, the Harrisons visited various other taverns and inns for meals or tea or coffee. One of their favorite dining spots was the Bunch of Grapes on Third Street between High Street and Mulberry, and they also tried the White Swan on Race Street, the Cross Keys on Third and Chestnut run by Israel Israel who had done so much for the victims of the yellow fever epidemics, the St. George and the Dragon on Mulberry at Second Street, and the Crooked Billet whose Sign of Crooked Sticks had attracted Benjamin Franklin on his first arrival, and still in operation the Tun Tavern on the waterfront known in earlier days as Peggy Mullan's Beefsteak House and where, it is said, the U.S. Navy and the U.S. Marine Corps were first organized in 1775. Several times they attended amateur music concerts at the Sign of the Rainbow on Race Street.

They liked to take little Betsy to P. Bossu's Ice Cream Parlor on Ramstead near Fifth Street. For other amusements they sometimes went to Peale's Museum, the "automations", "tumbling feats", "ballon ascensions", the "panorama", and walks in the parks when weather permitted.

On Sunday mornings, the Harrisons chatted with friends in the churchyard of Christ Church where they regularly attended.

Again Harrison frequented the library whenever he could and continued his reading of history, and Anna, too, found this a pleasant and instructive place to spend time when she could. Both liked to read and then discuss with each other what they had read.

William Henry Harrison was present for the opening of the session of Congress on December 2, and he listened to John Adams' address on the State of the Union the next day. As a territorial delegate, Harrison was in a unique position. No one ever had held such a position before. He could not vote, but he could speak and propose legislation. His sponsor, Robert Goode Harper, presented him to the House and even sponsored a bill to extend to him the franking privilege. All the members were cordial, and they accepted him as one of their own.

The House went into mourning on December 18 on receipt of the news of the death of Washington. The House turned its attention to a resolution on slavery. Other subjects of prolonged and at times heated debate were the Republican attacks on the Alien and Sedition Acts, a Disputed Elections bill sponsored by the Federalists, Republican attacks on the provisional army being raised for possible war with France, and the National Bankruptcy Bill. Harrison followed all these with interest, though he was glad he did not have to cast a partisan vote on these issues. He did find a new admiration for his colleague, John Marshall, who, though now rising to a place of prominence in Federalist party circles, voted with the Republicans to repeal an "obnoxious section of the Sedition Law." The only Federalist to vote for this resolution, his vote provided the margin of victory for the Republicans. Marshall was known to harbor no Republican doctrines, nor any sympathy for the Republican leader, Thomas Jefferson, but in this case he could not vote against his own convictions.

On December 24, Harrison got his chance to open his drive for the measure for which he had been elected—a new land law. On that day he addressed the House on the need for improving the system for the sale of public lands in the Northwest Territory. He offered a motion that a special committee be appointed to study the matter and bring in recommendations. The motion was adopted, and he was made chairman of the special committee.

Harrison worked hard with the committee. He impressed upon the members the fact that the current system was not working, that it was a system more suited to establishing a landed gentry than for the purposes for which the Revolution had been fought.

On February 18, 1800, shortly after his twenty-seventh birthday, Harrison was able to report out a bill from his committee. This provided that the public lands should be sold in half sections, i.e., 320 acres, at a price of $2.00 an acre. Payment could be accepted at one-twentieth down, one-fourth in forty days, and the balance in installments in two, three, and four years, at six percent interest. Land offices would be opened at Pittsburgh, Marietta, Chillicothe, Steubenville, and Cincinnati. The House approved the bill on April 28. The Senate made some amendments to the effect that lands east of the Muskingum were to be sold in sections (640 acres), and those west of that river one-half in whole sections and the other half in half-sections. To the price was added $6.00 a section for survey. Final approval came on May 10.

In his instructions from the legislature Harrison had one embarrassing item to contend with—he was instructed to get from Congress an act conveying a so-called "college township" to the legislature from the Symmes purchase—a township owned by the Judge, but upon which, according to the legislature, he had reneged. This put Harrison in the position of going against his father-in-law. He did not mind doing that, but he did not want in any way to hurt Anna, even though she insisted that he should not be governed by any supposed feelings on her part. For whatever reason, Harrison accomplished nothing on this point.

But there was another matter on which he did move and which, as it turned out, had an important bearing on his own future—the division of the Northwest Territory. This, too, was at the initiative of the group at Chillicothe headed by Thomas Worthington, a group now being referred to as the "Virginia Group." Their object was to get a line drawn far enough to the west so that Ohio, divided from the rest of the territory, soon would have sufficient population to be admitted as a state. Worthington himself went to Philadelphia to urge this division.

Governor St. Clair did not oppose division, but he wanted the line drawn in such a way that neither part would qualify for statehood for some time. St. Clair found support in the federal Government by suggesting that early statehood was being promoted by a group of Republicans who then would be able to add their strength to the Republicans in Congress. St. Clair sent a letter to this effect to Secretary of State Timothy Pickering who showed it to Harrison. The delegate did not want to damage his standing with the Federalist Administration, and he showed the letter to Worthington.

Finally, they were able to work it out. Harrison, again as chairman of a special committee, already had brought out a bill to reform the superior courts in the Territory, but he recommitted it and then brought out the bill for division. After prolonged delays, discussions, and proposed changes, the bill was approved largely in the way the "Virginia Group" wanted it. The new territory, including all the Old Northwest west of Ohio, would be the Indiana Territory.

As the congressional session was winding down early in May, Harrison returned to the hotel one evening with even greater news for Anna. They would not be in Philadelphia for the next session of Congress, desirable though that might be. They would be going west again, but this time to the farther west. They would be going to Vincennes, on the Wabash. President Adams was appointing him Governor of the new Indiana Territory.

Before leaving Philadelphia, Harrison wrote a long letter to the Cincinnati *Western Sky*, with copies to the other newspapers in the Territory, to explain the new land law and the division of the territory, and he reviewed briefly the other acts of the session.

Now there would be a chance for a visit to Berkeley. They spent a pleasant summer there. Anna had a chance to meet many of Harrison's family and friends for the first time, and he enjoyed the chance for a reunion. The children enjoyed their hours at play on the plantation. Anna admired the great house, and Harrison promised her that one day they would have one like it.

Anna was expecting their third child, and in late August Harrison took her to Richmond where a physician's care would be available. On September 5, Lucy Singleton was born.

Two months later they went by coach, via Cumberland, Maryland, to Wheeling, and from there took a river boat down the Ohio. After a visit at North Bend, they went on to Lexington, Kentucky, where they spent several winter weeks at the home of Peyton and Maria Short.

After Christmas, Harrison decided that he would move on as quickly as possible to Vincennes while his family remained in Lexington until the more favorable weather of spring. With a saddle horse, a pack horse, and a black servant on a third horse, he set out during the "January thaw." Crossing the river by ferry at

Louisville, he took the path known as Clark's Trace through the woods to the west. They slept on the ground at night, but suffered little from the cold in what was relatively mild weather for that time of year on the Ohio.

They arrived at the new territorial capital on Saturday, January 10. John Gibson, an able veteran of the frontier who, as Secretary of the Territory, had been in charge since the effective date of the new territorial government (July 1, 1800) and had been waiting for the arrival of the Governor. Gibson was a tall, distinguished looking man whose facial features seemed more suited to a professor than to the rugged frontiersman and warrior he was known to be. He had served as interpreter for the old Mingo chief, Logan, and in fact at one time was married to the sister of that chief. Harrison found the Secretary at the tavern. As Gibson doffed his hat he revealed a bald head which seemed altogether in keeping with his other professorial features.

"Welcome to the capital city of the Indiana Territory!" he exclaimed, with a sweep of his arm to indicate the town which consisted mainly of a double row of log houses, mosty white-washed, each with its fenced-in garden and orchard. "All the local citizens have been looking forward to your arrival, Governor. They are mighty proud to be the capital of a great Territory."

"Thank you, Colonel Gibson, I am mighty grateful for your looking after things until I could get here," responded Harrison.

Just then an older man came up to the tavern. He had come in response to a message from Gibson, and the Secretary led the way outside to meet him.

"Governor Harrison," Gibson said, "may I present Colonel Francis Vigo?"

"How do you do?"

Gibson went on to explain, "Governor, you should know that this is the gentleman who gave such critical assistance to George Rogers Clark in the capture of Vincennes. It was he who carried the vital information that the British had recaptured Vincennes to Clark at Kaskaskia, and it was he who financed Clark's expedition across the Illinois country to retake Vincennes."

"Oh, yes, I have heard about that," Harrison acknowledged. "The pleasure is all mine in making your acquaintance."

Vigo smiled and said, "Governor, the people of Vincennes have been awaiting your arrival with great anticipation."

"Thank you."

Vigo continued. "They have been especially concerned about a place for you and your family to live, and I want you to know that by special effort I have just finished a house of my own which I would like to put at your disposal until you can get a place of your own."

Harrison raised his hand as though to decline, but John Gibson caught his eye and flashed a signal through the expression on his face that the Governor ought to accept. Harrison took Vigo's hand and said, simply, "That is very kind of you, sir. We shall be honored to take advantage of your offer and hope that we can be into a place of our own before too long."

The new Vigo house was a large two-story frame house of early American type, painted white, with green shutters and with a veranda all around. On arrival at the house the men alighted and walked into the great parlor, a large room paneled with alternate blocks of walnut and ash, which extended all across one side of the house.

Gibson explained to Harrison that the builder had been given an extra premium of twenty guineas to hasten the completion of the house so that it would be ready for occupancy by the time of the Governor's arrival.

While Vigo excused himself, Harrison asked Gibson to remain in the parlor. "It appears that you have things going well, Colonel Gibson," Harrison said. "I want you to know that I appreciate it, and I look forward to working with you."

"Thank you, Governor. I am anxious to do whatever I can to help. Please let me know if you want anything or if you have any particular thing you want done."

"Yes, and thank you for that. Tell me, what is the population of this place?"

"It's just about 600."

"Oh? I thought it must be larger than that."

"Actually back in 1787 it was supposed to have 520 French adult males and 103 American adult males. It has been losing some population since then, mainly on account of the Indian troubles, but now I expect the population to grow again since it is a territorial capital."

"Yes, I should think so, although you know we still are way out in the middle of Indian country, even after the Treaty of Greeneville."

"Yes, I guess that's right."

Harrison went on to explain further. "The Treaty recognized our claim to Vincennes all right, as well as to a number of other posts throughout the territory, and it guaranteed routes of communication by river or trail to all of them. But all the rest belongs to the Indians and is not open to settlement."

"I'm afraid that may be hard to control," Gibson said. "There are a good many squatters out there right now."

"How do the French get along?"

"Oh, there's a little friction between the old French population and the new American settlers, but nothing serious. And somehow the French seem to get along better with the Indians than do the Americans. For some reason the Indians seem to trust them more, don't see them as much of a threat."

"Ah, interesting."

"Some of the French have intermarried with Indians, and they content themselves with a pleasant, and I must say indolent, existence, and they spend most of their time in trading, drinking, general merrymaking, and quarreling. One problem is that they thus have allowed themselves to be reduced to poverty, and many have sold out their lands, cheap, to incoming Americans."

"Where are the Indians in the area, and who are they?"

"Well, mainly the Sac and Foxes, the Kickapoo, the Piankeshaw, and the Weas, between here and Ouiatenon. There must be several hundred right here in the vicinity."

"Ouiatenon, that's about a hundred miles up the river, isn't it?"

"Yes, that's right. And on the upper Wabash and the Mississinewa there are Miamis and Potawatomis and Shawnees."

"Yes, I guess we had better keep an eye on all of them, in spite of the Treaty."

"Yes," agreed Gibson. "But maybe because of the Treaty."

"You think some of them are not accepting the Treaty?"

"I understand there are some dissidents and die-hards at work among the Shawnees, especially, but also among some of the others."

"What kind of defense do we have?"

"We have a small garrison at the fort, just north of town, Fort Knox, a company of the 4th Infantry under Captain Honest F. Johnston."

"Honest John, eh? I hope he is."

"Indeed. I also have been trying to organize the militia since my arrival in July."

"Good. We must keep that up." Harrison paused and then said, "Colonel Gibson, I wonder if it would be possible to find the three territorial judges and have them come on over here Monday morning."

"Why, yes, I can try."

"I think we ought to get our legal system organized right away and decide what laws we need to adopt."

An hour later Gibson returned to report that he had found all three judges, and they all would be present on Monday morning.

At the appointed time on Monday, the three judges arrived. All were acquaintances of Harrison and appointed upon his recommendation—Henry Vanderburgh who had been a representative from Vincennes and president of the Legislative Council of the Territorial General Assembly at Cincinnati at the time of Harrison's election as delegate to Congress, William Clark (not the same as the one Harrison had known in the Army), and John Griffin. After exchanges of greetings, Harrison called to order his first session of the Territorial Court.

"As you know, gentlemen," he said. "We constitute the sole law-making authority of the Territory. Of course we must follow the provisions of the Northwest Ordinance of 1787, for in creating the Indiana Territory Congress stipulated that that ordinance should continue to apply to the new Territory. And of course we are bound by other acts of Congress. For direction of military and Indian affairs, we look to the Secretary of War. For other relations with the Federal Government we look to the Secretary of State."

"But our immediate task is to adopt such laws as we think are required for the internal government of the Territory. Here we have a free hand, limited only by the Constitution and the acts of Congress, to adopt any law of any of the states and to make that law a law of the Territory."

"Are there any questions?"

Vanderburgh spoke up, "Yes, Governor, should we assume that all the laws previously in force for the Northwest Territory remain in force for the Indiana Territory?"

"That seems reasonable to me. Are there any objections to that?"

All agreed, and the Governor asked the Secretary to make that a matter of record.

The session continued for two weeks, and at the end of that time the group had adopted six laws, three resolutions, and one additional act. One of the laws adopted was from the code of Pennsylvania to set up a system of local courts for the Territory.

Harrison quickly learned that most of his day-to-day, routine business had to do with land claims. With these, as in all other matters, his word was final.

Harrison at first appeared in breeches and buckles and silk stockings for formal occasions, but somehow these seemed out of place on the frontier even though he insisted that he was going to bring culture and refinement to the West. But he sensed that breeches and silks were regarded a Federalist affectation, and he was sensitive about being identified as a Federalist where most of the voters were Jeffersonian Republicans. True enough, he owed his appointment to Federalist friends and a Federalist President, John Adams, but now Mr. Jefferson had been elected President. Now Harrison favored more and more the dress associated with Republicans. He usually would be seen in pantaloons and Hessian boots.

While giving his attention to matters of the territorial government, Harrison did not neglect either his family or outside activities. About the first of April, Harrison returned with the horses to Lexington to bring his family to Vincennes. For this expedition, Anna's stepmother had done major preparatory work. She supervised the packing of Anna's things at North Bend and then the stowing of them on a big flatboat. She herself, in the company of two "gentlemen" escorts, an overseer and a cook, in addition to the two hands to work the boat, embarked on the boat on April 15. Harrison and his family waited at Louisville for the boat. Anna was happy to see her stepmother and expressed her appreciation for all she had done.

"I think we could use you to help organize the Territory," Harrison said.

"Thank you, William, I think it is exciting to prepare an expedition like this."

"Now here, we shall have to get our things around the falls," Harrison observed. "I think we'll have to transfer to keel boats. It is difficult going, trying to pole a flatboat upstream, and we have a long way to go upstream on the Wabash."

"I'm sure," Mrs. Symmes agreed. She laughed and added, "One might as well try to move an island upstream."

They waited in Louisville a week for keel boats, but this gave an opportunity for a good visit. Then they transferred to two keel boats, one for the passengers, the other for the freight. It still was a slow trip, and they did not reach Vincennes until May 14.

On their arrival, John Gibson hurried down to the riverfront to

meet them. He had a whole column of horses and carts drawn up
to take the Harrisons and their baggage to their dwelling.

"It's beautiful!" Anna exclaimed as they drove up to the Vigo
house. "It's beautiful!" she exclaimed again when she saw the
paneled interior walls of the big parlor.

That spring Harrison acquired 300 acres of prairie farm lands
between the town and the forest, and he immediately set about
fencing it in. He planted crops of wheat and corn and barley and
tobacco. Going out to the field one morning he said to Anna, "You
know, as Voltaire said, 'Let us cultivate our garden.' "

"And how soon do I get my garden?" she demanded.

"Soon," he always said. "Soon."

Harrison early made the acquaintance of the military commander, Captain Johnston, and a few weeks later reported to a
friend, "We generally spend half the day together making war
upon the partridges, grouse and fish...."

In the next year when the brother of Daniel Boone started a
settlement on the Blue River called Wilson's Springs, Harrison
built a grist mill and saw mill there.

With a rapidly growing family, and anxious to build a respectable house as soon as possible, Harrison was concerned about his
income. His farming, his own land activities, and his mills were
ways to supplement his governor's salary, though this was far
greater than anything he ever had received in the Army. At
$2,000 a year he was receiving as much as had Arthur St. Clair
as governor of the whole Northwest Territory.

Much as he enjoyed the activities of government and politics,
much as he liked farming and hunting and fishing, Harrison's
favorite time of day was in the evening when he could play with
the children, read to them, and bid them good night, and then
have a quiet hour with Anna.

She adapted very well to the frontier. She had enjoyed life in
Cincinnati and North Bend. She had enjoyed life in Philadelphia.
Now she was learning to enjoy life in Vincennes.

"Are you happy here, my dear, or at least content?" Harrison
asked her earnestly one evening.

"Of course," she replied without even thinking. Then, more
thoughtfully, she went on. "This is far different from Philadelphia, isn't it? No roads that go anywhere, no big theatres or
ballrooms, a little tavern or two, of course, no newspaper. Do you
know what the old settlers are thinking of when they talk about

going to the city? New Orleans!"

"Yes, you're right. It is a big change."

"But maybe I've just been spoiled a bit by Philadelphia. After all, this is not very different from Cincinnati, is it?"

"No, just a little farther from Philadelphia, and not all the river traffic that you see on the Ohio. You know that Vincennes is much older than Cincinnati. In fact, it is older than Richmond."

"Is that an advantage?"

"Sometimes, yes, sometimes, no."

"But now my old man, Henry, is all of twenty-eight years old. Twenty-eight, and the Governor of a great Territory. I'll bet you are the youngest governor in the whole country!"

"Is that an advantage?"

"It is for me."

Harrison walked over to her, bent low, and kissed her on the cheek. She returned a kiss to his lips.

Harrison was proud of his wife as a woman, as a mother, as a homemaker, as official hostess. Her beauty did not have that striking quality which arrested all eyes on first contact. But it had a richness and a depth that grew in knowing her. Harrison, to be sure, had been attracted to her when he first saw her, though he was not sure that she outshone either Sarah Cutler or Hettie Morris. But now after six years, he was sure that she was the most beautiful woman in the whole world. Anna always had been quite proper in manner and deportment—first as befitting the daughter of a judge, then as befitting the wife of an officer of the Legion of the United States, then as befitting the wife of a member of Congress, and now as befitting the wife of the Governor of a great Territory. Her refinement had become all the more impressive the farther west she had traveled.

CHAPTER VIII

Busy Beavers

1

"Watch for the beavers," Tecumseh whispered to his twelve-year-old son, Pachetha, as they crept through the woods toward the creek. The creek was fresh with the waters of spring as it flowed toward the White River not far from the village that some of the Shawnees were sharing with the Delawares. "Stop. We wait here," Tecumseh said a few minutes later. "These are poplar trees, the kind the beaver likes best. He likes the bark and the little branches to eat and the big branches and trunk to make his dam."

"Why does he make a dam, Father?" the young lad asked.

"To make a lake where he will build his wigwam."

"Why does he want his wigwam in a lake?"

"To be safe from his enemies and to be close to a place where he can store food."

"Why does he store food?"

"He works all summer to store branches from the trees so that he will have something to eat in winter when the ground is covered with snow and the tree branches are not good food. Now let us look to see if we can find a beaver at work cutting down a tree."

"Listen, Father, I hear a strange sound, there."

"Yes, it is the sound of a beaver at work. There he is, look! At the bottom of that tree."

"That little animal that looks like a squirrel?"

"Yes, but he is much bigger than a squirrel. Come, let us see if we can get much closer. Take care. Make no noise. When he works, we walk. When he stops and looks, we stop and look so that he will not hear us. Keep very low so he cannot see us. And we must keep the wind in our faces so he will not smell us."

Carefully they crept closer.

"Look," Tecumseh whispered. "There are two of them. One works on the tree while the other watches, then they trade places."

Soon the stalkers were close enough to see the animals very clearly, the small front paws which the beavers used almost as hands, their larger back paws with webbed feet, and their broad, flat tails which they were using to brace themselves. The tree was as big around as a man's leg and as tall as four men.

The Shawnee father and son lay quietly, watching, watching, acknowledging with a smile to each other from time to time their recognition of the beavers' accomplishments. Before the sun had moved an hour, the creaking sound of falling timber reached their ears.

Then they watched the beavers trim the upper branches for a meal, and then saw them begin dragging the tree away. The Indian watchers followed at a safe distance to avoid detection and saw the beavers, with great, persistent struggle, get their tree to the bank of the creek and then drag it into the water. It floated downstream for the distance of a hundred paces to where obviously a dam was under construction. There the beavers went to work to make their new acquisition a part of their dam. They dived beneath the water to secure branches of the tree to others already in place, and then they brought up rocks and mud to make it all watertight.

Pachetha walked down the bank of the creek. Losing his footing on slippery mud, he promptly, if unintentionally, sat down at the water's edge. Though startled, he sat still, for he looked out and saw a beaver swimming directly toward him. It was a big beaver. It swam right up to within an arm's length of the boy, and then just stopped in the water and looked up. Big, beady, black eyes looked up as though to inquire if the Indian lad was all right. The beaver stayed there, head and back exposed above the surface of the water, and just stared for fully a minute. And then, apparently satisfied, the animal suddenly turned about, and with an enourmous flop of his big, flat tail, spraying water all over Pachetha in the process, dived beneath the surface and was gone.

Tecumseh told his son that now they would return to the village, but they would come back in six days to see what the beavers had done by then.

During the interval Pachetha practiced at stalking. Sometimes under the watchful eye of his foster mother, Tecumapease, he and several other Shawnee and Delaware boys of his age would play at having one close his eyes while the others would see how close they could approach him before he heard them. Pachetha was the champion when it came to this kind of contest.

At other times he would go out into the nearby woods to see how close he could come to a rabbit, and then a squirrel, and then, the most difficult of them all, a turkey.

But he was most fascinated by the beavers, and he was glad when the time came to return to their dam. This time Tecumseh led his son directly to the dam. They were astonished to see the dam nearly completed. It was almost as high as Pachetha's head and extended all the way across the creek and up its sloping banks. It was as long as fifty steps of a man. Already a small lake was forming behind it. In the lake was the beavers' house.

"You see the beaver's wigwam, out in the water?" Tecumseh asked.

"Yes, Father. But where is the door? How do they get in? Is it on the other side?"

"No, it is under the water. They can enter their wigwam only by swimming under it and going up through an open place in the floor."

"Why do they do that?"

"So their enemies cannot get to them."

"Do they have blankets to sleep?"

"They do not have to have blankets, but they make soft beds from the shredded bark of trees."

"The roof of their wigwam has a hole in it. Will they fix it?"

"No, they leave that little hole to let fresh air into their lodge."

"But where are the beavers? Are they hiding?"

"They may be cutting more trees, or they may be sleeping. They like to work at night. We shall remain here after the sun sets to see if they come out then."

Patiently, Pachetha and his father watched a colorful sunset. Lying on the ground, Pachetha fell asleep. He awoke as his father shook him. "Look!" his father said. "Two beavers are swimming through the water. Let us see where they go."

In the twilight they had to look sharply to keep the beavers in sight. They saw them leave the water and climb up the bank. Cautiously the Indians followed. A little distance beyond where they had watched previously they came upon a little ditch. It was in fact a little canal in which a whole series of little dams had been built. In about an hour the beavers could be heard coming down the canal. They were floating a log down the waters of the canal. At each of the dams they dragged the log out, and then tugged it around and into the water of the next "lock" until they finally got it down to the creek. They floated it down and anchored it to the dam as a completion of the final layer. Then they went scurrying through the water with small branches and twigs in tow, but they were carrying these upstream from the dam and then disappearing under the water.

"What are they doing now?" Pachetha wanted to know.

"They are storing food. Those twigs and little branches are their food. They store it where they can swim to it from their wigwam without being seen."

"Beavers are very wise."

"Yes, my son, they are very wise. You see how they work together to cut and pull the big trees and build their dam and their wigwam? You see how they work very hard, and you see how they work together to protect themselves from their enemies and to provide food?"

"Yes, Father, they are very wise and very busy animals."

"Yes, they build better dams and better canals for their logs than men do for their canoes."

"A beaver is a good animal. Someday when I have a son I would like to name him Beaver."

"Beaver is a good name, but when you choose a name it should come from an *unsoma*."

"What was your *unsoma*, Father?"

"Mine was a great shooting star, like a panther passing across the sky."

"And you are Tecumseh. Why am I Pachetha?"

"Because a few days after you came, a cat came to the wigwam with its prey."

"Is cat a good name?"

Tecumseh could not help remembering his preference for Lynx or Wildcat, but he responded positively, "Oh, yes. Yes, it is a good name. A cat is very clever and has special powers."

"What kind of powers?"

"It is said that a cat has many lives."

"Is it true?"

"We cannot be sure, but often when everyone thinks he has been killed, or has gone away, he comes back. A cat can always find his way back to the wigwam."

"Yes, that is true."

"And a cat can see at night."

"Yes, he can see at night."

"And he is so skillful in stalking that he can catch a bird. Can you catch a bird?"

"No, Father, I cannot come close to a bird. Yes, the cat is very clever. He does have special powers."

"Yes, when you were born a cat carrying a bird came to the wigwam. That was your *unsoma*."

"Could this be an *unsoma*, to watch the beavers working?"

"Perhaps it could. Perhaps it could if we can learn from them how to work together and how to protect ourselves from our enemies."

2

As Governor of the Indiana Territory, William Henry Harrison found it useful to cultivate friends among the Indian leaders and to renew older friendships. One of these was a Delaware village chief with whom he had become acquainted during the negotiations for the Greeneville Treaty. On several occasions, the Governor took the trouble to visit this old chief at his village near the White River, near the eastern boundary of the Territory.

Arriving here one day in May, 1802, Harrison was appalled to learn that a council of Delaware chiefs had voted to accept the charge of the tribe's medicine man that the old chief, Harrison's friend, had been guilty of practicing sorcery, and they had condemned him to death. Harrison felt helpless to interfere with the tribal custom and procedure, but he did go to the wigwam of his friend to offer condolences.

Harrison found the old chief, now grown rather fat and flabby, dressed in his finest deerskins and feathers, and in unbelievably courageous spirits, though his wife showed signs of despair. The Chief's main concern was for his ten-year-old son. Harrison took the hand of the Chief, and then of the boy, and promised that he would look after the young one. The Chief gave a smile of thanks and said that he was ready to go.

Two warriors escorted the Chief to a small knoll at the edge of the village. All the men of the village, together with visitors from other villages and from other tribes, had gathered to witness the execution. Without instructions or compulsion the Chief turned his back on the crowd and looked into the setting sun. As the executioner raised his tomahawk, the Chief turned his head slightly and caught a glance of his son. The momentary glance turned to a sightless stare as the executioner plunged the tomahawk into the Chief's skull.

For a moment Harrison thought of himself as a Pontius Pilate. Here he was, the "procurator" in an American colony who thought he should not intercede in the practice of an alien people to impose his own sense of justice. He found no fault in this man. Yet he let the people have their way. He left this man to his own people to be executed.

After watching a brief burial ceremony, Harrison took the Chief's little son and put him up on his horse. The boy grasped tightly to the saddle and buried his tearful face in a coat as they set out through the early night toward Vincennes.

The boy's name, like that of his father, was Beaver.

CHAPTER IX

Dreams of Empire

1

"'To promote this disposition to exchange lands, cultivate the Indians' relationship with the Government factories, and be glad to see the good and influential individuals among them run into debt, because we observe that when these debts get beyond what the individual can pay, they become willing to lop them off by a cession of lands.' That's what he says, gentlemen, what do you make of it?"

William Henry Harrison, meeting with a group of his closest associates in the parlor of the Vigo house in April 1803 to discuss Indian policy, was reading from a letter dated February 27 which he had just received from President Thomas Jefferson.

Harrison looked in turn to John Gibson, the fifty-three-year old, professor-looking veteran of the frontier who was the Governor's right hand man as Secretary of the Territory; Francis Vigo, Italian born, Spanish-trained, at fifty-five the gray-haired venerable dean of the community; and Benjamin Parke, a twenty-six-year-old lawyer who had come to Vincennes from Lexington, Kentucky, early in 1801 and just recently had been appointed attorney general. Parke was nearly six feet tall, of slender build, and looked the part of a classical philosopher. His personality was much warmer and more forceful than his coolness of manner and appearance suggested.

"Read that last part again, Governor," Gibson said. "I'm not sure I got that last part."

Harrison looked back at the paper in his hand and re-read, "'Be glad to see the good and influential individuals among them run into debt, because we observe that when the debts get beyond what the individual can pay, they become willing to lop them off by a cession of land.'"

"Well, I'll be damned," Gibson finally burst out, "sounds like he wants us to trick them out of their land, doesn't it?"

"I don't care if he is a Virginian," Parke spoke up. His blue eyes sparkled beneath his neat brown hair. "I think he's gone too far this time. Clearly he wants more land from the Indians, but this is a hell of a way to go about it — urge them into debt over their heads at Government trading posts and then accept a cession of land in payment. Oh, there's nothing illegal about it, but somehow that does not sound like the Jefferson of equal rights and justice and all that."

Vigo had remained quiet for some time. Now he volunteered, "Oh, no doubt that would work in some cases; it's not difficult to skin an Indian in trading, especially if you offer him *l'eau de feu*, but it would lead to lots of discontent in the long run."

"But why in the world would the great President of the United States be urging this kind of devious tactic?" asked Parke.

Harrison had been listening with interest to the responses. He said, "Well, I suppose we shouldn't make too much of this particular thing, but I confess, it did strike me as a bit strange, coming from Mr. Jefferson. I am sure we can do much better by negotiating treaties for additional lands from the Indians. Oh, we'll get some resistance, but I'm sure it can be done. I think, frankly, that Mr. Jefferson has no stomach for war, and he doesn't want to risk further hostilities with the Indians. Everyone knows he is a shrewd and a tough politician, and I guess this is the way a shrewd and tough politician operates sometimes. But really, we should read this in connection with the policy which he laid down in his message to Congress in January. Ben, would you see if you can find the copy of that message? Let's have a look at it too."

Parke went to the records in the corner of the room and presently returned. "Here it is," he said.

"Read it out," said Harrison.

Parke explained, "This is from a confidential 'Special Message to Congress Recommending a Western Exploring Expedition, dated January 18, 1803'" and then began reading, "'The Indian tribes residing within the limits of the United States, have, for a considerable time, been growing more and more uneasy at the constant diminution of the territory they occupy, although effected by their own voluntary sales; and the policy has long been gaining strength with them, of refusing absolutely all further sales, on any conditions; insomuch that, at this time, it hazards their friendship, and excites dangerous jealousies and perturbations in their minds to make any overture for the purchase of the smallest portions of their land.'"

"Well, he's right about that, all right," said Harrison.

"Apparently he has been getting our reports," added Gibson.

"Go on, read on," Harrison said.

Parke continued reading: "'In order peaceably to counteract this policy of theirs and to provide an extension of territory which the rapid increase of our numbers will call for, two measures are deemed expedient. First: to encourage them to abandon hunting, to apply to the raising of stock, to develop agriculture and domestic manufactures, and thereby prove to themselves that less land and labor will maintain them in this, better than in their former mode of living. The extensive forests necessary in the hunting life will then become useless, and they will see the advantage in exchanging them for the means of improving their farms and of increasing their domestic comforts.' Well, that's a tall order, isn't it?" Parke commented.

"It makes sense as a general principle," Harrison observed. "The question is, will it work? Can we make it work?"

Gibson questioned further, "Can you change the whole manner of living of a whole people like that?"

"Of course you can," commented Vigo. "We see examples all the time. The real question here is time. Do our people have the patience to allow all the time needed to bring something like this about?"

"That's the key," Gibson went on. "There are lots of examples of Indians who have become fairly good farmers. We have several right in this vicinity. But few have really prospered, and it would take a lot of time to persuade a whole tribe, much less a dozen tribes, to take up this mode of living—more time than we have, I'm afraid."

"I'm afraid you're right about that," Harrison said. "And even if we had a lot of time, I'm not sure the tribes ever would buy it. It would take some real persuasion. Go on, Ben, what was the next point?"

"'Secondly: to multiply trading-houses among them, and place within their reach those things which will contribute more to their domestic comfort than the possession of extensive but uncultivated wilds. Experience and reflection will develop to them the wisdom of exchanging what they can spare and we want, for what we can spare and they want. In leading them thus to agriculture, to manufactures, and civilization; in bringing together their and our settlements, and in preparing them ultimately to participate in the benefits of our government, I trust and believe we are acting for their greatest good.'"

Gibson interrupted, "Clearly Mr. Jefferson is urging a policy of assimilation."

Harrison said, "John, you more than anyone else around here know the life of the Indians. Do you think assimilation a feasible policy?"

"It may be over the long run, but I doubt it for the immediate future. The tribes are very proud, and they don't take lightly the prospect of just disappearing, and the chiefs are very jealous of their positions."

"All that is true, but I think Mr. Jefferson sees that as the solution," Harrison went on.

Parke asked, "When you say assimilation, do you just mean cultural assimilation, that is, Indians living in the same way as White men, and living peaceably side by side, or do you mean total mixture of the races?"

Harrison stood up, walked around slowly, looked out the window, and returned to his chair. He explained, "Jefferson advocates intermarriage, mixture of the races. On more than one occasion he has told Indian representatives, 'Your blood will mix with ours and will spread with ours over this great island.' But again, John, you are the expert on this sort of thing; you have lived with them, even had an Indian wife."

"Yes, I did live with them for a time, though not by my own choice. But I must say, an Indian woman can make a wonderful wife—anxious to do the man's bidding, willing to do all the work around the house, to cultivate the crops, and so on. I must tell you, these people have some strange ways, but they are just as intelligent as anyone. A number of Indians have married white women, and sometimes that works out and sometimes not. But half-breeds are generally held in low respect among the Indians as well as among the Whites, so I'm not really sure whether or not it would work. Somehow White men who have joined the tribes, those who may have been captured when they were young boys, may be adopted by the tribes, and they get along as well as anybody."

"How about their children?" asked Randolph. "Does the taint of the half-breed apply to them?"

"No, strangely it doesn't," replied Gibson. "It's not a matter of blood so much as it is circumstances. The lowly regarded half-breed is the one who was raised in a White community and then comes back as a trader or something. He is looked upon with suspicion, as a part-Indian who is trying to use his Indian connection for the advantage of some sharp White trader."

"Isn't a mixture of the races what the Spanish have in Mexico?" Parke asked.

"Yes, they do," Vigo responded.

"But has that worked to the advantage of anyone?" Parke asked.

"How do you mean?" asked Vigo.

"Well, it does not strike me that there is any superior civilization in Mexico," Parke answered. "Actually from what I have heard and read, it would seem that the Aztec Indians had a civilization in some ways superior to what you find there now."

"Then it must be the Spanish strain that has led to the deterioration," Gibson suggested.

Everyone greeted this with a light laugh as Vigo responded quickly, "Oh, now, I would not say that!"

"Well, look at it this way," persisted Parke. "Would you say that the Spanish culture, civilization, mode of life in old Spain is superior to what you now find in Mexico?"

"Yes, I would say so," Vigo granted.

The others nodded in agreement.

"All right," said Parke. "Would you say that the Aztec civilization in Mexico was superior to what you find there now?"

"Probably in some ways, at least," granted Gibson. No one else protested.

"Then look at what you have," said Parke. "A relatively high Spanish civilization mixes with a relatively high Aztec civilization, and the result is a mixed civilization and people lower than either one of them."

"I think we had better get back to Mr. Jefferson's paper," said Harrison. "Isn't there more?"

"Much, much more," Parke said.

"All right, let's have it. Go on."

Parke again took up his reading: "'In leading them thus to agriculture,' let's see, I already had read that; he was speaking of the advantages of multiplying the trading houses. Here it is here, 'At these trading-houses we have pursued the principles of the act of Congress, which directs that the commerce shall be carried on liberally, and requires only that the capital stock shall not be diminished. We consequently undersell private traders, foreign and domestic; drive them from the competition; and thus, with the good will of the Indians, rid ourselves of a description of men who are constantly endeavoring to excite in the Indian mind suspicions, fears, and irritations toward us. A letter now enclosed, shows the effect of our competition on the operations of the traders, while the Indians, perceiving the advantage of purchasing from us, are soliciting generally our establishment of trading-houses among them. In one quarter this is particularly interesting. The legislature, reflecting on the late occurrences on the Mississippi—'What is he talking about here?" Parke asked, as he looked up inquiringly from his reading, "What late occurrences on the Mississippi?"

Harrison explained, "First of all, the action of the Spanish in suspending our right of deposit at New Orleans. That is very important in providing a means for the people of this area to get their produce out to foreign markets. Secondly, there was the news late last year that Spain had retroceded the whole of Louisiana back to France. That means that instead of a rather passive Spain controlling the territory to the west of us, including the west bank of the Mississippi and both banks at its mouth around New Orleans, we have a vigorous, ambitious, and aggressive France to deal with in that quarter."

"Yes, I see." Parke went on: "'—the late occurrences on the Mississippi, must be sensible how desirable it is to possess a respectable breadth of country on that river, from our southern limit to the Illinois at least, so that we may present as firm a front on that as on our eastern border. We possess what is below the Yazoo, and can probably acquire a certain breadth from the Illinois and Wabash to the Ohio—'"

Harrison interrupted, "There he's talking about us, right here, wants to get from the Indians a breadth of land from the Illinois and the Wabash to the Ohio. Go on, Ben."

"'But between the Ohio and the Yazoo—'where's the Yazoo?" asked Parke.

"That's the river that flows southward from somewhere below

the southern boundary of Tennessee, through the Mississippi Territory, to the Mississippi River near the place called Walnut Hills, and a little above Fort Nogales."

"Wherever that is. Yes, I see about where you mean." Parke continued, "'Between the Ohio and the Yazoo, the country all belongs to the Chickasaws, the most friendly tribe within our limits, but the most decided against the alienation of lands. The portion of their country most important for us is exactly that which they do not inhabit. Their settlements are not on the Mississippi but in the interior country. They have lately shown a desire to become agricultural, and this leads to the desire of buying implements and comforts. In the strengthening and gratifying of these wants, I see the only prospect of planting on the Mississippi itself, the means of its own safety. Duty has required me to submit these views to the judgment of the legislature; but as their disclosure might embarrass and defeat their effect, they are committed to the special confidence of the two houses.

"'While the extension of the public commerce among the Indian tribes may deprive of that source of profit such of our citizens as are engaged in it, it might be worthy of the attention of Congress, in their care of individual as well as of the general interest, to point in another direction the enterprise of these citizens, as profitably for themselves, and more usefully for the public.'"

Francis Vigo looked up from a thoughtful pose and interrupted, "Now, here is what I have been wondering about. There are going to be a lot of unhappy traders if the Government runs them out of business with its own trading posts, but now it appears that Mr. Jefferson intends to point them farther west."

"Yes," said Parke. "Listen: 'The river Missouri, and the Indians inhabiting it, are not as well known as is rendered desirable by their connections with the Mississippi; and consequently with us. It is, however, understood that the country on that river is inhabited by numerous tribes who furnish great supplies of furs and peltry to the trade of another nation, carried on in a high latitude, through an infinite number of portages and lakes, shut up by ice through a long season.'" Parke paused to suggest, "I guess when he speaks of 'another nation' he is referring to the British in Canada?"

"Exactly," Harrison acknowledged. He got up and poured a glass of cider for everyone as he continued speaking, "You see the English, coming down from Canada and having a lucrative trade on the upper Missouri, even though that territory belonged to

France or Spain, so why shouldn't our own traders get in on it? Go on, Ben."

"Yes. 'The commerce on that line could bear no competition with that of the Missouri, traversing a moderate climate, offering, according to the best accounts, a continued navigation from its source, and possibly with a single portage, from the western ocean, and finding to the Atlantic a choice of channels through the Illinois or Wabash, the lakes and Hudson, through the Ohio and Susquehanna or Potomac or James rivers, and through the Tennessee and Savannah rivers. An intelligent officer, with ten or twelve chosen men, fit for the enterprise, and willing to undertake it, taken from our posts, where they may be spared without inconvenience, might explore the whole line, even to the western ocean; have conferences with the natives on the subject of commercial intercourse; get admission among them for our traders, as others are admitted; agree on convenient deposits for an interchange of articles; and return with the information acquired, in the course of two summers. Their arms and accoutrements, some instruments of observation, and light and cheap presents for the Indians, would be all the apparatus they could carry, and with an expectation of a soldier's portion of land on their return, would constitute the whole expense. Their pay would be going on whether here or there. While other civilized nations have encountered great expense to enlarge the boundaries of knowledge, by undertaking voyages of discovery, and for other literary purposes, in various parts and directions, our nation seems to owe to the same object, as well as its own interests, to explore this, the only line of easy communication across the continent, and so directly traversing our own part of it.'"

A wasp cautiously entered the realm and settled on the bald head of John Gibson. The old Indian fighter held steady, not a move. Everyone else gasped and stopped talking. In hushed silence, the wasp explored the whole area and then, giving up, flew away.

"Ah, nerves of steel, that's what it takes!" exclaimed Harrison.

"God, I was afraid that either I was about to lose my scalp again or, more likely, gain a double goose egg here, and not golden ones either," Gibson laughed. "It's that damned cider. Don't get cider on your hand and then rub your head."

"Sometimes passive resistance is best after all, isn't it?" Harrison looked back to Parke. "Ben, I don't think you're attracting any stingers yet; read on, before one takes after you."

" 'The interests of commerce place the principal object within the constitutional powers and care of Congress, and that it should incidentally advance the geographical knowledge of our own continent, cannot but be an additional gratification. The nation claiming the territory, regarding this as a literary pursuit, which it is in the habit of permitting within its own dominions, would not be disposed to view it with jealousy, even if the expiring state of its interests there did not render it a matter of indifference. The appropriation of two thousand five hundred dollars, 'for the purpose of extending the external commerce of the United States,' while understood and considered by the executive as giving the legislative sanction, would cover the undertaking from notice and prevent the obstructions which interested individuals might otherwise previously prepare in its way.' There," concluded Parke.

"*Dios mio!*" Vigo exclaimed. "What was the date of that message?"

"January 18th," answered Parke.

"*Dios mio!* Does this mean that Mr. Jefferson has designs on the whole of Louisiana?"

Harrison responded, "Not necessarily designs on acquiring it, but certainly on opening up trade there. But to get back to our Indian policy. In his letter of the 27th of February, Mr. Jefferson also says, 'The crisis is pressing. Whatever can now be obtained must be obtained quickly. The occupation of New Orleans, hourly expected, by the French, is already felt like a light breeze by the Indians. You know the sentiments they entertain of that nation. Under the hope of their protection, they will immediately stiffen against cessions of land to us. We had better therefore do at once what can now be done.' There is one other basic document that governs what we can do."

"You mean the Constitution?" asked Parke.

"I mean what is in effect the constitution for our Territory —the Northwest Ordinance of 1787."

"What does it have to say about Indians?" inquired Parke.

"Just this." Harrison opened a desk drawer and took out a document. He glanced over the paper and then read:

Article 3. The utmost good faith shall always be observed towards the Indians; their lands and property shall never be taken from them without their consent; and, in their property, rights, and liberty, they shall never be invaded or disturbed, unless in just and lawful wars authorized by Congress; but laws founded in justice and humanity, shall from time to time be made for preventing wrongs being done to them, and for preserving peace and friendship with them.

"Well, that's pretty clear, isn't it," remarked Parke.

"It is if everyone can agree on what constitutes 'justice and humanity,'" Harrison responded. "And if we can figure out what constitutes their consent in giving up lands. Does it mean the consent of the chief or chiefs in a particular area, or all the chiefs in a whole region, or all the warriors, or what?"

"And I would even wonder about the invasions of their territory. Did Congress authorize a lawful war for the expeditions of Clark and Harmar and St. Clair and Anthony Wayne, and all the others?" asked Gibson.

"Not explicitly," admitted Harrison, "though you might say they were authorized by the congressional appropriations which financed them. Rather more questionable might be some of the forays which the Kentucky militia and others seem to be in the habit of making on their own."

"But you can't stop the settlers from defending themselves," Gibson countered.

"No, no, of course not," Harrison agreed. He went on, "But you know that Northwest Ordinance is a remarkable document."

"How do you mean?" Parke asked.

"You, as a lawyer, must be acquainted with it," Harrison rejoined.

"Oh, yes, I'm acquainted with its general terms. It is stated well, but I see nothing especially remarkable in it beyond what you find in most of the state constitutions."

"There is one aspect that is very remarkable."

"What is that?"

"It's the whole concept of territorial government and the expectation of statehood. Come to think of it, when I went to Congress as delegate from the Northwest Territory, I may have been the first representative in history from a dependency to the supreme legislative body at the seat of government. That was completely beyond the British comprehension. If the British had had a 'Northwest Ordinance,' the American Revolution might have been avoided. The American colonists thought of themselves as Englishmen, Englishmen equal to those in the mother country. To Great Britain, the colonists were subjects to be ruled for the good of the mother country. Protests against 'taxation without representation' fell on deaf ears in London. The British Government operated on no other assumption than that the colonies would remain in a permanent state of dependency. That is the way it always has been with empires—the Persian, the Macedonian, the Roman, the Russian, the French—all of them. But now the United States adopted an unprecedented policy that the colonies should become equal states. Here we are governing a colonial territory of the United States. We shall have a delegate in the national Congress who, even though he has no vote, will have a full voice. Right now we govern this territory through a federally-appointed Governor and judges, but soon we shall have an elected legislature, and one day additional states will be admitted from this territory. Ohio probably will be admitted this year. Others will follow—the Ordinance said up to five. And each of these states will have the same status as the original thirteen."

"Yes, I must grant, that is remarkable," agreed Parke.

"Now, where does all this leave us with our Indian policy? If the Northwest Ordinance assumed that five states would be carved out of the Territory, then it had to assume that all those areas would first be settled. Clearly there was no thought that this vast extent of land would be left solely to the Indians."

"Obviously not," agreed Gibson.

"The question is, how do we permit or encourage the extension of White settlement while protecting the rights of the Indians?" Parke asked.

"The only way I see is by continuing to purchase the Indian lands, and then opening them up to settlement," was Harrison's reaction.

"Then we're back to your old question of who represents the Indians," said Gibson.

"But aren't the Indians going to object to a steady advance of White settlers?" asked Parke. "What if they simply refuse to sell, then what?"

Harrison responded wryly, "In that case I guess it is up to us to persuade them, and to deal with the ones who are willing to be persuaded."

"How, by getting them into debt, as Jefferson suggests?" asked Parke.

"Not necessarily," responded Harrison. "I think we can do it by offering payments and annuities to the tribes."

"But where does that leave the Indians who depend on those lands?"

"But who is to say that the Indian is any more entitled to seek a livelihood there than anyone else?" countered Harrison.

"Well, presumably the Indian is the original owner, and he has a right to it until he voluntarily gives it up," Parke came back.

Harrison offered refills of cider as he said, "But how can we say who is the original owner of anything? I guess the only original owner of anything was Adam in the Garden of Eden, and he got thrown out. Everywhere any race now lives once belonged to someone else. Look at the Angles and the Saxons and the Jutes in England. What about the Celts there? What was the way of the Israelites in going into the promised land? I don't recall any programs of assimilation or grants for the Canaanites. And what about the rights of the Philistines? Look at the Indians themselves. The Iroquois chased the Shawnees out of Pennsylvania, and then they came into territory already occupied by the Miamis, and so on. Nobody seems to get excited when the Red men encroach on each other, but if the White man comes in, then that's different." Harrison returned to his chair.

Parke interjected. "As far as ownership is concerned, we need to make a distinction between two different definitions of ownership. One refers to the sovereign ownership of the state, we might say, and the other to the prescriptive ownership such as a farmer holds to a piece of land. The difference is between *jurisdiction* and ownership in *fee*. When we say that Spain or France 'owns' the Louisiana Territory, we mean that that nation has acquired sovereignty over it. When it changes from one of those nations to another, that does not affect the property rights of a particular individual in New Orleans, nor St. Louis. Now with the Indians it becomes more complicated, because they don't recognize individual property rights. For them the land belongs to the whole tribe, or a whole group of tribes. The chief may parcel out tracts for planting corn or building wigwams, but that does not mean that the individuals own it. The United States has sovereignty over the whole Indiana Territory, for instance, but so far we operate on the assumption that the Indians retain ownership of the land until the Government has acquired title to the land from them, and individuals can acquire title to that land in the first instance only by purchase from our Government. Is that right?"

"You present the matter very well," Harrison granted.

"Except for the further complication of the squatters," Gibson added. "Very often settlers will simply move into the Indian lands. Sometimes they will improve the land—clear, build a cabin, maybe a barn and some fences—and then sell the improvements to a rightful purchaser, and move on. But some refuse to move at all. The squatters create real problems with the Indians and later with those who have purchased the land at a Government land office."

"Then I say, why not follow the letter of the Northwest Ordinance and the Treaty of Greeneville and hold up on further moves into the Indian lands." responded Parke.

"Which?" asked Harrison, "encourage the population of new states in the Northwest or just give up that prospect on account of a few thousand savages?"

"What are our alternatives?" Parke asked.

"Well," said the Governor, "let's see. One, assimilation. We push Jefferson's project of the factory system, by which we mean trading posts and try to induce the Indians to become civilized farmers when, as Jefferson points out, they will need much less land. Our factory at Fort Wayne is working fairly well, and the Indians do well in growing corn, but they show no disposition to settle for that. Second, we simply could launch a war of annihilation and drive them out. Third, we could do what would amount to the same thing, adopt a policy of removal—grant them lands near the Mississippi, in the territory south and west of the lakes and then move them there, forcibly if necessary. Fourth, we might try to freeze the status quo at the Treaty of Greeneville line plus our more recent acquisitions."

Parke spoke up quickly, "I say hold the line where we are. That's the only way to observe 'the utmost good faith,' isn't it?"

Harrison went to a shelf and took down a book. "Listen to this," he said. "This is what Sir Thomas More says in his *Utopia*: 'But if so be that the multitude throughout the whole island pass and exceed the due number, then they... build up a town under their own laws in the next land where the inhabitants have much waste and unoccupied ground, receiving also of the inhabitants to them, if they will join and dwell with them.... But if the inhabitants of that land will not dwell with them to be ordered by their laws, then they drive them out of those bounds which they have limited and appointed for themselves. And if they resist and rebel, then they make war against them. For they count this the most just cause of war, when any people holdeth a piece of ground void and vacant, to no good for profitable use, keeping others from the use and possession of it.'"

Parke responded, "God, I never realized that More was so unfeeling for the rights of the natives; but then, this is not Utopia."

Harrison asked, "Then how do we stem the tide of White immigration? Do we turn the Army on our own people to protect the line of the Indian lands?"

"Do what Washington suggested for the squatters," Parke came back. "Give them fair warning and then leave them to the mercy of the savages on whose lands they are encroaching. They are victims of the fear which they have created."

"That would be pretty tough, wouldn't it, Ben?"

"Not any tougher than it's going to be if we follow a different policy."

"What do you think, John?" the Governor asked.

Gibson replied slowly, "I think we probably should continue to acquire additional lands by treaty and try to avoid the use of force. I'll grant to Ben that we should treat the Indian justly, and I guess in the long run, if we can maintain peaceable relations, Jefferson's idea of civilization might work out. But if any Indians accept our ways of life, we must give them protection." Gibson paused and in a low voice went on, sadly, "I was in command at Fort Pitt when the Christian Moravian Indians came there for protection. I appealed repeatedly for government assistance but got none. So I sent the Moravians back to their homes, unharmed, but on their own. It was only a few days later that all of them were massacred. Massacred, all of them, for no reason, by our frightened White Christian settlers."

Harrison commented, "I agree we should avoid force if we can, and we should provide protection, certainly, but we have to meet force with force. What makes the Shawnees so violent and warlike? Have they always been like that?"

"No, no they haven't," Gibson replied. "I understand that Pere Marquette reported years ago that they were a very peaceful tribe, but the others took advantage of that, pushed them off their land from one place to another."

Harrison turned to Francis Vigo and said, "Colonel Vigo, why is it that the French settlers in this area seem to get along better with the Indians than do our American settlers?"

"Oh, I think it's mainly because they constitute less of a threat and maybe have a little more flexible attitude. The Indians see the present White settlers as just the advance element of a flood of immigrants in the future. They see no such number of Frenchmen waiting to move in. And the French were content to settle in a few villages and farm the land around and trade with the Indians. Every American wants his own separate farm, and they want to spread all over."

Harrison refilled the cider glasses and then said, "Our aim always must be to advance the interest of the United States, but at the same time we are bound to treat the Indian justly and fairly, although Machiavelli would say that if we achieve our object the means will matter little." Harrison picked up an old volume from his desk, thumbed the leaves until he found his place and then read: "'In the actions of all men and especially princes, . . . the end is all that counts. Let a prince then concern himself with the acquisition or the maintenance of a state; the means employed will always be considered honorable and praised by all, for the mass of mankind is always swayed by appearances and by the outcome of an enterprise.'"

"I'm sure he's right," said Gibson.

"I'm afraid he is," agreed Parke. "But all the same, I think it's a pretty cynical attitude to assume that the end justifies the means. Carried far enough that can excuse the most gross injustices. After all, aren't the means what politics are all about? Most of us can agree on broad objectives for the country. The means to be employed are the bases of differences. When someone says, 'Oh, we agree on the basic objectives, we only disagree on the ways to achieve those objectives,' that is not necessarily just a minor disagreement. That can be a very major difference."

"I'll grant you that," Harrison conceded. "That's why I suggested that we must proceed in a way to respect the rights of the Indians." The Governor noticed a scowl forming on Ben Parke's brow. "What is it, Ben? I was trying to agree with you on that point."

"Yes, sir, I know, but I was just thinking that there can be danger even in a just and compassionate treatment of the Indians."

"How do you mean that?"

"Well, now, just think about it. Machiavelli said, 'The end justifies the means.' I would reject that, but at the same time I would suggest that it is conceivable that sometimes people make an assumption that 'the means justify the end,' and that too can be pernicious and dangerous."

"Well, go on, how's that?"

"I mean it may be possible to treat the Indian with compassion, and humanity, and then let that demonstration of concern justify taking his land away from him and destroying his culture."

Harrison thought about that for a moment, and then said, "You may have a point there; in fact it may be worse than that—it may be that with no unjust intention at all and with complete compassion, we devastate the Indian just the same. Or perhaps just in an unthinking or wreckless way we do harm without intending to do so. I have come to the conclusion that sometimes the very proximity of the White man seems to have an unfortunate effect on the Indian. As I have said on previous occasions, I can tell at once upon looking at an Indian whom I chance to meet whether he belongs to a neighboring or a more distant tribe. The latter is generally well-clothed, healthy, and vigorous; the former half-naked, filthy, and enfeebled by intoxication, and many of them without arms excepting a knife which they carry for the most villainous purposes. I tell you the best thing we could do for the welfare of the Indian would be to prohibit the sale absolutely of intoxicating liquors to him."

Gibson interjected, "I'm afraid there's a lot to the old saying, 'The Indian the White man despises is the Indian the White man has made.'"

Parke was quick to see this, and he went on to say, "Yes, yes, I see that. In the long run, what really is the difference for the Indian nations? If the White settlers murder the Indian or the humanitarian befriends him and tries to help him, the result is the same—the destruction of the tribe. The Christian missionaries are destroying Indian culture just as surely as was Wayne's Legion."

With a smile of understanding and appreciation, Harrison brought the meeting to a close. "I did not intend to consume your whole afternoon, Gentlemen, but for me at least it has been very helpful and worthwhile. I would only add this one further thought. Here we are on the frontier. We are on the outer frontier of Gaul, as it were, and I don't want to be caught in the situation of opening the frontier to barbarian invasions which might threaten the American empire. Thank you. Thank you for all your help."

2

At the urging of Thomas Jefferson just now, Harrison's approach to the Indian problem was to redouble his efforts at extinguishing Indian titles to lands through treaties agreed to by responsible representatives of all the tribes concerned in a particular area.

First he turned his attention to getting a permanent treaty to validate the preliminary one which he had persuaded a group of chiefs to sign at Vincennes late in the preceding summer to recognize the claims of the United States to a large tract of land around that city. This had been an effort to transfer what Harrison perceived as old French claims to the area. But this flew in the face of guarantees of the Treaty of Greeneville, and the whole prospect was making the natives restless again. Harrison had had trouble in getting any agreement at all in his negotiations at Vincennes. A main facilitator for him had been Captain William Wells, Indian agent at Fort Wayne. Wells was one of those who as a young White boy had been taken captive by the Miamis. After growing up in the Indian ways, he left and served as a scout for Anthony Wayne. Then he went back to Fort Wayne and married a daughter of Chief Little Turtle. Now he, like his father-in-law who had given up warlike resistance since the Battle of Fallen Timbers and the Treaty of Greeneville, urged the Indians to accept White man's civilization.

The preliminary treaty at Vincennes—preliminary because the Indians refused to accept anything else—had defined a tract extending around Vincennes to an extent of twenty-four leagues long and twelve leagues wide. This went far beyond the small enclave provided for in the Treaty of Greeneville, and none of the Indian leaders was anxious to concede as much. The preliminary Vincennes treaty provided that four chiefs—Little Turtle and Richardville of the Miamis, Winamac of the Potawatomis, and Topenebee of the Delawares—should meet with Harrison at Fort Wayne this spring to sign a permanent treaty.

Noting the widespread opposition, Harrison was sure that he would need more than the four designated chiefs if the tribes were to accept the validity of the treaty. He had little success in persuading the leaders even to attend the Fort Wayne council until he let it be known that the annuities would be distributed only upon their attendance.

Harrison made the long ride up to Fort Wayne in June. Black Hoof was there with a group of Shawnees, but Tecumseh would have no part of it. All the tribes concerned were well represented —the Delawares, Potawatomis, Miamis, Kickapoos, and the smaller tribes of Weas, Eel River, and the wretched Piankeshaws, who allowed the four designated chiefs to speak for them.

Harrison opened the conference with a long, flowery speech in which he recited the benefits which the Seventeen Fires had bestowed upon his Red brothers, and in which he appealed to them not to bring tears to the eyes of their Great White Father by showing hard feeling or by refusing to make a peaceful agreement.

He went on in his gentle speech to demand acceptance of the cession of land agreed to in the preliminary treaty signed at Vincennes. This brought a storm of protest. The Shawnees walked out. The others said they would not sign away such a vast area of their hunting grounds. It took days of wrangling, but Harrison persisted. His persistance and his arguments became effective only after he threatened to withhold annuity payments until an agreement was signed. At last everyone agreed to sign. Harrison returned in triumph to Vincennes with confirmation of 1,152,000 acres of land around Vincennes without having to commit any further payment at all. The Indians returned to their villages amidst a great deal of disgust and dissatisfaction.

One morning in August, 1803, Harrison was meeting again with Vigo, Parke, and Gibson in his Vigo house office. He had just received official word of the Louisiana Purchase. Jefferson would lay the treaty before the Senate within a few weeks.

"Colonel Vigo, maybe Jefferson really did have designs on the whole of Louisiana all along," Harrison said.

"Yes," Vigo responded, "certainly his plans for an exploratory expedition rather seemed to indicate that."

"Maybe this will take off some of the pressure for additional Indian cessions," Parke said.

Harrison thought for a moment and then responded, "I doubt it. On the contrary, I gather that Mr. Jefferson will be just as anxious for those cessions as before. Indeed this may make that policy more possible, for now we shall have a vast new territory into which the Indians can move. Obviously he was planning to send an expedition of exploration through the territory before he had any idea it would be our territory, which of course it will be now unless the Federalists are able to block ratification of the treaty in the Senate."

"If they block the treaty there will be war or secession or both," opined Gibson.

"Some of the eastern Federalists are threatening secession of New England and New York if the treaty *is* approved," said Harrison.

"Oh, that's a lot of linsey-woolsey to try to frighten the Senate into rejecting the treaty. But if it is rejected, I'm thinking some of these western folks are liable to raise forces of militia and descend on New Orleans on their own," Gibson said.

Harrison came back, "I wouldn't doubt that, but I don't think it'll come to that. The treaty will be approved, and we'll have all Louisiana without a fight. Think of that. That doubles the size of the country. I understand that two of my old comrades of the First Regiment, William Clark and Meriwether Lewis are already preparing the expedition which Congress authorized in response to that confidential message of Mr. Jefferson."

The Kaskaskia tribe had almost disappeared from the Illinois country, but Harrison found enough of them in August 1803 to sign away seven and a half million acres of land extending westward from the Little Wabash River to the Mississippi and Illinois rivers, and from the Ohio northward all the way to the Kankakee.

A year later Harrison was able to negotiate a treaty with the Delawares for the cession of another million and a half acres south of Vincennes to the Ohio River. In return he granted work horses, cattle, hogs, and "implements of husbandry" to the value of $800 in addition to an annuity of $300 a year for ten years, and he recognized the Delawares as sole owners of the great tract in the southeast between the Ohio and the White Rivers in spite of substantial claims of the Miamis and the Potawatomis to that area. To guard against possible future objections to this cession, Harrison also got a treaty from the Piankeshaws to relinquish any claims they might have in the area.

While all this public activity was going on, so too was the work on the Harrisons' new house. Truly a mansion, it was near enough to completion to allow them to move in during the summer of 1804.

One afternoon shortly after they had moved in, Harrison went out to their little house behind the mansion where he found Anna hard at work in supervising the laundry and the kitchen and getting ready to go out to her garden. She was expecting another child within six weeks or so, but she remained active.

"Anna, Darling, I have special news," said Harrison.

"Oh, Henry, is someone sick? Is everyone all right? Have you news from Father?"

"No, no, no, nothing like that. It's just about the Territory."

"Oh, what about it? Your reappointment for another term is all right, isn't it?"

"Yes, yes, of course. But our domain is being extended. It's being extended all the way out to the Stony Mountains."

"How far is that?"

"A thousand miles and more west of the Mississippi."

"A thousand miles?"

"A thousand miles."

"My goodness, that's as far as from Vincennes to Philadelphia, isn't it?"

"Yes, farther."

"What is it?"

"Well, you know the Louisiana Purchase of last year. Well, they are organizing the southern part, from New Orleans about as far up as the Arkansas River as the Territory of Orleans. All the rest of it they are designating as the District of Upper Louisiana and attaching it to the Indiana Territory."

"My goodness, Henry, that Louisiana Territory is as big as all the rest of the United States, isn't it?"

"Yes, it is."

"And you are to be governor of all that? My goodness. That must be just about the biggest territory anybody has ever been governor of. Oh, Henry, will we have to move?"

"No, no, I think not. I expect this is only a temporary arrangement. Too vast a domain for any one man to look after, but I shall be having to go to St. Louis, on the Mississippi, very soon to accept jurisdiction and begin setting up some kind of a government structure for people who so far have never lived under a democracy."

"I can see that will be very important."

"Yes, very."

"But, Henry."

"Yes, my Dear."

"Henry, does this mean that you will not be here for the birth of our child?"

"Well, I'm afraid I shall have to leave the last week of September. Do you think that will be too soon?"

"I'm afraid so, and I do so want you to be here."

"I wish so too, but there is much to be done, many other people involved, and I hope we can avoid crossing Illinois in the winter."

"Oh, I would not want you to do that. I understand. I know you must do your duties."

"Thank you. You know John Scott will be here—as usual. He's probably on his way now."

"Yes, I trust we can count on him again."

"And Anna, is it agreeable to you to name this one in honor of our good doctor friend?"

"What, *John*? Do you forget we already have a John?"

"Of course not, but this will be John Scott Harrison, no need for confusion with Symmes."

"Or maybe it will be Jane Scott Harrison. Have you thought about that?"

"Oh yes, I've thought about it, but this one is going to be another boy."

"Oh, you think so. Well, if you're so sure about that, of course it will be John Scott. Of course."

On Saturday, September 29, Dr. John Scott arrived. He was delighted to find the Harrisons in their new Berkeley-like mansion, Grouseland. He was impressed with the structure and furnishings of the house and with the accommodations of his guest room.

At dinner in the new dining room that afternoon, he explained that it had been a little awkward for him to get away from Lexington this time.

"Oh, we are so glad you did," Harrison said. "So glad you could keep to your biennial schedule. If you had not, it would have been very awkward for me because I have to leave on Monday to go out to St. Louis."

"Why to St. Louis? Surely you don't have to worry about the Spanish and the French now that all that territory is ours."

"No, no, they are attaching Upper Louisiana to the Indian Territory for the time being, and I must go out and get some kind of government structure set up."

"Oh, that is exciting! But I'm afraid it will be a few more days yet for Anna."

"I was afraid of that."

Anna spoke up, "But John, what was your problem? You were saying that it was a bit awkward for you to get away this time."

"Yes, you see, we too are expecting a child just now, and Alice thought it would be a good idea for me to be there."

"Oh, I can understand that," Anna said. "I'm so sorry to have taken you away!"

"Oh, that's all right," Scott assured her. "She'll be in good hands. And I'll not have to go through the ordeal of waiting while someone else tends her. And you know what we are going to name him?"

"You say *him?*" Anna protested. How do you know it's going to be *him?*"

"Well, we already have a girl, and I just feel sure that this one is going to be a boy."

"All right," Harrison asked, "what is it going to be, Thomas Jefferson?"

"No, it's going to be William Henry Harrison Scott. What do you think of that?"

"Zounds!" Harrison exclaimed. "Sounds great. That's great!"

"Yes, it's great," Anna agreed.

Scott explained, "My wife suggested it. Said that way she always would remember where I was when he was born!" He laughed, a little nervously. The Harrisons joined in the laughter with rather more spontaneity.

"But now we have one for you," Harrison said. "What do you think our new boy is to be named?"

"Oh, a boy is it? Surely he will be named Benjamin."

"No, we'll save that for next time. He is going to be John."

"John? But you already have a John."

"We have a John Cleaves Symmes Harrison. This one is to be John Scott Harrison."

"Well, I'll be damned. Oh, excuse me. By Jove, isn't that something! That's great! He'll probably grow up to be President of the United States or something."

"Oh, don't forget William Henry Harrison Scott on that score. We just hope our John Scott grows up to be as fine a man as Dr. John Scott," said Harrison.

"Hear, hear," agreed Anna.

Harrison lifted his wine glass and said, "A toast! A toast to the future of the future William Henry Harrison Scott and John Scott Harrison!"

"To their health and to the health of both their mothers," added Scott.

And they all drank.

Early on Monday morning the Governor's official party gathered at Grouseland for the trip to St. Louis. There were the three judges of the Territorial Supreme court—Vanderburgh, Griffin, and Davis; William Prince, attorney; Joseph Barron, interpreter; and Colonel Francis Vigo. A detachment of dragoons from Fort Knox joined them as escort. When all was ready, Harrison shook hands with John Scott and thanked him again fo being there. All the walking children, including Beaver, the Indian boy, had gathered on the lawn, and he told each one good-bye individually. Then he went to Anna. "Do be careful," he said, "and thank you for all your help, and good luck with little John Scott. I'll be thinking of you all the way, and I'll be getting back as quickly as I can. And remember, I love you. I do, you know."

"And I love you. I do, you know," Anna responded, and taking a deep breath for an added boost of courage, she said, "Do be careful."

Harrison mounted his white Andalusian and waved to all the family and Scott. Then he called out, "The goose honks high! Westward—ho!" He sent four horsemen out to the front to reconnoiter the route and provide security. The rest followed down to the river to cross by ferry, and then they set their course west across the Illinois prairie.

It took nearly a week to reach Cahokia on the Mississippi. As they approached, a cavalcade of citizens came out to meet them and escort them into the town. After an overnight stay there, they took the ferry across the Mississippi. On the opposite side a welcoming party from St. Louis waited to escort them into that town.

Harrison found St. Louis a very attractive town. He and Vigo accepted accommodations at the elegant home of one of the leading inhabitants, Auguste Chouteau. The judges were taken in by other leading residents, and the other civilians had good accommodations at the local taverns. The soldiers were quartered at the local barracks.

Within a few days Harrison had made many new friends. From them he learned details of the fitting out of the Lewis and Clark expedition which had left St. Louis the preceding May. He learned something of what the Spanish and French policies had been. And he learned a good deal about the Indians of the area.

On October 12, he formally accepted jurisdiction. Captain Amos Stoddard who had been in St. Louis since March as United States military commandant, had the one hundred men of his garrison drawn up on one side, their uniforms neat and their weapons glistening in the sun. Opposite was the French garrison, men of the Louisiana Regiment under Colonel Charles Dehault Delassus. On signal the Tricolor came down, and the Stars and Stripes went up. There were cheers and handshakes all around. Afterward Colonel Delassus presented an exquisite

Limoges platter to the Governor for him and "Mrs. Harrison." The Governor accepted it with profound thanks and with a promise to prepare it carefully for the return trip. Stoddard already had been through this exercise on March 10 when the French flag on the portico of Charles Gratiot had been lowered and the Stars and Stripes raised. But now this formality in the presence of the civil Governor made it all seem very official.

That evening Harrison wrote a brief letter to Anna in which he said:

> I trust that by now our John Scott Harrison has arrived, and I hope that you both are well.
>
> St. Louis is an attractive town, rather more elegant than Vincennes, I confess. Few log houses or even clapboard are to be seen here. Most of the houses are stone. They are nice; a few are splendid, though I have seen none for which I would trade Grouseland.
>
> I must say the ladies are remarkably handsome, gentle, and well bred, and the society altogether a polished one.
>
> Now I must be about the business at hand which may take another three or four weeks. Be assured I shall fly back to you at the earliest opportunity.

Harrison encouraged an easy access that the local inhabitants had not been used to. He spent a good deal of time in issuing licenses to traders, and he even waived the customary fee. He was careful to issue no license to anyone who was a British subject or who was suspected of being a Tory.

Meeting with the three judges, he reorganized the court system and the militia, and then they drafted a new legal code based on the laws of the Indiana Territory. The Governor issued a proclamation to provide for the division of the new territory into five districts—St. Louis, St. Charles, St. Genevieve, Cape Girardeau, and New Madrid. These would be, in effect, embryonic counties, each with a seat of justice.

While in St. Louis, Harrison found that he needed to attend to other Indian matters, and he seized an opportunity for another great cession of Indian lands. Some members of the Osage tribe, known for their belligerency, came into town to make various demands, but they were dismissed with presents and warnings.

Then one day, in the room which he was using as a temporary office, Harrison received the Sac chief, Keokuk, and four other leaders of the allied Sac and Fox tribes.

"We bring Sac warrior who killed with tomahawk a White Man," the chief announced.

Harrison needed more information. Sensing that there were likely to be strong feelings in the town against the Indian, Harrison ordered him put in jail pending further inquiry.

Auguste Chouteau explained to Harrison that the incident had occurred at a dance at one of the frontier cabins. A White man supposedly had made improper advances toward an Indian girl and threatened to take advantage of her. This Indian had come to her rescue with a tomahawk. Chouteau said that he had had dealings with these people before and perhaps could make a deal with them which would include the transfer of some large tracts of land. This aroused Harrison's interest at once.

"I have a claim to some old Spanish grants," Chouteau explained. "I would like to bring that in for survey and sale, but the Sacs and Foxes are sitting on some of it and have never yielded. Actually much of the land they claim is unoccupied."

"What do you think it will take to get it?" Harrison asked.

"Well, let me do a little preliminary work. My brother and I can work out some trade in goods for them. Then maybe you could agree to return the prisoner to them and offer some kind of annuity such as have been granted other tribes."

"All right, see what you can do. Let me know the results."

Chouteau and his brother extended credit of over $2,200 to the visiting Indian leaders and encouraged them to use the credit to buy all kinds of items from shiny medals to fine coats—and whiskey. Then Auguste Chouteau promised the Indians that the prisoner would be released to them, and their large debt would be cancelled if they would agree to cede a large tract of land to the United States.

Harrison agreed to meet with the groups as a council to negotiate a treaty. Here Harrison was able to pull off the greatest coup of all his Indian negotiations. In return for an annuity of $1,000, with a promise that the Indians would be allowed to continue to have the privilege of living or hunting on the lands as long as they remained in the public domain, a promise to request a pardon for the prisoner, and forgiveness of their debt to the Chouteau brothers, they signed over fifteen million acres of land. This comprised all of the Illinois country between the Illinois and Fox rivers on the east and the Mississippi on the west, and north to the Wisconsin River. West of the Mississippi it included a large tract between the Missouri River and the Jefferson River.

Harrison made the request for the pardon to President Jefferson. He knew it would take several weeks to get a reply, but he was confident that the President would approve his recommendation.

But just a few days later the Indian prisoner broke out of the jail and was shot dead by a sentinel.

When the Sac and Fox leaders returned to their villages with news of the treaty, the shooting of the prisoner, and the whiskey, there was an uproar throughout the tribes. Black Hawk, a young, self-proclaimed Sac leader, insisted that the five chiefs could not give away land that belonged to all the Sacs and Foxes, and he advised his tribesmen not to accept the annuities. A delegation of indignant village chiefs and warriors hurried up to the nearest British camp to review their complaints and seek support.

For his part, Harrison was satisfied that he had gained a great advantage for the United States in a reasonable and fair agreement. Most pleased of all was Auguste Chouteau. He even had offered Harrison a partnership in some of his enterprises, but the Governor had quickly declined.

On his return to Vincennes in mid-November, Harrison was delighted to find that little John Scott Harrison, born on October 4, was doing very well, and Anna was up and about and looking after getting things arranged in their new mansion. Thankful that he had been able to overcome the recalcitrance of many Indian leaders in obtaining the land cessions that he had so earnestly sought, he now turned his attention to other pressing matters.

As for the Indians, he sympathized with Jefferson's project for a "factory system" which would offer goods to Indians on attractive terms while forcing out of business unscrupulous private traders. Most of all, this was to be one of Jefferson's main civilizing influences. Unfortunately for that purpose the system had not been extended, but Harrison tried to see to it that the one "factory" in his area which held some promise, the one at Fort Wayne, would flourish. In the earlier years, goods had been sent out by War Department officials with little regard to the needs or desires of the Indians. Now the Indian agent, or "factor," had been brought more directly into the system for ordering goods. The idea was for the trading post, after an initial capital allowance, to operate with neither profit nor loss, but to exchange goods for items which the Indians would bring in. During these years the agent noted those items which were most useful for purposes of trade, those which were of doubtful use, and those altogether "useless or extravagant." Among the "useful" items were such things as cotton hose, shawls, gartering, women's cloth hose, calico, flannel, broadcloth, wool hats, brass kettles, beaver traps, tin kettles, spades, Britannia ware, camp kettles, candles, candle holders, soap, claw hammers, tin cups, harness, saddles, rifles, gunpowder, shot, flints, razors, seeds, nail rods, shoes, bandannas, blankets, and diapers.

Of "doubtful use" were such items as oven stoves, stove pipe, sheet iron, coffee, silk, spectacles, mirrors, and scythes. "Useless or extravagant" items included such as writing paper and ink, ivory combs, ostrich feathers, Jew's harps, flowered cream jugs, white butter boats, wine glasses, and chocolate.

So far the territorial government of Indiana had been operating in what was called the "first stage," where the Governor and the judges made the laws, and outside that, the Governor wielded virtually dictatorial powers. But there had been a growing agitation for advancement to the second grade which would allow for the election of a legislature. Congress had exempted the Territory from the requirement of the Northwest Ordinance that there had to be a population of at least 5,000 free adult males for that status. Harrison had discouraged any change in status until 1804 when he agreed to put the matter before the voters. Out of 400 votes cast, 269 were for advancement. Accordingly, in December Harrison proclaimed that the Territory had reached the second grade, and he called for an election for January 3, 1805, to choose nine members for a House of Representatives. The Council, or upper house, was to be appointed by the President of the United States from a list of nominees (at least ten for a Council of five) submitted by the lower house.

Jefferson asked Harrison himself to make the choices for the Council from the list of nominees presented by the Representatives, being guided only by three principles: (1) to reject dishonest men, (2) to reject those called Federalist, even though they might be honest, and (3) to reject land-jobbers. With all this, Harrison came up with one Federalist among the five he chose. Wayne County, the area around Detroit, had not participated in the election, and in that same month of January, Congress provided for a separate Michigan Territory. Still the Indiana Territory extended west to the Mississippi and north to Canada. As Harrison had anticipated, the District of Louisiana had been organized as a separate territory, with General James Wilkinson as governor.

When the Indiana Territorial General Assembly met for its first session, on the upper floor of a two-story frame building in Vincennes in July 1805, Harrison greeted it with his first annual message. It was a group of twelve men—seven elected members of the House of Representatives and five members of the Council.

The Governor greeted the legislators cordially and then proceeded with his discourse. At the outset he alluded to the recent acquisition of Louisiana:

> The mighty river which separates us from the Louisianans will never be stained with the blood of contending nations; but will prove the bond of our nation, and will convey upon its bosom, in the course of many thousand miles, the produce of our great and united empire . . . . And if, in the immense distance. . .other laws and other manners prevail, the contrast. . .will serve the useful purpose of demonstrating the great superiority of a republican government, and how far the uncontrolled and unbiased industry of the cautious and measured exertions of the subjects of despotic power.

And then Harrison turned to the area of his greatest concern—relations with the Indians:

> The interests of your constituents, the interests of the miserable Indians, and your own feelings will sufficiently urge you to . . . provide the remedy which is to save thousands of our fellow creatures. You are witnesses to the abuses, you have seen our towns crowded with furious and drunken savages, our streets flowing with their blood, their arms and clothing bartered for the liquor that destroys them, and their miserable women and children enduring all the extremities of cold and hunger . . . . A miserable remnant is all that remains to mark the names and situation of many numerous and warlike tribes. . . . Is it then to be admitted, as a political axiom, that the neighbourhood of a civilized nation is incompatible with the existence of savages? Are the blessings of our republican government only to be felt by ourselves?

The legislature responded promptly with an act to prohibit the sale of intoxicating liquor to the Indians, but the law was not to take effect until the legislatures of all adjoining states and territories—Kentucky, Ohio, Michigan, and Louisiana—had enacted similar measures. Harrison sent copies of the law to the governors of those states and territories and urged them to take similar action. But he was unable to make that effective. There already was a federal statute prohibiting the sale of intoxicants to Indians, but that had been interpreted as applying only to Indians in their nonceded homelands. This then left out all the trading posts and the towns and villages where liquor might actually be available.

Another burning issue before the legislature was slavery. The Northwest Ordinance contained a clause "forever prohibiting slavery" in the Territory, but Harrison had recommended that Congress temporarily suspend this clause. Harrison was not insensitive to the evils of slavery, but he had been reared at the Berkeley plantation where slavery was an accepted aspect of the economy and where his contacts with slaves always had been friendly and considerate. He also had developed sympathies for emancipation, as in his youthful participation in the abolitionist society in Richmond, and from Quakers and others, including Benjamin Rush, in Philadelphia, from whom he had been subjected to anti-slavery ideas. Actually he thought emancipation as inevitable, but thought that it should be gradual with some assurance of compensation for the owners and with regard for the interests of the freed slaves. But at this time and place, he thought that some allowance for slavery would be beneficial for the development of the Territory. Indiana was being settled mainly from the South rather than from the East. Most of the people were coming from Virginia, North Carolina, and Kentucky —all slave-holding states—via the Ohio River. Moreover he saw slavery as a way of providing some of the labor needed so acutely for developing this vast region.

Already, there were about two hundred slaves in Indiana, mostly around Vincennes and the Illinois towns. The Northwest Ordinance was not made retroactive, so that those people who held slaves in the Territory before 1787 were allowed to retain them, though they could not buy nor sell them.

In 1803, Harrison and the three judges had adopted a law authorizing a species of indentured contracts which had the effect of allowing settlers to bring in slaves under the guise of indentured servants, though there could be no slave trade, and Harrison strictly forbade people's taking their servants to Kentucky for trade. Actually Harrison himself had brought three household slaves from Virginia as indentured servants.

In 1802, he had presided over a convention which adopted a resolution to petition Congress to suspend operation of the slavery prohibition clause of the Northwest Ordinance, but this was not acted upon at the time.

Harrison reckoned that ninety percent of the voters of the Territory favored slavery. In the House of Representatives now meeting the count was six to one in favor of slavery, and now the legislature itself adopted a resolution to request Congress to suspend the prohibition against slavery for a period, but again Congress refused to act. Jefferson generally ignored any suggestions along those lines that he received from Harrison.

Benjamin Parke, chosen by the legislature to be the territorial delegate in Congress, was troubled by the whole question of slavery. He raised the subject with the Governor one afternoon in the Grouseland office.

"Governor, I'm not quite sure what to make of the whole slavery controversy. Arguments in the local paper and in the campaigns for legislators have been getting pretty heated."

"So I have noticed," Harrison acknowledged.

"I see our biggest problem out here as being relations with the Indians, but I'm not certain that can be separated entirely from our attitude toward Negroes."

"How's that?"

"Well, do we assume that all other races are inferior to the White, or only some? Do we treat one in a way different from another?"

"It's not a question of superiority or inferiority, but a matter of difference. I don't know whether one is inferior to another. I just know they're different. There are obvious physical differences, in color if nothing else. And it's pretty obvious to me that there is some kind of physical difference about the Indian that makes him unable to hold liquor. It's not just one or two here and there; it's all of them."

"I can't disagree on that. But otherwise are the Red and Black races inferior?"

"As I said, I don't know. I just know they're different. I often allude to the barbarian tribes of Europe. Now that was not a matter of race. Who was any whiter than the Germanic tribes— the Franks, and the Goths, and the Angles and Saxons, and all the rest. It was just a question of the degree of their cultural development. Once they came into contact with Rome they developed very rapidly, and then went on to further development on their own. Maybe the Indians can do that, and maybe they can't. Maybe the Negroes can do that, and maybe they can't."

"Of course, that is impossible to tell, I guess," Parke said. "But what does all this say to the question of whether or not we should admit slavery?"

"You know, one interesting thing, attempts to make slaves of the Indians always have failed, while the Negroes, when treated properly, make excellent workers as slaves."

"But don't they make just as good workers as free men?"

"Sometimes yes, sometimes no. Ben, I really don't like slavery, and surely it will be ended one day. But we have to start where we are. And we have to exercise the same care with respect to Negroes that we were talking about one day with respect to the Indians—we have to be careful not to let humanitarianism kill them."

"I remember the question about killing the Indian culture, but that's not the same for the Negroes."

"No, it's not the same, but for the individuals it can be just as dangerous. Why do you think so many slaves, or former slaves, are coming into the Territory?"

"Because their owners want their services. It's a question of economic advantage."

"That's true of some of them, but for others, for other Negroes I mean, it is a matter of protection. Some of them who actually have been freed prefer to attach themselves to families for their own protection."

"Why is that?"

"Well, they don't have the wherewithall and the training or experience to go out on their own. And much as I hate to say so, a lot of them who are freed are kidnapped and sold back into slavery and sent off to God knows where. They would much prefer to stay with people they know, with people who will protect them from being shanghied."

"Well, I guess that's right. But I sense a growing anti-slavery sentiment. Where is that coming from?"

"Partly on moral grounds, from some of our Evangelical churches, and others, and for that I have a certain sympathy. The other is more of an economic matter. Many Northerners seem to think that everybody in the South has slaves. Now Ben, I know you are from New Jersey—so is my wife—but you spent five or six years in Kentucky, and you know that that is not true."

"Of course not. In fact it strikes me that a good many of the settlers coming in now have never held slaves, and in fact one of their motives for coming is to get away from slavery. If they wanted a slave territory they could go to Mississippi."

"Exactly. Many of these are small farmers and tradesmen who do not want the competition of slave labor with their own labor, so they oppose slavery altogether."

"Yes, I can see that. So, where does that leave us?"

"I would be willing to see slavery allowed for ten years or so mainly to protect the slaves and to help develop the territory, and failing that, to continue our indenture laws to provide that protection. As for the broader picture, I would look some time in the future for some kind of gradual, compensated emancipation."

"With the Black man adopting the White man's ways and living alongside him peaceably?"

"I would think so. What do you think?"

"I guess I could go along with that, but I would hope that we could find some way to avoid the forcible return of fugitive slaves. If they run away, obviously they don't want the protection or subsistence of their masters and ought not be made to return."

"We don't do that now in this Territory."

"But I am always seeing notes in the *Gazette* where people offer rewards for the return of runaway Negroes."

"I'm afraid you're right about that, and I agree it ought to be stopped, but there is another problem with that."

"What is it?"

"Simply that a lot of those runaways are not runaways at all—they're victims of kidnapping."

"Oh, I see that does complicate the problem."

"Indeed."

"But with those reservations and the approach which you suggest, I guess I could be a strong and forthright pro-antislavery man!"

As a new delegate to Congress in the next session, Parke was appointed to a select committee chaired by James M. Garnett of Virginia to study the requests from the Indiana Territory for a temporary suspension of the prohibition of slavery. Although a similar committee under the chairmanship of John Randolph of Roanoke (without representation from Indiana) in 1803 had voted negatively on Harrison's request, Parke, together with some sympathetic colleagues, was able on this occasion to persuade the committee to Harrison's view. The report of the committee stated:

That having attentively considered the facts stated in the said petitions and memorials, they are of the opinion that a qualified suspension, for a limited time, of the sixth article of compact between the original States and the people and States west of the river Ohio, would be beneficial to the people of the Indiana Territory. The suspension of this article is different from that between slavery and freedom, inasmuch as it would merely occasion the removal of persons, already slaves, from one part of the country to another. The good effects of this suspension, in the present instance, would be to accelerate the population of that Territory, instead of seeking as they are now compelled to do, settlements in other States or countries permitting the introduction of slaves. The condition of the slaves themselves would be much ameliorated by it, as is evident, from experience that the more they are separated and diffused, the more care and attention are bestowed on them by their masters, each proprietor having it in his power to increase their comforts and conveniences in proportion to the smallness of their numbers.

Then in its actual recommendation the committee adopted the following resolution:

Resolved: That the sixth article of the ordinance of 1787, which prohibits slavery within the Indiana Territory, be suspended for ten years, so as to permit the introduction of slaves, born within the United States, from any of the individual States.

The House, sitting as a committee of the whole, accepted the recommendation of the special committee. However, the House of Representatives in formal session then rejected its own recommendation.

3

Tecumseh was sitting on the ground beside his brother, Laulewasika, at the edge of their village on the upper White River. Tecumseh had about given up on trying to make a warrior out of his one-eyed, rotund younger brother. Better to encourage his interest in learning to be a medicine man, he thought. But Tecumseh did appreciate the sharpness of his brother's mind, and he liked to test ideas on him.

"My Brother," he said, just to get attention.

"Something troubles you," Laulewasika responded to prove that he was awake. "What is it?"

"I wonder what happens to us."

"What, to you and me? Oh, you are strong, you will find plenty of game."

"No, I mean all of our Red People. The White Devil Harrison makes more and more treaties. From a few old and weak chiefs he pretends to buy more and more of our hunting grounds."

"My Brother speaks true words."

"I told our friend, Blue Jacket, that the treaty he and all the others signed with the White Chief Wayne at Greeneville was no good. It would not be the end. There will be no end until all our land is gone or until we find a way to stop them before all our land is gone."

"But, my Brother, how can we stop White Devil and his Long Knives before our land is all gone? There are more Blue Coats than leaves on the trees."

"The only way is for all Red Men to stand together. My vision quest, many summers ago, told me that. The White Buffalo told me that."

"That may be the only way. But is it enough? Against White Chief St. Clair, Red Men fought together with Little Turtle and Blue Jacket, and won. Against White Chief Wayne at place they called Fallen Timbers, Red Men fought together and lost. It was not enough."

"But many of the Red Men were cowards and ran home before the battle. And later Red Men stood together at place called Greeneville and all signed treaty—gave White Wayne everything. No good, no good. White Men always want more."

"My Brother speaks true words, but what is to be done if standing together is not enough?"

"It is not enough for a few tribes to come together only to make battle and then go away."

"Tell me what you are thinking."

"All Red Men must come together for all time. We must have great union of all our nations, to make one big nation, like the union of the Seventeen Fires."

"My Brother is dreaming. All the chiefs do not like one big nation. Each one wants to keep his little nation under his rule. All sachems want to continue to be sachems."

"If they cannot come together and give up little fires, there will be no sachems. The only rule will be the White Man's rule."

"My Brother speaks wise words, but the sachems and the war chiefs will not listen."

"Then they will lose their ears to the Long Knives!"

"My Brother speaks wise words, but little sachems and chiefs do not like wise words from other men. They prefer their own stupid words."

"Yes, my Brother speaks true. If chiefs will not listen, we must appeal to the warriors. To the warriors, they will listen."

"Yes, sometimes warriors will listen, but sometimes they prefer stupid words of our chiefs to wise words from other nations."

"But they must listen. And we appeal to the women too. They will listen. They will listen, because they vote for peace, and the only way to have peace is to have a union of all Indian nations so strong that White Men will not go on war path. White Men will not attack when they know Red Men are strong enough to destroy them, like that!" Tecumseh clapped his hands loudly.

Laulewasika got up and walked slowly away. He returned shortly with his lighted pipe.

"Ah, my Brother is ready to smoke peace pipe already?" Tecumseh asked.

"This is just pipe. I am ready to smoke peace pipe when we are strong enough to keep our lands."

"My Brother speaks wisely."

"But tell me my Brother, how do you form the great union of all the Indian fires?"

"First we make our plan, and then I go to all the tribes to explain it to them. I visit all the people, not just the chiefs. I explain it to the warriors and to the women and ask them all to join the Great Indian Union."

"First, before you explain it to all the young warriors and old women, explain it to your young Brother."

"Yes, but first let us have our supper."

The brothers walked over to the wigwam of Laulewasika where his wife, Melassa, had prepared broiled squirrel and corn meal mush. They ate silently. Tecumseh was always especially glad to have a bowl of mush because this was supposed to be the favorite food of the buffalo. After all had finished, the brothers sat by the outside fire. Laulewasika smoked his pipe as both gazed thoughtfully at the embers.

Laulewasika spoke. "My Brother has been thinking by the fire many sleeps. Explain your plan for Great Union of all Red Men. It must sound good to me if it is to sound good to all people."

"Listen!" Tecumseh poked the coals of the fire with a long stick. He picked up a small stick and handed it to his brother. "Break it," he said.

Laulewasika did so.

Tecumseh picked up two sticks of the same size. "Now hold the two sticks together and break them."

Again Laulewasika did so.

Then Tecumseh picked up a dozen similar sticks and bound them together. "Now break," he said.

Laulewasika could not do so.

"You see, you cannot break many sticks when all are tied together."

"That is true."

"In same way, when all Indians are bound together, White Men cannot break them."

"Yes, that is true. But how do you tie all Red Men together?"

"All believe in same Manitou, and want to please him, yes?"

"Yes, that is true."

"So we make rules, the same, for all Indians to please Manitou —give no more land to White Men—drink no more firewater— always speak truth—always be brave."

"Yes, that is good, but how do you make rules?"

"By Great Council of warriors chosen by all the tribes."

"How chosen, by chiefs?"

"No, not by chiefs, by warriors and women of each tribe. Great Council chooses Great Chief over all the tribes."

"Chiefs of tribes will not like Great Chief to rule them."

"Warriors must agree. Village chiefs will stay the same. Chief of all Shawnees does not tell village chief what to do in village. Same way, Great Chief of all Red Men will not tell village chief what to do in village."

"Who will be war chief?"

"Great Chief will be war chief and peace chief, no difference."

"Will Tecumseh be Great Chief?"

"Only if Great Council chooses."

"Who is Great Chief before Great Council is chosen?"

"Tecumseh."

"Good. And Great Council will choose Tecumseh for all Indians. After Tecumseh will son become Great Chief?"

"Great Chief will not be by family. Always will be chosen by Great Council."

"That also is good. How many nations will join Great Union?"

"More than five times number of fingers on my hands. I go to visit the nations of the Iroquois in north, by the great lakes and the great river — the Mohawks and Oneidas and Onondagas, and Cayugas and Senecas. I visit our friends here, by Maumee and Mississinewa and Wabash—the Delawares, the Miamis, the Potawatomis, the Eel River Miamis, the Illinois, the Kickapoos, the Weas. I go north and visit the Hurons, the Ottawas, the Chippewas. I go farther toward setting sun of summer and visit the Winnebagoes, the Menominees and the Sacs and Foxes. I cross the big river toward the setting sun of autumn and visit the Poncas and Pawnees, the Iowas and Omahas, the Sioux, the Missouris, Osages, the Kansans, the Wichitas. I go toward the setting sun of winter and visit the Quapaws, the Yazoos and

Natchez, the Kitchais. I go toward the mid-day sun of winter and visit the Cherokees, the Choctaws, the Chickasaws, the Biloxis, the Alabamas, all the Creeks, and then the Seminoles, the Catawbas, the Santees."

"My Brother knows where are many nations."

"Yes, many nations, and all see White Man coming to steal their land."

"How many warriors?"

"Great Indian Union, like Blue Coats, will have more warriors than there are leaves on the tree. As many as with Blue Jacket as many times as my fingers and toes."

"With many warriors, can stop Long Knives."

"Yes."

"It will take many moons to visit all the tribes, to make the Great Indian Union."

"It will take many summers. Maybe five summers. Maybe ten summers. But we must be patient. Always patient, must not make war before we are ready."

"Long Knives will make war when they see Indian Union becoming strong."

"My Brother speaks wise words. Long Knives must not know what we do."

"White Man will know. Always spies, always traitors."

"We must be very careful."

"Will Great Indian Union make war on White Men, send them back across big water?"

"No, it is too late. It is too late to push back. We try to live in peace, but we give no more land. Treaty made at Greeneville with White Chief Wayne was bad news. Blue Jacket and Little Turtle sign. Tecumseh refuses. But now we must accept. But let that be the line. We give no more."

"But little chiefs sign new treaties for presents from Seventeen Fires."

"We must stop them. All land not already given to Seventeen Fires belongs to all Indians. Manitou has no boundary lines. Animals have no boundary lines. Red Men have no boundary lines."

"My Brother speaks well."

"Look," Tecumseh said. He pulled a burning ember from the fire and laid it on the bare ground. Soon it flickered out. "You see? Now look." He took five or six embers and stacked them together. Soon they burst into flame. "You see? Together we make bright fire. Separate, we die."

"It is true."

"We must make rule that all land belongs to all Indians. We must stop where one day Delawares sell land and another day Miamis. If more hunting grounds are to be given away, all the tribes must agree."

"And all must agree to make Great Union."

"Yes. When many tribes have agreed, many more will join. When we are very strong it will not be necessary to make war. Long Knives will not make war when they know we are strong enough to destroy them. We do not want war. We want only our villages and our hunting grounds."

"My Brother speaks wise words. I will try to help. My Brother makes Great Union appear good. Only little chiefs will try to stop it."

"And the White Devil, Harrison."

"Yes, the White Devil, Harrison."

4

"Well, my Dear, I have another important bit of news," William Henry Harrison said to his wife as he came into the back sitting room one afternoon in August 1805.

"Well, where are you off to this time, New Orleans or somewhere?"

"No, my Dear, we are having a special guest, with your concurrence, of course."

"Who, Daniel Boone or Simon Kenton?"

"No, no."

"Or some Indian chief."

"No. The Vice President of the United States."

"The Vice President? George Clinton?"

"No, I should have said ex-Vice President."

"Oh, you mean Aaron Burr?"

"Yes, Aaron Burr."

"The murderer of Alexander Hamilton?"

"According to some people's definition."

"I guess according to the New Jersey grand jury."

"Yes, that's right."

"What's your opinion?"

"I think it was a very unfortunate incident. I think Hamilton was foolish for accepting the challenge, and Burr was culpable for issuing the challenge, and culpable for shooting him. Nevertheless, the Senate of the United States continued to accept him as presiding officer and Vice President of the United States."

"Well, I'm not sure I can be civil to him under our roof."

"Of course you can."

"What is he coming out here for?"

"Oh, he's been travelling all through the West, down to Kentucky and Tennessee, all the way to New Orleans. He'll be coming here from St. Louis."

"Probably travelling all around here because he doesn't dare go back to New York or New Jersey. If you ask me, he can't be up to any good."

"I don't know what he's up to, but we'll find out in about three weeks, I guess."

On September 23, Aaron Burr arrived in Vincennes. Travelling by horse for this part of his journey because the water was low in the Wabash at this season, Burr presented a figure of elegance and charm. Governor and Mrs. Harrison welcomed him to Grouseland with all the hospitality for which they had become noted.

In the parlor, at the dining table, or at his ease, Burr remained a sparkling and affable conversationalist, and a model of deportment and manners.

At the dinner table the conversation turned to the war in Europe, the potential of the Louisiana Purchase, and only in general terms to politics. Then Harrison asked, "Where have your travels taken you on this trip?"

"Well," Burr answered, "I had a very plesant voyage by ark down the Ohio. Had several days in Lexington and Frankfort, and then on to Nashville where I had a delightful few days with Andrew Jackson. Jackson thinks that war with Spain is likely. Says when the time comes he's ready to lead a force to take Texas."

"Yes, I am sure he would. Andy always seems ready to go to war at the drop of a hat." Harrison commented.

"Perhaps so, but it may come to that. Then I went on down to New Orleans, enjoyed the hospitality of Edward Livingston's galleried house in the *Vieux Carre*. And I must say, Governor, you have a fine house here. I can't say that Vincennes benefits much in comparison with Lexington or St. Louis, but I must say, this house is as fine as any of them."

A dessert of apple pie slowed the conversation somewhat. Then Burr went on, "I was glad to see the Louisiana matter brought to a successful conclusion. I wasn't sure Mr. Jefferson was going to be up to it. It would have been a shame to let that vast empire get away, to fall into unfriendly hands."

"Yes, I guess Mr. Jefferson had some qualms about the constitutionality of what he did."

Anna volunteered, "My husband always has been a strong supporter of Mr. Jefferson, as was his father before him."

"Yes, of course," Burr acknowledged. He returned to the question, "But I never quite understood Mr. Jefferson's doubts about the Constitution. He said the Constitution had no provision for annexing foreign territory. But the Constitution clearly gives the President and the Senate the power to conclude treaties, which the Louisiana Purchase was, and it clearly gives Congress the power to admit new states into the Union, and where are new states to come from if not from foreign territory?"

"Yes, I think you're right about that," Harrison agreed. "I see no constitutional problem."

"There's bound to be a great future out in the country of the Southwest," Burr went on.

"No doubt. But wherever we go we must deal with the Indian problem," Harrison said.

After dinner, while Anna went back to look after the children, Harrison showed his guest to the study where they continued their conversation. Burr took from his pocket a letter and handed it to Harrison. "General Wilkinson, at St. Louis asked that I deliver this letter from him on my behalf."

Harrison read it silently, though carefully:

"I will demand from your friendship a boon in its influence coextensive with the Union; a boon perhaps on which the Union may much depend; a boon which may serve me, may serve you and deserve neither. If you ask, what is this important boon I so earnestly crave? I will say to you, return the bearer to the Councils of our Country where his talents and abilities are all important to the present moment. But, you continue, how is this to be done? By your fiat! Let Mr. Parke adhere to his profession; convene your Solomons and let them return him to Congress. If you taste this proposition, speak to him, and he will authorize you to purchase, if necessary, an estate for him in your territory."

Harrison was taken by surprise by this suggestion and felt a little embarrassment now in facing Burr directly. Finally, he said, "Colonel Burr, I never realized that you had an interest in representing the West, and particularly the Indiana Territory in Congress. How does this come about?"

"I have long had an interest in the West and my recent travels have only heightened that interest. But as for representing the area in Congress, that is a notion that holds more fascination for General Wilkinson than for me. He seems to think I could perform some useful service in Congress, and this would be a way of getting there. Actually my attention now has been turned more in the other direction."

Harrison remained noncommital.

About a year later Harrison began to hear rumors that Burr was involved in a conspiracy aiming at an invasion of Mexico and possibly attempting to unite that with a section to be detached from the United States to make an empire of his own. Troubled by all this, Harrison sent a confidential associate, Judge Waller Taylor, to Jeffersonville to see what he could find out.

One evening Harrison reported to Anna, "Mr. Burr has suggested that he may want to visit us again this fall."

"What, that murderer and traitor! What did you say?"

"I have not said anything, but damn him, if he comes this way again I'll hang him from the highest sycamore tree!"

In November, Harrison received a letter from Burr in which the latter said,

All reflecting men consider a war with Spain to be inevitable; in such an event, I think you would not be at ease as an idle spectator. If it should be my lot to be employed, which there is reason to expect, it would be my highest gratification to be associated with you.

Burr enclosed a copy of Andrew Jackson's order mobilizing the militia of middle Tennessee, and suggested that Harrison might want to take similar action in Indiana Territory.

A month later another letter came from Burr in which he took pains to deny the rumors circulating about his supposed plans to detach a part of the Union. He had nothing more in mind, he insisted, than many others had had in heading a small expedition to seek lands in Texas.

In January Judge Taylor sent a detailed report on all the rumors about a supposed "Burr conspiracy." Harrison had seen enough. Yet he offered protection for some of those who had been associated with Burr. Stoutly he came to the defense of Major Davis Floyd of Jeffersonville who actually had been indicted for his alleged complicity with Burr.

5

Shortly after outlining his plans for Indian union to his brother, Tecumseh began to visit neighboring tribes to impress upon them the need for all Red Men to stand together against the Long Knives. Some were skeptical. Some were enthusiastic. Some were hostile.

One evening as Tecumseh and Laulewasika sat by their fire, a visitor arrived. It was Winamac, a chief of the Potawatomis. Tecumseh greeted him cordially and offered food. They smoked pipes for a while. Winamac said, "Plan for Red Men to come together and fight Long Knives is bad business."

"My Potowatomi Brother speaks in strange words. All Indians stand together or all Indians die!"

"Too many Long Knives. Too many Blue Coats. Seventeen Fires gives us food, gives our people things they need. Only way to live is to live in peace with White Man."

Laulewasika spoke up, "The way of the White Man is not the way of Manitou."

"Manitou tells me, live in peace."

"Only Red Men who live in peace with White Men are Indians who receive presents for selves, but do nothing for our people."

Winamac insisted, "All Red Men can do same. Get help from Seventeen Fires, live in peace."

"Never!" Tecumseh exclaimed. "Chiefs who accept presents from White Men's government are selling their own people."

"No, they make it better for own people, because Long Knives do not make war."

"All chiefs must be loyal to Red Men. All wariors will stand together. If chiefs stand outside, they stand by themselves."

"I go now," Winamac said, and he departed.

In the weeks that followed, Tecumseh found that Winamac was following him from village to village, trying to undo what he had accomplished toward persuading the tribes to accept the idea of an all Indian union.

One evening a warrior came to tell Tecumseh that Winamac wished to see him again.

"No!" exclaimed Tecumseh. "Winamac is damned traitor. If he comes this way again I will throw tomahawk!"

Laulewasika said to his brother, "We have to stop White Devil Harrison. Now Red Devil Winamac is helping him!"

CHAPTER X

Religious Ferment

1

"Come quickly, Tecumseh! Come quickly! I fear our brother is dead!"

Tecumseh ran out of his wigwam and followed Tecumapease at a run to the wigwam of their brother, Laulewasikaw. Inside they found their brother lying on his back beside the fire. His wife, Melassa, crying with grief, was bent over him, and several other men and women who had responded to her cries for help were surrounding them.

"Too much firewater," one of the neighbors said.

Tecumapease could detect no sign of breathing. Cold water and hand slaps to his face brought no response.

"No, it is not firewater this time," Tecumseh said as he conceded the opinion of some of the others that the man was dead. Tecumseh and Tecumapease led Melassa outside the wigwam while the others covered the body to wait for half a day until they could begin the purification. Then Melassa, Tecumapease, and Tecumseh would return to begin washing the body in preparation for the two-day waiting period before the funeral. It was a cool, April day.

"What happened?" asked Tecumseh. "Had he been sick with the White Man's fever as so many of our people this year?"

"No," Melassa replied. "He had been working with the sick people, and he was saddened because he had not been able to help them. But he was not sick."

"Had he been drinking firewater?"

"Many times, yes, but today, no."

"But what happened to him just now?"

"He was sitting beside the fire with blanket over his shoulders, his pipe in his hand. He was just reaching with the other hand to get an ember from the fire to light his pipe when suddenly, without any sound or warning he fell over on his side. His eyes were closed, and he did not breathe. I ran out to get some of the men and women to come. They turned him on his back, called to him, slapped his face, and rubbed his hands, but still he did not breathe. Now we can do nothing. He is dead. He is in the hands of the Master of Life."

"I am afraid we have neglected our brother," said Tecumapease with some feeling of remorse. It was evident to everyone that she always had favored Tecumseh in their early years, and she felt a tinge of guilt over her lack of attention to Laulewasikaw even though the latter now was thirty years old and had had a wife and a wigwam of his own for four years.

Laulewasikaw never had attained the stature of any of his brothers. He lacked the skills as well as the physique that would have enabled him to become an accomplished warrior. Considerably shorter than Tecumseh, he was rotund and rather flabby. Loss of an eye while he was engaged in a war game as a youth had left him with an appearance that was more grotesque and fearsome than his manners and demeanor warranted. He was bright enough intellectually, but he had never developed the skills to be a good hunter or a successful warrior. He resented the name by which he was known and with which he was teased by his associates, "Laulewasikaw," meaning "Loud Mouth." He was self-conscious about his lack of accomplishments and his lack of any significant role in any of the battles which his tribe had fought. He was a little envious of the respect and admiration paid his brother, though he himself shared fully in that respect and admiration. His kinsmen as well as his adversaries had regarded him as sly, slippery, and excessively clever.

He had felt keenly the loss of his father and two brothers in battle and the absence of his mother.

For some time Laulewasikaw had shown a greater interest in learning the skills of a medicine man and the ways of a holy man than in those of a warrior. Lately he had developed some skills in prescribing medicines and cures for various ailments. He had learned about herbs, cures, and incantations from Penageshea, an old shaman who had been living in the village. At first rejected by the old man, Laulewasikaw had persisted until finally the old shaman agreed to instruct him.

Ordinarily, to become a medicine man one had to serve an apprenticeship of several years and then be chosen by the village or tribal council. The old shaman's death the previous year had left a vacancy, but it also had left Laulewasikaw short of training. Mainly on account of his debauchery and his braggadocio combined with his ineptness in the woods or on the battlefield, he had been regarded as something of a buffoon, and certainly not one to be taken seriously. Any words of wisdom from his mouth had been those of a court fool.

"Melassa! Come, Laulewasikaw lives! He lives!" called those who had been preparing for the funeral. Tecumseh and Tecumapease rushed with Melassa back into the wigwam. Actually several hours of mourning and hopelessness now had passed, but when they got back inside they found that their husband and brother indeed was sitting up. He shook his head as though dizzy and then opened his eye.

While his family and neighbors gathered around he told his story. Their amazement at his return to life became even greater as they listened.

"My Brothers and Sisters, I was dead, but the Master of Life has returned me to life. I have been on a great journey. While I was dead the Master of Life sent two young men who carried my soul to the spirit world. They carried me to a mountain top where I was able to look into heaven. It was a paradise filled with game and with abundant cornfields where our good brothers and sisters who have gone before us could enjoy a life of abundance without enemies, without sadness. Our bad brothers and sisters were allowed only to look at the great paradise, then they had to move on to another place where eternal fires were burning in a huge wigwam. All the sinners had to suffer punishment in the fire. Those who drank firewater were forced to swallow molten lead until flames burst out of their noses. The worst sinners were burned to ashes. After the sinners had paid the price for their wrongs, they were at last allowed to enter paradise, but never would they be able to enjoy it fully as did the good Indians."

"My Brothers and Sisters, I am a changed man. Never again will I drink the White Man's whiskey.

"The Master of Life has chosen me to lead all our people, all the Red Men, to salvation that they may avoid the eternal fire and enjoy the eternal paradise. No longer will I be called Laulewasikaw. From this day I shall be known as Tenskwatawa—the 'Open Door'."

Through the rest of that spring and summer of 1805 Tenskwatawa experienced several more visions, and he developed more his new religious doctrines—essentially to reject the ways of the White Man, to partake no more of the White Man's whiskey, to return to the old ways of Indian life. With all this Tenskwatawa prevailed upon the village and then the tribal councils to recognize him as prophet, and while he was known to his close associates and family as Tenskwatawa, he was becoming known far and wide simply as The Prophet.

Tecumseh at first was not impressed by his brother's claims, and for a time he remained indifferent to his doctrines. But as the summer passed, Tecumseh's interest rose. Recognizing the sincerity with which The Prophet not only expressed but practiced his doctrines, and realizing how they might provide a spiritual undergirding for his own political doctrine of uniting the tribes to save the Indian way of life, Tecumseh accepted his brother's religious doctrines as his own. Soon their White enemies would be thinking of them as a kind of Moses and Aaron.

In August of that year Tecumseh went with The Prophet to establish a new village at Greeneville, in Ohio. There Tecumseh would organize the village to take care of the physical needs, and The Prophet would be able to devote himself to their spiritual needs. But now he was looking far beyond the local residents who accompanied them. Greeneville would become a center to which members of all the tribes might come to hear the word and then return to their own villages to spread the new dispensation among their brethren.

In November Tecumseh went with The Prophet to Wapakoneta, Black Hoof's village on the Auglaize River, where The Prophet delivered long discourses to delegations of Senecas, Wyandots, and Ottawas, as well as Shawnees.

The Prophet said to them, "I have been sent by Manitou, the Master of Life, because the Red Men were wandering away from their old customs. At first I forgot that this was my mission. Motchemenetoo, the Devil, spoke to me with a forked tongue. At first I believed him. I drank the White Man's firewater and became very bad. Then one day Manitou, the Master of Life, took me back to our Grandmother's home, and he said to me, 'How are you getting on with the work which you were to do?' Then I remembered what I had been doing. Then the Master of Life said, 'Is it for this that I created you?' Then he took my mouth and showed it to me, and I saw that it was crooked and sticking out in all directions.

"Then he took my understanding and showed it to me, and he said, 'Did I create you thus?' Then he showed me my ears, and they were all crooked and ragged. Then he took out my heart and showed it to me. It was all wrinkled and bad to look upon. 'Did I create you thus?' he asked."

"'Now you will return to your people and do better next time,' the Master of Life said. I did not come back to look for revenge. I came back to tell of the mysteries of life, of how an eternal paradise awaits for all good Indians who give up their bad ways and follow the way of the Master of Life and the Great Spirit, and how all bad Indians who continue to follow the bad advice of Motchemenetoo, the Devil, must burn in fire to suffer for their wrongs before they can enter the great paradise.

"Will you give up the bad ways of Motchemenetoo and follow the good ways of Manitou?"

"Yes! Yes! Yes!" shouted his listeners. Some of the women began to sway back and forth in a cluster dance. Others began to dance in circles in a frenzied outburst to the accompaniment of wild whoops.

"Then you must give up the White Man's fire water. You will drink no more."

"Drink no more!" they shouted.

"You must give up White Man's goods and White Man's tools and guns."

"Yes! Yes!" The whole throng seethed with excitement.

The first converts were, in one sense, the most improbable —the young drunkards, habitual thieves, and adulterers—but they also were the ones with most reason to be fearful of the threatened torment in the eternal fire. The greatest resistance came from the older chiefs who saw all this as threatening to their own control.

Those who dared speak out against The Prophet he denounced as witches and condemned them to death by burning. He also demanded that the old medicine men give up their medicine bags or face the same fate, for in them lay possible rivals to The Prophet's spiritual leadership.

Early in his campaign he called upon the Delawares to execute a group of those in their midst who were guilty of witchcraft, and they obediently followed his order. This exercise began with the roasting of an old woman. For four days Delaware warriors roasted her slowly over a fire, demanding that she give up her charm and medicine bag. Just as she was dying she cried out that her grandson, then out hunting, had the charm. Warriors went out to find the young man, and they brought him, bound, back to the village. He admitted that he had borrowed the charm once and had used it to allow himself to fly through the air over Kentucky and to the Mississippi River one night before his bedtime, but he insisted that he then had returned it to his grandmother. After much argument, he finally was set free.

The next day a council deliberated on the case of the venerable chief, Tatepocoshe, and after full discussion, it decided that he too should die. The old chief put on his finest apparel and insisted on helping build his own funeral pyre. Out of deference to his age and position, the executioners allowed him the mercy of a tomahawk to his skull before they put his body on the fire. Next was an old prophet who was called "Joshua" who also was granted the benefit of a tomahawk before burning.

Then the wife of Tatepocoshe and his nephew, a lad who had been converted to Christianity and given the Christian name of "Billy Patterson," were brought in for trial. Both were condemned. The lad was burned alive as he prayed and sang Christian hymns.

While the old chief's wife waited in the council house, together with the council and onlookers, for the pyre to be built for her, a young man of about twenty suddenly jumped up, calmly walked over to the lady, took her by the hand and led her outside. A few minutes later he returned and called out, "The Devil has come among us, and we are killing each other. This must stop!" He resumed his seat in the midst of the crowd while the astonished council members went into a flurry of consultative activity. The shock was such that they adjourned the meeting, and that ended the spate of executions for witchcraft.

When The Prophet heard about the suspension of executions by the Delawares, he was concerned about the challenge that this might pose to his authority and his claim to religious leadership. He told Tecumseh what had happened.

"Who was the young brave who interfered?" Tecumseh asked.

"One who is called Peshewa—Wildcat."

"Peshewa, Peshewa. He did act as a Wildcat. But my Brother, I believe he was acting according to word from Manitou."

"What, to defy my instructions?"

"My Brother, when I was a very young man Manitou told me that it was bad to torture and execute prisoners. I listened to him, and I told warriors. Our brother, Chiksika was there. They all believed me. They all vowed never to torture or execute prisoners again. Now my Brother, I believe Manitou has spoken to us through Peshewa. We must listen. We will be stronger if warriors join us because they believe your wise words, not because they fear executions. It is better that they fear burning in eternal fire, not burning in our fire."

The Prophet said nothing for a long time, and then without turning his head he said simply, "My Brother has spoken wisely. He gives good advice from Master of Life."

Governor William Henry Harrison was appalled when the news reached him in Vincennes about the witchcraft executions among the Delawares. Immediately he dispatched John Conner as special messenger with a forceful draft to be read out to the tribe at Little Munsee, the village of the Delawares on the White River:

My Children: — My heart is filled with grief, and my eyes are dissolved in tears, at the news which has reached me. You have been celebrated for your wisdom above all the tribes of red people who inhabit this great island. Your fame as warriors has extended to the remotest nations, and the wisdom of your chiefs has gained for you the appellation of grandfathers, from all the neighboring tribes. From what cause, then, does it proceed, that you have departed from the wise counsels of your fathers, and covered yourselves with guilt? My children, tread back the steps you have taken, and endeavor to regain the straight road which you have abandoned. The dark, crooked and thorny one which you are now pursuing, will certainly lead to endless woe and misery. But who is this pretended prophet, who dares to speak in the name of the Great Creator? Examine him. Is he more wise or virtuous than you are yourselves, that he should be selected to convey to you the orders of your God? Demand of him some proofs at least, of his being the messenger of the Deity. If God has really employed him, he has doubtless authorized him to perform miracles, that he may be known and received as a prophet. If he is really a prophet, ask of him to cause the sun to stand still—the moon to alter its course—the rivers to cease to flow—or the dead to rise from their graves. If he does these things, you may then believe that he has been sent from God. He tells you that the Great Spirit commands you to punish with death those who deal in magic; and that he is authorized to point them out. Wretched delusion! Is then the Master of Life obliged to employ mortal man to punish those who offend him? Has he not the thunder and all the powers at nature at his command?—and could he not sweep away from the earth a whole nation with one motion of his arm? My children; do not believe that the great and good Creator of mankind has directed you to destroy your own flesh; and do not doubt but that if you pursue this abominable wickedness, his vengeance will overtake and crush you.

The above is addressed to you in the name of the Seventeen Fires. I now speak to you from myself, as a friend who wishes nothing more sincerely than to see you prosperous and happy. Clear your eyes, I beseech you, from the mist which surrounds them. No longer be imposed upon by the arts of an impostor. Drive him from your town, and let peace and harmony once more prevail amongst you. Let your poor old men and women sleep in quietness, and banish from their minds the dreadful idea of being burnt alive by their own friends and countrymen. I charge you to stop your bloody career; and if you value the friendship of your great father, the President—if you wish to preserve the good opinion of the Seventeen Fires, let me hear by the return of the bearer, that you have determined to follow my advice.

When Delaware messengers brought a copy of Harrison's message to The Prophet at Greeneville, and some began to question the truth of his teachings and the authenticity of his claims, he was delighted to see the Governor's challenge. He had learned, whether by conversations with astronomers who had gone through the area, or contacts with missionaries, or by direct divine revelation, that a total eclipse of the sun was to occur at noon on June 16.

On June 6, The Prophet assembled his followers and told them, "The Great White Chief has asked that I show signs that I represent the Master of Life. Some of you have asked questions about the truth of my teachings. Now, I tell you that in ten days the Master of Life will send a Black Sun, that you might believe. Go tell your brothers and return to this place before midday in ten days."

On June 16 The Prophet remained out of sight, in his lodge, while a large crowd gathered. Then, as the darkness came at noon, he came out and stood on a stump.

"My Brothers!" he cried out in a loud voice. "My Brothers, you have asked of me signs that you might believe that I speak truly the word of Manitou, the Master of Life. I told you that one day I would bring darkness over the sun. Now the time has come. Did I not prophecy truly? Behold! Darkness has shrouded the sun!"

The Indians fell down on their knees, their faces to the ground. And there was much crying and wailing and gnashing of teeth.

Then The Prophet spoke again, "Fear not, my Brothers. Fear not, for I shall restore the light to the sun."

Presently the shadow of the eclipse passed away, and the Indian multitude rose up rejoicing—they danced about, shouted, and swore allegiance to the great Prophet.

Soon word of the miracle and the words of The Prophet had spread all the way around the Great Lakes and west to the Mississippi.

In April 1807 about four hundred Indian religious fanatics assembled at Greeneville to hear more advice from The Prophet. He took advantage of the situation to summarize his whole doctrine in a long oration.

He said, "My Brothers, if you will follow the way of the Great Spirit and the Master of Life, you must follow these commands from Manitou:"

"First, no whiskey or other firewater may be tasted for any reason whatsoever.

"In the future no Indian may take more than one wife. Those who now have two or three may keep them, but it would please the Great Spirit if you have only one wife.

"No Indian man shall be running after women; if a man is single, let him take a wife.

"If any squaw behaves ill by not doing proper work or taking care of her children, the husband has a right to punish her with a rod, but when that is done, then husband and wife must look each other in the face and laugh, and let no ill will last.

"Indians must marry only Indians. There must be no inter-marriage with White People. All Indian Women who are living with White Men must be brought back to their own families and friends. Their children will be left with their fathers so that the Indian nations may become pure again."

"All medicine bags and medicine dances and songs must be abolished. Medicine bags will be destroyed in the presence of an assembly of all the People, when everyone must make a confession, in a loud voice to the Great Spirit for all bad deeds done in their lifetime.

"No Indian is to sell any provisions to any White People, though small presents may be given.

"No Indian is to eat food cooked by White People, or eat provisions raised by White People, as white bread, beef, pork, chicken.

"No Indian is to sell any skins, or furs, or other items, but only may offer them in trade for other things.

"Americans must be kept at a distance, though French, English, and Spaniards may be considered as friends.

"All items of White Men's dress must be given back to White People at the first opportunity, and not more than one dog or cat may be kept.

"Bows and arrows will be used to hunt animals. Firearms may be used only to defend ourselves against the White Man.

"Always remember to respect the elderly and to see that they have good food and shelter, and everything possible for their health and happiness.

"Prayers are to be repeated morning and evening for the earth to be fruitful, for the fish and game to be plentiful, and for the fire and the sun to be benevolent.

"Indians who refuse to follow these rules may be condemned to death."

Again, fanatical followers began to shout and dance. The Prophet called for quiet and continued.

"My Brothers, we must return to the ways of our fathers. We must reject the ways of the White Men and recover the greatness of our own Indian nations. And now, let me repeat to you the great rules which our fathers taught us:

"Do not kill or injure your neighbor, for it is not him that you injure; you injure yourself. But do good to him, therefore add to his days of happiness as you add to your own. Do not wrong or hate your neighbor, for it is not him that you wrong; you wrong yourself. But love him, for Manitou loves him also as he loves you."

The Prophet raised his hand and called for the blessing of Manitou.

This was the signal for the commencement of the great ritual dance. The men stripped themselves naked, painted their bodies in elaborate colors, picked up war clubs, and then danced in a great circle in honor of the perfect oversight of Manitou and their commitment to his rules.

The next spring no less than 1,500 Indians came from all over the Northwest during the month of May alone to hear The Prophet. Large collections of Indians always were matters of concern to the White settlers, the Indian agents, and the Governor.

One day an Indian brave ran up to tell Tecumseh that a messenger had arrived from the White Warriors at Fort Wayne. Tecumseh summoned a council. They sat down to listen to Anthony Shane, half-breed messenger of Captain Wells. The messenger said that it was desired that they come to Fort Wayne to hear a message from their great father, the President of the United States.

Tecumseh rose and spoke coldly, "Go back to Fort Wayne and tell Captain Wells that my fire is kindled on the spot appointed by the Great Spirit above, and if he has anything to communicate to me, he must come here."

Shane then explained that it was hoped that the Red Men of this village might accept the assistance of the United States in finding new lands, as this was located in the lands given to the White Men in the Treaty of Greeneville.

Tecumseh replied, "These lands are ours. No one has a right to remove us, because we were the first owners. The Great Spirit has appointed this place for us on which to light our fires, and here we will remain. The Great Spirit and the animals of the forest know no boundaries, nor will his Red Men know any. If my father, the President of the Seventeen Fires, has anything more to say to me, he must send a man of note as messenger. I will have no further communication with Captain Wells."

Then The Prophet spoke, "Why does not the President of the Seventeen Fires send us the greatest man in his nation? I can talk to him—I can bring darkness between him and me; nay, more, I can bring the sun under my feet, and what White Man can do that?"

A few weeks later a messenger arrived from Governor Harrison with an address for the Indians at Greeneville. Patiently The Prophet, surrounded by a group of followers, listened to the reading.

My Children, I have heard bad news. The sacred spot where the great council-fire was kindled, around which the Seventeen Fires and ten tribes of their children smoked the pipe of peace—that very spot where the Great Spirit saw his red and white children encircle themselves with the chain of friendship —that place has been selected for dark and bloody councils.

My Children, this business must be stopped. You have called in a number of men from the most distant tribes to listen to a fool, who speaks not the words of the Great Spirit, but those of the devil and of British agents. My children, your conduct has much alarmed the white settlers near you. They desire that you will send away those people, and if they wish to have the imposter with them they can carry him. Let him go to the lakes; he can hear the British more distinctly.

The Prophet stepped forward to dictate a reply:

Father, I am sorry that you listen to the advice of bad birds. Father, these impeachments I deny and say they are not true. I never had a word with the

British, and I never sent for any Indians. They came here themselves to listen and hear the words of the Great Spirit. Father, I wish you would not listen any more to the voice of bad birds.

2

"I tell you, Billy, I never saw anything like it, never. The religious frenzy of that Cane Ridge revival meeting swept our people by the thousands. They would fall to the ground in a trance and appear to be dead, sometimes for hours, and then would rise up and proclaim that they had been reborn." Dr. John Scott, in Vincennes in May this time on his biennial visit to deliver another child for the Harrison family, was speaking to William Henry Harrison in the study of the Grouseland mansion.

"Yes, I have heard some of the folks around here speak of it, and some have gone from here to attend other camp meetings since then. Let's see, when was that big one?"

"About four or five years ago, I guess. Yes, five years ago in August."

"Yes, I remember, you mentioned it when you were here two years ago for the birth of John Scott, but then I was about to leave for St. Louis and we didn't have time to talk much about anything. Well, we had a Presbyterian preacher arrive here several months ago, Thomas Cleland. You know him?"

"No, but I think I've heard of him all right."

"Well, anyway, I went over to hear his first sermon—over in the old Indian lodge. I guess this was the first regular Presbyterian sermon ever preached in Indiana, which pleased Anna. I gathered that he had been influenced by the Cane Ridge meeting, and some of the others since then, and I have just been wondering what went on there."

"There was an earlier camp meeting over in Logan County which I heard about, and it sounded so fascinating that when I heard they were having another one in Bourbon County I decided to ride over and have a look. What I saw was beyond any imagination."

"What did they do, meet in a big tent?"

"They started out with one big tent, but no tent could have been found to hold that crowd. They had other tents, all right, lots of tents, but they were for sleeping. All the activities were out of doors, so you can bet their first prayers were for fair weather."

"I guess a downpour would not have bothered the Baptists. They believe in total immersion."

"I guess not rain nor wind nor lightning and thunder would have stopped any of them, but they did have fair weather though it was hot."

"So what happened? What did they do, exactly?"

"Well, I tell you it was like a gigantic picnic, church service, and frolic all going on at the same time and continuously for over five days. The crowd began to gather on Friday afternoon, and the thing went until the next Thursday morning. I went over on Sunday and stayed twice as long as I intended. When I arrived, preaching and eating and talking were going on everywhere. People were in a jovial, holiday mood, young and old, rich and poor, all kinds of people. Everyone greeted everyone cheerily, and everybody offered everybody food. People would stand around in circles of a dozen or so, singing hymns, so crowded that one circle would rub against the next. Then a preacher would come along and get up on a stump or a log, or the back of a wagon, and start preaching while as many as could get within earshot would crowd around. A dozen preachers would be in action at once. Methodists, Presbyterians, Baptists, they all participated. They would get the people stirred up to a frenzy. People would start going through all kinds of bodily exercises—screaming, yapping, barking, flopping, flouncing, head twisting, jerking. Some would start running and others dancing. Sometimes sinners would be seized by jerking, and they would be cursing and swearing, but the only way they could stop it was by long praying. Sometimes, just an arm or a leg would jerk; sometimes, the head; sometimes, the whole body. When a whole crowd would get started it created a wild spectacle. Right with hardened and grizzled sinners would be young dandies and belles. It was quite a sight to see proud young gentlemen and young ladies, dressed in their silks and jewelry and prunella from head to toe, seized by the jerks. With the first jerk or so their fine caps, bonnets, and combs would fly off, and then their long, loose hair would crack like a wagoner's whip! There must have been ten or fifteen thousand people there on that Sunday, and it seemed that most of them got involved in these wild gyrations. After their jerking or barking or running, many of them would let out a wild, piercing scream and then fall to the ground. They would lie there as though dead, sometimes for hours. They finally got a system to carry these people over to other preachers who then would pray with them and hear their confessions. This was conversion. The success of meetings was counted in the number of falls recorded. They say that three thousand were brought to the ground at Cane Ridge."

"How long did this go on, 'til supper time, or 'til dark?"

"There wasn't any supper time and no ceasing for dark. Some individuals would crawl into tents or wagons to sleep at night, and some would sleep in the daytime. Lots of folks would come just for a day or two and leave, and others would come in. Actually, the nights were more spectacular than the days. Scores of big fires, hundreds of lanterns and thousands of candles lit the whole area. Shadows of the trees and of the gesturing preachers and of the flopping and jerking multitude played upon each other in grotesque combinations. And this night great numbers broke into wild dancing—friends, couples, or complete strangers would embrace each other as long friends, and then go into the dancing. Sometimes a couple—a couple of strangers even—would fall to the ground together in such complete compassion and excitement that they would roll to the shadows and confirm their love in a most intimate way."

"No!" exclaimed Harrison.

"Oh, yes, I wouldn't say how many went to that extreme, but there were a good many, I'm afraid."

"Well, for the great majority, do you think any of this did any good?"

"That's hard to say," Scott replied as he thought about it. "I'm not much inclined to these emotional outbursts and find them a little ridiculous, but I'm inclined to say that it does do some good. I must say that I have seen a good many men known to be drunkards and gamblers and horse thieves come out changed men. I'm sure a lot of them become backsliders, but if even a few of them can be reformed in that way I guess it may be worth it. They say that Barton Stone who was more or less the instigator of the Cane Ridge meeting is quite a reasonable fellow. In fact, he is so reasonable that he is in trouble with his own presbyter, and I understand he may be going out on his own with his 'New Lights.' When ten or twenty thousand people will ride horses or drive wagons over the rough roads for those distances, obviously there is something there that attracts them."

"Maybe part of it is simply in being a part of that big a crowd. Out on the frontier a person feels all alone, or one of only a handful of people in a settlement. There, he is one of thousands, with no place for loneliness."

"Yes, that may be a part of it. Religion is a strange drawing card, isn't it?"

Two weeks later Harrison was beating his usual path in the upstairs hall as he awaited the birth of their fifth child when John Scott came out from the bedroom to announce the arrival of a new son. Harrison hurried in to greet Anna and the new baby with as much excitement as on the first such occasion. Then, turning to the doctor, he said, "John, do you know what we are naming this one?"

"No, I suppose Benjamin?"

"Right. Right you are!"

Harrison had some doubts himself about the great revivals and camp meetings, but he welcomed the organization of churches as stabilizing influences in the communities. He was troubled by the extent of bickering going on in Vincennes. Fisticuffs were common, and sometimes there were duels. The Quaker, Dr. McNamee made charges against John Badollet and Nathaniel Ewing. General W. Johnston attacked Dr. Samuel McKee, and so it went. Even Benjamin Parke, irked by criticisms of Governor Harrison that William McIntosh had been mouthing, delivered this broadside through a letter to the *Western Sun*:

Circumstances have recently occurred which authorize me in pronouncing and publishing Wm. McIntosh an arrant knave, a prostigate villain, a dastardly cheat, a perfidious rascal, an impertinent puppy, an absolute liar, and a mean cowardly poltron. B. Parke.

Parke even challenged the Scotsman to a duel, but McIntosh did not accept it.

Until 1806, the only church in Vincennes was the Catholic log church of St. Francis Xavier. This was the church built under the leadership of the renowned and revered missionary, Father Pierre Gibault. In its belfry hung the "liberty bell of the Old Northwest"—the bell which had tolled in 1778 when the local French inhabitants, under the leadership of Father Gibault, had aligned themselves with the American colonies against the British.

Even the Catholics in the area had been without spiritual leadership for a number of years, but recently an outstanding priest, Father John Francis Rivet, had been in their service and that of the entire community. Since there was and had been no other church, the Governor and Mrs. Harrison frequently had attended the mass under his direction at St. Francis Xavier, and Harrison had developed a high regard and friendship for him. A refugee from the French Revolution, but a priest highly respected in his home diocese, Father Rivet had brought a refinement of culture, eminent learning, and high character so badly needed in this frontier community. Harrison had been so impressed with his qualities that he had persuaded the Federal Government to recognize him as a primary agent in their efforts to educate the Indians toward civilization. For his part, he had held Harrison in high regard and had spoken of him to the people as "their true and just friend." Father Rivet's death in February 1804 left a void not only in the Catholic community, but for all of the communities in the Vincennes area.

Protestant churchmen, or at least those who had been churchmen in the eastern states, were uneasy about the vices of Sabbath-breaking in Vincennes, the profane swearing, the whiskey drinking, and the gambling that went on. For them, the Catholic Church offered little hope, for the French Catholics rode, fished, danced, played cards, played billiards, and had parties on Sunday. Whether to inform or to obscure, the local newspaper office offered for sale, over a considerable time, *The Real Principles of Roman Catholics; In Reference to God and the Country*, by The Rev. Stephen Theodore Rudim.

Thomas Cleland found some sympathetic ears for his sermons, and he urged the organization of a local church. Samuel B. Robertson was able to do this with the organization in 1806 of the "Church in Indiana," with a little log church about two miles north of the borough. This was the first Presbyterian congregation in Indiana, and a year later Samuel Thornton Scott became the minister, the first settled Presbyterian minister in the Territory. Scott, like Father Rivet, became a local favorite, and even the Catholics, without a priest since the death of Rivet, appreciated his presence.

In 1808 the Territorial legislature chartered the Wabash Baptist Church. In May, 1809, the Mariah Creek Baptist Church was organized. In the same year the Methodists sent the Reverend William Winans who held his first service in a small room of a private house. This was at night, and Governor Harrison held a candle while the new minister read his text.

These Protestant groups differed sharply in theology and structure, though all had shared in the Cane Ridge and other revival meetings. The Presbyterians here still clung to the strict Calvinistic doctrines of election and predestination. The Baptists were equivocal on Calvinism, though all held to the essential doctrines of separation of church and state, baptism by immersion for accountable believers only, individual conversion as a condition of membership, individual responsibility to God, and a congregational form of government. They opposed an educated and salaried ministry; they would accept anyone who had received a "call" and could demonstrate his talents. The Methodists had developed as dissenters out of the Church of England and held to the Arminian (in contrast to the Calvinistic) tradition, with emphasis on free will, and they maintained an episcopal structure in church government.

About this same time a more peculiar colony of two dozen adherents from Ohio appeared about sixteen miles up the Wabash from Vincennes. These were members of a sect named the United Society of the Believers in Christ's Second Appearing. Other settlers referred to them as "Shakers" on account of their devotional dancing, jitters, handclapping, and "speaking in tongues" which they exhibited while at worship. Their opposition to marriage as the root of all evil and their dedication to celibacy, abstinence from liquor and tobacco, vegetarianism, and communal property holding provided other bases for other settlers to regard them as "peculiar." Tales of obscene practices followed them. They were accused of seizing and beating children because "the devil was in them," and of breaking up families for their beliefs. They rejected literature, learning, and amusements, but they did gain a reputation for cleanliness, industriousness, and skilled farming.

3

Harrison always had had an interest in religion. He was interested in its effects on people, and he was interested in it as a guide to his own thinking. Since becoming the head of a family he had developed the habit of reading from *The Bible* each evening before retiring. He liked to read some history, and perhaps the newspaper, and then *The Bible*. Best of all, Anna liked to do the same things, and he always enjoyed the discussions that she generated.

On this evening she called his attention to a piece in Elihu Stout's weekly newspaper, *The Western Sun*. "Henry, see if you don't think this is pretty well stated. It's called 'The Moralist; Thoughts on Religion.'" She read:

THE MORALIST
Thoughts on Religion

Errors and mistakes, however gross in matters of opinion, if they are sincere, ought to be pitied and not punished or laughed at. The blindness of the understanding is as much to be pitied as the blindness of the eyes; and it is neither laughable nor criminal for a man to love his way in either case. Charity bids us endeavour to set them right by argument; but at the same time forbids either to punish or ridicule their misfortunes.

Every man seeks for truth: and God only knows who has found it. It is unjust to persecute, absurd to ridicule people for their several opinions, which they cannot help entertaining upon the conviction of their reason; it is he who acts or tells a lie, that is guilty, and not he who honestly and sincerely believes the lie. The object of all public worship in this world is the same; in the great Eternal Being who created everything. The different manners of worship, are by no means subjects of ridicule. Each thinks his own the best; and I know no infallible judge in this world, to decide which is the best.

"Well, I must say," Harrison responded. "I don't agree with Eli Stout on some of his political support, but I cannot disagree with him on that. Well stated, I would say, well stated, indeed."

"I think so, too," agreed Anna, "but the real question is whether or not that holds for everybody or just for Christians?"

"For everybody, I would think."

"Yes. Here is an earlier one, rather clever, that he had picked up from somewhere else, probably from the Mohammedans, who try to express their moral doctrine in a kind of proverbial chain of parallels:

There are five things which a wise man will ground no hopes on: the color of a cloud, because imaginary; the friendship of the covetous, because mercenary; beauty, because frail; praise, because air; and the pleasures of this world, because deceitful."

"Yes, I guess that is pretty wise too, isn't it? Except that part about beauty being frail; I don't believe that, because, my Dear, your beauty grows with each year; it becomes stronger with each child. There's nothing frail about that."

"Now, Henry, careful, you know praise is only air."

"And I don't agree with that one, either."

Both resumed their reading until Anna interrupted again.

"Henry."

"Yes?"

"What about the Indians?"

"What about the Indians?"

"Oh, I mean their religious beliefs. Is it absurd to ridicule them for their opinions?"

"I wouldn't ridicule them, though I guess I wouldn't put much stock in some of them. For instance a young Delaware man, on seeing his grandmother being roasted alive as a witch who refused to give up her charm, said that he had borrowed the charm one night to enable him to fly over Kentucky and to the Mississippi River and back before his bedtime. Can you believe that?"

"Believe what, that he said it or that he flew to St. Louis? Well, of course, it does sound a little ridiculous, doesn't it, but then, you know, some of our Catholic friends say that back in the 14th Century there was a nun who flew to Rome."

"Who was that supposed to be?"

"I'm not sure, but it may have been St. Catherine of Siena. Anyway, they say she flew to Rome to see the Pope."

"Do you believe that?"

"Course not, but some of those folks really do. Probably she reported it from one of her trances, like she reported talking to Jesus."

"Well, maybe the Indian boy just dreamed he flew to St. Louis."

"Probably so. But why is it, when an Indian boy flies to St. Louis to see his grandmother, that is just a pagan fantasy, or a dream, but when a nun flies to Rome to see the Pope, that is a Christian miracle or a prophetic vision?"

"Yes, you may have a point there."

"What about the one they call The Prophet, the Shawnee Prophet? Does he really believe all those things he teaches, or is that just a cynical way of attracting a following?"

"I'm really not sure about that. I'm sure he believes some of the things he says. In fact so do I, but some of it is superstition, and probably some of it is simply a cynical appeal for power. But we had better take it all seriously."

"What did you mean about some of his teachings that you believe?"

"That Indians should not drink firewater, for a starter. I don't know what it is, but Indians simply cannot hold their liquor.

They develop a craving for it, and when they get hold of it they just go crazy. That's the way lots of unscrupulous traders take advantage of them. If The Prophet is able to get his followers to give up whiskey, then I have to hand it to him for that."

"Is that all there is of substance to his doctrine?"

"Oh, no. One which actually predates him, but which he reemphasizes, is what one might almost call a Shawnee 'Sermon on the Mount.' It goes something like this: 'Do not kill or injure your neighbor, for it is not him that you injure, but yourself. But do good to him, as you will add to your own days of happiness as you add to his. Do not wrong or hate your neighbor, for it is not him that you wrong, but yourself. But love him, for Manitou loves him also as he loves you.'"

"Oh, that is remarkable, isn't it? It seems to me that a good deal of what The Prophet preaches has something the same as Christianity."

"Yes, I suppose it does, in a way."

"Then what is the real difference, the really essential difference between the Shawnee religion as he preaches it and Christianity?"

"Well, I suppose first of all the idea that his appeal makes no claim at being universal. His 'neighbors' are only the Red men. His is a pan-Indian appeal, not an appeal to all mankind. He has no apostle to the Gentiles. He is not trying to convert White men to his doctrine. He is not attempting to convert Rome."

"No, I suppose not. What else?"

"And secondly, the idea of Christian love. He urges a certain harmonious consideration among the Indians and a certain high moral code in dealing with each other, but when it comes to dealing with White men, it is simply a question of getting away with what you can, or treating them like they treat you. The idea of loving your enemy is completely foreign to him."

"Yes," Anna countered. "Yes, Christians profess that, but I'm not sure how much they practice it."

"Certainly the way he has gone about executing nonbelievers and witches is not very compatible with Christian ideas, is it?"

"What about the burning of Joan of Arc? What about the Spanish Inquisition? And what about the trials and executions of witches in Salem, Massachusetts—all done in the name of Christianity?"

"Yes, I'm afraid you're right about that. But to my way of thinking, all those were aberrations, while for him it seems to be a part of his central doctrine. You see, Jesus himself never executed anyone, nor ever suggested that heretics and witches ought to be burned. The Prophet has done so."

"I'm not sure that makes much difference to the victims. He surely has not executed anything like the number they did in Salem, has he?"

"No, so far as I know he has not. I have tried to do all that I could to put a stop to that."

"I am glad for that, Henry, and I think the country is glad, too. From what you have told me in the past about The Prophet, he seems to have reformed his own life, and I guess he deserves some credit for that."

"That is true. From one caught up in drunkenness and debauchery and licentiousness and lewdness to one who has reformed into a model of personal conduct, he almost reminds one of St. Augustine. Or even St. Paul who experienced a spectacular conversion and changed his name as he became the greatest supporter and strength for those whom he had been persecuting."

They returned to their reading. Harrison picked up his Bible and more or less at random, opened it to the thirteenth chapter of Mark.

"What are you reading?" asked Anna.

He read, "But in those days, after the tribulation, the sun shall be darkened, and the moon shall not give her light," and he laughed.

"Why do you laugh?" she demanded.

"Don't you remember, I told you, how the Shawnee Prophet darkened the sun at midday?"

"Oh, yes, yes."

"I surely played into his hands on that one. I forgot all about the eclipse when I urged the Delawares to challenge him to give signs of his authority, such as making the sun stand still. I tell you, that made believers out of lots of them."

Anna laughed softly at that. But she had more questions. "Henry, I wonder sometimes about all those camp meetings, those big revivals where hundreds or thousands of people get caught up in a frenzy, and shout and jump around, and carry on in all sorts of ways. How is that really different from all those Indian dances which we think of as pagan rituals?"

"I'm afraid they do have a lot in common. I guess the revivals do some good in reforming some of the sinners and in getting churches started, but I tell you, Anna, sometimes they almost make me lose faith in popular government."

"How is that?"

"Oh, so many of those preachers are so smug and self-righteous. They claim to have all the answers. And the people jump up and down, and shout 'Amen!.' They don't think about it. They just accept whatever the most eloquent and dynamic preacher of the moment says. So many of the preachers are quick to demand tolerance for themselves, but they are mighty slow to recognize it for anybody else."

"Henry, I think it's past our bedtime. Otherwise I might get the jerks and fall on the floor, or something."

As was their custom, they knelt beside the bed, hand in hand, for their nightly prayers, first Anna and then Henry.

CHAPTER XI

Continuing Education

1a

Tecumseh slowed the progress of his birch-bark canoe as he paddled up the Little Miami River on a June afternoon in 1806. Finding the little inlet with some slanting, overhanging trees on the east bank that he was looking for, he guided his light craft to the spot. Putting the canoe parallel to the bank, he stepped out and pulled the canoe up after him. He carried it up the slope and turned it upside down against some small trees. He picked up a rolled buffalo skin and a pouch of wild strawberries and walked up to the clearing and then up the river. Within a few minutes he came to a grove of buckeye trees and listened for the trickling water of a spring. Then he paused for a long draught of the clear, cool water as he remembered previous stops at the place which held such special meaning for him—the place of his birth thirty-eight years ago.

He walked up again through the clearing toward the site of the old village of Chillicothe where he had spent several happy and exciting years of his boyhood in spite of the attacks of the Long Knives. He looked over to his right in search of the log cabin of the White Man, James Galloway and his family. Somewhat to his surprise he saw a log house considerably larger than the cabin he remembered from his last visit of nearly four years ago.

As he continued walking he thought about the Galloways. He remembered when he first met them as they arrived to settle on this place nine years ago. At first he had been a little bitter about their coming into this land, though he knew it was well within the area that the misguided leaders of the various tribes had given up by the Treaty of Greeneville. He had been rather bitterly amused at learning that Galloway had discovered this plot of ground as a member of Clark's army that had burned old Chillicothe. But he was pleased in a way that Galloway was planning to make this his permanent home and was not simply what the Whites called a "squatter" who was rushing in to make a few improvements just to divide the land into smaller pieces to sell to more and more White settlers.

He had found the Galloways unusually thoughtful and considerate, and almost without thinking, he had returned their proffers of friendship. In those early days Tecumseh even had helped in clearing the land and in building the log cabin. On many evenings he had smoked the peace pipe with James Galloway in front of the fireplace. He valued the friendship because of the obvious respect that the Galloways had for the Indians, and he valued it further as a way to learn to know the White Man better—to know his language, his customs, his beliefs. He found all this fascinating in itself, but he also knew the value this would have in his dealings with White leaders as he sought ways to save Indian lands from further White encroachment.

Out of deference to what he had sensed as the sensibilities of his White friends during previous visits, Tecumseh carried no weapon other than his war club, and he wore a neat suit of light doeskin—pantaloons, tunic, and moccasins—and no feather in his turban, nor rings in his ears or nose.

As he approached the house, Tecumseh could see James Galloway coming out. Almost at a run Galloway came, hand raised in a wave, and then grasping hand and shoulder of the visitor in a cordial welcome. Tecumseh stepped back to look at Galloway, a man of the same height, but of considerably more weight and with graying hair.

Putting his arm around the shoulder of the Indian, Galloway led him to the house.

"You have much bigger wigwam," Tecumseh observed. "You have bigger family now?"

"We have one new son since you were here last," Galloway answered with a smile. "But two older sons have gone away and built their own houses."

Tecumseh nodded his understanding.

The house was built of hewn logs and was two stories high, with windows of glass. As they entered, Tecumseh noticed immediately that he was in a large parlor or sitting room, with a big fireplace, separated by a wall of slender logs and plaster from the kitchen and dining room where, of course, there was another big fireplace. The hard-packed dirt floor of the old cabin had given way to a pinion floor of split logs. The sitting room was furnished with several chairs, some wooden benches with backs on them, a table, some chests of drawers, and long book shelves the full length of one of the side walls. Many books as well as objects of stone and clay pottery rested on the shelves.

Galloway's wife, Rebekah, came to greet Tecumseh. She bade him have supper with them and expressed a sincere hope that he would remain with them for several days. He thanked her, handed her his pouch of strawberries, and tossed his buffalo hide into the corner beside the fireplace.

A seven-year old girl came into the room from the kitchen, and without even thinking, Tecumseh smiled and greeted her, "Becky!"

"No, no," her mother corrected him. "This is Ann. There is Becky."

Fifteen-year-old Rebekah Galloway—named for her mother—came in, her blue eyes sparkling in a sense of excitement that matched the smile on her lips, her auburn hair neatly brushed, her skin scrubbed to show its fair complexion, her gray dress clean except for a few food spots which showed that she had been working in the kitchen.

"Becky, I forget that you have grown into a woman during my absence!" Tecumseh said with a soft laugh. "Yes, now you are a beautiful lady."

Young Rebekah fought back a blush as she stammered, "Tecumseh looks the same!"

The visitor was reintroduced to the other young members of the family: John, twelve, and Andrew, ten, and he met the baby, Anthony, aged two. The two older sons who still were at home, William, now twenty-one, and Samuel, nineteen, came in several minutes later from the field where they had been working.

"We still have your special chair for you," the elder Galloway said as he pulled up a wooden ladder-back arm chair with tightly woven cane bottom.

"Thank you," Tecumseh said as he sat down in the chair. He smiled again and said, "Only here does Tecumseh sit in chair; at all other places he sits on Mother Earth, or he sits on buffalo hide on floor; only here does he sit in chair, but it is good."

Mrs. Galloway and the two girls returned to the kitchen. The boys went outside. From his bedroll Tecumseh took out a long pipe and presented it to Galloway as a "souvenir of friendship." The bowl of the pipe was carved from stone, and it was fitted with a long wooden stem decorated with white feathers, as a peace pipe. Galloway filled the pipe with tobacco and lit it with a firebrand from the kitchen. He offered it to Tecumseh for the first smoke. The two men sat in front of the fireplace—without any fire—and smoked and talked until supper was ready.

At five o'clock Becky called everyone to the dining table. Tecumseh again was impressed by the size of the room, the fireplace, and the heavy oak table. Utensils hung on pegs over the fireplace, but those that had been used for the meal remained on the hearth, or suspended from sturdy metal arms beside the fire. Father took his place at the head of the table with Mother opposite. The others sat on benches on either side of the table. Tecumseh was given the place of honor on Mrs. Galloway's right. Young Becky sat on the right of Tecumseh. When everyone had been seated, Mr. Galloway said grace. At the same time Tecumseh gave thanks to Manitou for the food. This was the signal for Father and Mother to begin passing the dishes and platters of food around the table counterclockwise. These included fresh fish, some strips of salt pork, beans, turnips, and corn bread. For drink there was fresh milk and buttermilk for everyone, and then cups of hot sassafras tea. For dessert, Mrs. Galloway brought out Tecumseh's strawberries. These needed no sugar, but a bowl of whipped cream turned them into a delicacy of unequaled taste.

This brought on the quoting of an old nursery rhyme by Becky:

> A man in the wilderness asked of me
> How many strawberries grow in the sea.
> I answered him, as I thought good,
> As many red herrings as swim in the wood.

Tecumseh smiled in polite misunderstanding. The others laughed gleefully.

At the end of the meal Tecumseh said a prayer of thanks to Manitou.

While Mrs. Galloway and the girls cleared the table and cleaned the kitchen as baby Anthony supervised from his cradle, the four older boys went outside with garbage for the hogs, and they penned up the two cows in the log shed, while Galloway and Tecumseh went to the other room to continue their conversation.

An hour later all the family gathered in the parlor for a devotional period. Tecumseh listened carefully with the others while Father read from *The Bible*. He read excerpts from the book of *Exodus*, of how the Israelites were delivered out of Egypt:

And Moses and Aaron went in unto Pharaoh, and they did so as the Lord had commanded: and Aaron cast down his rod before Pharaoh, and before his servants, and it became a serpent. Then Pharaoh also called the wise men and the sorcerers: now the magicians of Egypt, they also did like manner with their enchantments. For they cast down every man his rod, and they became serpents: but Aaron's rod swallowed up their rods.

And the Lord said unto Moses, Pharaoh's heart is hardened, he refuseth to let the people go.

"Who were Moses and Aaron and Pharaoh?" Tecumseh asked.

"Moses was a great prophet and leader of the people of Israel, many, many years ago, in a land far beyond the big water," Galloway explained. "And Aaron was his brother who spoke for him. Pharaoh was the great evil ruler or chief of the land of Egypt where for many years he had held the children of Israel in bondage."

"Who was the Lord?" Tecumseh asked.

"The Lord is God."

"Like Manitou?"

"Like Manitou."

"My brother is a prophet. He too can do magic when it pleases Manitou."

Galloway read on:

And Aaron stretched out his hand over the waters of Egypt; and the frogs came up, and covered the land of Egypt. And the magicians did so with their enchantments, and brought up frogs upon the land of Egypt.

Then Pharaoh called for Moses and Aaron, and said, Intreat the Lord, that he may take away the frogs from me, and from my people; and I will let the people go, that they may do sacrifice unto the Lord....

And Moses and Aaron went out from Pharaoh: and Moses cried unto the Lord because of the frogs which he had brought against Pharaoh. And the Lord did according to the word of Moses; and the frogs died out of the houses, out of the villages, and out of the fields. And they gathered them together upon heaps: and the land stank.

But when Pharaoh saw that there was respite, he hardened his heart, and hearkened not unto them; as the Lord said.

"Pharaoh does not speak truth. He makes promise and then breaks word." Tecumseh noted.

"Exactly," said Galloway.

"Like White Chief with Red Men," Tecumseh said.

Galloway went on to read of the plague of lice, and of flies, and the murrain of beasts so that all the cattle of the Egyptians died, but none of those of the Israelites; and of Moses sprinkling ashes toward heaven which became boils upon all the Egyptians and upon the beasts; and of the plague of hail and fire. Pharaoh again promised to let the people go if this were stopped, but when it was done, had a change of heart and would not let them go. And then the plague of locusts, and then the three days of darkness, and each time Pharaoh promised to let the people go, and then went back on his word.

By this time the younger children were nodding to the approach of sleep, while the older ones were dreaming of other things, but Becky followed everything with close interest, and Tecumseh listened in fascination.

Galloway lit some candles to continue his reading.

"Many times White Chiefs say, we make treaty. We take no more land. Indian Chiefs agree to make peace and move away. Then White Chiefs have change of heart, and want more land." said Tecumseh.

"I'm afraid that has happened sometimes," Galloway acknowledged. He returned to his reading—of the slaying of all the firstborn of Egypt, and of Pharaoh at last letting the people of Israel go:

But the Egyptians pursued after them, all the horses and chariots of Pharaoh, and his horsemen, and his army, and overtook them encamping by the sea....

And when Pharaoh drew nigh, the children of Israel lifted up their eyes, and behold the Egyptians marched after them; and they were sore afraid: and the children of Israel cried out unto the Lord ....

And Moses stretched out his hand over the sea; and the Lord caused the sea to go back by a strong east wind all that night, and made the sea dry land, and the waters were divided. And the children of Israel went into the midst of the sea upon the dry ground: and the waters were a wall unto them on their right hand, and on their left.

And the Egyptians pursued, and went in after them to the midst of the sea, even all Pharaoh's horses, his chariots, and his horsemen....

And Moses stretched forth his hand over the sea, and the sea returned to his strength when the morning appeared; and the Egyptians fled against it; and the Lord overthrew the Egyptians in the midst of the sea. And the waters returned, and covered the chariots, and the horsemen, and all the host of Pharaoh that came into the sea after them: there remained not so much as one of them.

Galloway explained briefly how the children of Israel had wandered through the wilderness, how the Lord had provided quails for them to eat in the evening, and manna as bread in the morning, and then how Moses went upon Mount Sinai to receive the Ten Commandments. After reading the Commandments, Galloway said a prayer. Then the children all went upstairs to bed—the boys in the room nearest the sitting-room chimney, the girls in the middle room, and his wife to the room over the kitchen. Galloway and Tecumseh lit a small fire and remained to talk a while longer.

"What are the Ten Commandments?" Tecumseh asked. "The rules of Manitou for all the people?"

"Yes, in a way. These are rules which all people follow who want to please God."

"I am not sure I understand all of them."

Galloway returned to The Book. "Listen—"

"'Thou shalt have no other gods before me.' There is only one God."

"You have no Grandmother spirit to help Master of Life?"

"No Grandmother, but there is Jesus who is Son of God."

"Is Jesus 'God'?"

"Yes."

"Then that makes two gods, Father and Son."

"No, we think of them as different parts of one God."

Tecumseh still did not understand this, but went on, "Do you have Evil Spirit?"

"Yes, Satan, or the Devil."

"Is he god?"

"No, he is not god."

"Does he have power over men?"

"Yes."

"Then he is god too."

Galloway shook his head and went on, "'Thou shalt not make unto thee any graven image, or any likeness of any thing that is in heaven above, or that is in the earth beneath, or that is in the water under the earth.'"

"It is forbidden to have totem pole?"

"Yes."

"Why?"

"We must never be led to substitute an image for the true Spirit of God."

"Yes, that is good. You explain to me before that early Christians made pictures of fish."

"Yes, but that was only a symbol for recognition, not something to be worshiped."

"Sometimes French people have crosses with image of Jesus. Sometimes carry little ones. Sometimes set big ones near trail. Why?"

"Those are as reminders. We are what are called Protestants, and we do not have many of those symbols."

Again questions remained in Tecumseh's mind, but he nodded for Galloway to go on.

"'Thou shalt not take the name of the Lord thy God in vain....'"

"What does that mean?"

"That means not to use the name of the Lord, God, to try to put bad curse on other men."

"What does 'in vain' mean?"

"That means useless, without effect."

"If it has no effect, then why is it important to forbid it? How does it make any difference?"

"Because it shows a bad attitude, an evil in a man's heart toward another man."

"Is it more bad for a man to show evil in his heart than just to have evil heart?"

"Evil thoughts alone do not make another man feel as bad as evil words do."

Galloway continued, "'Remember the sabbath day, to keep it holy.'"

"Why?"

"This is the day to remember the Lord."

"I think one should remember Manitou every day."

"True, but this is a special day for worship and a day of rest. It goes on to say, 'The seventh day is the sabbath of the Lord thy God: in it thou shalt not do any work, thou, nor thy son, nor thy daughter, thy manservant, thy maidservant, nor thy cattle, nor thy stranger that is within thy gates.'"

Tecumseh smiled. "It is good. It is all right for squaw to work. It is good for man to rest, let squaw work so it is possible to eat that day."

Galloway searched the passage again to see if there was some mention of wife. Finding none, he went on, "Honor thy father and thy mother."

"That is good."

"'Thou shalt not kill.'"

"Then how did the people eat the quails which the Lord sent? Is it forbidden to hunt?"

"No, this means to kill people."

"Then why did the Lord slay all the firstborn of Egypt? And why did he drown all the Egyptian warriors in the sea?"

"Those were for protection of children of Israel."

"Is there another god to protect the Egyptians?"

"No, but they were doing evil. It probably is better to think of this as 'Thou shalt not murder.' Do you see the difference?"

"Yes, one nation of many men may make war on another nation, but one man does not make war on another man. Go on."

"'Thou shalt not commit adultery.'"

"I do not know what that means."

"That means that men must not run after women who are not their wives and possess them."

"Yes, that is very good. Go on."

"'Thou shalt not steal.'"

"That is good."

"'Thou shalt not bear false witness against thy neighbor.'"

"Tell lies about neighbor? Say he did something bad which he did not do?"

"Yes, you understand."

"It is good."

"'Thou shalt not covet thy neighbor's house, thou shalt not covet thy neighbor's wife, nor his manservant, nor his maid, nor his ox, nor his ass, nor anything that is thy neighbors.'"

"What is 'covet'?"

"That means to want very much. To have an extreme desire for something."

"Do the White Men covet the Red Men's land?"

"I'm afraid some of them do."

"Do some of the White Men want the Indian Women?"

"Sometimes some of them do. But the rules say they should not."

"They are good rules. But many White Men do not keep the rules."

"Do all the Red Men keep all the rules of Manitou?"

"No, they do not. What do you call the book you were reading?"

"*The Bible.*"

"Yes, I know *The Bible*, but what do you call this part?"

"This is called *Exodus*, which means the exit, or going out of the people of Israel from Egypt where they had been in bondage many years."

"It is a very good book. We too have a story of the sea parting to allow our people to pass in ancient times. And the commandments are very good. It is a very good book."

Galloway invited Tecumseh to make his bed by the fireplace and went upstairs. The Shawnee unrolled his buffalo hide and lay upon it. He thought for a long time about the things he had heard and then fell asleep.

The next morning Tecumseh gathered with all the family for a breakfast of mush and milk. He told them that this was his favorite food, not only because he liked it, but because it was supposed to be the favorite food of the buffalo which was his guardian spirit. But with maple syrup and milk, he found it especially delicious.

Tecumseh went with Galloway and William and Samuel out to clear a field and to put up rail fences. There were two tasks for clearing. One was to girdle trees, to deaden them, in an area where a new field was to be developed. The other was to fell trees in a patch that had been deadened three years earlier. The Galloways accomplished the latter in a spectacular way. With axes they carefully chopped at the trunks of half a dozen deadened trees that were standing close together. They chopped lower on the side of the trunk in the direction they wanted the tree to fall, and they cut them almost through, almost until they were ready to fall. Then James Galloway himself very carefully finished cutting the last tree. He calculated carefully the direction he wanted to make it fall, and then applied the last few blows of the axe. With a creaking that crescended into a crash the tree fell against the next one in such a way as to knock it down, and it fell against the next, until all six went down like dominoes.

At noon Rebekah and the girls had dinner ready. It was bacon and fried mush with maple syrup, and milk to drink.

Becky asked her father if she might take the two horses to ride over to show Mr. Tecumseh the church. He had no objections. Tecumseh welcomed the chance for such an excursion.

Becky mounted the sorrel mare and Tecumseh the bay stallion. They set off at a canter until they reached the woods, and then slowed to a walk. Along forest trails and across clearings they rode for about an hour, varying the gait with the terrain and the whim of the moment.

"There," Becky called out. "There is our little Presbyterian Church."

They rode up to the log church, dismounted, and tied the horses to a rail. The building, about thirty feet long by twenty feet wide, was of rough hewn logs, notched at the corners, and with plaster between. The gabled roof was of wooden shingles. There was a stone foundation, and three stone steps leading up to the door near the right end of the side they faced. A single glass window was near the other end of this side. A walk around the building revealed two glass windows in the end wall as they walked around counterclockwise, two windows in the long wall opposite the door, and a big stone chimney on the other end wall.

The door was hinged by sections of hollowed logs mounted with large wooden pinions to form hinges. They opened it. Inside they could see beams of large, rough hewn logs and rafters that were flat on top and round underneath. A big stone fireplace was at one end, with a pulpit in front of it. The floor was of heavy boards varying in width from eight to ten inches. Rows of benches, with aisles in the center and on either side, provided seating for the congregation.

Becky and Tecumseh sat on opposite benches, half facing each other across the center aisle.

"This is medicine lodge where people come to pray to Master of Life?" asked Tecumseh.

"In a way," replied Becky. "The people come here each Sunday to pray and to sing songs, and to listen to the minister tell how to be a good Christian."

"I thought these were Presbyterian. Now you say Christians."

"Yes, there are many kinds of churches, but they are all Christian, like there are many tribes of Indians who have different ways of worshiping the same Manitou."

"Yes, but I still do not understand about your God. Sometimes people say you have one God, sometimes three or four."

"Yes, we speak of God the Father, God the Son, and God the Holy Spirit—three aspects of the same God."

"Like we have Manitou who is the Master of Life, and Wishemenetoo who is the Great Good Spirit and who is under

Manitou, and also another, Inumsilafewanu, also Great Spirit, but is our grandmother. You see, Shawnee also have three."

"Yes, I see. We call our God, three in One, the Trinity."

"Why do you say one God?"

"It is one God, three in One. Some explain this as being God the Father who is the Creator of the Universe and the great Creative Power; God the Son was manifest in Jesus Christ who was sent to dwell in this world and then was crucified—"

"What is 'crucified'?"

"Killed on a big cross."

"Who killed him?"

"His people."

"Why did they kill him?"

"Because he was such a good Man. He preached good will and peace to all."

"I do not understand. Why would they kill a good man who advised peace?"

"Old chiefs urged them because they were afraid the people would follow Jesus, and then the old chiefs would lose their power and authority."

"Oh, yes, that I can understand, but if Jesus was God, how could they kill a god?"

"Jesus was God who had taken the form of a man. Does not the Master of Life or the Great Spirit sometimes take the form of an animal or a bird?"

"Yes, that is true."

"And if someone should kill that animal or bird, that would not kill the Great Spirit, would it?"

"That animal or bird would not be killed; but yes, if it was killed, that would not kill the Great Spirit."

"Jesus was killed on a cross, and then he was resurrected, restored to life, and now some speak of him as God the Son dwelling within man as the internal inspiration of man, acting through the intellect and the will."

"You speak in big words for young girl."

Becky laughed and went on, "And God the Holy Spirit might be thought of as the Spirit of love and the outside inspiration of man. You see, in this way, the Trinity might represent our relation to the world or the universe, to ourselves, and to others."

"I am not sure I understand everything, but it is good. My Brother, Laulewasika, died, and after a few hours was restored to life. He had been shown paradise for good people and place of suffering for bad people. Now he is called by a new name, Tenskwatawa. Some people call him The Prophet."

"Do you believe he died and went to heaven and hell, and then came back?"

"Did not your Jesus?"

"Yes, but he was God."

"Is it not within the power of God for others to do the same?"

"Anything is within the power of God."

"And don't you also have an Evil Spirit?"

"Yes, Satan, or the Devil."

"He is like our Motchemenetoo, the Bad Spirit."

"But God can overcome him."

"Yes, Manitou can do so. And if people obey your Ten Commandments, they all go to paradise?"

"Not necessarily."

"What else is necessary? What must one do?"

"Our church believes there is nothing one can do to guarantee going to heaven."

"Nothing? It is all the same for good men and bad men?"

"God's grace is so vast, that no one could do enough to earn it. It is a gift of God."

"A gift? Does he give it to everybody?"

"No, not to everyone. Only to some."

"What happens to the others?"

"They go to hell and burn in the fire."

"How long?"

"Forever."

"They never can be admitted to paradise?"

"No."

"Which ones are chosen to go to paradise?"

"We don't know."

"Does he love all his children?"

"Of course."

"But he will choose only some of them to enjoy paradise and will make all the others suffer in fire?"

"Yes."

"That is not a good god. I prefer Manitou. He will let even the bad people, after they have suffered for their bad ways, he will let them enter paradise. That is better."

"You see, everyone is a sinner. No one deserves anything, but God just gives a gift to some of them even though they do not deserve it."

"Why not a gift to all the people even if they do not deserve it? Why doesn't he at least allow the good ones to earn their way?"

"It is not always clear to me," Becky said frankly, "but our minister has explained that if one could earn his way by his works, then that would reduce our highest ethical conduct to mere prudence. That means that we would do everything in the hope of earning a reward."

"Is not that good?"

"It may be good, but it is much better if one does good things only because they are right, only because he loves others, and not just because he hopes to earn a reward or to escape punishment. That is the way of children."

"Yes, I understand that would be very good, but I think it is better to have some way to make bad men change their ways."

"There is, by love."

"But many times men act like children, and must be punished."

"Yes, that is true in this world. We must have laws and punishment, but God has a higher way."

"Not if he lets good men burn in hell forever."

"Let us return to our wigwams, Mr. Tecumseh," said Becky.

They rode back by a slightly different route, pausing now and then to admire the wild flowers, to watch a bird, to look at a waterfall in a creek. They were back in time for Becky to help with the last phase of preparation for supper.

After the meal, Becky helped clear the table, and then as the others went about chores, she joined Tecumseh in the sitting room.

"You understand and speak English very well, Mr. Tecumseh," she said.

He smiled and responded, "But I must do better, and I must learn to read and write better."

"I will help you," she said. She went to the corner bureau and returned with pencil and paper. She wrote a column of words and showed them to him. "Now look at each word and say it, and explain what it means."

The Indian glanced at the list of words:

bow	fast
bough	raft
tough	bright

trough	cite
through	site
though	right
thought	rift
ought	write
draught	tongue
tow	argue
two	ague

Tecumseh started reading down the list. "*Bo*, that is for shooting arrows."

"Good. It may also be a stick with hairs for playing a violin. And, pronounced *bow*, it may also be the front of a boat."

"I thought that was a *prow*."

"Yes, same thing. Now look again: b,o,w. When pronounced bow it also may mean to bend over."

"But how am I to know which of those things it means when I see it?"

"It depends on what other words are with it. If you are talking about hunting with arrows, you know it is *bo*. If you are talking about a boat, you know it is *bow*. Go on to the next word."

"I'm not sure I remember the sounds of all those letters. Is it *bug*?"

"No, it does look as though it could be, doesn't it? This is pronounced like *bow*."

"No, we already finished *bow*. I know that. What is: b,o,u,g,h?"

"That also is pronounced *bow*, and it is the limb of a tree."

"Oh, I had forgotten. I know *bough* of a tree, but did not know how the word looked. All right. Now the next one must be *tow*. but I do not know what that could mean."

"No, t,o,u,g,h is pronounced *tuf*."

"Oh, *tuf*, that means strong, hard."

"Yes. Now look at the next one."

"*Truf*."

"Almost, but not quite. It is pronounced *trof*."

"Yes, something to hold food or water for horses."

"Yes. Now be careful about the next one."

"I guess it should be *thruf*, but I don't know what that means."

"No, it is pronounced *thru*."

"Oh, you mean like someone threw a rock?"

"No, that sounds the same, but that word is spelled: t,h,r,e,w. This word, t,h,r,o,u,g,h, means something like riding through the forest."

"Or someone is finished, he is through?"

"Yes, good! Now look at the next word."

"*thuf*. I do not know that meaning."

"No, that word is pronounced *tho*. As when you might say, 'He is strong, though he is short.' It may be about the same as *although*."

"Yes, I understand the meaning, but why do you say *tuff* for tough, and *tho* for though?"

"That's English for you. I guess it is because of the way they have come down through different languages."

"All right, now, the next one must be *thuft*; no, it must be *tuft*, like a piece of hair," Tecumseh said proudly.

"Good try, but no, that word is *thawt*; you know—"

"Yes, what one thinks."

"Good. Now look carefully at the next word."

"You always make one that looks like the other one be different. Let's see, this one must be *oft*, meaning frequently."

Becky laughed aloud at that.

Noting her laugh, Tecumseh said, "Is it *aft*, the back of a boat?"

"No, but it is wonderful the way you are trying. This one really is pronounced like the one above. It is *awt*, meaning—"

"Should or must."

"Good! Now try the next word."

"Is it *draft*?"

"Yes! Good, you got that one. That can be a drink of water or a current of air through the house, or a drawing, or a writing."

"Oh, too many things for one word."

"Yes."

"The next is *tow* or to, yes, to, like fingers on my feet."

"No, that is spelled: t,o,e. This is pronounced the same way, but means to pull, like you tow a boat. And now: t,w,o?"

"*Twoh*?"

"No, no, we pronounce that word *tu*."

"Oh, yes, it means also."

"No, that is spelled: t,o,o. This one is for the number two, like: one, two, three, and so on."

"All right. I know the numbers, but I cannot spell them. Why do you have to spell them? Why not just write the figure?"

"You can if you want to. It's just that sometimes one makes a bad mistake in reading a number that is not made properly."

"And *fast*, that is running quickly."

"Yes, but if someone is stuck to the ground and cannot run at all we say he is *fast*. And *fast* may mean going without food, but we may also speak of someone who carouses all the time and is loose in morals as being *fast*."

"Oh, my little Becky, how do you learn all that when you are so young? How can anyone learn the English language?"

"You do very well," she reassured him.

He knew *raft* and *bright*, had to have help with *cite* and *site*, thought *right* was *rift*, and knew *write* from *right*. When he came to *tongue* he said, "The next is *tung*," and he stuck out his tongue. When he came to *argue*, he said, "*Arg*, I don't know."

"It is pronounced *argu*."

"Oh, yes, dispute."

"Good."

"And *agu* is the fever."

"Good."

Once done, Becky asked him to repeat the whole list. He did so without a mistake either in pronunciation or meaning. Most of the next day Becky continued with her help sessions in reading and writing.

After supper they turned to books. "You have many books," Tecumseh observed.

"Yes, Father brought most of them by flatboat to Kentucky, and then by pack-horse up here. He tries to buy two or three new ones each year. I have read about all of them, some of them two or three times."

"My people do not write letters or make books. It is a great loss. Someday they must learn to do so."

"Yes. For me, life would be dull without letters and books."

"Which books do you like best?"

"I like all of them. The best are the plays of a great English writer Shakespeare, though I do not know many of the words he uses. You will like the histories."

"What are histories?"

"True stories of the nations—their great leaders, their civilizations, their wars."

"Yes, I like to learn of other nations."

"There are many nations beyond the seas, and there were many others in ancient times."

"When are ancient times?"

"Many years ago, many summers. Maybe more than two thousand years ago. Count the fingers on your two hands as many times as there are fingers. That makes one hundred. Do that as many times as there are fingers, that makes one thousand."

"Yes, I know what is one thousand."

She went over to the bookshelf and took down a copy of Sir Walter Raleigh's *The History of the World*.

"First I shall read about the Greeks."

"Who were the Greeks?" Tecumseh wanted to know.

"They were the people who lived in Greece."

"In Grease? I thought you called bear fat and hog fat grease. Did they live in that?"

"No, no, I'm not sure why it was called Greece. It sometimes was also called Hellas, and the people the Hellenes. Now listen." She began reading from the book:

So died Epaminondas, the worthiest man that ever was bred in that Nation of Greece, and hardly to be matched in any Age or Country: for he equalled all others in the several virtues, which in each of them were singular. His Justice, and Sincerity, his Temperance, Wisdome, and high Magnanimity, were no way inferior to his military virtue; in every part whereof he so excelled—

"How did he die?" asked Tecumseh.

She turned to the preceding page:

This was the last work of the incomparable virtue of Epaminondas, who being at the head of that warlike troupe of men, which broke the Lacedemonian squadron, and forced it to give back in disaray, was furiously charged on the sodaine, by a desperate company of the Spartans, who all at once threw their darts at him alone; whereby receiving many wounds, he nevertheless with a singular courage maintained the fight, using against the enemies many of their own darts which he drew out of his own body; till at length by a Spartan called Anticrates he received so violent a stroke with a dart that the wood of it brake, leaving the iron and a piece of the tronchion in his breast. . . . Epaminondas being brought to his tent, was told by the physicians that when the head of the dart should be drawn out of his body, he must needs die. Hearing this he called for his shield, which to have lost was held a great dishonor: It was brought unto him. He bade them tell him which part had the victory; answer was made that the Beotians had won the field. Then said he, it is fair time for me to die, and withall sent for Jolidas and Diophantes, two principall men of war, that were both slain; which being told him, he advised the Thebans to make peace, whilst with advantage they might, for they had none left that was able to discharge the office of a General. Herewithall he willed that the head of the weapon should be drawn out of his body; comforting his friends that lamented his death and want of issue, by telling him that the victories of Leuctra and Mantinaea were two fair daughters in whom his memory should live.

"Yes, he was a great man," Tecumseh said.

Then she read of Alexander the Great. Tecumseh was impressed by Demosthenes and his "Philippics" in which he tried to warn the Greek city states to unite to defend themselves against the coming attack of Philip of Macedon, father of Alexander. But he also was impressed by the way Alexander was able to unite the Greek cities—all the tribes—even if by force—and then spread the Greek culture through the eastern Mediterranean world. Tecumseh followed with special interest Alexander's great victory over Darius at Arbela where Darius, fearful of surprise, had had his troops in their armor all day and all night while Alexander had rested his men and given them food.

He pondered the author's appraisal of Alexander:

Howsoever it were, Alexander's former cruelties cannot be excused, no more than his vanity to be the esteemed son of Jupiter, with his excessive delight in drink and drunkenness, which others make the cause of his fever and death. In that he lamented his want of enterprising, and grieved to consider what he should do when he had conquered the world, Augustus Caesar found just cause to deride him, as if the well governing of so many nations and kingdoms as he had already conquered, could not have offered him matter more than abundant to busy his brains withall. That he was both learned and a lover of learning it cannot be doubted.

Later Becky read some excerpts from two books which had only recently arrived. Both were written by William Russell in the form of a series of letters to a young nobleman. One volume was *The History of Ancient Europe*, and the other was *The History of Modern Europe*, from the decline and fall of the Roman Empire to the Peace of Paris of 1763.

Then she took down Thucydides' *History of the Peloponnesian War* and read a few passages. One was from a speech of Pericles, the Athenian leader:

If you yield to them in a small matter, they will think you are afraid, and will immediately dictate some more oppressive condition; but if you are firm, you will prove to them that they must treat you as their equals.

"Pericles was a wise man," Tecumseh said. "Will you read that again?" He listened intently, eyes closed, to a rereading. Then he said, half to himself, "That is good advice for my Red Men—if you yield to them on a small matter they will only come back with greater demands. Yes, my little Becky, if Red Men give up land to the White Men, the White Men soon come back demanding more."

She read another passage, this time an excerpt from a speech of Archidamus, the Spartan King:

Do not take up arms yet. Let us first send and remonstrate with them: we need not let them know positively whether we intend to go to war or not. In the meantime our own preparations may be going forward; we may seek allies wherever we can find them, whether in Hellas or among the Barbarians, who will supply our deficiencies in ships and money . . . . And we must develop our own resources to the utmost . . . . Perhaps too when they begin to see that we are getting ready, and that our words too sound a note of war, they may be more likely to yield; for their fields will be still untouched and their goods undespoiled, and it will be in their power to save them by their decision. Think of their land simply as a hostage, all the more valuable in proportion as it is better cultivated.

If you begin the war in haste, you will end it at your leisure, because you took up arms without sufficient preparation.

"Archidamus was a wise man," Tecumseh said. "He too gives good advice for my Red Men."

Becky went on to read of the Athenian expedition to Sicily. Tecumseh interrupted as she read from a speech of Nicias:

The Greeks in Sicily would fear us most if we never went there at all, and next to this, if after displaying our power we went away as soon as possible. Men, as we know, respect most what is remote and least liable to have its reputation put to the test.

"More good advice for my Red Men."

1b

After the birth of Benjamin Harrison at Vincennes on May 29, 1806, Anna Harrison suffered an illness of over a month. During the whole time William Henry remained at home close to his wife. He continued to look after special matters from his Grouseland office, but he devoted most of his time in supervising household activities, looking after the children, and visiting with Anna. When she was too weak to read, he read to her from *The Bible*, from Seneca, from the histories, and from *The Western Sun*. All these provided a great deal for discussion and, as Anna's strength returned, her participation in discussion became more animated. Her first worries were for her children, but she found more and more worrying time to apply to the country, to the Indians, to Europe, and to Christianity. Fortunately, baby

Benjamin grew strong rapidly and escaped the treacheries of early life that she feared for him.

Harrison always enjoyed these hours with Anna. One evening he ran up to her to assure her that the children were all right, and then he picked up his volume of Seneca's *Epistles* and began to look through some of the notable maxims of that Roman stoic. "Here, do you know this one 'You roll my log, and I will roll yours.'?"

"That's good advice for raising houses on the frontier, but isn't that what they do in Congress all the time?"

"The basis of politics, isn't it? Now this, 'What fools these mortals be.'"

"Sounds like Shakespeare."

"So it does, but please remember, Seneca antedated Shakespeare by fifteen hundred years. Ha, and here's a good one, 'I was shipwrecked before I got on board.'"

"That's the way I feel," said Anna.

Harrison read on, "'Man is a reasoning animal'—that sounds a little like Aristotle—'That most knowing of persons,—gossip'— My dear is he saying there that women are more knowledgeable than men?"

"Oh, Henry!"

"'It is better, of course, to know useless things than to know nothing.'"

"Now he's saying that men are more knowledgeable," Anna came back.

For their evening Bible reading Harrison turned to the tenth chapter of *Exodus* which included the Ten Commandments. As he read, "'But the seventh day is the sabbath of the Lord thy God: in it thou shalt not do any work, thou, nor thy son, nor thy daughter, nor thy manservant, nor thy maidservant, nor thy cattle, nor thy stranger that is within thy gates,'" Harrison paused and remarked, "What a relief that is!"

"What do you mean, 'relief'?" asked Anna. "You've read that many times before. What do you find different now?"

"I just never noticed before that this makes no mention of 'thy wife' in there. Fortunately, she is excused from the prohibition against working so the rest of us can eat on the sabbath."

"Oh, you silly goose, of course the wife is included."

"Show me, where? I see daughter and maidservant, but I see no mention of wife."

"Well she's included by what John Marshall calls implied powers."

"How do you figure that?"

"Now, Henry, you know that she is one of the parties to whom the whole thing is addressed."

"Of course not, this was addressed to the heads of families—to the men."

"But when a woman reads it, 'Thou shalt not' refers to herself, not to some man somewhere."

"You know in those days women kept their faces behind a veil. It says 'thy daughter,' but says nothing about thy wife. And look on to 'Thou shalt not covet thy neighbor's house, thou shalt not covet thy neighbor's wife'—now, do you think it's addressed to wives when it says, 'Thou shalt not covet they neighbor's wife.'? Really, now."

"All right, all right. So you are saying these don't apply to wives, then I guess we are to assume that it's quite all right for a wife to kill, to steal, to bear false witness—to commit adultery."

"Now you are going too far!" Harrison laughed, walked over and patted Anna's cheek. "It is great to see you feeling so much better," he said. "It is, you know."

Harrison kept up his own continuing education in his reading of history and military affairs and in his reading of *The Bible* as much for recreation as for learning. But he felt a strong sense of urgency to bring learning of all kinds to the frontier. He was sure that educated people got more enjoyment out of life than did unlettered ones, and he was sure too that thinking men—and women who could share ideas with them—could contribute much more to the community than could ignorant ones.

That summer Harrison pushed for the organization of a circulating library and a university. He was going to bring culture to the banks of the Wabash or know the reasons why not.

In July he met with a group of citizens who responded to his call at the tavern of John D. Hay to discuss the organization of a circulating library. Harrison himself accepted the chairmanship, and his good friend, Benjamin Parke, was chosen secretary. All of the thirty to forty men present were interested in the project, but many had no clear conception about how it would work.

"We should form a company to be responsible for the operation of the library," explained Harrison.

"Where do we get the money, from the legislature?" Someone wanted to know.

"No, we shall have to operate at first by private subscription. We shall have to have enough interest to buy books and to support a part-time librarian."

"How much will it cost?" asked another.

"You mean for total expenses or for the individual subscriber?"

"I mean how much is it going to cost me to be a subscriber?"

"That is something we shall have to agree upon. I should think something equal to perhaps the cost of two books to join, and then dues of about half that a year. You see, if you were to buy just two books in a year, that would cost you about five dollars. Now if you paid that same amount to a library with everyone else, you could have access to fifty books for the same price."

"Then you will have to be a member to use the library?"

"No, I would say not. Let others use it by putting up the price of any book they borrow until they return it and charge a small service fee."

"That doesn't seem fair somehow."

"The idea is to make books available to all the people as well as to each other. The system works well in Philadelphia, very well indeed."

"This ain't Philadelphia."

"Neither was Philadelphia before they had a library!"

"Where are we going to put the library?" asked John Rice Jones.

"Someday it should have its own building, built for the purpose, but in the meantime I shall be glad to have it in the basement of Grouseland."

"Sure, so the Governor can have first chance at using it?" asked Dr. Elias McNamee.

Harrison responded, "Doctor, if you have in mind any better place that can be had as cheaply, I'll be glad to concur."

"Oh, no, Governor, I think we should all appreciate the offer," McNamee said lamely.

It took a couple more meetings for all the details to be worked out, but finally on August 2 the group agreed to an organization and the rules and regulations to govern the library. Subscriptions were to be at five dollars, payable either in specie or in acceptable books. Annual dues would be two dollars. Harrison bought two shares. Among the thirty charter subscribers, in addition to Harrison and Parke, were Dr. Charles Smith, Colonel Francis Vigo, Elihu Stout, John Rice Jones, Henry Vanderburgh, and most of the other leaders of the community. The legislature granted a charter to the company, and soon the library was in operation under the direction of Peter Jones as librarian.

In the same session of the legislature that fall, Harrison persuaded the representatives to charter Vincennes University. Funds would come from the sale of lands of a township that Congress had granted Indiana Territory in 1804 "for a seminary of learning." In its resolution for incorporation the territorial legislature stated, "for as much as literature, and philosophy, furnish the most useful and pleasing occupations, improving and varying the enjoyments of prosperity, affording relief under the pressure of misfortune, and hope and consolation in the hours of death," Vincennes University should be incorporated. The trustees were directed "to use their utmost endeavours" to persuade the Indians to send their children to the University, tuition and maintenance to be provided by the institution. Further, the trustees were directed to establish a seminary for the education of females as soon as funds were available. For initial construction and support the legislature also authorized a $20,000 lottery. Professors and students were to be exempt from miliary duty.

The course of study was to include logic, rhetoric, the law of nature and of nations, natural philosophy, mathematics, and the Greek, Latin, French, and English languages.

Harrison was chosen unanimously as president of the Board of Trustees. Other Trustees who met in an organizing meeting on Saturday, December 6, included Judge Parke, Waller Taylor, then chancellor (presiding judge) of the Territory, John Badollet, registrar of the land office, and Nathaniel Ewing. Almost at once the Trustees arranged to sell some of the land granted it, to arrange for the lottery, and to begin construction of a building. Construction began in the following year of an attractive brick building some sixty-five feet long. The attraction of students would take a little longer.

One other step for cultural advancement in Vincennes in 1809 was the organization of a Thespian Society for the promotion of the dramatic arts.

2a

During a year busy with meetings with various tribes as well as the usual hunting, Tecumseh stopped at the Galloways' for brief visits of only a few hours the three or four times he came to the vicinity. He always promised that he would return, and he always looked forward to keeping those promises.

One bright, warm day in late June, 1807, this time coming from the north, he paddled down the river with a second canoe—a new, well-made birch bark—in tow. As he approached the Galloway house shortly after midday, Becky came running out to meet him.

"Miss Becky," he called out to her.

"Mr. Tecumseh," she said with a broad smile as she came up and shook his hand.

"I have come for a few days more of Miss Becky's school, if it is still in operation."

"Of course it is. I am so glad you have come."

"Are the others here?"

"Mother and Ann are in the kitchen. Father and the boys are in the field. Come in, please, come in."

Tecumseh exchanged greetings with the senior Rebekah and Ann, and accepted their usual invitation to stay over. He presented Mrs. Galloway with a bag of a dozen squirrels, and tossed his buffalo hide roll into the corner. Then he asked her, "Do you think Becky can be excused from her duties for a little while?"

"Mr. Tecumseh, when you are here, her duty is to look after our guest."

"I want to show her something down at the river."

"We shall have supper before the sun goes down."

Already Becky was waiting in anticipation. At a quick pace they walked to the river bank where he pointed to the new canoe. "It is yours," he said.

"Oh, Mr. Tecumseh," she gasped. "It is beautiful! How did you get it here?"

"I tow it—t,o,w. I tow it by the bow—b,o,w."

She laughed. "Show me how to paddle it."

"Yes," he said with a grin. "Now we have Tecumseh's school." Handing her a paddle he said, "First you will be in front—in bow. You sit facing back so you can watch me. Later we both paddle together. Then we come back, and you sit in back—in stern—and paddle."

"Whatever you say, teacher," she said.

Tecumseh put the canoe in the water and held it while Becky got in. She sat on the front seat.

"It is better at first if you sit on bottom of canoe, not on seat," he said. "Then it is not so easy to roll over."

She complied. He took his place at the stern and shoved off. Assuming a kneeling position, on both knees, and half sitting on the narrow thwart, he began paddling with strong, steady strokes upstream. "See I put my right hand on top of the paddle and my left down almost to the blade. I keep my left arm pretty straight all the time. I put paddle in water as far forward as I can reach, and then while I pull with my left hand I push my right hand, at top, toward the front."

He took several slow, deliberate strokes in demonstration. Becky nodded her understanding. "Now when I am in stern I must steer canoe, make it go straight, or make it turn. You see as I finish stroke I turn paddle and push it through the water away from canoe. This makes it go straight." He demonstrated the "J" stroke several times. Then he went on, "But if canoe turns too much, or if you want to make it turn quickly, paddle on other side. Also, as you glide through water you can turn paddle and use it like a rudder."

Again Becky nodded her understanding. "Yes, Yes," she said. "It is very simple. Let me try."

Tecumseh took the canoe back to the bank where he helped Becky turn around and step over the thwart. She knelt on both knees, partially sitting on the front thwart, and as they turned toward midstream she put her paddle into the water. She did so without pulling on it, and immediately it got away from her and dropped into the water. She was glad Tecumseh could not see the sheepish look on her face.

Quickly he swung the canoe around and recovered the paddle. As he was about to hand the paddle back to her, Becky stood up and turned around to receive it. Before he could even cry out his warning, she was in the water. She gave out a loud cry of surprise which quickly turned to nervous laughter as Tecumseh jumped in beside her. The water was only waist deep for her, and he held to the canoe with one hand as he grasped her arm with the other. He joined her in laughter as he led her to the bank. He put the canoe a few feet out of the water, and then, with both hands, helped her up the grassy bank and into the sunlight. As her wet dress clung tightly to her body, he could not help but see that she had developed into more of a woman than he had previously noticed. Her wet hair, stringing down her neck and sticking to her face, framed a countenance of greater beauty than he had noticed before. In spite of his wet legs he felt a glow of warmth within to match the warmth of the sun on his shoulders. He felt a little self-conscious in noticing the physical attributes of his young friend that had mostly escaped him until now.

"You finish your first lesson very quickly," he laughed.

Although she really did not feel cold in the warm sunshine, Rebekah was conscious that her teeth were chattering violently. Steadying her lips, she spoke out, "Oh, no. We will continue. I must run to the house and change my dress. You wait. When I fall from a horse, I must get back on and ride again immediately. When I fall from canoe I must try again immediately."

Tecumseh looked down to avoid her eyes. He glanced at the canoe and saw that her paddle was missing. He looked out to the river just in time to see the paddle about to float out of sight downstream. "You go for dress; I go for paddle," he said as he ran down to put the canoe in the water. With long, strong and rapid strokes he went after the paddle and recovered it.

Half an hour later Becky returned in a dry dress and with a linen towel formed into a turban around her hair. Now Tecumseh had her practice the motions of paddling while yet on the bank. Then they returned to their places in the canoe and began paddling upstream.

"Now hold your paddle tight," he warned.

"Yes, teacher," she said.

"And do not stand up in the canoe."

"No, teacher."

Very soon Becky caught the gist of the bow stroke.

"Very good," said Tecumseh. "Now you are ready to try paddling from the stern."

"Good," she said. She started to rise up as though to exchange places with him.

"No, no!" he shouted. "Do not stand!"

She was back on her knees before he finished his warning.

"How many dry dresses do you have?" he asked.

"If I get this one wet, I shall paddle in a wet dress," she said.

He guided the canoe to the bank and there they traded places. They continued upstream. Tecumseh faced forward so that he could paddle, but he turned his head with each stroke to watch her.

"Remember to turn your paddle to the side and push away from the canoe to make it go straight when I am not paddling."

"Yes," she answered, and tried with some success.

"Now we turn around," he said. "You push with your paddle, and I pull with mine, and we turn around very quickly."

Having brought the canoe about, Tecumseh turned about on the thwart and sat on the bottom of the canoe, facing Becky. He accomplished this maneuver without even rocking the canoe.

"Now Tecumseh rests and looks at the trees and the water while woman works," he said. Actually he kept his eyes on Rebekah most of the time, and he gave little directions and corrections to help her improve her stroke. It was not difficult for her to paddle downstream, and she very quickly mastered the "J" stroke to keep on course. She shifted the paddle to the right side from time to time, as much to rest her muscles as to correct the direction of the craft. As she got the feel of it she relaxed, and each stroke became a greater pleasure in her sense of accomplishment and in allowing her to take in the beauty of the flowers and trees along the riverbank. She went far beyond their landing place, and then, again with Tecumseh's help in the bow, came back upstream. They landed and took the canoe out of the water.

"Oh, it was wonderful!" exclaimed Becky. "It is such a beautiful canoe. Thank you so much."

"I made it for you," said Tecumseh. "You have helped me so many times in learning better English."

"I am always glad to help if I can, and you don't have to bring presents."

"I make canoe for you."

"Oh, you made it yourself. That is wonderful! I shall always keep it as a souvenir, even when it will no longer float."

Tecumseh smiled again. "I am glad you like it," he said. "You learn very quickly. You learn canoe more quickly than I learn English."

"You learn English more quickly than I do," she said.

When they returned to the house the others were there. Tecumseh exchanged greetings with them. Becky excitedly told about her new canoe.

"Miss Becky is a very good pupil with canoe. She learns very quickly," Tecumseh said. "She also enjoys the water—." He stopped as he caught a sharp glance and shake of the head from Becky. Evidently she had not told her mother about her fall into the water.

While supper preparations proceeded, Galloway brought out his Indian pipe and, as on many previous occasions, the two men sat and smoked and talked in front of the fireless fireplace.

The supper featured broiled squirrel and brown gravy made with milk and flour and beef grease. As always, Tecumseh asked a blessing before the meal and gave thanks afterward.

For the evening devotional hour Galloway first read the 19th Psalm:

The Heavens declare the glory of God; and the firmament sheweth his handiwork.

Day unto day uttereth speech, and night unto night sheweth knowledge . . . .

And Tecumseh thought about his learning with Becky.
And then Galloway read from the book of *Job*:

Then the Lord answered Job out of the whirlwind, and said, Who is this that darkeneth counsel by words without knowledge? Gird up now thy loins like a man; for I will demand of thee, and answer thou me. . . .

And said, Hitherto shalt thou come, but no further: and here shall thy proud waves be stayed.

And Tecumseh wondered how he could say this to the White Men.
And Galloway read from the third book of *Proverbs*:

Happy is the man that findeth wisdom, and the man that getteth understanding . . . .

She is more precious than rubies: and all the things thou canst desire are not to be compared unto her.

Length of days is in her right hand; and in her left hand riches and honor.

Her ways are ways of pleasantness, and all her paths are peace.

And Tecumseh thought about how he needed wisdom to carry through his plans for all the Red Men. But then he thought that these words really spoke of Rebekah Galloway.

James Galloway then led all the family in the Lord's Prayer, and they retired, leaving young Rebekah and Tecumseh to continue their lessons.

Before they turned to other things, Tecumseh asked Becky to explain for him the Lord's Prayer that the family had just said. She thought for a moment, and then repeated, "'Our Father, who art in heaven, hollowed be thy name.' You know about God the Father, like Manitou."

"Yes, I know that."

"This is just an expression of respect for his holiness. Then it says, 'Thy Kingdom come.'"

"What is that?"

"This is the Kingdom of Heaven or the Kingdom of God. It's not like a nation of the earth. It means to make the earth like paradise, with peace, and love, and no strife, and no want."

"Yes, that is good."

"Then it says, 'Thy will be done on earth as it is in heaven,' that is, making earth like paradise, with everyone doing God's will —like all people following the rules of Manitou."

"Yes, yes, it is good."

"And then, 'Give us this day our daily bread.'"

"Yes, I understand very well."

"'And forgive us our trespasses as we forgive those who trespass against us.'"

"What is 'trespass'?"

"Here it means any wrong that a person does to another person. Strictly, trespass means walking on someone else's land without their permission."

"You mean like White Men come on Red Men's land without permission?"

"If the Indians owned the land, that would be trespassing."

"Many White Men trespass. I do not mean your family, Miss Becky, foolish chiefs give away this land to White Men. The treaty was not good, but you follow rules. But many White Men cross line even given in bad treaty. They trespass."

"Yes, they trespass," conceded Becky.

"And they only have to say this prayer to Master of Life to be forgiven?"

"For a person to be forgiven he must have a contrite heart. He must be very sorry that he did what was wrong and make promise not to do it again."

"White Man all time trespass, say he is very sorry, ask for forgiveness, and then goes and trespass again when he wants more land from Indian. That is bad rule."

"I'm afraid some may do that, but that does not please God when they do same thing over and over. That is not good."

"That is not good. And it says we should forgive those who trespass against us. How can we forgive White Men for taking our land? What are we to do? That is bad rule."

"It means we should not hold a grudge, should not always be mad at people for evil they do us."

"Then there will be no end of the evil they do us. It is bad rule."

"In many of our churches, especially in our Presbyterian churches they say 'debts' instead of 'trespasses'."

"Oh, that is better," said Tecumseh. "I know what are debts. This means when Red Men owe much money at Government stores or trading posts, White Men will forgive, and so do not have to pay? That is much better."

"Well, not exactly. Here it is supposed to mean the same as trespass — any wrong against another person."

"I prefer White Men forgive Red Men's debts than Red Men forgive White Men's trespasses."

Becky smiled in futility and went on, "'And lead us not into temptation,' that is, do not make attractive things which we should not do; don't make us want to do things that are wrong."

"That is good rule."

"—'but deliver us from evil'—"

"Good."

"'For thine is the kingdom, and the power, and the glory forever,' that just acknowledges the overall and continuing power of God."

"Yes. It is a good prayer. Except for trespass on land of other people."

Glad to get away from further difficult theological explanations, Becky turned to other things. She read several of Aesop's *Fables* —"The Wind and the Sun," "Belling the Cat," "The Fox and the Grapes." Tecumseh took special delight in these. He especially liked "The Four Oxen and the Lion," with its moral, "United we stand, divided we fall." When she finished "The Bundle of Sticks," with its moral, "Union gives strength," he told her that this was his favorite of all. He explained how he had learned this on his vision quest.

It was late when she said they must stop for tonight. "And thank you again, Mr. Tecumseh, for my beautiful canoe. We must go out in it again tomorrow!"

"Yes, and you are welcome, Miss Becky. And thank you again for all your help. All those stories were good, very good."

"Your English has improved so much that now it is easier for you to understand all the stories."

"Thanks to you."

"Good night, Mr. Tecumseh."

"Good night, Miss Becky."

On succeeding days Tecumseh spent the mornings with the men in the fields, with more clearing and fence building, building sheds or small barns for the animals and, even though he felt this really was woman's work, hoeing the corn fields to get out the grass and wild flowers, and coax moisture up through the ground. In the afternoons he went canoeing or riding with Becky, and once simply walked with her through the woods, pointing out the plants whose roots or stems or leaves or flowers were good for medicine, which were good for food, which were poisonous, which were good for pain. In the evenings she continued her reading to him, with frequent pauses for discussion—selections from *Robinson Crusoe, Gulliver's Travels,* the *Song of Roland,* and finally, with some misgivings she read a part of Bunyan's *Pilgrim's Progress.* He seemed to like each one better than whatever had just preceded it. He would like to have continued indefinitely, but he felt duty bound to return to his people and continue his work among them. At the end of a week, early on a clear morning, he took his leave with a promise to return "before the snow comes."

CHAPTER XII

Schools of Romance, Literature, and Politics

1

During the next three months, Tecumseh visited some of the tribes in the vicinity and then returned to Greeneville where he and The Prophet received and addressed an almost constant stream of visitors. On September 16, a commission of two officers—Thomas Worthington and Duncan MacArthur—sent by Governor Thomas Kirker of Ohio arrived to make inquiries about the activities at Greeneville. Both Tecumseh and The Prophet greeted them courteously and assured them of their peaceful intentions. The brothers invited the visitors to stay and observe a big Indian council that was then assembling.

The White Men invited the Indian council to send a delegation back with them to Chillicothe (a "newer" Chillicothe, on the Scioto River, then serving as the state capital of Ohio) to meet with the Governor personally. Tecumseh, together with Blue Jacket; Roundhead, a chief of the Wyandots, and The Panther, a chief of the Unami tribe, allied with the Delawares, agreed to go. Stephen Ruddell went along as interpreter.

At Chillicothe the Governor called a mass meeting of local settlers and invited Tecumseh to speak. He did so with magnetic effect. Using his translator only occasionally, Tecumseh spoke in a way that reassured everyone and left the crowd in high spirits. The Governor dismissed the militia companies that he had assembled.

Worthington invited the Indian leaders to a reception and banquet at his mansion, "Adena," on the evening before their departure to return to Greeneville.

Tecumseh and his colleagues were impressed as they rode their horses up the hill to the crest where the Worthington mansion overlooked the whole town and the valley. It was a big stone house, set on a flat lawn shaded by large oak trees and formal gardens styled after those the Worthington family had known in Virginia. General Worthington and his wife and daughter greeted the Indian and White guests as they arrived. Worthington explained that many of the fruit trees on the grounds were those he had brought from Philadelphia seven years ago, when he had gone to the national capital in support of a land bill which the territorial delegate, Mr. William Henry Harrison, now Governor of Indiana Territory, was sponsoring.

Tecumseh felt altogether at ease at this affair, and with his assurances, his companions were able to enjoy themselves as well. After courses of fish and roast beef and potatoes, and then fruits and melons, heaped upon "the pyramid table" which the guests approached in buffet fashion, the waiters brought out coffee for everyone. In the serving, they overlooked Chief Panther. Tecumseh and the other Indians noticed this right away, and they began to tease Panther as the "coffeeless Chief," and as a crude fellow who must have offended their hostess. All the other Indians joined in the banter. But then Tecumseh noticed looks of wonder and uneasiness on the faces of the White people. He promptly and quietly notified the hostess. This was a great relief to Mrs. Worthington, who was wondering about what had caused the disturbance. With her own hands she served Panther and refilled his cup as long as he would accept it.

Again Whites and Indians alike were impressed by the good will and real enjoyment of the occasion. All the way back to Greeneville—a trip of about seven days—Tecumseh and the others were teasing Panther as the Chief without coffee.

Within only a few days after this trip, Tecumseh was getting ready to start on another—this time up the Little Miami River to the "Old Chillicothe."

Tecumseh beat the snow by two months when he returned to the Galloways' in mid-October. He was ahead of the snows, but not of near freezing weather. This time before he could sit in front of the fireplace and smoke with James Galloway, it was necessary to lay a fire.

This was a task for William and Samuel. First they brought in two green buckeye logs, each so big that it took both of them to carry it in. They put first one and then the other in the fireplace, and pushed them all the way back to the clay backwall, one log on top of the other. Then they pushed the big andirons, or "dog irons" up against the backlogs. Next they laid a fairly big green log across the front of the andirons. This would keep burning logs from rolling out and, being elevated on the andirons, would allow a draft. The men built the fire of dry sticks and small logs between those big logs. That done, Samuel brought in a shovel full of live coals from the kitchen, and within minutes a big fire was warming the whole room. Now it was for young Andrew to keep the fire going by adding small dry logs as needed. The backlogs threw out lots of heat once the fire was well started, and they could be expected to burn slowly for several days. Now Tecumseh and the senior Galloway could sit in front of the fire and have their smoke and talk.

Such peace and quiet had lasted only a few minutes when Becky came in to invite Tecumseh to come back to the kitchen to watch operations there. When the Indian excused himself, Galloway went on staring at the fire, daydreaming, as though he did not even notice.

In the kitchen Tecumseh could see that the grouse he had brought this time was on the menu. Hanging on one of the cranes in the fireplace was a pot in which lye hominy was cooking. Tecumseh was familiar enough with this Indian dish. He knew that the grains of corn had been soaked in lye recovered from wood ashes, and then had been boiled until the hulls had come loose, so that they could be rubbed off by hand. The kernels were soaked in cold water to get the lye out, and then were put in a pot of water to cook. In another pot potatoes were boiling. These were less common for him. Pumpkin, familiar to him, was stewing in the third pot. Becky was at work on a special treat —wheat biscuits. It was only in the last year that Galloway had tried to grow any wheat. Previously the ground was too rich, and the wheat would grow up in straw and fall over without yielding any grain. Now they could have a small field, and they ground flour for small quantities of bread, biscuits, and pie crusts. Becky mixed with the flour, some corncob ashes, to serve as baking powder, and then added milk and a little salt to make dough. She cut this into biscuits and put them in the Dutch oven.

On a side table there was a big wooden bowl heaped with paw

paws from the nearby forest and apples from trees that "Johnny Appleseed" had planted. Two peach pies were cooling on the table.

Tecumseh always preferred corn bread to wheat bread, but he found the biscuits, hot and covered with melting butter, especially delicious. He wondered if this was because he had seen Becky make them. But everything tasted especially good this evening—the broiled grouse, the hominy, mashed potatoes, stewed pumpkin, smearcase, biscuits with apple butter, sassafras tea, and then delicious peach pie. Each took a paw paw or an apple into the sitting room. After the tables had been cleared, each went to an activity beside the fire—Mother to spinning thread from flax, Becky to weaving, Ann and Andrew to ciphering on their slates, William and Samuel to chewing tobacco, Father and Tecumseh to smoking, while the farmer read again from his well-worn Raleigh's *History*. There was little talking, but everyone obviously enjoyed being beside a warm fire on a cool evening. After an hour or so, Father led a short devotional period with readings from the Sermon on the Mount which Tecumseh thought "very good," and then all the others cleared out to leave Becky and Tecumseh to their lessons.

This session Becky was determined to introduce Shakespeare's plays. On this evening she began with *As You Like It*. This went very well.

Tecumseh could identify with *The Tempest* on the next evening. The third evening she read *Julius Caesar*. Tecumseh already was familiar with the historical character, and this only added to his admiration of the Roman leader, but made him wonder about assassination.

On the next evening she read *Hamlet*. Tecumseh from the very beginning found this the most fascinating of all. He missed the plays on words, but he caught and felt the sense of tragedy. Becky concentrated on the reading, but Tecumseh's eyes, like his mind, wandered from time to time. Briefly he caught her eye and felt a surge and throb in his throat as she read:

> Doubt that the stars are fire;
> Doubt that the sun doth move;
> Doubt truth to be a liar;
> But never doubt I love.

And he nodded in agreement as she read:

> To be honest, as this world goes, is to be one man picked out of ten thousand.

He laughed at the lines,

Polonius. What do you read, my lord?
Hamlet. Words, words, words.

And he was impressed by the lines,

Guildenstern. My lord, we were sent for.
Hamlet. I will tell you why; so shall my anticipation prevent your discovery, and your secrecy to the king and queen moult no feather. I have of late,—but wherefore I know not,—lost all my mirth, foregone all custom of exercises; and indeed it goes so heavily with my disposition that this goodly frame, the earth, seems to me a sterile promontory; this most excellent canopy, the air, look you, this brave o'erhanging firmament, this majestical roof fretted with golden fire, why, it appeareth nothing to me but a foul and pestilent congregation of vapors. What a piece of work is a man! How noble in reason! how infinite in faculties! in form and moving how express and admirable! in action how like an angel! in apprehension how like a god! the beauty of the world, the paragon of animals. And yet to me what is this quintessence of dust? Man delights not me; no nor woman neither, though by your smiling you seem to say so.

At this point Tecumseh interrupted to inquire, "When he speaks of the greatness of man, does he mean all men, or just some men? Does he mean only White Men?"

"All men, I should think." Becky smiled and added, "And surely Indians."

"And women too?"

"Of course."

When she came to the end of the long reading,

> ...Bear Hamlet like a soldier to the stage;
> For he was likely, had he been put on,
> To have prov'd most royal.
>   And for his passage
> The soldiers' music and the rights of war
> Speak loudly for him!
> Take up the bodies.
>   Such a sight as this
> Becomes the field, but here shows much amiss?

Tecumseh could not but wonder how often brave warriors become involved in such tragedies—how it seems to be impossible for them to get out of the entanglement, no matter what they do. He wondered if whole nations might suffer such a tragic fate.

As he arose he said that he would have to be leaving early the next morning.

Becky looked sad. She extended her hand. As he grasped it he said, "In a Shawnee village when a maiden gives her bare hand to a warrior, it has a special meaning."

She extended her other hand, and he took that also. "I'll be back in spring," he promised.

"I hope so," she said. "I'll be up for early breakfast tomorrow. Good night, Mr. Tecumseh."

"Good night, Miss Becky, and thank you, thank you many times."

She went to the stairs, paused long enough to look back and smile over her shoulder, and disappeared.

The next morning silvery ice needles of a hoary frost sparkled outside in the rising sun as Tecumseh joined the family for a breakfast of fried eggs, fried mush and maple syrup, with milk to drink. Immediately thereafter, he departed.

For Tecumseh the spring seemed at the same time to be rushing past him and to be just dragging on. As he tried to meet with one group after another to explain his plan of Indian union, the time rushed by. There never seemed to be enough of it. When he thought about his promised visit to the Galloways, time seemed to drag.

More and more he found himself thinking of visiting again with the Galloways. And when he thought of the Galloways, his thoughts first and foremost were of young Rebekah. He looked forward again to having an opportunity to learn better the language of the White Man. He looked forward to hearing more of their history and their great stories. He admired the way the White Man had mastered the art of writing so that it was possible to read advice and history and stories which someone had written many years ago. In admiring the White Man's writing, he admitted to himself that the White Man was the equal of the Red Man, and in this respect, at least, the White Man had achieved a kind of superiority. But he knew that the Indians could do as much, for he had done well at learning the language and its letters.

The more he had heard about the wars and the empires of great White chiefs of the past, the more fascinated he had become. Now he looked forward with a real sense of intellectual excitement and challenge to learn and know more. As he thought about it, he began to realize that in his recollections, the readings tended to be those of Rebekah most of the time. Indeed he had to admit to himself that though he enjoyed the readings and explanations of her father, he much preferred those of Rebekah.

Near the middle of May the oak leaves had reached the size of squirrels' ears, and it was time for the women to be planting the corn. Tecumseh was able to put his canoe in the water and paddle downstream toward "Old Chillicothe." The water was fairly high from the spring rains, and the current was swift. For that he was glad. Still he paddled hard to overtake his thoughts of anticipation. Why was his anticipation so much greater on this than on previous such occasions, he wondered. Simply to wonder was to find the answer. He knew very well that the answer was Rebekah Galloway, and he was troubled. But a troubled heart would not stay his further contemplation and meditation about the beautiful, dynamic, intelligent White maiden. The more he thought, the more his heart was troubled. He knew that his admiration for Rebekah, and his abiding friendship for the little girl who suddenly had grown up, had developed into true devotion and love. He wondered if she would consider marrying him.

The very thought startled him. He was surprised at his boldness, even in his own mind. He began to slow the stroke of his paddle, that he might postpone a confrontation rather than hasten just another friendly meeting. The excitement of anticipation began to give way to dread and doubt. By the time he had reached the great sycamore tree opposite the Galloways' house, he was ready to turn about. Instead he drifted on past the landing place. Then he had to turn about if he were to see the Galloways at all—especially *the* Galloway. He did so.

He made his way close to the bank where the current was not so strong. Then he began to think of the great differences in the ways of life of the White Man and the Red Man, and he wondered how it would ever be possible for this White girl to give up her strong house; her books; her white bread and chicken and pork and beef and milk; her pretty dresses; and become a Shawnee squaw. He lifted his paddle as he thought and drifted back out to midstream, where the current caught him and swept him back downstream. With strong strokes he fought back and with some effort recovered his position. He thought of the difference in age between him and Rebekah; he knew that his age was closer to her father's than to hers. Again, he lifted his paddle in the thoughtlessness of deep thought, and again drifted downstream. Again he recovered and paddled back. He repeated the performance as he thought of his own mission to unite the Indians, and to lead them in their defense against the Whites' taking more of their lands. Could a White woman possibly help with those plans, or would she always be an obstacle to their accomplishments?

In recognizing all the doubts, Tecumseh recovered his self

assurance. He knew that there would be great obstacles, but he was confident that in overcoming them he could grow stronger, and this marriage could be good. His greatest remaining doubt was whether Rebekah would be able to overcome those that she would have, and whether her father's doubts could be overcome.

As he came to the landing, Tecumseh felt a strange fatigue. He seldom felt tired even after all-day journeys on horseback or on foot. Now he was not sure whether this was the result of his strenuous and repeated paddling againt the strong current, or whether it was a kind of exhaustion growing out of this troubled and emotional thinking. Probably both, he decided.

His strength returned with his composure as he approached the house. He was glad to find James Galloway alone in the parlor of the log house, and he was glad for the chance to sit quietly in his favorite chair. Galloway brought out the souvenir pipe and lighted it. The two sat in front of a small fire and smoked without words, beyond greetings, for several minutes. They talked about the growing restlessness among the Indians and fears among the White settlers that there would be attacks and war. Tecumseh granted that there would be war if White settlers persisted in moving beyond the Greeneville Treaty line. Galloway expressed a sense of helplessness in being able to do anything about it. The men returned to their smoking, in silence, for another twenty minutes or so.

Then Tecumseh went straight to the matter that he had been thinking about all along. "Mr. Galloway," he said. "I wish to speak to you about a matter—"

"Yes? What matter?"

"About Rebekah."

"About Mrs. Galloway? Does she have some problem I don't know about?"

"Oh, no sir, I mean young Rebekah, Becky."

"Oh, yes? What about Becky?"

"Well, sir, I know all the differences in the ways of life of Red people and White people. I know that. I know the difficulties of one understanding the other, but, sir, I have learned to know and admire Becky very much. She is a wonderful young woman. I wish your permission for her to be my wife."

There, he had said it. Tecumseh felt more uncomfortable than in facing a battalion of Long Knives, but he maintained his composure through the surprise he could see on the face of James Galloway. The latter refilled and relighted the pipe, and sat without a word for another fifteen minutes.

Tecumseh had learned long ago that a long delay usually results in bad news. He braced himself for a negative response.

"My dear fellow," Galloway responded at last. "All of us admire you very much. For a long time you have been a good and trusted friend. But, my dear fellow, do you really expect our little Becky to give up her big house, her books, her white bread and pork and beef and milk, her pretty dresses, to become an Indian squaw, planting the corn, building the wigwam, and all the other work while you are away on your travels?"

"She would not be an ordinary squaw, Mr. Galloway. She would be my queen!"

Galloway smiled and said, "Chief, that must be up to Becky herself. I shall harbor no personal objections. I shall neither encourage her nor discourage her. I shall only endeavor to be sure that she understands all the problems and weighs them all carefully."

"Oh, thank you, Mr. Galloway, thank you, thank you!" Tecumseh said with as much excitement as he ever permitted himself in company. "I shall speak to her at once. I shall speak to her but will not expect a quick answer. I know she, too, needs time to think."

After the supper and the family devotional hour, as Becky was looking through the books to choose something for their reading, Tecumseh asked her to go for a walk with him down to the river. It was a pleasant evening, and she was glad to get out for a while.

They walked down to the great sycamore. Becky seemed more dynamic, more cheerful, more enthusiastic—and beautiful— than ever. Tecumseh did not want to dampen that cheerfulness and enthusiasm. His first move brought quite the opposite result. He drew from his shirt a heavy, beautifully carved and decorated, silver comb.

"A souvenir, for you," he said.

"Oh, thank you, Mr. Tecumseh," Becky responded in an enthusiastic outburst as she threw her arms around his neck and quickly stepped back.

After a long pause, when he looked at the sky, the trees, the wild flowers, everywhere but at her, he looked directly into her eyes, and holding her steadily in his spell, he said, "Miss Becky, I have come to admire you very much. You are very intelligent, very considerate, very beautiful." Her eyes waivered for a moment and then returned to his. He went on, "You are a very nice young woman, and I wish you to be my wife."

Now it was Becky's turn to show surprise, though hers was less noticeable and less prolonged than her father's had been. Her eyes shifted to the ground, to the trees, to the sky.

"Oh, Mr. Tecumseh," she said. "You are a wonderful person, a wonderful friend, and I feel a very deep devotion for you. You flatter me."

"What is that?"

"You flatter me—you speak better of me than I deserve—you honor me, and I am very appreciative. But do you expect me to be able to adopt the way of living of the Red People?"

"You can do it."

"But Mr. Tecumseh, I have heard that Indian men take many wives. I never could share a man with other wives."

"No, Miss Becky. It is true that many years ago some men took more than one wife. Most of them were following their duty to take as his wife the wife of a brother who had died. Now only few do, and only those who follow that duty. The word from Manitou now is one wife."

"And I have heard that word from Manitou is that Indian man must take only an Indian woman for his wife."

"That is true unless one prays to Manitou and Wishementoo, and Inumsiilafewanu, and receives special permission. I pray very long. I am sure I receive special permission."

"But Mr. Tecumseh, it would be very difficult for me to leave our house for a wigwam, to give up my books, my white bread and chicken and pork and beef and milk, to give up my pretty dresses and my family, and go to plant corn, to grind corn, to cut wood, and to build wigwams while you are away on your travels."

"My dear Miss Becky, you will live in very big wigwam, like your house, a strong wigwam at Tippecanoe."

"Where is Tippecanoe?"

"Where Tippecanoe meets the Wabash, as far from here toward setting sun as from here to big Ohio River. My dear Miss Becky, you take books with you, and you must remember what you taught me from the Shakespeare: 'And this our life..Finds tongues in trees, books in running brooks, sermons in stones, and good in everything.' You will teach Indian children; you will have many pretty things like canoe and like silver comb and pretty Indian dresses; you will not work like common squaws. You will have others to do work; you will teach many children the English; and you will help Tecumseh; you will be my queen."

"Oh, Mr. Tecumseh, you are a wonderful man. But it is very difficult for me. My father and mother will think I am too young."

"Your father says you may decide. You are very young, but many Indian wives are as young. That is something, as you say, you will grow out of."

Becky took the hand of Tecumseh, and they resumed their walk. They walked a little farther downstream and then turned back toward the house. They looked at the big red sun setting behind the hills beyond the river, sending waves of color all across the western sky. As they turned they saw the full moon, big and orange, rising in the east.

"Isn't it beautiful!" Becky whispered softly.

"Everywhere is beautiful where you are, Miss Becky."

They walked on without words, but with a shared sense of hope against known obstacles, and a faith in overcoming those unknown.

Presently Tecumseh said, "Miss Becky, I want you to think about what I have said. I do not want you to answer now. Think about it. Then give me your answer."

"Yes, I will think about it." She squeezed his hand. "Come back when the moon is full again, and I shall give you my answer."

"Yes, that is good. I return when the moon is full again."

When they got back to the house they joined in conversation with the family as though nothing unusual had happened, and then Becky read some of Isaac Watts, *Divine and Moral Songs for Children*, and then some of Shakespeare's sonnets, including:

> Lord of my love, to whom in vassalage
> Thy merit hath my duty strongly knit,
> To thee I send this written ambassage,
> To witness duty, not to show my wit:
> Duty so great, which wit so poor as mine
> May make seem bare, in wanting words
>   to show it,
> But that I hope some good conceit of thine
> In thy soul's thought, all naked, will bestow it,
> Till whatsover star that guides my moving
> Points on me graciously with fair aspect,
> And puts apparel on my tatter'd loving,
> To show me worthy of thy sweet respect:
> Then may I dare to boast how I do love thee;
> Till then, not show my head where thou
>   mayst prove me.

Finally she turned to Christopher Marlowe —

> Come live with me, and be my love;
> And we will all the pleasures prove
> That hills and valleys, dales and fields,
> Woods or steepy mountain yields.
>
> . . . . .
> By shallow rivers, to whose falls
> Melodious birds sing madrigals.
> And I will make thee beds of roses
> And a thousand fragrant posies.

Tecumseh asked Becky to read that one again while he watched the words very closely. Then he took the book and read it to her, read it without a flaw. And she melted in quiet tears.

Tecumseh kept up his front of an ordinary visit, with no undue haste in departing, and Becky did nothing to hint anything to the contrary.

Returning to the vicinity of the Tippecanoe, Tecumseh got a party of a dozen warriors and hurried up the Wabash to near Fort Wayne, down the St. Mary's and the Maumee to Lake Erie. He went to the Wyandot village near Brownstown to urge his project of union, and then he crossed the river to Amherstburg to call on the Indian agent of the British at that place to solicit his assistance.

As the full moon of June was rising, Tecumseh returned to the Galloways'. He arrived free of self doubts and anxiously awaiting the word from young Rebekah. Even so he followed the usual pattern of talking with James Galloway, mostly about alleged attacks of one kind or another in various parts of the country and prospects for long-term peace. This went on until Becky interrupted to suggest that Tecumseh come with her for a ride in her canoe.

By now the sun was fully down and the moon fully up. Becky sat in the bow of the canoe, facing the stern, and she let Tecumseh do the paddling. The water of the river ran quietly now, and Tecumseh handled the paddle so deftly that one could not even hear the dripping of water as he lifted the paddle out of the water and carried it forward for another stroke. They glided upstream, in and out of shadows and moonlight, where the croaks of frogs and the chirping of crickets were the only sounds to be heard.

Rebekah looked with a smile just as the moonlight caught her face fully and added sparkles to her eyes. She said, "Tecumseh, I have been thinking very hard all month. I do want to marry you"

Tecumseh did not reveal the sudden sense of elation that he felt. His first impulse was for joy, but her tone cautioned him to wait.

"I will marry you, Tecumseh, if you will come live with me and be my love. I will marry you if you will adopt the dress and way of life of my people."

Tecumseh said nothing, though deep within, his acute elation had given way to chronic disappointment.

Becky went on to answer his unspoken protests, "Tecumseh, you are a great man. You can be a great man in councils of the Seventeen Fires. You can be a great leader who will become a spokesman for your people with the great White Father. Adopt the White Man's ways, and you will be listened to. Speak the ways of peace, and they will listen. Speak the ways of war, and they will reply only with guns. By war there can be no end. You turn back the Long Knives today, there will be more tomorrow."

Still Tecumseh said nothing. Becky went on. "Some day this will be a very great nation, greater than the empires of Alexander the Great or Caesar or Napoleon. If Red Men and White Men can join together to become one people, then all of our children will be great people in a great nation. You and I can help to make your people and my people one people." After a pause, Becky continued," It just struck me: I could be a White Pocahontas, and you a Red John Rolfe. Do you know about them?"

"Indian Woman who married White Man long ago?"

"Yes, yes, he was one of the early English settlers. She was the daughter of the great Chief Powhatan. Later she adopted the White Man's religion. She became a Christian. And do you know what her Christian name was?"

"What was it?"

"Rebekah!"

"Ah, Rebekah, Rebekah."

Tecumseh thought about all these things as he brought the canoe to land by the great sycamore. As they walked toward the house, he took Becky's hand and said, "My dear Miss Becky, you speak very well. You do me honor to be my wife under any condition. In one moon—at the next full moon, I return with my answer."

The next four weeks were weeks of soul searching for Tecumseh. Years earlier he had turned away from marriage with Mineshelana out of concern that this might detract from his possible mission for his people even though his plan had not yet formed. Later he had taken Monetohse in marriage with unfortunate results except for a fine son. And then there had been Mamate, poor Mamate. Now he was facing a temptation that would jeopardize all he had been trying to do.

With some misgivings he broached the subject to his brother while they were discussing plans for their new town on the Tippecanoe. The Prophet's reaction was quick and to the point. "My Brother, how can we persuade our people to return to the ways of our fathers when you think of adopting the ways of the White Man? Brother! Already you make trouble by visiting with White People and eating White food."

Tecumseh answered slowly, thoughtfully. "My Brother, we must be friends to good White Men. Most White Men are bad. They deserve to be treated like bad dogs. But from good White Men we can learn much, and they can help in our struggle with the Long Knife dogs. My Brother, when we visit good White Men we eat their food. When good White Men visit our village we give them Shawnee food; we do not give them White Man's food."

"My Brother speaks true words, but we must be careful, for all our people take all that we do as the way they should do. If you take White Woman as wife, that will be very difficult. I have been telling all Red Men that they should put away White Women. I say that Red Men should take only Red Women for wives. If we are to save our nation we must forbid marriage between the races."

"Blue Jacket was a White Man. He took Indian squaw. He was great war chief"

"Yes, Blue Jacket became true Indian. That was not same thing."

"Some people think the best way to save our people is to mix the races, that together we can make a greater nation."

"My Brother does not believe that. He knows how difficult to bring all the tribes into Indian union. How much more difficult to bring White Men and Red Men into same union."

"Yes, very difficult."

"And if Tecumseh turns into apple Indian like Little Turtle and Winamac—"

"Don't mention traitor Winamac at same time."

"If Tecumseh takes White Woman and adopts White Man's way, then Tecumseh the Indian is dead. He is lost to his people. That is the same as dead."

"My Brother speaks good words. I must think. I must ask help of Manitou."

Ever since his vision quest, Tecumseh, when facing a great decision or a time of crisis in his life, had found it helpful to walk alone in the woods in quest of an omen for guidance. Now he spent a whole day walking, thinking, walking, meditating. He felt a temptation to settle in a White village. He searched for some way to reconcile the differences, to find a way to make the White Rebekah want to share in the Indian world. He came back to the need to be strong to save the world of the Indian. As evening approached he came upon a clearing. Some black crows flew over. Then a white pigeon flew low, over his head, causing him to look upward. There in the pale blue evening sky was a white cloud clearly in the form of a buffalo. A white buffalo, his guardian spirit. Rays of the setting sun turned the buffalo cloud red. Surely this was a sign to him. Surely he must follow his guardian spirit to lead his Red people.

His duty now clear in his own mind, Tecumseh returned to Canada, to Amherstburg, to meet the British Lieutenant governor, Francis Gore, and several Indian agents. In a council which followed, the British made clear to all the western tribesmen that they could expect assistance in food and ammunition.

At the full moon of July, Tecumseh was back at the Galloways'. This time Becky was looking for him, and she came running out to meet him. She seemed to be in especially good humor, eyes sparkling in face of all smiles. He arrived early enough in the afternoon for a walk with Becky before supper. They sat for a while under the great sycamore, seeking its shade from the July heat.

A bee flew around Tecumseh's head, and Becky began reciting an old nursery rhyme:

> Bless you, bless you, burning bee,
> Tell me when my wedding be;
> If it be tomorrow day,
> Take your wings and fly away.
> Fly to the east, fly to the west.
> Fly to him I love best.

She laughed, and he smiled, and then she recited another:

> The cock and the hen
> The deer in the den,
> Shall drink in the clearest fountain.
> The venison rare
> Shall be my love's fare,
> And I'll follow him over the mountain.

"I wish," he said.

"I'm thirsty," Becky said. "Let's to the spring to fetch a pail of water."

On returning to the house, she left him long enough for his usual introductory smoke with her father. Galloway did not mention the proposal of marriage. He took up his usual concern about possible hostilities.

At this point Tecumseh said, "My Friend, I give you my word that none of my people ever will harm this house or any member of your family."

"I appreciate that," said Galloway. "I know I can trust your word."

The next day after the noon dinner, Tecumseh followed Becky outside. They sat on a log in front of the house. Each looked at the ground, or straight ahead.

"My dear Becky, I wish you would come with me and be my queen."

"I want to be with you, but I would feel so strange in an Indian village that I could not be a good wife for you. But you, you are able to live at ease anywhere. Look to the paths of peace, and live as great White men do."

"My dear Becky, I have thought long and hard. The Great Spirit has told me that I must stay with my people. They have much need. I must do what I can to bring them together so that they may be strong enough to live."

Becky's smiles were gone now, and her lips quivered ever so slightly.

Tecumseh went on, "My dear Becky, an Indian who takes on White Man's ways is like an oak tree that is struck by lightning —it is no longer one good tree, but two worthless ones—no good to either side. As Red Man who takes on White Man's ways is an apple Indian—red on the outside, but white on the inside, and left alone, will soon rot."

They rose, and Tecumseh grasped both of Becky's hands in his. Looking into her eyes, he said, "You have been a wonderful teacher. You are a wonderful person. I will never forget. But now I must return to my people."

Becky did not turn away as traces of tears began to well in her eyes. Tecumseh looked into her eyes quietly and intently. Then he turned and walked toward the river. Walking with firm step and steady stride, head up and shoulders erect, he never looked back. He was walking back to his own rendezvous with destiny. That destiny was with the defense of his own people, not for the satisfaction of his personal pleasure. He knew that he would never see Rebekah Galloway again, and for that he was sad. But he felt a sense of relief in knowing that he had done the right thing. And for that he was glad.

2

While William Henry Harrison continued his interest in reading the classics and the scriptures, and while he continued his interest in the advancement of learning in Vincennes, his sternest school was the school of politics.

One warm afternoon in September, 1807, when Harrison returned to his office from the noonday dinner with his family, he found Nathaniel Ewing waiting. Ewing was the receiver in the Vincennes Land Office where he worked closely with John Badollet who was the registrar. Harrison could see that Ewing was agitated.

"What is it, Nathaniel?" asked Harrison as he waved Ewing to a chair.

"Governor, I'm afraid we have trouble in the Land Office."

"What kind of trouble?"

"Well, you know that young Jonathan Jennings we have in there as clerk?"

"Yes, bright lad, isn't he?"

"Well, he's trying to stir up trouble, even claims I'm involved in illegal speculation, and if you ask me, he'll be after your hide next."

"Hell of a shallow, self-seeking fellow, isn't he?"

"Well, yes, I would say so," Ewing responded. "He's only twenty-three years old, but his cockiness makes up for his youth, and his conceit for his lack of experience. He's only been here a little over a year, but he's lost no time in jumping into politics and land. And did you ever notice the furrows in his brow? His eyebrows slant upward toward the center of his forehead, and these, together with his habit of wrinkling his forehead when he is talking to you, give his countenance a look of inquiring innocence which mask his inner craftiness for the unwary."

"Ha, yes," responded Harrison. "But what kind of so-called illegal activity is he talking about?"

"He claims our companies are in collusion to eliminate competition and hold down bidding at the public auctions."

"Did he tell you that?"

"Oh, no, it's that Doc Sam McKee and a few others mostly. I think Jennings feeds them the information, and then they make the charges."

"What kind of charges, exactly?"

"Well, they say we engage in swapping sections, for instance, where the companies come to an agreement to parcel out the sections, and then not bid against each other. Or several speculators agree among themselves not to bid on a section. Then one of them gets it at the minimum price, later sells it at a higher price, and divides the proceeds among all the group. Or sometimes one of the group bids up the price on a piece of land so high that it scares everybody off, then he forfeits on his purchase, and it goes back on sale at minimum price when nobody knows about it except the members of the group who have stuck around."

Harrison permitted himself a wry smile. "Well, have you been involved in any of that sort of thing?" he asked.

"No, of course not. At least not exactly."

"How do you mean, 'not exactly'?"

"Well, being right there in the Land Office, sometimes I can see what is going on and take advantage of it. Once or twice when they have run the price up and then forfeited, of course I did not go home. I was right there, and once or twice I stepped in and picked it up before the speculators could get back to it."

"Bravo!" Harrison laughed. "And I must admit once or twice I have been able to take advantage of situations like that. But I can see how someone might scream when they get beat out of something by someone right in the Land Office. I suspect, that it would be well to avoid being identified as having an interest in a company known to have a purpose of lessening competition."

"Yes, I suppose so. But Governor, how is anyone to get ahead around here without some land?"

"Yes, you're right. Long ago I saw the necessity of acquiring land. Without that I would never have been able to pay for this house."

"I dare say. Of course when some speculators get beat at their own game they think that is *prima facie* evidence that there has been some finagling going on."

"And of course all Jennings is after is votes and influence."

"In Virginia they used to talk about the 'landed aristocracy.' Here I guess we have to contend with the landed politicians."

"Oh, Jennings is after the 'Virginia aristocracy' which he says is running Vincennes and the Indiana Territory. Of course he probably was born in Virginia, too. Says he doesn't know whether he was born in Virginia or New Jersey. He'll probably claim whichever one he thinks will do him the most political good at the moment. Anyway, he says that in this Territory it is simply a contest between the Virginia aristocracy and the common man."

"But what do we do about these charges?"

"We have a public hearing and lay them to rest," Harrison promised.

The matter went to court, and Harrison's testimony was instrumental in getting acquittal for Ewing.

But the Governor himself was not off the hook. Dr. Samuel McKee wrote a long letter to the *Western Sun* in which he launched a broadside attack against the fraudulent operations of land companies. In this he expressly exempted Harrison from any blame. But that lasted only a few days. A week later he followed up with a blast at the Governor himself for alleged involvement in companies engaged in such operations. Harrison repudiated the charges in an answering letter in the newspaper, and then he brought out witnesses to support him, and before whom McKee conceded the Governor's innocence.

One night the children seemed especially restless. While Anna went in to see about the baby, Benjamin, Harrison picked up three-year-old John Scott and carried him downstairs. While the boy fussed, the father tried to comfort him, walking back and forth in the hall. Then suddenly there was a sharp crack over their heads and a sound of splintering wood. Immediately Harrison fell to the floor with little John Scott under him. Looking up, Harrison could see by the dim candle light a hole in the shutter of a parlor window opposite the hall entrance.

"What was that?" Anna cried out as she ran down the stairs

with baby Benjamin in her arms.

Without saying anything Harrison got up and ran over to her with John Scott. "Wait here on the steps," he said. "Stay away from the windows."

Harrison raced to his study, took down his loaded rifle from the mantle, and ran out the front door. In the half moonlight he could see what appeared to be an Indian, crouched low, slipping away. Harrison fired a shot into the air. The shot turned the stealth into full flight as the intruder mounted a horse and raced for the woods.

"What was it?" asked Anna when Harrison came back into the house.

"It looked like an Indian. He ran away in a big hurry, so I think we have nothing more to fear from him."

"Who do you think it was?"

"I don't know what to make of it. Probably some drunken Indian on his way home from the tavern."

"Or some assassin who is unhappy about something."

"Perhaps. But in that case we don't know whether he was sent by some disgruntled tribe or whether he was acting on his own, perhaps trying to get revenge for some relative who was killed. "

"Or hired by some of those White scoundrels who are after you."

"There's no way of knowing. I say, let's just not worry about it and see if we can get some sleep."

Another source of embarrassment was the rather bizarre Davis Floyd affair. Floyd had been involved at Jeffersonville in helping fit out the Burr expedition. For that involvement he was indicted in 1807 for treason. Harrison publicly advocated Floyd's innocence, but the jury found him guilty, and he was sentenced to three hours in jail. Thereafter, he made his way to Vincennes and almost immediately the legislature elected him as its clerk. A writer to the *Western Sun* denounced this in the strongest terms. He wrote that the Governor,

As a 'pillar of good government,' should have stood firm and not have condescended to have stooped from his dignified station, especially to attempt to screen from the righteous indignation of an incensed and injured people, (or from the malice of a secret foe) a marauding minion of a second Cataline.

And of the legislature, he declared that this was a "Burrite Legislature" and:

·...What could possess the men who voted for him? Surely they were *bewitched, bewatled, or discomgarigamfrigated.* It's clear enough they were infected with the Burrite mania. I'll wager my new Suwarrow boots that if the business was to do over again they would act very differently.

About the same time sentiment was growing in the Illinois country, mostly in the western settlements near the Mississippi, for separation from Indiana Territory. Harrison opposed this and became involved in a political tussle. A friend of his in the Kaskaskia Land Office, Michael Jones, exposed fraudulent land claims on the part of some of the leaders of the anti-Harrison faction. But this only brought forth demands for his own ouster. Those in the legislature favoring separation, in opposition to Harrison, were able to elect one of their own number, Jesse B. Thomas of Dearborn County, in eastern Indiana, as territorial delegate to Congress in 1808. In Congress Thomas pushed immediately for separation. He was armed with petitions which were referred to a committee of which he was made chairman, and early in 1809 he won congressional approval. This was occasion in Vincennes for hanging the territorial delegate in effigy. But the deed had been done, and Illinois was organized as a separate territory.

Congress also in 1809 enacted a law that provided that the territorial delegate now should be elected by popular vote rather than by legislature, and the Legislative Council, the upper house of the legislature also should be elected by popular vote. Almost immediately, Jonathan Jennings offered himself as a candidate for delegate and began a popular campaign. Harrison put forward his fellow Virginian and good friend, Thomas Randolph, whom he had just recently appointed attorney general of the Territory.

Randolph was a fiery new recruit of the "Virginia coterie" in Vincennes. A second cousin of John Randolph of Roanoke, he was born in Richmond, Virginia. He was an honor graduate of the College of William and Mary. After graduation he had read law, and he had served a term in the Virginia House of Delegates. At thirty-eight now, he was two years older than Governor Harrison. With a long queue hanging down his back and ringlets of brown hair bordering his high, broad forehead, he looked too much the aristocrat and intellectual to have an immediate appeal for the common man. His large mouth and firm lips, between a long, slender nose and a slender chin, gave him the appearance of an orator, which he was. His average height and slender build did not give him the appearance of a firebrand, which he also was. In the year since coming to the Territory—for which he had given up the offer of a lieutenant's commission in the Army—he had become a close friend and associate of the Governor.

In the race for delegate to Congress, the waters were muddied a bit by the entry of a third candidate, John Johnson, also from Virginia, also now a lawyer in Vincennes, and a frankly pro-slavery man.

Slavery turned out to be the most discussed issue in the campaign for delegate. Jennings vigorously attacked slavery, and urged no modification of the prohibition of it in the Territory. Randolph tried to escape the brush of being painted proslavery— though his position was similar to Harrison's in favoring modification of the prohibition for a specified number of years. But he resisted the proslavery label even to the extent of challenging to a duel one of his opponents who accused him of it. Johnson openly espoused slavery.

But the election turned more on the essential non-essentials of campaigning. Randolph, riding the trails and traces of Dearborn County in the eastern part of the territory, came upon a farm where a logrolling was going on. He stopped and chatted with voters at the farmhouse for a few minutes, and then rode on. A day later Jennings came by; he went right in to help with the logrolling, and then joined the men in tossing quoits and throwing the maul—and allowed them to beat him narrowly. At another place he grabbed an ax and helped erect a log cabin in record time. He sent to voters handbills which, treated with grease, became window panes in cabins throughout much of the Territory.

Harrison did what he could to help Randolph. The Governor took the stump as far away as Corydon. He sent letters of support to people where he thought they would do the most good. He pledged one hundred dollars when a subscription paper was circulated in Vincennes to urge the sending to Congress a man who would support the interests of Vincennes and Knox county. But all the while Jennings was dubbing Randolph the "Governor's man" and the "agent of the Virginia aristocrats" in Vincennes.

In a close contest where few voters participated, Jennings won a narrow plurality with 428 votes to 402 for Randolph and 84 for Johnson. Randolph carried Vincennes and Knox County by 231 to 44, but Jennings gained enough in the outlying counties of Clark and Dearborn (in the southeast and east) to overcome that.

Actually the proslavery Johnson siphoned off enough votes from Randolph in Knox County to throw the election to Jennings.

There were enough disputed votes, mainly in Dearborn County, to change the outcome. Randolph appealed the decision to Congress. Both Randolph and Jennings made their way to Washington to appear before a special committee. The committee brushed aside the disputed votes and went to a more basic question of whether the election itself was legal. As attorney general of the Territory, Randolph naturally had to argue that the election was legal. But the committee voted that it was not legal and recommended that the seat be declared vacant. A committee of the whole agreed with this, but then the House of Representatives in full session rejected the earlier action and seated Jennings.

The election left a wake of hard feelings between the two candidates and their friends and supporters.

Judge Waller Taylor wrote to Randolph: "He [Jennings] is a pitiful coward, and certainly not of consequence enough to excite resentment nor any other sentiment than contempt. He may rest in peace for me. . . . I expect, before you receive this, you will have passed through the list of your enemies in asking them over the Wabash to partake of your company and the amusement you wish to afford them. I make no doubt they will decline your invitation. I hope the junta will be put down like Lucifer, 'never to rise again.'"

Randolph did indeed extend to one of his tormentors an invitation to meet him on the other side of the Wabash. On learning from the editor of the *Western Sun* that the author of some anonymous letter in the paper against him was a Dr. Elias McNamee, he sent to him a direct communication by Major Jonathan Taylor, demanding redress.

McNamee responded with the statement, "I must leave you to seek that redress you may think most proper."

Randolph wrote back on the same day, "I hope a polite invitation to meet me on the other side of the river Wabash, in the Illinois Territory, will be accepted."

Instead of accepting, McNamee went straight to Judge Vanderburgh and swore out a warrant "that Thomas Randolph, of the county of Knox, Esquire, hath challenged him to fight a duel, and that he hath good reason to believe, and doth verily believe, that the said Randolph will take his life or do him some bodily harm."

Randolph was arrested and put under bond. Most embarrassing to him was that McNamee turned out to be a Quaker who had strong religious as well as legal scruples against dueling. Randolph nevertheless delivered himself of another long tirade against McNamee in the *Sun* which ended with the statement, "In taking leave of you, Dr. McNamee, as a scoundrel no longer worthy of my notice, I pronounce you a base slanderer, an infamous liar, and a contemptible coward."

The third candidate, John Johnson, appeared on the streets carrying a heavy hickory stick that was intended for Randolph according to some of the latter's friends. Urged by them to look out for his defense, Randolph carried a heavy stick one evening, and then, thinking this all foolishness, threw it away. He was glad that he had done so when he found out that Johnson was carrying his stick only for defense on the basis of some false rumor that Randolph was out to get him.

But this was not all. About this same time a group against Harrison, the "junta," led by William McIntosh, John Rice Jones, and Elijah Bachus, became more active. This pained Harrison especially because both McIntosh and Jones had been friendly in earlier years and indeed had served in his administration shortly after he first took office as governor—McIntosh as treasurer of the Territory and Jones as attorney-general—,but their attitude changed about 1805. They opposed the move to advance the government of the Territory to the second stage. They also were interested in land speculation and from time to time they made accusations that Harrison had cheated the Indians in his treaties with them for the cession of lands. They further accused Randolph of being a pro-slavery man.

All this led to further outbursts between Randolph and McIntosh which ended up in a serious altercation. McIntosh struck Randolph in the back with a dirk. Randolph was carrying only a small pocket knife which he used to cut McIntosh across the face. The wound to McIntosh was superficial. That to Randolph kept him near death for several weeks.

Harrison was deeply disturbed by the Randolph-McIntosh affair, especially since it appeared to have resulted, at least in part, from Randolph's loyalty to the Governor.

Still, Jonathan Jennings continued to be the major political thorn in Harrison's side. Jennings never hesitated to use his closely won position as delegate in Congress to embarrass the Governor.

Harrison welcomed a chance to express his feelings to Anna in one of their evening sessions.

"I tell you, Anna, that Jennings fellow has no substance, no substance at all," he said.

"I guessed as much," she said. "He's been in Vincennes two years and already he's acting like he owns the place."

"Yes, indeed. Oh, he's a clever politician, all right, with a certain surface of brightness, but he's like a shallow pool in the sunlight—a reflection of brightness, but no depth. Tom Randolph, on the other hand, is like a deep well in the shade. He doesn't shine very much, but he has great depth, great substance, and he's great to have around. He has lots of good ideas and is no 'yes' man; he doesn't try to express opinions just to please you, but of course, that's what a lot of the voters want. Tom would make a great senator if we could just make him a good enough politician to get elected. But whatever it may be, I'm sure he has a great future. Jennings, I'm afraid, is one of those bright young men who is all show and no know. I'm afraid he is one who can get elected, but then has nothing to offer when he gets there."

"And Henry, I'll tell you something else. I cannot *abide* that Mrs. Jennings."

"But my Dear—"

"No, no. I'm sorry, but I cannot abide her for a minute."

"But my Darling—"

"Yes, Henry?"

"There is no Mrs. Jennings. The young man has not as yet persuaded anyone to accept that station."

"Oh, oh, I'm sorry. What was I thinking of? Well, I wish there were a Mrs. Jennings, for if there were I just know I could not abide her." She laughed.

So did he.

"Well, I hear Jennings is planning to move back to Clark County soon, anyway," Harrison said.

"It can't be any too soon, if you ask me," responded Anna. "But on the other hand, is that good or bad? He may do even more mischief over there where it won't be so easy to keep an eye on him."

"That's what I was thinking. Undoubtedly the reason he's moving is political. Everything he does is politically motivated."

"Sure enough."

"Well, that's where his political base is. You saw how few votes he got in Vincennes and Knox County in the contest for delegate. I have an idea he figures he can do better over there."

Meanwhile Harrison tried to see to it that the University and the Library and the cultural societies continued their slow beginnings.

In 1807, Jonathan Jennings had become clerk of the University Board of Trustees. This was too much for Harrison. Within a few months he supported a motion to inquire into the conduct of Jennings and then resigned. Early in 1808, after a new clerk was chosen, Harrison returned to the Board.

A petition by the Trustees to Congress for more funds for the university got a negative response in committee, but the building proceeded anyway. In February 1807 the Trustees had bought the necessary land for a building. They bought an initial tract from Judge Vanderburgh, then, by trading a part of this for two lots from Colonel Vigo and adding a third lot from Vigo, they acquired the rectangular plot they wanted between Hart and Sixth Streets. In the next year they let the contract for construction of a building to Joshua Bond who had been on George Rogers Clark's expedition. This first building was to be a handsome brick structure, 65 x 40 feet, two and one-half stories high, with full basement. It was to have seven rooms on the first floor and nine on the second.

Instruction—mainly in the elementary branches—began in 1810 under the Reverend Samuel T. Scott, Presbyterian minister. They were unable to attract Indian students as they had hoped, and funds were not available for opening a female branch. The building was not finished for another two years, though the territorial legislature was able to hold its session there in June 1811. That fall The Reverend Henri M. Shaw entered into an agreement to move his Episcopal School into some of the rooms, and the church was granted permission to use one of the rooms for its services.

The Library, too, was off to a slow start, but already by the spring of 1808 it had close to two hundred books. Among the titles on its shelves were Leland's *Philip of Macedon*; Robertson's *History of America, and Dictionary of Arts and Sciences*; Guthrie's *Grammar*; Blair's *Lectures*; Vattel's *Law of Nations*; Witherspoon's works; Morse's *Geography*; Pinckerton's *Geography with Maps*; Goldsmith's *Animated Nature*; Vailow's *Husbandry*; Priestley's *Lectures*; Tucker's *Slavery*; Smith's *Wealth of Nations*; Voltaire's *Philosophical Dictionary, and Hapless Orphan*; Knox's *Essays Beggar Boy, Daughter of Adoption, Mysteries of Adolpho, Beauties of History, and Vagabond*; Goldsmith's *Roman History, and Lectures on Female Education;* Locke's *Essays; Arabian Nights, Fool of Quality*; More's *Utopia; Joan of Arc, Robinson Crusoe; Military History*; *Horace* in French, *Principles of Literature in French*; and Seneca's *Morals.* The final volume in John Marshall's five-volume *Life of George Washington* became available in the autumn of 1807, and the Library had ordered it immediately.

Harrison was a chief organizer and first president of the Vincennes Historical and Antiquarian Society in 1808. In 1809 he organized the Society for the Encouragement of Agriculture and the Useful Arts and served as its first president. This was the first agricultural society in the whole area of the old Northwest Territory. It disseminated information on various aspects of agriculture, sponsored agricultural fairs, and offered prizes for bumper crops.

CHAPTER XIII

Tales of Two Cities: Spring and Summer

1a

Vincennes—It was a town of log houses and rows of white clapboard, mostly single story. But the clapboard outnumbered the rustic, and the old outnumbered the new. In times of low air pressure and light winds, a stench of horse manure and buffalo dung, cows and hogs, chickens and skunks, green wine and corn whiskey, rotting wood and mildewed cloth, seventy-year-old privies and unwashed people, hung heavily over the town. By day flies swarmed from one to the other, and by night mosquitoes took their place.

When it was dry, it was dusty; when it was wet it was muddy, and at all times it was musty.

The stench was moderated in spring and summer by honeysuckle and clover, in autumn and winter by smoke from pine logs and oakwood, and in all seasons by the broiling, braising, boiling; the frying, stewing, roasting; the baking, toasting, warming, of meats and fish and game; of roots and greens and fruits; of breads and cakes and pies, from four hundred kitchens.

Sounds of life filled the air—the cock's crow in morning, the crow's caw at midday, the whip-poor-will at eventide; the howl of the coyote by the light of the moon, the screech of the owl by the dark. There were the clucks and quacks and honks of domestic fowls, and the coos and chirps and songs of wild birds; the frequent bark of a dog close at hand, the less frequent howl of a wolf in the outer land. The days echoed far-off musket shots of hunters in the woods and nearby hoofbeats and creaking wagon wheels, of parades of footsteps and slamming kitchen doors. There was the church bell on Sundays and dinner bells everyday; cow bells in summer and sleigh bells in winter, and always the ring of the blacksmith's anvil. In counterpoint were the cries of frightened and disgruntled children and the laughs of happy and mischievous ones, the war whoops of imaginary Indians, and the drill calls of real militiamen.

1b

Tippecanoe—known generally as Prophet's Town—It was the chief Indian town of the whole territory. Rows of sturdy wigwams, bark on poles, or skins on poles, spread out in lines and circles beside the open field around the big log council house. There were more of bark than of skins, and the new outnumbered the old. The grass was heavy, and it seldom was dusty or muddy. Smoke from four hundred fires, in wigwams and outside, added a deeper hue to the blue haze rising from the Wabash and the Tippecanoe.

The smell of marsh grass and pine trees, of burning oak and sycamore, of birch bark and maple sap, and of corn, corn, always corn, boiling, parching, drying, grinding, baking; the greasy smell of opossum and bear fat, oil lamps and oil skins, drying hides and soaking yarn, rotten fish and green saplings, all drifted in differing mixes on every breeze.

Trees and grass and habits of movement muffled the sounds of hoofbeats and footsteps. There were drill calls of imaginary militiamen and whoops of real Indians at war games. The whirr of arrows countered the whirr of wild geese. The chatter of people was less than the chatter of squirrels, but at times of prophetic orations and ritual dances the sounds of the multitude drowned all the sounds of the forest. But at night all fell silent, a silence made more so by the howl of a wolf or the cry of a night hawk, and by the popping sounds of growing green cornstalks, when the shine of the pale moon made pale faces of them all.

2a

Vincennes, in a way, comprised two towns—the old French quarter and the newer part settled by Americans, most of whom had arrived in the last decade or so. The French houses were in narrow streets along the Wabash River. Their construction was in the French way—logs, either round or hewed, set up on end, the cracks between them filled with a mortar made of clay and straw. The roofs were either thatch or hewed shingles. The walls in many cases were covered with stucco as in France, and most, whether stuccoed or not, were whitewashed with a lime obtained by burning mussel shells from the river. Most of the houses were one-story high, and most were of similar design, with a central hall running through from front to rear. Each had its own patio which, in many cases, ran all the way around the house, with vegetable and flower gardens enclosed with pole fences.

The earlier American settlers also had log cabins, but their logs, round, notched, were laid horizontally. The more primitive cabins had no windows, and only an opening in the roof to allow smoke from the fire to escape. More common in town now were log houses with logs hewed to a flat surface, roof of split shingles, a good fireplace and chimney, a puncheon floor (of split logs with the flat surface up), and glass windows. But now most of the newer houses were of frame and clapboard construction, painted white. Within a few years there were a hundred of these in addition to the older French houses. With the coming of the territorial government, a number of the newer arrivals: doctors, lawyers, and other professional people, built brick houses.

When an immigrant farmer arrived to settle on a farm in the vicinity, he would first build a temporary shelter, perhaps a lean-to of logs and brush, and then would set about clearing the land and building a more permanent log cabin which later would be improved to a more spacious and comfortable log house.

While the American farm settler liked to live on the land that he cultivated, the French followed the European custom of living in town and going out to their fields each day. These French had developed a substantial prairie below the town where each had a grant of about eighty acres, each tract in a narrow strip two acres wide so that it could have frontage on the river. There were seventy of these tracts plus a four-acre plot set aside for the church. The tracts were not fenced, but were separated by turning rows so that each farmer could identify his parcel and cultivate it without getting in the way of his neighbors. There they grew corn, wheat, barley, tobacco, squash, melons, and some rye, rice, and hops. The French had had years of attention to develop good orchards of apples, peaches, pears, cherries, and currants.

Streams filled with fish and forests and prairies filled with game: deer, elk, bear, squirrels, rabbits, and turkeys, prairie chickens, quail, grouse,pheasants, and ducks; and wild fruits and nuts: grapes, persimmons, paw paw, black walnuts, hickory nuts, hazel nuts, chestnuts, pecans—all these added to the quantities and varieties of foods available.

Most farmers grew some flax, and some even tried cotton. A number grew hemp along the river. Farmers brought produce to market, and grain to be ground, in small two-wheeled, wooden carts, called caleches by the French, tied together with rawhide and drawn by one or two Spanish horses or "Indian ponies,"or they simply tied their bags to the back of a horse. Some farmers used a kind of wheel-less wagon, a wooden sled or "mud boat" with heavy wooden runners. Others used a more simple Indian-type travois for dragging loads across the ground. A gristmill had been operating in the town for many years. This also served as a social center where farmers, waiting their turns to have their corn and wheat ground, had considerable time for visiting with each other. Recently a sawmill had been added where logs could be brought in to be cut into boards. Some of the more recent settlers had built stills so that they might offer whiskey to compete with the local wine and beer. Most farms in the vicinity had a smokehouse for curing pork and beef.

For laundry, the few great houses had separate buildings where servants soaped, boiled, and scrubbed the clothes and then hung them out to dry. Most of the newer American settlers performed these activities out-of-doors in fair weather, and in their kitchens in bad weather. Many of the French women still took their clothes down to the river and scrubbed them on rocks along the water's edge. For ironing, everyone used a battery of irons heated in the fireplace. With wooden handle, they would clasp one iron to use on the clothing while the others heated, and then, when the first iron cooled, switch the handle to a second.

Several stores offered merchandise from Pittsburgh, Philadelphia, and Baltimore, and from Europe. C. Smith Co., successor to W. Bullitte and C. Smith, dealt in fine cloths from the East, and Owen Reilly offered president cord, constitution cord, twilled coating, and moleskin. The establishment of the seat of government had brought more merchants and artisans. Soon there were cabinet makers who were turning out fine furniture from the local cherry and black walnut woods, and blacksmiths and others who were producing farm tools and nails as well as andirons, pot hooks, spits, tongs, and shoe scrapers. There were saddlers, gunsmiths, cobblers, tailor shops, milliners, a wheelwright, a tanner, a silversmith, an apothecary, and even a limner.

Carpenters, masons, shoemakers, and other skilled workers earned about one dollar a day. For their food they paid three cents a pound for pork, four or five cents a pound for beef, and five dollars a barrel for flour.

While in the earlier days the inhabitants had been content with coonskin caps and buckskins and homespun suits and dresses, now, in the capital city, the more prominent gentlemen wore fine coats, silk ruffles, knee breeches with silver buckles and lace stockings for receptions and other special occasions, while the ladies had dresses of English muslin, French silk taffeta, and Irish linens.

Four or five taverns and inns were operating in the town at most times, of which the most popular was Graeter's. This was operated by Frederick and Christian Graeter who had come to Vincennes from Alsace-Lorraine before 1800. There, the price of a meal was twenty-five cents and lodging was half that amount. Whiskey was twenty-five cents a pint; punch and brandy toddies were one dollar a glass or a dollar and a half for a bowl. A special drink of the house was a spice and sugar concoction called *sangaree*. Billiards was available at twenty-five cents for three games, or one game at one-third that amount. In 1808 Graeter and Woodcock opened a new house of entertainment at the Sign of the Ferry Boat.

Another favorite tavern was that of Hyacinthe Lasselle. This was in a large, two-story building with big dining hall suitable for banquets and balls. Another was that of Permanes Beckes (at the Sign of Thomas Jefferson) which Beckes had taken over from Peter Jones when the latter became the Governor's secretary in 1807. Other, smaller taverns, were operated by John D. Hay and John McCandless.

As early as 1807 local inhabitants could find entertainment at a theatrical exhibition.

But Vincennes still was an isolated outpost. Roads out of the town went nowhere. Travel and transportation to and from the town had to be by horseback or river boat. Vincennes and the immediately adjacent area were still an island in the midst of what had been recognized in the Treaty of Greeneville as Indian hunting grounds. The only overland connections with the outside world were the buffalo traces and Indian trails which a thin stream of immigrants and visitors had followed. It was a hundred miles to Louisville over the trail referred to as Clark's Trace through woods and swamp lands. It was a three-day trip under the best of conditions, and one had to carry with him food and forage for that time, for there was no place for replenishment. At night there was no question of looking for a good inn, for there was none. Lodging was simply on the ground.

In the opposite direction, it was a forty-three hours' ride through woods and over prairies covered with grasses ten to twelve feet high in summer and swept by cold winds and snow in winter, to Kaskaskia on the Mississippi. At infrequent intervals in some years, Rangers patrolled these routes for the safety and welfare of travelers.

Several ferry boats facilitated the crossing of the river, though, in times of low water, most people, whether on horse or on foot, simply waded across. One of these was a current-powered ferry. A heavy line, with a big iron ring on it, had been secured to a big tree on either bank of the river. At midstream the line still was eight to ten feet above the level of the river. To the ring on this line another line was attached, the other end snapped to the bow of the boat. Then as a rudder kept the boat headed toward the opposite shore, the current pushing against the boat caused it to be forced across as the iron ring slipped along the line. Poles forced the boat on for the last few feet. Then, its passengers and cargo unloaded, it was ready for a trip in the opposite direction.

One of the most important acquisitions in the coming of age of Vincennes was the newspaper and printing shop. Elihu Stout established those in 1804. Early that spring he went to Frankfort, Kentucky, and bought a printing press which he sent to Vincennes by river. It arrived three months later. On July 4, from his little office on East St. Louis Street, he issued the first copy of the *Indiana Gazette*. Eighteen months later the shop burned, but soon the newspaper reappeared as the *Western Sun*. It was offered at a subscription price of $2.50 which might be paid in cash or in beef, pork, bacon, corn, whiskey, wheat, sugar, potatoes, butter, eggs, tobacco, salt, tallow, flour, or oats, delivered at the office. Over a period of years, Stout made an annual trip to Georgetown, Kentucky, to get paper, ink and other supplies. He took three horses on these trips—one to ride and two to carry his purchases.

The building which the Territorial Government occupied, where the court sat and later the House of Representatives met, i.e., the capitol building, was a two-story frame structure on the southwest side of Main Street, between Second and Third Streets. It was a trim building with internal chimney and fireplaces, doors at either end of a one-story porch in front, with windows between, and with two windows at the front of the upper story.

The building which overshadowed all the others in the town was the Governor's elegant brick mansion, "Grouseland." Harrison had intended from the outset to build a house as soon as possible, and shortly after his arrival he had purchased forty-nine acres of land from Colonel Vigo. This was a plot bounded on the west by the river, on the east by a lane known as Elm Road, and on the north and south by what became Hart and Locust Streets respectively. But Vigo's title to the land was not clear, and it took Harrison a year to settle that.

Harrison's ambition had grown with each day of delay. When the building was started in 1802, he was determined to bring a little of the James River to the Wabash. Here would be his frontier Berkeley manor house.

He had contracted with Samuel Thompson for the brick, some of which was made locally and some brought in from Pittsburgh at a price of four hundred acres of land worth about a thousand dollars. He had brought in glass and hardware from Pittsburgh, and several workmen skilled in bricklaying and carpentry came in from Kentucky. The great oak beams, the yellow poplar boards for the floors, and the black walnut for the woodwork came from the adjacent forest and local sawmill.

The house was two years in building, and when completed it impressed everyone who saw it. It was easily the largest building in the town, and indeed was the greatest house in the Territory. Of two-story brick construction in a modified Georgian style with hipped roof punctuated by four tall chimneys, it clearly showed the influence of Berkeley. Perhaps the most striking departure from the general style of such houses was its west side wall, the one toward the river. This was shaped in a great arc, both stories, so that the windows on that side were given the effect of a gigantic bay window which provided a sweeping vista of the river, upstream and down.

A two-story veranda, supported by two tiers of white columns formed an imposing portico at the main, south entrance to the house. The front door opened into a great central hall, much as at Berkeley. Rugs of oriental design covered the floor and a runner of similar design carried up the open stairway. An arch of white woodwork was near the middle of the hall. Plain paper of a light lemon hue covered the dado opposite the stairway, between the dark baseboard and the white chair rail, and a figured paper in matching colors covered the much higher expanse of wall from the dado to the white ceiling. Similar papers, separated by a dark handrail covered the wall beside the stairs, opposite the white balusters and dark handrail on the other side. The stairs went straight up to a landing midway to the second floor. A floor clock stood on the landing. There, the stairs curved to the right, and then back toward the front to reach the upstairs hall. A crystal lamp hung from the ceiling of the main hall.

To the left, or west, of the hall was the big parlor. This was the room where windows in the curved side gave the best view of the river. Oriental rugs covered the floor. The windows were covered with white, floor-length shears and blue silk draperies topped by full blue valances. Draperies and valances alike were trimmed with gold fringes. The walls were covered with smooth paper of light gold color, bordered with blue flouncing along the cornices all around the room, matching the valances of the draperies. A crystal chandelier, carrying six tall tapers, hung from the center of the high, smooth white ceiling. The fireplace was in the middle of the south (front) wall, a wall without windows, though, on the outside walls, shutters indicated, falsely, that there were windows on either side of the interior chimney. Fireplace and borders were in white. A big round pedestal table stood at the center of the room, and by reason of some of the conferences held around the table, the room came to be referred to as the "council chamber." Sofa, chairs, end tables, and candle tables were situated around the walls, and a walnut chest was in the little alcove beside the fireplace. In the corner opposite the hall door and the fireplace was a small, rectangular piano, one that had been built in New York over fifty years earlier. The Governor's office was in the room adjacent to the parlor, at the northwest corner of the house.

Across the hall from the parlor was the dining room. Here the long dining table and most of the other furniture was of native cherry. The walls were blue with white chair rails and blue dado, bordered with gold flouncing around the cornices to match the gold valances of the draperies. Separated from the dining room by a lateral hall that connected the central hall with an outside door on the east side of the house and across the central hall from Harrison's office, was a large warming kitchen. Its brick walls and big fireplace were painted white. Big, exposed beams in the ceiling gave an impression of sturdiness. Ordinarily food was prepared in the kitchen of the smaller house in the rear and then brought to this kitchen for finishing and to be kept warm until time for it to be served.

Off the central hall upstairs were three large bedrooms and a nursery. In the master bedroom two high four-poster beds, with white canopies, extended at right angles to each other from the two blank walls. The master bed had heavy posts of elaborately carved walnut. It had a low footboard, the better to accommodate the long frame of the Governor. The other was less massive, of cherry, with high footboard. Anna used this one during the weeks surrounding child-bearing and during illnesses. A cradle at the foot of this bed provided a place for a newly-born infant until he or she was ready to go into the nursery. The room was furnished with two rocking chairs in front of the white fireplace, with cherry candlestand between, where William Henry and Anna spent many hours reading and discussing, intimidated only by the big clock that stared at them and tryannized over them from the mantle. Blue and beige oriental rugs gave a special aspect of decor to the surroundings. There were ladder-back chairs beside the beds, chests of drawers, blanket chests, mirror, corner wash stand, and towel rack. The high ceiling was white, and the walls were covered with paper printed in beige figures. Sheer white curtains covered the long windows at front and side. They were trimmed with off-white straight, floor-length draperies and valances. The guest rooms were furnished similarly, though less elaborately. They had figured pull-back draperies at the windows.

An unfinished attic provided ample storage above, and a full basement finished in brick had additional rooms with fireplaces for servants' quarters.

Immediately behind the main house, separated from it by only a few feet, was a smaller house which contained, in addition to the kitchen, a family dining room, and several more bedrooms. As the children outgrew the nursery they were assigned back bedrooms here, with a nurse nearby to look after them. All together, there were twenty-two rooms and thirteen fireplaces in the house.

The inhabitants of Vincennes looked upon the Governor's mansion, not with envy, but with pride. It seemed to symbolize the strength and significance of the territorial government, and it added to their own feeling of truly being a part of a capital city.

2b

While Tecumseh and a few others went on ahead with the horses, The Prophet was busy with a band of sixty to seventy followers on the Mississinewa River building canoes to descend to the Wabash and the Tippecanoe. One day he looked up to see the familiar figure of Little Turtle, chief of the Miamis.

Walking up directly to the Shawnee holy man, Little Turtle went straight to the point. "You must not go to the Wabash. Black Hoof, Tarhe, Five Medals, all say this is bad business, and you cannot go."

The Prophet stood up straight, defiantly, and said, "I must go. It is the will of the Master of Life."

Little Turtle warned him, "If you continue, our chiefs and their warriors will cut you off. Your scalp will hang in their lodges."

Unmoved, unintimidated, The Prophet, in a strong voice, denounced the Miami chief. "I am saddened that the great chief who led our people to a great victory against St. Clair and his Long Knives now speaks the way of the Long Knives. I will go to the Wabash and the Tippecanoe, and it is not in the power of any man to stop me. The Master of Life wants all Red Men to assemble at the mouth of the Tippecanoe. There, at a new village they will be able to watch the boundary line between the Red Men and the White Men, and if any White Man puts his foot over that line the warriors will easily push him back. When the corn is ripe, all our people in all our nations will be united, and the chiefs of the Seventeen Fires will no longer be able to cheat them out of their lands. Instead of trying to stop us from this great mission, Little Turtle, you and your warriors should be going with us. You are like a ripe apple. Your skin is red, but inside you have turned white. Now, come with us, or go!"

With no further word, Little Turtle and his party of half a dozen warriors departed. The Prophet knew that he was on

strong ground. He knew that Little Turtle represented a group of
"government chiefs" who, allowing themselves to become dependent on U.S. Government handouts, had become spokesmen for
the United States in helping to preserve their government
annuities and to preserve their influence within their own tribes
which depended largely on those payments.

On his side, The Prophet had the support of one of the most
powerful men in the whole region of the lakes—Main Poc of the
Potawatomis. It was he who had suggested that The Prophet and
his followers leave Greeneville and go to the Tippecanoe in the
lands of the Potawatomis. Born without thumb or fingers on his
left hand, Main Poc claimed that this was a special mark of
distinction from the Master of Life, and he had managed to
acquire the status in his tribe of *wabeno*, or "firehandler." Much
to the consternation of the government agents, he sympathized
with the Shawnee Prophet.

At Greeneville, The Prophet had been hard-pressed to feed the
many visitors who came long distances to hear his revelations.
Moreover, Greeneville was well within the area given up by the
Treaty. On the Tippecanoe he would be much closer to many of
his most ardent supporters such as the Kickapos and the Weas.
There, instead of being a drain on his meager resources, they
might be able to add to them.

Now, in April 1808, The Prophet and his followers moved on.
Floating down the Mississinewa and then the Wabash, they
looked in eager anticipation as they approached the mouth of the
Tippecanoe. Finding a good spot a mile farther downstream, they
landed. As they walked up through the woods, all were impressed
by the attractiveness of the place with its good trees and grass,
good water, and connecting streams that would make it easy to
travel great distances. As they walked on, the younger warriors
were amazed to see ahead of them trees without trees beyond.
They had spent their whole lives in the forest, a forest interrupted only now and then by small clearings. They had imagined
the whole world covered with trees, but here they were coming
upon an openness previously unknown to them. At the edge of
the forest, they looked out upon a sea of grass, as far as they
could see, and overhead only the vast, open sky. They felt as
though they were standing naked before Manitou. They felt a
sense of awe but also a sense of expansiveness, as though they
could ride out from here and be in touch with all of mankind.

Tecumseh and his brother had been in communication with

British officials in Canada and had been invited to come to Amherstburg, across from Detroit, for a conference. Tecumseh agreed to go to Canada while The Prophet remained to receive the influx of pilgrims which already was beginning and to supervise the construction of the new village which soon would be known far and wide as "Prophet's Town."

The village was laid out in a pattern of neatness and utility unusual for the Shawnees, and the wigwams and lodges were built with a sturdiness that suggested more than usual permanence. The bark wigwams were in orderly rows along the northwest bank of the Wabash, about a mile below the mouth of the Tippecanoe. They began about fifty yards from the river and extended up the slope through the woods to the adjoining prairie, where several wigwams were built in concentric circles around the great council house. The wigwams of Tecumseh and The Prophet were on a little knoll where they commanded a sweeping view of the Wabash in both directions.

While the men cut trees and stripped bark, the women, with some help from the men in setting the pole frame, did most of the work in constructing the wigwams. They looked for elm and birch trees for the bark. They stripped the bark from the standing trees and laid it flat on the ground under the weight of several logs, where it was left to dry to an extent. While the bark was drying they cut poles from straight young saplings and stripped the bark from them to discourage insects. They set the poles in the ground to form a frame. Three forked poles were set to support the long center pole to which all the side poles were bent and attached with strips of bark or leather thongs. Then to these they attached other long poles, the same length as the center pole and running parallel to it. They picked up the sheets of bark while they were still pliable and laid them on the cross poles. The bark was held in place by other poles laid across on the outside and tied securely to the poles within.

The building of the *Msikamekwi*, or council house, was a cooperative effort of many hands. It was a big, sturdy log structure, about 175 feet long and fifty feet wide, with gabled roof of hewn shingles. Two openings were left in the roof for the escape of smoke from the council fires. It had doors at each end but no windows. Inside, a series of three flying cross timbers, each supported by a pair of heavy timbers firmly planted in the ground, in effect posts and lintels, made a column of square arches for use in various ceremonial activities. Here is where

Tecumseh and The Prophet would meet their followers and where the tribesmen would join in special rituals on occasion.

Two other "public buildings" were to be noted. One, near the council house, was The Prophet's medicine lodge. This served as his temple and chapel. At the opposite end of the village on a low bluff overlooking the river was the "House of the Stranger." This was built of logs and bark and was the Shawnees' equivalent of a tavern where the large number of visitors could find sheltered lodging.

It took two months to complete the basic construction of Prophet's Town, and already the population had doubled the number of those who had originally moved here. By early autumn the number had reached 800 and still was growing rapidly.

At the same time cultivation went on. The prairie offered great rich fields where the women planted many acres of corn and beans and pumpkins and squash and melons, but mostly corn. The prairie also offered rich growths of grass useful for the large number of Indian ponies and horses kept there.

Prophet's Town was at an almost ideal site for communication with the Indian world. By canoe it was possible to go up the Wabash and its tributaries such as the Mississinewa and the Salamonie to Ohio, or to take a very short portage near Fort Wayne to St. Mary's River and down the Maumee to Lake Erie. Or one could go up the Tippecanoe north and northeastward until close to the Kankakee, and then go westward to the upper Illinois country, or continue upstream through a chain of sizeable lakes. Downstream, of course, there were many tributaries of the Wabash flowing across the southern part of the Territory, and then the great Ohio to the Mississippi.

A good trail, only about three feet wide but hard-packed and free of brush, ran from Prophet's Town southwest along the Wabash. Most people came to call this "Tecumseh's Trail," though Harrison sometimes referred to it as the "Appian Way." A similar trail ran along the western bank of the Tippecanoe up to the mouth of the Monon.

Prophet's Town had all the promise of becoming the capital of a pan-Indian confederation and a base of operations and training for its defense.

3a

In the spring of 1808, the growth in population and visitors at Prophet's Town were outrunning the supply of food. While Tecumseh was off on his mission to Canada, The Prophet decided to seek assistance from the White Chief himself, Governor Harrison. His immediate reference would be to give further response to the letter of the Governor that John Conner had delivered at Greeneville two years earlier. The Prophet decided that for this first contact he would remain in Prophet's Town, but would send a delegation under Blue Jacket to deliver his message to the Governor in Vincennes.

Harrison greeted the delegation on June 21 at Grouseland and invited them to deliver their message. First they presented a copy of the message that the Governor had sent by Conner, and Blue Jacket then recited the message from The Prophet:

"My Father, the paper which I now deliver to you is the speech you sent to us by Conner. When it was delivered, we were surprised to find that we had been so much misrepresented. The chief, The Prophet, has sent us to speak to you in his name.

"My Father, it never was my intention to lift up my hand against the Americans. On the contrary, we had determined to follow the advice of the Great Spirit who has told us that our former conduct is not right; and that we ought to live in peace upon the land which he has given us. This is our positive determination, and we are resolved not to listen any longer to bad advice.

"My Father, you have always told us to let you know what is doing amongst us, and I now inform you that I sent word by Conner that we were shortly to move to the Wabash. We have lately done this, and I now send some of my chiefs to visit you and to inform you that the bad reports you have heard of me are all false, and I beg you not to believe them.

"My Father, as a proof of our sincerity we have brought our women and children to reside near you. I am now very much engaged in making my new settlement, but, as soon as it is completed, I will pay you a visit to remove every bad impression you have received against me.

"Father, I hope what I now say will be engraven on your heart. It is my determination to obey the voice of the Great Spirit and live in peace with you and your people. I do not mean to do anything to risk the safety of our children, but on the contrary, to multiply them as much as possible. This is what the Great Spirit has told us repeatedly. We were all made by him although we differ a little in color. We are all his children and should live in peace and friendship with each other.

"Father, believe what I say; it is the truth. The Great Spirit has told us not to lie; you must know I did not make my own head and tongue; they were made by the Great Spirit, and I cannot lie without offending him.

"Father, in consequence of our removal we are in great distress; we hope that you will assist our women and children with a little corn. We are now planting and hope to have plenty when it is ripe.

Harrison arose from his chair and replied: "My Children, I have listened to the speech you brought me from the Shawnee chief or Prophet and now return to you my answer to which I request you to pay particular attention that you may truly repeat it to him."

"It is true that I have heard a very bad report of you—not only the White people in your country but many of the tribes, your neighbors, have taken up very unfavorable opinions of your intentions. It is believed by them that you are endeavoring to alienate the minds of the Indians from their great father, the President of the Seventeen Fires, and once more to bring them under the influence of the British, and I must confess that I have myself given credit to this report. But the solemn assurances which you now give me that you have no other object but that of making your people happy and living in peace with all mankind have in a great measure removed my prejudice, and if your subsequent conduct agrees with your present professions you may rest satisfied that you will continue to enjoy the favor and protection of the Seventeen Fires. Very different, however, will be your lot if you permit yourself to be seduced by the British agents, by those enemies to your repose and happiness who have so often deceived you and led you into difficulties and danger. You need only to recollect their conduct to you during the last war in which you were engaged with the Seventeen Fires, to know the manner in which you will be treated should you again open your ears to their counsel. It was by their persuasions that you took up the tomahawk, but they abandoned you as soon as distress came upon you and left you to the mercy of those very enemies whom you had provoked and injured to gratify their revenge and malice. How different has been the conduct of the Chief of the Seventeen Fires towards you. Like a true father he watches over your happiness and gives you the same advice that you say you have received from the Great Spirit—that is to have pity on your women and children and live in peace with all mankind. War he detests and never engages in it but in his own defense, nor will he ever condescend to ask the assistance of his Red children, confident in his own strength and knowing the calamity which war always brings on those who engage in it without sufficient cause, he is desirous that his children should remain at peace in their cabins. If any of the nations which reside beyond the great waters should provoke him to war, he is sufficiently able to punish them. He wants the aid of no power on earth and relies on his own strength and the favor of the Great Spirit who always takes the side of the injured.

"Your Father, the President, will be much pleased when he hears your determination to continue under his protection and to shut your ears against the bad talks of the people on the other side of the lakes, and I shall take care to express to him my belief in your sincerity. But I must candidly inform you that it is his positive determination, in case any of the tribes who became his children by the Treaty of Greeneville should lift up the toma-hawk against him, that he will never again make peace as long as there is one of that tribe remaining on this side of the lakes. He gives them their free choice either to live by his side in peace and happiness and receive from him every necessary aid for pro-viding a comfortable and certain subsistence for their women and children or to suffer all the calamities which the number and strength of his warriors will enable him to inflict. I do not say this with an intention to insult you. I know that the Shawnees and other tribes who have joined you are brave warriors, but the Long Knives are not less brave, and you know their numbers are as the blades of grass on the plains, or as the grains of sand on the river shore. Be wise then, and show the people who are endeavoring to seduce you that you have sense enough to distinguish the path that leads to happiness from that which would conduct you to certain misery and ruin.

"With respect to your religious opinions, they shall never be the cause of dissension and difference between us. The mild religion which we profess will not permit us to use any other means than argument and reason to induce others to adopt our opinions, and it is an inviolable rule with the Seventeen Fires to permit every man to worship the Great Spirit in the manner he may think best. I shall say nothing upon the subject of your settlement on the Wabash as that country is the property of the Miamis and we do not wish to interfere with you."

Blue Jacket responded immediately, "Father, when I return to my village with your answer every man, woman, and child will rejoice to find that you are still their friend."

Harrison then asked about the "religious opinions and pretentions" of The Prophet.

Blue Jacket answered, "I have now listened to that man for upwards of three years and have never heard him give any but good advice. He tells us that we must pray to the Great Spirit who made the world and everything in it for our use. He tells us that no man could make the trees and the plants and the animals, but that these must be made by the Great Spirit to whom we ought to pray and whom we ought to obey in all things. He tells us not to lie, to steal, not to drink whiskey, not to go to war but to live in peace with all mankind. He tells us all to work and make corn."

Harrison said that in order to assist in that work he would give them a plough and some hoes.

Obviously pleased, Blue Jacket said, "Father, you can give us nothing that will be more acceptable to us. We are not now ashamed to work and make corn for our women and children."

Before the delegation departed, Harrison also arranged to give them a quantity of corn to carry back to their village.

Harrison felt reassured by the meeting. He saw that the teachings of The Prophet could be an asset in improving relations with the Indians. He told Elihu Stout, "I believe The Prophet is an influential fanatic who may be a useful instrument to forward the benevolent views of our Government in introducing amongst the Indians the arts of civilized life."

In Prophet's Town, both Tecumseh and The Prophet were delighted. Tecumseh had returned from Canada with assurances of British assistance, and now the delegation had returned from Vincennes with assurances of the Long Knives' friendship and assistance, not to mention a supply of food when supplies were running very low. The two leaders agreed that this would be a good time for The Prophet to visit the White Chief in person to consolidate their gains. A message to Vincennes brought a response that the Governor would indeed be pleased to receive

The Prophet at the middle of August.

Harrison told his aides to prepare for the conference. "And oh, Tom," he said to Thomas Randolph, "be sure to have plenty of whiskey on hand here. That ought to be a good test of The Prophet's powers. If he can keep his followers away from that firewater, he must be a prophet."

On the fifteenth of August, The Prophet arrived at Vincennes with over two hundred disciples. They made camp along the river, just above the town. The next day, as townspeople stopped to look in amazement, the Shawnee holy man, with a retinue of thirty warriors, marched through the town to Grouseland. Wearing light doeskin pantaloons and moccasins, a brown, armless, fringed linen hunting shirt, an open orange and blue turban, a ring through his nose, a thin mustache above his lips, three feathers through one ear lobe and medallions hanging from both ears, with medallions and strings of beads around his neck, a pair of broad silver bracelets on each arm, his one good eye, his left, looking ahead, he left no doubt among the curious onlookers as to his identity.

Harrison himself was curious to meet this strange Indian evangelist about whom he had heard so much. He greeted him cordially in front of Grouseland and invited him to a chair on the lawn. John Gibson, Joseph Baron, Thomas Randolph, and several other men were beside the Governor. They went out to greet the Indian followers of The Prophet, to engage them in conversation and to offer them refreshment. Baron offered whiskey to each of them. Not one accepted.

The Prophet addressed the Governor with a long speech:

"Father, I have had no other intention but to introduce among the Indians those good principles of religion which the White People profess. I heard, when I settled on the Wabash, that my Father, the Governor, had declared that all the land between Vincennes and Fort Wayne was the property of the Seventeen Fires. I heard that you wanted to know, my Father, whether I was god or man, and that you said if I was the former I should not steal horses. I heard this from Mr. Wells, but I believe it originated with himself."

"I told all the Redskins that the way they were in was not good, and that they ought to abandon it; that we ought to consider ourselves as one man, but we ought to live agreeably to our several customs, the Red People after their mode and the White People after theirs; particularly that they should not drink whiskey, that it was not made for them, that it is the cause of all the mischiefs which the Indians suffer. Determine to listen to nothing that is bad. Do not take up the tomahawk should it be offered by the British or by the Long Knives.

"Brother, I speak to you as a warrior. You are one. But let us lay aside this character and attend to the care of our children, that they may live in comfort and peace."

During a two-week stay in the area, The Prophet met several more times with the Governor who continued to be favorably impressed with what he heard. Even more impressive were The Prophet's daily religious meetings with his followers. With expressions and gestures that firmly held the attention of his listeners, he repeatedly denounced the use of firewater and professed the ways of peace in the name of *Manitou* and *Wishemenetoo.*

At the conclusion of the conference, Harrison again gave the visitors food and tools. He reported to Secretary of War Henry Dearborn, "The influence which The Prophet has acquired will prove advantageous rather than otherwise to the United States."

4

"I say, Governor, where did you get this beer?" asked Dr. John Scott with a broad smile, as he held out his glass for a refill, while the Harrisons and the Scotts sat on the Grouseland lawn overlooking the river on a warm afternoon in September.

"Made it myself," replied William Henry Harrison as he refilled Scott's glass from a pitcher.

"Well, I didn't know you were a brewmaster in addition to all your other talents. Where did you learn that?"

"Self-taught. I ordered a book from Albany last winter, and when it got here I put it to use. Anyway, this beats that spruce beer they used to give us in the Army, doesn't it?"

"I'll have to agree with that," Scott said. "You grow your own hops, I suppose."

"That's right. And the barley, too. Right out there on my little corner of prairie land."

"And you have plenty of water right here in the river."

"I dare say the Wabash would make pretty good beer. I'm sure it would be especially tasteful in late summer when the water stagnates among the weeds. No, I should think you would appreciate the good spring water that goes in it."

"Oh, I do, I do. I must say it is very refreshing on a day like this."

Anna Harrison and Alice Scott contented themselves with cool apple juice.

Anna turned to the doctor and said, "John, I'm so glad you are here in such good time this year. I thought you were not going to make it in time for Benjamin."

"No, you crossed me up on that one. You had established such a regular pattern of September or October that it did not occur to me he would be arriving in May. And here I am, in September again, but now you tell me I am three or four months ahead of time."

"But John, and Alice, we are so glad you are here. Why don't you just move to Vincennes? We have been urging that for years."

Alice spoke up quickly, "I guess I would see more of my husband if we just moved here as long as you keep on having children as fast as you do, and as long as he insists on bringing every one of them into the world."

"But look what a fine job he has done," said Harrison.

"Oh, yes, you have six now, don't you, six healthy ones."

"Yes, little Benjamin is the sixth," Harrison responded. "Some of the folks refer to my father as Benjamin the Fifth, just to distinguish him from all the Benjamins before him. Of course that made my oldest brother Benjamin the Sixth, but our little Benjamin is also Benjamin the Sixth, Benjamin the Sixth Child. And now we await for number seven. But you only have the two children, don't you?"

Alice shot back, "What more could you expect with my husband all the time going off to Vincennes? If there were fewer Harrisons maybe there would be more Scotts!"

"Oh, there are already so many Scots that they have their own country, and half of them have come over here. What would we do with any more?"

The doctor chimed in, "I guess you already have a Harrison county, don't you? Are you trying for a whole state now?"

John and Alice Scott and their daughter and son, aged six and four, were house guests at Grouseland for several weeks this fall.

Alice was of somewhat larger build than Anna Harrison, and she had light brown hair and brown eyes. She was talkative and witty, and also reliable and sincere. John was three inches shorter than Harrison, of slender build, with thin wavy hair of dark brown, and blue-gray eyes. He was studious and had a voice deeper and more resonant than might be expected from one of his size and build.

Harrison had enjoyed John Scott's company ever since their meeting in the Army. Although they had been widely separated for most of the last eight years, Harrison always considered him one of his closest friends, and always looked forward to his biennial visits. Now they were so often seen together around Vincennes that the people of the town referred to them as "David and Jonathan."

The Scotts stayed longer than they had intended, but after all, the doctor did have to await the arrival of the new baby. Mary Symmes Harrison was born on January 22, 1809.

There was a January thaw which allowed the Scotts to find a boat to get them back to Louisville from whence they could get a coach to Frankfort. But the rest of the winter was a cold one, and heavy snows persisted for weeks at a time.

5a

After the long, hard winter, the people of Vincennes greeted the spring with even more enthusiasm than usual. The first festival of the year, celebrating the return of life to the earth and when Christians commemorated the crucifixion and resurrection of Jesus of Nazareth, was Easter. The time for the observance of Easter varied from year to year. It was reckoned as the first Sunday after the first full moon after the vernal equinox.

Actually, this celebration began with a festive occasion which had become traditional in the French community. This was known as "Mardi Gras" or "Fat Tuesday." This was the day before Ash Wednesday which marked the beginning of Lent, a season of forty days—forty to serve as a reminder of the forty days that Jesus fasted in the wilderness—before Easter. This year, 1809, Mardi Gras, or "Shrove Tuesday," fell on February 15. The weather was cold, but the celebrants tried to overcome that with their enthusiasm, and Graeter's tavern cooperated with a good supply of stimulants.

While most of the others watched, the French inhabitants, at least the more hardy among them, formed at the St. Xavier Church for an afternoon parade. Ahead of the procession, a farmer, in the old Parisian tradition, drove a fat ox down the street. Then came the parade of masked people, dressed in colorful and grotesque costumes representing all kinds of animals and birds and spirits. Some of the neighborhood Indians joined in the parade, and it was hard to tell the difference. It ended at Graeter's Tavern. Those who could make it went back to the church for a feast, while others waited. The French ate rather better than their Anglo-American counterparts. For their feast, they had soups and fricassees and gumbos in addition to a very tender roast beef which had been marinated in wine. All of them spent most of the night in the taverns, drinking and singing and dancing to the strains of the fiddlers' music.

William Henry Harrison and the older children watched most of the parade and then hurried back to the warmth of Grouseland. There they entertained a large number of guests—the Parkes, the Vigos, the Taylors, Thomas Randolph, and a dozen others—at a pancake supper in recognition of the traditional English "Pancake Tuesday." It was Anna's first day "out" since the birth of Mary Symmes.

After this celebration, presumably marking the end of the winter carnival season, came six weeks of fasting for Catholics and Episcopalians, though other Protestants paid little heed to that aspect.

Easter, April 2, still was early in the season, but a warm, spring day broke the siege of cold weather.

The Harrisons, including all six of the children who could walk, attended services at the Presbyterian Church. Anna had a new dress for the occasion. It was blue muslin with a short waist and very narrow skirt. She wore a dark cape to protect her from the cool air. Her gray Roram felt hat, with purple and green feathers and gold band, hid most of her new coiffure, though dark curls, only on the left side, came down almost to her shoulder. Harrison had a handsome new wool great coat, beaver top hat, and boots in the new style of differentiation for right and left foot.

At the church service everyone who had been baptized and who had confirmed belief in Jesus Christ as Lord and Saviour were invited to partake of communion. In this ceremony the minister asked blessing for unleavened bread, and then said, "The Lord Jesus the same night in which he was betrayed took bread, and when he had given thanks, he brake it, and said, 'Take, eat; this is my body which is broken for you. This do in remembrance of me.'" And then all of the people ate a morsel of the bread.

Then the minister continued, "After the same manner, also he took the cup, when he had supped, saying, 'This cup is the new testament in my blood. This do ye, as oft as ye drink it, in remembrance of me.' For as often as ye eat this bread and drink this cup, ye do show the Lord's death till he come."

After an Easter dinner of ham and stewed apples and cakes, the Governor and his lady received callers in the afternoon.

They were more grateful than ever for an hour to relax that evening in their bedroom. They sat in their respective rocking chairs and took long breaths of air.

Harrison, noticing Anna's new "one-sided" hair-do, and always mindful of how she loved to sit in her chair and have him comb her hair, often for as long as she could persuade him, volunteered, "My dear, would you like for me to comb your hair?"

"Please do," she called as she tossed it across the room to his lap. Anna had succumbed to the new fashion and cut her hair short, to be covered with a wig which would take much less time and trouble to keep neat and orderly. Almost as soon as she had done it, she regretted it, but not nearly so much as her husband did. Still he could not deny the convenience of her new arrangement. Actually she had two wigs, One for dress on special occasions, the one with long curls in a one-sided effect, and the other for daily wear, done in small, tight curls in a kind of "poodle-dog" effect. This one Harrison did not care for at all.

"Oh, Henry, it is such a convenience, but I promise I'll have my own hair grown out by the time we have our next baby."

"In that case, let us make that as soon as possible!" He admired rather more her new dress. "What a relief it must be to get rid of all those hoops and bustles and everything."

"Oh, yes, and the corsets, too. And all those extra petticoats."

"Yes," Harrison laughed. "They can't accuse us of having petticoat government now, can they?"

"I guess not."

"But of course there may be other problems?"

"Like what?"

"Do you realize how many women in hoop skirts have had their skirts catch fire when they unknowingly passed too close to a fireplace?"

"Oh, yes, I'm sure that was a hazard," acknowledged Anna.

"But I recently read in the paper an account of the new fashion in London. It said that in one year in London eighteen ladies caught fire, and eighteen thousand caught cold!"

"Oh, Henry."

With spring came the opening of the river. It amounted to another holiday when all the town turned out to see the first flotilla of flatboats and barges laden with furs, salt pork, venison, hams, whiskey, and peach brandy start down the river for New Orleans.

Within the next few weeks, a number of men would be off to visit their friends "in town," all the way down to New Orleans, or up the Wabash and the Tippecanoe to the portage at Fort Wayne, and then down the Maumee to Lake Erie—Lake Ontario —and the St. Lawrence to Quebec.

5b

At Prophet's Town, the principal festival of spring, for celebrating the beginning of a new year, was the Spring Bread Dance, sometimes referred to in French as *le Feu Nouveau*, and the first football game. The time was the time of the first full moon after the arrival of spring, but this was not reckoned according to any set calendar. The arrival of spring was taken as the time when the bluebirds returned from the south, and when the wild geese and wild ducks departed for the north, when buds appeared on the trees and the first flowers appeared in the woods. This usually was in April (according to the Christian calendar), though the persistence of the cold winter made it a little later this year than usual, the first of May.

Prophet's Town was not, strictly speaking, a tribal village. It welcomed all tribes. But the rituals and dances and games generally followed the Shawnee tradition, with certain modifications in keeping with the position and teachings of The Prophet, and with certain additions out of deference to their great leader, Tecumseh.

After the first full moon of spring had shone on the Wabash, The Prophet called the people together to announce that the time had come for the Bread Dance by which to honor Manitou, the Master of Life, and their Grandmother, Wishemenetoo, the Great Spirit, to thank them for seeing their people through another winter, and to ask their blessing for the planting of crops in the new year. Tecumseh appointed a group of twelve men to serve as the hunters for the feast, and Tecumapease appointed twelve women who would serve as the cooks and make other preparations. He also appointed Wabethe—the Swan—(now in her fifties) the wife of Blue Jacket, to be "Queen" of the football game.

Wabethe attended to the making of the football. She took two round pieces of tanned buckskin, eight to ten inches in diameter, and carefully sewed them together except for a three-inch opening on one side. Then she turned it inside out in order to protect the seams, stuffed it tightly with deer hair, and then sewed the opening.

At the same time some of the twelve women whom Tecumapease had appointed were making a prayer hoop. For this they took an oak sapling about nine feet tall, trimmed it, peeled the bark, and shaved it to a thickness of about one inch. Then they bent it into a circle and tied the small end where it overlapped the larger, as a symbol of growing. The hoopmaker carried the hoop into the Medicine Lodge and laid it in the center of the floor. Wabethe took the football in and placed it in the center of the hoop. Then all twelve women filed in and seated themselves in a semicircle around one side of the hoop. Each attached a small buckskin packet containing a particular kind of seed: red corn, white corn, yellow corn, ordinary squash, small native squash, brown beans, red beans, white beans, pumpkin, cucumber, watermelon, muskmelon. The women then filed out of the lodge, and the twelve men filed in. They sat in a semicircle on the opposite side of the hoop from where the women had sat, and they tied four items to that side—a tuft of skunk fur, racoon fur, deer hair, and a turkey feather. The head man put the hoop around his neck, picked up the football, and led the men outside. He handed the football to Wabethe who fell in behind the column of men, and the twelve cooks followed, single file, behind her. As the column walked out, the whole village followed en masse to the game field, a broad, open field just beyond the ceremonial grounds. En route the head man hung the hoop on the limb of a tree as a sacrifice.

Wabethe proceeded directly to the field and stood on the sideline midway between the two ends while the teams formed.

The football game was a religious occasion, but for the Shawnee such an event was supposed to be joyful and cheerful and merry, one that would please the Master of Life.

The contest was a match of men versus women. Everyone who

wished to do so could play, and everyone else watched with almost as much animation.

The field was in the form of a square about eighty yards in each direction. Two stakes, set about twenty feet apart, marked the goal at each end, east and west. There were no strict boundary lines, but the ball had to pass between the stakes from the front to be a score. Rules established by long tradition required the men and boys to advance the ball only by kicking it, while the women and girls might throw it, run with it, or kick it. On the other hand, if a woman were holding the ball, a man might grab it or knock it from her grasp, or if she were running with it, a man might impede her progress by holding or even tackling her. The side which first scored ten goals or the side which had scored the most goals at sunset (about two hours after the starting time), when the game had to stop, was the winner.

A matronly woman chief of the Delawares was designated the score keeper. She sat on the ground where she had in a little bowl twenty grains of corn. Whenever anyone scored, she would put down a grain of corn on her right or left side to show which side had scored. The losers would have to gather the wood and build the fires for the feast and dances which would follow three days later.

About sixty players, ranging in age from eight to seventy, volunteered for each side. They took their places, the women with their backs to the sun, defending the west goal, and the men facing the sun. Tecumseh stood at the front and center of the men, Tecumapease at a similar position with the women.

All became quiet as Wabethe raised the ball to signal that the game was about to commence. She tossed it high into the air toward the center of the field, to the accompaniment of a great roar of anticipation by participants and spectators alike as the players struggled for possession.

A gust of wind curved the ball in the direction of the women. Tecumapease grabbed it and immediately threw it to a younger girl. But Tecumseh had anticipated this move. He quickly knocked the ball from the girl's hands to the ground, and maneuvering it with great agility from one foot to the other, he went flying down the field while most of the defenders looked on in such awe that they were helpless. Without any interference he ran straight to the goal and kicked the ball through. Then, having made his point, the Chief retired to the sideline to watch the remainder of the game.

Again Wabethe tossed up the ball at the center of the field. Again, but with a great deal more effort, the men scored. Next time, a young lad was going down the field, kicking the ball as he went, when one of the strong girls simply ran over and jumped on the ball and fell on it. In doing so she absorbed a kick from the boy's moccasin-covered foot, but she quickly tossed the ball to another strong girl who ran with it down the sideline and then over to the goal, where she threw it in.

After half an hour the men were leading 3 to 2, and by now most of the younger children, fatigued from constant running and yelling, had joined the chief on the sidelines.

On one occasion a young woman fell on a loose ball and then just lay there crouching over it, holding so tightly that no one could touch it; then two warriors simply picked her up, ball and all, and carried her across the goal line for a score.

The men were ahead by three goals, 7 to 4, at the end of an hour, with about an hour yet remaining before sunset. The men, much faster and stronger, had dominated most of the game, but as time went on the endurance of the women became more apparent.

"Throw the ball high! Throw it high!" called Tecumapease. The women responded in throwing the ball to each other in high arcs which resulted in sun-blinding the men as they tried to follow it, and then a girl would grab it and run it to the goal. By these and other devious means, they managed to tie the score at 8 to 8.

At this point a seventy-year old squaw got the ball at midfield, and a seventy-year old warrior took after her. All the others parted and shouted encouragement as they let the elders go after it. Finally, the man caught the woman and stopped her with a stand-up tackle. Then he grabbed the ball from her hands and pulled with such force that he reeled back, off balance. She pushed him to the ground. As he hit, he dropped the ball. She picked it up and tossed it to one of the girls, amidst wild cheering. The girl ran with it, dodged, ran back toward her own goal, and then, at the urging and direction of Tecumapease six girls formed a column behind her as she started toward the far goal. As a man grabbed her, she tossed it off to the next girl, now running up beside her. This one in turn ran about ten steps when she was grabbed, and then she tossed it off to the next girl coming up on her right side. In this way, the column of six girls was able to take the ball all the way to the goal line and make another score.

The men caught the next toss-up and began kicking the ball from one to another until a woman intercepted it. Then she began running around in circles until about thirty women gathered all around her. They concealed the ball completely as Tecumapease took it and tucked it under her skirt. Then one after another of the other women, pretending to have the ball, began running down the field, each with a group of men in pursuit while Tecumapease very unobtrusively trotted in a wide arc to the goal, and, with a loud whoop, threw the ball in. That completed the victory. Now the men would be stuck with a task for which they were relatively unaccustomed—gathering the wood and building the fires for the big celebration.

Immediately after the football game, the twelve hunters, each carrying only a pouch of parched corn for food, left on horseback in quest of game for the feast. For this occasion the game would include only deer, squirrel, turkey, and grouse.

At sunrise on the third day after the departure of the hunters, the people gathered at the ceremonial grounds adjacent to the Medicine Lodge to greet them on their return. As they came in with their bags of game, the twelve women cooks took the game, dressed it, and put it on to cook.

The hunters formed a single file behind their leader and walked over to where four singers, each with a water drum, waited for them. The water drum was made by stretching and tying a soaked and wrung-out buckskin over a flat-bottomed crock or section of hollow log sealed at the bottom. The drums were partially filled with water, so that the tone of each differed according to the water level. A piece of charcoal, symbolic of the sacred fire, also was put into the water of the drum, and this contact of fire and water, known as important truth bearers, would help carry the prayers to Manitou. The drumsticks were of black walnut with a rounded knob on each end. The singers also had rattlers made of gourds or turtle backs to accompany their music.

As the singers began their series of songs to the beat of their drums, the hunters moved slowly in a circle to perform their preliminary dance. They continued that dance, stepping first on the ball of one foot and then the heel, and then the ball of the other foot and then the heel, until the singers completed their series of four sacred songs. Then the women brought out breakfast for them.

In the late morning, the women cooks brought out the roasted venison, the baked turkey and grouse, the fried squirrel, and several kinds of corn bread—some which had been wrapped in corn husks and boiled, some which had been fried in big skillets, some which had been baked in reflector ovens—and laid it all on white linen cloths at the center of the grounds. Then they covered the food with other cloths. The people gathered around, and The Prophet stepped up on a low log platform to offer the prayer.

"Oh, Manitou, our Master of Life, we look to you to guide us in the planting of our corn and beans and pumpkins and melons, that we may have abundant crops for food for our people. We also pray that you will put more birds and more animals in the forest, and more fish in the rivers, so that our hunters may find them for food for our people. We also thank you, our Master of Life, for all the game that our hunters have found in the great winter just passed. We hope that we may act in a way that will be pleasing to you, and we ask your help in the year ahead in making our people safe from the attacks of enemies, rich in food and good health, and free in their hunting and in their wigwams, until the time when all may enjoy the everlasting bounty and safety of your paradise."

At this point, all the women moved to form a compact group in front of the singers, and, standing in place, they swayed right and left as they joined in another series of sacred chants. After this, each of the two preparatory groups, the twelve hunters and the twelve cooks, went out to form circles around the food, the men on the inside, the women on the outside. Many of the other people then followed the lead of those two groups in the dance as the singing and the drum beating went on and on.

Then it was time to eat. The twelve hunters distributed the bread, and the twelve cooks distributed the meat.

At dusk the losers in the football game lit up huge fires all around the ceremonial field to give plenty of light. Now painted in red and with decorative feathers and other ornaments, everyone began dancing as the singers took up their long, rhythmic chants and drum beating again. The people were in a holiday mood. The men would go into a dance, and the women would call out, "The women conquered the men in football, as in everything else!"

The women would go into a dance, and the men would shout, "The men will conquer all!"

As the drums sounded the rhythm, BOOM, boom; BOOM,

boom; BOOM, boom; BOOM, boom, the dancers followed, TOE, heel; TOE, heel; TOE, heel; TOE, heel.

Later dances were in slower, more deliberate rhythm, with a loud beat on the drums, followed by three soft beats—BOOM, boom, boom, boom, BOOM, boom, boom, boom. Following the rhythm of the drums, the dancers would plant their toes on the loud beat and then move the heels up and down on the soft beat, first the left and then the right—LEFT, two, three, four; RIGHT, two three, four; LEFT, two, three four; RIGHT, two, three, four—on and on around the circle.

As the night went on, the occasions became more frequent when men and women danced together. For these dances the woman usually would choose her partner by lining up behind the brave that she chose. She always carried a handkerchief over her hand as she grasped hands with the others in going around a circle, but a few young women could be seen here and there who offered their bare hands to the braves in front of them. This was a signal that they would accept the attention of the particular one, with a possible hope of marriage.

With fires glowing brightly and the late-night half moon shining, the dancing continued until sunrise. Then the weary revelers returned to their respective wigwams. At dawn, Wabethe planted the twenty grains of corn that had been used to keep score at the football game. That was the signal that all planting could begin.

In the festivities of the Spring Bread Dance, the people at Prophet's Town looked forward with hope to escape from a disastrous winter. In December, many of them had been reduced to eating their horses and dogs. In February and March, many of them had succumbed to whooping cough, another of the dreaded White Man's diseases that ravaged the Indians. Strangely, the malady had affected mainly the northern tribesmen who had come to Prophet's Town. While the Master of Life had taken 160 Ottawas and Chippewas, he had claimed only five Shawnees. To them, this meant either that The Prophet had lost his powers, or that he was using them selectively in favoring his own Shawnees. When the bluebirds heralded the arrival of spring, the Ottawas and the Chippewas, frightened and disillusioned, followed the wild geese back toward the Lakes.

6

In the late spring of 1809, William Henry Harrison was worried by continued reports of hostile plans and activities at Prophet's Town. Hearing rumors that The Prophet was planning an immediate attack against Vincennes, the Governor called out two companies of militia. Harrison sent two spies, in the guise of traders, to Prophet's Town, and they returned with reports of some hostile activity there, but reports also of the defection of the Ottawas and Chippewas. Tecumseh now was in the Illinois country.

For his part, The Prophet took pains to defend himself against attacks by the dissident tribes, and to allay American suspicions. For the first, General Hull at Detroit came to his rescue when the American commander in the North warned the Ottawas and Chippewas against attacking the Shawnees. For the other part, The Prophet accepted an invitation to visit the new agent at Fort Wayne, John Johnston, whom he was able to impress with his peaceful intentions. Now he felt the need for another call upon the Governor at Vincennes.

In late June the Shawnee holy man arrived in Vincennes with forty followers. Going directly to Grouseland, he found Harrison rather cooler than on their previous meeting. This time as The Prophet repeated his assurances, Harrison remained skeptical.

"Why is it," the Governor wanted to know, "that you have seen fit to meet and counsel with large numbers of Red men of other tribes who are known to be hostile to the Seventeen Fires?"

"My Father, it is true that I have met with tribes who were hostile to the Seventeen Fires and to my White Father. They were made hostile by the Red Coats. I met with them to advise them that they should not listen to the Red Coats and should not make war against the Long Knives."

"But my Brother," Harrison came back, "why did you not inform me? Why did you not report to us this conspiracy by the Red Coats, the British?"

"My Father, it was not necessary, because I was able to convince them to give up their hostile intentions."

"And what is your brother, Tecumseh, doing on the Mississippi?"

"My brother, Tecumseh, still seeks to unite all Red Men, but my Father, it was only by him that the tribes near the Mississippi, the Winnebagoes and the Sacs and Foxes were persuaded not to attack the White fort called Fort Madison, as the Red Coats advised them to do."

Harrison still was not convinced.

The conversations dragged on for ten days. At the last one, The Prophet spurted out with some feeling, "I hate, I despise your feast days, and I will not smell in your solemn assemblies. Though you offer me your meat and corn, I will not accept them; neither will I regard your fat beasts. Take away from me the noise of your songs, for I will not hear the melody of your viols. But let judgment run down as waters and righteousness as a mighty stream!"

Those words struck Harrison forcefully. He could not get them out of his mind.

That evening Anna asked him, as she was want to do, "Well, Henry, how did you get along with The Prophet this time?"

"I tell you, Anna, this man is a fanatic, and he is gaining a big following. He may be dangerous."

Anna, smiling indulgently, said, "It seems to me the Romans once said that about a prophet in Palestine, that he was a fanatic, was gaining a big following, and might be dangerous."

"Surely you are not comparing this pagan savage to Jesus Christ!"

"No, of course not, not for us. But for the Indians there might appear to be some similarities."

"I tell you, Anna, this man is a liar and a rascal."

"Oh, that's a little different from your opinion of last year when you thought he might be useful in controlling the Indians."

"Yes, it is. Now, after all of his solemn promises of peace I see evidence of all kinds of hostile intent and conspiracy. I must say that my suspicions have been more strengthened than diminished by every interview I have had with him since he has been here."

"What is it? Have he and his followers taken up firewater again?"

"No, no they haven't, and I do have to give him credit for that. It's just that he keeps bringing in these hostile tribes and seems continually susceptible to British manipulation."

"Then it's the British who may be more successful in using him to control the Indians?"

"Well, not exactly, but more and more they seem to be in cahoots." Harrison paused a moment and then went on, "But I must say he made a very impassioned statement at our last meeting. I can't get it out of my mind. It sounds very familiar."

"What was it?"

He started out, "I hate, I despise your feast days...."

"Mmm," she pondered. "That sounds a bit like one of the Old Testament prophets, doesn't it?"

"Mmm, Old Testament; yes, I think you're right." Harrison picked up his Bible and began thumbing through it. "But which one? Which one?"

"Sounds like Amos to me."

Harrison turned to that book and began scanning the pages. "Yes, here it is, in the Eighth chapter." He read it to her. Then he repeated the last verse—'But let judgment run down as waters, and righteousness as a mighty stream.' Yes, I must say, he has learned some things pretty well from some of those missionaries, hasn't he? But I must say too, I think The Prophet could have written this himself. But I keep thinking about it, and I keep asking myself, what is righteousness? Let righteousness run as a mighty stream, but what is it?"

"I guess that's what the whole Good Book is about, isn't it?"

7a

The principal summer festival in Vincennes was the Fourth of July. This year, in keeping with the custom, the military company from Fort Knox and companies of volunteer militia paraded, and all the people gathered near a spring about three-quarters of a mile up the Wabash from the town. The sun was hot, and people sought shade where they could, but all were in a holiday mood. The ladies had tried to outdo each other in preparing roast beef, chicken, pork, turkey, wheat bread, corn bread, cakes, and fruit pies for a big dinner at noontime. For the ceremonies of toasts and orations that followed, Governor Harrison acted as president, and Secretary Gibson as vice president. As an opener one of the volunteers of the Vincennes Light Infantry sang a song which he had written for the occasion:

> Proclaim loud the day
> The Sons of Liberty
> With hearts of freedom and boast
> Our great Jubilee.
> Be mindful the praise,
> Ever view what it cost
> What perils, what tortures,
> What blood hath been lost.

Chorus
Be this happy theme
To posterity joined
Whilst ages endure,
And the sun circling round.

Then the crowd joined the Governor and the Secretary in drinking seventeen toasts.

"The United States—may the principles which gave birth to this memorable epoch in her history, descend unsullied from generation to generation, until nations shall cease to exist."

"The patriots of '76—may their fame be as lasting as the principles they established."

"The heroes of the Revolution, their arms defended, and their blood sealed the liberties of America—shall they not live in the hearts of their countrymen?"

"The Congress of the United States—wise, dignified, and patriotic; let the good of the nation be its leading star."

"The memory of Washington—the glory of ancient and modern heroes sink before the lustre of his name—they fought for empire or fame—he, to wrest the sceptre from a tryant."

"The President of the United States—a successor worthy of Jefferson."

"The Sage of Monticello—author of the Declaration of Independence—his public services entitle him to the gratitude and love of a people who value the independence and happiness of their country."

"The militia of the United States—arms in the hands of its citizens is the sure and natural defense of republics."

"The Army and Navy of the United States."

"The Embargo—wise in its policy, happy in its effects."

"A friendly adjustment of our differences with all nations upon honorable and equal terms."

"The Legislature of Indiana—may local politics and party considerations never influence its proceedings."

"The Volunteer Battalion of Knox County—the honors of their country and the smiles of the fair shall reward their sacrifices and their gallantry."

"Republics throughout the world."

"The American Fair."

From there followed a siege of toasts offered by "volunteers"—to "Govenor Harrison—the friend of the people—his virtuous administration and public services merit the plaudits of his countrymen and cast a shade over the political schemes of his enemies."—to the Secretary of the Territory—to Judge Parke, and Judge Vanderburgh.

Harrison added two toasts of his own—"the people of Indiana—may they estimate the merits of their officers by the performance of their duties, not by the opinions of partymen and zealots."—and to "Ephraim Jordon—the major of the Volunteer battalion—he was ready; why did not the enemy appear?"

A Delaware Chief known as "Captain Bullit" offered a toast —"Health and prosperity to the gentlemen present."

At the end, some unknown supporter of Harrison offered this toast to the Governor's most bitter political enemy—"Jonathan Jennings—the semblance of a delegate—his want of abilities, the only safety of the people." Groans rippled through the crowd at that one.

Jennings, only a few weeks previously, had won the election for territorial delegate in Congress over Thomas Randolph, Harrison's close friend and attorney-general.

The Fourth of July toast became a subject of controversy in the local newspaper. Elihu Stout, the editor, insinuated that the toast had been dictated by Randolph or Harrison himself. Not so, maintained a firm Harrison supporter who wrote:

I have hitherto remained a silent, tho' not disinterested spectator, of your feeble and ineffectual efforts to sully the fair name of Governor Harrison, and Thos. Randolph, Esq., two as respectable citizens as Indiana ever has, or probably ever will possess—it is not my design to write a panegyric on the virtues of those gentlemen, their characters need not such a prop; they are founded upon the broad basis of moral and political rectitude, and will be held in veneration by the friends of Independence, when Scotch tories, and apostate republicans are buried in oblivion, or remembered only with merited execration.

The writer went on to say that the toast "was not dictated...by governor Harrison or Mr. Randolph, but was given by a private citizen, as I believe under a firm persuasion that Jennings was the humble tool of a base and designing faction."

Summer was a time for fun and games as well as for hard work on the farms and in the gardens. The seven Harrison children were in constant motion around Grouseland, and often they attracted the children of friends and neighbors in the town to join in their activity. The boys played marbles and leap frog. They competed in the hop, step, and jump, and in the high jump, and they made up games of town ball, a variation of English cricket played with a ball and bat on a field marked with a batter's box and four bases.

The Indian boy, Beaver, slept with the servants, but he often joined the Harrison boys at play. This summer, by his own wish, he left to rejoin his people on the upper Mississinewa.

Older men in the town competed in all kinds of contests from marbles to pick-up horse racing.

One Saturday afternoon, Harrison was out riding around the outskirts of Vincennes when he came upon a crowd of men who were shouting and jumping as horsemen took turns in rushing by a tree and trying to grab a goose that was suspended from the limb of a tree. Coming closer Harrison could see that the feathers had been picked from the neck of an old gander, and then grease had been applied to the neck. The goose was tied by the feet to the limb. As it came a man's turn, he would jump on a horse, bareback, and as members of the crowd gave the horse a sharp lick, he would go off with a start, and the rider would try to grab the goose by the neck and pull its head off. Several tried without being able to get a firm hold.

As Harrison rode up, one of the young men shouted, "Hey, Governor, the goose hangs high, what!"

Harrison laughed. He watched the next competitor get a firm hold of the gander's neck, but it was too tough for him, and he fell off the horse. This disqualified him. The next rider was successful in pulling off the head. Harrison grimaced at the sight.

After the cheering had subsided, Harrison called out, "Boys, may I propose another contest as an alternative?"

"What is it, Governor?"

"I'll challenge you to spearing rings."

"How's that?"

"First let's get some tree branches and bend twigs into rings about this big." Dismounting from his horse, Harrison took a twig and formed a ring in demonstration. He continued, "All right, let's make several."

Willing hands followed his instructions. Now, getting back up on his horse, he suspended the ring from the tree limb with a length of thong from his saddle. "Now, lads, I need a pole about six feet long—let's strip that sapling over there."

In minutes the fresh, green pole was in Harrison's hands. He rode up twenty-five yards, turned, and came back at a full gallop. He thrust the pole at the ring and barely missed as a gust of wind blew it to the side.

"Anyway, you see the object," he explained. "Everyone who wants to take a few practice runs should do so. For this it's better if you saddle up. Let the goose be the prize. The winner will be the one who spears the most rings in three tries—and you have to be at a full gallop!"

Harrison waited until the others had finished. Of the eight who took part, four failed every time, three got one, and one got two. Harrison promptly completed his turns with three. And he rode off with the goose tied to his saddle.

Later, on the other side of town, up near Fort Knox, Harrison came upon an even larger group of men engaging in their favorite sport—shooting at marks. Soldiers from the fort and local citizens all were participating. Harrison always encouraged this because he was anxious to do all possible to have an effective militia as a defense force, and he considered marksmanship some of the best training of all. He was pleased to see that many of the men were shooting well, though none was doing as well as he thought he should.

"If someone will lend me a rifle, I'll challenge your winner. I'll put up this goose against your side of beef."

"You mean the loser gets the goose, Governor?"

"The loser has to take the goose."

The marks had been made by mounting strips of white paper in a cross, an X, on a board, and the X enclosed in a circle about eight inches across. The agreement was for five shots each. The score would be determined by measuring the total distance of the bullets from the center of the X. The range was one hundred yards.

Steven Spencer, a farmer and hunter, was the winner so far. While he prepared his rifle, Harrison looked over several that were offered to him and chose one that he liked.

"Since this weapon is unknown to me, may I try it out first?" he asked.

"Of course," Spencer said. "Shoot as many practice shots as you want."

Harrison carefully measured the powder and poured it in the chamber, took a greased patch and ran it down the barrel, and rammed home the wad and the ball with the hickory ramrod. He checked the flint, then took careful aim and squeezed the trigger. He fired three shots and then went down and inspected the results. He had a good shot group, but all were wide of the mark, about eight inches to the left—not even within the circle. Now he took a stick and measured the precise distance from the center of the mark to the center of his shot group. Then just as carefully, he took the stick and made a scratch at exactly that distance to the right of the target. He mounted another target so that the center of the cross would be exactly where he had made the scratch. Now he was ready.

"What you doin', Governor, which one of them targets are ya shootin' at ?" someone wanted to know.

"I'm intending to hit the target which you put up, but to do that I'll need to be aiming at the target on the right."

"Well, I always make a little allowance for the wind and so on, but I never seen nothin' like that," said Spencer.

Deliberately and carefully, Harrison fired his five shots. A couple of the men ran to the target. "My God," one of them yelled, "I don't believe it." They brought the board back to show everyone. "Look! The Governor has put five right at the middle!"

"Hell, Governor, they ain't nobody gonna beat that," Spencer conceded. "Gimme the damned goose."

Harrison tied the beef behind his saddle and rode home.

Summer was a time for fun and games in Vincennes, but late summer also brought the ague and fevers. This year it seemed that a third of the population was affected. Harrison and his wife recalled the accounts of yellow fever in Philadelphia, and they worried about Vincennes, and they worried about their children. First to be affected in the Harrison household was little Lucy Singleton, now nine years old. She suffered alternately from chills and fever. Some recommended sweating and snakeroot and a purge of white walnut bark, peeled upward. Others urged soaking in a wet sheet and carrying her out-of-doors to induce a chill. Still others urged bleeding and calomel.

Harrison had little faith in any of these. He told his friend, John Scott, that he believed the chances of the patient in that country were directly proportional to the distance away from doctors. Scott agreed with Harrison, and for Lucy he simply prescribed rest in a well-ventilated room, frequent sponge baths in cool water, and drinking lots of sassafras tea and fruit juices. Actually Lucy avoided the crisis common to many victims of the fevers and escaped with a mild case. So too did the other Harrison children, and the youngest were not bothered at all. But many older folks in the town suffered worse, and many of those died.

People looked to all kinds of explanations of the cause for this annual assault, but most often blamed was the putrid water of the river. The *Western Sun* carried a strong editorial:

The inhabitants of this town have been frequently severely afflicted with the ague and fever, billious complaints, which commonly occur in the months of August and September; and it is now well known by every person of the least observation that they are to be attributed, in a great measure, to the putre-faction of the grass growing in the river opposite to the village.

A great depression of the river which generally occurs in August, almost suspends the motion of its waters, about a mile in length, and in width, about half the river. In this part of the river the grass grows luxuriantly; and as soon as it begins to float on the waters, it putrefies, and becomes the source of all the agues and fevers that afflict the town.... Who, and where are the trustees of the town? What are they doing, and what is their duty?...

Harrison read this with some interest and asked Scott his opinion.

"Well, I'm thinking there just may be some connection with the river and the low water, but I'm not sure what. I don't think it's the grass, at least not the grass itself. It may be something in the grass."

Scott was making his rounds at Grouseland, looking after the sick children.

"Well, looks like there may be some hope for the horses, anyway," Harrison said as he picked up the newspaper. "Here is an item taken from the *Lynchburg Press.* That's Virginia, you know. It says:

It is now sufficiently certain that horse botts, or grubs, by which so many horses are annually destroyed, are produced from eggs or nits, which are deposited chiefly on the inside of the knee, and back part of the shoulder of the horse, by a certain species of fly, which is called *Oestrus equi.*

"Well, think of that," responded Scott. "Maybe we can learn something from the horse doctors."

"I always said you had to be smarter to be a horse doctor than a real doctor, anyway," Harrison remarked. "Because a horse can't tell the doctor what's wrong with him."

"Yeh, yeh, and maybe smarter yet to be an Indian doctor, huh? But really, I suspect we should be paying more attention to flies and various flying insects as carriers of disease in some way or another."

Meanwhile Harrison kept on with his various Indian negotiations. After the last visit of The Prophet, he was more sure than ever that he should treat with the tribes separately and not recognize Tecumseh, nor The Prophet, nor anyone else as the leader of them all.

In late August he arranged for a meeting with the Miamis, Potawatomis, and Delawares to purchase a tract of land along the Wabash and some sections in eastern Indiana. Since the strict influence of The Prophet would not be present, Harrison issued his usual proclamation:

Whereas, conferences are about to be commenced in the town of Vincennes, with certain of the Indian Tribes, on subjects interesting as well to the Territory, as the United States—and whereas the laws of the Territory authorize and empower the Governor of said Territory to prohibit the sale of any ardent or intoxicating liquors to the Indians, pending any Treaty or Conference.—Now, therefore I have thought proper to issue this my proclamation prohibiting the sale or disposition of any spirits or other intoxicating liquors to, or amongst the Indians, on any pretence whatsoever, in the Town of Vincennes, or within thirty miles of the same.

7b

While the Shawnees and visiting and allied tribesmen entered into their football games with enthusiasm and glee, the games themselves had religious significance. They were seen as being pleasing to the Great Spirit and to the Thunderbirds who would bring rain and promote the growth of the crops. Therefore, they ended their season of football about June 21 so that they would not risk inviting summer storms. The final game had about the same kind of ceremony attached to it as did the first.

This time, however, the sky was cloudy, and Tecumapease was unable to use her sun-in-the-eyes strategy. The men won the contest 10 to 4. At the end of the game, Wabethe, accompanied by The Prophet, carried the ball to the center of the field. There she opened the seams of the ball, raised it over her head, and spilled the deer hair to the wind, while The Prophet spoke an eloquent prayer for the success of the crops.

That was the end of football, but men and women, boys and girls, took up many other activities during the summer. The boys ran foot races, rode ponies, wrestled, and shot arrows at hoops. A favorite game of skill for many, old and young alike, was the rolling game. For this they laid out a smooth court about fifty feet long and four feet wide. Within this court they dug a small hole at each end, and four irregular rows of three holes each. The object was to roll little balls or marbles made of smooth stones or peach seeds into the holes. One player stood at each end and tried to roll his marbles into the hole at the far end, and in the other holes in the two rows farthest from him. The holes were assigned varying values with those at the end worth the most. These were indicated by dropping a certain number of grains into the respective holes.

But a large share of the games at Prophet's Town were of a kind that would develop strength and endurance and war skills—running, riding, shooting. Frequently large groups of warriors would engage in war games through the woods and along the streams.

Tecumseh was away on his missions much of the time, but, when he was present, he liked to go around and challenge winners in whatever competition might be taking place, and whether it was shooting rifles and muskets, or shooting bows and arrows, or a hunting contest for squirrels, or the rolling game, he invariably won.

The first harvest festival of the summer was the Green Corn Dance in mid-August. This was when the corn had filled out but was soft with milky kernels, good for roasting and eating from the cob. The Green Corn Dance was similar to the Bread Dance, except that the food which was brought to the center of the ceremonial grounds was not the meat and bread of the spring, but muskmelon and watermelon and roasted green corn, and huge kettles of corn soup. After the ceremonial dances and the feasting, social dancing again continued all night.

A few days after the Green Corn Dance was the Buffalo Dance, developed by Tecumseh in honor of his guardian spirit, the buffalo. All other dances were said to have been handed down by the Great Spirit, but the buffalo dance was handed down by Tecumseh, though this, too, honored the Great Spirit.

The Buffalo Dance took place on the football field rather than on the ceremonial grounds by the Medicine Lodge. For this occasion hunters brought in buffalo meat or venison for a feast. The dance itself was around a fire crane from which were suspended two big kettles of cornmeal mush—supposedly a favorite food of the buffalo. The mush in one was sweetened with maple syrup, while the other was without either sweetening or salt.

Tecumseh appointed twelve hunters to act as "buffaloes." The leader painted his face red; the others painted theirs blue. Each painted a figure of a bull's head on his bare chest so that his breast nipples appeared to be the eyes of the buffalo. The leader put on a headdress made of buffalo hide with horns on the sides.

Three musicians this time began beating on their water drums as they chanted a series of songs. This was the signal for all the women who wished, to join a cluster dance, swaying right to left as they sang, in front of the musicians. After that the "buffaloes" came out in single file and walked across the field to face the music. When all were ready the leader gave three loud whoops, and then all gave whoops. Immediately, the drums started and the singers began their songs as the "buffaloes" danced in file, stomping hard in their toe-heel right, toe-heel left step. When they were half way around, a column of women costumed as "buffalo cows" joined the dance, coming up on the right of the men to form an outer circle. As they took a second tour around, volunteers from the crowd joined in. After four episodes of this kind, the men went to the kettle of unsweetened mush and dipped their hands in for a taste. Then, as the women, the "cows," tried to taste the mush, the "bulls" by butting with their heads or pushing with their shoulders, tried to keep the women away. This turned into a frolic that ended with many women slipping up to the mush for a handful to rub over the back or chest or head of a man. This finished, a dozen women cooks came out to serve bowls of sweetened mush first to the regular dancers, then to the volunteer dancers, and then to the spectators.

There followed another night of social dancing.

In Prophet's Town, the late summer also brought the fevers —usually associated with contact with the White Men. The Prophet performed intonations and prayers for all his people. But he also prescribed roots and herbs.

Pachetha, Tecumseh's son was striken and under The Prophet's direct supervision, Tecumapease gave him Jimson weed seeds as an additional sacred boost, and then a series of teas brewed from Boneset leaves, Dogwood bark, yellow root, and Ginseng roots. All these seemed to have good effect, for the lad recovered in good order.

Blue Jacket, the man who, as a White boy had been adopted into the tribe and then had become one of the greatest of the war chiefs, was not so fortunate. After surviving many battles and bullets from the Long Knives, the great war chief succumbed to the fevers. The whole town was thrown into mourning, most of all Tecumseh who had looked to Blue Jacket's late acceptance of his cause as a source of great strength in building his confederation. Deeply, too, did the Prophet mourn because, in addition to a personal regard for Blue Jacket, he feared once more an erosion of respect for his powers on the part of Blue Jacket's followers.

CHAPTER XIV

Missionary Journeys

1

"**L**isten! My Brothers! Listen! I come to urge you to join all Red Men in stopping the Long Knives who keep coming to steal their lands." Tecumseh was speaking to a large council of Menominees, near the shore of Green Bay in the Wisconsin country, in the autumn of 1808.

"Listen! My Brothers! You see how the Delawares, the Wyandots, the Miami, the Shawnee, the Potawatomi, and all the others are pushed farther and farther out of their hunting grounds. Soon they will be here. All Red Men must stand together to save their homelands. We cannot wait for our sons to do it. Then it is too late. It is better to fight your enemies when they are far away, not when they are burning your villages."

The warriors nodded to each other in agreement and leaned forward to hear every word as Tecumseh went on for an hour.

"White Men make many promises; they are no good," he cried. "White Men make many treaties; they are no good. All the treaties are bad treaties. But White Men break them, and then they are very bad treaties."

"The White Chief, the Mad Man, Wayne, made treaty at his Fort Greeneville. And he said, 'This, Indian Brother, is the last treaty, there will be no more war.' Such lies make the puke burn in my throat. Since the treaty of the Mad Man Wayne, the new

White Chief Harrison makes more treaties. But it is never enough for the White Men. They pay no attention to treaty lines. My Red Brothers, take the husks from your eyes and see that the White Men want all of the Red Men's land. They want all our hunting grounds, all our homelands. If you do not join your brothers to stop the Long Knives, very soon you will have no where to go but in the big lake."

The warriors looked out toward the bay, shook their heads, and began giving shouts of approval. They became quiet as Tecumseh spoke again. The Shawnee leader spoke in a voice whose strength and resonance commanded immediate attention. His words alone created respect. His voice regardless of words aroused admiration. Together, voice and words gave him domination over any gathering.

He continued, "Already the Long Knives have their Fort Dearborn on this lake. Already, in the Mad Man Wayne's treaty, bad chiefs give away the land at the mouth of Chicago River. Soon there will be more White Men's wigwams. Will they be content to stay behind the line of that treaty or of the next treaty? Or the next? My tongue swells with laughter of ridicule."

"Listen! My Brothers! It is easy for a little child to break one hair from a horse's tail; the strongest warrior — even the strongest horse — cannot break a thousand horse hairs woven into a rope. Together, all Red Men can be strong. Separate, they will be weak. Let us stand together. All Red Men!"

By now the warriors were shouting. Members of Tecumseh's party led off in their national dance. Afterward, many of the warriors said that they were ready to move to Tippecanoe. Others said they would come at the signal.

Tecumseh was pleased to find such a favorable reception here. He had been rather disappointed with the response he had received among many of the tribes close to his home area. In a way it seemed strange that those more remote from the danger were more willing to fight than those closer to the danger. But that did not seem so strange when he remembered that the tribes west of the lake had so far escaped much of the the corruption by the Whites. They had not yet been bought by government subsidies, and their leaders had not yet been bought to become the tools of the government.

When Tecumseh left to visit a neighboring tribe to the south, the Winnebagos, many of the Menominees followed him. They wanted to hear him again. And they listened to the second round with as much fervor as they had to the first. And when he moved down closer to the Chicago settlement to visit in turn villages of the Sacs and Foxes and of the Potawatomis, numbers of the earlier groups followed. The snowball effect continued on through other Winnebago and Potawatomi villages and those of the Kickapoos west of the Wabash. In each place some warriors agreed to move with their families at once to Tippecanoe. Others said they would come later. Most of the remainder said that they would come any time that they received from him a black wampum war belt or some clear signal such as the shaking of the earth from Manitou.

With the approach of winter, Tecumseh did not tarry long at Prophet's Town, but set out in the company of a Shawnee village chief, called Captain Lewis, and a small party for northeastern Indiana and northwestern Ohio, to the people whom he knew best, many of whom were giving him the greatest difficulty. He stopped briefly to visit with his friends among the Miamis and the Delawares, many of whom were still noncommittal, but he devoted his greatest attention to the Senecas and the Wyandots. The Senecas had lost a good deal of their former power and prestige in moving about, but the Wyandot tribe retained such prestige that he was especially anxious to sway its members to his support. They shared with the Delawares the prestige of being regarded as "wise uncles" of all the tribes of the area, and they had custody of the orginal document of the Treaty of Greeneville.

As he rode across northern Ohio, Tecumseh's thoughts turned to Rebekah Galloway. In a way, he still wished that he had found a way to persuade her to come away with him. Then, in a way, he almost regretted having raised the question at all, for that had ended the series of long visits that he had come to enjoy, and the long sessions of learning the White Man's language and history and stories that he had come to value so much, as well as to enjoy. But these thoughts did not deter him from his course. He reassured himself that it was better this way so that he could give his full attention to what he felt Manitou had called him.

Tecumseh had arranged for the Wyandots and the Senecas to meet with him in a great council at Sandusky in late January of 1809. When he entered the great council house about noon for the main session of this assembly, he found it filled with warriors and the chiefs. As he rose to speak he sensed a coolness which had not been present west of the Wabash and west of the Great

Lake. In all the eloquence he could summon, he told them, "My Brothers! Listen! You know that the treaty of the Mad Man Wayne is no good. Look! See how many White Settlers already live across the line of the Treaty. Look at the other treaties the White Chief Harrison made with some of our chiefs who gave away more land, more land that was not theirs to give. And if we do not unite to stop them, the Long Knives will not stop until they have all our land, and we have no place to go but in the stinking lake."

"Listen! My Brothers! Come to the Tippecanoe. There is land better than the land here. There is more fish in the rivers, more animals in the woods, more grass for your horses. The Wabash and the Tippecanoe are farther away from the White settlements, and your women and children will be safer there. Give up your land here which now is becoming crowded, and come with us to the Tippecanoe where you can live in greater contentment."

This time there were no nods, no shouts of approval, just silence. Presently Tarhe, the Crane, an old government chief of the Wyandots rose to reply. Tecumseh knew that he had followed the Americans' line since being in their pay, but he also knew that the old chief still carried embers of resentment from The Prophet's witch hunt among the Wyandots three years previously. Tecumseh also knew that the Wyandots and Senecas had lost their zest for resistance as a result of their losses at Fallen Timbers.

Tarhe spoke, "My Children, my Brother Tecumseh and his brother who calls himself The Prophet, want us to come to Tippecanoe only to satisfy their own ambitions, only to help them for their own purposes. We stay here now. We wait a few summers. If the hunting grounds and the land and the rivers there are as good as they say, we will hear about it. If we find that our Red Brothers on the Tippecanoe are happy and contented, then we shall probably join them there."

Tecumseh was disappointed even though he had not expected full support here. At least he could take consolation in seeing that Tarhe had not been hostile, and indeed had left the door open for joining the others at Tippecanoe at a later time. Tecumseh had trained himself to be patient. He avoided controversy and just thanked the chief and the warriors for listening to what he had to say. He spent several more weeks among the Wyandot and Seneca villages, but with little success as far as immediate support was concerned.

After a few weeks back at Tippecanoe, Tecumseh, with essentially the same party as on his previous trip, set out on horseback the first of April to ride across the prairie to the vicinity of the Mississippi. In visits with Sacs and Foxes and Winnebagos in that area, he found the same kind of enthusiasm that he had encountered with their brother tribesmen farther north. Indeed, now he faced the problem contrary to the passivism of the Wyandots and Senecas—too much enthusiasm. Many of these rash young warriors wanted action now. Here Tecumseh had to use all his persuasive powers to turn them away from an attack upon Fort Madison, an outpost at the mouth of the Des Moines River that the Long Knives had erected in the last year.

Tecumseh returned to Tippecanoe in time for the Spring Bread Dance and the first football game. Shortly, thereafter, reports that young warriors of the Illinois tribes were lurking around Fort Madison and sniping at members of the garrison took him hurrying back to the Mississippi. There he remained, recruiting more followers, but counseling peace, until the end of July, 1809.

2

Harrison's negotiations with Indian leaders at Vincennes, in late August and September, laid the groundwork for a treaty to be signed at Fort Wayne. Following up his earlier accretions of Indian lands, Harrison now was going after the rich lands right up the Wabash valley in the heart of what Tecumseh (and the Treaty of Greeneville) regarded as Indian country. But Tecumseh had no part in these negotiations. The relatively small number of Shawnees who had followed Tecumseh and The Prophet to Tippecanoe were newcomers. Harrison chose to deal with friendly chiefs of the Wea, Miami, and Eel River (a branch of the Miami), Potawatomi, and Delaware tribes. The earlier treaty of 1805 had recognized the Miami, Wea, and Eel River tribes as sole owners of the land in question, but Harrison brought in the Potawatomis and Delawares to add their support for a treaty, and to preclude any claims on their part in the future. Since the Delawares and Potawatomis had no claim anyway, they were glad for this chance to get an extra annuity. The Miamis, who did have a strong claim, were more difficult. Harrison's pleas for gratitude to the White Father for all the benefits he had provided had little effect. The offer of an immediate payment in a supply of goods as soon as the treaty was signed, together with a promise of a permanent annuity of $500, had greater effect.

This done, Harrison began preparations to go to Fort Wayne to meet with all the tribes concerned.

"This could be Indiana's Treaty of Greeneville," he said to Thomas Randolph one morning in his Grouseland study.

"Meaning that everyone will be there, everyone will sign, and they'll agree to the cession of a big slice of land across central Indiana?"

"Yes, that's about it."

"Including Tecumseh? And The Prophet?"

"What do you mean, including Tecumseh? And The Prophet?"

"I mean as a signatory to the treaty. Aren't they the key to the whole project?"

"They have no legitimate claims as sachems or anything else. We certainly don't want to add to the prestige of that charlatan prophet. They have only a small following among the Shawnees and a few other tribes. To bring them in would only add unnecessarily to their strength."

"But Tecumseh has been out gaining support from the other tribes. I don't see how he can be ignored."

"If we should bring him in to these negotiations he would wreck everything."

"I should say that if we *don't* bring him in, he will wreck everything. He has been going around preaching to the Indians not to give up any more land."

"I tell you, he has no claim to be their chief."

"Doesn't he have as much claim to be chief as Blue Jacket did?" Randolph persisted.

"Oh yes, I suppose so."

"Wasn't Blue Jacket a signatory of the Treaty of Greeneville?"

"Yes, he was."

"Don't you think that may have been a key to the success of that treaty?"

"Yes, I suppose you're right about that. It was then that he agreed to bury the hatchet, to step aside as war chief, and let the peace chiefs take over."

"Might not the same be done with Tecumseh?"

"I doubt it. I want to bring in every chief and all tribes that have any legitimate claim to this land. Of course Tecumseh contends that no single tribe or group of tribes has a claim to any of it. His position is that all the land belongs to all the tribes."

"All the more reason for getting him to sign."

"But he would not do it. Not at any price I could think of. No, he would rather hold out and be in a position to contest it."

"Is he being invited to the negotiations?" Randolph wanted to know.

"Oh no, he would only make trouble. Our best bet is to get these negotiations all settled before he even is aware of them."

John Gibson came in to inquire about some papers and about the proclamation for the next session of the legislature. Harrison gave his instructions on that, and then said, "John, we were just discussing the up-coming negotiations at Fort Wayne."

"Oh yes, I trust everything is in order?"

"Oh yes, we're about ready. We'll be leaving on the first. You got word to John Johnston to assemble everybody on the 15th?"

"Yes. I trust all the tribes will be there."

"I hope so."

"Will Tecumseh be there?" Gibson asked.

"Not if I can help it."

"Why not?"

"In the first place he is no legitimate chief, and in the second place he would be a trouble-maker and would probably upset the whole thing."

"Blue Jacket was not a sachem either, just a war chief, but I would say he was important for the Treaty of Greeneville. Tecumseh is probably just as important now. If he is not a party, and big concessions are obtained, then he is going to be a trouble-maker for sure. He will never accept it."

"Our position has to be that it makes no difference if he does not accept it," Harrison said.

"But that might mean war," said Gibson.

"I hope not."

Gibson left to tend to other duties. Harrison turned back to Randolph and said, "I guess John shares your views on Tecumseh."

"I'm glad someone does," smiled Randolph. "I'm going to feel uneasy as long as he is out there arousing opposition."

"We just have to make support for this treaty so overwhelming that his opposition will not upset matters. We do want to be very careful in the way we negotiate this." Harrison leaned back in his chair and thought for a moment. Then he continued, "You know something, I never felt very good about that treaty we signed with the Sacs and Foxes at St. Louis back in '04."

"Why is that?" asked Randolph.

"Well, we got a big piece of land all right, but the way the Chouteau brothers plied them with whiskey and got them into debt left me a little uneasy."

"Then why did you sign it?"

"Well, it seemed exactly what Mr. Jefferson wanted, and it was done more or less in the way he advised."

"Who are you to say that Mr. Jefferson's judgment is better than your own?"

"And who are you to say it is not, aren't you his kinsman?"

"His kinsmen, especially the Randolphs least of all, say that he is wise above all others."

"But he was our chief, and if we didn't keep him happy, he might have found someone else to put in our places. Then where do you think Tecumseh and his followers would be?"

"Probably right down their throats."

"Well now, I'll probably be away for over a month. It'll be up to you and John Gibson to mind the store."

"We'll get along fine, if we can keep out of the way of Tecumseh — and Jonathan Jennings."

"Indeed."

On Friday, September 1, Harrison mounted his sorrel horse and with his secretary, Peter Jones; his interpreter Joseph Barron; a Frenchman; two Indian guides; and a personal servant, set out for Fort Wayne. They followed a recently cut road eastward toward Cincinnati as far as the Dearborn County line which was close to the Ohio border, and thence northward to Fort Wayne. This route, forming a right angle, lay almost wholly within areas that had been ceded by the Indians.

As he rode toward Fort Wayne, Harrison could almost feel Anthony Wayne looking over his shoulder. He was thinking about how he would visit the various tribes in advance of any general session, and as Wayne had done before Greeneville, would try to get their general assent in advance.

Arriving at Fort Wayne on the 15th, after two weeks in the saddle, Harrison found that the Delawares, with John Conner as interpreter, were arriving at the very same time, though two of their principal chiefs, the Beaver and Hockingpomscon, were absent on a visit to Detroit.

Other tribes arrived during the next few days. On the morning of the 16th, Winamac arrived with a party of Potawatomis.

Harrison was disappointed to learn that the head chief of the Potawatomis, Topenebe, and Five Medals also were off on a visit to Detroit and had authorized their son and nephew respectively to act for them. The Eel River Tribe and more Potawatomis arrived that evening. The next day several smaller groups arrived, and Harrison sent a message to Little Turtle urging him to come. Little Turtle responded that he would arrive in two days. Harrison also sent a messenger to Detroit to hasten the arrival of the chiefs who had gone to that place.

The principal chief of the Miamis, Richardville, had sent word that he was unable to attend on account of illness. Harrison sent Joseph Barron to go the sixty miles to the Miami towns to see if Richardville really was sick and, if not, to try to persuade him to come.

Days of waiting gave opportunities for visiting and for preliminary negotiations, but also allowed some feelings of nervousness and apprehension to develop. At one point some of the young warriors began running about with a rumor that a detachment of American soldiers was on the way to attack them. They finally settled down when Harrison and the chiefs assured them that that was not true.

When a delegation of Potawatomis approached the Governor with a request for a little liquor, Harrison refused with a declaration that all liquor casks would be kept shut up until the business at hand had been completed.

On the 18th, Harrison had a most interesting conference with a deputation of Delawares. They represented members of that tribe who had migrated west of the Mississippi. Now they had come all the way here to urge their Delaware brethren who remained to join them in the Far West. To many, the great Louisiana Territory was the answer to the Indian problem. The absence of trees on the Great Plains indicated that this was a desert land, largely unsuited to White settlement, but with a vast area abounding in game which should be a suitable homeland for the Indians. If they could be persuaded to move out there, that would remove their friction with the White settlers east of the Mississippi. Now here was a group of Indians themselves urging that course. Harrison promised that he would do all he could to promote their object, and in return he elicited from them a promise to support his proposed treaty among their brethren.

By the evening of the 18th, the number of Indians who had gathered were numbered at 892. The next day, Little Turtle arrived as he had promised, and more Miamis and Potawatomis arrived. Harrison made the rounds of the various camps to explain what he had in mind for a treaty, and to solicit the support of the tribes. A Mohican chief, called Captain Hendricks, reported that the British agent had advised all the tribes never to listen to any proposition to sell their lands to the United States.

On Wednesday, the 20th, Harrison had a conference with all the Miami and Eel River chiefs. He pointed out to all of them that it would be highly advantageous to them if they would persuade the Weas, a kindred tribe to the Miamis and the Eel Rivers, to leave their lands along the Wabash which were close to the White settlements. If all the Miamis could move closer to the center of their present lands, it would make them a much more respectable nation. By selling their lands close to White settlements, lands already exhausted of game and no longer of real use to the Indians, they all could enjoy a much larger annuity. He asked them to consider his proposals coolly and deliberately.

That evening, William Wells, who had remained while the Miami chiefs conferred among themselves, reported to the Governor that they had determined on no account ever to part with another foot of land. Harrison knew that this might mean trouble. He also thought that the chiefs might have taken this hard position mainly to raise the price they might get. He was further reassured when Joseph Barron returned that same evening with the news that Richardville, the chief sachem of the Miamis, really was confined to his sick bed, but that he had sent word to all the other chiefs to comply by all means with the Governor's wishes.

On Friday, the 22nd, Harrison called for all of the chiefs and headmen to meet in the Council House. With John Conner, William Wells, and Abraham Ash as well as Joseph Barron sworn as true interpreters, the Governor delivered a long speech to explain his objectives. He explained the advantages that all would enjoy by selling a large tract of land in the southwest and a somewhat smaller tract in the eastern part of the territory. In the west, the line would begin on the Illinois boundary at a point about midway between the Ohio River and Lake Michigan and run southeast to the treaty line of 1805. This would add a great deal of the land of the Wabash and of the West and East Fork White River valleys. The other piece would be a tract, rather wider, to the north of the present Dearborn County. He emphasized the importance of the annuities without which they were unable to clothe their women and children. He explained that the wars in

Europe had depressed the value of their peltries, while the rise in the prices of goods that they needed made it more difficult for them to provide for their families. He said that the sale of their land would not prevent their hunting upon it as long as the game lasted. Now the game was no longer plentiful, and it was absolutely necessary that they adopt other means for their support. Cattle and hogs required little labor and offered the surest way to substitute meat for the game which unfortunately had been largely destroyed simply for their skins. Their desire for hunting still could be satisfied, if they would prevent their young men from hunting at improper seasons of the year. He told them that they were too apt to blame the White settlers for the scarcity of game and their poverty, when the real cause was their own foolishness in listening to the advice of British traders, who urged them to kill the wild animals for their skins alone, when the flesh was not wanted. That this was the cause of their scarcity was evident from the fact that much greater quantities of game were to be found to the south than to the north of the Wabash where no White men, other than traders, ever were seen. He noted that the Weas inhabited the tract along the Wabash, that now was wanted for purchase, were poor and miserable because of their nearness to the Whites, to whom all of the proceeds of their hunts and part of their annuities went for whiskey. They would be much better off if they moved closer to the center of the Miami nation.

A Miami chief, Owl, responded, "Father, we are happy to hear your address. We shall take what you have said into consideration and will return an answer to you."

The next day Harrison had a private interview with Little Turtle. This Miami chief reported that in a council of the chiefs, the Potawatomis had supported the Governor's proposals fully, and the Delawares had seconded them, but the Miamis had remained silent. Little Turtle said that he would do all he could to persuade his fellow chiefs to agree to the proposed treaty, but many difficulties remained in the way. These had to do with the amount of money that might be granted and the amount of increase in the annuities.

That evening all the Miami chiefs called upon the Governor, at his lodging in the fort, and spent the evening with him. This time, when they requested a little liquor for their young men, he allowed two gallons for each tribe. Although Harrison usually was very strict about allowing any intoxicating beverages for Indians, and especially when engaged in negotiations, he also allowed a little wine for his guests on this evening — just enough

to mellow them to that pleasant state of agreeableness; not
enough to carry them into that obnoxious state of negative
rancor.

Late that evening, after everyone else had gone, Winamac
came to Harrison's quarters. The Potawatomi chief told the
Governor that he had come to make him sleep well. Harrison
would be pleased to know that the Indians would accede to his
proposition.

But that was not the word the next day. When the chiefs met
to decide upon their answer to the Governor, the Miamis declared
that they were determined not to sell another foot of land. They
declared that the Whites were continually buying their land at
far less than the real value, and it was time to stop the
encroachments of the Whites. The Potawatomis bitterly criti-
cized the Miamis and urged the sale so that they might benefit
from the greater annuities. They had always agreed to the sale of
land for the benefit of the Miamis, and now the Miamis should
agree to a sale for the benefit of the Potawatomis. The Delawares
remained neutral in this discussion.

Harrison called a general council to meet in the Council House
on the 25th, where he addressed the gathering:

"My Children. My heart is oppressed. If I could have believed
that I should have experienced half of the mortification and
disappointment which I now feel, I would have entreated your
Father the President to have chosen some other representative to
have made known his wishes to you. The proposition which I
made to you I fondly hoped would have been acceptable to all,
because I knew it would be beneficial to all. Why then this
disagreement amongst you? Is there some evil spirit amongst us
that has set brothers against brothers and the children against
the Father? The wind I hear has blown from the north. No good
has ever yet come from that quarter. If we who inhabit this great
island, who were born here, are not friends to each other, who
will be our friends?

"Believe, my Children, the people upon the other side of the Big
Water would desire nothing better than to set us once more to cut
each other's throats. Miamis, be not offended with your brothers
the Potawatomis. If they have discovered too much eagerness to
comply with the wishes of their Father, look at their women and
children; see them exposed to the winds and the rain and, as they
will be in a short time, to the snows of winter. Potawatomis, do
not suffer your love for your Father and your own distresses to
make you angry with your brothers the Miamis. Chiefs and

warriors of the Delawares, I have put confidence in you and you have not deceived me, you have united with your children, the Potawatomis, to accomplish the wishes of your Father. He will remember you for it. Your brothers on the Mississippi shall also feel good effects of your Father's affection for you. I promise you that the Osages shall not molest you in your hunting grounds.

"My Children, the Miamis, what disconcerts you? Have you not always received justice from the hands of your Father?

"Potawatomis and Miamis, look upon each other as brothers and at the same time look upon your grandfathers, the Delawares. I love to see you all united. I wish a strong chain to bind you all together in the bonds of friendship. I wish to hear you speak with one voice the dictates of your heart. All must go together. The consent of all is necessary.

"This is the first request your new Father, President Madison, has made to you; it will be the last. He wants no more of your land. Agree to the proposition which I now make you and send on some of your wise men to take him by the hand. He will set your heart at ease. He will tell you that he will never make another proposition to you to sell your lands."

Little Turtle then got up and spoke, "We have listened to what our Father has said. Potawatomis and Delawares, we have heard him say that you united for the purpose of complying with his wishes. I am sorry that he has met with so much difficulty. Father, it appears that the thing is now left with the Miamis. They will withdraw and consult together and, after they have made up their minds, you shall hear our answer."

The debate among the Miamis continued over the next three days. Most vehemently opposed were the Miamis from the Mississinewa villages. At one point the leaders from those villages said that they no longer would consider the others their brothers and, with a shout of defiance, all their warriors marched to the Council House to tell the Governor what they had done. He chastised them for their rashness and made them promise to come to him with their complaints and not to direct any more insults to their brother Miamis.

By now, the total number of Indians that had gathered had grown to 1,380. At another general council on the 29th, the Owl, a Miami chief first spoke:

"It has pleased the Great Spirit to unite again all who were present in the bonds of friendship. You have told us not to let any person have our lands but consider well before we sell them. This was good advice. You know when things are scarce they are dear.

You know the price of land. We are willing to sell you some by the acre for the price it sells for amongst yourselves. The land you want on the Wabash we have nothing to say to, at present, as the Weas are not here. If people have anything that they do not want, they will part from it easily. We yet find game on this land. When there is none, we will let you know. Father, at this Council you have told the Miamis to speak. We therefore expect that you will be governed by what they say. When you spoke to us, you wished that we would comply. We now wish that you would comply with what we wish. We do not wish you to go home unsuccessful. We will let you have some land near Fort Recovery. The land on the Wabash, our younger brothers occupy. Don't be dissatisfied. This is our determination. We have disputed about your proposal, but our disputes were fortunately settled yesterday."

Harrison then gave a two-hour speech in which he contrasted the history of the United States in their treatment of the Red people with that of Great Britain. The Americans never had asked the Red Men to fight their battles for them, he said. He went on, "No other power but the United States ever has made treaties with the Indians for their lands. Other civilized nations considered the lands of the Indians as their own and appropriated them to their own use whenever they pleased. Treaties made by the United States with the Indian tribes are considered as binding as those made with the most powerful kings on the other side of the Big Water.

"With respect to your selling land by the acre, that is entirely out of the question. If the United States were to agree to it, you have no one that could survey it for you, or who could tell whether it was accurately done or not. If it was sold by the acre we would only take what is good and leave the rest in your hands. When it is bought in large quantities, you are paid for good and bad together, and you all know that in every tract that is purchased, there is a great portion of bad land not fit for our purpose. This idea must have been suggested by some person who is as much your enemy as he is the enemy of the United States."

Harrison concluded by saying that he had waited long enough. The next day he would bring the form of a treaty that he would like for them to sign. If they would not agree to it, he would extinguish the council fire.

The Governor's most consistent supporter, Chief Winamac of the Potawatomis, then addressed the group:

"Father, all the Potawatomis address you. Listen to what they say, which comes from them all. Father, the Potawatomis are of the same opinion that they have ever been, that your proposition is right and just. We all know our Father never deceived us. We therefore agree to his proposal."

At this point the Mississinewa Miamis all walked out.

A Delaware chief arose and remarked that the Delawares had always kept fast hold of the chain of friendship that united them to the Seventeen Fires at the Treaty of Greeneville. He said that they always listened to the voice of their Father, and that they were willing to agree to his proposals.

After the session, Harrison remained troubled about the Mississinewa Miamis. The interpreters and others around the fort doubted that they ever could be brought around. Harrison kept wondering if something else was bothering them, something other than their expressed demand of two dollars an acre for the land. He decided to find out.

The next morning at sunrise, alone except for Barron to serve as interpreter, Harrison went to the camp of the Miami and Eel River tribes. He assembled all the chiefs in the tent of Peccan, the principal chief present, and said, "I visit you here, not as the representative of the President of the United States, but as an old friend with whom you have been acquainted for many years, and who always has endeavored to promote your happiness by every means possible. I plainly see that there is something on your hearts that is not consistent with the attachment which you ought to bear to your great Father. I fear that you have been listening to bad birds. I come to hear any cause of complaint that you may have against the United States."

The first thing that surfaced was the old question about sole ownership of the lands of the Wabash. The principal chief of the Eel River tribe drew out a copy of the Treaty of Grouseland and said, "Father, Here are your own words. In this paper you promised that you would consider the Miamis as the owners of the land on the Wabash. Why then are you about to purchase it from others?"

Harrison explained that he was not going back on that. He would even give all the money intended for the Potawatomis and Delawares for this to the Miamis, if they insisted, but they knew what trouble that would cause. "It is my intention," he said, "to draw up the treaty in such a way that the Potawatomis and Delawares would be considered as participating in the advantages of the treaty as allies of the Miamis, not as having any right to the land."

Evidently it was a matter of pride, for almost at once Harrison could see a lightening of the countenances of those about him. He invited all the other chiefs to voice any complaints or grievances. Several raised old incidents relating to being cheated by White traders. He promised to do what he could to obtain redress, but he held firm on attempts to raise the price. Finally Peccan told the Governor that he might return to the Council House, and that shortly they would be there with good news.

Harrison hurried back to prepare the treaty. He had a separate article for the Miamis for the protection of the Kickapoos in the Wabash area. He brought the treaty before a full assemblage of all the chiefs and warriors. It was signed without a single objection, except for an objection by Little Turtle to a provision that gave the Mohicans the right to settle on the White River. Peccan and Little Turtle of the Miamis signed, and so did Five Medals and Winamac of the Potawatomis, and Chief Anderson of the Delawares.

The treaty was signed on September 30th. During the next three days, Harrison devoted himself to what probably had been a major consideration in obtaining agreement to the treaty, the distribution of the annuities for the current year. He knew that for numbers of the tribal chiefs and their followers, the promise of American annuity payments held more attraction than the dreams of Tecumseh.

On October 4, Harrison and his little party set out on the return trip. This time they took the shorter route through the Indian country. On the 6th, they arrived at the Mississinewa where they called upon Richardville. The Grand Sachem of the Miamis received Harrison and his party cordially and gave his complete approval of the treaty as it was explained to him. At the Eel River village on the Petit, Harrison met some Weas. He sent them to collect the Wea chiefs for a special follow-up conference at Vincennes.

Harrison arrived back at his home on October 12th. Anna and the children had been looking for him daily, but not with any more anticipation than he had been feeling. He was tired after the long trip and the drawn-out conferences and speech-making, but he stayed up late that night to exchange bits of news.

On the 15th, the principal chief of the Weas, Lapoussier, arrived at Vincennes with fifteen of his tribesmen and made camp at the edge of the town. Three days later Little Eyes arrived with some others, and then a chief called Shawnee with a small party, and finally Negro Legs. By the 22nd, a total of sixty-one had arrived.

On the evening of the 24th, Harrison assembled all the visiting Indians for a preliminary council in the parlor of his house (a room thereafter referred to by family and friends as the "council chamber"). He greeted them all cordially and then stated very frankly, "I wished to see you all here to discover whether you were in a condition to understand the important business I have to bring before you." There were smirks and grins on the faces of his visitors.

He went on, "I had shut up the liquor casks, but I am sorry to say that some bad White men have disregarded my proclamation and have secretly made available the means of intoxication. I am glad to see, however, that you all have kept your heads. I hope that you will not drink any more until our business is finished. Tomorrow I shall explain to you the proceedings of the council at Fort Wayne."

The next day all the Wea chiefs came in promptly as requested, and he brought out the treaty signed at Fort Wayne and explained it to them. He also suggested to them the advantages of moving their tribe from the vicinity of Vincennes to an area closer to their older brothers, the Miamis. They were especially glad to hear that they would share in the annuities. The conference continued through the next day. After some further explanations of the treaty, and a special plea by Negro Legs that something be done to curb the sale of whiskey to the Red Men by White Men who thereby took from the tribesmen much of their annuities and goods essential to their livelihood, all the chiefs and head warriors present added their marks to the treaty.

The Treaty of Fort Wayne opened another three million acres for White settlement, some that was among the richest in fish and game and soil of any part of Indiana.

Harrison was pleased with the result.

Tecumseh was furious.

3

If there was some question in the minds of some people about who really was in charge of operations at Tippecanoe before the Treaty of Fort Wayne, Tecumseh left no doubt in anybody's mind afterward.

Here was exactly the kind of treaty he had been warning against. The old Treaty of Greeneville had been in effect superseded by a "new Greeneville" treaty for the Indiana Territory. It was another example where some chiefs, influenced by government presents and annuities, had given away land belonging to all the Indians. In this case it was not simply a matter of Tecumseh's and The Prophet's withholding their assent; they had not even been consulted. Indeed, the White Chief Harrison had done his best to conclude the treaty behind their backs, without their even knowing about it. Tecumseh had admitted that it was too late to push the White settlers back behind the Greeneville Treaty line, but it was not too late to nullify the Fort Wayne Treaty. He would redouble his efforts at forging his Indian union. If war should be necessary to prevent this latest encroachment from going into effect, he would try to see to it that the Indians were prepared to stand together to defend themselves. His next effort would be to seek support in the South and West. Captain Lewis had promised earlier that he would go along on a mission to the Creeks and Cherokees, but now he stepped aside in favor of Little Blue Jacket, son of the late war chief. Tecumseh also prevailed upon a cousin of his, Sikaboo, to go along as interpreter. Sikaboo had been born among the Creeks and had lived with them until his parents moved north to join the Shawnees in Ohio. He was about the age of Tecumseh and had a reputation as a brave warrior, an eloquent orator, and as one of the "minor prophets" among the Shawnees. His gift for languages—he was fluent in English, Choctaw, and Muscogee as well as Shawnee—gave him great influence in the Indian councils.

Tecumseh picked twenty Shawnee warriors known for their strength and bravery. He saw to it that they all dressed similarly in buckskin hunting shirts, cloth flaps, with buckskin leggins, and ornately fringed and beaded buckskin moccasins. All, except Tecumseh, wore plumes of eagle and hawk feathers in their cloth and silver headbands. The leader wore two long crane feathers — one white for peace among the Indians, the other dyed a bright red for war against their enemies. All of them wore three silver bracelets on each arm—one around the wrist, one around the forearm, and one around the upper arm. Tecumseh, Sikaboo, and Little Blue Jacket wore silver gorgets suspended from their necks. For weapons, each carried a rifle and in his belt a tomahawk or war club, and scalping knife.

Early one morning, a few days after the Fall Bread Dance in 1809, they mounted strong horses. Putting the rising sun behind their backs, they set out across the prairie first in the direction of

St. Louis. In five days they reached the Great River and ferried across to visit their kinsmen Shawnees and Delawares who had gone out from Ohio twenty years ago. Tecumseh even hoped that he would be able to see his mother and sister, though he had heard indirectly that his mother had died. This he verified. His sister had married a Shawnee warrior but now lived in a remote village far to the west.

Tecumseh and his party turned south. They moved down through the foothills of the Ozarks to the Arkansas country where they met with small groups of Osages. The Osages greeted Tecumseh's appeal with the indifference of ignorance and the ignorance of remoteness. Here Tecumseh had to exercise care, for he knew that the Osages were hostile toward the Kickapoos and the Sacs and Foxes who were among his staunchest supporters. After only a few days which accomplished nothing, he turned eastward to the Mississippi.

It took three days to build rafts big enough and sturdy enough to ferry the horses as well as the men across the great river. Now, in the northern Mississippi Territory, they were in the country of the Chickasaws. The Chickasaws, like the others of the "Five Civilized Nations" of the southern Indians, had been fairly successful in adopting the mode of settled farmers. Many lived in substantial log houses, complete with fireplace and chimney, like those of the White settlers, and their villages and towns were more or less permanent. They cultivated crops with skill and showed signs of adapting to new conditions which might enable them to survive in a White Man's world.

For his part, Tecumseh held no illusions about the permanency of the Indian villages in the face of White encroachments. He found his way to the house of a local Chickasaw Chief, known as George Colbert, to try to persuade him to use his influence with his people in promoting the project of Indian unity and a common stand against the White Man. Colbert was not interested. He said that the Chickasaws had been able to live in peace with the Whites, and he was not going to do anything that might involve them in war. Seeing that further argument was futile, Tecumseh moved on.

He and his party crossed the Oktibbeha Creek into the Choctaw country. They took the trail known as the Six Towns' Trail southward until they came to the home of the Choctaw mingo or sachem, Moshulitubbee, about seven miles beyond the Noxubee River. Here Tecumseh remained for several days while a number of Choctaw mingoes and warriors came to see him, but he won no converts.

Moshulitubbee sent along a warrior to act as guide as Tecumseh's party went on beyond Ben Dick Creek to the village of a noted warrior, Hoentubbee. Here, after several days, a large council of Choctaws assembled. Both Moshulitubbee, mingo of the northeastern district, and Pushmataha, mingo of the southeastern district, were there. Tecumseh and his warriors put on war paint—semicircular steaks of red paint extending along each cheekbone from the eyes, a small red dot on each temple, a large red spot on the breast. They went into their national dance to whip up enthusiasm, and then Tecumseh rose to address the crowd with Sikaboo acting as interpreter.

He said, "The White race is a wicked race. Since the day when the White race first came in contact with the Red Men, there have been continuous aggressions. The Red Man's hunting grounds are rapidly disappearing, and the Red Men are being driven farther and farther to the west. That has been the fate of the Shawnees, and surely that will be the fate of the Choctaws and Chickasaws and the Cherokees and the Creeks. The mere presence of the White Man is evil for the Red Man. His whiskey is destroying the bravery of our warriors, and his lust is corrupting the virtue of our women. The only hope for the Red Man is to stand together in war against the White Man.

"My Brothers! Red Men must give up making war against other Red Men. Follow the white feather of peace toward all other Red Men. Reserve the red feather of war for the White Man. Join in a union of all Indians!

"And My Brothers! In all wars, even with the White Man, we must give up the torture of prisoners. We must give up the killing of women and children. Those are the ways of cowards, not the ways of brave warriors."

After Sikaboo had finished the translation in his very eloquent way, Pushmataha rose to reply, "My People must not think of going on the war path against the White People. Choctaws have always lived at peace with the White Men, and they will continue to do so. They never have shed the blood of White Men in war. The advice to cease war among the Indian tribes and the advice not to kill women and children is good advice. But my People must not listen to the talk of Tecumseh and make enemies of the White People."

Tecumseh replied with some bitterness, "Why are you willing to make war on your Red brothers, but not against the Whites who are your real enemies? Remove the husks from your eyes and see! You cannot trust the White Man. You have good land here. You are allowed to cultivate good crops. Do you think your sons will be allowed to do so? You are blind. You are blinded by false hopes. Even if you help the White Men they will not spare you. If you do not join in a union to defend all Indian lands, there will be none. When your sons are men they will have no land. They will have no home. They will have no nation."

Still no one offered to join Tecumseh in his project, though Hoentubbee did become an admirer and friend.

Next Tecumseh and his party went to Yazoo where the local mingo was Tanampo Eshubbee. Here another council, with another dance, another talk by Tecumseh in the same vein as the previous one, and a similar reply by Pushmataha had essentially the same results.

Tecumseh tried again at the most noted and most populous of the Choctaw towns, Mokalusha. The town extended north and south a distance of three miles, and half that east and west, on a plateau above the headwaters of the Talasha Creek. The log houses were in neat rows, interspersed with fields of corn and other crops. During the growing season the boys of the town would herd the cattle and horses on the range outside while the women tended the crops and the men hunted. Now in winter, all were drawn in more closely. A crowd of warriors and many of the same mingoes as at previous meetings assembled on a hillside at the edge of the town. Again the Shawnees went into their dance, Tecumseh and Sikaboo delivered their oration, and Pushmataha his reply. There was sufficient interest for a crowd to gather, but they seemed to be there more out of curiosity than out of concern about Tecumseh's message.

Disappointed but undaunted, Tecumseh led his party down the east side of the Talasha Creek to Chunky town, near the confluence of Talasha Creek and Chunky Creek. On their arrival, Tecumseh and Sikaboo called upon Pierre Juzan, a French-Indian known for his influence. Juzan operated several trading houses among the Choctaws, and he had a comfortable house with garden and apple orchard at Chunky town. He listened to Tecumseh's pleas for assistance in uniting the Indians against the Whites only with growing indignation.

The next day Tecumseh learned that Juzan had informed Oklahoma, a noted mingo from Coosha, who happened to be in town with a number of his warriors, of the object of Tecumseh's visit. Oklahoma, a brother of Juzan's wife and a nephew of Pushmataha, had become outraged and ordered his warriors to prepare to make war against the Shawnees. In addition, Tecumseh learned, Juzan had sent word to the mingo of the district, Iskifo-Chito, Big Axe, and urged him to prepare for war against the Shawnees.

This was the supreme irony, Tecumseh thought. He had come to urge peace among all Red Men that they might combine their strength against the Whites, and here he himself was being threatened with war. Anxious to avoid any conflict, he called his warriors together and quietly withdrew from the place.

After a few other local excursions, Tecumseh arranged for a final council with the Choctaws at a second residence of Moshulitubbee. To reach the site Tecumseh and his group went back up the Six Towns Trail until they crossed the Noxubee River, and then took another trail to the northeast to their destination. Here they waited while all the principal mingoes and hundreds of warriors gathered. The council met under a big red oak tree on top of a hill about five hundred yards from the house of Moshulitubbee.

After the Shawnees' dance, Tecumseh, with the aid of Sikaboo, made essentially the same speech he had given to the previous councils. Pushmataha did not make his reply until the next day, but when he did it was with an added note of rancor and threat. He concluded by saying that any warrior who followed Tecumseh and joined in hostilities against the Whites, if he were fortunate enough not to be killed in battle, would be executed upon his return home. The other mingoes followed with speeches in which they concurred that any warrior who followed Tecumseh would be put to death.

After the council, the mingoes had a private conference and then informed Tecumseh that if he did not leave their country forewith he would be put to death. Little Blue Jacket let them know that if any harm came to Tecumseh, he, Blue Jacket, and the Shawnee warriors would see to it that every mingo present would die. They protested that they intended Tecumseh no harm if he moved on, and they appointed a noted and highly trusted warrior called David Folsom to lead an escort party to see the Shawnees safely across the Tombigee River.

Tecumseh showed no undue haste, but presently he and his Shawnees, joined by Folsom and his Choctaws including Hoentubbee, all mounted on horses and fully armed set out to the southeast toward the Alabama country. Arriving at the Tombigee, they camped until they could make rafts by tying logs together with grapevines. While Folsom and his party remained on the west bank, the Shawnees launched their rafts. The warriors sat on the rafts, and while some paddled others held the horses by the bridle and made them swim.

That night a marauding band of Creeks crossed the river and stole a number of horses from Folsom's camp, led them away to a swamp, and then laid an ambush along the path. The next morning the Choctaws, missing the horses, went in pursuit. Running into the ambush they ran back to their camp and began returning the fire as the Creeks took possession of a hill to the south of the camp. Hearing the firing, Tecumseh took his warriors back across the river and went to the aid of Folsom. The fighting went on all day until, about sunset, Tecumseh led his warriors, together with some of the Choctaws, on an assault up the hill. They put the marauders to flight. Folsom and his party then crossed the river. Folsom had been painfully wounded, and he returned to his village. The other Choctaws remained on that side of the river where they wreaked revenge on several Creek villages and, quite by accident, found their horses which had been stolen.

Tecumseh and his warriors took no part in this but went on southeast to contact the Seminoles around Pensacola. The Seminoles, the most ferocious of all, were a relatively new tribe that had developed out of a mixture of Creeks, remnants of several smaller tribes, and runaway slaves. They gave Tecumseh a rather more friendly ear. The idea of making war against the Whites was not unwelcome to them, though they were not prepared to make any direct commitment to support Tecumseh.

After many weeks of effort with almost nothing to show for it, Tecumseh decided it was time to return north. The discouragement he had received was not enough to daunt him. He had the character and determination to persevere against adversity. The experience simply reemphasized for him the enormity of his task. He returned to his homeland, via Tennessee, Kentucky, Illinois, more determined than ever to hold out against the Treaty of Fort Wayne and any other encroachments on the Indian lands.

CHAPTER XV

Tales of Two Cities:
Fall and Winter

1a

Sensitive and far-reaching negotiations with the Indians, local political controversies, matters of military preparation, claims and counter claims on land titles, land surveys in the face of Indian threats, sickness in town and family—all these weighed heavily on the shoulders of William Henry Harrison at his beloved Grouseland in Vincennes in the early autumn of 1809. Yet with it all, he managed to maintain a light and optimistic air, a lilt in his stride, a smile for his friends, and a smile for his foes. He regretted that he had less time now with his family, but with fewer hours, he was determined to make the most of each.

Whether early or late, in good weather or bad, Harrison always started his morning with a shave. With a big bowl of warm water, a razor sharpened on the leather strop which hung on the washstand, a lather spread with a brush of hog bristles, he rather looked forward to this morning chore. Whether as army officer or public official, he always had been careful about his appearance. He recoiled a little at the long hair and scraggly beards of the backwoodsmen and said he always felt a great advantage over them in time for concentrated thinking. He got some of his best ideas while shaving. He rather pitied those who thought that they had no time for shaving. That was like saying they had no time for thinking, and that was a pity.

Anna looked forward to the fall as a time when the fever season should be past and when her activities could be a little more regularized. She loved tending her gardens, her kitchen garden and her flower garden, but she also enjoyed doing many other things—drawing, pottery making, sewing, cooking new recipes, whenever time from other duties would allow.

But Anna Harrison was a perfectionist. So much so that sometimes she would complete a project — the making of a dress, the drawing of a landscape, the moulding and painting of a jar— to the point of perfection. Then, instead of stepping back to admire the beauty of her work, to sense the satisfaction of a task well-done, she would proceed to improve it until she had ruined it. But that was not the end of it. She had that rare perseverance and sense of mission to start all over again. From scratch. At once.

Anna had little time for diversions for her own pleasure, but she enjoyed nearly everything she did. Of all her duties: serving as official hostess, supervising all the cooking and the care of the house, sewing, tending garden, laundry, and all the rest, the one to which she attached the greatest importance was the education of her children. She always had appreciated the advantages of her own education, and she was determined to impart as many of these as possible. She always spent at least a couple of hours a day directly in this kind of activity, whether with several of the children together or individually. Often she said to them, "Live today to build beautiful memories for tomorrow."

For the more formal aspects of instruction in reading and writing and ciphering, she was able to engage a tutor. Several other families took advantage of her offer to share these services. As a result, a number of the neighboring children joined with the Harrison children at Grouseland for school on a more or less regular basis. They often met in the basement of the mansion, though in fair weather they were as likely to meet on the lawn.

This she always regarded as an interim arrangement until the "Jefferson Academy" which the Governor and judges had established several years earlier could have a building and teachers of its own. Now she was interested in the plans of Dr. (M.D.) William F. Thompson to open a school in his house in Bufferon Township in January (1810) where he promised to offer instruction in reading, writing, arithmetic, geography, English grammar, and the Greek and Latin languages.

Harrison, too, took these matters seriously. Frequently he would offer some instruction of his own in history or literature, often at the dinner table. He always enjoyed the gatherings with the family at dinner and supper in the family dining room off the kitchen in the smaller house, and he would mix efforts at humor with instruction and small talk. These were welcome interludes between conferences with Indians and conferences with politicians, between listening to conflicting land claims and demands for special favors.

September and October were special birthday months for the Harrisons. Anna and William Henry always resisted the temptation—though the thought occurred to them every year—to consolidate the celebration of all the birthdays to one or two occasions. Even William Henry, Jr., who celebrated his seventh birthday anniversary on September 3, and Lucy who celebrated her ninth on September 5, each had his and her own distinctive recognition. Everyone was especially grateful this year for their recovery from the fever. Betsy, the oldest, was thirteen on the 29th. The other two boys had birthdays in October—John Scott was five on the 4th, and John Cleves Symmes, usually called "Symmes," was eleven on the 28th. Harrison made it a tradition to see that his own favorite, grouse, was served for a birthday dinner, and Anna always made a special cake. Harrison always brought some kind of special gift for the child, but he always had a bouquet of flowers for Anna. He said that a birthday was a time for rejoicing in the arrival of the particular one to join the family, but the mother was the one who really should be honored.

One evening at supper in October, between birthday celebrations, Harrison started off with some of his customary historical queries. "Who was Julius Caesar?" he asked.

"He was the Roman who conquered Gaul," Betsy quickly responded.

"Good. Who discovered the Pacific Ocean? Let Symmes answer this time."

"DeSoto," came the reply.

"No, he discovered the Mississippi River. Do you know, Lucy?"

"It was Magellan."

"Well, that's a good answer, but someone ahead of him."

"I think Lucy is right," Betsy volunteered.

"No, no, someone saw it before Magellan."

"The Chinese, of course," said Betsy.

"Yes, but I mean the first European."

"Marco Polo."

"Actually I don't know whether he saw it or not, but I mean who saw it first from this side."

Betsy grinned and said, "The answer is Magellan, before the Chinese or Marco Polo, or any of those."

"No, No. I'll have to tell you. It was the Spaniard, Balboa."

"Yes," said Betsy. "But what did he call it?"

"Well, he saw it from the Isthmus of Panama, and he called it the South Sea."

"Yes, Daddy, he called it the South Sea, but who named it the Pacific?"

"Why Magellan did."

"There you are!" Betsy came back triumphantly. "There wasn't any Pacific Ocean until Magellan, so he had to be the first one who saw it, at least he was the first one who saw it as the *Pacific*."

"Well, my Betty, I'll have to grant you a point on a technicality. You should make a lawyer someday or at least a lawyer's wife."

"I plan to," she said.

"Plan to what?"

"Be a lawyer's wife."

Anna took a turn at questions, directing her attention to five-year-old John Scott.

"Johnny, can you tell us who is the president of the United States?"

"What's a president?" he asked.

Harrison prompted him. "He's the head man, like a chief of the country."

Little John's face brightened. "Tecumtha," he said.

Amidst rounds of laughter, to the boy's embarrassment, Harrison explained, "No, no. Tecumseh is a great Indian chief all right, but he is not president of the whole United States." "It's Mr. Thomas Jefferson," William Henry, Jr., volunteered.

"That's almost right," Harrison said. "He was until last March, but now it is—"

Lucy filled in, "It is Mr. Madison, James Madison."

Anna returned to John Scott. "Now, my boy, tell me, who is the Governor of the Indiana Territory?"

"Mr. Jennings?" he replied with some uncertainty.

"Oh, you silly goose," Betsy said. "It's your father. It's Mr. William Henry Harrison, Senior."

"It's not fair," little John protested. "You ask me all the hard questions."

Harrison turned to another vein. "Oh, I heard that a gentleman and his servant stopped overnight at Graeter's Tavern one night last week, and the gentleman told the servant to awaken him at six the next morning. At four o'clock the servant wakened the gentleman. 'Why?' the man asked. The servant said, 'Sir, to let you know that you still have two hours to sleep.'"

A chorus of "Oh, no," greeted that, except for young William Henry who asked, "Daddy, who wakened the servant?"

Neither dismayed nor dissuaded, Harrison went on, "Two men were riding along one day, and they saw an eagle soaring overhead. Both took careful aim and fired their rifles and killed it. An Irishman was passing by, and he said to them, 'You might have saved your powder and shot, for the very fall would have killed it.'"

"Oh, Daddy," said Betsy.

"Oh, Daddy," said Lucy.

"Oh, Daddy," laughed Anna.

Undeterred, Harrison tried again. "There was an Irish sailor riding a horse through town the other day. He stopped for a few minutes to look for his direction. Flies were bothering the horse and, trying to beat them off, he caught one of his hind feet in the stirrup. The sailor said, 'How now, Dobbin, if you're going to get on I'm getting off, for I'll not be riding double with you.'"

This brought laughter all around, and the children were excused from the table.

Harrison picked up the newspaper and began hurriedly reading. "Well, I see Mr. Stout is upset this week by the carelessness of some of the boys shooting at marks. Seems some stray bullets have been whistling down the streets, so that sometimes a person is not safe on the streets or even in his house."

"Is that so?" asked Anna.

"I 'spect it is. I like for the boys to improve their marksmanship, but there's no excuse for such carelessness. He goes on in the same editorial to complain about the carcasses of dead dogs and even horses being left in the streets. I don't know whether or not the carelessness of the shooters is the cause of the latter, but I agree that the Town Trustees had better do something about cleaning up the streets."

"And I see there was a horrid murder over at Patoka. Seems Moses Hopper had some objections to John Tweedle calling on his daughter, so he blew his brains out, literally. Zounds! I'm glad Judge Symmes didn't have a gun when I approached him."

"Oh, Henry."

"And here, did you see Tom Harden's notice?"

"No, is it about Mary?"

"It's about Mary all right, says, 'Whereas my wife Mary Harden has absented herself from my bed and board, and deserted her infant children, this is therefore to forewarn all persons from harboring her, or dealing with her in any wise, as they are assured it is not my intention to discharge any debts of her contracting, until she returns to her duty.'"

"Well, I can see where she might want to flee Tom Harden's bed and board, but I cannot forgive her for fleeing from her children."

"Quite, quite. Oh, I must say, Stout always seems to dig up something for his weekly 'Poetical Asylum.' Would you grant him 'political asylum'?"

"Sometimes yes, more often no. What is it this time?"

Harrison read:

> A bosom should remain unseen,
> Hid from the lawless glance;
> No charm there is, so great I ween
> Which fancy's dream cannot enhance.
>
> The fancy robe, and bosom bare,
> Wither the bud of Virgin shame,
> The sleeveless arm and forward stare,
> Ill become a virgin's name.
>
> I love to see the maid aspire,
> By other arts to please,
> I love the simple neat attire,
> Combining elegance with ease.

"Oh, Henry. Who wrote that one?"

"Anonymous."

"I should think so. Probably Stout himself. Henry, do you think I wear my gowns too low?"

"My dear, your gowns are beautiful, and you are beautiful in them or out of them."

She laughed while Harrison was reading another item. He turned back and said, "But here is one that does fit. It's signed 'Senex,' and its 'On Education.' Listen:

During the periods of infancy and early childhood, the education of boys is chiefly, while that of girls is almost exclusively, devolved on the mother. She is their first friend and possesses their earliest love. She dispenses their food, dandles them in her arms, and assiduously guards their waking hours and their slumbers....

The father is less domestic—Worldly cares engross his mind; necessary business calls him from home; and the kindnesses he bestows on his infant offspring are more indirect, and therefore less obvious and impressive. The mother's constant presence and endearing attentions...give her peculiar advantage for daily pouring into their minds the precepts of wisdom... Those first impressions which a child receives from the mother, are a fort of indelible characters. They are deeply engraven on the heart, as 'with a pen of iron, and with the point of a diamond.'

Emelia (read 'Anna') possesses both youth and fortune. Youth still blooms in her countenance. Her manners are easy and graceful. She is capable of shining at balls and attracting around her a fluttering crowd of admirers. But 'well ordered home' is her delight. She soothes the cares and multiplies the comforts of the man to whom she has pledged her vows. The daily comforts of her little nursery are her delightful talk. She is amused with their innocent prattle. With secret rapture she marks in them the dawn and progress of reason, and the still brighter dawn of virtue. She guards them with vigilance, and guides them with discretion; prudently checks the wayward propensities, 'confirms the generous purpose,' watches the most happy moments for making useful impressions, gratifies their curiosity, patiently answers their questions, 'teaches the young idol how to shoot, pours the fresh instruction o'er their minds.'...

Is there under heaven a sight more charming, than that of an intelligent, and virtuous mother, assiduously instructing her infant offspring, and using her daily endeavours both to inform their minds and fashion their hearts...

She is rearing flowers that will never fade!

Harrison put the paper down and said simply, "That's my Anna."

The greatest community festivity of the fall was muster day for the militia. According to the law of the Territory, every able-bodied citizen between the ages of eighteen and forty-five was a member of the militia. The organized militia was made up of volunteers who formed the companies and the battalion, who reported for training drills, and who were immediately available for call in case of emergency. On muster day, all the men turned out to answer to their names. This meant a holiday from work and other activities. Practically everybody in town turned out to watch the call of the muster roll, and then they watched while the battalion put on extensive and elaborate drills, in close order formation on parade, and then in extended order, in combat formations. Harrison was pleased with this performance.

At the end of October, the Harrisons invited the parents of the neighborhood to bring their children to Grouseland for a Hallowe'en Ball. Festivities began in the afternoon with various contests such as "bobbing for apples" in a tub of water; trying to obtain, by biting, apples suspended by strings from a tree limb; and, blindfolded, trying, with a stick, to break a bag of candies suspended by a string from a limb. Then everyone, old and young alike, put on costumes with masks, to represent witches and goblins and ghosts and wild animals and birds. Prizes of cakes and cookies went to those judged to have the most original and the most expertly done costumes.

As the young revelers circled around, Anna Harrison looked up at William Henry and said, "Henry, what's the difference between this and what the Indians do?"

Harrison smiled broadly and answered, "There's a big difference; if Indians were doing it, we would call it a pagan ritual!"

It all ended with rounds of dancing on the lawn and eating refreshments of ham and bread and fruit and cakes.

This preceded a special holy day called All Saints Day, a day of obligation for the Catholics, mostly in the French community, and also a prescribed holy day in the Episcopal Church.

For the Harrisons, the greatest family and religious holiday of the fall was Thanksgiving Day. Settlers from New England brought the tradition of the New England Thanksgiving with them, and some of the other families observed it on the same or on a different day. The Harrisons followed the observance as established by the Episcopal Church on the first Thursday in November, November 2, this year. Harrison always was at pains to explain to those of New England background that the first Thanksgiving was at Berkeley Plantation, before the Pilgrim Fathers had even left England. The date of that Berkeley Thanksgiving was December 4, 1619. Actually that day of Thanksgiving was for safe arrival in the New World. The more traditional Thanksgiving celebrations were more in keeping with the harvest-home celebrations of England. This was in effect the American equivalent of the harvest festivals of many lands from ancient times.

This year the Harrisons invited the Gibsons, the Parkes, the Vigos, and Thomas Randolph to share Thanksgiving dinner with them at Grouseland.

All the guests arrived early. By nine o'clock all the men were off on their horses, heading toward the woods for what had become the traditional Thanksgiving hunt. On this occasion the deer were relatively safe. What amounted to a keen competition among the hunters was for rabbits and squirrels. Though Harrison really preferred to chase grouse on the prairie, this was the preferred season for rabbits and squirrels, and actually Harrison did just as well as anyone in the woods. They chided Randolph for being too impatient, firing at long range and scaring the game away. The old timers, Gibson and Vigo, had the best results, with Parke and Harrison not far behind. All together they had an impressive bag of game to present on their return to the house about noon, where the ladies had been visiting as they prepared the dinner.

Anna had been working with the cooks for days in advance to begin preparations. Wild turkey was the main feature of the menu, though of course the rabbit and squirrel had to be added. Corn, green beans, squash, and yams filled out the main courses, and for dessert there was pumpkin pie, mincemeat pie, and apple pie.

For this occasion the whole group, including the children, the smaller ones at a separate table, went to the formal dining room. Before the dinner was served, Harrison read the appointed lessons from the Episcopal Prayer Book, from the Eighth Chapter of Deuteronomy:

> For the Lord thy God bringeth thee into a good land, a land of brooks, of water, of fountains and depths that spring out of valleys and hills; a land of wheat, and barley, and vines, and fig trees, and pomegranates; a land of oil olive and honey; a land wherein thou shalt eat bread without scarceness, thou shalt not lack any thing in it; a land whose stones are iron, and out of whose hills thou mayest dig brass.
>
> When thou hast eaten and art full, then thou shalt bless the Lord thy God for the good land which he hath given thee....

At this point, while all bowed their heads, Harrison read a prayer from his Prayer Book:

> "O most merciful Father, who hast blessed the labours of the husbandman in the returns of the fruits of the earth; We give thee humble and hearty thanks for this thy bounty; beseeching thee to continue thy loving-kindness to us, that our land may still yield her increase, to thy glory and our comfort; through Jesus Christ our Lord. Amen."

By this time the little ones were getting restless and impatient to eat, but warning frowns from mothers kept everyone quiet. When all had been served, Harrison said Grace: "Bless. O Father, thy gifts to our use and us to thy service; for Christ's sake. Amen."

Eating rather stifled conversation for a time. After everyone had had second helpings, the pace of talk quickened with the slowing pace of eating. By desert, small talk had almost been exhausted. The children were excused to go out-of-doors, while the ladies withdrew to the parlor and the gentlemen were left to consider matters of world affairs.

"Do you think there will be war?" asked Benjamin Parke.

"With whom?" Thomas Randolph inquired. "Do you mean with the Indians or the English or the French?"

"Well, I was thinking with the French, with Napoleon, I guess," replied Parke.

Harrison grinned and said, "Maybe we'll have war with all those, and at the same time."

"That's not a happy prospect," Randolph said. "Don't you think we could find some way to take them one at a time?"

"As between France and Great Britain, where are our interests?" asked John Gibson.

Harrison reflected a moment and said, "Our interest is in maintaining freedom of the seas. Who threatens that most?"

"Surely the British with their Navy in cutting off our trade with the Continent," Randolph ventured.

"But if Napoleon triumphed over the British, then he would have control of the sea and cut off our trade with Great Britain, and our trade with the British is greater than with all the Continent," Harrison said.

Parke asked, "But the big question right now is, is the embargo working?"

Harrison replied, "Oh, it's working all right, you can see that by how many people are unhappy with it. I guess if it does nothing else it helps us avoid incidents on the high seas which might lead to war. However, they say the British have started impressing some of our citizens. They claim, that they are still British, so they just take them off of our ships and put them in their Navy."

"That's a hell of note," said Randolph. "We surely can't let them get away with that."

Harrison came back in another direction. "The big question, I think, is, who is most likely to stir up the Indians?"

"That's easy," Francis Vigo responded. "With the French now out of Louisiana, and the British in control of Canada, you can see what the possibilities are."

"It's more than just possibilities," Harrison said. "We have plenty of evidence that the British, based in Canada, have been behind a good deal of the Indian troubles lately. We probably ought to march up to Canada and clean their nest out."

"And by the way," Parke asked, "how do prospects look for reappointment of the Governor?"

Randolph answered quickly, "I should say excellent, excellent indeed. You should see the resolution that the legislature adopted. I guess it should be in the paper this Saturday, anyway it recommends the reappointment of William Henry Harrison because 'they are sensible that he possesses the good wishes and affection of a great majority of his fellow citizens; because they believe him sincerely attached to the union, the prosperity of the United States' and so on; and 'because they believe him in a superior degree capable of promoting the interest of our territory' and so on; 'from his long experience, laborious attention to our concerns, influence over the Indians,' and so forth."

"Bravo!" cried Parke. "But tell me, Tom, how do you know all that?"

"Well, I helped write it!"

"That's good, damned good."

Harrison laughed and poured each a glass of peach brandy. As he did so, he related, "Three gentlemen were over in the tavern the other afternoon, and one called for a dram because he was hot. His companion a little later said, 'Bring me another, because I am cold.' And the third, who had been sitting quietly called out, 'Bring me a glass because I like it!'"

This evoked laughter from the group, and then Randolph said, "Recently I have noticed that some of our ships have been released by the French, but now the Barbary pirates in Algiers are after them."

"Seems we're always in hot water somewhere, doesn't it?" observed Harrison.

"Rather more reassuring were the reports in the *Western Sun* about manufacturing in the western country," Gibson said, "about the stream-driven gristmill at Pittsburgh, the ironworks there, the extensive paper mills in Kentucky and Western Pennsylvania (for which the women are urged to save all their rags), the new cotton mill in Cincinnati which makes cotton cloth from raw cotton, the extensive shoe factories, the harness and saddle makers, the powder mills, and the manufactories for rifle and musket balls."

"That is most impressive," said Harrison. "Actually, the interruption of trade with England and Europe may be a boon to these industries. This may give them a chance to show that maybe Alexander Hamilton was right after all in urging manufactures."

"Now if we only could have a few years of peace, maybe we really could develop economic prosperity," said Vigo.

"Yes, yes," echoed Parke and Randolph.

"What do you mean, peace?" asked Harrison. "War is what has stimulated most of this."

1b

As summer drew to a close Tecumapease was just as busy as ever. With her making of clothing, preparing food for her family, keeping the wigwam attractive and in good repair, looking after the sick in her family and others, her greatest concern of all was for the training and instruction of the children. Although Tecumseh's son was now fifteen years old, she continued to look after him much of the time. When Tecumseh was there, Pachetha stayed with him in his wigwam, but most of the time the Chief was away. Pachetha always looked forward to being with Tecumapease, and Tecumapease still had children of her own, older and younger than Pachetha, to look after. In them all she tried to instill a sense of honor, a respect for other people, a quality of bravery based on strength of character, and an awareness of the importance of learning the arts of war from her husband and from other respected warriors in the village.

Although the Shawnees and their allies in the Tippecanoe area still relied more on hunting than on cultivation for their subsistence, their festivals related to the planting and harvesting of crops.

The year had been a good one for the corn, and the people at Prophet's Town looked forward to celebrating in the Fall Bread Dance. This was timed for the week of the first full moon of autumn, this year about mid-October.

It was the season of summer days and winter nights. Clear skies admitted the warm rays of the sun, but then held no cloak against early frosts. Sun and frost brought bright colors to the leaves along the Wabash and dull color to the grass of the prairie.

Since the football game was seen as a ritual to appeal for rain, it would not do to have a football game at harvest time. Instead, the fall festivities opened with a men-versus-women dice game. Just as for the Spring Bread Dance, twelve men had been chosen as hunters to bring in meat, and twelve women had been chosen as cooks to prepare the food. These groups of twelve constituted the opposing teams for the dice game, though each could enlist the support of as many others as wished to play.

The game began just seven days before the Bread Dance itself was to be held. Again Wabethe presided. Along the edge of the football field, about mid-afternoon, she brought out a blanket and a large wooden bowl in which she had placed six peach seeds, each rubbed smooth and painted red on one side and blue on the other. She folded the blanket and set the wooden bowl at the center. The people gathered around and began shouting in excited anticipation as Tecumseh and Tecumapease came up to start the game. Tecumapease had the first turn. She knelt to the ground, grasped the bowl, and gave it a sharp up-and-down jerk to make the peach seeds jump a few inches into the air and then fall back onto the flat bottom of the bowl. Wabethe saw that all six of the seeds had come up red. There was wild screaming among the women. This meant that Tecumapease had scored five points. The old squaw who was acting as scorekeeper noted this by setting down five of her counting sticks on her right side. She had a total of one hundred sticks, and the side first to win all of these won the game. As in the football game in the spring, the losers had to gather the wood and build the fires for the dance.

Having scored, Tecumapease could take another turn, for a player continued to shake the dice until he or she had lost a point—a failure to score meant a point for the other side and allowing a player on that side a turn at the dice. On this try, Tecumapease had five red, and one blue turn up. This gave a score of one point. On the next, she had neither all of one color for five points nor five of one and one of the other for one point. This meant she had to give up one point to the men, and now it was their turn. Now Tecumseh would lead off. He had four straight of five and one for a total of four points, and then he had to turn it over.

Tecumapease kept playing for the women until she had lost a total of five points, regardless of the fact that she already had won more than that. Then another woman took her place—in this case the head woman of the twelve cooks.

The game went on until sunset, when the men had an advantage of thirty points to twenty. Play had to stop at sunset, but since neither side had won all the sticks, it would be resumed the next morning.

With only an interval at midday for eating and resting, the game went on all the next day. At the end of that day the women had built up an advantage of 90 to 10. The next morning the men regained ten, but then the women began winning again, and they won the game before noon.

The hunters then set out on their quest for game, the cooks began to make their preparations, and the remaining men and boys began to collect wood.

The Bread Dance itself was much the same as in the Spring—the dance of the hunters, the dance of the cooks—all to the singing and the beating of water drums by the four musicians—the women's cluster dance, the men in a counterclockwise circle, the women in a circle, both in concentric circles.

But the food was ever so much better. The hunt had been as successful, and the meat, broiled over hot coals or roasted in damp corn husks or stewed with corn and beans, was even more delicious. The bread was of much greater variety and of much better taste. Some breadcakes were wrapped in wet corn husks and baked in hot ashes. Again, some were made into blue biscuits, the corn flour being mixed with a small bit of ashes from bean husks, made into dough, and dropped into a kettle of boiling water. Big cakes of corn bread were baked in iron skillets over the coals. A special delicacy was made by pounding grains of corn to break the outer skins, then lifting these grains in a basket to let the chaff blow away, and then the kernels boiled in water to a heavy white fluid, after which pounded pecans or hickory nuts or walnuts were added, and the whole cooked together. In addition, there were kettles of hominy and of succotash and of squash and pumpkins.

When all was prepared, The Prophet uttered a long prayer of thanksgiving to Manitou and the Great Spirit, thanking them for the bountiful crops and promising that their children would try to act in a way pleasing to them.

After a feast in which everyone ate above capacity, the night dances began to the light of the big fires. Then came the social dancing, women behind the men of their choice, all through the night when, before morning, the dancers were approaching the fires more for warmth than light.

It was an occasion of such merriment, and of such a joyful nature, that it was bound to be pleasing to the Great Spirit. Yet there was just a touch of dread. This was autumn. It meant that winter lay just ahead. Winter was a time for departures of the hunters, for separation, and often a time of discomfort in the wigwams of Tippecanoe.

The Prophet was worried about disaffection among his followers, and he was worried, in spite of the abundant crops, about having enough food to see all the people through the winter.

Tecumseh was thinking about more far-ranging travels to elicit other tribes and groups to their project for an Indian confederacy.

2a

Winter was a time of indoor activity in Vincennes except for a number of farmers and traders who then became trappers. Shops and stores and taverns were as busy as ever, though activity slowed at the gristmill and river traffic practically closed. In the homes it was a time for spinning yarn, weaving cloth, and making clothing. Kitchens were popular gathering places for their warmth and their hot food. And winter was the time for the greatest holiday festivities of the year, Christmas.

Christmas was not just a day, but a season, and it extended from Christmas Eve, December 24, to Twelfth Night, January 6. All the members of the Harrison household looked forward eagerly to this Christmas season, and in only a few years they had adopted customs of observance which already had become traditions with them.

Shortly after supper on Christmas Eve all the family gathered in the parlor beside the fireplace, even baby Mary in her crib under the watchful eye of an attendant. All who could had helped decorate the house with sprigs of cedar, spruce, pine, holly, and mistletoe. A huge Yule Log in the fireplace gave added light and heat, and additional candles at the windows brightened the corners. The round table in the center of the room bore a large bowl of popcorn balls, a bowl of red apples, and plates of maple sugar candy and molasses taffy. The younger the children, the more anxious they were to get the preliminaries over so that they could get to that table.

First they had to join in the singing of two favorite Christmas songs and to listen to the reading of the Christmas story. Anna went to the piano. The songs were always the same two. The first was to a melody from an opera by Handel:

> While shepherds watched their flocks by night,
> All seated on the ground,
> The angel of the Lord came down
> And glory shone around And glory shone around.

The other was one which was sung to an old melody called *Greensleeves*. Father William Henry explained that this hymn was supposed to have been written by King Henry VIII of England who had become King just three hundred years ago:

> The name-day now of Christ we keep
> Who for our sins did often weep;
> His hands and feet were wounded deep,
> And his blessed side with a spear;
> His head they crowned with thorn
> And at him did laugh and scorn,
> Who for us good was born:
> God send us a happy New Year!

"Good!" said Anna with a broad smile. "That is a good one to help us get the New Year started too."

"Now is it time for popcorn balls?" asked little John Scott with a cry of expectation.

"Just a minute, Son," cautioned William Henry. "First we must read the Christmas story. What's the Christmas story, Billy?"

"The story of the birth of Jesus," William Henry Junior responded in a demonstration that last year's coaching had had some effect.

"And about shepherds and wives' men and camels and donkeys and Frank Inz and Myrtle, and everything," added little Lucy.

Harrison opened the big family *Bible*, and began reading from the Gospel of St. Luke:

> And it came to pass in those days, that there went out a decree from Caesar Augustus, that all the world should be taxed....
> And she brought forth her first born son, and wrapped him in swaddling clothes, and laid him in a manger....

After completing the passage relating to the visit of the shepherds, Harrison glanced quickly at this wife and then began reading from a verse further on:

> And there was one Anna, a prophetess, the daughter of Phamuel, of the tribe of Aser: she was of a great age, and had lived with a husband seven years from her virginity.

Anna Harrison nodded with a laugh as her husband turned to the Gospel of St. Matthew to read the account of the wise men from the east who had seen a star in the east and had brought gifts of gold and frankincense and myrrh.

"Now is it time?" asked John Scott.

"Now it is time," his father said. "Let us all have some Christmas goodies." For drink, a servant brought in some hot apple juice, and everyone began talking and eating in good cheer. Even little Mary cried out, and Anna had to take her aside to another room.

In the quiet of their bedroom, Harrison embraced his wife and said, "Merry Christmas, Darling. Merry Christmas, my young Anna."

She laughed and said, "Merry Christmas to you, again and again, my Love."

They sat for a while to relax and "unwind."

Anna looked over toward her husband, her forehead furrowed in thought, and said, "Henry, I've been wondering about some of that scripture. The Christmas story, I mean."

"What is it?"

"Well, I don't want to be questioning the divine word, but it always has bothered me just a little, that part about no room in the inn, and having to stay in a stable, I mean."

"What about it?"

"Well, why was it that they had to go to Bethlehem?"

"To be taxed."

"No, I mean, why particularly Bethlehem?"

"Because that was the city of David, and Joseph was of the house and lineage of David."

"Exactly, so that means all the people there were his cousins and aunts and uncles, doesn't it?"

"Why, I guess that's right."

"And you mean to tell me that not one of those relatives would give a place for this woman, their kinsman, who was about to have a baby?"

"Mmm, apparently not."

"Even if she were not their relative, don't you think they would have found a place for her? Did you ever hear of any of the inns in Vincennes turning anybody away, or any inn in Cincinnati, or Lexington, or anywhere else in this country?"

"No, I can't say that I have."

"And they get overcrowded, too, sometimes, don't they?"

"Yes, they do."

"And then what?"

"Well, they just make room, even if some have to sleep on the floor, and even strangers have to share the same room, even strange men and women."

"So, there you are!"

"Oh, but I doubt if a woman would want to give birth to a baby in those surroundings."

"Course not. But do you think she would want to give birth in the surroundings of a stable? For a woman in her condition, you know that any of our innkeepers would clear out a room and make those people double up in other rooms. So there you are. And anyway, why did Jesus have to be born in a manger?"

"I suppose to demonstrate humble origins to show that he would be accessible to all people."

"Humble origins? Then why did he have to be born to the house and lineage of David?"

"Anna, I have a confession to make about another aspect of that which has always bothered me."

"Oh, yes? What is that?"

"It's the whole thing about Mary's going to Bethlehem. It says that a decree went out from Caesar Augustus that all the world should be taxed. Now if this was a decree for the whole Roman world, you would think that there would be mention of it elsewhere. But I have searched all the ancient histories I could find, and I can find no trace of it other than in the Gospel. There's no mention of it in any records, even in Rome itself."

"That is strange."

"And if all the world were to be taxed, and everyone had to go to his own city, to the city of his forefathers, the whole world should have been in motion. Every province would have a greater congestion of traffic than Philadelphia at the time of Ben Franklin's funeral, or at the time of a balloon ascension."

"I guess so."

"But there is no evidence in anything I have read that there was any such movement. Actually, in all the accounts of any Roman census that I have seen, people did not have to go to their forefathers' city. They were counted and taxed where they lived. And in addition to that, it was the men, the heads of households, who were counted and taxed. There would have been no need for Mary to go to Bethlehem even if there was some unusual ruling that Joseph had to go."

"I must say, that is all very mysterious."

"Quite. But the real question is this: Does it make any real difference?"

"How do you mean that?"

"I mean, does it make any difference to the essential teachings of Christianity whether Christ was or was not born in a stable in Bethlehem?"

"What teachings?"

"The central teachings of loving the Lord thy God with all thy heart, strength, and mind, and loving thy neighbor as thyself —including loving your enemies."

"Certainly not. In fact, I would feel much better about it if I didn't have to base it on such a curious account as you have explained it."

"And so would I."

"Oh, Henry, it is Christmas Eve. Let's pray to the Lord to forgive us of our doubts."

"Let us pray to him to thank him and praise him with a faith that is *stronger because of our doubts.*"

"Amen."

Light flurries of snow were blowing outside when, on Christmas Day all the family gathered in the formal dining room at two o'clock. It was one of the few times during the year when the family alone used this room. Right away the young ones began asking about presents.

"There will be no presents until everyone eats a good dinner," Anna said firmly.

The table was filled with food. At one end, at Father's place, was a big roasted goose. At the other end, around Mother's place, were bowls of mashed potatoes, sweet potatoes, succotash, squash, and brown beans. Harrison said grace and then began carving the goose.

"Hey, Papa," Symmes called out.

"Yes, son, what is it?"

"Hey, Papa, the goose hangs high, what?"

William Henry Harrison laughed and said, "Right you are, lad. Now, would you like the left leg?"

"Sure, but what's the difference?"

"You mean you can't tell right from left?"

"Not in a cooked goose!"

"Well, a traveler lately arrived at Beckes' Tavern—the one at the Sign of Thomas Jefferson—and he said that in many of his late arrivals after a long journey, he enjoyed the luxury of a bit of ham and the left leg of a goose. 'And what is so luxurious about the left leg of a goose?' his friend wanted to know. 'Well!' he said, 'when I get there it is the only leg that is left!'"

"Papa, I'll have the first leg, if you don't mind," Symmes came back.

"All right, there you are." Harrison passed the plate down for Anna to fill with vegetables, and then it came to rest in front of Symmes. The other plates followed quickly, and as soon as Mother had taken a first bite, all began eating.

It was Betsy's turn to put in her two-cents' worth:

> "Goosey, goosey gander
> Whither shall I wander?
> Upstairs and downstairs,
> And in my lady's chamber;
> There I met an old man
>   Who wouldn't say his prayers;
> I took him by the left leg
> And threw him down the stairs."

"I guess that served him right, didn't it?" Harrison remarked. He looked at his wife and said, "And Mother, or should I say, 'Mother Goose'? What do you have to say to all this?"

Anna laughed and said, "I always say, 'What's sauce for the goose is sauce for the gander.'"

"Oh, yes, yes," responded Harrison. "And what I always say is, 'Don't kill the goose that laid the golden egg.'"

"What goose laid a golden egg?" Little William Henry demanded to know.

"Well, Billy, once upon a time, in a time long ago and a land far away, a man found that a goose of his had laid a golden egg. Thinking to find much more gold he killed the goose and opened it up and found nothing." responded Harrison.

"So did he eat it for Christmas?"

"Probably that was all he could do with it."

"Wasn't one golden goose egg enough to buy a sled and lots o' maple candy, and ice cream, and everything?"

"Of course it was, but you see he was very greedy. He was not satisfied with that. He wanted more and more of everything, and he ended up having nothing."

"'Ceptin' one gold egg and a Christmas goose."

"Yes, except one gold egg and a Christmas goose, neither of which lasted him very long, I can tell you."

Betsy chose the moment to enter a complaint. "I'll tell you one thing; if we don't get a better fire in our bedroom, I'm going to be covered with *goose pimples*."

"Yes, me too," her sister Lucy agreed, "I always get covered with them chilly bumps or goose pimples whenever I go to bed."

Anna responded, "Yes, my dears, a warm bedroom in winter is the greatest luxury on this earth. I guess most of the people in this part of the world go to bed with goose pimples. But you usually are spared the worse torture—getting up in the morning with no fire."

When everyone had finished, Ella, the dining maid, cleared the table and brought in a white-frosted cake with lighted candles on it.

"Whose birthday is it?" asked little Lucy.

"It's Jesus' birthday," John Scott answered quickly.

"Good," his mother said, "Don't you remember, we always have a birthday cake so that we will remember that it is Jesus' birthday."

"How old is he?"

"Well he was born over eighteen hundred years ago, but now he lives with God the Father in heaven, and he lives in the hearts of us all, and time does not mean anything there. He never grows old. We put on candles just to remember him and honor him."

"And look what we have to go with the cake!" exclaimed Anna as Ella returned with a big bowl. "It's ice cream!"

"Oh, goodie, goodie!" nearly everyone shouted.

"This is one time we are glad it is cold outside, otherwise we wouldn't be able to freeze the ice cream."

"Then what would we do?" asked John Scott.

"Then we would just have to drink it," she said. "Betsy, can you remember the first time you had ice cream?"

"I'm not sure exactly when the first time was, but I can remember having it in Philadelphia."

"Yes, and so did Symmes, but he will not remember."

"No, but I remember it in Vincennes, and I'm always glad when we have ice so we can have more."

After dinner all the family adjourned to the parlor to receive their gifts. Each child had an item of clothing—a dress, a shirt, pantaloons, shoes—but more interesting was a special toy or artifact for each. Betsy had a peg game which she prized. Symmes had a heavy all-wood sled, and William Henry Junior had a little two-wheeled cart equipped with a tongue for pulling and a seat for a passenger. The boys immediately agreed that they would pull each other on the sled when there was snow and on the cart when there was not. Lucy got a rag doll. John Scott received a toy birch-bark canoe, which he found he could sail in a tub of water if he put pebbles in the bottom of it to keep it from rolling over. Little Benjamin received a small Indian ball, one made of soft doeskin and stuffed lightly with animal hair, which he delighted in hurling about without damage to anything. And even baby Mary had a present—an Indian gourd rattle which pleased her as much as it distracted everyone else.

The rest of the afternoon was devoted to trying on clothes and playing with toys. The boys rushed outside to find a beautiful snow too light for the sled, too heavy for the cart, so they used both.

Greater events came to Grouseland with New Year's. New Year's Eve was the time for a Ball which local citizens regarded as the social highlight of the whole year. Christmas decorations, replaced and refurbished, still were up all over the house. Lighted candles were at every window, and the chandeliers were filled with candles with servants about to replace the candles as necessary. Guests came to refer to the whole thing as the "Ball of the Hundred Candles."

Anna had worked for weeks with the musicians, and now they were in their places in the bay window—two violins, a viola, a French horn, and a snare drum. The rug had been taken up, and the furniture pushed to the walls in that room, and the central hall had been cleared as well. Small tables had been set up in the upstairs hall and in the dining room for those who wished a game of cards or chess.

Guests began arriving about seven o'clock, and during the next hour at least eighty crowded into the mansion. They were in formal attire—most of the men in breeches and silk stockings, ruffled shirts, and dark coats; the women in gowns of silk and satin and muslin in the current mode without hoops and bustles. Anna Harrison was stunning in a lavender satin brocade with figures in blue silk and wearing her stylish one-sided coiffure. Most of the professional people and merchants of the town were there—doctors, lawyers, members of the legislature, the judges and other local officials. Six officers from Fort Knox were there in splendid uniforms, and several officers of the militia were in uniform. The Harrisons greeted the Jonathan Jennings with the same cordiality that they showed the Scotts, the Parkes, the Gibsons, and the Taylors. Thomas Randolph was there with Catherine Lawrence, a step-daughter of General James Dill and a grand-daughter of General Arthur St. Clair.

At eight o'clock, the dancing began with an old-fashioned minuet that attracted few dancers but created a pleasant atmosphere. An old version of the *Quadrille* brought greater response. Then, of course, the Harrisons insisted on the *Virginia Reel* to everyone's delight. *Contre-danse* consumed the rest of the time until a break at nine-thirty for supper.

For this, two servants brought from the warming kitchen to the dining room an emornous Yorkshire Christmas pie. A bushel of flour had gone into the thick crust and it had been filled with a boned whole turkey, a goose, a chicken, a partridge, and a pigeon, with appropriate seasoning of nutmeg, mace, cloves, salt, and pepper, and enriched with four pounds of butter. The thing had been baked for over four hours in a hot oven. The dancers greeted it with exclamations of delight. On the side was a *wassail bowl* filled with a mixture of hot ale, spices, and toasted apples. A little later several plum puddings which had been "ripening" since Thanksgiving were brought out.

Guests joined in a loud singing of the Wassail Song —

> Wassail, wassail, all over the town
> Our toast, it is white, our ale it is brown,
> Our bowl it is made of the white maple tree
> With the wassailing bowl we'll drink to thee.
>
> And here is to William and to his left ear
> Pray God send the Governor a happy New Year,
> And as happy New Year as e'er he did see;
> With the wassailing bowl we'll drink to thee.
>
> And here is to Anna and to her right eye,
> Pray God send our master a good New Year's pie
> And as good New Year's pie that may we all see;
> With the wassailing bowl we'll drink to thee.

After an hour for eating and visiting, the Harrisons called for attention, had the musicians play a German waltz tune. *Ach! du lieber Augustin*, and proceeded to whirl around the floor in demonstration of the German waltz. Others quickly joined in, and this became the most popular dance of the evening.

Some of the Methodists and Presbyterians and Baptists were scandalized by all of this, but several came and enjoyed themselves anyway. Catholics and Episcopalians enjoyed it all immensely, without qualms.

Precisely at eleven-fifty, Harrison signaled the musicians to stop playing and the drummer to "roll off" for attention. He called upon the military officers to pick up muskets—muskets which had been loaded only with powder and paper wad—and he led them out the front door to the edge of the lawn, lighted by candles in storm globes. At exactly midnight, on his order, they fired a volley that reverberated across the valley. Inside, everyone raised glasses to drink a toast for prosperity and peace in the new year—1810. And gentlemen kissed their own and others' wives in greeting and best wishes.

Then to the accompaniment of the musicians, everyone joined in singing *Auld Lang Syne*. That ended it.

Almost at once, servants appeared to clear the food and restore order to the rooms. Others would finish their work the next morning in preparation for yet another big event—the New Year's Reception. For this the musicians returned to provide background music, the *wassail bowl* was refilled, bowls of eggnog and grog set out, and plates of small pieces of fruit cake and plum pudding. This was open house for the whole community, and it seemed that everyone was there—many of those from the previous evening—so they could meet the voters—and artisans, tradesmen, hunters and trappers, Indians—all were there in their finest, whether imported or homespun. It was something of an ordeal for the Harrisons who stood in a receiving line all afternoon, and William Henry insisted on shaking hands with everyone.

Before they collapsed in bed that night, Anna, still in good spirits, said, "Henry, you know this town has shown a lot of progress since we have been here, and you are responsible for most of it."

"Oh, I wouldn't say that. But you know something—think about it—to the extent that is true at all, you know who really is responsible?"

"Who?"

"Think about it. Now just think of some of the things we have here — a library, a university now chartered, an agricultural society, a historical and museum society, an organized militia, plans now to form a fire company, a fairly well-functioning post office, a newspaper that's pretty good — who does all that make you think of?"

"Benjamin Franklin."

"Of course, and we even have Philadelphia to thank for our introduction to the German waltz and even for the idea of an official New Year's Reception. And now they are even laying out

the streets and numbering the houses according to the Philadelphia model."

"I guess maybe our time in Philadelphia was fairly well-spent
after all."

"Yes, I would say so, but you know something else?"

"What?"

"Think of all those things you mentioned, add to that all the
laws that have been adopted since we have been here and all the
treaties with the Indians; somebody has opposed every one.
Somebody has opposed every one of those measures and activities and organizations and institutions. Every one."

2b

"Indian summer"—those warm days of late November and
early December following the first hard freeze—provided a
postscript of summer delight all along the Wabash. But Indian
winter could be a time of suffering in the villages.

It was the Shawnee custom for families to move out of their
tribal villages to scattered locations for better prospects in
hunting. Winter hunting was a necessity for providing food at a
time when the ground was frozen and the trees were bare. It also
was a desirable time for fur animals, for then their furs were
thicker and more valuable.

This winter many families moved out of Prophet's Town for
the winter hunt. But more remained, depending upon hunting in
the vicinity. Many had come close to starvation in the previous
winter, but this year it was better. The Master of Life had seen
fit to make the crops plentiful, and he also had seen fit to direct
several pack trains of foodstuffs from the British to Tippecanoe.
With these supplies Tecumseh and The Prophet were able to
offer sustenance to all the additional tribesmen who answered
Tecumseh's call to come together to oppose the latest encroachments as set down in the Treaty of Fort Wayne.

In the wigwams there always were the fires to be tended, food
to be prepared, clothes and bedding to be made and mended, but
often there were times of uncreative inactivity. This was especially difficult for small children for whom the weather often was
too bitterly cold for outdoor play and the wigwam too limiting.

Frequent dances and games in the big Council Lodge relieved the monotony for many of the people and helped to build community spirit among members of different tribes.

When he was not off visiting other tribes, Tecumseh often sat in the Council Lodge with the chiefs and leaders and warriors of all the tribes at Tippecanoe.

"Will there be war again?" one of the Delaware chiefs asked in one of those council meetings.

"The Long Knives have made it certain," was Tecumseh's reply. "They have made it certain unless they give up their claims to the Red Man's land along the Wabash—the claims they make in the big steal that they call the Treaty of Fort Wayne."

"What can we do when all the chiefs sign the Treaty at Fort Wayne?" asked another.

"All chiefs did not sign at Fort Wayne," Tecumseh responded. "Tecumseh did not sign. Tecumseh will never sign treaty to give more land to White Man."

Grunts of approval greeted that statement.

The war chief went on, "I have told my Brothers many times. Do not trust word of White Man. Every time they sign treaty they say this will be enough. But soon they return with demands for another treaty to steal more land."

"But how is it possible to stop the Long Knives?" another chief asked.

Tecumseh said with firmness, "Long Knives will be stopped when all Red Men fight together. Brothers, listen! Have Long Knives ever defeated Red Men when numbers were the same? No. Remember the Long Knives of Harmar? Remember the Long Knives of St. Clair before Little Turtle turned into a red apple, and when the great Blue Jacket helped lead us—when the Long Knives were destroyed!"

"Brothers, listen! Red Men suffered from Wayne's Long Knives because some of our people became cowards and went home. In that battle, there were two White Men for each Red Man."

"Brothers, listen! When there is one Red Man for each White Man, Red Men always win. Now we must teach all of our sons to be good warriors and all of our good warriors to be great warriors."

Later all the warriors in the village were invited to come to the Council Lodge. Tecumseh repeated his pleas for unity, his hostility for the White Man, his confidence in the superiority of the Red warriors, his warnings of continuing White encroachments.

"The White Men speak with forked tongues," he cried. "The White Men are tools of Motchemenetoo. The Master of Life has set us here, and here we will stay!"

This touched off a war dance in which all the men participated, stomping round and round the lodge for nearly an hour.

Tecumseh rose again and spoke briefly, "My Brothers! We must be ready for war path. But it is not time yet to take up the tomahawk. Manitou wants us to live in peace with all people. First we try to persuade White Chief to give up claims to lands of Red Men. First we bring all Red Men together. Then we go on war path to push White Men back to line they agreed to in old treaty."

CHAPTER XVI

Equal Justice

1

E arly the next spring Red Bird, a Wea squaw, was planting corn in a small field not far from their wigwam in an isolated village thirty miles or so north of Vincennes. A papoose on her back and two young sons at her side, she worked diligently to complete her task before her husband, Long Hare, returned from his hunt in the forest.

Sensing the approach of a stranger, she looked up to see Willie Jones. She had seen him in the area many times before. He was a trapper and trader who spent much of his time in trading with the Indians. His appearance seldom changed — long, unkempt hair, coarse, straggly beard, a frayed slouch hat, a dark linen shirt crusted with oil and grime, and thread-bare pantaloons to match. As he approached, his eyes glistened beneath bushy eyebrows, and his face broke into a grin of informal greeting.

Red Bird had caught his eye many times previously as he passed by, though he never had stopped before. She was still slender and handsome. Middle age had not yet had its broadening effect upon her. Just becoming noticeable was her fourth child.

Willie Jones came to within a few feet. He asked her to come along with him. He wanted to show her something; he had a gift that she would have to choose from among several prize items which he had been saving.

The Indian woman did not respond. He repeated his offer more earnestly and again more urgently with no different result. Then, he suddenly grasped her wrist and bent it over his forearm to force her to walk away with him. One of her sons scurried away and disappeared into the woods. To the other she cried out, in her native tongue, "Tell your father! Tell your father!"

Before the boy could turn Jones pulled a big pistol from his belt and shot him dead.

A two-hour struggle brought Jones and his quarry to his cabin at the near edge of a tiny settlement five miles down the river. He was sweating and panting, in part from exertion, in part from lustful anticipation. Inside the cabin he paused only long enough to take a long draught of whiskey from a jug on the shelf.

Quickly, though clumsily, he threw his victim onto his cot. His grasping hands and hot breath muffled her cries. As he gazed into her dark eyes he was attracted, not by their beauty, but by their terror and supplication. She fought back frantically. With strong hands and sharp fingernails she scratched deeply his arms and chest. She scratched furiously at his throat and face, and he liked it. Each movement of her struggle only heightened his delirium as he ravished her again and again. With her forced submission he could feel the exhilaration of dominance. For an instant he was king of all he surveyed.

Exhaustion at last overtook him and he let up. He gave respite. But only for a moment. With another draught of whiskey he returned to the attack. Now there was less struggle. But he found new delight in sensing the flow of warm blood as Red Bird began hemorrhaging. So absorbed was he in his purient adventure that he was aware of no sounds, no sights, no smells other than those of Red Bird.

He did not sense the approach of Long Hare who, being warned by his son on his return from hunting, had run the whole distance to this place. The Indian flung open the cabin door without regard to noise or disturbance. Seeing immediately what he had been fearing most, he raised his tomahawk and with a mighty blow sank it squarely into the skull of Willie Jones. As Jones fell dead his blood gushed out and mingled with that of Red Bird's and with that of her unborn child. Quickly Long Hare dragged the body to a corner. In only a few seconds he scalped it and threw the scalp into the fireplace.

Picking up his semiconscious, bleeding wife, he called to his son to pick up the papoose. Carrying wife and baby sister, they returned swiftly to their wigwam.

Less than two days had passed when a constable and a party of gunmen rode up and placed Long Hare under arrest for the murder of Willie Jones.

At the trial the prosecutor maintained that there was no justification for the Indian's violent act. Willie Jones, he suggested, had not shot the Indian boy intentionally; apparently the boy had grabbed the pistol, and it had gone off accidentally. And as for any indiscretions of Jones with the Indian squaw, they had only the words of Indians that anything had happened at all. And if it had, it probably could be attributed to bad whiskey rather than to any evil intention.

"None of this could excuse cold-blooded murder," the prosecutor cried out. "How can any of our homes and families be secure if an Indian can enter and kill a man in his own house?"

The jury deliberated only ten minutes to return a verdict of guilty. Long Hare was executed by firing squad that same evening. The prosecutor had won another case. Red Bird had lost her husband, her unborn child, a son, and her physical and emotional well-being. But that was the end of that.

2

A few weeks later three local men—Jack Henderson, Caleb Smyth, and Joe Johnson—were out hunting a few miles east of Vincennes. As they walked through the woods Henderson, a few yards in the lead, signaled," Halt," and called in a low voice, "Look at that Indian!"

Looking across a slight clearing all could see an Indian about two hundred yards away. He had just shot a deer and was kneeling to reload his musket.

"Let me have him!" Henderson said in a loud whisper.

"You wouldn't shoot a sitting duck or a sitting rabbit, would you?" Johnson asked in feeble protest.

"Duck, no. Rabbit, no. Indian, yes," responded Henderson.

Johnson proposed to give the savage a fair chance. "Let me shoot over his head, and then you see if you can get him on the jump."

"Okeh, shoot!"

"And, if you miss him, I get a chance," chimed in Smyth as he readied his rifle.

Without careful aim Johnson fired in the general direction. Startled, the Indian looked around just in time to meet the bullet from Henderson's rifle. Almost simultaneously Smyth fired. "Just wanted to make sure," he said.

As they walked forward to reclaim the Indian's deer they saw the bushes move and then two other Indians jump up and run off.

"Damn! Damn! Damn!" cried Henderson. "Now we all three have fired, and we let those other damned varmints get away before we can reload. Damn!"

Those other Indians reported back to their village chief what had happened, and they identified the three men whom they had seen frequently in the area.

At the trial the three admitted their identity but argued that they had fired in self-defense. Their defense attorney put it, "What were Indians doing so near the White settlements? Why was this particular Indian kneeling except to take careful aim at our friends here? How are our families and our homes to be secure if we allow these savages to roam at will? Didn't one of them just a few weeks ago murder Willie Jones in his own house?"

The jury deliberated only ten minutes before coming in with a verdict of "Not guilty" for all three men.

3

The Wabash Baptist Church, chartered in Vincennes a couple of years earlier, still maintained the fervor of recent converts. In order to renew its dynamic energy in spreading the word and extending its influence, it scheduled a two-week series of revival meetings in early summer. Each evening the faithful would meet to cleanse their souls, persuade the errant to mend their ways, and urge newcomers to join in the experience of spiritual rebirth and salvation.

One evening, Harrison suggested to his wife that they attend a session. She readily agreed. They had heard reports of the meetings, of course, but both were curious to see for themselves what went on there. Moreover they thought it a good thing to show their personal support of the churches in the area. He put on his beaver hat and she her white calash bonnet. He brought around the two-wheeled gig, which they drove the two miles to the church.

At the evening service which gathered a half hour before sunset, they were treated to a session of congregational singing, long prayers, scripture readings, and a longer sermon. In this discourse the preacher varied his dramatic presentation from low whisper to high shout in warning of damnation and eternal punishment in hell fire and brimstone for the wicked, and the prospect of everlasting paradise without work or pain for the righteous.

Then the preacher invited the members of his flock to testify— to offer public testimonials to their witness of the goodness of the Lord and to make public confession of their sins. Harrison glanced at Anna with a feeling of selfconsciousness and just a little discomfort, but they held their places in respectful silence. Brother Will Adkins stood up to express thanks for a good crop this year and to ask the Lord's oversight for Bessy Barkley who was suffering from the ague and for Robert Barkdull who was suffering a broken leg which he had sustained when a tree fell on it.

Sarah Greene arose, her worn and pale countenance even more strikingly so in the dimming sunlight that reflected off the dingy walls. "I want to confess that at times I have complained about the work of bearing and raising eight children while looking after house and garden, but I ask forgiveness, 'cause I really am thankful for my family." A chorus of "Amen" resounded approvingly.

Everett Hughes, practically in tears, got up and said, "I hope the good Lord will forgive me for drinking so much corn likker; I swear I'll cut down from now on."

He was hardly finished when George Stookey jumped up to say, "I just want to assure Brother Hughes that that corn likker was only half as bad for him as he thought it was, 'cause I filled the jugs half with water afore I sold 'em to him, but I pray the Lord to forgive me for charging the full price."

Harrison, head bowed, put his hand to his face to conceal an involuntary smile, and he nudged Anna with his elbow. Without turning her head, she responded by rolling her eyes toward his.

A lad confessed to stealing a square of maple sugar. A farmer owned up to having coveted his neighbor's house, his ox, and his ass.

Then John Beaman stood up. He fidgeted for a while and then in a faltering voice began his testimonial. "I have asked the good Lord for forgiveness for my sins, and I do proclaim my thanks for his loving kindness and mercy [choruses of 'Amen, Amen']. Last winter I fell on evil ways. While Robert Russell was away to run his traps—while he was away—I slept with his wife—three times." All eyes turned to Ella Russell who sat with her husband on the other side of the church. She kept her head bowed while her neck and cheeks reddened. Her husband grabbed her arm, and while the congregation sang the "invitation hymn," during which new converts walked down the aisle to make their confessions and to accept church membership, the Russells marched the other way, out the door.

When it was all over Harrison and Anna shook hands all around, paid their respects to the preacher, and drove home. They exchanged few words until they were within the safe confines of their big house. As soon as they were in their own room, Anna gasped, "Well, I never! I never heard the likes of that before!"

"Zounds!" her husband exclaimed. "That revival meeting is a better source of news and gossip than either the *Western Sun* or the Graeters' Tavern. I know confession is good for the soul, but don't you think they carry it a bit too far?"

"I thought I was at a comic opera for a while," said Anna. She laughed. "Goodness, goodness, goodness. But then I thought, this is no comic theatre, this is real! Now I'm not sure which is worse, what some of those people have been doing or their telling about it in public."

"Well, I guess the doing may have been bad enough, but we shouldn't hold their confessions against them. After all, they were baring their hearts, acknowledging their sins, and begging the Lord for forgiveness. At least that is commendable. Think of all the folks out there who do as bad, or worse, and never have a change of heart, never go near a church."

"Yes, I suppose so," said Anna. "Still I'm a little uncomfortable about it. How do you think that poor Ella Russell feels? How can she face the people in town after that public humiliation?"

"Well, we'll see, I guess."

The next day Robert Russell took down his musket, loaded it with nails, glass, and lead, and with a double charge of powder. He marched over to the Beaman place where he found John in the garden. When the latter saw Russell coming at him, he turned to flee. But the blast of the musket caught him full in the back. Bleeding from multiple injuries, he was carried into the house by neighbors. Russell followed him in to tell him that he was sorry. Beaman whispered that he, too, was sorry for what he had done, and then expired.

Russell was arrested and tried for murder. The court found that he had committed a crime of passion which was justified in the circumstances, and the jury gave a verdict of "Not guilty."

4

On hearing the news of the Russell trial, Anna Harrison asked her husband one evening, "What do you think the result would have been if Russell had been an Indian?"

"Execution," Harrison acknowledged.

"Is there one law for the Indians and another law for the White people?" she asked rhetorically.

"There shouldn't be, but actually that is one of the factors which complicates our relations with the Indians."

"Has it always been so?"

"More or less, I'm afraid. You remember not long ago when that Italian innkeeper killed a Muskoe Indian right here in town. I ordered his arrest and trial, but of course the jury gave a verdict of 'Not guilty' with scarcely any deliberation at all. And remember those two Weas who were wounded badly by a local White settler about twenty miles from here, and of course he went unpunished. And over at Cincinnati some time ago several Shawnees were murdered when they were on peaceful trading missions, and the Federal officials could get no convictions."

"Yes, I remember that Father wrote about that. But what about the other side? What happens when the Indians commit crimes against the White people?"

Harrison thought a moment as he put a stick in the fireplace and answered, "I'm afraid White man's property is fair game for many of them, though I must say, they take things into their own hands on the side of justice sometimes. Recently, you know, I demanded that the Delawares hand over one of their tribesmen named White Turkey. He had robbed one of our settlers by the name of Vawter. They simply refused my request, though I repeated it several times. They said that they were not going to hand over any of their people until some of the White men had been punished for the murder of Indians. And they didn't. Later, then, I heard that they executed White Turkey themselves."

"And I've heard lots of complaints about horse stealing," Anna went on.

"Yes, and on both sides. The difference is, that when their horses are taken they often are sent to Kentucky, and the Indians never see them again. But if we determine that Indians have stolen horses or other property, we can at least make compensation by taking it out of their government annuities. But even worse are cases of kidnaping. I understand that at times in the past in Ohio, hunters have stolen Shawnee children, little ones less than six years of age, and taken them back to be adopted in farm families or apprenticed to tradesmen."

"How awful!" gasped Anna. "That would be a terrible blow for anyone, but for the Shawnees, they are supposed to have such strong family ties—"

"But some of that goes on the other way, too. Sometimes Indians kidnap White children. They made one of them into a great war chief — one called Blue Jacket."

"I'll declare."

"But very often the White settlers retaliate by killing Indians, while the Indians, though just as belligerent, have less opportunity."

"Is there nothing to be done about this unequal treatment?"

"We must try, but I'm afraid it's too much in the attitude of our people. I'm afraid that hasn't changed since I reported to Henry Dearborn seven or eight years ago that a great many of our frontier inhabitants consider the murdering of Indians meritorious in the highest degree."

"And that's a pity."

"And I shall go on reporting that the Indians often are abused and maltreated by our citizens, and that it is very rare that they obtain any satisfaction for the most unprovoked wrongs. I grant that the Indians bear these injuries with a patience which is astonishing." Clearly he was troubled by the situation.

So was Anna, for his troubles were her troubles. "Just laws unjustly enforced are not just at all, are they?" she observed. "Indeed, I should think that no laws at all might be better."

"Spoken like a true judge's daughter," Harrison said with a smile. Then, with a deep frown, he went on, "Yes, yes, of course. The laws of Solon or Lycurgus are of no account if they are not justly applied. We need a Pericles to enforce them."

"Henry, my dear, don't you have to be the Pericles of the frontier?"

"But this is different. Much as I wish to set things right, I cannot interfere with the operation of the courts."

"Why not let the trials be before judges only, without these juries of biased men?"

"But we can't do that. The Constitution in the Bill of Rights guarantees trial by jury."

"But I thought those provisions of the Constitution applied only to the Federal Government, not to the states."

"Yes, my dear, but this is Federal territory. And anyway our constitution for the Territory is older than the Federal Constitution."

"How is that?"

"What amounts to our constitution is the Northwest Ordinance of 1787."

"Yes, I remember."

Harrison went down to his study and came back with a big law book. He opened it and began to read:

" 'The Inhabitants of the said territory shall always be entitled to the benefits of the writ of *habeas corpus,* and of the trial by jury.'

"See? It goes on —

" 'No man shall be deprived of his liberty or property but by the judgment of his peers or the law of the land.' "

Anna protested, "Do you call it a trial by his peers to have White men sit as a jury for Indians? Why not let Indians sit on the juries? Why not let them sit on the juries for White criminals?"

"Can you imagine the outcry that would bring? All the settlers in the area would be after my scalp. Anyway, Indians are not really citizens."

"Not citizens? Why not?"

"Different civilization, that's all."

"What do you have to do to be a citizen?"

"Generally, be born here."

"Where in the world do you think that they were born?"

"Well, they have their own tribal governments. They are sort of like aliens in our territory."

"But subject to our laws."

"Of course, all aliens on our territory are subject to our laws."

"Somehow that just doesn't seem right."

"Would you have the Indians take over the government of the Territory?"

"No, of course not, that wouldn't be right either. There just ought to be some way to live and let live—peaceably."

"That's just what we would like to find. But now I'm afraid you're not only asking for a Pericles, but for a Solomon."

Harrison put the book down on a table and returned to his chair.

He turned again to Anna. "My dear, you never have harbored the fear of the savages that many of our women folk have, have you?"

"Why, should I?"

"No, no. I think you're quite right. We can't always be sure about some individuals, but on the whole I think you're quite right. I'm reminded of an incident which John Conner tells about. He was up north walking along the trail between the White River and the Mississinewa when he came to a small clearing where an isolated cabin stood. He stopped to ask for some water and found a young White widow living there alone with two small children. After visiting her briefly he asked, 'Ma'm, aren't you afraid, living here alone in this country?' 'Oh, no,' she said. 'If some passerby or intruder threatens me I only have to cry out, and immediately three or four Indians will come running from the woods to my rescue!'"

Anna laughed. "I do believe it," she said.

CHAPTER XVII

Worlds in Collision

1

One afternoon in June, William Henry Harrison dropped into the Graeter Tavern looking for a game of pool. Ordinarily he did so two or three times a week, except when he was out on the trail or involved in some prolonged negotiations. There he found Elihu Stout, editor of the newspaper, who was in the habit of playing even more frequently. Stout could be found there almost every day of the week except when the legislature was in session and when he was especially busy at printing the legislative journals and acts in addition to his weekly newspaper and various private orders for job printing.

The two men had played several rounds when they were interrupted by a terrific noise from the barroom—a noise of moving bodies, breaking wood and glass, and animated voices. Harrison stepped to the doorway just in time to see three men come together in a wild altercation. He stepped back to avoid flying objects as the combatants hurled bottles and tumblers at each other. Other men, lining the walls in amazement and excitement, urged them on.

Harrison recognized the fighting men immediately. One, George Cooper, was an Anglo-American, recently arrived from Kentucky, who was farming a place a couple of miles down the river. Another, Jean Martin, was a long-time resident of the French community, a trapper and trader. The third was a Kickapoo Indian who had lived among the Whites for some time and was thought to be a fairly reliable person, except when he got hold of firewater. Drunken brawls were common enough, but this had a special twist.

"Damned frog eater! Damned snake in the grass!" Cooper cried out.

"Damn *yanqui*! Damn *sauvage*!" yelled the French Creole.

"Damn *whoreson*! Damn *Tota*!" whooped the Indian shrilly.

Each grabbed a weapon. The Indian slammed a chair to the floor and picked up a leg from the broken pieces. The Frenchman pulled out his hunting knife. Cooper grabbed a beer bottle, broke it on the bar, and held the jagged glass at the ready position. He rushed to the Indian and swung the broken bottle toward the Redskin's throat. His blow glanced off to the shoulder as the Frenchman's knife dealt a glancing blow across his jaw, and the Indian landed a glancing blow to the back of the Creole's head.

"This is the damndest thing I've ever seen," muttered Harrison to Elihu Stout who now was standing cautiously in a half crouch beside him. "Each one has taken on two adversaries. This is a real triangular war where there are no allies, only enemies. Look at that."

"Well I'll be damned," Stout acknowledged.

As though in a circle dance of some kind, the three reversed directions at the same time and threw blows at the other adversary with similar results all around. Then with much shouting they all went to the floor in a wild melee. They abandoned their weapons for close-in combat. First fists, wildly flailing in all directions, and then frantic grasps of wrestling. Cooper got a half nelson on the Indian; the Redskin applied a firm toe hold to Martin, and the Frenchman had a hammer lock on the Anglo-American's other arm.

In the wrestling, flinging, pounding which went on furiously for another ten minutes, each combatant became a caricature of the three cultures which came together at Vincennes. The whiskey had dissolved the thin veneer of western culture which the Indian had acquired, and he was reduced to all the savagery which his enemies imagined. Exertion had turned his copper skin a true red. In the Creole's perception, the hunting knife had become a rapier in his hand though now he was forced to fight more clumsily for his honor. To his enemies he was a cunning fox bent upon destroying them by craft and design. George Cooper was simply defending himself against unprovoked attacks, though the others saw him as a schemer bent on running away with their goods and bludgeoning them with superior height and weight.

By this time Harrison decided that the contest had gone beyond the bounds of common decency. He called to one of the interested onlookers to hurry out and get a constable. When he returned a few minutes later the fight had subsided from mutual exhaustion, though all were trying to keep up the battle.

"Let's lock them up in the old fort for the night," Harrison ordered, "in separate cells. Tomorrow morning let them go, one at a time, at one-hour intervals."

Feeling a little weary by the excitement, Harrison waived Stout to a table and then joined him. The bartender, Rufus Hadley, came over with a glass of red wine for each and said, "Be my guest."

"Rufus, how in hell did this thing get started?" Harrison inquired.

Hadley drew up a chair and sat down with them.

"To peace and tranquility," smiled Harrison as he raised his glass, and Stout raised his to meet it.

"Well, Governor, I don't know who started it, but they was arguin' over women. Women—that was what set 'em off."

"What women? How could that be, here," he asked.

"Well, near as I can figure it out from what they said and from what some of the other boys here said, it all came from a whole lot of confusion. You know Frenchy is married to an Indian woman, and when the Indian saw him walking up the street with her last evening, when he was comin' in from huntin', he thought he saw him with his own squaw. And George Cooper has been curryin' favors with the whore Daisy Ellis, and he thought the Frenchman was trying to gain some time with her which she owed Cooper. Frenchy and Cooper saw the Indian with his squaw, and Frenchy thought it was his wife, and Cooper thought it was Daisy. And Frenchy and the Indian saw Cooper come into the tavern with Daisy, and each one thought it was his wife. If you ask me, we have too many black haired women in this town, and too few women all together, and they don't always stick very close to their own kind of clothes either. Reckon these guys all must have pretty bad eyesight if they can't tell their own woman a hundred yards away, although I guess that corn whiskey makes all of them a little blurry-eyed."

"I dare say," Harrison laughed. "But it all is very confusing to one who has had nothing more than a glass of wine—I guess somebody ought to go up to the jail and set them straight on the facts—if that's possible."

The bartender returned to his place. Harrison turned to his billiards partner and said, "Eli, isn't that just the way of people—always fighting for they know not what?"

"Isn't it the truth," agreed Stout. "Here each one suffered injury for unfounded accusations built up in the others' minds. Each one imagined the worst of the other two, and nobody took the trouble to check the facts."

"But the damndest thing," said Harrison, "is this each against all situation. Each one took on two enemies. If they are anywhere near evenly matched, there's no way anybody could win. To win, somebody had to overcome not one but two foes." Harrison paused to reflect as he sipped the last of his wine, then went on, "Eli, can you imagine this sort of thing ever happening among nations? Can you think of any example in history of a triangular war where each of three nations was at war with the other two? I don't mean two against one. We have lots of cases of that. I mean where each one takes on two enemies."

Stout thought for a minute or two. "Right off, I can't think of any," he finally said. "There have been cases where a country has changed sides, first fought one and then the other, but I can't think of any triangular war in the past such as you suggest. But we are getting mighty close to it right now."

"What do you mean?"

"Why, I mean the U.S. and France and England. With all those decrees of Napoleon and the British orders in council, with both of them interfering with our shipping, I wouldn't be at all surprised if we declared war against both of them. Then you'd have your triangular war all right."

"Maybe that wouldn't be such a bad idea," Harrison concluded. "If we really went into it, then nobody could win. It would be a draw, and everybody would have to settle for the *status quo ante bellum*. With peace restored between England and France, then neither would be interfering with our ships; but maybe even more important than that, neither of them would be in a position to threaten us or our interests because they would know that they would be running the risk of another triangular war which neither of them could win!"

"By God, Governor, you may have something there," admitted Stout. "Before I take an editorial stand on what we should do about the French and British violations of our rights and which one is worse, I'll have to think about that."

"You know something, Eli, it's conceivable that we could face a situation something like that with the Indians."

"How do you mean?"

"I mean if Tecumseh should succeed in putting together his confederation of all the tribes, they might be moved to fight both us and the British here in the Northwest and Upper Canada, while at the same time we go to war with England. Think about that for a moment."

"My God!" was all Elihu Stout could say.

Later that evening after supper and after visiting with the children, Harrison went to their upper bed chamber, as he always did, put on his nightshirt, and sat in his rocking chair to read awhile. He read a few verses at random from *The Bible*, but he was not concentrating. His thoughts kept returning to the tavern brawl and to the idea of a triangular war.

When Anna had seen all the children to bed, she brought in a plate of hot biscuits covered with butter and honey and a pitcher of cold milk. Setting these on the candlestand between them, she brought over two glasses and took her place in her rocker. Harrison told her in detail about the three-way fight. At first she gave it only the passing attention of just another of the drunken brawls which were all too numerous. Then her interest picked up as he explained the apparent cause as being based upon mistaken identity of women. She found that a little amusing, if disgusting, and wondered aloud whether something more might have been involved than the matter of women for the result to have been so bitter and so violent.

"Oh, I don't know," said Harrison. "Guess there aren't many things men would fight more violently for than women."

"Oh, you think so?" asked Anna, with a smile of affected coyness.

"Well, what else?"

"Well, what did your Machiavelli have to say about how a prince should get along?"

"Mmm," Harrison reflected for a while and then responded. "Well, for one thing he said to avoid earning the hatred of his subjects. A prince must respect the honor of their wives and their property—"

"Yes, wives and property—" Anna interrupted.

Harrison continued, " 'and it is certain that men sooner forget the death of their relations than the loss of their patrimony;' yes, you may have something there."

"Has any of them threatened any of the property of the others?"

"Well, now that you mentioned it, I have heard some complaints that Martin was doing some trapping down on Cooper's place, and Cooper claimed some time ago that some Indians were shooting deer on his place, and he claims some of them were trying to steal his horses. And the Frenchman claims some Indians ran his traps ahead of him and even stole some furs out of his drying shed. And of course the Indian resents any White men coming into his hunting grounds — so there you are."

"You see?" Anna affected a certain smugness. "You see, there is more to it. It probably doesn't matter much whether this particular Indian was guilty of the things alleged. It was just that in fighting him they were fighting all Indians, and he in turn was fighting all White poachers. Add to that the rivalry between Cooper and Martin for limited animal resources, and there you have a basis for real war."

"Yes," Harrison agreed. "You have put it well. In a way, I suppose you might say all men's hopes and fears were at war with each other in these three men. Maybe you are suggesting that the women were the immediate cause of the war, but that there were more remote or fundamental causes."

"Exactly. To look a little further, just what are the basic things for which people or even nations struggle?"

"That's a good question. Think about it. We have already suggested the honor of their wives and supposedly self-defense. Put all that together and you have the matter of safety. People want to be secure from pillage and violence. They want their families to be safe from harm, their children safe from kidnapping, and then, we said property. We're really talking about the means for livelihood. Everyone wants a certain amount of prosperity, and certainly the rivalry of nations on the seas is based upon that. What else?"

"It seems to me that there is a third matter which may be most important of all."

"What's that?"

"What slogan is at the masthead of Elihu Stout's *Western Sun*?"

"Liberty."

"Of course!"

"You won't believe it, but do you know what verse I just happened to be reading in *The Bible* before you came in?"

"What?"

"This verse in the eighth chapter of the Gospel of St. John, 'Ye shall know the truth, and the truth shall make you free!'"

"Amazing!"

"Now it seems to me that perhaps we have been saying that the American saw in the Frenchman a rival for economic gain and in the Indian a threat to his safety. At the same time, the Frenchman saw that rivalry and a threat to his freedom from the American, and the Indian saw threats to his freedom and economic goods from both of the others. In fact, the more you think of it, each one saw in each of the others threats to his freedom, to his prosperity, and to his safety."

"And to the honor of his wife or woman," Anna added.

Harrison sat quietly, reflecting for a while. Less obviously, Anna was thinking too. Finally, Harrison broke the silence, otherwise disturbed only by the rustle of trees in a light wind outside, with another question, "What are the very basic things that all people want?"

Without hesitation Anna replied, "Love—"

"Well, yes, I suppose so—love, deference, recognition—what else?"

"They want to have plenty to eat, a roof over their heads, enough clothes on their back to be warm and comfortable, and perhaps, above all, good health. Have I left anything out?"

"Yes, I think so."

"What?"

"One is adventure. I mean the thrill of discovery of a new land or a beautiful landscape—"

"Or a work of art—"

"Or a good book—new ideas, learning something new, whether from school or friends or whatever—growing in one's capacities." Harrison paused again and then went on, "And perhaps most of all the thing we were just talking about, what people were seeking when they came to this country and when they fought for the Revolution."

"Of course, liberty."

"Yes, freedom. That is what makes possible the adventure I have been talking about."

"But just what is freedom? What does that mean?"

"It means for Elihu Stout to have the right to print in his newspaper whatever he wants, and for anybody else to write back a letter and have it printed, as you see every week. The Bill of Rights. I guess in a broader sense it means the right to do what you want when you want."

"I'm not sure how much freedom anybody has according to that. How much freedom does a housewife have when she must be up early preparing meals, looking after half a dozen children, making and mending clothing, tending garden, keeping the house in order, and all the rest of it. When can she do what she pleases?"

"Of course there must be limitations on freedom, because people want those other things we have been talking about, food and clothing and shelter. But there is a big difference between whether people are all bound to the soil like the serfs of Russia and whether they are free men to work for those things in their own way."

"Or slaves in America?" Anna knew she was touching a tender spot but didn't see how that could be ignored.

"Yes, but that's a little different. We have to start from where we are and go from there, but freedom to move about doesn't mean anything if you don't have the wherewithall. Is a slave really free if you condemn him to starvation and freezing on his own? What would happen to the Negroes if you set them all free?"

"What *would* happen to them? I suppose they would go to work for wages like everybody else."

"No, they would never make it. Someday maybe, but not now. They would not be able to get those other essentials you are talking about."

"I wouldn't be sure. There are several free Negroes in this area who are doing as well as the slaves. Our own servants do very well, and they serve us well. We don't have to own them."

"Of course not, but many of them cannot function that well on their own, at least not yet."

Anna took another tack and pressed on. "Is freedom something special to us or do all people want it?"

"Of course all people want it—but only a few have obtained it. Only a few have been willing to fight and die for it."

"Sometimes I wonder if everybody really does want it. Some people don't want the responsibility that goes with it. I think some really prefer to be led around rather than to have to bear the responsibility of making their own decisions."

"You may be right about some, but surely the main stream is in the other direction. We also have to recognize other constraints on freedom."

"Like what?"

"Well, duty for one. A soldier's duty, a citizen's duty to his country, a person's duty to his or her family."

"What else?"

"Well, as the saying goes, 'One man's freedom ends where another's nose begins.' We have to recognize rights of others. Freedom must be bounded by justice."

"Yes," Anna said. "Well put. But to get back to the broader question. Are Americans really any more free than anybody else?"

"Certainly Americans are more free than the serfs of Russia; they are more free than the subjects of the German princes; in fact they probably are more free than most other people."

"What about the Indians? Are they free?"

"What do you mean?"

"Well, it seems to me that they move about quite a lot, and they go hunting and fishing where they want, and they build their wigwams where they want, and they do what they please when they please."

"In a way they do, though they also must work long hours to produce the food and other things they need."

"Yes, but their women do most of that, so that leaves the braves really free, doesn't it, except when White settlers or somebody moves in on their territory?"

"I suppose they do have a certain rustic freedom, but they lack that opportunity for individual growth—the freedom of the mind, the freedom of thought that comes with a more advanced civilization."

"What else is essential for freedom?" persisted Anna.

"Oh, as our Bill of Rights says, freedom of speech and assembly, the press—"

"Does free speech include The Prophet?"

"Surely."

"Then why do we worry about trying to stop him?"

"He is getting too many followers. They may become a serious threat to our security."

"Oh, then freedom of speech is all right so long as it has no results."

"No, I wouldn't say that exactly, but that like any other freedom has to have limits. We can't have people preaching sedition and rebellion, for instance."

"What, like James Otis and Sam Adams and Patrick Henry?"

"When it comes to that, then we have to be prepared to take our chances."

"Anything else essential for freedom?"

"Anna, you are a true gadfly, but it's great. It's important to think about these things. Yes, of course I think a republican government, participation in a popular republican government, or as Pericles termed Athens, a democracy, is the essential element in maintaining political freedom."

"How did Tecumseh get to be a chief? Was he born to it?"

"No, he is not a hereditary chief. He was not born to it. He is only a Shawnee war chief."

"Isn't a war chief important?"

"Well, yes, he is in charge in time of war. And I must say Tecumseh is very important, apparently the head man now."

"How did Tecumseh get to be war chief?"

"Well, according to their regular procedure, the leaders voted on it."

"Oh, and how was the great chief of the Indiana Territory chosen?"

Harrison grinned slightly and said, "He was appointed by the Great Chief of the Seventeen Fires—in fact by two successive Great Chiefs of the Seventeen Fires."

"Oh, so he was not chosen by vote of the people."

"You know that will come later when the Territory becomes a state."

"And another thing. Do the women participate in the Indian's government?"

"Which Indians?"

"The Shawnee."

"Why yes, they do. In fact in some cases the women choose the war chief."

"Isn't that interesting! And what about the women in Indiana Territory or the women in all of the Seventeen Fires? Would you say they have as much freedom as the Shawnee women?"

"Well, surely, they are a part of a republican system through the participation of their husbands."

"Why not let the women vote the same as the men?"

"That would be an unnecessary duplication. Either the woman would duplicate her husband's vote or she would cancel it. Neither would be good."

"Don't you think women should participate in the government itself?"

"They have too many other things to do. Anyway, I'm not sure their temperament is suited for government affairs."

"Why not? Anne and Elizabeth did all right for England, and Catherine for Russia, and Maria Theresa for Austria and Hungary, not to mention such in the ancient world as Cleopatra and Zenobia."

"Granted. All those you mention were truly exceptional, very exceptional. But surely you are not suggesting that women should go into the ministries of government or places of military leadership."

"And why not?"

"What if there is a crisis of some kind, or the enemy is coming, and it is their 'falling off the roof time,' or they are out having a baby?"

"Oh, Henry, don't be ridiculous. If they're having a baby, that's no more serious than a man's having the gout or an officer being wounded, and I don't hear about women being involved in drunken brawls. What if the enemy is coming, and somebody like your Captain Smith is out with his sergeant's wife?"

"Better than if the sergeant's wife had been in command of the company."

"As for women in the Army, what about all those women who were with St. Clair's expedition?"

"Yes, that just proves my point. Look what happened to St. Clair's force, cut to pieces. I'm afraid a lot of the soldiers were giving more attention to those women than they were to their weapons or the Indians. I'm afraid a lot of those women got themselves killed, and for what?"

"And as for military leaders, I guess Joan of Arc did pretty well for the French in driving out the English. And don't you remember Zenobia of Palmyra? She defeated about everybody around her."

"Yes, of course, but those were extraordinary cases. Very extraordinary."

"Extraordinary, indeed! Henry, I'm not suggesting that women ought to go in the Army, or that they ought to try to be soldiers or sailors. I'm not suggesting that they ought to try to put themselves in the places of men. Obviously God made men stronger than women, and naturally there are some things that men can do better than women, and some things that women can do better. Just look at the Indians. Seems to me that women do about all the work, except hunting and fighting, and sometimes they even do some of that, and you said yourself that the Shawnee women have a strong voice in their councils and sometimes may even choose the chiefs. All I'm saying is that it seems to me that we should always be willing to take advantage of women's intelligence, and we should keep the way open for those 'special' and 'extraordinary' cases."

"My Darling, I'm always grateful to be able to take advantage of your intelligence."

"Oh, go on!"

"My Dear, all that you say is very interesting, but what has it got to do with women in general?"

"Don't you think women are equal?"

"Of course I don't think women are equal. You are more beautiful and more intelligent than any other woman I know."

"Oh, you silly goose, that's not what I mean."

"Pray tell, what do you mean?"

"I mean that all people should have, as the French say, 'Liberty, equality, fraternity.'"

"Of course women are free and equal, like anybody else, but that doesn't mean they have to vote or run for office."

"Do you remember the essays which Elihu Stout put in his paper last fall?"

"About what?"

"About 'Female Influence.'"

"I may have seen it. Didn't pay too much attention."

"Well I have it here." Anna dug out from the corner a scrap book in which she had dropped all kinds of loose clippings, letters, and other items she wanted to save for future reference. "Here, listen to this." She read:

The early ages of the world, present the female character in a state of extreme humiliation. . . . Superior strength, pride or temper, in the one sex, took advantage of the delicate dependence of the other, and the virtue of the latter was unable to gain an ascendency over the roughness of the former. . . . Homer considers Helen. . . of little other value than as a part of the goods stolen with her; and the same author celebrates Penelope for refusing suitors in the absence of Ulysses, not because she loved her husband supremely, but because, in thus doing, she preserved to his family the dowry she brought from her father, Icarius.

The early ages of the Roman empire presents the same subordination of the sex; but after the conquest of Carthage, the improving state of society, and of science, brought them forward to a degree of imminence; and for many ages, the Roman women were respected throughout the world.

Anna looked up. "Henry, the way you like to cite Roman examples and quote Roman leaders, I hope you will remember this."

"Aha, maybe you have discovered there the reason for the fall of the Roman Empire," her husband quipped.

"Nonsense. Listen." Anna resumed her reading:

In the reign of Tiberius, when heavy contribution was laid on the women they sought a *man* to defend their cause, but no man would consent to reason against those who had the power of life and death. The daughter of the celebrated Hortensius appeared. She revived the memories of her father's abilities, supported with eloquence, argument, and ability, her own cause and that of her sex. The triumviers blushed and revoked the orders. Hortensia was conducted home in triumph, and had the honor of having given, in one day, to men an example of courage, to women a pattern of eloquence, and to tyrants a lesson of humanity....

After the subversion of the empire, the barbarians, who spread conflagration and ruin—who trampled on the monuments of art—who spurned the appendages of elegance and pleasure, introduced into Europe that spirit of gallantry and subordination to female merit, which now so characterizes their amusements and their courts.

That system which now teaches to consider the woman as equal, which powerfully influences customs, manners and policy, in both hemispheres; which exalts the human character by softening the empire of force; which mingles politeness with the use of the sword, which delights in protecting the weak, and in conferring that importance which nature or fortune have denied, was first introduced from the frozen shore of the Baltic and from the savage forest of the north.

The barbarians who overran Europe, carried their opinion with their armies and thus the influence of the women is discovered to have originated; not in the depravity of sense nor in the caprice of fancy; but in the natural untaught manners of the barbarians.

Anna paused again. "What do you think of that, Henry? Do you think it possible that we might learn something like that from our barbarians?"

Harrison winced just a little as he said, "Anna dear, one thing I dread above all else is a barbarian invasion."

"Let me read just one more paragraph," and she read on:

The influence thus gained and avowed began to extend itself, and to form a foundation upon science and religion; upon mental as well as personal attractions. Under the auspices of an improving state of society and of laws highly favorable to the sex, have flourished that simplicity which is the best index of an elegant and cultivated mind, that taste for refined literature which charms in the possession and stimulates to instant improvement...

"It goes on, but that should give you the idea. Pretty good for a little ol' frontier newspaper, isn't it?"

"Yes, it is, very impressive."

"Isn't it interesting to see a similarity in the place of women in the barbaric tribes of north Europe with those of the Indian tribes of North America?"

"Yes, it is. I just hope the comparisons don't go too far. I hope they don't include massive invasions of our frontier—and the sacking of our Rome!"

Harrison picked up a book which he had been rereading from time to time. "When it all boils down," he said, "I think I like best the picture of democracy which Pericles gives in his funeral oration, as recounted by Thucydides":

Our form of government does not enter into rivalry with others. We do not copy our neighbors but are an example to them. It is true that we are called a democracy, for the administration is in the hands of the many and not of the few. But while the law secures equal justice to all alike in their private disputes, the claim of excellence is also recognized; and when a citizen is in any way distinguished, he is preferred to the public service, not as a matter of privilege, but as the reward of merit. Neither is poverty a bar, but a man may benefit his country whatever be the obscurity of his condition...

"And then, here:"

An Athenian citizen does not neglect the state because he takes care of his own household; and even those of us who are engaged in business have a very fair idea of politics. We alone regard a man who takes no interest in public affairs, not as a harmless, but as a useless character; and if few of us are originators, we are all sound judges of a policy. The great impediment to action is, in our opinion, not discussion, but the want of that knowledge which is gained by discussion preparatory to action. For we have a peculiar power of thinking before we act and of acting too, whereas other men are courageous from ignorance but hesitate upon reflection.

"Great," Anna said. "You have read that before, several times, but each time it sounds better. Each time it seems to mean more. I wish that Jonathan Jennings with all his talk about the Virginia aristocracy in Vincennes could hear you read that!"

"Yes, yes. Then, for Pericles, freedom finally comes down like this."

Esteeming courage to be freedom and freedom to be happiness, do not weigh too nicely the perils of war.

2

William Henry Harrison reflected frequently on what the policy should be toward the Indians. He maintained a conscious concern for the welfare of the Indians, but he also worried about the safety of the White settlers, and their welfare, and deep within he harbored that dread of a barbarian invasion. One afternoon he sat in his office at Grouseland with the territorial secretary, John Gibson, discussing matters in general.

Tecumseh reflected frequently on what the policy should be toward the White Men. He recognized the concerns of the White settlers for their safety, but he worried about the safety of the Indian villages, and deep within, he harbored a dread of a White Man's war of annihilation. That afternoon he sat in his wigwam at Prophet's Town with his brother, The Prophet, discussing matters in general.

Vincennes
    Harrison: "I tell you, John, I keep worrying about the Indian situation. What do they want? What else can we do? We give them extra food; we pay them subsidies; we give them animals."

    Gibson: "Yes, what more do they want?"

Prophet's Town
    Tecumseh: "My Brother, our people only want to be left alone in their hunting grounds. The miserable payments which the Long Knives give are nothing."

    The Prophet: "Truly, nothing."

Vincennes
    Harrison: "And why do they keep attacking our people?"

    Gibson: "To steal horses and children and whiskey."

Prophet's Town

Tecumseh: "Our warriors attack the White Men only to protect our villages and our hunting grounds. Why do the White Men keep attacking our people?"

The Prophet: "To steal horses and children and corn."

Vincennes

Harrison: "But my friend, there is something deeper at work here. If it were just a question of outrages, reparation could be made. The real problem is the occupation of the land itself."

Gibson: "The question is, who has the right to the land?"

Prophet's Town

Tecumseh: "How can the White Men deny that the Red Men were here first? How can they say that this land should belong to them?

The Prophet: "Do they say that because they burn our villages and rob our crops that they all belong to them?"

Vincennes

Harrison: "Granted, the right to the land is a complicated question. But we have recognized the Indians' claim. Our position is that France first established sovereignty over this Territory which she ceded to Great Britain by the Treaty of 1767, and which Great Britain ceded to the United States by the Treaty of 1783. Nevertheless, we recognize that the Indians have a certain claim to ownership. Therefore we have not allowed any grants of land, or purchases, by our people of land that has not been secured by treaty from the Indians."

Gibson: "The trouble is, how do you know which Indians have the claim? They move all about, and very often more than one tribe will claim the same area. They don't even recognize each other's rights."

Prophet's Town

    Tecumseh: "This land belongs to all of the Red Men, not just to one nation or to two or three or four nations, but to all the nations. It cannot belong to the White Men unless all of the Red Men's nations agree."

    The Prophet: "The land is the land of all the Red Men."

Vincennes

    Harrison: "We try as best we can to recognize the rights of all nations involved. Look at all of the tribes represented in each of our treaties."

    Gibson: "How can we do more than that?"

Prophet's Town

    Tecumseh: "And the White Chief pays bribes to a few old chiefs to persuade them to agree to his treaties, or the Long Knives make war on our people to force their leaders to make treaties. Their treaties are false! They had no right to make them."

    The Prophet: "The treaties are pieces of paper which are no good."

Vincennes

    Harrison: "I look at the treaties as being perfectly binding. I don't know what else we can do."

    Gibson: "What else?"

Prophet's Town

    Tecumseh: "The treaties are no good. Even the White Men do not think they are good. Why must they always make new treaties? They draw a line and say they want only the land on the other side. Always they come back to make another line, to take more and more of the Red Men's hunting grounds. This must stop. A wise man on the other side of the Great Water said if you give in to your enemies on one thing, they will come back for more."

    The Prophet: "The White Men always come back for more."

Vincennes

Harrison: "I know some of the Indian leaders are never happy with the treaty settlements. We just have to do the best we can. But I tell you, if they keep collecting up on the Tippecanoe we may be in for some real trouble. We may have another Pontiac conspiracy on our hands."

Gibson: "Indeed."

Prophet's Town

Tecumseh: "Yes, the only thing we can do is bring all the tribes together; we must all act together, even as the great Chief Pontiac tried to do."

The Prophet: "How did the great Pontiac go wrong? What was his big mistake?"

Vincennes

Harrison: "Pontiac very nearly pulled it off. That was back during the French and Indian war, and he arranged to have some tribe attack each of the English forts in the Northwest country, usually by gaining entry through some kind of ruse. They got all the forts except Detroit and Fort Pitt, and then the French signed peace with the English, and the English sent out the expedition to the Ohio country under Henry Bouquet which put an end to the matter. Pontiac might have been successful if he could have taken Detroit and then concentrated his forces."

Gibson: "But I wonder if even then he could have been successful in the long run."

Prophet's Town

Tecumseh: "Under Pontiac the tribes fought separately. They must fight together. And at Detroit Pontiac was betrayed by a Red Woman."

The Prophet: "And if they all fight according to the wishes of the Master of Life, they can keep their hunting grounds."

Vincennes
   Harrison: "Sometimes I feel like we're operating a Roman proconsulate, guarding the frontier against barbarian invasions. I don't want us to be cast in the role of opening the frontiers of the empire and allowing the barbaric horde to sack the Imperial City."

   Gibson: "I trust there's no danger of that."

Prophet's Town
   Tecumseh: "Sometimes I feel that we are waiting in our city like an ancient man across the waters called Demosthenes, waiting for our city, and all the Red Men's cities, to be overwhelmed by a new Alexander."

   The Prophet: "You talk in strange words, but they are wise words."

   Tecumseh: "Or maybe we can be like the forest people across the waters and capture the great 'Imperial City!'"

   The Prophet: "Now your words are foolish words."

Vincennes
   Harrison: "The real question is, can war be avoided? If we make peace with the Miamis, the Shawnees make war, and so on."

   Gibson: "Maybe in that sense it would be better for us if they were all united in a confederacy; then at least we would have to treat with only one entity."

Prophet's Town
   Tecumseh: "Maybe war will not even be necessary if we can bring all of our people together. A great Greek King said, 'They will fear us most if we never come.' If we bring all the Red Men's nations together, and if we have many warriors at this place and remain very strong, the Long Knives will not dare attack. In effect we can hold Vincennes

	hostage, and they will not leave it unguarded."
The Prophet:	"But we can never be safe until the White Man is eliminated from our country. Is there any other way?"
Vincennes *Harrison:*	"You know something, John? In a way I would fear them most if they never came. If they assembled a huge force at Prophet's Town and then never came out, what would we do? They would be a constant threat even to Vincennes. No settlers would dare move near the place, and there would be nothing we could do about it unless we went up there and cleaned them out."
Gibson:	"I see what you mean. But isn't some kind of more durable and acceptable pacification possible?"
Harrison:	"What are our choices?"
Prophet's Town *Tecumseh:*	"The White Men's choices are either to give up trying to take our hunting grounds and let us live in peace or annihilate us."
The Prophet:	"There is no other way."
Vincennes *Harrison:*	"Are we simply to tell our settlers that they must give up their lands which the Indians claim? Are they to give up their dreams of opening new lands?"
Prophet's Town *Tecumseh:*	"The White Men must give up their claims to the hunting grounds of the Red Men."
The Prophet:	"By all means."
Vincennes *Gibson:*	"How can we do that? Are we to leave the continent empty when it could be supporting a great civilization? All the Indians, themselves, came from somewhere else, and in many places the tribes that arrived

later drove out tribes that had been there earlier. The Shawnees themselves were driven out of Pennsylvania by the Iroquois, and the Shawnees were notably aggressive against other tribes in Kentucky. Should all the continents have been reserved for use of scattered savage tribes and the animals with whom they shared them? Is Europe worse because the Romans civilized it?"

Harrison: "It seems to me there are two alternatives in our approach to the Indians."

Gibson: "What are they?"

Harrison: "Assimilation or removal."

Prophet's Town

Tecumseh: "I suppose the White Men want us to live as they do or leave the country."

The Prophet: "Live as White Men?"

Vincennes

Gibson: "Do you think assimilation really is possible with an inferior race like the Indians?"

Harrison: "Why do you say they are an inferior race?"

Gibson: "If they are equal why have they not already civilized the continent? Why have they not achieved a civilization to equal that of Europe?"

Harrison: "Maybe they just got a late start. Undoubtedly, all of our ancestor peoples went through nomadic and hunting stages before they became farmers and mariners and builders of great cities. Mr. Jefferson has complete faith in assimilation—even including intermarriage of our races. He says it is inevitable, just a matter of time. It's for us to do what we can to hasten it along."

Gibson: "And how does he propose to do that?"

Harrison: "By persuading the Indians to become yeoman farmers and traders, to cultivate the land for most of their food instead of only a small part of it. You know they can grow corn and beans and pumpkins very well. If they devoted themselves to that as civilized farmers, each with his own piece of land, then they would not need these huge tracts for hunting grounds. And Mr. Jefferson also thinks we should spread the system of government 'factories' or posts, like the one at Fort Wayne, where the Indians can do their trading, trading their furs and hides and handcraft items, and even corn, for all kinds of manufactured goods at fair prices. A part of the reason for their unrest always has been the trading practices of the private traders among them who are more interested in plunder and profit than in the welfare of the Indians."

Prophet's Town

Tecumseh: "The White race is a wicked race. Since the day when White people came in contact with Red people they have been the cause of miseries. They have driven the Shawnees and all our brothers farther and farther away as they steal our hunting grounds."

The Prophet: "The mere presence of White Man has been a cause for evil to the Red Man. His whiskey destroys the bravery of our warriors. His lust corrupts the virtue of our women. His diseases kill our old people and children."

Tecumseh: "They want us to adopt their ways, to live as White Men live."

The Prophet: "Never! We must follow the way of Manitou and and not the way of the White Man's false gods. We must follow the way of our fathers."

Vincennes

Gibson: "And what if the Indians don't want to live like White Men? What if they won't do it?"

Harrison: "They will eventually. For the ones who cannot or will not live as civilized farmers, then it is a matter of removal. They must move westward, westward beyond the

Mississippi. There in the Louisiana Territory there is such a great area that they can have several generations to become civilized and assimilated."

Gibson: "It will never work. Have you ever seen any civilized Indians? I mean whole tribes?"

Harrison: "I think the Iroquois have shown a capacity for it and look at that group of Delawares in western Pennsylvania and Ohio who accepted Christianity. They lived in a very civilized manner."

Prophet's Town
The Prophet: "Some of our Delaware brothers tried to live as White Men. They accepted the White Man's gods, and cultivated the land, and buried their tomahawks. And what happened to them?"

Vincennes
Gibson: "They were massacred, completely wiped out by White men."

Prophet's Town
Tecumseh: "They were murdered by White Men, for no reason."

Vincennes
Harrison: "True, unfortunately it is true, they were massacred by White men for no reason. Granted, our problem is as much one of persuading the White men as the Indians to accept this solution. But John, the country has a great future. One day there will be great cities and manufactories here. That is bound to be true."

Gibson: "Yes, that is bound to be true—and the Indians can be a part of of all that?"

Prophet's Town
The Prophet: "The White Men will build more of their stinking cities, crowded with sick people, many people who cannot hunt and cannot grow corn and will not have enough to eat, their people working like slaves who can-

not move from one place to another. Manitou made the Red Man first. This is his homeland. We must return to the ways of our fathers before the White Man brought all his troubles."

Tecumseh: "All the nations of Red Men must fight together to save their homeland and to save their way of life."

3a

William Henry Harrison and his wife, Anna, stood alone in the west great room of their Grouseland manor after the departure of several guests and friends on a sunny Sunday afternoon in June. Anna stepped to the bay window. "Look what a gorgeous sunset," she said.

William Henry joined her. He grasped her hand as they looked out. Over the trees along the Wabash, the clear sky was a deep, bright red, all along the horizon, and extending upward ever so slightly less brightly the crimson faded into a lighter red, and then successively into hues of yellow and green and blue and violet and then pink.

"Magnificent!" he whispered. "Magnificent! Eventide, the closing down of one day, and time to be thinking of the next."

Gazing out the window, Harrison said, "Out there is the future, the West. Anna, what a wonderful thing it is to bring sons and daughters into a world full of such promise. Look how our country already has developed since Jamestown. But this is only the beginning."

Anna remarked simply, "It is beautiful, and the beauty of the evening is made ever more beautiful by the hope of tomorrow."

"Anna, someday, someday soon, this country right where we're standing will be thriving. Eli Whitney's development of manufacturing guns with interchangeable parts gives new substance to Hamilton's report on manufactures. Surely there will be great factories here. Jefferson keeps emphasizing improvements in agriculture. And soon there will be rich farms throughout the Territory. John Fitch's steamboat will show the way for bringing steamboats to the Ohio and the Mississippi and the Wabash. The balloon ascensions in Philadelphia show the possibility of man's taking to the air. Soon this Territory will become a state—a state just as great and equal with the older states,

Virginia and Massachusetts and Pennsylvania, and there will be many more equal states farther west. This right here, the Northwest, one day will be the heartland of America."

"It is a great country, with a great future, Henry."

"I think about all that, and I wonder what our sons and daughters will be doing."

"I wonder. What would you like for our sons to be?"

"To be men of courage and hope and uprightness. I hope they will see their future right here, in the West."

"Who knows, maybe one of them will be President of the United States."

"Or maybe one of the sons of one of them will be President of an even greater United States, for I see this great progress growing. And we are a part of all that." He paused in reflection for a minute or two. "Anna, what a wonderful thing it is to bring our sons and daughters into a world full of such promise—with a real hope, with an assurance, really, that they will have a better world than their father and mother had—with a real faith in the prayers of our Prayer Book, 'world without end.'"

"And with the support of great faith in our nation and great faith in the Almighty." She picked up a Bible from the table and read from *Isaiah*:

The Lord, the everlasting God, creator of the wide world, grows neither weary nor faint; no man can fathom his understanding. He gives vigour to the weary, new strength to the exhausted. Young men may grow weary and faint, even in their prime they may stumble and fall; but those who look to the Lord will win new strength, they will grow wings like eagles; they will run and not be weary; they will march on and never grow faint.

3b

Tecumseh and his sister, Tecumapease, walked slowly together out to the edge of Prophet's Town and looked across the prairie toward a magnificent sunset. Over the broad grasslands the sky was a deep, bright red, all along the horizon, and extending upward ever so slightly less brightly as the crimson faded into a lighter red, and then successively into hues of yellow and green and blue and violet and then pink.

"What a beautiful, beautiful sunset, my Brother," said Tecumapease

"Beautiful sunset, my beloved Sister, the ending of the day. Time to think of the next day. But if tomorrow has no hope, the sunset is robbed of its beauty. Without a bright future, how can life have meaning? What is today if there is no tomorrow?

Without a past the present has no meaning; without a present, there will be no past; without a future, the present is nothing."

"My Brother, look at the great grasslands where we plant our corn. Turn, look at the great forest where we get our meat and our clothing and our wigwams. Look at the great rivers which give us our fish and our furs."

"Yes, my Sister, and the White Men would take them all from us."

"But Manitou will look after his people."

"My beloved Sister, Manitou gives us life, and he provides the things for us to make our living and make ourselves strong. But we must find the way to do it. We must do it."

"My Brother, what do you want your son to be when he becomes a man? Surely he will be a great war chief like his father."

"Not a war chief. Our wars must be all finished before he becomes a warrior."

"What then?"

"Just to have a chance to become a man. Just to be alive. If we have not been able to stop the invasion of our hunting grounds, there will be nothing. My beloved Sister, it is a sad and terrible thing to bring a son into a world without promise, into a world which can only be sadder than his father's—into a world that is ending. It is sad, very sad, to have no promise for our sons for tomorrow, no sunrise. You see what happens to our people when the White people approach. Things were much better in the old days. We must stop the White Man and persuade our people to return to the old ways which were good. The greatest hope for our sons is not in a future dominated by the White Man, but in a return to the glorious past of our own people."

Tecumapease held both hands of her brother and looking into his eyes said, "My Brother, you give our people hope."

He turned back toward the sunset, now fading, and said, "My beloved Sister, the sun is setting over our people. The sun is setting at Tippecanoe. Can we hold back the sun?"

CHAPTER XVIII

Meeting Engagements

1

The outstanding social event for Vincennes in the summer of 1810 was the June wedding of Thomas Randolph and Catherine Lawrence.

With the concurrence of the bridegroom, the bride and her mother accepted the invitation of the Harrisons to make Grouseland the site of the wedding. William Henry arranged for Samuel T. Scott, the Presbyterian minister, to officiate, but to read the Episcopal ceremony.

Well before eleven o'clock on the day of the wedding the great house was filled with over 150 guests. Harrison assumed the role of a military field commander in getting everything organized and moving on time. Attended by Benjamin Parke and Waller Taylor, the bridegroom entered the great parlor from the Governor's office and took his place near the minister who stood in the alcove formed by the bay windows.

Then, to the strains of violin music, the bridal attendants came down the stairway to the central hall, marched on into the parlor and took their places opposite the bridegroom and his attendants. Then, here came the bride, gracefully down the curving stairway to the landing, around the turn, and on down the stairs to the hall. She wore a dress of white satin, with shell trimming around the neck and on the sleeves, and white gloves and white shoes.

419

Her blonde hair was braided down the back, with Grecian curls bearing white rosebuds around her crown. She carried a bouquet of pink and yellow roses. Proper sighs and gasps of approval greeted her as she came into sight. At the foot of the stairs her stepfather, James Dill, met her and escorted her to her place in the parlor.

After the ceremony all the guests joined the wedding party and the families for a big wedding feast on the lawn. Improvised serving tables, formed by putting boards on wooden horses, but covered with linen, creeked under the weight of roast beef, pork, and turkey, and huge bowls of potatoes, beans, cabbage, baked custard, pickles, corn bread and wheat bread. For seasoning there was catsup and pepper-sauce and for desert stacks of cakes, pies, and doughnuts. Beverage tables held bowls of punch and bottles of wine, cider, and corn whiskey. The men and boys were seated on benches around several tables first, and after they had finished, the women and girls had their turn.

The festivities went on most of the afternoon, but Randolph and his bride, after she had changed her clothing, slipped out to his gig and drove off to their new house on Hart Street.

But that was not all of it. About ten o'clock that night a crowd, mostly young people, gathered outside their house for a *charivari*—called shiveree—or "belling." Each person had armed himself with a bell, a horn, boards to clap together, or other noisemakers. Now all joined together to allow no peace for that quarter of the town, much less for the newlyweds.

Randolph and Catherine stepped out on their little porch to greet well-wishers and revelers. This brought excited cheers and yells, but no respite. When the couple returned into the house the noise only became louder. Then they returned and handed out cookies for everyone. But the crowd would not disperse until Randolph strode out on the porch, bade them good night, and then fired his musket into the air over their heads.

The next day the newlyweds opened their house to a number of invited guests, including the Harrisons and all the territorial officials, for an infare.

2

Throughout the spring and early summer of 1810, reports came to Harrison of warlike activities on the Tippecanoe and of plans for Indian attacks against White settlements throughout the Territory. Winamac, the friendly Potawatomi chief, reported to the Governor that Tecumseh and The Prophet were preparing to strike at many White towns. When all was ready, their first attack was to be against Vincennes. Then in turn they planned to capture Fort Wayne, Fort Dearborn and Chicago, and then St. Louis. Grosble, chief of the Piankeshaws, came with tears in his eyes to beg the Governor to move his little tribal remnant across the Mississippi to escape the war that he was sure was coming. Confirming Winamac's report, Grosble added that The Prophet, after the manner of Pontiac, was planning to enter Vincennes in the guise of friendship and then give the signal for a massacre.

Harrison sent Michael Brouillette, a French trader of Vincennes, up to Prophet's Town for direct observation. Brouillette came back with a report that Tecumseh and his brother were determined not to allow any survey of the lands of the "New Purchase" (from the Treaty of Fort Wayne) to be made.

Harrison asked Brouillette to deliver the annual salt shipment—part of the annuity payment—to Prophet's Town and to other villages on the upper Wabash.

Brouillette collected a crew to load a pirogue and with the load of salt set off up the river. At Prophet's Town, they dropped off a few barrels of the salt and went on up the river to make their other deliveries. On returning to Prophet's Town, they noticed that the barrels of salt remained untouched where they had left them. On landing, they were told by some warriors that The Prophet refused to accept the salt.

The boatmen were reloading the salt when Tecumseh strode up and grabbed the men by the hair and with a violent shake, asked them, "Are you Frenchmen or Americans?"

"Frenchmen," they all replied, whatever claim they might have to share Brouillette's national origin.

Tecumseh let them go, saying only, "We want no more presents from Long Knives. When we take presents, Long Knives always say we are selling land. No more!"

By the time the visitors could get back to their boat, several Indians were plundering Brouillette's cabin. Finally the boatmen persuaded them to leave and hurried out to midstream to return to Vincennes as quickly as they could.

Harrison had not made public any of the reports that had come to him, and he had done nothing to lend credence to any of the stories about an impending Indian attack. But rumors of such were rife from many sources. When Brouillette's boatmen returned and spread their story through the town, that was all the credence many of the local inhabitants needed. Now outcries of fear and demands for action reached the Governor.

Harrison called a public meeting to assure the people that prompt measures for defense were being taken. "Then why don't ya call out the milishy!" someone cried.

"All right, I will," he said. "I'll call out two companies, and I hope that you who are concerned here will be willing to serve."

Whatever might happen, Harrison did not want to be caught unaware. He asked Touissant Dubois, another trusted French trader and guide, to go up to Prophet's Town for further observation and report. He asked Francis Vigo to go up to the Miami villages to see if there was truth to a report that a band of Wyandots was trying to get them to join the Tippecanoe confederation, and if so, to do what he could to stop it.

At Prophet's Town, Tecumseh told Dubois that the Red Men had been cheated out of their lands, that no sale of land to the White Men was good unless all the Red Men agreed. The Shawnees and the other tribes at Tippecanoe had not agreed. The chiefs who had given up their lands at the Fort Wayne Council had no right to do so.

Vigo returned with a report that apparently only one Miami chief was supporting Tecumseh, and there appeared to be no danger just now from that direction.

Harrison knew that the focus of his concerns must be on the Tippecanoe. Now he sat down and composed a sharp letter to The Prophet. Harrison decided to send the message by his most trusted interpreter, Joseph Barron who, while delivering the message, would at the same time keep his eyes and ears open to find out actually what was going on up there.

On July 24, 1810, Barron arrived at Prophet's Town. He was impressed with the neat, busy town. A warrior led him to the place where The Prophet, surrounded by a number of followers, was seated. Here Barron was left standing about ten feet from The Prophet while the latter, without any sign of recognition, stared at him coldly. After some time, The Prophet spoke: "For what purpose do you come here? Brouillette was here; he was a spy. Dubois was here; he was a spy. There is your grave! Look on it!"

At this point Tecumseh came out of one of the wigwams and greeted Barron coolly but told him that his life was in no danger and asked him the object of his visit.

Barron then read the Governor's letter to him:

William Henry Harrison, Governor and Commander-in-Chief of the Territory of Indiana, to the Shawnee Chief and the Indians assembled at Tippecanoe: Notwithstanding the improper language which you have used towards me, I will endeavor to open your eyes to your true interests.

Although I must say that you are an enemy to the Seventeen Fires, there is but little harm done, which may be easily repaired. Don't deceive yourselves. Do not believe that all the nations of Indians united are able to resist the force of the Seventeen Fires. I know your warriors are brave, but ours are not less so. Our blue-coats are more numerous than you can count. Our hunters are like the leaves of the forest or the grains of sand on the Wabash. Do not think the red-coats can protect you. They cannot protect themselves. Brothers, the citizens of this country are alarmed. They must be satisfied that you have no design to do them mischief, or they will not lay aside their arms.

Tecumseh replied: "The Great Spirit gave this great island to his Red Children. He placed the Whites on the other side of the water. They were not contented with their own but came to take ours from us. They have driven us from the sea to the lakes. We can go no farther. Our father tells us that we have no business upon the Wabash, the land belongs to other tribes. But the Great Spirit ordered us to come here, and here we will stay.

"But I am pleased to receive the Governor's message. I never have been to see him, but I remember him as a very young man sitting by the side of General Wayne. I have never troubled the White People much, but now I will go to Vincennes and show the Governor that he has been listening to bad men."

"I am sure the Governor will be pleased to receive you," said Barron.

"I shall bring thirty of my principal men to Vincennes with me, and as the young men are fond of attending on such occasions there may be a hundred in all."

"And you may expect to see more than that," The Prophet added.

Tecumseh invited Barron to lodge with him in his wigwam that night. Their conversation continued through much of the night.

"We have no intention of going on the warpath against the Long Knives," Tecumseh reassured his guest.

"I hope that is true," Barron responded. "The Seventeen Fires do not wish to make war against our Red brothers. I hope our nations can always be friends."

Speaking lowly, slowly, in the darkness of the summer wigwam, opened to the night songs of the cat birds, the hoots of the owls, the crepitation of growing corn, and the distant howls of coyotes, Tecumseh said firmly, "It is not possible for the Red Men to remain friends with the Seventeen Fires unless they give up their ideas of extending their settlements always farther and farther to the north and to the west."

"This is big country. There is much, much land, plenty of land for all," said Barron.

"That is not true! That is not true. Already the game becomes scarce in our forest, the fish scarce in our rivers."

"You must plant more corn; then there will be plenty food for all."

"We plant much corn, but it is not enough. And Red Men must decide how much corn to plant on our land, not White Men decide."

"It is difficult for White Men to know which land belongs to Shawnee, which to Wea, which to Miami."

"That is what makes it difficult for us to be friends. White Men must understand that land does not belong to one nation of Red Men here and another nation there, must understand that all the land belongs to all the nations, all the tribes. Must understand that land cannot be sold unless all agree. White chiefs must understand this, or it is not possible to be friends."

"White Chief Harrison always makes treaty with all the tribes, not just one. He makes treaties with all tribes having any claim to the land."

"He did not make treaty with Tecumseh at Fort Wayne."

"He did not make treaty with Tecumseh because Shawnee never have lived on land he was purchasing."

"Tecumseh does not speak for Shawnee. Tecumseh speaks for many tribes. Little Turtle signs treaty for Miamis, but he has no right. He signs because Government gives him presents."

"I hope we can be friends and there will be no war."

"We do not want war, but we want our lands. Chief Harrison made good speech that you bring. I will go to see him to make peace if he will let us keep our land."

When Barron returned with his report to Vincennes, Harrison who never had been quite sure who was in charge at Prophet's Town, The Prophet or Tecumseh, wrote to the Secretary of War,

No particular answer was returned by Mr. Barron. It is to be brought by the brother of The Prophet who will be here in a few days. The brother is really the efficient man—the Moses of the family. I have not seen him since the Treaty of Greeneville and should not know him. He is, however, described by all as a bold, active, sensible man daring in the extreme and capable of any undertaking.

3

Two weeks later while Harrison was welcoming a newly arrived company of regulars and setting them to work at trying to restore old Fort Sackville in the town, and militiamen were returning to their homes to tend their crops, a flotilla of war canoes carrying 400 Indian warriors was streaming down the Wabash from Prophet's Town. Tecumseh, with an unexpectedly large retinue, was on his way. They arrived on Sunday, August 12.

As the canoes, with the mass of warriors in paint and full battle array, approached Vincennes, excited citizens ran through the streets fearful of an attack. A militia company formed in the streets. The Indians filed up to an area outside the town to make their camp, and Tecumseh, with forty warriors, marched through the streets toward the Governor's house. A man from the Governor's staff met them and showed them the way. Tecumseh himself still was dressed very neatly in buckskin coat and pantaloons.

Harrison had set up seats on the portico of his house with the intention of holding the conference there. With the Governor awaiting the Chief were John Gibson, Thomas Randolph, Joseph Barron, as well as the judges of the Supreme Court, Army officers, a sergeant with twelve regulars from Fort Knox, the Methodist minister, and a number of local citizens, and Winamac and a few of his Potawatomi followers.

Tecumseh advanced to within about fifty yards of the Governor and halted. Harrison sent Barron to invite him and his party to join them on the portico. But Tecumseh refused. He indicated that he would prefer to hold the conference in a grove of trees a short distance away. Harrison replied that he had no objection, but that there were no seats there.

Tecumseh said, "It will only be necessary to bring enough chairs for the White Men. The earth is my mother, and on her bosom will I repose."

The people settled. Harrison spoke a few words of welcome and invited Tecumseh to state any complaints openly. There should be no concealment betweeen the White Chief and as great a warrior as Tecumseh. "Let all transactions take place in an open path and under a clear sky," the Governor said.

After a week of preliminaries, Tecumseh summarized his position in a long speech on Monday, August 20. Speaking in his native Shawnee language he said, "Brother, since the peace was made you have killed some of the Shawnees, Winnebagos, Delawares, and Miamis. You have taken our land from us, and I do not see how we can remain at peace if you continue to do so. You try to force the Red People to do some injury. It is you that are pushing them on to do some mischief. You endeavor to make distinctions. You wish to prevent the Indians doing as we wish them—to unite, and let them consider their lands as the common property of the whole. You take tribes aside and advise them not to come into this measure. And until our design is accomplished, we do not wish to accept your invitation to go and see the President. You are continually driving the Red People. When, at last, you will drive them into the Great Lake where they can't either stand or walk.

"Since my residence at Tippecanoe we have endeavored to level all distinctions—to destroy village chiefs by whom all mischief is done. It is they who sell our lands to the Americans. Our object is to let our affairs be transacted by our warriors.

"Brother, this land was sold and the goods that were given for it were only done by a few. The treaty was afterwards brought here, and the Weas were induced to give their consent because of their small numbers. The treaty at Fort Wayne was made through the threats of Winamac. But in the future we are prepared to punish those chiefs who may come forward to propose to sell the land.

"Brother, do not believe that I came here to get presents from you. If you offer us any, we will not take them. By taking goods from you, you will hereafter say that with them you purchased another piece of land from us. I wish you, Brother, to consider everything I have said as true, and that it is the sentiment of all Red People that listen to me." Tecumseh sat down on the grass.

Harrison looked over at Winamac who was lying on the grass a few feet away and saw that he was holding a pistol in such a way as to conceal it from the Indians. The guard now retired to the shade of some other trees.

Harrison arose and replied to Tecumseh: "When the White men came to America, the Miamis occupied all the country on the

Wabash, and the Shawnees lived in Georgia, from which place they had been driven by the Creeks. It is ridiculous to say that the Indians are all one nation. If the Great Spirit had meant it to be so, he would not have put different tongues into their heads. The Shawnees have no right to come from a distant country and control the Miamis in the disposal of their property. And while other civilized nations have simply taken land from the Red Men by conquest, the United States always has made treaties and made payments for the purchase of land. It always has been the desire of the White Father of the Seventeen Fires to treat his Red children fairly."

The Governor sat down to allow the interpreter time to explain his words to the members of the different tribes. But Tecumseh jumped to his feet and, speaking strongly, said, "You do not speak the truth!" Then noticing Winamac, Tecumseh poured a torrent of invective and abuse upon him as a "traitor to all Red Men."

Surprised at the violent gestures, Harrison looked over at Winamac. The latter was priming his pistol. John Gibson said to Lieutenant Jennings, "Those fellows intend mischief. You had better bring up the guard."

Harrison saw the other Indians seize their tomahawks and war clubs and spring to their feet around Tecumseh. Harrison freed himself from his armchair and drew his short dress sword to defend himself. Captain Floyd drew a dirk, and Winamac cocked his pistol. The citizens withdrew hurriedly, but many of them picked up stones or bricks. The Reverend Mr. Winans ran into the Governor's house and came out with a deer gun and placed himself at the door to stand guard for the Governor's family. The guard came running up and was about to fire when Harrison ordered them not to do so. Then he turned to Tecumseh. "You are a bad man," he said. "I will have no further communication with you. You came under protection of the council fire, and you may go safely, but you must return to your camp at once."

At dark two companies of militia marched into Vincennes to reinforce the local garrison. In order to make an appearance of strength they made frequent changes of guards, and one company marched round and round near the edge of town. Indian fires burned brightly in the background.

The next morning Tecumseh sent a messenger to the Governor to apologize for his anger during the preceding day and to request another conference. Harrison consented, and the conference resumed in much of the same setting.

Now very dignified and collected, Tecumseh denied any intention of attacking the Governor. Then the Indian leader continued his address: "Brother, there are many White people among you who are not true Americans, they are endeavouring to fill the minds of the Indians with evil towards the United States of which I shall now inform you. The person that informed me was a man of sense.

"Brother, he said to us, that when you first began to bring about the last treaty you observed the greatest secrecy, after which you went to Fort Wayne and there made the treaty equally secret, declaring that you did not think it necessary to call upon us, but that you were determined to confine us to a small piece of land, and that you would bring all the tribes who listen to me, to abandon myself and The Prophet, and then you would know what to do with us.

"Brother, this person came to our village shortly after the Treaty of Fort Wayne and said to us—'Laulewasika [The Prophet] and you Tecumseh, you may believe what I say to you, it is not me alone who speaks to you. I am the agent of a large party of White people who are your friends and will support you. They send me here to inform you everything that that man, the Governor at Vincennes, is doing against you; but you must observe great secrecy and by no means inform him of us, or we shall be hung. I was at the Treaty at Fort Wayne and heard the Governor say that The Prophet was a bad man and that he would prevent traders from trading at his village [The Prophet's]; or if any did go, they should sell their goods so high that the Indians could not purchase them, and consequently must suffer.'

"Brother, this man further represented to us that you were yet to remain in office two years and would be succeeded by a good man who was a true friend to the Indians, that you would offer us goods [annuities] but by no means to accept of them, that in order to induce us to take them you would offer us horses with saddles and bridles plated with silver, that all the goods and even the provisions that you give to the Indians are with the intention to cheat them out of their lands, that it was the intention of the United States to oppress the Shawnees, before long the White people would push their settlements near to them and oblige them to use the ax instead of the rifle—therefore he recommended to us to take nothing from you.

"Brother, another American told us lately at our village, that you were about to assemble the Indians at Vincennes, for the purpose of making proposals, for more land, that you were placed here by Government to buy land when it was offered to you, but not to use persuasions and threats to obtain it.

"Brother, this man told me that I must go to Vincennes and make my objections to the purchase of land from the Indians, and not be afraid to speak very loud to you—that when you wanted land you were very smooth with the Indians, but at length became very boisterous.

"Brother, after my hearing this so often, I could not help thinking otherwise than you wished to sow discord amongst the Indians. I wish you, my Brother, to let alone those distractions you have always been endeavouring to establish among the Indians. It is doing them a great injury by exciting jealousies between them. I am alone the acknowledged head of all the Indians."

At this point, Harrison interrupted to ask Tecumseh to state explicitly whether surveyors who might be sent to survey the lands in the New Purchase would be interfered with by the Indians, and whether the Kickapoos would accept their annuities which were now available.

Tecumseh responded, "Brother, when you speak to me of annuities I look at the land and pity the women and children. I am authorized to say that they will not receive them.

"Brother, they want to save that piece of land. We do not wish you to take it. It is small enough for our purposes. If you do take it, you must blame yourself as the cause of trouble between us and the Tribes who sold it to you. I want the present boundary line to continue. Should you cross it, I assure you it will be productive of bad consequences."

Now leaders of the Wyandots, Kickapoo, Potawatamie, Ottawa, and Winebago spoke in turn. They said that their tribes had joined the great confederacy, and they would support the principles laid down by Tecumseh, who was their leader.

Harrison agreed to transmit a statement of their claims to the President of the Seventeen Fires and to inform them of his reply. He said that he was certain, however, that the President would uphold the fair purchase of the Wabash lands, and the rights of the United States would be supported by the sword. He suggested that Tecumseh go himself to see the Great White Father and hear his decision with his own ears.

Except for Sunday, and for one day when it rained, the conference had gone on daily for ten days. In the privacy of his office, Harrison discussed Tecumseh's remarks with Joseph Barron.

Barron reported, "When I talked with Tecumseh privately the next day, he told me that it was probable that he had been deceived by White people, that he had been told by some of our citizens that the people were equally divided, that only about half supported the Governor, and about half supported Tecumseh's position."

"Where would he get that idea?" asked Harrison.

"Well, he said that half of the people were opposed to the purchase of Indian lands and the other half, with the Governor, wanted to drive the Indians to extremities."

"Now, you know that is not so. I wonder if that damned Jennings has had anything to do with this."

Barron went on, "He even said that he had been told that you had purchased the lands without the consent of the Government, and against the wishes of half of the people who did not want the land as they already had more land than they could occupy. Tecumseh took this to be true, because he sent some of his men to reconnoiter the settlements, and he found that the lands toward the Ohio were not settled at all."

"No, you know who is behind this. You know who does not want us to purchase these lands from the Indians because he claims to own large tracts of it that he got from the French. It's that damned Scotch Tory, McIntosh!"

"No doubt," Barron agreed. "And of course the man he was referring to as giving him the information about the Treaty of Fort Wayne had to be the agent up there."

"Yes, of course, that damned William Wells."

Harrison reported to Secretary of War William Eustis,

"The information which was given him [Tecumseh] came I am convinced from a small factious party here headed by a scotch tory who would not hesitate to adopt any measure that would be likely to do me an injury. Independent of his hatred to the American government and individually to myself, he is very much interested to prevent the settling of the new purchase as he is the owner of a large quantity of land, purchased for a song from the ignorant French. The person alluded to by Tecumseh as giving him the information from the Treaty of Fort Wayne is beyond all doubt Wells!!"

4

That fall Tecumseh was out making the rounds again to solicit support, this time in the northeast. In northwestern Ohio, he was disappointed in still being unable to persuade Black Hoof's Shawnees to join him. He had rather more success as he travelled all across Ohio, south of Lake Erie, and into northwestern Pennsylvania, among the Ottawas, Potawatomis, Winnebagos, and Sacs and Foxes.

Most encouraging of all was his visit to Canada. Over 160 of these tribesmen, including thirty-three women and children, went along with him when he visited the British 100th Regiment and the British Indian agent, Matthew Elliott, at Amherstburg.

Elliott always had been supportive, but now Tecumseh found him especially friendly. Elliott had lived among the Indians and he had married a Shawnee woman. His devotion to the Indian cause may have been greater than official British policy warranted, but Elliott provided substantial quantities of clothing and ammunition and promised later shipments of goods to Prophet's Town for trade. Even more important, Tecumseh came away with a conviction that the British looked with favor on his project for Indian union.

Tecumseh boycotted a meeting which Governor William Hull of Michigan Territory had arranged at Brownstown, the Wyandot village south of Detroit. He heard from the government chiefs whom Hull had told that Tecumseh had proclaimed himself spokesman for all the Indians.

He also boycotted a meeting of some 1,700 Potawatomis, Delawares, Miamis, and Black Hoof's Shawnees at Fort Wayne, under the auspices of the new agent there, John Johnston. This was a meeting for the distribution of annuities. Tecumseh was pleased to learn that Peccan, Miami chief from the Mississinewa River, had protested the payments for lands given up by the Treaty of Fort Wayne, and had said that the Miamis had been coerced into signing the treaty and did not consider it valid.

5

William McIntosh persisted in defamatory remarks about the Governor. The "Scotch Tory" accused Harrison of defrauding the Indians in the various treaties, dealing only with chiefs to suit his own purposes to the exclusion of the real chiefs and even of profiting from the large quantities of Indian goods that had been drawn.

McIntosh sent to Jonathan Jennings, in Washington, accusations that Harrison was guilty of bribery and collusion in public land sales. Jennings was only too glad to refer these to members of Congress and to the President, though without result. Jennings proclaimed to his friends that Harrison's political career was ended, and he, Jennings, proposed to lay the groundwork for impeachment proceedings.

Harrison decided to have a showdown. He called Thomas Randolph into his office one day and said, "Tom, that damned McIntosh won't let up. The more I try to settle the question of the Indian lands the more he hollers 'Fraud'."

"Yes, I've been hearing some of his talk," Randolph said. "He's a damned Scotch Tory, and he means no good, Governor. You know he has no scruples. He has no religion, but he does have a bunch of mulatto children by his Negro housekeeper. But what's really bothering him?"

"Money, what else?" Harrison answered. "He's afraid that the opening up of the lands in the New Purchase will keep the price of his land down. He was out to make a killing at the expense of the settlers."

"Of course, and now that won't be so easy."

"I've half a mind to take him to court," Harrison said. "I hate to get involved in this sort of thing, but if I remain silent and let him go on broadcasting his lies, he'll undermine my whole position. It will cause the people to lose confidence and then I won't be able to accomplish anything."

"Of course you're right," Randolph agreed. "I say sue the bastard. Sue him for slander."

Harrison thought a while. "Do you have enough to go on?" he asked.

"We've got enough to hang him."

"Witnesses?"

"Certainly—witnesses to swear that he said those things, and witnesses to swear that you did what was right in all those cases."

Harrison thought some more and then said, "All right, we'll do it. Go to it."

Randolph enlisted two other able lawyers in the town: General W. Johnston (that was his name, "General Washington Johnston") and Ellis Glover, to help prepare the case.

It went to the Supreme Court of the Territory. There, of the three judges, two disqualified themselves as being friends of one or the other of the parties to the suit, and this left the most recent arrival, Waller Taylor, to carry on alone though he too was a friend of both Harrison and Randolph.

To assure an impartial jury Judge Taylor named two elisors who chose a panel of forty-eight citizens from whom the jury would be drawn. The plaintiff and the defendant each struck twelve names. The twelve jurors were drawn by lot from the remaining twenty-four on the panel.

The trial was ready to begin at ten o'clock on that warm April morning, the 11th, (1811), in a crowded courtroom. After a series of witnesses had sworn to the slanderous statements that McIntosh had made, and then a whole series of witnesses from Vincennes and Fort Wayne had testified as to the integrity of the Governor's actions, the defense shifted ground. They began to ask questions about the Governor's civil administration.

Randolph objected. The judge and the jury upheld the objection. But Harrison said to let them ask anything they wanted to. With twenty-five witnesses put on the stand, the trial went on until an hour after midnight. By the end, the defense counsel was pleading simply for a mitigation of damages.

It took the jury one hour to return a verdict in favor of the plaintiff. Harrison had asked for damages in the amount of $9,000, but he was pleased to accept the jury's award of $4,000. As it was, McIntosh asked for a new trial on the ground of excessive damages, but the court refused.

Harrison arranged for the transfer of a large share of McIntosh's land to pay the award. A little later, McIntosh moved across the Wabash River to the Illinois Territory where he joined a group of European Free-Thinkers in building a new town that they called Mount Carmel.

About the same time, Harrison brought suit against Isaac Darneille, an Irish lawyer and land speculator of Cahokia, with similar results. Darneille had published a series of scurrilous attacks on the Governor in a book called *The Letters of Decius* that created a sensation in the Territory for a time. The trial was essentially a contest between the land speculators and Indian traders, on the one hand, and the Governor on the other. In this case, the supportive testimony of William Wells brought him back into the good graces of the Governor.

Victory brought no sense of delight for Harrison. He continued to be deeply troubled by petty intrigues of many of his constituents. At times he brooded, but only briefly. Privately he wondered whether his prospects for achievement were worth enduring the torment of his detractors.

In public he never failed in his optimism and determination. Sometimes he felt that he had persuaded an enthusiasm in his supporters, such as Randolph and Parke, that was greater than his own. And this affected his whole attitude. It was in a way a kind of "virtuous circle"—having implanted an optimism and positive outlook in his friends, he did not dare let them down by admitting the kinds of doubts that he had put to rest in them. Thus in his case, flashes of pessimism quickly gave way to his more characteristic optimism.

6

Again this spring, Harrison was worried by reports of warlike activities and plans in Prophet's Town, and several instances of the murder of White settlers by Indians in Illinois.

This time, when he sent the boat up the Wabash with the annuity salt, The Prophet seized all of it. John La Plante, in charge of the boat, returned with a report that about a hundred warriors were presently in Prophet's Town, and Tecumseh was expected at any moment with large reinforcements from the lakes. A Kickapoo chief warned of impending war. Governor William Clark of the Missouri Territory reported that the Sacs in his area had accepted a black wampum belt for war. An interpreter at Chicago reported that Indians in Michigan were bent on war.

Harrison felt frustrated, not sure which way to turn. He wanted to be prepared for war, but did not want to take any action that might precipitate it. He did not want simply to sit in Vincennes, with inferior forces, and await attack. He decided to send a sturdy militia captain, Walter Wilson, with Joseph Barron as interpreter, to Prophet's Town with a message for Tecumseh and The Prophet.

After five days in the saddle, Wilson and Barron arrived at Tippecanoe. Wilson delivered to The Prophet the message from Harrison:

Brothers, Listen to me, I speak to you about matters of importance, both to the White people and yourselves; open your ears, therefore, and attend to what I shall say,

Brothers, this is the third year that all the White people in this country have been alarmed at your proceedings. You threaten us with war, you invite all the tribes to the north and west of you to join against us.

Brothers, your warriors who have lately been here, deny this; but I have received the information from every direction. The tribes on the Mississippi have sent me word that you intended to murder me, and then to commence a war upon our people. I have also received the speech that you sent to the Potawatamies and others, to join you for that purpose; but if I had no other evidence of your hostility to us, your seizing the salt which I lately sent up the Wabash is sufficient.

Brothers, our citizens are alarmed, and my warriors are preparing themselves; not to strike you, but to defend themselves and their women and children. You shall not surprise us as you expect to do; you are about to undertake a very rash act. As a friend, I advise you to consider it well. A little reflection may save us a great deal of trouble, and prevent much mischief; it is not yet too late.

Brothers, what can be the inducement for you to undertake an enterprise where there is so little probability of success? Do you really think that the handful of men that you have about you are able to contend with the power of the Seventeen Fires, or even that the whole of the tribes united could contend against the Kentucky Fire alone?

Brothers, I am myself of the long knife fire. As soon as they hear my voice, you will see them pouring forth their swarms of hunting-shirt men, as numerous as the mosquitoes on the shores of the Wabash. Brothers, take care of their stings.

Brothers, it is not our wish to hurt you; if we did wish it, we certainly have power to do it. Look at the number of our warriors to the east of you, above and below the Great Miami, to the south, on both sides of the Ohio and below you. You are brave men, but what could you do against such a multitude? We wish you to live in peace and happiness.

Brothers, the citizens of this country are alarmed. They must be satisfied that you have no design to do them mischief, or they will not lay aside their arms. You have also insulted the government of the United States, by seizing the salt that was intended for the other tribes; satisfaction must be given for that also.

Brothers, you talk of coming to see me, attended by all your young men. This, however, must not be so. If your intentions are good, you have no need to bring but a few of your young men with you. I must be plain with you; I will not suffer you to come into our settlements with such a force.

Brothers, if you wish to satisfy us that your intentions are good, follow the advice that I have given you before; that is, that one or both of you should visit the President of the United States and lay your grievances before him. He will treat you well, will listen to what you say, and if you can shew him that you have been injured, you will receive justice. If you will follow my advice in this respect, it will convince the citizens of this country and me that you have no design to attack them.

Brothers, with respect to the lands that were purchased last fall, I can enter into no negotiation with you on the subject. The affair is in the hands of the President, and if you wish to go to see him, I will supply you with the means.

Brothers, the person who delivers this is one of my war officers and he is a man in whom I have entire confidence. Whatever he says to you, although it may not be contained in this paper, you may believe comes from me.

My Friend, Tecumseh, the bearer is a good man and a brave warrior. I hope you will treat him well since you are yourself a warrior and all warriors should have an esteem for each other.

Showing no reaction, The Prophet had a warrior show the visitors to the House of the Stranger where they were given lodging for the night. They were pleased with the cabin, but a little apprehensive about what might be in store for them. They were not reassured by the unfriendly gestures of the village squaws when they filed past the cabin under the leadership of The Prophet's wife.

About midnight they were surprised by the arrival of Tecumseh. The chief told them that the Council had decided that the two men should be handed over to the village women to be disposed of as they wished, and he had not been able to overrule them. However, he had seen the message from the Governor and he wished to respond. He would give them the message and then would lead them out to safety.

By a dim candle, Barron wrote down Tecumseh's message and handed it to Wilson. Then, about midnight, the chief led them quietly through the town to a spot where a warrior was waiting with their horses. Tecumseh told them that he would arrive in Vincennes within eighteen days, "To wash away all bad stories, and I will bring with me only a few warriors."

Back in Vincennes Captain Wilson delivered to Harrison the message from Tecumseh:

Brother, I give you a few words until I will be with you myself.

Brother, at Vincennes, I wish you to listen to me whilst I send you a few words, and I hope that they will ease your heart; I know you look on your young men and your women and children with pity, to see them so much alarmed.

Brother, I wish you now to examine what you have from me, I hope that it will be a satisfaction to you, if your intentions are like mine, to wash away all these bad stories that have been circulated. I will be with you myself in eighteen days from this day.

Brother, we cannot say what will become of us, as the Great Spirit has the management of us at his will. I may be there before the time, and may not be there until the day. I hope that when we come together, all these bad tales will be settled; and by this I hope your young men, women, and children will be easy. I wish you, Brother, to let them know when I come to Vincennes to see you, all will be settled in peace and happiness.

Brother, these are only a few words to let you know that I will be with you myself, and when I am with you, I can inform you better.

Brother, if I find that I can be with you in less time than eighteen days, I will send one of my young men before me, to let you know what time I will be with you.

Tecumseh

7

When Tecumseh made ready to leave Prophet's Town for Vincennes on July 15, he planned to take with him twenty-four warriors in eight canoes, but he found that many others wanted to come along. He made no objection when his brother and many of the warriors wanted to bring along their women and children. Indeed he thought this might be an impressive demonstration of his peaceful intent, a reassurance to nervous Long Knives who dreaded an Indian attack.

Instead, Tecumseh's host, now grown to 300, alarmed the Long Knives even though they moved slowly and deliberately, some by canoe while others rode or walked on the "Tecumseh Trail," in order not to surprise anyone. About seventy-five miles upstream from Vincennes, they halted for several days.

When spies reported to Harrison the size of the Indian party, the Governor sent Captain Wilson up the river to inquire of Tecumseh why he was bringing all these numbers and what his intentions were.

On the 25th Captain Wilson met Tecumseh at Bosseron, about twenty miles north of Vincennes, where the Indians were camping on the east side of the river. Wilson reported that the Governor was astonished that the Chief was bringing so large a force when he had been asked to keep the numbers small and had given his promise to do so. Tecumseh's response was that he had chosen only twenty-four warriors to come with him; all the others had followed by their own accord. He assured Wilson that there would be no trouble.

But near panic was spreading among some of the people of Vincennes. Elihu Stout allowed himself to print in the *Western*

Sun a warning that Tecumseh and his "insolent banditti" intended to burn Vincennes and massacre all the inhabitants.

When Tecumseh arrived at Vincennes on Saturday, July 2, nearly 800 troops of the regular army and militia were patrolling the streets. Harrison hoped to start the conference on Monday, but Tecumseh insisted that he could not be ready until Tuesday. He asked Harrison if he intended to have a large body of armed troops at the conference. Harrison replied that there would be only a token force of 25 or 30 dragoons, dismounted. In that case, Tecumseh stated, his warriors would leave their muskets at the camp.

On Tuesday, Tecumseh arrived at Grouseland with about 180 warriors carrying no firearms, but with tomahawks, knives, and war clubs in their belts, and some with bows and arrows. The Prophet remained to keep order and to discourse their followers in the camp. Tecumseh and his warriors took their places about in the same way as for their first conference a year earlier.

In his opening remarks, Harrison said, "Brother, our people have been much alarmed by the murders of innocent White people in Illinois.

"Brother, our people here are alarmed when you bring so many warriors when you promised to bring only a few.

"Brother, I am ready to listen to anything that you or any of the other chiefs have to say, but I can enter into no negotiation regarding the new purchase. That is now entirely in the hands of the President, but you may be pleased to go and see the President himself and hear his determination from his own mouth."

Here of course Harrison was declaring "non-negotiable" the very reason for the unrest that Tecumseh and The Prophet had been stirring up—indeed the very reason for the conference itself —the Treaty of Fort Wayne.

Harrison continued, "And I also must require an explanation for the seizure of the salt which was sent for all the tribes on the Wabash who were entitled to the annuity."

In his response, Tecumseh referred to the last point first, "Brother, the salt which you mention was taken this year. I was not present either when the salt arrived this year or when it arrived last year, but it is impossible to please the Governor. He was angry last year when the salt was refused. He was equally angry this year when the salt was taken."

Before there was time for much more of an exchange, a downpour of rain set in, and Harrison agreed to Tecumseh's request to adjourn the conference until the next day.

It was two o'clock before the Indian group arrived the next day. This time, Tecumseh stepped aside in favor of the Wea chief who reviewed all the treaties that Harrison had made on behalf of the United States with the Indian tribes. Then he said that at Fort Wayne the Miami chiefs had been forced by the Potawatomis to sign the treaty, and that an inquiry should be held to find out who had held the tomahawk over their heads, and to punish him (presumably Winamac).

Harrison replied at once that no one had held a tomahawk over anyone at Fort Wayne, and he asked the Miamis present to verify this. Then turning back to Tecumseh, he said,

"Brother, it is within your power by a single act to demonstrate the truth of your professions of friendship for the United States, and your desire to preserve peace. Deliver up the two Potawatomis who murdered the four White men on the Missouri River last fall and who, I know, are now in your camp."

Tecumseh responded with a long speech in which he said, "Brother, Listen! After much trouble and much difficulty I have at last brought all the northern tribes to unite and to place themselves under my direction. The White People are unnecessarily alarmed by these measures. They really mean nothing but peace. The United States has set for me the example of forming a strict union amongst all the fires that compose their confederacy. The Indians do not complain of this. Neither should my White brothers complain of my doing the same thing among the Indian tribes. As soon as this council is ended I will go to visit the southern tribes to get them to unite with those of the North.

"To your demand for handing over the Red Men who killed the Whites, I must say they are not in this town as you believe. It is not right to punish them. They ought to be forgiven, as well as those accused of killing White People in Illinois. I have set an example of forgiveness of injuries which you ought to follow. The Ottawas murdered one of our women and the Osage murdered one of my relatives, but I have forborne revenge against them, and I even took the tomahawk out of the hands of those who were ready to march against the Osages."

Harrison returned to his central question: "Are you determined to prevent the settlement of the New Purchase?"

"Brother, I hope that no attempts will be made to settle those lands until I return in the spring. A great number of Red Men and their families are coming to settle on the Tippecanoe this fall, and they must occupy much of that tract as a hunting ground. Even if they did no other injury, they might kill some of the cows and hogs of the White People, and you know that will cause a disturbance.

"Brother, listen! I wish everything to remain in its present situation until I return in the spring. White Man's settlements must go no farther, and no revenge must be sought for injuries while I am away. When I return, I will go see the President and settle everything with him.

"Brother, the affairs of all the tribes in this area are now in my hands. Nothing can be done without my approval. I will send messengers in all directions to prevent the warriors from harming the White People. I truly regret the murders which may have resulted from the wampum belt that I sent."

The conference went on for five days. Throughout the time, Harrison made a military presence known in order to avoid any surprise attack. Benjamin Parke frequently paraded through the streets his troop of dragoons mounted on fine horses with great effect. Three companies of infantry were marched about in relieving each other in such a way as to create the impression that they were four or five companies.

On the evening before his departure, Tecumseh made a personal call on the Governor.

Harrison asked, "Brother, did your statements at the council represent your true intentions?"

Tecumseh replied, "They certainly did. It is with great reluctance that I would make war with the Seventeen Fires. If you will persuade the great President to give up these lands lately purchased and agree never to make another treaty without the consent of all the tribes, I will be a faithful ally. I would rather be a friend of the Seventeen Fires, but if they do not agree to our rights I may have to join with the English."

Harrison repeated his assurances to communicate with the President, but said there would be no change.

"Well," said Tecumseh. "As the Great Chief is to determine the matter, I hope the Great Spirit will put sense enough into his head to induce him to direct you to give up this land. It is true, he is so far off, he will not be injured by the war. He may still sit in his town and drink his wine, whilst you and I will have to fight it out."

Harrison spoke again. "If war comes, I have one proposal to which I hope you will agree: that is to stop the cruel mode of warfare which Indians are accustomed to wage against women and children and those unable to resist."

"To that, Brother, I can agree."

It was growing dusk now, and a full moon was rising.

Tecumseh added, "I wish all to remain quiet until my return. Then I will visit the President and settle all differences with him."

Harrison replied, "The moon which we see would sooner fall to the ground than the President would suffer his people to be murdered, and he would put petticoats on his warriors sooner than give up a country which we had fairly bought from its true owners."

The conference with Tecumseh did little to allay the fears of the people of Vincennes. On the contrary the impression of Indian union that he created only heightened their apprehensions.

On one evening, while that conference was in session, a number of the local citizens held a public meeting where they adopted resolutions for publication in the *Western Sun* and prepared a petition to President Madison. They applauded the steps being taken by the Governor for defense, but they urged that further steps be taken immediately to break up the Indian confederacy that Tecumseh was organizing.

8

From their confrontations with each other and from their respective approaches to great projects, it was clear that both Tecumseh and Harrison were cast in the heroic mold. Each was willing to undertake great deeds and to accept responsibility for what he did or failed to do. They were willing to face the consequences of their actions without either trying to shift blame to others or trying to run and hide.

The Prophet, on the other hand, affected an acceptance of responsibility with a certain arrogance that served as a defense against his own lack of self-confidence. Yet his religious convictions were genuine enough, and these elevated his feelings of inferiority and his arrogant manner to traits of substance in offering leadership to followers who were desperately searching for some basis for confidence of their own.

Harrison, after his direct experience with Tecumseh, saw him as more straightforward, more reliable, and a lot more skillful and clever. He saw him as something of an egotist and something of an opportunist in winning adherents to his cause.

Harrison now saw The Prophet as less reliable, more cunning than clever, and a complete opportunist and cynical charlatan, one who shaped his religious doctrines and practices to fit his own personal or political objectives. He regarded him as rash and sometimes daring, but never as a warrior.

Tecumseh saw Harrison as a straightforward, reliable, and generally honest man who would resort to any means to acquire the Indian lands that he wanted for his government. The Prophet thought him altogether egotistical and cynical, one who espoused high principles only because that suited his objective in ever extending the power and influence of the United States over the continent.

CHAPTER XIX

Peaceful Pursuits

1

Upon conclusion of the conference with Governor Harrison, Tecumseh prepared to embark immediately on his projected trip to try again to enlist the support of the southern tribes for his proposed union for a common stand against the Whites. He had a long conversation with his brother, The Prophet, to implore him to hold things together and to risk no open conflict during Tecumseh's absence.

Tecumseh picked up a big supply of bundles of red sticks that The Prophet and his helpers had been preparing during the preceding weeks. In the center of each bundle was a stick of red cedar about a foot long and half an inch thick. The sides were cut flat, and on one side carved figures represented a message for all Indians to assemble near Detroit with the speed of lightning when they felt the trembling of the earth which would be a sign to them. Then all together they would recover the lands that the Whites had stolen from them. The red sticks around the center sign stick represented months. At each full moon, one of the red sticks would be thrown away, and when all were gone the time for the great sign for all Indians to assemble would be at hand. Most of the bundles had six or seven red sticks in them, but some had only three or four. The differences allowed for the different times when the bundles would be given to the different tribes.

For this trip, Tecumseh again chose Sikaboo to go along as interpreter and prophet, and Little Blue Jacket again would be the Chief's principal aide. But this time, the party would be a mixed group, the more to emphasize the theme of unity among the tribes: three Shawnee warriors (in addition to Tecumseh and his two assistants), six Kickapoos, and six Sacs and Foxes. Some weeks earlier, a number of Creeks had visited Tippecanoe, and now two of these Creek warriors accompanied Tecumseh as guides.

Early on August 5, as The Prophet made ready to return to Prophet's Town, Tecumseh and his party embarked in three big war canoes and began paddling down the Wabash. The water of August was barely deep enough to carry them, but it improved with every league, and they made good time toward the Ohio.

Tecumseh always had counseled patience in building his Indian union. Now he had a feeling that time was running out. His last conference with Harrison had impressed upon him a conviction that the next year would be the year of decision. He felt sure that Harrison would try to precipitate an incident or even attack during his absence. He had told the Governor that he planned to return in the spring. Now the troubled war chief was determined to return in four or five months rather than in the eight or nine he had indicated. He hoped that would be in time, but first he must do all that he could to gain additional support.

They went down the Ohio as far as the mouth of the Tennessee and visited briefly the villages in the Chickasaw country west of Kentucky. Then they paddled back up the Ohio to the Cumberland and up the Cumberland all the way to Nashville. Here Tecumseh arranged to trade the canoes and some furs and other goods for horses. By the 8th of September, they were in Nashville and continuing on to the southeast.

On this trip Tecumseh and his party were going about the reverse of the route they had followed on the previous southern trip. This time the Shawnee leader was most anxious to get to the Creeks and the Seminoles. Except for the little skirmish with the band of horse thieves, he had missed the Creeks previously, and he had had a very brief encounter with the Seminoles. Now he would go directly to the Seminoles and then to the Creeks. Later, as time permitted, he would visit the others.

Among the Seminoles, Tecumseh had no trouble in arousing their sympathy for a stand against the Whites, but their leaders wondered why they should follow Tecumseh. It so happened that Tecumseh had learned through some British agents that a load of

British supplies was on the way to the Florida coast west of Pensacola. He announced to his listeners that he came with the blessing of the Great Spirit and, in just two days, the Great Spirit would send a great canoe filled with weapons and ammunition and food and clothing for his Seminole children. It came to pass as he had predicted, and this was enough to consolidate support in that quarter.

About the first of October, Tecumseh made his way to the Creek town of Chief Red Eagle. Walking through the town Tecumseh noticed a very striking Creek woman. She returned his glance with a look of recognition. Almost with a start he recognized her as Mineshelana. She came out to welcome him warmly. She explained that her husband was away with a group of warriors on a short hunting trip but would return in two days.

"Who is your husband?" Tecumseh asked.

"Red Eagle," she replied.

For only an instant, Tecumseh was tempted to throw discretion to the wind and take her away, but better judgment prevailed. He knew there could be no more certain way of wrecking his whole project. How foolish, he thought. He had not taken her with him when he could have, when she had urged him to, but he had refused because he was afraid it might interfere with his future work among the tribes. Now, when such a course would completely wreck all that work by incurring the enmity of a whole nation whose support he desperately needed, how could such a thought have entered his mind even for a moment?

Because she was just as beautiful and just as helpful and considerate as ever, and she was the most unselfish person he had ever known. What a contrast with Monetohse! he thought. Though friendly and cordial, Mineshelana made it clear that she had great respect for Red Eagle, was entirely devoted and faithful to him. This only made Tecumseh appreciate her qualities all the more. Now he did feel a sense of regret that he had not made her his squaw and taken her with him. But then he had been too young to be wise. Now he was too wise to act young. Yet he could not dismiss thoughts of what might have been. How much better he might have been able to do his work if he always had been able to return to a neat, well-supplied and warm wigwam, kept so by Mineshelana. What greater hope for the future he might have if he had many sons and daughters in her care!

"I am glad to see you," she said with a smile.

"And I am glad to see you," he repeated. "You are a good woman. A very good woman."

She smiled again. Then her face turned more solemn. "Have you come to make war on the White Man?" she asked.

"I have come to urge all Red Men to unite together, to be strong, so White Men will not keep taking the lands of the Red Men."

"I understand," she said. "You are a very good man. You want to help all Red People."

"Yes, I want all Red People to help each other."

"You speak wise words. I will speak to Red Eagle. He will help. I know he will help." She smiled again.

"I hope so," said Tecumseh. "But is he not part White Man?"

"Yes, he is," she answered. "His father and mother were White, but one grandmother was Creek. His name was William Weatherford, but now Red Eagle. He is a good man. He thinks like Creek. Are there no Shawnee warriors who had White parents?"

Tecumseh smiled and pointed across the way. "You see that young warrior?"

"Yes."

"That is Little Blue Jacket. His father was Blue Jacket who was a White Man. His name was Marmaduke Van Swearingen."

Mineshelana laughed.

Tecumseh went on, "He was adopted by the Shawnee as Blue Jacket and became a great war chief."

Two days later, Red Eagle returned. He reflected Mineshelana's cordiality, and he fulfilled her promise with his own promise of assistance. Tecumseh gave him several bundles of the red sticks to hand out to all the village chiefs in the area. The red sticks were sought as marks of distinction for followers of Tecumseh. Soon they lost their value as special signs of time. Instead of throwing away the sticks month by month, the village chiefs soon were distributing them to all the warriors, and when the supply ran out, as it did almost immediately in any village, warriors who had been left out began making counterfeits. Not everyone wanted to be known as a follower of Tecumseh, but with the encouragement of Red Eagle most of them did. Soon they all came to be known as the "Red Sticks" to distinguish them from those who had resisted the influence of Tecumseh and Red Eagle.

Tecumseh encountered greater difficulty as he and his party moved on to the town of Tuckabatchee on the Tallapoosa River where Chief Big Warrior presided. This was to be the major meeting with all the Creeks. Red Eagle and a party of his warriors and their families went along, though with less enthusiasm than they had displayed previously. Big Warrior had called a general council, and as was common for such occasions, white traders and other visitors as well as warriors and their families from all the villages came until a crowd of nearly five thousand had gathered.

On the second day of the council, Tecumseh and his warriors, impressive in their similar dress of buckskin, eagle feathers and war paint (Tecumseh had two feathers, one red and one white) and their firearms and war clubs and tomahawks, marched into the town square. After a turn around the square, they went to a big cabin set aside for them, and that night reappeared to lead a war dance.

Tecumseh was determined that he was not going to make his spiel in front of White Men. Each morning, Sikaboo would announce that his chief would speak at noon, and then each noon he would announce that the speech had been put off until the next day. This went on until the U.S. agent, a Colonel Hawkins, finally departed. The next day Tecumseh made a grand entrance with his warriors and delivered his speech to the assembled multitude:

"My Brothers! Listen! Look back. See how the White Men have taken your lands. You think they are finished? No! They always want more.

"Now you think you have good houses. You have good fields of corn. But listen! The better you make your houses and the better your fields of corn, the more the White Men will want them. Then, you will be forced to leave all you have built and to start again.

"The Long Knives soon will be at war again with the English. That will be the time for all Indians to come together to recover their lands.

"My Brothers, you are becoming weak in sitting on the land and planting corn like women. You must find the bravery and the independence of your fathers.

"All Red Men must unite together to defend their homelands from the Long Knives. It is easy to break one stick. It is not possible to break many sticks bound together."

One of the chiefs present, a mixed-blood called Moniac, rose to object. He said, "We are at peace with the White Men, and it is better to remain so. The Creek people are doing well. It would be bad policy to take sides between the English and the Americans, but, if we must, it would be better to take the side of the Americans."

Tecumseh replied, "You are blind! Your sons will have no land here. If you help the Americans, they will not help you. They only want your land. The English have no claim to the land against the Americans. They will let you keep your land if they defeat the Americans. That is the only way.

"Tonight, watch! You will see the fiery arm of Manitou across the sky. And remember! I am Tecumseh, the Shooting Star."

Tecumseh was referring to the great comet that had come into view in late August and had just now, October 15, reached its greatest brilliance.

After sundown that evening, Tecumseh and his warriors led off the dancing in the square. At the outset, he pointed upward to where the tail of the comet arched across the clear sky and cried out, "Behold, the fiery arm of Manitou!"

The next day Tecumseh went to the lodge of Big Warrior. Tecumseh presented a bundle of sticks, a piece of wampum, and a tomahawk. The Creek chief accepted these things, but Tecumseh, sensing that he was not a real supporter, said, "After I visit the other nations, I will return north and go to Detroit. When I arrive, I will stomp my foot on the ground, and the whole earth will shake until all the houses of Tuckabatchee fall down!"

Moving on, Tecumseh was disappointed in his short contact with the Cherokee. This was the most pro-American tribe of them all, and they were noted for their prowess in earlier days, but he decided he had not the time to make any effective impression upon them. His rule of politics was to "seek friends where you already have them," rather than to devote too much time and energy to those who were hostile. On the other hand, he did find a much more favorable reception among the Chickasaws and the Choctaws than he had had two years earlier. This led him to believe that his message then had had some effect, in spite of the hostile reaction of a number of the leaders.

Finally, he went back to the Mississippi for another visit with the Osages on both sides of the Great River. From there he would work his way up the river and return to Tippecanoe by way of Illinois.

2

Tecumseh and The Prophet and their followers were hardly out of sight of Vincennes when Harrison began to move to unsettle them.

"Now is the time to strike, while Tecumseh is in the South; now is the time to root up his conspiracy," the Governor said to his good friend and attorney general, Thomas Randolph, in a morning conference in the Grouseland office. Randolph was troubled by the prospects of war. He even was troubled by the idea of trying to undo the work of Tecumseh, and he was troubled about the long-term prospects for the Indians.

"But, Henry, why move at all just now? Why break up Tecumseh's confederacy?"

"Because that is the greatest source of danger for our people in this country."

"Are you proposing to go on the warpath, to attack the Prophet's Town?" asked Randolph.

Just a trace of a pained expression flashed across Harrison's face. Then he replied, "I'm not proposing to go to war. I hope that won't be necessary."

"Then what are you proposing?"

"To go up there, make a show of force, and try to persuade the various tribes to depart peaceably from that place."

"You mean there won't be any war if they just give in without a fight?"

"Well, damn it, Tom, we can't have a hostile military base up there. Look." Harrison got up and pointed to a rough map on the wall. "Look. It would take two or three weeks at least for us to move any kind of a military force up there, weeks of hard marching and dragging up supplies. But in only a matter of a day or two, coming downstream in their war canoes, they could swoop down upon us before we could have sufficient warning to defend ourselves. I tell you they have a great strategic advantage in that location."

"Yes, I see that. But why should they want to swoop down upon us?"

"Supposedly to reclaim the land which they claim was unfairly taken from them."

"Then it seems to me our course ought to be to persuade them of the fairness of the arrangement."

"How do we do that?"

"By making a fair arrangement."

"But how can you do that when people like Tecumseh maintain that everybody has to agree to it? You know you never can get everybody to agree to anything. What greater concurrence could you expect than we obtained for the Treaty of Fort Wayne or than Wayne obtained for the Treaty of Greeneville?"

"No, I grant those were very impressive," Randolph said. "Still there was one big omission at Fort Wayne."

"What was that?"

"Tecumseh."

"Oh, damn."

"Well, I'm still wondering why you did not have Tecumseh as a party to the Fort Wayne Treaty."

"First, his Shawnees are late comers to the Wabash valley. Secondly, he doesn't represent even all of the Shawnees. Thirdly, I doubt very much if he would have come."

"Blue Jacket came to Greeneville, didn't he?"

"Yes, but he had none of those grandiose ideas of Tecumseh's in trying to form a great conspiracy."

"What do you mean, conspiracy?"

"To threaten the U. S. Haven't you heard of the conspiracy of Pontiac?"

"Of course, but this is very different. Pontiac did have a secret conspiracy going. Tecumseh is quite open. He simply wants to bring the Indians together in a confederation. As he says himself, he only wants a united Indian nation, just as the United States brought together the separate states to form a Union. As he asks, why should we object to that? Why should we object to the Indians forming a union after the very model that we have provided?"

"Because if they ever succeeded in forming an effective union, they would be a real and continuing menace to the United States."

"Not unless they saw us as a real and continuing menace to *them*."

"Tom, I'm afraid it's not that simple."

"What do you mean?"

"Consolidation of the tribes could be very dangerous because then, instead of warring among each other, they all would be warring against the U.S."

"Why should they go to war at all if we treat them fairly?"

"You must understand that very often the Indians have no political objectives for their wars. It is difficult for us to conceive of war without a political object, or at least as an attempt for economic gain of some sort. For the savages, war is a kind of necessary sport. The savage mind requires a certain element of excitement, and they find it in warlike activities. The savage cannot be at rest. He cannot be happy unless he is acted upon by some strong stimulus like war. Their men are not referred to simply as men. They are always warriors or braves. For them there is no greater prize than an enemy's scalp. This is a kind of proof of their manhood. And I tell you, tranquility between neighboring tribes will always be a sure indication of war against us."

"Well, I can see there may be something in what you say," Randolph conceded. "In fact I suppose there is a little bit of that craving for excitement in all men. Some find it in going to sea, some find it in exploring the wilderness, some find it in smoking opium, some in going to war."

"And some find it in politics and dueling," Harrison added.

Randolph flinched, flashed a grin and went on, "Maybe all men share some of this, but the veneer of civilization modifies the expression of it. Tecumseh must have that. He certainly does not believe in the excitement of torture or of firewater. And he certainly does not have to prove his manhood."

"But many of his followers do."

"Still, even if your purpose is a peaceful one in approaching the Indians on the Tippecanoe, I don't see how you can have any kind of meaningful agreement without Tecumseh."

"I'm afraid the only way we can persuade the allied tribes to leave is *without* Tecumseh."

Randolph protested, "But Tecumseh is the key to the whole situation. I say make him an ally rather than an enemy. He has never broken his word. He never allows his warriors to massacre women and children nor to torture nor kill prisoners. The Prophet persuades them to let whiskey alone."

"We treated with him in two conferences," rejoined Harrison. "They led to nothing. He will not compromise."

"What kind of compromise? He opposed the Treaty of Greeneville, but I'm sure he would accept that now. What he is so opposed to now is the Treaty of Fort Wayne. Would not a fair compromise be to go back to the Treaty of Greeneville"?

"You know the White settlers never would stand for that, the way they already are pouring into the lands of the Fort Wayne Treaty and beyond."

"I say give him a chance. He asked that we do nothing in his absence. He said that when he returned in the spring, he even would be willing to go see the President to settle differences. It seems to me the least we can do is to honor our promise to do nothing until he returns."

"I made no such promise."

"But he could draw an inference of one, which amounts to the same thing."

"When he returns he will be stronger than ever, more independent. One must never negotiate from a position of weakness."

"But you are asking him to."

"What would you have me do?" Harrison asked, a little brusquely.

"Give him a chance. Let him unify and organize his people but make them our allies. If we are not very careful, we shall drive him into the arms of the British. He will make an ally of England rather than of the United States. Then where will we be if war comes with England?"

"I must say, I wouldn't be surprised to see it come to war with England, even within the next year or so. That's why we've got to break up Tecumseh's confederation now. We never have had the Indians do our fighting for us. And the English have all the advantage in promising them assistance in their fight against us. The Indians want to recover land from us. The English are not in that position, though some day they will be, as settlement moves westward in Canada."

Randolph got up and paced the floor. He looked out the widow in a long gaze of thoughtfulness. Patiently, Harrison waited to hear what else he might have to say. After several minutes of reflection, Randolph turned back from the window.

"Ever since our discussions about Jefferson's Indian policy, I keep thinking about a possible middle way."

"How is that?"

"I mean something between forcible expulsion or annihilation and what amounts to forcible assimilation."

"What would that be?"

"Some kind of peaceful tolerance, to let time do its work."

"And what form would that take?"

"I say let's reaffirm the Greeneville Treaty. Let the Indians know that their lands north and west of that treaty line will remain inviolate."

"I doubt if you can do that," Harrison said. "We must press westward. This is where the future of our nation lies."

Randolph protested vigorously, "Why? Why must we? The land is finite; it must have some bounds. If we move on to the west, eventually we will encounter the Stony Mountains, and if we go beyond those, then we encounter the Pacific Ocean. Why not settle for the Wabash? Why cannot the march of civilization stop as easily on the banks of the Wabash as on the shores of the Pacific?

Why cannot all the territory north and west of the Greeneville line be reserved to the Indians? Leave to them the rich Wabash valley. Leave to them the Great Lakes. Let Tecumseh have his confederation, if he can. Let that be the instrument for deciding and ruling the hunting grounds of the Indians. Then we would have to deal with only one central authority rather than with dozens of separate tribes."

"You seem to take everything into account except the American settlers."

"We keep telling the Indians they would not need all that land, if they would just settle down to agriculture and animal husbandry instead of depending upon hunting, which requires great expanses of land. Well, surely the White farmers don't need all that land either since they do depend upon domestic animals and cultivation of the soil."

"You have a point there, except that the number of settlers keeps increasing so rapidly that we can't keep up with them."

Randolph kept pressing. "Look how things are changing," he said. "Franklin's experiments with electricity, Whitney's manufacturing with interchangeable parts, the steamboats which soon will be appearing on the Ohio and the Mississippi. You know, the way White men live a hundred years from now will be as different from the way they live now as the way White men live now differs from the way the Indians live now."

"I dare say."

"Then why not let the changes come in a way that will benefit both races—not have only one change for the better while the other deteriorates."

"And how do we do that?"

"Let the Greeneville Treaty line remain firm. Indians who wish to join the American community on this side of the line should be free to do so as individual land owners. Those who want to continue in their own way of life should be free to do so in all the area on the other side of the treaty line. That area should be guaranteed against further White settlement. Let the two civilizations flourish side by side in mutual tolerance. What we need is a hundred years' truce. In that time, with peaceful tolerance, my guess would be that a large share of the Indians would voluntarily join the American community. The American nation would be the richer by peaceful and friendly contact with a culture rich in its own right. Christians should mean what they say when they say that 'all men are brothers.' The Shawnees should see that their ethical doctrine—their 'Sermon on the Mount'—should extend to all people, not just to their own kind. In a century or two then we should have that great amalgamation that Jefferson dreamed about, simply as a matter of mutual tolerance and continuing progresssive change. Civilization should always mean life, not death."

Harrison looked up with a smile and said, "Well spoken, I must say. I am inclined to agree with you except for two important details."

"What are those?"

"Well, I think Tecumseh's confederation would hinder, rather than encourage, the process you envisage."

"On the contrary, I think something like that would be essential to make the whole thing work. But what is the other?"

"The line of demarcation. We have gone too far beyond the Greeneville Treaty line. Even the Fort Wayne Treaty line is too close in. But I think there might be a real possibility if we expand our horizon."

"What is that?"

"I think Louisiana is the answer to our problem. There is a vast area that could be set aside for Indians who do not wish to join the American community. I would be willing to set aside all the territory northwest of Green Bay in the Wisconsin country, down to the Mississippi, and then everything west of say, the Missouri River and the 95th meridian." Again Harrison pointed to the map.

"Yes, that might do it," conceded Randolph, "if the Indians were given a free choice. But do you think even that line could be held against the encroachment of White settlers in years to come?"

"That of course remains the big question, but for now I say, 'On to Tippecanoe.'"

That afternoon Harrison called in Peter Jones, his secretary, and dictated a letter to Secretary of War William Eustis:

My letter of yesterday will inform you of the arrival and departure of Tecumseh from this place and of the route which he has taken. There can be no doubt his object is to excite the southern Indians to war against us. I do not think there is any danger of further hostility until he returns: and his absence affords a most favorable opportunity for breaking up his confederacy, and I have some expectations of being able to accomplish it without a recourse to actual hostility.

The implicit obedience and respect which the followers of Tecumseh pay to him is really astonishing, and more than any other circumstance bespeaks him one of those uncommon geniuses which spring up occasionally to produce revolutions and overturn the established order of things. If it were not for the vicinity of the United States, he would, perhaps, be the founder of an empire that would rival in glory Mexico or Peru. No difficulties deter him. For four years he has been in constant motion. You see him today on the Wabash and in a short time hear of him on the shores of Lake Erie or Michigan or on the banks of the Mississippi. Wherever he goes he makes an impression favorable to his purposes. He is now upon the last round to put a finishing stroke to his work. I hope, however, before his return that that part of the fabric which he considered complete will be demolished and even its foundations rooted up.

3

Over the next several weeks, Harrison devoted himself to organizing forces, arranging for supplies, building wagons, and drilling militiamen.

In his quest for peace by preparations for war, Harrison was to an extent simply reflecting the mood of the West. And to an extent he was creating that mood. The conference with Tecumseh at Vincennes had done nothing to overcome the suspicions of White settlers of an Indian conspiracy, nor to ease their fears of attacks and massacres. Continuing crises with Great Britain over interference with commerce on the high seas and impressment of American seamen only added to worries in the West that the British were instigating the Indians to attack American settlements and were providing them with the means to do so. In congressional elections of 1810 and 1811, the voters, mainly in the West and South, had turned out many of the older "submission men"—nearly half of the members of Congress—and replaced them with young "War Hawks."

Public meetings in Ohio, Kentucky, and Tennessee fanned the flames of war. Kentuckians openly espoused an invasion of Canada on their own authority. William Clark, Harrison's old comrade in the Army at Fort Washington, co-leader of the Lewis and Clark expedition and now Indian Agent at St. Louis, stated that he believed a crisis to be "fast approaching." Governor Ninian Edwards of the Illinois Territory warned that "partial war" would continue as long as the savages were allowed to assemble at Prophet's Town. The Indiana Territorial legislature adopted a resolution commending the Governor for his prompt and decisive action at the time of the conference which probably had spared Vincennes from destruction and its inhabitants from massacre. It further resolved "that a temporizing policy is not calculated to answer any beneficial purpose with savages."

Harrison sent a letter to the Indian Agent at Fort Wayne, John Johnson, asking him to warn the Indians against any hostile acts and urging him to send delegations of friendly Indians to Prophet's Town to try to discourage any further warlike activities there. He stated further:

> You will be pleased also to state, in all your communications with the Indians upon this subject, that the war that may be waged against us by any of the Tribes shall be the last that they shall ever make, as it is the positive determination of our Government after having so long and so sincerely laboured for their advantage to open their eyes to their inferior condition and to provide the means of their improvement and civilization that they will not again suffer themselves to be imposed upon by the professions of those who have so often deceived but that the War, once begun, will be pursued to the utter exterpation of those who shall commence it or until they are delivered to such a distance as to preclude all probability of their again annoying us.

Harrison was glad to learn that the 4th U.S. Infantry Regiment already was on the way in response to some earlier incidents in Illinois. But he was annoyed by the caveat that only one company was to be at his disposal, while the remainder of the regiment was to hold up at Newport, Kentucky, opposite Cincinnati, unless it was "indispensibly required."

Harrison ordered the mobilization of the Indiana Territorial militia and sought authority to accept volunteers from Kentucky. He already had determined in his own mind that the 4th Regiment of regulars was "indispensible," and in the third week of August, accompanied only by an aide, two riflemen, and his orderly, he set out by horseback for Jeffersonville to meet the regiment in person. On the way, he sought out officers of the militia and urged them to get their units organized and on to Vincennes.

At Jeffersonville, Harrison found that the regiment was held up, by failure of supplies to arrive on time, while the water level was falling to a point which threatened the navigability of the keel boats by which the troops were travelling. While waiting, Harrison reviewed militia units in Clark and Harrison counties. When he crossed the river for a visit to Louisville, Kentuckians greeted him with offers to march anywhere, so long as it was north and preferably all the way to Canada. He declined offers of volunteer infantry from Kentucky, explaining that he had enough in Indiana, but he did write to Govenor Charles Scott of that state for permission to accept a detachment of mounted riflemen from Louisville. In his excitement the commander of the Louisville troop, Captain Peter Funk, rode in such haste to Frankfort with the letter that on arriving at the destination his highly valued horse dropped dead.

At last on September 3, the 4th Regiment, reduced by sickness and desertion to a strength of about 400, arrived in ten keelboats at Jeffersonville. Harrison invited the regimental commander, Colonel John P. Boyd, to join him for the overland ride to Vincennes while the boats continued on down the river to the Wabash. Harrison welcomed the chance to trade war stories with the colorful colonel who was noted for his exploits in India where he had commanded an army of native mercenaries, mounted on elephants, in the service of the Nizam of Hyderabad.

While the regulars struggled with their heavy boats up the low waters of the Wabash, militia units were converging on Vincennes. They went into camps between the town and Fort Knox.

Harrison was at the river to greet the 4th Regiment when the regulars landed their boats at sunset on September 19. They had paused downstream to change into their clean, gaudy uniforms. Smartly dressed in dark blue tail coats, with brass buttons, light blue, tightly fitting pantaloons, shiny black boots, tall shakos with colorful plumes, the men formed up into their companies. With drums beating and flags flying, they marched through the town, much to the excited amazement of the local citizens. The militiamen, garbed in soiled deerskins and linen hunting shirts, with coonskin or bearskins caps, and tomahawks and knives at their belts, greeted the regulars with such whoops and yells that some of the latter thought they had indeed landed in the midst of the savages themselves.

One of the staff officers of the regular regiment was Lieutenant Colonel Zebulon Montgomery Pike, lately returned from an expedition to the Far West when he had discovered the peak bearing his name and during which he was at one time reported to have been killed.

One additional company of regulars, about forty men, came from the garrison of Fort Knox, a company of the 7th Infantry under the command of Captain Albright.

Colonel Joseph Bartholomew arrived from eastern Indiana with three companies of infantry, sixty mounted riflemen and a troop of dragoons. Captain Funk arrived from Louisville with his troop of forty mounted Kentucky riflemen, with a promise of more to follow in a month. Accompanying him was the attorney-general of Kentucky, Joseph Hamilton Daveiss, who had fought at Fallen Timbers and who was a colonel in the Kentucky militia, but without a command. He had come as a volunteer private. Harrison promptly made him a major and set him over all the dragoons and mounted riflemen, somewhat to the chagrin of another experienced Indian fighter and good friend, Captain Spier Spencer, who was there with his mounted troop of "Yellow Jackets." Another Kentuckian, Samuel Wells, who had a commission as a brigadier general in the militia of his own state, also arrived to offer his services as a private, and Harrison promptly appointed him a major too.

Militia units from Vincennes and Knox County comprised about 350 infantrymen under command of Major Waller Taylor who actually in civilian life was chancellor (presiding judge) of the Territory, and about sixty dragoons under Judge Benjamin Parke, a captain of militia.

As Governor of the Territory, William Henry Harrison was Commander in Chief, and he held the rank of major general in the militia. This did not mean, necessarily, that he had to take the field himself in leading an expedition into the Indian country. He might have assigned the command to the veteran Colonel Boyd. A number of the other officers had had more experience. To be sure, Harrison had been a professional army officer for seven years and had risen to the rank of captain. He had had invaluable experience as an aide to General Wayne, though he never had commanded anything either in extensive combat or on an extensive expedition in hostile country, but the thought did not even occur to him that he would not take personal command. He had full confidence in himself, and he commanded the confidence and respect of his subordinate officers and men.

For his personal staff as aides for this expedition Harrison chose Major Taylor, Major Henry Hurst, a Vincennes lawyer, and Colonel Marston G. Clark, a member of the territorial legislature. As Harrison was completing these arrangements, Thomas Randolph came in to see him.

"Governor, I'm going to Tippecanoe with you," said Randolph.

"Well, Tom," Harrison gasped, "I have been assuming that you would be here to help John Gibson mind the store. I'm afraid there's no time to get a commission for you, anyway."

"I don't need any commission," insisted Randolph. "I'll go just as I am."

"But what about Catherine and what about your duties here? Somebody has to stay here. Anyway, I thought you were opposed to the whole idea of going up to Prophet's Town."

"I still don't think much of the idea, doubt that it will do any good, but I have been having an uneasy feeling that the Indians will be after you, and I think I had better go along to help look after you. Catherine will be all right, same as Anna and all the others. And Gibson can look after the business here all right. Anyway, if I'm going to be a successful politician, I've got to have a war record."

"Oh, Tom, your arguments overwhelm me. God knows I could use you and would appreciate having you along. And I do appreciate your views on the Indian matters. That makes your willingness to go along now all the more impressive."

"Somebody's got to see to it that the Indians are treated fairly in any treaty or other arrangement."

"Well, Tom, get yourself ready. You'll come along as aide to the Governor."

Harrison had hoped to have his little army move out by September 19, but the 4th Regiment only arrived that day, and failure of the government contractor to deliver the necessary flour and beef on time caused a delay of another six days.

But the days of waiting were not wasted. They were devoted to drilling. On the 22nd the militia paraded on the big prairie north of the town, and Harrison put them through tactical maneuvers in attacking and changing directions. The performance left something to be desired, but it hardly was surpassed by the evolutions of the regulars. Evidently Colonel Boyd's experience in moving elephants had been of little use in preparing him to maneuver partially trained infantry.

Harrison hoped to get more rifles for the militia. Many of the militiamen simply refused to carry muskets. One of the main objections to the rifle that Ordnance Bureau chiefs had held for a long time was the slowness in loading. It was more difficult to ram home the wad and ball down a rifled barrel than down a smooth bore. Much of this difficulty had been overcome when, many years earlier, someone had introduced the greased patch.

Now one of the militia battalions here assembled had come up with a method of loading that enabled the men to load and fire at a rate at least one-third faster than the others. Developed by the battalion major, this method was based upon the use of a metallic cartridge. In this procedure the rifleman carried his cartridges in leather bands buckled on front. The cartridge was a tin "Julie" or tube, rather than the more common paper, which held exactly the right charge of powder with ball and patch on top. The lower opening of the cartridge was closed with a wooden stopper attached to the tube with a string to keep from getting lost. When ready for use the rifleman drew out the cartridge from his belt and turned it over as he took the ball and patch in his left hand. Holding the cartridge in his right hand, he removed the wooden stopper with his teeth. He primed the weapon with a little powder and then, holding his finger over the end of the cartridge to prevent loss of powder, placed it in the muzzle to let the powder pour in. Then, with the left hand, he put the ball in patch in place while with the right he put the tube in his pouch—or threw it to the ground when in a big hurry—and with the ramrod forced the ball and patch down against the powder.

While all this was going on, Harrison was careful to impress upon the Secretary of War the importance of using all the militia, rather than only four companies as the Secretary had suggested earlier. The Governor elicited testimonials from both Judge Parke and Judge Taylor. The latter put down as his opinion that to dissolve The Prophet's combination would require "a force that would awe the turbulent and refractory, confirm the timid and wavering, and insure protection and safety to the friendly and well-disposed."

Parke warned, "The smallest reversal of fortune on the part of the Government would instantly unite all the Indians against it, and a five years' war would scarcely be sufficient to restore peace on the frontier."

Harrison summarized his own views for the Secretary as follows:

My own opinion is that with this force we might march to the upper line of the New Purchase, erect a fort and return with safety. It would however present the Indians a great temptation and the defeat of this Detachment would give to the Prophet's party an eclat that would enable him to effect his purpose of uniting all the Tribes in a war against us. The appearance of a military force in the neighborhood of the Indian towns will produce a good or an ill effect in proportion to the operation it will have upon their fears. A small body of men will excite their contempt, a large one (such as they will think themselves unable to resist) will not only deprive them of a wish to measure their strength with ours, but will cause all those who waver to decide in our favour and even many of those who are now in close union with the Prophet will think of nothing but retracing their steps and submitting to a compliance with our just demands. Our Friends will be enabled to speak out openly as such and be freed from the necessity of skulking about the woods (as at this moment) for fear of their lives. You will see below that Mr. Dubois reports that almost every Indian from the country above this had been or were then gone to Malden on a visit to the British agent. We shall probably gain our destined point at the moment of their return. If then the British agents are really (as I most sincerely believe) endeavouring to instigate the Indians to make war upon us, we shall be in their neighbourhood at the very moment when the impressions which have been made against us are most active in the minds of the savages. In your letter of the 17th July, you enjoin it upon me in the most peremptory manner "not to attack the Prophet without having a force that would ensure success". The injunction appears to me to include a prohibition of placing myself in a situation with a military force where I could be attacked with success, as the consequences in either case would be nearly the same. Upon the whole I think that the preservation of peace which is the great object of the President (and certainly of myself also) would be jeopardized by the employment of any force which the Prophet might think himself able to contend with. I do not think him much of a warrior, but he is certainly daring, presumptuous and rash. In proportion to the strength of our Detachment not only the relative but the actual numbers of his followers will be decreased and if such a force as I could raise in two weeks was to go up and erect a Fort upon the reservation at the old Wea Towns I would pledge my reputation for judgment and a knowledge of the Indian character that four fifths of his followers would instantly abandon him. And being once undeceived with regard to his ability to defend them, they would never be brought to unite with him again.

Anna Harrison was thankful for the delays. She dreaded his being away, as always. She dreaded now more than ever that he was likely to be involved in battle against the Indians, and she knew, in spite of all his reassurances, that that meant danger, but now she had another dread. Their eighth child would be due in about a month. Now it seemed likely that her husband would be away at that time.

"Henry," she said to him one evening as the time drew near for his departure, "do you really have to go just now? Don't you think the troops need just a few more weeks of drills?"

"Yes they do, but I'm afraid there's no time to lose."

"Henry, don't they know that September and October is baby time for us?"

"It did used to be, didn't it? And now again!"

"And I missed you very much when John Scott was born, when you were off to St. Louis."

"That was seven years ago, and you never have forgiven me for that, have you?" smiled Harrison. Anna smiled too, but he could see that she was smiling through tears.

"No, I haven't," she said. "Or rather I should say I have never forgiven Mr. Jefferson for making you go at just that time."

Harrison had seldom seen Anna in tears. Seeing them now sent waves of feeling all through him. He felt caught in a tremendous tug of war, one force drawing him off perhaps to real war, the other desperately trying to hold him to the peace of home. A struggle between public duty and family duty.

He grasped both of her hands and looked into her sad eyes. "My Darling, you know I would rather be here than out chasing Indians. I would rather be with you than with anyone else or anywhere else. But maybe by going out now, we can make it possible for us and for all the other people around here to be at home more, and for all the families to be together in safety."

Anna sensed how her husband felt torn, and she wanted to spare him that. She knew that he faced difficult days ahead, and she wanted to help him face them, not make it more difficult.

"I know you are right, my dear," she said. "I know these things must be done and events don't wait on our personal calendars or conform to our personal preferences. All of us are in it, and we all have to do our part."

Harrison looked into her eyes and gained strength from the brightness he saw there. He embraced her warmly and felt more strength.

"Here, let me help get your uniforms and everything ready." She went scurrying about with a feigned light-heartedness that was contagious.

4

While Tecumseh toured the South, The Prophet, in Prophet's Town, pushed preparations for possible conflict. The Prophet's efforts and the earlier excursions of Tecumseh were bearing fruit in the assembly of tribes at Tippecanoe. Nearly 1,200 active warriors, in addition to the women and children, now were at Prophet's Town and in satellite villages of the various tribes. The leaders included the wise and widely respected White Loon of the Weas, and his Wea comrade, Negro Legs; Big Man and Peccan of the Miamis; Stone Eater of the Kaskaskias; Shabonee, an Ottawa but now a chief of the Potawatomis; Oscemit, of the same tribe; and, most surprising of all, Winamac, with his large following of Potawatomis. In addition to those tribes, warriors also were there from the Wyandots, the Kickapoos, the Winnebagos, the Chippewas, the Eel River Tribe, the Sacs and Foxes, and, of course, the Shawnees. There were a few individual Delawares and even a few Creeks.

Added to supplies of food and implements from the American annuities, the tribesmen at Tippecanoe had great quantities of rifles, gunpowder, flints, blankets, shirts, and cloth from British sources at Amherstburg. All this was in addition to the greatest harvest ever of corn and beans and squash and pumpkins and melons from the fields around Prophet's Town.

Almost daily the warriors engaged in war games, and The Prophet harangued councils of chiefs and assemblies of warriors. He emphasized how the Long Knives had grown weak and how the Great Spirit would show the Red Men to victory when the time came.

On one such occasion, Chief Shabonee added his observation on the Long Knives: "Their hands are soft; their faces are white. Half of them are calico peddlers; the other half can only shoot squirrels."

As a way of testing their skills, a group of young warriors approached The Prophet one afternoon in early September, to request his permission for them to make a foray down to the White settlements to see if they could get away with stealing a horse apiece. The holy man was pleased at the respect they showed his leadership, and he also was pleased to see the intertribal nature of the young adventurers: one Eel River, one Potawatomi, one Wyandot, two Kickapoos, and two Shawnees. The Prophet listened gravely, but sympathetically. When he gave his blessing, the young warriors gave a great war whoop and set off.

Five days later, they all returned jubilantly, each astride a horse and telling how they had taken them from under the very noses of the Whites, without being detected. A day later, fifteen White Men rode into Prophet's Town and demanded to see The Prophet.

"We have come to get the horses which some of your young braves stole from us," their spokesman said.

"Horses, horses?" responded The Prophet with a look of wonder.

The men looked about. "Yes, right over there—those horses."

"Oh yes, yes," The Prophet laughed. "I'm afraid some of our young men were involved in a youthful prank. It was only a joke. Go, take your horses."

The White Men gave no sign of seeing any humor in the situation. Grimly they seized the horses and led them away.

The Prophet retired to his wigwam for meditation. He emerged an hour later with a revelation which he explained to an assembly of the people who gathered around him.

"The Great Spirit has told me that those horses belong to us, and if anyone goes after them they will not be harmed."

Fifty warriors answered the challenge. They jumped on their horses and with loud whoops, charged off after the White horsemen. The warriors rode on until well after dark when they spied the campfire of the White Men. Throwing caution to the wind, the Indians rode boldly into the camp and at rifle point demanded the horses. They took not only the seven horses that previously had been stolen, but also the fifteen that the other men had been riding.

Returning in triumph to Prophet's Town, they were told that it always would be easy to overcome the White Men when the Great Spirit gave her blessing.

5

John Conner returned to Vincennes from a spy mission to Prophet's Town and reported to Harrison. There were a thousand warriors, of many tribes, at Prophet's Town, and greater stocks of supplies than he ever had seen before.

"But Governor, wait till you hear this. Guess who has joined them up there."

"Don't tell me Tecumseh is back already."

"Oh no, not that, but someone just as surprising."

"Tell me, man, who?"

"Winamac."

"Winamac! Zounds!" cried Harrison. "Who can you trust these days?"

"Tecumseh," said Conner.

"Tecumseh what?" Harrison responded, only half concentrating on what Conner had said.

"Tecumseh, I said, you can always trust him."

"Oh yes, Tecumseh," laughed Harrison. "You're right about that. There never is any doubt about where he stands, is there?"

"No doubt at all, always squarely against us."

"But, John, this Winamac business could be serious. I don't like it. I don't like it at all," Harrison said.

"No, I suppose not. But I doubt that you will find him any more formidable than White Loon or Shabonee, or some of the other chiefs they have up there."

"No, I suppose not. But Winamac has been one of our most faithful supporters and allies throughout the last five or six years. Think of it."

"Yes, that's true. It's a pity that he has gone over."

Harrison thought a while and then said, "He's a damned opportunist. That is the only explanation for his behavior, a damned opportunist."

"Yes, I suppose so."

"You can't tell me he has been persuaded at last by the eloquence of Tecumseh, or by the magic of The Prophet any more now than a year ago or two or three years ago."

"No different."

"Of course not. It's just that he is a damned opportunist, and that is bad news."

"How's that?"

"Why, don't you see, man, he aligns himself with the side he thinks is going to win. He has been so impressed by all the tribes and chiefs gathering at Prophet's Town that he thinks they are going to win. That's bad news for us. A chief known to be unfriendly with them, who has had the opportunity to observe everything carefully, now thinks they are going to win. Damn it, John, that's a bad sign, and I don't like it."

"Yes, Governor, I see what you mean."

"What that means is that we have got to have this thing settled before Tecumseh returns. When he gets back with more followers from the South, and when he finds Winamac in his camp, there will be hell to pay for us."

"God, you're right."

"Zounds!"

CHAPTER XX

The Battle of Tippecanoe

1

While he awaited the arrival of supplies, and while the troops continued to go through training exercises, Harrison issued his orders for the march formation.

He organized the force into two provisional brigades. The first comprising the 4th U.S. Regiment, the U.S. Rifle Company (armed with muskets); and the mounted dragoons of Captain Benjamin Parke of Vincennes and Captain Spier Spencer of Corydon, and the small detachment of Kentucky dragoons under Colonel Joseph H. Daveiss, was under the command of the commander of the U.S. Regiment, Colonel Boyd. All the other militia units were placed under the command of Colonel Joseph Bartholemew.

The arrival of a boatload of flour on September 24th brought the total rations on hand to 12,000. A ration being food for one man for one day, and the strength of the force now at one thousand, this meant food only for twelve days. Nevertheless, with assurances that more flour would be coming up the river shortly, that same day Harrison sent the mounted troops on ahead to Bosseron, twenty miles to the north where they could find better forage for their horses while providing security. He gave orders for the main body to be prepared to march at ten o'clock the next morning.

466

Company commanders were enjoined to inspect all weapons and to hold an inspection every morning of all ammunition, flints, priming wires, and breeches to see to it that weapons were in good functioning order. Each man drew twenty-four rounds of ammunition, three flints, and a priming wire. All arms and accoutrements for the sick would be boxed and stowed on boats. Each man was to have two days' rations cooked and packed in his haversack. Militiamen had no tents, but for the regulars one wall tent was allowed for the officers of each company, and one common tent to each six men. A wall tent and a common tent were allowed for the medical detachment of the regular regiment.

The army would march in a column of twos, with command group and supply trains near the center, and with security detachments to front, flanks, and rear. Specific instructions were given for the column to face right to meet any attack from that direction, to face left for an attack from the opposite direction, for the five leading battalions to deploy to the front in case of an attack there, and for the five in the rear to face about and deploy to the rear in case of attack from that direction.

There were no women. Harrison was bound and determined that there would be no such following as had accompanied St. Clair in his disaster. A number of the wives of the regular officers were in the habit of following their husbands as far as possible. Some of them had come to Vincennes. Harrison welcomed them there, but that was as far as they could go.

When Harrison heard that the wife of Lieutenant Josiah Bacon, a quartermaster in the 4th U.S. Regiment, was ill, he visited her at her sickbed in Lasselle's Tavern. He found her suffering from ague, homesick for New England, not much impressed with Vincennes, worried about her husband, and worried about Indian attack while the troops were away. She was sharing the room with another officer's wife and both kept loaded pistols at the bedside. But for all her misery and all her worries, Mrs. Bacon was highly impressed and pleased that the Governor and Commander-in-Chief should call upon her.

Some of the officers brought along younger brothers or sons as a part of their commands. Spier Spencer brought his fourteen-year-old son to serve as orderly and drummer for the "Yellow Jackets."

Incidents in the vicinity continued to keep the whole area alert. Thirty-five miles to the southeast, Indians stole the horses of a Captain William Piatt and a companion who were on their way from Louisville to join the army at Vincennes. The next night Indians stole horses from the Bosseron settlement twenty miles in the other direction. Three men who went after the horses were lucky to escape with their lives when they hid in a swamp from pursuing Indians.

A deputation from Prophet's Town, headed by an old Kickapoo chief, arrived with professions of peace. In addressing the Governor, the old chief said, "Father, I am astonished at seeing your preparations for war. These have excited great alarm among our people. Our women and children are in tears. My heart, and the hearts of all the people who follow The Prophet are warm toward the United States. We have no other object than peace, but Father, we want to know what are your intentions."

Harrison replied, "It would be with great reluctance that your Father would draw the sword against his Red children, but the injuries that our people have suffered are such that I can no longer put up with them. The army will march in a day or two. I shall go up the valley of the Wabash, and if you are inclined to join our friends who are endeavoring to have the persons taken who have killed our people, and to restore the stolen horses, you may meet us on the way."

"Father," the chief replied, "the time is too short. Nothing can be done this fall. You must wait until the spring. Then, we will get all the Red Men together and try to find out who has injured your people."

"The army will march today," Harrison responded peremptorily. "The distance they go up the Wabash will depend entirely on the Indians themselves. If they will not deliver up those who have murdered our people and restore the stolen property, we must take upon ourselves the trouble of finding them even though that might mean some injury to innocent persons."

"Father, I do not know where the murderers are, but I will do all I can to find them and to return the stolen horses. I will go back to the Prophet's Town and then return to meet you."

A heavy rain was falling on September 25, and Harrison decided to postpone the march of the main body one more day. He announced, however, that the march would begin the next morning whatever the weather might be.

Thursday, September 26, 1811, dawned clear and cool. At last the expedition for Tippecanoe was ready to leave. Bidding goodbye to his children and to his anxious wife who was expecting their eighth child within a month, Harrison mounted his gray Andalusian mare and rode out to join his troops. They were nearly one thousand strong: about 250 regulars of the 4th U.S. Infantry, including mounted riflemen; about 150 Kentucky volunteers; and about six hundred local Indiana Territorial militiamen. A wagon train, under guard, carried provisions; and a herd of cattle and hogs provided fresh meat. Other supplies were in boats.

Under the eyes of a sizeable crowd of onlookers, the units formed. The order of march was, first, a detachment of mounted riflemen, guards on the flanks, and the infantry in single file on each side of the road with the men spaced about ten feet apart. The baggage wagons, the field staff, and then the cattle and hogs moved along the road between files of infantry.

Harrison sent a patrol of mounted scouts out to the front and gave the order to march. To the huzzahs of the populace, the long column started to move.

Lifting his hat, Harrison shouted, "The goose honks high! Let's go!" And he galloped up to the head of the column. There he waited for each unit to march by. The thirty-eight-year-old Governor and Commander-in-Chief presented a striking figure, tall and slender, wearing a calico hunting shirt trimmed with fringe, dark pantaloons and Hessian boots, and a round, black beaver hat ornamented with an orange ostrich feather. Once all the units were in motion, including the wagon train, Harrison galloped on up to the head of the column again.

Though for the Kentuckians and the U.S. regiment, it was much of the same old thing as the former's march from Louisville and the latter's march to Pittsburgh, for the Indiana militiamen and the local garrison company the first day's march was something of a lark. Drummers at the head of each column tapped a regular beat to help keep the units moving at the same speed and not become too dispersed. Some of the Regulars made some feeble attempts at singing a few verses of "Yankee Doodle," and "The Girl I Left Behind Me," and then, with a little more fervor, "Hail Columbia." Then the Indiana militiamen, bringing up the rear, offered with booming voices a refrain which soon dominated the whole column:

> The sons of The Prophet are
>   brave men and bold,
>   and quite unaccustomed to fear,
> But braver by far are the men in the rear
>   of our own tried and true brigadier!

Succeeding rounds came up with revised versions, until the final one came out:

> The sons of The Prophet
>> Are poor men and cold,
>> And always accustomed to fear;
> The brave and the true
>> Are the red, white, and blue,
>> And the ones who stayed home to make beer!

Marching up the Wabash, Harrison felt a certain satisfaction in bringing to a climax the pacification of the Indians by a showdown at Prophet's Town. He still felt a certain dread of barbarian invasion. Now, marching into the heart of the barbarian country, he could not help thinking of his several readings of accounts of the Roman general Quintilius Varus who led his three legions into an ambush set by the barbarian German chief, Arminius, in the Teutoburg forest where the Roman legions had been annihilated. And Harrison remembered how the Emperor Augustus, on hearing the report, had cried out, "Quintilius Varus, give me back my legions!" Harrison hoped that Mr. Madison would have no cause to cry out for his legions. No, he confidently looked forward to this meeting, as Caesar had in going against Vercengetorix and the Gauls.

To newspaper readers in the East and to foreign observers, this would be a parade of wooden soldiers, faceless, nameless, homeless. To the Anglo-American citizens of Vincennes, it was the departure of husbands and sons and fathers and friends to protect them from the ravages of the savages. To the French *habitants*, it was a matter of some indifference with a possibility of being precursor to a blow against "Perfidious Albion." To Harrison, it was an expedition to forestall barbarian invasions against the Empire. To the Indians of Prophet's Town, it would be a hostile incursion into their hunting grounds and against their central town.

By noon the column was about eight miles out. The men halted for an hour for a dinner of corncakes and beef. By sundown they had made over twice that distance, to Bosseron Creek. Those who had tents pitched them in company rows. Many of the militiamen, having no tents, cut saplings and brush to make lean-tos. The General's marquee, a big tent with sides that could be rolled up, was pitched near the center of the camp. This done, the men had a supper of broiled beef and corn bread for which groups of six formed together for the preparation and cooking.

The camp guard was formed by two captain's guards consisting of one captain, two sergeants, two corporals, and forty
privates each; two subaltern guards consisting of one subaltern,
one sergeant, one corporal, and twenty-one privates each; one
corporal and three privates for a contractor's guard, and one
subaltern, one sergeant, one corporal, and twelve privates for the
guard of the Commander-in-Chief. A field officer of the day was
in overall charge of security.

Succeeding days had less and less of the aspect of a holiday.
Steps became heavier with each mile, and each campfire brought
a greater longing for return to homefires, but now the leaves
were turning, and spirits of the men rose with the color and good
weather. The autumn leaves of maples, oaks, elms, and sycamores surrounded the whole column with bright hues of reds,
yellows, and orange in all shades. Along the river line a light haze
added a touch of blue and purple.

Within five days, the expedition arrived at an area of high
ground along the Wabash which the commander of the scouts
and guides, Captain Dubois, explained was called by the Indians,
"Bataille des Illinois," and by the French, "Terre Haute." Here
the expedition took a welcome stop of several weeks. It was a
relief from walking, but not from work, for the men immediately
fell to work in cutting timber and preparing logs for building a
fort between hours of long military drills.

During the evenings, Harrison liked to walk around the camp
and visit with the men. He came upon one pair of soldiers who
were regulars of the 4th Regiment, Private George Bentley and
Private Charles Coger. They were comparing notes on some of
the company commanders that they had known in earlier years.
Harrison overheard them as Bentley said, "We used to have a
captain by the name of Thomsen who was always giving us an
order to do something we already were doing, or were just about
to do. I would be on my way out to get some wood, for instance,
and he would say, 'Oh, Bentley, would you bring in some of that
wood?' or I would be going to pitch his tent for him, and he would
say, 'Oh, Bentley, would you pitch my tent, right over here?' We
all got to calling them kind of orders 'Captain Thomsen orders.'"

"Hah," Coger responded. "I used to work for a captain who
was always giving another order to do something before we had a
chance to do something he had ordered before. In my case he
would say, 'Oh, Coger, would you gather up some wood?' and I
would grab my axe and start for the wood, and, before I could get

to it, he would say, 'Oh, Coger, let's pitch my tent right here,' and as I would start toward the tent roll he would call out, 'Oh, Coger, don't you think you had better water the horse right away?' Sometimes he would even get the platoons all tumbling over each other as he would keep giving them new orders. We all called them kind of orders 'Captain Roecker orders.'"

Harrison came up laughing and said, "Both of those sound just like my wife! A Captain Thomsen order and a Captain Roecker order, eh?"

The men laughed and then the General said, "But take it from me, a 'General Harrison order' is one to be done straightaway, without any questions."

"Yes, Sir," both the soldiers responded.

Over in another area, the area occupied by Barton's Company of the 4th Regiment, Harrison came upon a young man sitting alone. He seemed to be troubled and said that his name was Lehman Welch. Harrison engaged him in some small talk about his family and where they were from. Then the young rookie said, "Are them Indians good with their bows and arrows?"

"Bows and arrows? My boy, they have as good muskets and rifles as we do," answered Harrison.

"How's that?"

"Oh, there's always some trader or skinflint willing to trade a rifle and ball and powder for a couple of beaver skins. I suspect the British up at Detroit are pretty active in supplying the Redskins with White men's weapons."

"Oh."

"Yes, my boy, they are good with bows and arrows, but they use them now mainly for sport and in hunting deer and buffalo, but when they're hunting White men they use powder and lead."

"Well, I'm sorta glad. I guess I'd rather be shot at with something I can hear."

"Yes, but you'd better worry more about their tomahawks and scalping knives. They can slip up on a man and crack his skull with a tomahawk before he knows what's about."

"Oh, oh."

"We've just got to be sure to stay alert. Shoot him first."

"Yes, Sir."

Harrison wandered over to where some junior officers, lieutenants and ensigns, were talking. A "veteran" lieutenant was imparting some of his special wisdom to his less experienced colleagues, "If you ask me, we'll be lucky if any of us get back alive. I hear there are thousands of Indians up there, and it wouldn't surprise me a bit if we got surprised by an ambush, just like St. Clair. We're sticking our necks out farther than he did." The lieutenant stopped short and came to attention as he saw Harrison.

The General looked at him coolly for a minute and then said, "Lieutenant, I'll say to you what the sea captain said to the mate, 'From now on I don't want to hear nothin' from you but silence, and damned little of that.'"

Days of waiting became days of discontent for many of the militiamen. They began to harbor fears for the future and homesickness for the past. Harrison patiently assembled the units from time to time and spoke eloquently of their duty, of the trust that their family and friends had put in them, and of their safety if all stood by each other and everyone did his duty properly. Without threats of punishment or coercian, Harrison defused sentiments for desertion. In the process his voice became familiar to everyone and he was looked upon with trust.

Harrison rejected the Machiavellian doctrine that it is better for a leader to be feared than loved. By banning annoying punishments that some of the noncommissioned officers had been using to tyrannize over their men, by searching out and dealing with all kinds of longstanding grievances, Harrison earned the respect and devotion of the regular soldiers as well as of the militiamen.

Several delegations of Indians arrived to confer with the Governor, but nothing modified his view of the hostile intentions of those at Prophet's Town.

On the night of October 20, while all was quiet around the camp, a shot rang out. A sentinel cried out in pain as a musket ball went through both thighs. The sentinel on his right saw the muzzle flash from a nearby bush, but when he tried to return the fire, his musket misfired twice and the intruder escaped. Quickly Major Daveiss formed his dragoons and rode out in pursuit. The men sprang from their tents and shelters to form a battle line, and Colonel Boyd and Harrison rode up and down the line to urge them to do their duty in case of attack. The greatest danger in this case turned out to be for the dragoons who, returning from their unsuccessful chase, were fired upon by some of the sentinels, though fortunately for them none was hit.

The fort completed, the soldiers congratulated each other on their work and the officers agreed that the fort should be called "Fort Harrison."

Harrison waited several more days for the arrival of two additional companies of mounted riflemen that he had ordered up, for the arrival of the boat with additional food supplies, and in vain for the return of a spy he had sent to Prophet's Town. He also had decided that boats would be too vulnerable to attack from this point, and he had ordered additional wagons from Vincennes to carry supplies.

Harrison met with his officers—Major Wells, Colonel Boyd, Colonel Owen, Major Taylor, Major Hurst—to plan the march to Tippecanoe. He said that they would leave the soldiers who had become too ill to march, and these men would garrison the fort. Colonel James Miller of the 4th Infantry, himself taken ill, would be left in command. Pointing to their location and the location of Prophet's Town on his map, Harrison explained that the Indians used two routes to travel to Tippecanoe. The one on the southeast side of the river was the shorter, but it was wooded and more likely to come under Indian attack. He said that they would move a short distance on that route, have it opened as a wagon road for a short distance, and then cross the river to march toward the prairie.

The expedition marched out from Fort Harrison, on October 29, in gay spirits as Harrison shouted, "Let's go! The goose honks high!"

There was much calling back and forth among regulars, Indiana militiamen and Kentucky volunteers. Harrison, conspicuous on his white horse, rode near the head of the column. Soon they were fording the river, and then there was rough ground and heavy woods, then a difficult ford and rough terrain at Pine Creek, and then, at last, the relief of breaking out into open country and looking at the tall grass of the broad prairie.

There was a two-day stopover for the building of a blockhouse at the point where the Vermillion River emptied into the Wabash. This would serve as a storage house for additional supplies that were to come up by boat.

In a letter to the Secretary of War on November 2, Harrison noted that the 4th of that month would be the anniversary of St. Clair's defeat. "Should we be attacked on that day, I hope to alter the color with which it has been marked in our calendar for the last twenty years," he wrote.

Day after day, the expedition moved on. Now along the low ridge lines leafless trees stretched their fingers toward the clouds. These were days of drudging, marching, walking, walking, walking. As the column approached Ouiatenon in the heart of the Indian country, excitement returned to the men. It was the excitement of anticipation, of facing a growing prospect of danger, rather than the more enthusiastic and carefree excitement that had accompanied their departure from Fort Harrison or their earlier departure from Vincennes.

On November 5, Harrison announced that Prophet's Town was not more than three miles away. Major Wells urged him to attack at once, but Harrison resisted. He said that they must wait to see if the Indians would give in peaceably. The troops continued to march until they met three Indians. Harrison rode up to hear what they had to say. They announced that they were sent to know why the army was marching upon their town. They said that The Prophet was desirous of avoiding hostilities, and that he sent a peaceful message to the Governor by the Miami and Potawatomi chiefs, but those chiefs went down the other side of the Wabash and thus failed to meet him. Harrison agreed upon a delay of hostilities, to the disappointment of some of his men.

Harrison then led his troops in battle formation — toward the Wabash to encamp for the night—the U.S. Infantry in the center and two companies of militia infantry and one of mounted riflemen on either flank forming the front line. This movement alarmed the Indians in Prophet's Town who could be seen preparing for defense. Some Indians ran out to demand that the army halt. Harrison explained that he was only looking for a campsite. He asked if there was any other good water except that of the river, and the Indians pointed toward a creek which they had crossed two miles to the northwest.

Harrison sent two aides, Major Waller Taylor and Major Marston Clark, to reconnoiter. They returned to report that near the creek they had found a place that had everything desired— "an elevated spot nearly surrounded by open prairie, with water convenient and sufficiency of wood for fuel." The troops arrived at the site. It was an elevated area, with some woods and a narrow creek running through it, separated from Prophet's Town by a marshy grassland.

As darkness fell, the troops prepared their defenses and made camp. Harrison cautioned his officers to maintain a heavy guard

and ordered everyone to be alert an hour before dawn. He led a
short religious service, where he used as his text the 19th verse
of the 10th chapter of the Gospel of St. Luke:

> Behold, I give unto you power to tread on serpents and scorpions, and over all
> the power of the enemy; and nothing shall by any means hurt you.

While the regulars pitched tents, the others prepared lean-tos
or prepared to sleep in the open, all on their weapons. They were
in position for perimeter defense. As had been the order on the
march, tents were placed in such a way that each man could take
five paces to the front of his tent and be in battle position, the
tents arranged roughly in a rectangle on what was in effect a
wooded promintory surrounded on three sides by swampland. On
the east, facing toward Prophet's Town which lay a mile and a
half away across the swamp, Indiana militia units were on the
flanks, three companies under Bartholomew on the right (south)
and Bigger's Company on the left (north), with six companies of
regulars of the U.S. 4th Infantry in the center. On the opposite
side, facing Burnett's Creek that ran through the swamp on the
west, were four companies of Indiana militia under Decker on the
left (south) and another four companies of the 4th Infantry on the
right. Mounted riflemen were stationed across the two narrow
ends of the rectangle, with Guger's and Robb's companies, under
Wells, on the north, and Spencer's riflemen and Warwick's
company on the south. Daveiss' dragoons were inside the northeast angle. The command group and supply trains were near the
center.

Late that night as Harrison conferred with Major Sam Wells
and Colonel Owen they heard a commotion outside. It was
Captain Walter Wilson with a frightened Negro driver, known as
Ben, in tow.

"What is it, Captain?" asked Harrison.

"I found this wretch lurking outside your tent, Sir, and late
this afternoon, he was seen off in the direction of Prophet's Town
talking with Indians. Frankly, Sir, I think he was about to try to
do you in."

"Well, I'll be damned," Harrison snorted. "Secure him, but we
have neither irons nor stockade. What are we to do, take some
men away from their other duties to guard him?"

"Secure him a-la-mode de savage," said Wells.

"Sure, I'll help," added Owens.

The two disappeared and returned a few minutes later with a split log with a pair of notches at either end. They threw the culprit on his back on the ground and then put his ankles in the notches of one of the split log halves and replaced the other half log on top. With a pair of forks driven into the ground, they secured this in place. Then they drove a stake into the ground above each of his outstretched arms and tied his wrists to them. In this spread-eagle position, he remained.

The officers, joined by Thomas Randolph, resumed their conversation in Harrison's marquee.

"Is that a sign that the Indians are about to attack?" asked Randolph.

"What, the treachery of Ben?" Harrison responded. "No, I don't think so. Not necessarily. Maybe The Prophet thought that if he could do his work, it would not be necessary to attack."

"What are the prospects for attack anyway?" asked Wells. "With all the activity we've been seeing, I shouldn't be surprised."

Owen wondered, "Don't you think their request for a council tomorrow is on the level?"

"Is ours?" Randolph came back.

"I hope it won't be necessary to fight, but we must not shrink from it," Harrison said. "We'll invite them to confer, as we have been doing, and if they accede to our requests, there need be no fighting."

"And what does that include?" asked Randolph. "Abandoning their town?"

"That's our danger spot, isn't it?" Harrison responded. "Actually I don't much expect an attack. If they wanted to attack us, why didn't they do it while we were moving across that rough, open country yesterday, or any of the last several days when we were more vulnerable? Now we are in a pretty good defensive position. Still we must be on our guard against surprise. We must avoid another St. Clair debacle at all costs."

2

In Prophet's Town, The Prophet called a council of war. At first the holy man was noncommital about launching an attack. He remembered Tecumseh's warning not to get involved in a battle, and he talked about delay. He suggested arranging a council with Harrison where two Winnebagos would be designated to stay behind after adjournment and assassinate the White Chief. But now Chief Winamac of the Potawatomis, long a foe of Tecumseh and The Prophet and friend of Harrison, but now a staunch supporter, demanded immediate action in the strongest terms. Otherwise he threatened to lead his warriors away.

The Prophet told the chiefs that the White Men intended to destroy them. "We must strike first, while the White Men sleep," he said. Two men wearing red coats had just arrived from Canada. They urged the Indian leaders to attack the Long Knives, but to do so at daybreak. The Indian leaders insisted that the attack be made at midnight when the Long Knives would be sure to be asleep and when their fires would be burning more brightly. Finally, they agreed that the attack should be made two hours before daybreak.

The Indian warriors assembled. The Prophet mixed a concoction and, after working up the religious fanaticism of the braves, proclaimed: "One-half of the White Men's army is dead, and the other half is crazy. It will not be hard for you to finish their destruction with your tomahawks. And the bullets from your fire pieces will destroy them, but I say to you, their bullets will drop at your feet as sand. In the night you will see with great light, while all is thick darkness to your enemies."

The Prophet looked out solemnly over the assembly of warriors. He fingered his necklace of deer hoofs. He held up his strings of sacred beans and went on, "Manitou the Master of Life will protect you. By Manitou I give you power over all the power of the enemy.

"The Master of Life will send rain to dampen the powder of the Long Knives, but your fire pieces will be good. The Master of Life demands that the White Chief die. If he does not die, the Long Knives can never be defeated. Your first attack must be against the wigwam of the White Chief in the center of the enemy's camp. When the Chief Harrison falls, all the other Long Knives will run and hide in the grass like young quails. There they can be captured and be made slaves to do the work of the women of our town and villages."

"I choose one hundred warriors for this special task. They must crawl like snakes through the grass and strike the sentinels and then rush forward boldly and kill the Great War Chief of the White Men. If you do that you will have a horseload of scalps and every warrior will have a new gun and many horses.

"All the warriors must creep through the wet grass where the horses cannot run. Some will go up one side of the camp and the others by the creek and up the steep bank through the bushes to be ready to use the tomahawk against the sleeping White warriors as soon as their Chief is dead. If any of our warriors are discovered as they creep up to the White camp, they must give a great yell, and then everyone will attack together. The Indian yells will scare the White Men and they will run up to the thick woods. You can take all their goods, and you can shoot them with their own guns from every tree, but the most important thing is to kill the Great White Chief."

Two hours after midnight seven hundred warriors assembled on the playing field at the edge of Prophet's Town. Although the Miamis were not participating as a group, White Loon, a Miami chief, would serve as the principal battle leader with the assistance of Stone Eater, another Miami, and Winamac. Shabonee, a thirty-six-year-old friend and lieutenant of Tecumseh, an Ottawa who was a grand nephew of the great Chief Pontiac, and now, having married a Potawatomi, had been chosen a peace chief of that tribe, would lead the special force of one hundred warriors to assassinate the White Chief.

Accompanied by an old Ottawa chief, Sabaqua and his son, Shabonee led his group out in single file across the field and the swamp, all the way around the southern tip of the high ground occupied by the Long Knives and along the bank of Burnett's Creek to an area below the northwest corner of the enemy camp. The Prophet followed this group up the creek about midway of the rear of Harrison's position, and then crossed over the creek to station himself on a big rock that projected out of the side of a bluff. Here he could overlook Harrison's camp, at least when there was light.

Winamac followed with a file of 250 Potawatomis, Ottawas, Chippewas, Menominees, and Wyandots. He placed his warriors along the southwest corner of the campsite. White Loon and Stone Eater led their group of 350 Shawnees, Kickapoos, Delawares, Winnebagos, Weas, and Saks and Foxes to positions all along the eastern front of the Long Knives' camp.

A cold drizzle began to fall. Just as The Prophet had promised, rain was falling to dampen the enemy's powder. Campfires were burning throughout the camp, again, as The Prophet had promised, light around the enemy so that they could be seen but complete darkness around the Red Men.

3

By the light of the campfires, lone sentinels were marching their posts around Harrison's camp in the drizzling rain that made the darkness beyond the fires almost total. Private Lehman Welch stood at his post near the northwest angle of the camp and listened. He could hear the rustling of grass. It seemed to be more than just the wind and the rain. He raised his musket and waited. But while he waited his adversary did not. While he looked into the darkness ahead, a Potawatomi Indian crept up toward his side where his figure was silhouetted against the fires, and from only a few yards away let fly an arrow from a sturdy bow. It caught Lehman Welch in the throat before he knew what was about. He fell without a sound, the first casualty of the battle.

Shabonee's special band of one hundred warriors had climbed up the embankment near the northwest corner of the Long Knives' camp. Half of them carried bows and arrows, the better to attack silently without giving away their positions.

Corporal Stephen Mars, standing guard in front of Captain Frederick Geiger's company of Kentucky riflemen, heard a rustling of the grass directly below him. Quickly he levelled his rifle and fired. A wild scream from an Indian, struck by Mars' bullet, rent the air. To his dismay, Shabonee knew that the scream would alert the enemy. He called out for all his warriors to attack. A musket shot almost immediately killed Corporal Mars. Fifty arrows flew through the darkness into the camp and then with shooting of muskets and loud yells, the group charged into the Long Knives' positions.

As one of the Indians suddenly came upon another sentinel, a Daniel Pettit, the latter jumped up and ran toward his main line as fast as he could, the Indian in close pursuit. As the Indian was about to overtake him, Pettit, cocking his rifle on the run, suddenly turned about, thrust the rifle into the abdomen of his pursuer and pulled the trigger. At the same instant the Indian fired his rifle, but its barrel was longer, and he was too close to get a direct hit, but the muzzle flash set fire to a handkerchief that Pettit had tied to his head. While the Indian fell, Pettit went running through the woods, a fiery halo around his head.

Two Indians got into Captain Geiger's tent but were killed before they could get to the captain.

It was a little after four o'clock in the morning when Harrison, drawing on his boots by the light of a fire outside the open side of his tent, was talking with his civil aide, Thomas Randolph; his two military aides, Colonel Owen and Major Taylor; Major Daveiss, commander of the dragoons, and Major Wells, commander of the Kentucky mounted riflemen. The orderly musician, the drummer, was standing by to beat reveille—three taps on the drum—at the word of the General. Harrison told him that that would be in two minutes, but the beat of muskets beat the beat of the drum by those two minutes.

Suddenly they heard a shot and then a loud Indian cry from the direction of the northwest corner of the camp. At once the officers ran for their horses, and the two unit commanders rushed to their battle areas.

Harrison ran out and called for his horse. His habit had been to ride his favorite horses, the gray mare and a sorrel stallion, on alternate days. This day he had been riding the gray mare and as was his custom, he had left her bridled and saddled for instant use when she was tied to a picket for the night, but now Harrison did not see her, and he called again to his orderly, George, to bring up the horse quickly.

George ran up and, trembling with fear, explained, "General, I tied the mare to a picket, just like you said, but she pulled it up and strayed away. The dragoon on sentry duty over there saw her and woke me up, and then I tied her to a wagon wheel over there, but General I can't remember which one, I just can't."

In consternation and with a grim sense of humor, Harrison cried out, "A horse! A horse! My Kingdom for a horse!"

The allusion was completely lost on the poor orderly, but not the urgency of the demand. He scurried about in search of the strayed mare or a suitable substitute.

Just then Major Taylor's orderly brought up the aide's horse. Taylor called out for Harrison to mount this horse, a bay, and he would get another. As Harrison did so, his other aide, Colonel Owen, came riding up on a white horse, and they rode off together toward the sound of the shooting and yelling. They had gone only a few yards when a musket ball struck Owen in the temple, and he fell dead. Harrison first thought that this must have been a stray bullet that had passed over the fighting infantry, but then it suddenly occurred to him that that bullet had been intended for him, that an Indian intruder, misled by the white horse, had taken Owen for him.

A few minutes later Taylor came riding up to join the commander. Harrison saw that he was riding his (Harrison's) gray mare.

"For God's sake, Waller, get off the gray!" Harrison shouted. "They've just shot Owen off his white horse. Go back and get another. There are several others of my own back there."

Without hesitation, Taylor turned about to comply. The other aide, Major Henry Hurst, came up on another bay horse, and they went on toward the action. Shortly Taylor was back, this time on Harrison's favorite sorrel. They made no effort to exchange mounts, but went on, riding each other's horse.

Shabonee and two of his braves had slipped through the defensive positions and reached the interior of the camp. One of them had indeed shot the man on the white horse, and they were sure that the White Chief Harrison had been killed, but soon Shabonee knew better. He recognized Harrison on a dark horse. The Indian chief was unnoticed as he stood very close to where the White commander rode by. Shabonee lifted his musket, but the Great Spirit pushed it down. He was unable to shoot the White Chief.

Harrison and his two aides quickly made their way to the area of the initial attack. He knew that the fires were an advantage to the Indians and ought to be extinguished, but whenever anyone approached one, he was sure to be a target. At the same time, it would have been nearly impossible for Harrison to find his way through the absolutely black woods without the light of the fires. Rain still was falling, but not hard enough either to extinguish the fires or to render the powder useless. Many of the fires had just been refueled in anticipation of reveille and what little breakfast might be found.

Harrison found the companies at the angle in disarray and the line broken. The men cheered when he made his presence known, and he reassured them with his strong, calm voice above the noise of battle. He sent Taylor off to bring up two companies from the center of the western line, where the terrain was more defensible and so far not under attack. As Taylor galloped off, his horse, i.e. Harrison's sorrel, was shot from under him, and in the fall Taylor was pinned under the animal. Harrison dispatched

Hurst on the same mission while a passing soldier extricated Taylor from his precarious position. Harrison turned just as a musket ball cracked through his hat. A little later his horse went down from under him, and he had to send for another mount. Now another bullet struck his saddle.

The two companies arrived quickly and went into position to support the companies of Barton and Geiger. Together they were able to eliminate the Indians who had penetrated, and to begin to restore the position.

By now firing had broken out on the other side, at the northeast corner and along the east front where a small company of U.S. riflemen, armed with muskets, and three companies of the 4th Infantry Regiment were under attack. Harrison hurried to that area. He found that Major Daveiss was forming his dismounted dragoons in rear of those companies, preparing to counterattack.

"Will you permit me to dislodge those damned savages behind those logs?" he called out.

After two refusals, Harrison directed him to take his dragoons out and attack a group of Indians who were pouring out a devastating fire from a clump of trees about twenty paces to the front. With only his favored detail of twenty men, men who had been chosen for their horsemanship as well as for other soldierly skills, Daveiss, conspicuous in a white capot, rushed out with his little detachment, all on foot. Almost immediately Daveiss was struck down, mortally wounded by a musket ball in his thigh.

But the infantry companies, encouraged by Harrison and by Colonel Boyd who were riding up and down the line, were standing firm. Almost immediately after the fall of Daveiss, Boyd sent Captain Snelling out with his company to attack the Indians in the grove of trees. This effort succeeded. Cheered on, Boyd shouted, "Huzza, huzza, my sons of gold, just a little more fire, and victory will be ours!"

The muskets of the regulars were loaded with twelve buckshot for each round instead of the more common musket ball, and this proved to be ideal for close-in fighting in the dark.

Using deer hoofs for signals, the Indians abandoned their fighting behind cover and advanced in wild charges. This was unsettling for the untried soldiers, but ironically, in depending upon the White Man's weapons—muskets and rifles—the followers of the Prophet had thrown away their greatest advantage. The firing of the weapons alerted the Long Knives at a range where they could retaliate in kind. Had the Red Men held to their old ways, with reliance on stealth and bows and arrows and tomahawks, they might have overrun the entire encampment and engaged the whole force in close hand-to-hand combat where firearms would have been useless and the advantages of surprise more enduring. In this way, they might have achieved a massacre that really would have matched that of Little Turtle against St. Clair.

The Prophet stood on his rock protruding from the side of a hill several hundred yards away. His position overlooked the battlefield perfectly, but through the darkness he could follow the action only by the gun flashes and by occasional silhouettes moving before the few fires which yet burned. The Prophet loudly sang a war song as he watched. Indian messengers told him that their braves were falling back and were being wounded. The Prophet told them to keep fighting, that soon everything would be as he said. Now he began singing more loudly than before. Back on the battlefield The Prophet's voice could be heard in the distance, during intervals between firing.

Harrison found a French lieutenant standing behind a tree. He reproved the lieutenant for getting behind shelter while his men were exposed. "I not behind de tree," the lieutenant said. "De tree before me. Dere was de tree; here was my position. How can I help? I cannot move de tree. I cannot leaf my position!"

A militiaman found his flintlock out of order. Disregarding the warnings of his comrades, he went back and relighted a fire where, with bullets cracking all about him, he worked until the weapon was repaired. Then he returned to his position.

In some places the Indians again pushed into the camp area. One of the chiefs went up to a fire to work with his flint, but a bullet struck him, and he fell forward into the fire.

Captain William C. Baen, who had joined his company at Fort Harrison, was standing near his tent along the main front of the 4th U.S. Infantry, when an Indian stole up beside him and caught him in the side of the head with a tomahawk. The captain ran around in a wild delirium for several minutes before a merciful death overtook him.

Thomas Randolph came riding up in search of Harrison. On finding him, he called out, "Governor, I've just completed the circuit. Cook and Peters are doing well in bolstering up Barton and Geiger up on the northeast corner. Wilkins has arrived to help restore the hole left by Robb on the northwest. The companies of the 4th Regiment are all holding well. But right now, Spencer is catching hell on the south flank. He needs help, and quickly!"

"Thanks, Tom," Harrison called back. "That's a big help. But what in hell happened to Robb? Did he get overrun?"

"Oh no, Sir, somebody told him to pull back and reform."

"Who told him that?"

"I don't know."

"Where is he right now?"

"He's back where the dragoons were, in a kind of reserve position."

"Good, let's get him down to back up Spencer."

Randolph did not answer. He fell from his horse. Harrison dismounted and ran to him. By the dim light of a fire Harrison could see a gaping wound in Randolph's chest. He was dead. Suddenly Harrison put his hand to his own chest as a sharp pain went through it. It was a sympathy pain. He jumped back on his horse. Sending Waller Taylor off to find Captain David Robb and his company of mounted rifles and send them to the aid of Spencer, Harrison sent word for Prescott's company of the 4th Regiment to pull out of the front line to reinforce further the vacancy left by Robb, and then he galloped off toward the right flank.

On arriving at the southern flank, Harrison found Ensign John Tipton in command of the whole line. Spencer, after refusing to give up command after he had been thrice wounded, had been felled by a fourth ball and had succumbed. His two lieutenants also had been killed, and Captain Jacob Warwick in command of a militia company on the right of Spencer, also had died after having a wound dressed at the aid station and then returning to his command.

Robb's company arrived in time to shore up the position here.

Now Harrison began to think of counterattack. He was confident that if the lines could hold until daylight, a counterattack would drive the Indians from the whole area. Preparatory to doing this, he pulled back three companies from the front (east) line, and one from the rear to form on the left flank, and pulled back two other companies to form on the right. Anticipating this action, Major Wells at daybreak charged northward with his infantry companies and a small detachment of dragoons. Raising "huzzas" and yells to match those of the Indians of two hours earlier, the infantrymen drove the Indians back at the point of their bayonets, and then the mounted dragoons pursued them to the swamp. Just a few minutes later Captain Robb, with the support of the two companies brought up for the purpose, charged and put to flight the Indians on the south flank.

On returning from the pursuit, many of the Kentuckians took scalps from the dead Indians that had been left on the field. Some of the scalps were cut into three or four pieces so that everyone in a unit could have a trophy to display on the ramrod of his rifle or musket.

Harrison called a council of the officers to determine what should be done next. No one could be sure that the Indians would not reform for another attack. There was a rumor that Tecumseh was on his way from the South with two thousand warriors.

The decision was to send the dragoons, mounted on their horses, into Prophet's Town the next day to see if indeed the Indians were reforming there, and if not, to destroy the town. Meanwhile the army would be put to work building breastworks of logs and earth, about four feet high, to provide protection in case of another attack. Food supplies would be sought since the cattle and hogs had run off, or had been driven off, during the battle. Thirty-seven dead Americans had to be buried, and 126 wounded, twenty-five so severely that they would die, had to be cared for.

Within an hour after the battle, the Harrison County Yellow Jackets elected Ensign Tipton to be their commander, and Harrison gave him a battlefield commission as a captain in the militia. Harrison took the fourteen-year-old son of the fallen commander of that unit, Spier Spencer, into his own tent.

Waller Taylor found the body of Thomas Randolph. He cut a lock of his fallen friend's hair and took a pin from his chest to take back to the widow. Then, to his surprise, he found the body of Colonel Isaac White, another friend and Masonic brother from Vincennes. He had these two buried side-by-side with Major Joseph Daveiss who, as Grand Master of Kentucky, was also Grand Master over the Lodge at Vincennes. Waller carved their initials in a tree over their graves.

That same morning, Harrison appointed a court martial to try Ben, the Negro driver who had been pinned to the ground all night, accused of giving information to the Indians and of plotting the assassination of the Commander-in-Chief. The court unanimously voted the death penalty.

Had this come to him simply as a piece of paper, Harrison probably would have approved it and ordered the sentence carried out, but in this case, the accused lay before him. Without crying out, without saying a word, he simply fixed his eyes upon the commander whenever he was in the vicinity. Harrison read pleas for mercy in those eyes, and he could not bring himself to give the order. Later that day he assembled all the commissioned officers and asked them to reconsider the case, and then he would be bound by their vote.

At this meeting, Captain Josiah Snelling, the senior company commander of the Regular regiment, stepped forward and said, "Brave comrades, let us save him. The wretch deserves to die; but as our commander, whose life was more particularly his object, is willing to spare him, let us also forgive him. I hope, at least, that every officer of the 4th Regiment will be upon the side of mercy."

Snelling was sufficiently persuasive for the vote to go in his favor, and Ben was pardoned.

That night Harrison's whole command remained on the alert for an attack. In position behind the breastworks, no man was allowed to sleep during the night. They were required to pass the watchword, right to left, every five minutes. It was a long, cold night.

The next morning (November 8), Harrison sent a detachment of mounted dragoons into Prophet's Town. They found there only an old squaw, too feeble to flee, too defiant to give up. They found a storehouse containing three thousand bushels of corn, beans, and peas. After collecting all the food and all the pots and pans and souvenirs they could carry, the dragoons put the whole town to the torch. Nothing was spared. The wigwams, the public houses, the storage house—everything was burned.

They carried the old woman back to camp, where they told her to look after a wounded chief who had turned up.

From a distance, the Indians looked on in horror and dismay at their burning town. The soldiers looked on with shouts of glee. The burning town sent smoke signals to the Indians to beware, to the settlers to rest assured. That night its glow continued to light the eastern sky.

4

On the other side The Prophet was in deep trouble with his followers. As the Indians retreated at daybreak on the 7th, he had left his observation post on "Prophet's Rock" and had hastened back to his village. There he had met throngs of disillusioned, angry warriors. The Prophet had promised immunity from injury, but forty of their comrades had been killed and another 120 wounded by the Long Knives' bullets.

A group of Winnebagos confronted The Prophet. "Why? Why?" their spokesman demanded. "Why were we misled to believe that the White Men were dead or crazy, when all were in their senses and fought like the Devil?"

"Death to Tenskwatawa! Death to the false prophet!" the Winnebagos cried.

Fearing for his life, the holy man explained, "The fault must be placed on my squaw. Without my knowledge she handled the sacred things when she was unclean. When she handled sacred string of beans and tried to help in prayers, that broke the sacred power."

The warriors mumbled in disbelief. The Prophet tried to rally them. "My Brothers, if you will attack again, I will not make same mistake. If you attack again, the powers of the Master of Life will protect you."

No one was persuaded. Warriors, with their women and children, were fleeing from the town. Some went north to find their way back to their old villages. Most crossed the Wabash first, to escape a feared attack of the Long Knives on their town. They took no time to gather food or utensils. They ran to the river with what they had and crossed the river, some by canoes, but most, simply by wading or riding their horses.

The Winnebagos bound The Prophet with rope and took him across the river to a temporary camp on the Wild Cat Creek about twenty miles to the east. After further taunts and threats, the Winnebagos abandoned their erstwhile holy leader to return to their homes in the West.

About the same time Winamac arrived at the camp with twenty of his Potawatomi warriors. Recognizing The Prophet sitting alone, his head buried in his buffalo robe, the Potawatomis began shouting in derision. Winamac strode up and said in a loud voice, "Tenskwatawa is a Shawnee squaw! He told us the bullets of the Long Knives would fall like sand; they killed our warriors. He said that the Long Knives would run away; they ran after us."

Slowly The Prophet turned his head and raised his hand for silence.

"The Great Spirit promised victory, and Tenskwatawa gave the message to his children. The Great Spirit did not lie. The Great Spirit did not make mistake. Tenskwatawa made mistake. He made mistake by giving his ring, his symbol of power to the great Winamac, that he might lead his warriors to victory. But Winamac knew nothing of power. He was not able to use secret symbol."

"Tenskwatawa has no power. He is false prophet!" Winamac cried.

"Return the ring, and Tenskwatawa will show great Winamac he does not speak truth."

The Potawatomi chief took the ring from his finger and flung it down at The Prophet. Tenskwatawa picked it up and put it on the middle finger of his right hand. He slipped over beside Winamac, and catching the rays of the morning sun, flashed the reflection into the eyes of his tormentor.

"Look, look upon the sacred symbol," The Prophet said as he waved his hand to and fro in front of Winamac's eyes. Helplessly the Chief followed the motion of the ring with his eyes.

"You are drowsy, drowsy. Sleep, sleep, sleep."

Suddenly, to the amazement of his followers the big chief slumped to the ground.

"See, the great Winamac is in my power from the Great Spirit. Unless I ask Great Spirit to awaken him, he will sleep forever."

The Prophet threatened to put all the warriors to sleep. They began shouting, "No, no!" Some fell on their faces to beg for mercy. Others ran away.

"Fear not!" The Prophet said. "I will restore the great Winamac." He clapped his hands three times and called out, "Winamac, awake! Winamac, arise!"

The Chief opened his eyes in a look of wonder. Slowly he realized where he was and arose. With no further words he put a blanket over his head and walked away, together with what following remained.

As the Long Knives departed, The Prophet made his way back

to a small satellite village near the site of Prophet's Town where he joined a few remaining Wyandots and Shawnees.

5

Back on Burnett's Creek, William Henry Harrison was anxious to get his little army moving back toward Vincennes. Though he regretted deeply the nearly twenty percent casualties that his command had suffered in a battle of two and one-half hours, and though he had suffered the loss of some close personal friends, he felt a certain sense of satisfaction in the achievement of a victory. It had been costly. It was a Cadmean victory, perhaps, but victory nonetheless.

Harrison sent an express to Vincennes to carry a report of the engagement and a list of casualties to John Gibson and to carry whatever letters the men had been able to prepare.

He was worried about the shortage of rations. Already horse carcasses had been recovered from the battlefield and prepared for food. He hoped that additional supplies could be obtained at the blockhouse on the Vermillion River. Moreover, he still dreaded another attack by reorganized Indians and perhaps by Tecumseh, who supposedly was on his way with reinforcements from the South.

It took all twenty-six available wagons to carry the wounded. This meant that most of the food supplies from Prophet's Town had to be left behind, and most of the officers' personal baggage had to be destroyed.

With the same kinds of security detachments to the front, flanks, and rear, as for the march up the river valley, the army moved out on the morning of November 9 for the return down the valley.

Harrison had declared that all possible precautions against surprise attack had been taken before the battle, but now he found an added measure. At each encampment on the return trip, there were to be no fires in the camp itself during the hours of darkness, but all night fires would be maintained out in front of the picket line, in front of the sentinels, all around the camp. In this arrangement, it would be the attackers who would be in the light of the fires while the defenders remained hidden in the darkness.

It took five days to reach the blockhouse on the Vermillion River. Five days of walking, walking, walking by battle-fatigued infantrymen made more fatigued by the nervous anticipation of new attack; five days of painful jostling for the wounded in the wagons as they rolled over the rough ground, five days of short rations and horse meat.

Here Harrison found Sergeant Reed, who had been left in command, fully in control. He was holding two deserters as prisoners. The men had fled their battle stations the moment the shooting started and, on arriving at the blockhouse, had informed the sergeant that the whole army had been annihilated, and advised him to take his small party and flee to Fort Harrison before the Indians came up. Instead Reed took the men prisoners and held his place. A few hours later Harrison's express had arrived with word of the victory.

Harrison also was pleased with the arrival of a boat with a good supply of rations. Colonel Miller had sent the boat from Fort Harrison just in time to meet the army here.

Here also the wounded were transferred from the wagons to boats for what would be a much more comfortable trip for the remaining distance to Fort Harrison and Vincennes.

The army arrived at Fort Harrison late on November 14. Harrison left Captain Snelling, the regular company commander who had so distinguished himself in the battle, in command of a garrison strong enough to repel attacks. Four days later, the veterans of Tippecanoe marched into Vincennes to the cheers and shouts of a crowd that had been alerted by the advance scouts, but amongst the crowd were silent women. The women had gathered—as women had gathered for ages to hear of their personal losses in war, in disasters at sea, or in times of natural catastrophe, while celebrations of victory went on, to watch in silence to see if loved ones were among the living, the dead, the sick, or the wounded. Anna Harrison was there, tears streaming down her cheeks in joy for the return of her husband, in sadness for the non-return of many friends.

The regulars were quartered at Fort Knox, while the militiamen were quartered in town until ready to move on to their home communities or, in the case of Knox country units, to be mustered out here. A general hospital was opened in the seminary building of the University to receive the wounded. Twenty-five of the wounded had died enroute.

5

At Grouseland, Harrison spoke to all the children collectively and then to each individually. Then he ran up to pay special respects to the youngest, Carter Bassett, the baby who had arrived on October 26 during the father's absence.

For days and days and miles and miles, Harrison had been looking forward to sleeping in his comfortable four-poster bed, but even more, he was anxious to visit with Anna. He heard the local news from her and then related the main details of the battle.

"When your express arrived, you can guess what a furor of excitement it created," she said after a while.

"I can imagine."

"We had heard of a few reports that there had been a battle, but no one was sure what had happened. Then when the express arrived everyone poured into the street. The courier was so overwrought that he could not distribute the letters. He simply thrust the whole bundle into the hands of one of the women, Mrs. Bacon."

"The wife of Lieutenant Bacon, the quartermaster in the 4th Regiment?"

"Yes, that's the one."

"Oh, I take it that she recovered from her fever all right."

"Oh, yes, she's quite all right, and Henry, she said that your calling on her before your departure did her more good than any doctor."

"I'm glad," Harrison said, "but you were saying —"

"Well, she was as overwrought as the courier. She could not see through her tears to read, and she handed the letters to another lady beside her who then hurriedly looked through them until she found one for Mrs. Bacon. Mrs. Bacon nearly fainted with joy when she recognized the handwriting of her husband. She quickly looked over the contents and read, 'my comrades acquitted themselves with much honour.' Then she turned to her companion and said, "When will brother cease to lift his hand against his brother and learn war no more?"'

"When we learn it well enough not to be open to attack," Harrison answered gratuitously. Then he said, "And do you know what The Prophet claimed to be the cause of his defeat?"

"What?"

"His magical powers had failed to work because his wife had handled his sacred string of beans when it was her falling off the roof time."

"Ha, indeed."

"Did you ever hear anything so ridiculous?"

"Oh, I don't know," replied Anna. "Some say that because a woman gave Adam an apple to eat, all of mankind fell. How can you beat that for the power of a woman?"

The next day Anna went along with her husband to see Catherine Randolph. This was something he dreaded, but it was something that he felt he had to do.

When they arrived at the Randolph residence, Catherine greeted them with a momentary flash of friendly recognition, and then a longer snarl of accusation before lapsing back into a stupor that had overcome her when she first heard the news of her husband's death. Their little daughter, just four months old, was crying in the next room, but she paid no attention.

With a feeling of inadequacy and helplessness, Harrison went into his recitation of what a fine man Thomas Randolph was, how he had rendered a great service to his country, and had died a true hero. She reacted with only faint glimmers of comprehension. Even had the circumstances been different, Harrison knew that he could find no words of condolence for Mrs. Randolph.

He could find no words of consolation for himself. He felt as though in the death of Randolph, he himself had died a little. He knew Randolph to have been a great advocate of his in Vincennes, and that created just that much pressure on Harrison to be as good a man as Randolph claimed him to be. Now that was gone. And by just that much, with the death of Randolph, Harrison had died in Vincennes; with the death of Spier Spencer, he had died a little in Corydon and Harrison County; and with the death of Joseph Daveiss, he had died a little in Kentucky.

6

Harrison was shocked a little by the wave of criticism that greeted him on his return. There were the cheers of the citizens to be sure, but there were also the barbs —

—He had been lured into a poor defensive position by the bad advice of untrustworthy Indians —partisans of The Prophet.

—He had been taken by surprise.

—He should have pursued the Indians after the battle and annihilated them.

—There had been no movement of the troops to meet the demands of the battle. They simply had stood and fought in the places where they were caught.

—Colonel Boyd, commander of the 4th U.S. Infantry Regiment and second in command of the total force, deserved the credit for whatever victory there was.

—The expedition had taken far too much time.

— Casualties had been unduly heavy.

In his own mind, Harrison was sure that all these criticisms could be answered, but he took the trouble to obtain depositions and letters from officers who were there to disprove them to the satisfaction of others.

No one regretted the casualties more than he, but he had been congratulating himself on being able to stand firmly in face of those casualties and then to counterattack and put the enemy to flight.

A few weeks after the return, Ben Parke walked into the Governor's office one afternoon and said, "Governor, to listen to some of the folks around here, you would think that we were defeated up at Tippecanoe."

"Ah, how so?" asked Harrison.

"Well, they are saying that there were more of our people killed than Indians, and so that gives the victory to the savages."

"Oh, damn," exclaimed Harrison. "I doubt that that is true, but even if it were, you know that is not a fair conclusion. Damn it, Ben, victory is not determined by the number of bodies left on the ground, but by who turns tail and runs; by who gains the objective."

"Of course," Parke agreed.

Harrison went on. "You know, Ben, at Fallen Timbers, under Anthony Wayne, we had 130 or 140 men killed or wounded, and I am sure that there were not more than twenty Indians killed. And Wayne had a force of nearly 2,000 dragoons and mounted riflemen in pursuit, but they were not able to catch the fleeing Indians."

"I'm sure that's right."

"And who doubts that that was a great victory? It led directly to the Greeneville Treaty, and it put an end to Indian hostilities for twenty years."

"Nobody can deny that."

"But Ben, there is one thing about Tippecanoe that bothers me more than that."

"What's that?"

"I'm afraid The Prophet and Tecumseh have been left standing, like the chimneys of a burned-down house that stand as the only survivors of the fire which they caused."

"Yes, well put," said Parke. "But I really don't think we have anything more to fear from them unless they somehow tie up with the British."

"And that, I fear, is a real possibility."

Parke was carrying some newspapers and some other papers. "Have you seen these?"

"I don't know. What are they?"

"Oh, some resolutions and so forth about the late action at Tippecanoe. One of them is from a so-called public meeting, which actually was a meeting of half a dozen men without any public notice, where Vanderburgh presided as chairman and John Johnson served as clerk."

"What were they up to?"

"Well, it's a resolution in praise of Colonel Boyd's conduct at Tippecanoe and of his gallant exertions that contributed so much to the preservation of so many lives."

"Well, I suppose there's nothing wrong with a little praise for Boyd. He deserves it," remarked Harrison.

"Of course, but don't you see, this really is a slap at you. Where is their resolution in praise of the Commander-in-Chief? But that's not all. Look what they have to say about the Militia. Listen to this: 'Those grave regular's expressions repeated with enthusiasm by that spirited but untutored militia who witnessed and emulated your cool intrepidity, evince at once the importance of the service you have rendered and the warmth of their gratitude,' and a little further on they say, 'Our fellow citizens will be convinced that valour without science cannot, however duly exerted, lead to certain success and may eventually cause a useless effusion of blood and that an armed force without military knowledge is little better than an inefficient multitude. They will learn to submit with cheerfulness to that discipline and subordination which alone can render its efforts consentaneous and irresistible.'"

"Well, I guess we'll have to grant some truth to the general principles stated there, but damn, there's no justification whatever for their criticism of the militia. Who acted better than Spencer's Yellow Jackets, or Robb's company, or Parke's dragoons?"

"Who indeed, thank you. But now listen to this. Here is a body of resolutions of a truly public meeting of officers and men of the militia of Knox County. It was a meeting at Beckes' tavern, with Luke Decker as chairman."

"And who was clerk?"

"One Major Benjamin Parke, Sir, and I can vouch for its authenticity."

"Well, go on."

Parke read:

At a numerous meeting, (public notice for that purpose being given) of the Officers and Non-commissioned officers, or privates of the Militia corps (Hargrove's company excepted) of the county of Knox which served on the late campaign under Gov. Harrison met at Beckes's Inn in Vincennes on the 7th December, 1811, Col. Luke Decker was appointed Chairman and Maj. Benjamin Parke, Clerk.

A paper purporting to be "an address from a number of the citizens of Vincennes and its vicinity" and signed by Henry Vanderburgh, as Chairman to Col. John P. Boyd, being read, the following resolutions were unanimously agreed to.

1. *Resolved unanimously*, that we cannot consider the said Address in any other light than as one amongst the *many* attempts which have flowed from the same source, to wound the feelings and injure the character of Governor Harrison.

2. *Resolved*, That the said Address in attempting to bestow the merit of the *masterly conduct* in the direction and maneuvering of the troops in the late action to any other than the Commander in Chief asserts a notorious untruth, which will be acknowledged as such by the whole army.

3. That our indignation is justly excited at the false and contemptuous manner in which the *Militia* who served under Governor Harrison are treated, in the said address; being there represented as an *untutored, undisciplined* band possessing indeed courage, but none of the other requisites of soldiers; and owing eternal gratitude to the Col. Boyd and his Regiment, for the preservation of their lives.

4. That the *Militia* which served under Governor Harrison were neither *untutored* nor *undisciplined*, but in common with the Regular troops, they shared the attention of the Commander in Chief, and that by his *personal exertions*, both the Militia and Regulars were brought to a state of perfection in that kind of maneuvering calculated for Indian warfare, and that they were enabled to perform all the directions of the Commander in Chief with promptness, facility, and precision.

5. That it is a notorious fact, known to the whole army that all the changes of position made by the troops during the action of the 7th ult. and by which the victory was secured, were made by the direction of the Commander in Chief, and generally executed under his immediate superintendence.

6. That we cannot but view as a most dangerous usurpation, the meeting of a few individuals, not more than from seven to ten, in a private house, without any previous or public notice being given and to pass resolutions and addresses in the name of a neighborhood. And we do further view the conduct of said individuals (almost every one of whom are the avowed enemies of the Commander in Chief — and several of whom have uniformly discountenanced and opposed every measure of the government, in respect to the Shawnee Prophet and his party, and none of whom were on the Campaign) in daring to speak in the name of the Militia, as highly presumptious and unwarrantable.

7. That it was owing to the skill and valor of the Commander in Chief that the victory of Tippecanoe was obtained.

8. That we have the most perfect confidence in the Commander in Chief, and shall always feel a cheerfulness in serving under him whenever the exigences of the country may require it.

9. That we would prefer serving under him to any person that could be designated by the government for that purpose.

10. That when commanded by him, honor will be achieved; and we have every confidence that victory will be obtained.

11. That in expressing the above opinions, in respect to the reprehensible conduct of the Addressers, we desire it to be definitely understood that we have no idea of wounding the feelings, or injuring the character of Col. Boyd that we are free to declare, that we believe his conduct during the action to have been that of a gentleman and a soldier.

12. That we feel the highest respect, and shall always recollect with gratitude, our brothers in arms, the Officers and Privates of the U.S. Troops. —*We have often heard. We have now seen what Yankees can do!*

13. That in obeying our country's call we shall feel a proud satisfaction in being associated with *Kentucky volunteers.*

14. That the above resolutions be inserted in the *Western Sun.*

"I must say, well written," Harrison exclaimed. "That really overwhelms that damned Vanderburgh resolution."

"I think so," smiled Parke. "And now hear this. Here is a statement adopted even before the Vanderburgh thing. Listen":

The undersigned Field officers during the action at Tippecanoe the morning of the 7th inst. desirous of stating their opinion with respect to the conduct of the Commander in Chief on that occasion, do hereby certify, that the Governor was calm and deliberate—that his orders were precise and distinct—that he performed duties that might have been devolved on subordinates—that he directed and marched reinforcements to points where aid was necessary and posted them himself—that he never avoided the post of danger. That the victory was obtained by his vigilance and activity—In a word that his conduct in every respect was worthy the General and the soldier.

JOSEPH BARTHOLOMEW *Col. 2d Ind. Reg.* LUKE DECKER *Col. 4th Ind. Reg. Infantry* G. R. C. FLOYD *Major 4th U.S. Inf. Com., Regt.*

SAMUEL C. WELLS *Major Gen. of the 6th Division of the Kentucky Militia. Now a major of the Mounted Rifleman, Indiana Terr.*

B. PARKE *Major Light Dragoon*

NOAH PURCELL *Major 4th Inf. Reg.*

"That is an impressive, representative group of officers, and I do appreciate that very much."

"And here is another. One from Sam Wells' mounted riflemen":

The mounted volunteer Riflemen met at Gen. Samuel Wells' on the 27th of December, 1811, for the purpose of partaking a dinner with the general. After appointing Capt. James Hunter chairman and Major Isaac R. Gwathmey secretary, a letter addressed to Col. Boyd with Henry Vanderburgh as signer — and also the resolutions adopted on the 7th of Dec. 1811, by the officers, non-commissioned officers and privates of the militia corps of Knox County, Indiana Territory were then read to Capt. Geiger and his company — when the following resolutions were unanimously agreed to.

1. *Resolved*, That we the volunteers who fought in the late battle on the Wabash under the command of Col. Frederick Geiger, do with heartfelt satisfaction, highly approve of the resolutions adopted by our brother officers and soldiers at Vincennes, on the 7th of Dec. 1811.

2. *Resolved*, That that part of the letter of Henry Vanderburgh, which says that the militia were an untutored and undisciplined band, is considered by us as a groundless and malicious falsehood, and is calculated to take from them (the militia) the never-fading laurels they won by their heroism, their bravery and their firmness.

3. *Resolved*, That we view the address of Henry Vanderburgh, as an unjustifiable attempt to wound the feelings of the Commander-in-Chief of the late expedition. And that we are ready and willing whenever our country calls, to volunteer under the same commander.

4. *Resolved*, that the Editor of the *Western Courier*, be requested to give the proceedings of this meeting publicity in his paper.

Harrison responded, "You know what I like best about that one."

"I dare say — willing to volunteer to serve again under the same commander."

"Undoubtedly."

"What higher tribute can one receive? Now, you must hear some of their toasts":

After Dinner the Following Toasts were drunk

1. Our departed heroes, who gloriously fell on the 7th of Nov. while fighting the battle of their insulted country, may their virtues ever be remembered and their patriotism imitated — *2 cheers*.

2. Governor Harrison, the brave and consummate general, he deserves not only the praises but the benediction of his country — *7 cheers*.

3. The British Agents at Vincennes, if any there be, may they call forth the just indignation of their countrymen, and be treated as traitors by every honest man — *4 hisses*.

4. The brave sons of Kentucky, when their country calls, may they not hesitate to volunteer their services — *An everlasting cheer.*

5. James Sommerville, a brave and intrepid Scotchman, whose heart was swollen with joy at the rapturous fount of liberty, while he manfully sacrificed his life for a boasted independence — *3 cheers.*

6. Stephen Mars, a Kentucky volunteer, who with more than Caesarian bravery fell heroically fighting for his country — *3 cheers.*

7. May the 7th of Nov. prove to our enemies that the spark of '76 is not yet extinguished — *9 cheers.*

8. May the United States no longer depend on fruitless negotiations but appeal to the God of Mars to compel her enemies to respect her rights — *6 cheers.*

9. The Eagle of America, when summoned from her peaceful rock, may she hurl destruction on the British Lion — *3 cheers.*

10. May the starry flag of 1812 float triumphantly over the ramparts of Quebec — *17 cheers.*

Harrison laughed and said, "I say, aren't they getting a bit bellicose toward the end there?"

"Fervent patriotism, that's what it is."

"But that talk of the British Lion and Quebec — I'm afraid it may come to that before another year is out."

"I wouldn't be surprised," Parke said. "And oh, there are some more complimentary pieces here—an article from the *National Intelligencer* printed in the *Sun*, resolutions of Congress, and so on."

"Fortunately, Waller Taylor made it to Washington with our dispatches."

After a pause, Parke returned to the question of the critics. "But Governor, you know all the critics. You know who the leading ones are."

"Oh, I suppose McIntosh — "

"That damned Scotch Tory."

"And John Rice Jones, and Eliza Bachus, and surely Jennings, and now, I'm afraid, Vanderburgh and Johnson."

"Yes. Now, what do all those people have in common?"

"I guess they don't care much for William Henry Harrison."

"Yes," said Parke, "but more specifically let me point out: number one, they all have ambition for personal gain, political or financial; number two, growing out of number one, they are all political opponents; and number three, none of them was at Tippecanoe; none of them saw or participated in the battle which they now affect to know so much about."

"Zounds! I guess you're right. I've been getting lots of letters with the same kind of sentiments you speak of. Here is one from

Andrew Jackson of Tennessee. He offers his congratulations, in a way, but he also urges acceptance of his help in case of any further trouble from the Indians. Frankly, I find that rather more galling than complimentary."

As time went on, Harrison reconciled himself to the fact that there would always be criticism of one in high office, and that criticism would always accompany triumph—criticism from rivals for political power, criticism from rivals for glory, criticism from little men trying to bring the subject down to their level.

6

During this time, Tecumseh and his party were riding across Illinois. As they approached Prophet's Town, Tecumseh saw the burnt ruins of the town which was to be the capital of his great confederacy. He had heard of the battle, but he was not prepared for this. Feelings of astonishment, disappointment, grief, and anger swept over him. Turning to Sickaboo he said bitterly, "Now, who are the savages?"

Walking quickly through the ruined town, Tecumseh went on to the adjacent Wyandot village where he found The Prophet, sitting in silence and despair. In anger, Tecumseh grasped his brother by the hair and shook him. "What have you done? What have you done?" he cried. "Why? Why?"

The Prophet lowered his head in remorse, an attitude in which he had had much practice during the last few weeks, and said, "What would you have me do? Turn over and play dead like a 'possum, or run away like a weasel? Would you have me invite the Long Knives to destroy our village without protest? Or would you have me stand and defend our houses and our children like a bear, or like a panther, My Brother, the Panther?"

Tecumseh, cooling his temper, remained quiet for a while. Then he turned and patting his brother on the shoulder, said, "No, you did what you had to do. We must fight like the bear and like the panther to protect our young. The coward Harrison waited until I was away. He spoke of peace, and I asked him to do nothing until I returned from my journey. And then as soon as I departed he made ready for war. The coward Harrison attacked behind my back. No, my Brother, you did what you had to do."

CHAPTER XXI

Paths of War

1

The Shawnees and their allies had suffered less at Tippecanoe than on several previous occasions at Piqua and Chillicothe, and certainly less than at Fallen Timbers. Indeed, for a time, the Indian threat was greater. Like the metastasis of a locally destroyed cancer, it had spread. At Tippecanoe, the Indians had been concentrated and could be watched at one place. Now scattered, they struck back in many places, much to the horror of the far frontier settlers.

Far more seriously, Tecumseh's dream of confederation was shattered. The tribesmen had lost faith in The Prophet's magic and with that had lost faith in union.

But Tecumseh himself was not one to lose heart. He immediately set about to put the pieces together. The Winnebagos, Potawatomis, and Kickapoos all had departed for their former villages, but Tecumseh gathered up the remnants of the Shawnee and Wyandot followers who remained in the vicinity and established a temporary village on the Wildcat Creek about fifteen miles east of the Tippecanoe site. He sent warriors back to Tippecanoe to search for food that the Americans might have overlooked, and he sent others through the woods as far as the Mississinewa in quest of game. He himself hurried to Detroit to see if he could get some assistance from the British.

On Tecumseh's arrival at Detroit on December 15, a great

earthquake struck. Late that night earth tremors shook the ground all the way from the Lakes down the Ohio and Mississippi valleys. The shock waves centered in the area south of where the Ohio joined the Mississippi. The town of New Madrid on the Mississippi in southeastern Missouri was totally destroyed. In the Creek town of Tuckabatchee, Big Warrior's town on the Tallapoosa River, every house fell to the ground.

The Prophet proclaimed that he had called forth the earthquake to destroy the Long Knives, though his detractors maintained that Manitou had taken revenge against the one who falsely claimed to be his Prophet. Tecumseh did not have to say anything. The Creek tribesmen were convinced that he had arrived at Detroit and stomped his foot on the ground. They vowed to come at his call to take up the tomahawk against the Long Knives. A number of them needed no further call. They gathered up their weapons and fled from their towns and villages to find the Great Chief who had threatened this calamity, to join him in his struggle against the Long Knives now.

More to the immediate point, Tecumseh was able to get a small quantity of lead and powder from the British. This was not for war but for the hunting necessary to enable his small band of faithful followers on the Wild Cat to survive another hard winter.

On instructions from Secretary of War Eustis, and welcoming a chance to gain time against any resumption of Indian hostilities by having the principal chiefs from each of the tribes away for several weeks, in January Harrison sent a message to Tecumseh and his brother to join other chiefs of the tribes of the Northwest in a delegation to go to Washington. Welcoming what seemed to him a tender of time while he was trying to get his followers reorganized, Tecumseh responded that as he had said previously, he would be glad to go to Washington to speak to The Great Father, but he could not possibly leave until the corn had been planted, late in the spring.

Harrison thought that an acceptance of the invitation by the various chiefs would be "conclusive evidence of their peaceable disposition," but he doubted that either Tecumseh or The Prophet could be persuaded to go, or at least without Harrison's providing a hostage to guarantee their safe return.

Already Tecumseh had dispatched riders to the Kickapoo and Potawatomi villages along the Illinois and to the Winnebagos in the Wisconsin country to ask them to return to the Tippecanoe to prepare for war.

To his chagrin, Tecumseh learned that Winamac, apparently disillusioned in his brief turn of support by the results at the Battle of Tippecanoe, was plotting with some of the government chiefs to assassinate both Tecumseh and Tenskwatawa. He took steps to foil that plot. Convinced that Winamac was possessed of a fickleness that responded to the winds of war, Tecumseh held to a hope that the opportunistic Potawatomis might be brought back into the fold when the time came.

For his part, Harrison was chagrined to learn that during the previous spring at a time when he was trying to prepare conferences with the Indians to preserve peace, men in his own town had been plotting to undermine his position. Captain Snelling at Fort Harrison passed on to him a report from Indians that some Wea chiefs, Laprousier together with White Pigeon, and a warrior called Piankeshaw Dick as interpreter, had been in a midnight meeting at the house of Joseph Basidon, with William McIntosh and Thomas Jones also in attendance. There McIntosh had persuaded the Wea chiefs to sign a declaration to the effect that their lands had been taken from them without their consent. This declaration then had been forwarded to Jonathan Jennings in Washington to use as he might see fit. McIntosh had impressed upon the Indians that he had spoken in their behalf at great personal sacrifice, at a cost amounting to $4,000. They promised to indemnify him if they got their lands back. Thomas Jones also came in for a promise of land, over 5,000 acres along Racoon Creek. The Indians were told that soon they would have a new Governor, and then this would be the Golden Age in the Territory.

Harrison took no notice of this report other than to confirm, in his own mind, the perfidy of his political enemies.

While the events at Tippecanoe had tarnished the image and reputation of The Prophet, Tecumseh gleamed as brightly as ever in the eyes of many tribesmen of all the neighboring nations. Many of them began returning to the Tippecanoe.

To reassure Harrison and again to buy time, in March Tecumseh sent a delegation of Kickapoo and Winnebago warriors to Vincennes to visit the Governor.

Harrison welcomed the delegation, as he had so many others before them, in the "Council Room" at Grouseland. Their spokesman made an impressive speech about their peaceful intentions.

Among other things he spoke as follows:

"Father—the Kickapoos' and the Winnebagos' intention was not to strike the White People, but The Prophet told them many lies and made them do it. Now, Father, what you tell me I will do. I will not strike the White People any more, you may depend on it. Father, not one White Man will be injured by the Kickapoos, Winnebagos, Potawatomis, or Piankeshaws.

"Father, The time The Prophet came to the Wabash he said that he had had communication with The Great Spirit. I came there to see him, for I thought he must be a good Indian to speak to The Great Spirit. The time I started from the big village, my heart was not to strike the White People, but to hear what The Great Spirit said to the Red Men.

"Father, I am sorry you lost some of your young men. You did not make the war yourself, the Red Men did it, but that bad man told them they must.

"Father, I love my women and children as well as I do myself and I wish you to love and take pity on them. I now hold the White wampum you gave me at Vincennes in my hand.

"Father, I throw the tomahawk on the ground. I shall no more make war with the White People. I bury the war club and tomahawk in pity to my women and children."

Harrison responded, "My Children, I am pleased to hear your professions of peace. I hope that the tomahawk will remain buried. But, my Children, why do your brothers on the Illinois and on the Mississippi make war on the White settlements? Why do they kill our women and children?"

The Kickapoo spokesman answered, "Our brothers have not received the word of peace. If our Father will provide horses, we will ride to them and tell them to stop. We will tell them to bury the tomahawk."

Harrison was so impressed by the apparent sincerity of his advisers that he gave them the horses they requested and bade them be on their way on their mission of peace. He also invited them to join with Tecumseh, The Prophet, and other chiefs for the visit to Washington. He suggested that all who were going to Washington would meet at Fort Wayne in April to prepare for the trip.

Harrison reported to the Secretary of War that the tribes now were "sincere in their professions of friendship and their desire for peace." He sent a message to Wildcat Creek to pardon the Shawnees and Wyandots who had followed Tecumseh there and even to forgive The Prophet. He asked Tecumseh and The Prophet to meet with the others at Fort Wayne preparatory to going to Washington. He also invited delegates from the Miami, Eel River, Potawatomi, and Delaware tribes to come to Fort Wayne for the Washington trip.

Tecumseh was having second thoughts about going to Washington. He always had looked forward to meeting The Great Father in person and now, mainly in the hope of persuading him to overturn the Treaty of Fort Wayne, but he did not like the idea of being away just now when he was in the midst of reassembling and reorganizing his followers. The bitter consequence of Harrison's invasion during his last absence was still fresh upon him, and he was reluctant to leave the town, just now rebuilding, at the mercy of Harrison. Although he had accepted a belt of wampum to indicate his acceptance of the invitation to go to Washington, he now returned it and remained in his village. Taking their cue from Tecumseh, most of the other chiefs failed to appear at Fort Wayne in mid-April as had been the plan. Only the delegates from the Miamis, Potawatomis, and Eel Rivers showed up, and they were so intimidated by the absence of the others and the attitude of Tecumseh that they refused to leave Indiana.

If the earlier acceptances of the invitation to go to Washington could be taken as a sign of peace, Harrison concluded that the refusal now to go should be taken as an opposite sign. He reported immediately (April 4) to the Secretary of War, "The hopes entertained of our being able to avoid a war with the Indians are entirely dissipated."

Instead of going to Washington, Tecumseh and The Prophet went back to Tippecanoe and began rebuilding Prophet's Town.

Where his whole effort had been to achieve an Indian union for effective self-defense, where his whole ambition had been in the service of his people and their defense, now Tecumseh felt a sense of pique, of personal injury and insult. His impulse was to gather all his braves and descend upon Vincennes. Only the burning of Vincennes could compensate for his injury and for the burning of his town, but he thought better of that when he saw the continuing negativism in many of the tribes. Defeatism was spreading amongst them. He must find a way for greater strength, and he must find a way to redeem himself personally.

Harrison dreaded an attack on Vincennes. He saw that as a very real threat if Tecumseh were allowed to recoup his strength. As long as the 4th Infantry remained, the place was fairly safe, but the pressure was on to move it out as prospects for war with Great Britain continued to grow. Additional companies of Rangers had been authorized, and they were fine for patrolling the trails and for giving protection to isolated farm houses and settlements against Indian depredations. They would not be of much use against a combination of several thousand Indians in a concentrated attack on the capital city.

Harrison also felt a sense of pique. He had been surprised at the criticisms levelled against him on his return from what he regarded as a highly successful expedition to Tippecanoe. Yes, he had gained a victory of sorts, but it had been too costly in American lives, and it had not been decisive. The Indian menace remained as great as ever. He conceded, in his own mind, that he had not been vigorous enough in following up his victory. Perhaps he had been guilty of the same mistake that Clark and the others on earlier occasions had made, to be content with burning the villages without destroying the enemy.

Now he longed for an opportunity to redeem himself. He was fully confident that he could do it. What he needed was a force strong enough to move back up through the Indian country and to destroy all the concentrations of Indians in the Territory. This was the only way to assure the safety of Vincennes, and this was the only way to secure his own reputation.

2

Early one afternoon Harrison left his office to look for Anna. He found her in her garden.

"Aren't you rushing the season a little?" he asked as he approached her.

She looked up in surprise and then with a smile, she said, "Oh, no, I'm just planning a little, trying to figure out what ought to go where this year."

"What would you think of giving up the garden this year?"

Now the surprise returned to her face. "What on earth for?" she demanded. "What do you mean? We *have* to have a garden if we are to feed everybody properly. Besides, I like the flowers, too."

"Of course," responded Harrison. "I was just wondering what you would think of taking the children for a visit to North Bend for a few weeks."

"Oh, that would be wonderful!" she cried. Then she paused in hesitation and asked, "What's the matter? Are the Indians getting ready to attack here?"

"Oh no, I don't think so. Not just now, anyway. I just thought it might be nice for the children to have a chance to get away for once, to visit their grandparents, and their aunt and uncle and cousins and friends. And I'm sure it would be nice for you to see your father and Maria and everything, and to have something of a change from the politicians and Indians of Vincennes."

"Oh yes, of course it would. But what about you? Could you come along?"

"You know my duties are liable to take me anywhere."

"Yes, I know, like to St. Louis when John Scott was born, and to Tippecanoe when Carter was born."

"Yes, that's true, I'm afraid," Harrison granted. "But now I'm trying to work it the other way. I thought perhaps you and the rest of the family could take a boat."

"Yes, how else?"

"I would ride across to review the militia in eastern Indiana and then come on down to join you. I'll try to stay there for a few weeks until we get a better idea of what's going to happen."

"Can you do that? Leave all the business at Vincennes, I mean."

"Of course. John Gibson can run things here. Anyway, I do need to get out and see our constituents in other parts of the Territory."

"Even with the best intent in the world, I suppose it is difficult to know exactly where you should be when who knows what may happen who knows where."

"Ha, well put, my Dear. But Anna, my Dear, I'll tell you something I've found out from all my experience."

"Yes, what's that?"

"No matter where I happen to be at any given moment, there always is someone who thinks I should be somewhere else."

"Yes, I'm sure."

"And no matter what I am doing at any given moment, there always is someone who thinks I should be doing something else."

"Oh my poor dear, how can you ever keep yourself together?" Anna responded in a half mocking, half sympathetic attitude.

Then she added, "Yes, I guess that's true even in my little world. Should I be with this child or that, preparing for a reception or going to the church, going to market or seeing that the laundry's done, teaching the children or planting the garden? Yes, I see what you mean all right, and when jealous politicians or army officers or Indians are after you, no wonder you must want to go to Ohio for a spell!"

"Yes, but actually there's more to it than that just now. There is some danger of an Indian attack, especially if we get into a war with England, which seems pretty likely now. The best way to forestall it is another expedition up the Wabash. But if war comes with England, then the biggest threat may be to Detroit and Fort Wayne. In any case, this may be a good time for you all to be in Ohio."

"I appreciate that, but don't you think if people see the Governor's family leaving, that that might lead to worry and even panic on the part of the inhabitants?"

"There's enough of that already, what with all the depredations across southern Illinois, all the way from the Mississippi to the Wabash. I've already told the Secretary of War that if he didn't get some reinforcements out here for the defense of this place, the whole lower Wabash valley would soon be depopulated."

"Yes, I suppose so, but we don't want to hasten the process. When were you thinking of our going?"

"I would say early next month as soon as I can arrange for a boat."

"That doesn't give us much time, does it? And how long do you plan for us to stay?"

"That's hard to say. I would say a few weeks at least, and if there is war, perhaps just stay there until it's over. I think we should pack our things for a long stay. We'll leave Joe and Eliza here to look after the house and garden, and Joshua can look after the animals. We'll take everybody else."

"Very well, we'll be ready."

"Let's tell all the children together tomorrow noon."

"Yes, let's do that."

At the dinner table at noon the next day, Harrison broached the subject. "How would you all like to take a vacation trip this spring?" he asked.

"Oh yes, yes," came back a chorus of excited responses.

"Where to?" John Cleaves, now thirteen and a half, asked, "Where to, New Orleans?"

"New Orleans?" Betsy, the fifteen-and-a-half-year old cried.

"No, no, not that far. To visit your grandparents at North Bend."

"Oh yes," came more excited responses.

"Where's North Bend?" asked young William Henry, now nine and a half.

"Why, that's right by Cincinnati on the Ohio River, over in Ohio."

"In the Ohio River?" laughed William Henry, Junior.

"No," his father laughed, "Ohio is a state, and the Ohio River runs along it."

"Is Indiana a state, Papa?" asked John Scott, age seven and a half.

"No, but it soon will be. Ohio is like Indiana, but just a little older and with a few more people."

"What's the Ohio River like?" William Henry, Junior, asked.

"It's like the Wabash, only much bigger."

"And we get to ride on it in a boat?"

"Oh, yes. In fact you'll take a barge from here down the Wabash to the Ohio and then up to Louisville, where you will probably change to another boat to get around the falls and then to go on to Cincinnati. In another year, you probably would be able to take a big steamboat. They had a steamboat on the Ohio last fall. It was called the *New Orleans*."

Young William Henry almost shouted in excitement, "Oh, did they? Did they? Can I ride on it? Can I? Can I?"

"Well, I doubt it," his father answered. "They had to wait for high water to get by the falls at Louisville and then it stayed on the Mississippi. But it won't be many years until there will be lots of steamboats on many rivers."

"What's a steamboat?" asked William Henry, Junior.

"It's a big boat with smokestacks, like chimneys, and a big paddle wheel at the back, or on each side, like the one at the mill, and the paddle wheels spin around, from the power from a steam engine, and that makes the boat go." Turning to his wife, Harrison asked, "Anna, dear, do you remember our steamboat ride?"

"Where?"

"On John Fitch's steamboat at Philadelphia."

With an expression of amazement Anna said, "Henry! What in the world are you talking about?"

"You know, that day we took the steamboat to Trenton."

"Henry, you know I've never been on a steamboat in my life! That must have been with some other girl."

With a sudden and embarrassing recollection that indeed on that occasion he had been in the company of Sarah Cutler, he shifted his eyes and dropped the subject completely. He was grateful when Lucy, the eleven-and-a-half-year-old daughter, asked, "What's Cincinnati?"

"Cincinnati is a town about like Vincennes, except it's a little bigger, and it is on a bigger river, and it sits on a steeper hill running up from the river."

"How long will we be there?" asked Betsy.

"I'm not sure, but you had better take all the clothing you'll need for different kinds of weather."

"Papa." Benjamin, the one who would be six in May, sought attention.

"Yes, son?"

"Can we take our ole Dan?" [Their collie dog]

"Oh, yes, I guess we can arrange to take him, if you'll promise to look after him."

"Oh we will, we will!"

"Betty, can you remember the boat ride when you came to Vincennes?"

"Barely," Betsy answered. "And I can remember just vaguely Philadelphia, and the ice cream parlor, and the long trip from Virginia to grandpa's, and then down the river to here. But how exciting it will be to ride on a big boat."

"And Cleaves, I doubt if you can remember anything about your former trip," observed Anna.

"No ma'm, I can't remember a thing about it."

"And all the rest of you were born right here in Vincennes," their mother went on, "so of course you have nothing like that to remember."

"Where was I?" asked Benjamin.

"You weren't here yet," his mother answered.

"Yes, but where was I then?"

"With the angels."

"I don't remember anything about that either. What are angels?"

"Oh silly," Lucy chimed in, "they are up in heaven with God, and they have wings, and they fly around and play the harp all the time."

"I wish I could remember them," said Benjamin.

"Oh dear, you really didn't exist then, at least not in the way you do now," his mother explained. "You see, you had not been born yet. You had not yet joined our family."

"When do we leave?" asked Betsy.

"We hope we can arrange it for the first week in May."

"I'll have to get a letter off to Grandfather right away to let him know we are coming," said Anna.

After the children had been excused, Harrison and his wife remained at the table for a while.

Anna said, "You know, I never realized until now what it must mean to have spent your whole life in one place without ever having a glimpse of the outside world."

"Do you feel a bit cooped up here?" Harrison asked.

"Well, yes, a little I guess, sometimes. Now, don't misunderstand me. I enjoy it very much here — this beautiful house, our wonderful children, a wonderful husband! But it would be nice to be able to see another city sometimes."

"Yes, of course it would, but at least we have had some opportunities for that. Do you realize that when you were Betty's age you had lived on Long Island; you had attended school in New York City, and had visited many towns, while she has had none of that?"

"And when you were Cleave's age you had been often to Williamsburg and Richmond and to many different plantations. Think of it, two of the children have been elsewhere but can barely remember, or cannot remember at all. All the others were born here and have never been any place else. A child cannot even stray far out of town for fear of being kidnapped by an Indian or something. Vincennes is a fairly nice town for the frontier, but can you imagine never having seen another place in your whole life?"

Near the end of April, Harrison announced at the dinner table that arrangements had been made for departure on the afternoon of Tuesday, May 5.

"Oh, my birthday!" exclaimed Benjamin.

After days of packing and anticipation, the Harrison family was ready for its big trip on the 5th. In spite of all the turmoil, Anna was careful to have a nice birthday dinner for Benjamin.

His father brought in grouse, and his mother baked her special cake and put six candles on it. Excitement was too high for much eating, but it was a memorable day for everyone.

About two o'clock on a cool sunny afternoon, they loaded up to leave the house — Anna and the nurse with baby Carter, three-year-old Mary Symmes, Lucy, and Betsy in a two-seated carriage, and the four boys and the servants with the baggage in two wagons. The Governor rode his white mare to escort the convoy down to the river. The boat was waiting. They stowed their baggage. Harrison gave each of the children a tight hug and a kiss on the cheek, his wife a fond embrace, and then promised to see them at North Bend in June.

As soon as all were on board, the crew cast off. Everyone was waving. Little Benjamin ran to the stern and shouted, "Hey, Papa, the goose honks high!"

Harrison raised his hand and called back, "Yo! The goose honks high!"

3

Largely at the instigation of a mixed-blood Wyandot, called Isadore Chaine, who had gained the backing of government chiefs, including Little Turtle and Five Medals, the Indian agent at Fort Wayne, William Wells, called a council of the tribesmen for mid-May. Nearly 600 assembled on the Mississinewa for the meeting. Chaine played the role of supporter of the Government and spokesman for peace, though he secretly hoped to bring Tecumseh into alignment with the British in Canada to oppose the Americans.

In a preliminary speech he said, "I have come to the Mississinewa to clean your paths and wipe the blood off your land, to take the weapons that have spilled the blood from you, and to put them where you can never reach them again. The Red Men should remain at peace. Even the Red Coats advise all Red People to be quiet and not meddle in quarrels that may take place among White People."

Tecumseh could see that these words fell on sympathetic ears. He knew that most of those who had assembled were those who had followed the government chiefs into reliance on the annuities. He rose and addressed the group, "Elder Brothers, we thank the Great Spirit for inclining your hearts to pity us. We now pity

ourselves. Our hearts are good; they never were bad. Governor
Harrison made war on my people in my absence. We hope it will
please Manitou that the White People may let us live in peace. We
will not disturb them; neither have we done it, except when they
came to our village with the intention of destroying us. We are
happy to state to our brothers present that the unfortunate
transaction that took place between the White People and a few
of our young men at our village has been settled between us and
Governor Harrison. And I will further state that had I been at
home there would have been no bloodshed at that time.

"It is true we have endeavored to give all our brothers good
advice, and if they have not listened to it we are sorry for it. It
has constantly been our misfortune to have our views misrepresented to our White Brethren. This has been done by pretended
chiefs of the Potawatomi and others, that have been in the habit
of selling land that did not belong to them to the White People."

But the reaction was cool. Tecumseh sensed that he had not
gained their support.

A Delaware chief interrupted to say, "We have not met at this
place to listen to such words. We would tell The Prophet that
both the Red People and the White People have felt the bad
effects of his counsels. Let us all join hearts and hands together
and proclaim peace."

Chaine met privately with Tecumseh to tell him that war
between the Americans and the British was imminent, and that
in spite of the peace talk among those meeting on the Mississinewa, it would be wise to return to Tippecanoe and prepare to
join the British as a way of defending Indian rights against the
Americans.

Responding to the words of Chaine and to a message which
Chaine had brought from the British Superintendent of Indian
Affairs, Matthew Elliott, Tecumseh spoke as follows:

"Brothers! We Shawnees, Kickapoos, and Winnebagos, hope
you will not find fault with us for having detained you so long
here. We were happy to see you and to hear your words and our
Father's words; and it would surely be strange if we did not
listen to our Father and our eldest Brothers.

"Father and Brothers! We will now in a few words declare to
you our whole hearts. If we hear of the Long Knives coming
towards our villages to speak peace, we will receive them; but if
we hear of any of our people being hurt by them, or if they
unprovokedly advance against us in a hostile manner, be assured

we will defend ourselves like men. If we hear of any of our people having been killed, we will immediately send to all the Nations on or towards the Mississippi, and all this Island will rise as one man. Then, Father and Brothers, it will be impossible for you or either of you to restore peace between us."

Tecumseh agreed with Chaine's assessment, and he returned to Prophet's Town to assemble arms and ammunition and food, and to attempt to regain the support of the tribes.

While hostile Indians continued their raids against isolated settlements and farm cabins in parts of Ohio, Indiana, and Illinois, others continued to make their way back to Tippecanoe. Even some of the Winnebagos who earlier had turned against The Prophet and threatened his life, now returned and set up a camp on the Wildcat Creek, near the Wabash and Tippecanoe. Large numbers of Kickapoos and a good many Miamis came. By the end of May some four hundred warriors were back in the vicinity of the rebuilt Prophet's Town.

With the continuing influx of tribesmen to the Tippecanoe area, supplies soon were running short. Tecumseh determined to turn again to the British for ammunition and food. He also was aware of the war fever in the United States, and he thought that hostilities between the Americans and the British in Canada might provide a way for recovery of Indian lands within the United States.

In mid-June, leaving The Prophet in charge at Tippecanoe, Tecumseh set out with a party of ten warriors for Canada. At Fort Wayne the Indian agent, Benjamin Stickney, detained them for four days while he tried to persuade them not to contact the British, but then he let them go on. Tecumseh arrived at Amherstburg in Canada near the head of Lake Erie, south of Detroit, on July 1.

4

In mid-June, leaving John Gibson in charge at Vincennes, Harrison set out only with his orderly and an escort of four mounted Rangers for Dearborn County. After inspecting and reviewing local militia units along the way and meeting with local officials to warn them to prepare for war, he arrived at North Bend on July 1.

It was a day of rejoicing in family reunion at the house of Judge Symmes.

The judge obviously had grown weaker in the last few years, but his wife was as radiant as ever and as enthusiastic as ever in welcoming everyone to her home. Harrison was glad to see Peyton Short and Maria who were there with their children from Lexington, but there was little opportunity at first for anything but the exciting accounts of their river voyage with which the Harrison children interrupted each other.

About five o'clock that evening, all joined for a big family dinner at two tables. Talk gave way to eating for a while, but then resumed with as great animation as before.

"Are the Indians on the warpath yet?" asked Anna.

"No, at least not generally yet, but raids and murders are still going on at isolated settlements, and I'm afraid that they are congregating again at Prophet's Town," Harrison said.

"Does that mean you'll be having to go back to Vincennes very soon?" Anna inquired.

"Not necessarily. It all depends on what happens with the British," Harrison responded.

"Do you think war with the British is likely now?" asked Judge Symmes.

Peyton Short responded quickly, "We already would be in it if our Henry Clay and Richard Johnson had their way. They've been preaching war in Congress ever since November."

"I shouldn't be surprised," Harrison added. "Unquestionably, war is upon us, and I've got to see what I can do to help get ready for it. While I'm here I want to get in touch with the new Governor down at Frankfort."

"Who's that?" asked John Cleaves Harrison who, in spite of his youth, was following the conversation with great interest.

"Isaac Shelby," explained Peyton Short, "just took office a month ago."

"But he's hardly a new one, is he?" put in Judge Symmes. "You know he was the first governor of Kentucky, back twenty years ago. Now he has just started a second term."

"Good man," Harrison said. "Had a fine war record as an officer in the Revolution and even served a year in the Virginia House of Delegates with my father."

"I didn't realize that. He also served in the North Carolina legislature, you know," Judge Symmes added.

"And I want to get in touch with Governor Meigs up at Zanesville or Chillicothe or wherever they've got the capital at the moment."

"I guess at the moment it's on the road, moving back from Zanesville to Chillicothe," the judge laughed, "though you know now the legislature has decided to move it up on the Scioto across from Franklinton. They're going to call it Columbus. That will be closer to the center of the state."

"What's the name of the Governor of Ohio?" asked Cleaves Harrison.

"That's Governor Meigs," Harrison said.

"Meigs what?" the boy asked.

"It's R. J. Meigs."

"What does the R. J. stand for?"

"R. J. stands for *Return Jonathan*."

"Return Jonathan?" exclaimed Betsy. "Wherever did he get a name like that?"

"From his father," explained Harrison.

"Yes, of course. I supposed he got it from his father and mother, but where in the world did they come upon a name like that?"

"As I said, from his father. His father's name was Return Jonathan Meigs. The Governor is Return Jonathan Meigs, Junior."

"Oh, I see." Betsy went on, "But then how in the world did his father come to be named that?"

"Well, I'll tell you," Harrison explained. "The name of the father of the first Return Jonathan was just plain Jonathan —"

"Ha, ha," Betsy laughed. "Just Plain is as funny a name as Return."

"No, silly, his name was Jonathan."

"All right, it was Jonathan."

"And once, while he was courting a young lady back in Connecticut, for some reason he decided it was all over, and he walked out of the house in something of a huff at something she had said. The young lady ran out on the porch, crying, 'Return Jonathan, oh please, return Jonathan.' He finally yielded to her appeal and came back and asked her to marry him. She was so happy that she vowed to name their first son, 'Return Jonathan.'"

Laughing, Betsy could not refrain from one further comment, "It's a wonder they didn't name him 'O. Please!'"

Betsy turned to young William Henry and laughing again, said, "Billy, tell us who is the Governor of the Indiana Territory."

Billy gave a sheepish grin and then laughed, and his eyes sparkled as he answered, "Tecumseh!"

Some of the "strangers" gave a startled look, and then joined everyone in the laughter.

John Cleaves Short had been following the conversation closely, but the more he looked at Betsy Harrison the more his interest shifted away from the conversation to her. She was his first cousin, and her father might still see her only as little Betty, but John Cleaves saw in her only a beautiful young lady.

At this point the ladies went to the parlor while servants began clearing the tables, the children scattered, John Cleaves Short and Betsy Harrison went off together, and the men went out on the veranda overlooking the Ohio River.

The judge and Peyton Short lit pipes.

"I must say Meigs has been very cooperative with Hull," Judge Symmes remarked.

"I understood he was in Ohio with a brigadier's commission raising an army," noted Harrison.

"Yes indeed," the Judge said. "Now he has a U.S. commission as brigadier general to go along with his territorial governorship, and he has a force of about 2,000 men from Ohio to help defend Michigan. Presumably he is marching toward Detroit right now."

"I guess he had a pretty good record in the last war, but I doubt that he is up to a major military operation now," said Harrison.

"Everybody doubts it, but there he goes," responded Symmes.

"Interesting how willing volunteers are to come from states not immediately threatened," Peyton Short said. "Look at the Kentuckians, they flocked to Vincennes, and lately you had to put a halter on them to keep them from taking off on their own to invade Canada."

"Yes," Harrison responded. "They know it's better to fight the Indians at a distance from your own homes, if possible. They also know that in war offense is the best defense. The best way to curb Indian attacks is to get them into Canada and attack them there."

A horseman came riding up to the house, dismounted, and walked swiftly to the veranda where the men were sitting. He was a messenger from Fort Washington.

"War has been declared," he announced. "Word came earlier today on the packet that Congress had declared war against Great Britain on the 18th of June 1812." The young man did not tarry but rode on to spread the news.

The men got up and walked around a bit, each trying to collect his own thoughts without saying anything. Then they returned to their chairs.

"Zounds!" Harrison said. "I wonder if ol' Hull knows he's marching straight into war."

"Well, he'd better," Symmes said. "I reckon the fat's in the fire now, all right."

Short said, "Wouldn't surprise me if some of the Kentucky boys were on their horses already, heading for Canada."

Harrison paused a long time in deep thought and then said, "Think of it, war with Great Britain. Why have we sided with the tyrant Napoleon against the great parliamentary democracy?"

"Oh the British may have a parliament, but they can be tyrannical enough—else why did we have to fight the Revolution?"

"Because they didn't know how to govern colonies; they had nothing like our Northwest Ordinance," said Harrison. "But to get back to the first question. What got us into this war?"

Short ventured an opinion that it was trouble on the high seas. "What you read most of the time in the newspapers is about the British Orders-in-Council interfering with our commerce, and about the impressment of our seamen."

"Yes, I suppose that's it," concurred Judge Symmes.

"No, not at all, as I see it," countered Harrison. "Of course that is what you have been reading about in the papers. Granted, interference with commerce hurts everyone, and the impressing of seamen is a true grievance, but those are not what got us into this war. Where do most of our seamen come from? From New England. And who carries on most of our commerce? New England. And where is the greatest opposition to this war? New England. Surely if those were the real causes of the war, the New Englanders would be advocating it."

"Then what do you think is the cause?" Short asked. "Surely you don't think it is any desire to help Napoleon and the French."

"No, I tell you the real cause is the British stirring up the Indians in the West. It is from the West that the War Hawks come. The people in the West have been getting more and more agitated about Indian depredations. They are convinced that the British are behind the Indian unrest."

"You may have a point there," Short conceded. "I'm sure the Kentuckians are a lot more concerned about the Indian menace than they are about having seamen impressed into the British Navy."

"Yes," Harrison went on, "and this may just give us the chance we need. I hope Tecumseh casts his lot with the English. I really do. I hope he calls his whole confederacy together and marches them all to Canada. The best thing for us would be to catch the Indians and British together, preferably in Canada, and then whip them all at once!"

At sunset Harrison found Anna, and they went out for a stroll through the garden.

"It seems so quiet and peaceful here," Anna said. "It just doesn't seem possible that we are in a war now."

"No, it doesn't," Harrison said. He clasped her hand as they walked on. "Maybe just the calm before the storm."

"Does it mean that you must hurry back to Vincennes?"

"No, I think not. That was my first thought, but the best defense for Vincennes and for all Indiana is an offensive into Canada. I feel that's where I should be. I think I'll just wait here, see how things go with Hull at Detroit, and wait for word from Washington. They know where I am, and you know they can get a message to me here much more quickly than at Vincennes."

"Oh, there's no question about that. Anyway I'm glad you'll be able to be with us here for a while."

"So am I. Now with the coming of war, I think you should plan on a long stay. Let's see if we can find a bigger house."

They walked on silently for a while, admiring the beauty of the flowers close by, the evening reflections in the river farther away, the mounting color in the sky. They turned back and looked at the house.

Anna said, "It just doesn't seem possible that it has been seventeen years since you came sneaking up here for a wedding."

"You mean since I came dashing up here for an elopement in your own house?" Harrison laughed softly and then added, "In some ways, when I think of all that has happened, it seems that it must have been much longer."

"Oh yes, she agreed, that's true, and when I think of eight children!" She paused again, took deep breaths of the evening air, and said, "But at this moment, this seems like heaven."

"What is your idea of heaven?" Harrison asked. "What do you think it will be like?"

"How should I know? We don't have much to go on, do we? Very little in the Bible and then of course the suppositions of Dante and Milton."

"No, I don't mean what do you believe about what others have said. How would you *like* for it to be?"

She thought a while and then said, "Well, one thing for sure, I would not want to spend eternity flying around over streets of gold and playing on a harp."

"Nor would I."

"And I don't see how it would be a paradise without some kind of work—at least something to give a sense of accomplishment."

"Yes, I think that's true, too."

Then Anna said, "I guess heaven for me would be Grouseland and Vincennes, with my husband and children with me, and only friendly Indians around; enjoying the good food, and seeing the others enjoy it; enjoying the beauty of the woods and the fields and the river, and the changing beauty of the seasons; being at North Bend with family and friends; and sometimes visiting Philadelphia and Virginia—and on and on."

"And then, what is hell?" asked Harrison.

"To have seen all those things and then lose them."

Harrison frowned and said, "Have we condemned the Indians to hell?"

It was time to get back to the house, to get the children gathered up and to bed, and then to continue the war talk a little while before it was time for everyone to go to bed.

For a time, the Harrisons and the four youngest children slept in the log house where the Harrisons had lived while he was Secretary of the Territory. The four oldest children slept in the big house. Anxious to have the family all together, Harrison and Anna decided to look for a bigger house. They found one to their liking in Cincinnati. It was a large, stone-front house on Broadway just below Fourth Street. This was in the most attractive residential section of the city, a city now grown to 3,500 people and 500 buildings.

During the next few weeks Harrison almost frantically worked at playing with the children. At thirty-nine, Harrison suddenly felt that time was running out, and now that war finally had come, he was sure that he must be a part of it. That was bound to bring separation, whether for only a few weeks, or for years, or permanently, no one could foresee.

Sometimes all of them would join in a game of town ball on the lawn or a game of "Andy over" around the shed. Sometimes he took them down to watch in wonder at the construction of a great steam mill, a building of stone to be 110 feet high, with walls ten feet thick. Sometimes he would take all those who could make it on hikes through the woods or down along the river.

Sometimes they would ride horses. Sometimes the whole group would go together. Sometimes he would take just one, and he was careful to rotate so that each child got a turn. On these walks through the woods, he got acquainted with them in a way that he had never known before.

In the evening, Harrison would read nursery rhymes and Aesop's Fables to the younger children and history to the older ones. Sometimes he even would make a sugar teat by shaping a piece of linen cloth around a finger, then filling the hollow so formed with sugar, holding it tightly at the upper end and dipping it in warm water to pacify baby Carter.

Never before, given all the demands of land and politics and war, had Harrison been able to devote himself to such activity for any prolonged time. He found himself looking forward to it each day. Then he began to wonder. Was he doing this for the welfare of the children and the relief of his wife, or was he doing this for his own enjoyment? Both, or all three, he thought, and what was wrong with that? Nothing was wrong with that, he was sure, but he came to realize a very important consideration that he had to be careful about. That was the self-reliance of the children and his own independence. He knew that the closer he became to them, the more difficult it would be for him to leave, both for them and for him. That did not bother him so much. He knew that closeness made it more difficult to leave, but it also made it easier to be strong and to carry on in the absence of loved ones. The other side of this two-edged sword was the danger of the children's becoming so dependent that they would lose their self-reliance. That was a value which he held for all his children, right up with courage and honesty. Indeed self-reliance, as he saw it, was a kind of expression of courage and honesty.

And a couple of times during this month, Harrison and Anna rode horses up to the creek that had been their secret rendezvous over seventeen years ago, for a private picnic of their own. There they remembered the past and dreamed of the future.

5

With the army of two thousand men that he had organized in Ohio, General Hull arrived at Detroit on July 6, just four days after he had heard that there had been a declaration of war.

His first move was to venture a sortie across the Detroit River into Canada, toward Amherstburg.

Tecumseh noted, with concern, the flight of Canadian militia-men who allowed Sandwich, opposite Detroit, to fall into the hands of the Americans together with large stores of supplies. The Americans came on, without opposition, southward to the Canard River, about half-way to Amherstburg, but the British held the bridges, and the Americans came no farther.

By this time a large number of warriors from many tribes had joined Tecumseh in Canada. Many were firm and staunch supporters, including Main Poc the aggressive Potawatomi chief from the Illinois country and a band of his belligerent followers. But Tecumseh knew that many of the tribesmen were playing the role of the coyote. They were giving only token or lukewarm support to whichever side appeared to be in the ascendancy at the moment. The initial retreat of some of the Canadian militia brought its toll of defections among the Indians. Chief Walk-in-the-Water took many of his Wyandots back across the Detroit River to Brownstown where, in council with other weak chiefs, he announced a policy of neutrality. They were even emboldened to send a deputation to Tecumseh to invite his participation in a council to consider neutrality.

His response was quick and firm—"No! I have taken sides with the King, my Great Father, and I will suffer my bones to bleach on this shore before I will recross that stream to join any council of neutrality."

Still Tecumseh, with the assistance of Main Poc, met daily with his followers, and was able to keep about three hundred of them in line. He was sure that the American force was weak, and he was confident that a victory or two would bring many of his Indians to his side.

Tecumseh was determined to find some kind of victory to bring this about. He entered into several skirmishes with Ameri-can reconnaissance patrols with indifferent success. Then on the 28th of July came news which helped change the whole situation. The American Fort Michillimackinac, on an island in the Straits of Mackinac which linked Lake Huron to Lake Michigan, had fallen to a combined force of Indians and British. The American lieutenant in command at the fort had not even heard that war had been declared when the Indians and British, outnumbering his garrison of 61 soldiers by ten to one, surrounded his fort and invited him to surrender. This was a key to the upper Great Lakes. It also was a key to the hearts and tomahawks of the Indian tribes that populated the area. Even the fickle Wyandots under Walk-in-the-Water returned to the side of Tecumseh.

Tecumseh rushed off messengers to allied tribesmen southwest of Lake Erie to attack Fort Wayne, to those around southern
Lake Michigan to attack Fort Dearborn, and to his brother, The
Prophet, at Tippecanoe to prepare to attack Fort Harrison and
Vincennes. For a moment the Shawnee war chief could see a
glimmer of hope in his scheme to unify the tribes and reclaim
their lands in Indiana.

On August 12, near Brownstown, Tecumseh, with only 24
warriors, ambushed and put to flight a detachment of 150
American troops that Hull had sent to escort a supply train from
the River Raisin. The Americans suffered more casualties than
Tecumseh's entire force; the Indians lost one warrior. Four days
later, another American force, this time of 600 men, marched out
to bring up the supply train. Again Tecumseh with British and
Indian reinforcements to make a total force of 400, stopped them
with greater losses than their own, and the supply train remained stranded at the River Raisin. Tecumseh suffered a
painful gunshot wound in his right leg, but it was not serious
enough to stop him.

All this brought more warriors flocking to Tecumseh. By
August 13, when Major General Isaac Brock arrived at Fort
Malden, Amherstburg, to take command of the force of British
regulars and Canadian militia assembled to meet the American
threat to Upper Canada, Tecumseh could offer the assistance of a
thousand Indians. Brock welcomed with enthusiasm the assistance of the great Shawnee chief who had become known to him
already as the "King of the Woods."

It was respect at first sight between the Indian Chief and the
British General. Tecumseh presented a striking appearance in
his neat, fringed deerskin suit and brightly ornamented moccasins, turban and single eagle feather. He wore three crowns
suspended from his nose, and proudly wore, attached to a string
of wampum around his neck, a large silver medallion of George
III which one of his ancestors had received from Sir Guy
Carleton. Brock was no less impressive, a very tall, slender figure
in double-breasted, red cutaway coat with gold epaulets, buff
breeches, and polished black boots.

"I desire with my soldiers to take lessons from you and your
warriors," Brock said, "that I may learn to make war in these
great forests."

Tecumseh smiled his assurance.

The next morning Brock met an assembly of all the Indian

warriors. To their shouts of approval, he spoke confidently and boldly of the victory that would be theirs if they fought with him against the common enemy.

Tecumseh responded, "Father! Our warriors of many tribes stand with you against the Long Knives! They are pleased that at last their Great British Father has awakened from his slumber and has sent a real soldier to lead his Red Children. Father! The warriors here are willing to shed their last drop of blood in the service of their Great Father, the King."

Main Poc and other chiefs added their words to support those of Tecumseh.

After the meeting, Brock invited Tecumseh and the other chiefs into his headquarters to discuss his plans for an attack against Detroit. Thrilled by such a demonstration of boldness and initiative, Tecumseh turned to the other chiefs after the conference and said, "There is a man!"

On his own authority, Brock appointed Tecumseh a brigadier general and gave him a red coat of a British officer.

Thinking that his best move would be an attack against Detroit, Brock called on Tecumseh to inquire of him the lay of the country and the best routes to follow. Tecumseh stripped a large sheet of bark from a birch tree and spread it on the ground. With four stones he weighted the corners of the bark, and then taking his hunting knife he drew on the bark a detailed map of the roads, trails, streams, woods, swamps, springs, hills, and ravines of the area. Brock had never seen anything like it. He decided to move up the Canadian side of the Detroit River and to have Tecumseh and his Indians cross the river first to attack the fort of Detroit from the rear while the British soldiers then crossed to make a direct attack on the fort. Tecumseh was in complete agreement.

On the 15th, after General Hull had refused an initial invitation to surrender, Brock had Tecumseh send one of his Indians across the river with a fake report which he was instructed to let fall into the hands of the Americans. The document referred to a force of five thousand Indians that was ready to descend upon Detroit. Then Brock put the red coats of British regulars on some companies of Canadian militia and had them parade in full view of Detroit to give the American commander an exaggerated impression of the number of regular troops opposed to him. While this was going on, shore batteries from near Sandwich and two gunboats began a bombardment.

Hull desperately tried once more to get a party out to escort the supply train, but it got lost in the woods.

Early the next morning Tecumseh led his Indians across the river while Brock readied his frontal assault. The attack was hardly under way when Hull, fearing a massacre, surrendered.

To show his appreciation of Tecumseh's outstanding performance, Brock took a silk scarf from his own uniform and put it around the chief's shoulders. Tecumseh was no less pleased with Brock.

The next day Tecumseh appeared without the scarf. He explained that he had given it to Chief Roundhead of the Wyandots who, he said, was more deserving.

Elated by this success, Tecumseh was able to gain reinforcements from among the Wyandots around Brownstown who had remained aloof from his efforts, and from Potawatomis and others from farther away who now saw hope in Tecumseh's cause as their own.

Later that month in a report to Lord Liverpool who just now had become British Prime Minister after serving as Secretary for War and the Colonies, Brock included this statement:

Among the Indians whom I found at Amherstburg, and who had arrived from distant parts of the country, I found some extraordinary characters. He who attracted most my attention was a Shawnee chief, Tecumseh, brother to the Prophet, who for the last two years has carried on (contrary to our remonstrances) an Active Warfare against the United States — a more sagacious or a more gallant Warrior does not, I believe, exist. He was the admiration of every one who conversed with him: from a life of dissipation he has not only become, in every respect, abstemious but has likewise prevailed on all his nation and many of other Tribes to follow his example. They appear determined to continue the contest until they obtain the Ohio for a boundary. The United States Government is accused, and I believe justly, of having corrupted a few dissolute characters whom they pretended to consider as chiefs and with whom they contracted engagements and concluded Treaties, which they have attempted to impose on the whole Indian race. Their determined opposition to such ficticious and ruinous pretensions, which if admitted would soon oblige the Indians to remove beyond the Mississippi, is the true ground of their enmity against the Americans. The jealousy, with which they view the British Merchants continue their commercial intercourse with the Indians, has likewise been attended with serious inconvenience. Under the difficulty the Merchant experienced, few goods could be introduced into the interior, and their own measures, the operation of the non intercourse, precluded even their own people from furnishing the Indians with clothing of the first necessity. The consequence has been fatal to many. Deprived of ammunition, the poor Indian was unable to provide the necessary quantity of food or even cover his nakedness with the skins of animals.

The Armistice concluded between His Excellency Lt. Gen. Sir George Prevost and General Dearborn [American commander of the Northern Department] has suspended all active operations. However wise and politic the measure must be admitted to be, the Indians who cannot enter into our views will naturally feel disheartened and suspicious of our intentions. Should hostilities recommence I much fear the influence the British possess over them will be found diminished: no effort however of mine shall be wanting to keep them attached to our cause. If the condition of this people could be considered in any future negotiation for peace, it would attach them to us forever. The reinforcements lately arrived from the Lower Province places this portion of the country beyond the likelihood of an attack. The enemy must increase his present force considerable before he can hazard an Invasion with a view of keeping possession of the country.

6

During the weeks of playing with the children and visiting with other family and friends, Harrison kept up on the news through two local newspapers in Cincinnati, *The Western Spy and Hamilton Gazette,* and the *Liberty Hall and Cincinnati Mercury*, through the *Western Sun* which he had forwarded from Vincennes and from official communications from Vincennes and Washington. From John Gibson and from the *Western Sun* he learned that the citizens of Vincennes had held a meeting on July 9 to endorse the declaration of war and to promise full support of its prosecution.

He also made contacts with the Governors of Kentucky and Ohio where militia units were mobilizing. He went to Frankfort, Kentucky, to make a personal call on the newly inaugurated Governor, Isaac Shelby, to make an appeal for raising and equipping a regiment to go to the defense of Vincennes. Shelby was sympathetic, and the raising of a regiment began.

Already Kentucky had mobilized four regiments which now were marching to Cincinnati under Brig. Gen. James Winchester who had been called out of retirement from Tennessee and given a commission in the regular army. The 17th U.S. Regiment also was mobilizing at Cincinnati to form a part of the force to reinforce the northern frontier.

On August 24, while Harrison was still in Frankfort, news arrived of Hull's surrender. It seemed clear to everyone that a force would have to be started northward promptly to the relief of Fort Wayne and the recovery of Detroit.

On the 25th, a caucus of Kentucky leaders met in Frankfort to consider the emergency. Meeting with Govenor Shelby were ex-Govenors Charles Scott and Christopher Greenup; Judge Todd; Samuel Hopkins, a member of Congress and a major general in the Kentucky militia, and Henry Clay, political leader and speaker of the U.S. House of Representatives. All members of the group were anxious to get a force moving quickly to meet the threat in the north, but they lacked confidence in General Winchester and even, for this particular task, in their own Samuel Hopkins. At the urging of Clay and disregarding the Kentucky law that required militia officers to be citizens of the state, they voted to give William Henry Harrison a brevet commission as major general of the Kentucky militia with the understanding that he would take command of the troops dispatched to the north. Hopkins would be given command of the force being raised to be sent to Vincennes.

Harrison rode to Cincinnati to assume command of the troops. In an awkward exchange of notes with Winchester, Harrison explained that the Kentucky troops had been given to his command and that while the regulars properly belonged to Winchester, in the interest of having a single command for the expedition, they too should come under this command. He proposed that Winchester take a subordinate role as commander of a "respectable brigade," but the old veteran declined this.

Discouraged by events all along the northern frontier, President Madison flirted for a time with the idea of appointing James Monroe lieutenant general and giving him command of all the armies in that quarter. Monroe had been serving effectively as Secretary of State. Harrison and others advised Madison that the western men would respond well only to a western commander in whom they had confidence.

Harrison was thrilled to learn that the commander of one of the Kentucky regiments, just arriving, was Dr. John Scott, his old friend who now was a colonel in the militia. As they came across the river, Harrison rode down to meet them. Recognizing his old friend in one of the boats as it landed, Harrison raised his hand and shouted, "Yo, Jonathan!"

And he laughed as the answer came back loudly, "Yo, David!" He grabbed Scott's arm as he came ashore and then rode beside him up to where the regiment was making camp near old Fort Washington.

"Hey, it's great to see a surgeon in command of combat troops!" Harrison said as they dismounted. "Now you can help create the casualties, and then go back and fix them up."

"I hope most of the casualties will be Indians and English-men," said Scott.

"I hope so," Harrison responded, "but I tell you, I'm afraid most of our casualties will be Kentuckians."

"I suppose so," Scott said, "but what especially do you mean now?"

"I mean thank God for the Kentuckians. Without the Kentucky militia we wouldn't have any army here. The War Department keeps promising regulars, but so far only one regiment. In a way, I'm glad, because the only commission I have right now is from Kentucky, so from my point of view it's a good thing that most of the troops here are Kentucky militia."

"Yes, I should say. But let me tell you, Henry, you are very popular in Kentucky. When it became known that the victor of Tippecanoe was to lead the Kentucky forces, everyone wanted to come."

"Thank you for that, and thank you most for your being here."

"Tell me, Henry, what's our destination?"

"First Fort Wayne. Then Detroit."

"Detroit, eh, good. We've got to get Detroit back. Then what?—I hope we're not in for some damned wild goose chase!"

Harrison came back, "If we are, we'll be after a Canada goose! I say, 'On to Canada!'"

"Ah, that's it," Scott responded enthusiastically. "On to Canada! That's what all our boys are saying."

"But I'm afraid it's not going to be as easy as they think."

"Why not?"

"Mainly the difficulty of getting our supplies up. I don't propose to go up there and get stranded on account of a lack of supplies."

"No, I hope not," agreed Scott.

Though he said nothing about it, Harrison was a little concerned about Scott's health. The doctor looked pale and weak in spite of his enthusiasm.

The two exchanged news about family and friends and then talked a little about the bad news that had been coming about all the efforts against Canada. Harrison acknowledged that time was short, but he insisted that Scott come up to see the family and have dinner with them the next afternoon.

That night, August 28, Harrison received a letter from Thomas Worthington with an enclosure from Captain James Rhea, commander of the Fort Wayne garrison. Rhea reported that a large body of Indians was there, and he was expecting an attack at any moment. Harrison wrote to the Secretary of War, "I shall lose not a moment in marching to his relief."

On the 29th, Harrison got the troops around Cincinnati in motion toward Piqua. There he would pick up more forces from the Ohio militia. Meanwhile he would have one more night with his family in Cincinnati and then would ride up the next day to overtake the column.

That evening in Cincinnati was one of strained nonchalance. Everyone worked hard at being blithe with only partial success. Among the children, the light chatter and nervous laughter helped hold back unseen tears. In Anna's eyes tears surfaced just enough to double the sparkle in her sparkling eyes, while her smiles deceived no one about her true feelings. Harrison on the other hand appeared a little more stern than usual, but that did not fool anybody either.

"You going out to look for Chief Tecumseh?" young William Henry asked his father.

"Yes, that's right, I'm going up to find Chief Tecumseh and Perfidious Albion," the elder William Henry answered.

"Who's Perfidy Albion?" asked the young one.

"Well, maybe I should say, 'Fee fie, fo, fum, I smell the blood of an Englishman.'"

The young one laughed and let it go at that.

Early the next morning Anna was up to make sure that her husband had everything he needed in his saddle bags. He already had sent a trunk along with the supply wagons. With a light, nervous laugh, she said, "Remember what Charles Lee said to General Gates after Burgoyne's surrender, 'Beware that your northern laurels do not change to southern willows.'"

Harrison smiled back at her and said, "I just hope that we can get this business finished soon so that we can all be together, can all feel safe and secure, and can trade our weeping willows for giant sycamores."

"I pray," she said.

"And I'll just say, remember the words of Beilby Porteus as my words,"

> "Love is something so divine,
>   Description would but make it less;
> 'Tis what I feel, but can't define,
>   'Tis what I know, but can't express."

That did bring tears to Anna's eyes. She held him, and he her, tightly. Then he was away.

Out on the lawn all the children, and Anna and her father and stepmother, and even the dog, Old Dan, had gathered. As Harrison mounted his horse, the children almost in chorus shouted, "The goose honks high!"

He lifted his hat, turned his horse twice around, and took off at a gallop.

Harrison overtook his column about midway between Cincinnati and Dayton on the evening of the 30th. When he arrived at Piqua, a message from the Secretary of War awaited him. It was notifying him that he had been commissioned a brigadier general in the regular army effective August 22. Just in time, Harrison thought. It probably would make no difference to the Kentuckians, but it might give him better standing with the regulars in his command. But as he read on, his preliminary elation gave way to disappointment. The second paragraph announced that Brig. Gen. James Winchester had been given command of the Northwestern Army. "Zounds!" Harrison thought. "Zounds!" Here was another Hull, somebody with a Revolutionary War record, but with no experience and no following in this country. Reading on, Harrison found that he could be second in command. Well, he would not do it. He would not put himself under Winchester's command. He would not accept the new commission.

Harrison issued a statement saying that as governor and commander-in-chief of the Indiana Territory, he assumed command of all troops in that territory, and that as a major general of the Kentucky quota he was assuming command of all the troops of that state north of the Ohio River except for the army of General Winchester.

From St. Marys, thirty miles north of Piqua, Harrison wrote to Winchester:

The Secretary of War, in a letter received from him since I saw you, urges me to join you,...with a reinforcement of the troops subject to my orders. As I have declined the appointment tendered me of brigadier, I cannot comply with his request, as the commission which I have is of higher grade than yours. I must, therefore, carry the wishes of the President into effect, so far as to place at your disposal the regiments of Barbee and Jennings, and the quota of this state, which I have heretofore required of Governor Meigs. I shall retain the separate command of the mounted men and Pogue's regiment and will communicate to you by an express the particular object at which I shall aim. Be so obliging as to send orders to Colonels Barbee and Jennings. The former is at Piqua, and the latter I shall place on the road to Defiance, as I have above intimated.

During the next week the expedition of about 2,200 moved northward to Piqua, then St. Marys, and then northwest down the St. Marys River toward Fort Wayne. Harrison sent a three-man patrol ahead to reconnoiter around the fort. These were William Oliver, one of his able scouts, and two Shawnee Indians, one called Johnny Logan who had been raised by Benjamin Logan after the boy's father, Chief Moluntha, had been murdered after surrendering. He had learned the White Man's ways and always had been loyal to the Americans. The other Shawnee was called Bright Horn.

Early on September 11, Logan and Bright Horn came riding at high speed into Harrison's camp and rushed directly to the commander.

"Many Indians about to attack fort," Logan reported.

"Who are they?" Harrison asked.

"Potawatomis and Ottawas," Logan replied. "We saw Chief Winamac and four other chiefs. They had said they wanted to talk peace but then changed minds. We think they were trying trick. Tecumseh sent them."

"Where is Oliver?"

"He stayed in fort," Bright Horn explained. "We all got in fort. Lieutenant Curtis in charge. He say Captain Rhea drink too much firewater."

"Damn!" Harrison exclaimed. "Go on."

Bright Horn went on, "Lieutenant say many Indians surround fort for seven days. Now he thinks they make big attack."

"They need help quickly, very quickly," Logan interjected.

Indeed the Indians were attacking as Harrison approached Fort Wayne. He could hear the firing and see smoke in the distance, but the firing stopped as he entered the village. The trading factory, most of the houses, and everything else outside the fort had been burned. But the fort itself, despite some charred walls, remained intact. The Indians fled at the very approach of this two-thousand-plus-man army.

Harrison gave all hands a day of rest. While there, he heard more disquieting news. The first was from Fort Dearborn.

On learning of the fall of Fort Michillimackinac, General Hull had sent a message to Captain William Wells at Fort Wayne that he should hurry to Fort Dearborn with orders to the garrison and settlers to evacuate the fort, and the little settlement of Chicago adjacent to it, before the Indians attacked there. Wells had arrived on August 14, about the same time as Tecumseh's messenger. Already about five hundred Potawatomis, Winnebagos, and Sacs and Foxes had the place surrounded. Wells had delivered the order to the garrison commander, Captain Nathan Held. A friendly Winnebago chief, Black Partridge, warned that "leaden birds had been singing in his ears," and it would be better for the garrison to remain in the relative safety of the fort. But the captain, assuming that he must obey orders, had his garrison of some fifty regulars, together with forty-six civilians, march out. Within minutes, the Indians fell upon them and hacked them to pieces. Wells, sensing torture if captured, blackened his face with damp gun powder and on his horse charged straight at the Indians. Chief Blackbird himself, a Potawatomi who was leader of the Indians, shot Wells. Warriors then beheaded the American agent and stuck his head up on a pole. Blackbird then proceeded to cut out Wells' heart, and he and his fellow chiefs ate it. Over half of the Americans were killed, and nearly all the rest taken prisoner. A couple got away and got to Fort Wayne to tell the story.

Harrison recoiled in disgust at the account. "God, those people are savages, aren't they," he said.

News from the Wabash was more encouraging. Anticipating further word from Tecumseh about an attack on Vincennes, and anxious to restore his own reputation, The Prophet had sent a party of Kickapoos and Winnebagos down the Wabash to attack Fort Harrison where Captain Zachary Taylor commanded the small garrison. After a ruse to gain entrance had failed, the Indians burned a gap in the wall of a blockhouse and tried to force their way in. But Taylor held firm. He directed a work party to build log breastworks across the gap and stopped all further attacks.

Harrison was planning to move from Fort Wayne northeastward down the Maumee River to Defiance, but he had to wait several days for the arrival of a convoy of supplies. During this time, he sent out a strong detachment to destroy the corn and other provisions at the Potawatomi town of Elkhart, about sixty miles northwest of Fort Wayne, and another to destroy the Miami village at the forks of the Wabash, about forty miles to the southeast.

The detachment for the attack on Elkhart was under the overall command of Colonel Samuel Wells, the officer who had served so well at Tippecanoe as commander of the Kentucky mounted riflemen. It was composed of three companies of Kentucky mounted riflemen under Richard M. Johnson who, like Hopkins, was a member of Congress who elected on this occasion to take the field; of the 17th U.S. Infantry Regiment; a hundred Ohio riflemen; and John Scott's regiment of Kentucky militia.

Although in poor health from the start, Scott had stood up well so far, but now his officers, anticipating the excessive fatigue he was likely to suffer, urged him to remain behind. He would not hear of it. Harrison assured him there would be no fighting in that direction.

Paying no heed, Scott mounted his horse and said, "As long as I am able to mount you, none but myself shall lead my regiment, to fight or not to fight."

The expedition to Elkhart was a success. There was no fighting, and it did destroy the village. It covered the sixty miles to the village in two and a half days, and the return in two, with only scanty provisions of food.

Indeed it was fatiguing, and Scott was barely able to make it. Still he remained, as the army began the next phase of its march.

Leaving most of the force on the Maumee under the command of General Winchester, Harrison went back to St. Marys and Piqua to arrange for moving up additional forces for the planned attack against Detroit.

Meanwhile in Canada, General Brock had been ordered to the Niagara area to help repel an American threat there, and Colonel Henry Procter was left in command of the British and Canadian forces in the Detroit-Amherstburg area. So far as Tecumseh was concerned, this was a serious turn for the worse. Procter did not inspire the confidence and the enthusiasm for daring enterprise that Brock had. Nevertheless the Shawnee war chief was determined to continue his efforts at mobilizing and leading Indians in cooperation with the British. He saw no other way of stopping the Long Knives. Now, at last, he could see some hope of accomplishing his great dream, and he was not going to allow anything to interfere with that, if he could help it.

When a message arrived from Winamac saying that his Potawatomis had Fort Wayne surrounded, and if they could get the assistance of more Red Men and some British soldiers and cannon, they could take the fort, Tecumseh urged that a force be sent at once.

Procter agreed to send Major Adam Muir with 250 regulars and militiamen together with 800 Indians under Tecumseh assisted by Main Poc, Roundhead, and another Wyandot war chief called Split Log. The force also had the support of three cannon.

When the expedition reached the Maumee River, Tecumseh and Muir learned that an American force under William Henry Harrison already had raised the siege at Fort Wayne. Tecumseh hoped that here might be a chance for him to meet Harrison head-on. While they paused to await more information on the extent of the force in front of them, some of their spies rushed into the camp with word that most of Harrison's army, now under a General Winchester, was approaching down the Maumee Valley, only thirty-six hours away, and its strength probably was twice that of the British and Indians. Tecumseh was rather more delighted than awed at the prospect, and he called emphatically for a stand to be made here and now. To his great satisfaction, Muir agreed.

The next day they deployed their forces in defensive positions athwart the Maumee just above the mouth of the Auglaize. But they waited in vain for the approach of their enemies. The Americans halted and went into camp while yet eight miles away.

Fearing a flanking attack during the night, Muir ordered a retreat to the mouth of the Auglaize. When they got there a number of the Indians were missing. Leaving Roundhead to decide with Muir on where the next defensive position should be, Tecumseh, in spite of his still painful leg wound, scurried through the woods to round up the missing warriors.

But Muir and Roundhead could not agree on a position, and Muir ordered a further retreat. When, later that afternoon, the British commander ordered the cannon put on boats and returned to Lake Erie, a general erosion of confidence set in. The Indians held an all-night council, and many of them decided to pull out. Against Tecumseh's protests, most of the Ottawas and Chippewas set out on their own retreat, all the way back to their villages.

Taking advantage of the retreats, the Americans had been moving again, and now they were within two miles. Tecumseh and Roundhead and Main Poc still wanted to stand and fight, but

Muir thought the odds too great. He ordered a general retreat to Detroit.

This was a blow for Tecumseh. He saw the reluctance to fight as a reflection of the change in command.

Back at Piqua, Harrison received a letter from the Secretary of War which indicated that there had been a change of heart in Washington about the command of the Northwestern Army almost as soon as the original appointment had been announced. The letter, dated September 17, was to confirm the appointment of William Henry Harrison as commander of that army. Apparently President Madison had been impressed by the action of the Kentucky caucus and by the protests from Kentucky and elsewhere that had greeted the appointment of Winchester. Harrison's command was to include all the regulars, rangers, and volunteers in the area; the militia of Indiana Territory, Kentucky, and Ohio, and additional troops coming from Pennsylvania and Virginia. The total strength was expected to reach 10,000. Now, he thought, at last he would be able to accomplish something.

Harrison realized, of course, that this created an awkward situation with respect to General Winchester. In a very tactful letter, Harrison wrote to Winchester of the new command structure. He expressed appreciation for all that Winchester had done and then said that he would be pleased if the older general would remain with the army as commander of the left wing. With a graciousness that was beyond Harrison when the situations were reversed, Winchester readily accepted this arrangement.

With reborn enthusiasm Harrison set about making plans and preparations. His earlier experience with Wayne, his dozen years of experience in administering a large territory, his experience in the Tippecanoe campaign, and the experience of others that he gained from reading history, all gave him a perspective for military operations on a grand scale and an appreciation for the time and space factors in war that escaped the other senior commanders, all of them much older than he, who now were directing this war effort.

Harrison's first concern was about logistic arrangements for the concentration of his forces at the rapids of the Maumee preliminary to an advance on Detroit. The right column, made up of units from Pennsylvania and Virginia, was to move to Wooster, about forty-five miles west of Canton, and thence to the upper Sandusky where they would be joined by a brigade of Ohio militia from the Western Reserve, under Brig. Gen. Simon Perkins, and then all were to march to the Maumee. On the way, these units were to build a series of blockhouses along the Sandusky to serve as supply bases, and they would try to build a fifteen-mile causeway across the Black Swamp toward the Maumee rapids. Harrison directed one government contractor to deposit 200,000 rations at Wooster and another to deposit 500,000 at the same place, and to obtain the means for transporting these to Detroit. In addition Harrison asked the commissary at Pittsburgh to send another 400,000 rations, artillery, and other supplies to Wooster. These were to be sent to Georgetown (Liverpool) on the Ohio River, and thence via Lisbon and Canton to Wooster.

The middle column consisting of 1,200 Ohio militia under Brig. Gen. Edward Tupper was to march from their present location at Urbana along General Hull's road northward to the rapids. Two hundred thousand rations were to be deposited at Urbana to be moved by pack horses in two trips to the rapids. Another 200,000 rations were to be deposited at a blockhouse forty miles north of Urbana.

The left wing, under the command of General Winchester, was composed of Col. Samuel Wells' detachment of the 17th U.S. Regiment and four regiments of Kentucky militia. They already were at Fort Defiance and they would move down the Maumee directly to the rapids.

Harrison was distressed to learn that when John Scott arrived at Fort Defiance with his regiment, he was too sick to function. He was too weak even to raise a protest when he was put in a litter and sent back to Kentucky.

Three hundred thousand rations, purchased by the commissary, would be deposited at Fort Defiance and another 200,000 at a blockhouse then under construction between St. Marys and Defiance.

A mounted force would operate directly under Harrison. His first thought was to send it northward from Fort Wayne up the St. Joseph's River, then eastward by the River Raisin, and then northeast for a direct attack on Detroit. Then he thought better of it. If the mounted troops were successful, they would be so far in advance of the infantry that they probably would not be able to hold Detroit long enough for the larger forces to arrive, and if they had to evacuate it, the Indian depredations in the area probably would be worse than ever. Harrison decided that it would be better to use the horsemen to sweep free of the Indians the western coast line of Lake Erie and the Detroit River.

While all this was going on, Harrison was pleased to learn that Governor Shelby had raised a force of 1,600 mounted riflemen in Kentucky under the command of Samuel Hopkins. That force now was on the way to Vincennes by way of Clark's Trace from Jeffersonville. Harrison sent instructions for them to chastise the Indians on the Illinois River in an effort to put an end to depredations in that area, and then to move against Tippecanoe to put an end to any further threats to Vincennes from that quarter. Harrison reckoned that, with the addition of Indiana Rangers and territorial militia, Hopkins would have a force of 2,400 men. Governor Shelby described Hopkin's force as the best he had seen "in the western country or anywhere else." The men were enlisted only for one month, but that should be sufficient time for them to accomplish their special mission.

Harrison followed all the activities with close attention. Reports of Hopkins' expedition turned out to be disappointing at first. Hopkins and his men arrived in Vincennes to a loud and enthusiastic reception by the local inhabitants. Then they moved with dispatch across Illinois, until the Indians set fire to the prairies. At this, they turned around and made for home. This left the people of Vincennes, not to mention those of Illinois, more worried than ever. John Gibson kept the Indiana Rangers on constant alert in patrolling the trails and isolated settlements of southern Indiana.

With great effort Hopkins was able to recoup his forces. He returned to Vincennes with 1,200 men and marched up the east side of the Wabash to Tippecanoe. The Prophet and his followers abandoned the area, and, for the second time, Prophet's Town was put to the torch and its stores of corn were confiscated or burned.

On November 19, Hopkins visited the old Tippecanoe battle-field of the previous year and found that the graves of the soldiers who had been buried there had been opened and the bodies scalped and plundered and the remains scattered all about the area. Hopkins had his men rebury them.

Three days later, an ambush set by The Prophet caught a patrol of Hopkins' force and killed eighteen of the Americans. An early blizzard on November 25 cancelled any plans for pursuit up the Tippecanoe River, and Hopkins marched back down the Wabash.

Harrison was pleased at the report that the Indians had been dispersed again from Prophet's Town, but he could not get from his mind the report of the desecration of the graves of his men who had fallen at Tippecanoe a year earlier.

About this same time, Harrison was saddened by news that his old and esteemed friend, John Scott, had died. Scott had arrived at his home in Frankfort, but then two days later had died. Harrison felt no loss greater during the war. It was as though he had lost a member of his own family. Now he felt that he himself had died a little more in Kentucky.

In late October, Tecumseh heard with dismay that General Brock had been killed while leading a successful counterattack against the Americans at Queenstown Heights. Depressed by the news of Brock's death, disappointed by Muir's retreat, and still bothered by his painful leg wound, Tecumseh declined to go along with a large foraging party back to the Maumee in late November. Instead, Winamac and several other chiefs accompanied Captain Matthew Elliott in leading the group. They had with them four hundred Indians. Foraging for food along the way, they went as far south as an old abandoned stockade that American soldiers had built several years earlier on Swan Creek, a few miles north of the Maumee Rapids. There they took shelter.

From the other direction, Harrison sent one of his most trusted scouts, the Shawnee Johnny Logan, together with two other trustworthy Shawnees, Bright Horn and Otter, the latter a grandnephew of Black Hoof, to reconnoiter the country around the Miami rapids. Logan and his companions reported to General Winchester at his camp northeast of Defiance. Then, on foot, they went on down the Maumee toward the rapids for a distance of nearly twenty miles.

At the stockade on Swan Creek, Captain Elliott and Winamac decided to take a party of five other Potawatomis for a reconnaissance up the Maumee beyond the rapids. They set out early in the morning on horseback. About noon the two parties surprised each other near Turkey Creek. Quickly regaining his composure, Logan extended a friendly greeting to Winamac and told him that the three Shawnees were defecting from the Long Knives and were on their way to join Tecumseh. Not convinced, Winamac had his men disarm the Shawnees. But after visiting for some time in the afternoon, he was persuaded to restore their rifles to the three.

Just before dusk four of the Potawatomis went off to look around in the woods while the others remained seated around a campfire. Taking advantage of the moment, Logan gave a signal, and the three Shawnees opened fire. Chief Winamac fell dead. Captain Elliott, slightly wounded, ran off through the woods. One more shot brought down the warrior who had remained with them. Bright Horn and Otter quickly, if clumsily, took the scalp of the Potawatomi chief as the other Potawatomis, attracted by the firing and Elliott's shouting, came racing back. They opened fire. A bullet shattered Bright Horn's left thigh. Logan and Otter fired back and killed two of the Potawatomis. As the two survivors fled, one of them paused just long enough for one last desperation shot. This caught Johnny Logan in the abdomen. Otter boosted Logan up on Elliott's horse and Bright Horn on Winamac's before he jumped on a third. Clinging desperately to their horses they rode rapidly through the night. They arrived at Winchester's camp about midnight.

The next day Johnny Logan died. The faithful Shawnee was buried with full U.S. military honors. Harrison promised that he would seek government protection for Logan's wife and several children.

Now Harrison saw a chance to cut off all the Indians on Swan Creek. They were, as he put it, in a complete *cul de sac* formed by the fifteen-foot deep creek. If Winchester could get a detachment there before the creek froze, it would be possible to cut off their retreat. But the Indians, with their chief leaders lost, had cleared out before any attack could be mounted against them.

Harrison moved his headquarters to Delaware, Ohio, near the center of the state, to look after further logistic and administrative preparations for his army. He did send off a detachment for another foray against the Indians in northeastern Indiana. On November 25, Lt. Col. John B. Campbell left Franklinton (opposite Columbus) with a force of 600 regulars and Pennsylvania and Ohio militiamen to attack the Delaware and Miami villages on the Mississinewa. Harrison thought the time ideal for such an expedition—dry weather, snow on the ground that would make it impossible for the enemy to hide, and a near-full moon that would permit night marches.

Marching by way of Dayton and Greeneville, Campbell arrived on the Mississinewa in mid-December. He proceeded to destroy three of the villages. But this provoked a strong counterattack. On December 18, a force of 300 Miamis and Munsees (a branch of the Delawares) struck back fiercely when it caught Campbell's force about eighteen miles east of where the Mississinewa emptied into the Wabash, about forty miles southwest of Fort Wayne. In spite of serious casualties and the loss of most of his horses, Campbell held his ground and finally drove the Indians off. With low supplies and few horses, and fearing possible Indian reinforcements, Campbell returned to Ohio. By the time they got back half were unfit for duty on account of frostbite.

Campbell's expedition and his victory in the Battle of the Mississinewa probably discouraged the further participation in the war of the Miamis and the Delawares of the region. In any case, Harrison was pleased with the results, and he lauded the force for its discipline and restraint as much as for its discipline on the march and its success in battle. In his report he said:

> The character of this gallant detachment exhibiting, as it did perseverance, patience, fortitude and bravery, would however, have been incomplete, if, in the midst of victory, they had forgotten the feelings of humanity. It is with the sincerest pleasure, that the general has heard, that the most punctual obedience was paid to his orders; not only in saving the women and children, but in sparing all the warriors who ceased to resist; and that even, when vigorously attacked by the enemy, the claims of mercy prevailed over every sense of their own danger; and this heroic band respected the lives of their prisoners. The general believes that humanity and true bravery are inseparable. The rigid rules of war may sometimes, indeed, make a severe retaliation necessary; but the advantages which attend a frequent recurrence of it, are very uncertain, and are not to be compared with the blessings which providence cannot fail to shed upon the efforts of the soldier, who is "in battle a lion, but, the battle once ended, in mercy a lamb." Let an account of the murdered innocence be opened in the records of Heaven against our enemies alone; the American soldier will follow the example of his government, and neither the sword of the one will be raised against the helpless or the fallen, nor the gold of the other paid for the scalp of a massacred enemy.

7a

In Amherstburg, Tecumseh was rather surprised when his brothers arrived with a small band of followers about mid-December. To Tecumseh's dismay, The Prophet explained how the Long Knives had destroyed the villages around Tippecanoe and stolen most of the corn. Now he was hoping to get some food from the British.

Tecumseh explained that the British were planning a spring offensive against the Long Knives, and he was concerned about bringing together all the Indians possible to assist in that effort.

In the meantime, the British were encouraging the Indians to return to their winter villages, to supplement their small food supplies by hunting, and then to return in the spring for the big battle. Tecumseh, with Procter's blessing, proposed to return to Indiana for the winter to bring more warriors for the spring. He asked his brother to accompany him.

Tecumseh hoped in the coming year to see the realization of the dream for which he had lived his whole life.

Near the end of December, Tecumseh and The Prophet set out on their recruiting journey.

For Harrison, logistics ruled out an autumn campaign against Detroit, and logistics complicated by the weather made a winter campaign questionable, but he would try.

Prospects had appeared very favorable in the first two weeks of December. At St. Mary's, on the St. Mary's River, quartermasters and infantry officers supervised the loading and launching of boats manned by soldiers who volunteered for this special duty. The first group comprised a large boat and sixteen pirogues loaded with flour and other supplies. Three days later, two large boats cast off with 398 barrels of flour, 32 barrels of whiskey, 72 barrels of salt, 20 kegs of gunpowder, 10 kegs of lead, 150 cannon balls, 1 box of cannister shot, 2 boxes of clothing, 10 bushels of oats, 5 iron bars, 5 steel bars, 3 coils of rope, and hospital stores. Additional quantities of flour, whiskey, salt, and clothing were sent down the Auglaize in pirogues and on rafts, and 700 hogs were sent on foot. All these were for Winchester's troops.

When the first boats had gone sixty miles (amounting to only twelve miles by land) and the second group had gone forty miles (nine miles by land) a sudden freeze caught them. The roads were so bad and the water so high that it was impossible to use wagons, and almost as difficult for packhorses. This meant that Winchester's men had to go for ten days with only short rations of salt beef and no flour at all.

Nevertheless, Harrison decided that he must concentrate his forces. On December 20 he ordered Winchester to move on to the rapids. Winchester got his force of 1200 men—the regulars under Sam Wells and the four regiments of Kentucky militia—in motion almost at once. On receiving word that Winchester was on the move, Harrison himself hastened northward toward the rapids.

Through two feet of snow, the men and horses tramped slowly down the Maumee valley. It was a march of the great unwashed, over whitewashed paths through the fog of war. The Kentucky militiamen looked more the part of hungry woodsmen, which they were, than of trained soldiers which they were not. Their dress was more fitting for a Kentucky summer than for a Canadian winter. Scarcely a great coat or cloak was to be found among them. Their frocks, made of shoddy cotton stuff of varying hues of dirty browns, dirty tans, and dirty grays and blues, hung to their knees. Their pantaloons were of the same material. Their heads were covered with slouched hats of mixed felt, worn bare by constant use. Long hair, uncombed and matted, fell over their cheeks. Some wore boots with little care. More wore shoes the worse for wear. Vermin were out of season, so accumulations of body oils could be welcomed as insulation against the cold. For further warmth, they wore filthy blankets wrapped around their loins, secured by broad leather belts into which had been thrust broad axes and long knives. Angled muskets or rifles drained the warmth from their shoulders as did the knives from their thighs. Some had a glove or two and some wrapped their hands with frayed cloth bands. Yet spirits rose when on the move, fed on a hope that wherever they went things would improve.

Arriving at the rapids on January 10, Winchester began laying out a fortified camp on the northwest side of the river. This was as far as Winchester was supposed to go. Here was where the whole army was supposed to concentrate, to launch its offensive for the recapture of Detroit, but a little White settlement called Frenchtown on the River Raisin, about thirty-five miles to the northeast, beckoned. Messages from the settlers expressed a hope for liberation and indicated that a force of only fifty Canadian militia and one hundred Indians held the place. They further stated that there were large quantities of food there that ought to be protected. The prospects of fresh food and warm houses, and the opportunity for action against a weak enemy, were strong incentives for the Kentuckians. Winchester shared those temptations. A council of war of the officers, over the strong dissent of their only regular army colleague, Samuel Wells, recommended attack.

Winchester decided to send half of his force on the venture. On January 17, Colonel William Lewis led off with 550 men. Colonel John Allen followed with another 110 a few hours later. The next day, Lewis captured the village with a loss of twelve killed and fifty-five wounded.

Worried that he might have overextended himself so close to the British headquarters at Fort Malden, Winchester himself went forward with another 300 men to reinforce Frenchtown. There, his defensive disposition was in forming a line on the north side of the River Raisin so that the men had their backs to the river, and he set up his headquarters on the south bank, 800 yards from the front.

But already Colonel Procter was on his way with about 1,200 British and Indians from Fort Malden which was only eighteen miles distant. In the absence of Tecumseh, the leadership of the Indians which comprised about half of Procter's force, was in the hands of Roundhead and Walk-in-the-Water. On the night of January 21, in a raging snowstorm, this force crossed the Detroit River on the ice. Opening with artillery fire, the British and Indians attacked in the darkness through a still-falling snow at four o'clock in the morning on the 22nd. Caught without warning by pickets or sentinels, the American right collapsed almost at once. Indians poured through to the rear and within ten minutes had scalped a hundred Kentuckians.

Winchester hurried up to try to rally his men, but to no avail. He was taken prisoner and surrendered his whole force there. However, Major George Madison had been able to repulse attacks on the left and he held out, in spite of Winchester's surrender, until Procter had promised humane treatment of prisoners, but then Procter put the prisoners to work pulling guns and wagons to relieve his horses, and quickly departed, leaving the wounded with the Indians behind. Crazed by captured whiskey, the Indians began scalping the wounded.

Procter, fearing that Harrison would be coming up with a strong force, hurried back toward Malden.

Harrison, now at the rapids with the remnant of Winchester's left wing, about 240 men mainly of Wells' regular and Scott's Kentucky regiment, received the news of the Frenchtown disaster late that same afternoon. Fearing that Procter would be coming on with his much larger force, Harrison burned Winchester's camp and hurried southwestward toward Defiance. Within thirty-six hours, the enemy forces were sixty miles apart.

When at last they could catch their breath, Sam Wells stopped in to see his old friend. "Well, General, where do we go from here?" he asked Harrison.

"Same as before, 'On to Canada!'"

"Good!" Wells responded with a forced enthusiasm. "Do you think we can get to Canada with our 240?"

"Why not? Winchester made it with his 900, didn't he? He's probably inside Fort Malden right now. No trick at all! Isn't this the damndest thing?"

"Don't we still have enough men in the other wings of the army to have a go at it?"

"Of course we do, and that's just what we're going to do."

A week later Harrison returned to the rapids with 2,000 men. Consulting his engineer officer, Captain Eleazer Wood who had been educated at West Point, Harrison chose an excellent defensive site on the southeast bank of the river and there began the construction of a well-planned fortification. In honor of the Governor of Ohio he named it Fort Meigs.

During the next week, additional units arrived to bring his total force to over 4,000. This, he thought, would be enough. His first thought now was not Detroit, but the British headquarters itself, Fort Malden. This was considerably closer, and he was anxious to catch up with Procter and his Indians in revenge for the Frenchtown massacre. He set February 11 as the date to move out.

The appointed day arrived with an ice storm. It was hardly possible for man or horse to stand, much less to walk on the rough terrain. The colder weather also brought cooler consideration of the situation. He really did not have his supply bases in the order that he wanted. The men did not have the winter clothing, wool blankets, and shoes that they needed for a winter campaign, and he really did not have as many men as he thought he needed. The more he thought about it, the less appealing a winter invasion of Canada seemed. He had just learned of the disastrous retreat of Napoleon's Grand Army from Moscow through the Russian winter. Somehow a Canadian winter seemed no more hospitable just now. He decided to cancel the whole thing and prepare for spring.

At Malden, Procter watched developments carefully. He was not sure whether the Americans would attack soon or not. The buildup at the Maumee rapids suggested that they would. In this respect he thought the weather was on his side. He had enough supplies on hand for the winter, and he knew the Americans would be hard-pressed to carry enough supplies over the ice and snow.

At Fort Meigs, Harrison worked strenuously to get things organized. He read grimly a letter written by one of the men who had been taken prisoner at Frenchtown and then had managed to escape:

I saw my fellow soldiers, naked and wounded, crawling out of houses to avoid being consumed in flames. Some that had not been able to turn themselves on their beds for four days...arose and walked....the savages rushed on the wounded, and in their barbarous manner shot, tomahawked and scalped them; and cruelly mangled their bodies while they lay agonizing and weltering in their blood. A number were taken towards Malden, but being unable to march with speed, were inhumanly massacred. The road was for miles strewed with mangled bodies — all of them left for birds and beasts to devour.

Harrison ordered a string of blockhouses to be built to serve as storehouses for supplies, and he ordered the continuing improvement of Fort Meigs. Then leaving Colonel Wingate in charge there, he set off to raise more men at Urbana, Springfield, Dayton, and Cincinnati.

CHAPTER XXII

Lake Erie

1

W illiam Henry Harrison's visit to Cincinnati, in March 1813, gave him a chance to communicate more directly and quickly with Governor Shelby of Kentucky for another levy of troops from that state. Not only did he need to replace the units that had been lost in the River Raisin, he also needed to replace the large numbers of men whose short-term enlistments had expired or soon would be expiring. The Virginia and Pennsylvania militiamen, currently at the Maumee Rapids, had expressed a determination to leave the very moment their time of service expired, even if no replacements for them had arrived by that time.

Hardly less important than the collecting of reinforcements at Cincinnati, was the opportunity it provided Harrison for a brief visit with his family on Broad Street. As he rode up to the house late one afternoon in the last week of March, young William Henry and John Scott, just returning from their lessons, saw him and came out to greet him with excited shouts, followed by Old Dan barking just as loudly in greeting. As soon as Harrison had put up his horse, he accompanied them to the house where Anna and the servants were preparing supper.

"Papa, papa, is the war over? Did we win?" asked John Scott.

"Papa, did you catch Tecumseh?" asked young William Henry.

"Did you catch King George?" John Scott continued.

"Just a minute!" The elder Harrison laughed. "How can I answer so many questions all at once?" He paused only a moment and went on, "But I guess I can answer all those at once. I'm afraid the answer to all of them is 'no.'"

"No? Why not?" both boys asked.

"What have you been doing all year?" asked young William Henry.

"Well, my lads, we have been having a few contests and trying to hold an army together, but I'm afraid it's going to take a little more time."

"How much time?" asked John Scott.

"Nobody can know that. Maybe if we're very careful we can have some results this year."

By this time they were approaching the door. Anna and the other children were running outside, without wraps, into a cold wind, but nobody noticed the cold wind in the warmth of the greetings.

During supper, Harrison recounted in over-simplified terms some of his adventures in leading an army to the approaches to Lake Erie, and then his own travels by horseback all around Ohio. Later, by the fireplace, the family continued the interchanges about the war. Anna sent word up to North Bend that her husband was home for a couple of days, and they all would be up to visit the next day. For now, Harrison was content to relax with his wife and children.

Anna's first concern was about his health which, he assured her, was good.

"Henry, was it awfully difficult?"

"It was difficult, but nothing we can't handle."

"We have heard the terrible news about the River Raisin. What happened?"

"I'm afraid the general in charge of the corps that was advancing down the Maumee stuck his neck out too far. He went far beyond where he was instructed to go, and then he failed to set up a proper defense."

"And what happened to him? Did you have to replace him?"

"We had to replace him all right. He was captured, taken prisoner."

"Oh, by the Indians?"

"Yes, but they turned him over to the British commander, which may not be any advantage."

"Oh, Henry, it's wonderful you could come home, even for a day or two," said Anna. "How did you manage it?"

"Well, I had to get out to see about reinforcements."

"You mean the losses on the River Raisin were that bad?"

"Well, that, and also the short-term enlistments of the militia are expiring."

"That must be a problem, I'm sure."

"Always. The enthusiasm of the volunteers for joining the army is exceeded only by their enthusiasm for getting back home."

"Indeed!"

"And I can understand that, but it makes it very difficult to fight any kind of war against a determined enemy."

The children now asked questions only occasionally, but they listened intently far beyond their usual bedtime.

Then Harrison stopped everybody with a statement in his matter-of-fact way, "And my dears, it appears that we may not be going back to Indiana, at least not for some time."

"Oh, Henry," Anna gasped. "Have the Indians captured or burned Vincennes?"

"Oh no, nothing like that, at least I hope not."

"Oh Papa," cried seven-year-old Benjamin. "I wanted to ride on the riverboat again."

"Well, I guess if we wait long enough you'll tell us what this is all about," Anna said impatiently.

"Well it's just this," Harrison said as he took a folded paper from his pocket and read, "'I have the honor to inform you that on the 2nd instant the President, by and with the advice and consent of the Senate appointed you a Major General in the Army of the United States.'"

"Major General!" exclaimed John Cleaves. "Daddy, that's great! Isn't that the highest rank in the whole Army?"

Harrison smiled broadly and said, "Well, there are half a dozen others appointed at the same time, but you're right, Cleaves, just now it's the highest rank in the Army."

"Oh, that's wonderful, Henry," Anna said, "but what has all that got to do with going back to Indiana?"

"Yes, Papa," said young William Henry, "what has that got to do with it?"

John Cleaves rejoined, "Yes, Father, aren't you already a major general in the Kentucky militia and a brigadier general in the U.S. Army? How does this change anything?"

Harrison explained. "You see, this means a major command, an army or a department or something. In the first place this means that I'm probably in the Army for the duration of this war, and then thereafter, if I stay in, I go where the President and the Secretary of War tell me to go."

"But when the war's over, why can't you go back to being Commander-in-Chief of Indiana back at Vincennes?" asked Anna.

"I'm afraid it's not that simple. Now they are thinking that one should not be a governor and a regular army major general at the same time."

"I don't see why not," protested Anna.

"Well, you can't be off fighting Indians or Englishmen or heaven knows what in some far quarter of the country and be very effective as a governor. Anyway, they've already settled that. At the same time they sent my name to the Senate for promotion to major general, they also sent the name of the man to be the new territorial governor of Indiana."

"And who might that be? Not that Jonathan Jennings, I hope," said Anna.

"No, it's a man by the name of Posey, Thomas Posey."

"Who's he?"

"He's originally from Virginia, but now a senator from Louisiana. I guess he's sixty or sixty-five years old. He was with the Virginia militia that served under Lewis in the Battle of Point Pleasant on the Great Kanawa, against the Shawnee Cornstalk. He served with Morgan's Riflemen in the Revolution, and then in the Continental Army, and he served with Anthony Wayne."

"Well, what do you think about stepping down from Vincennes after twelve years?" asked Anna.

Harrison thought about it for a few minutes and then said, "Oh, I'll miss it all right. It was always exciting. There always was a sense of performing a real and necessary service for the people on the frontier. And there is something exciting about being a part of a great beginning, a territory that soon will be a state. And I enjoyed our house, Grouseland, with all our family there, maybe more now in retrospect than when we actually were there. But then—"

"But what?" asked Anna.

"But then in a way it is kind of a relief to be rid of all the political controversy and back-biting that goes with it."

"Yes, I'm sure."

"It was a situation where political enemies made every military victory a defeat, every Indian treaty a sell-out—I'm not sure whether a sell-out to the Indians or the Whites—where they saw every effort at peaceful settlement as weakness and every measure for the improvement of the Territory as a device for personal aggrandizement. And now, when most of our friends are off serving their nation or the Territory in the war, our political enemies remain behind to make political hay. It's not always easy to be sure which are friendly Indians and which are hostile, but that is more certain than being able to count on certain political friends, so-called, and the constant maneuvering of political enemies."

"Whew! That was a mouth full!" exclaimed Anna.

"Well, Mother, what do you think?"

"Oh, I am happy to be wherever you are and wherever we can have the children with us."

"Suppose you could have that either way. Would you prefer being here or at Vincennes?"

"Oh, I miss our beautiful house very much."

"Well, we can build another right here. We can extend our little house at North Bend into a big house too."

"In that case, I guess maybe it would be better to be close to family and friends here than among political enemies there."

"Yes, I suppose so."

"But, Henry—"

"Yes?"

"You said Indiana soon will be a state. By all counts you should be the first governor of the state. Aren't you going to try for it?"

"With a war on, who knows where I'll be at the time? And with all the back-biting going on, with Jennings free to play politics while I'm out playing war, I doubt if I would stand a very good chance."

"Oh surely, after twelve years, you have a great following there."

"I'm not sure about that now. I like to hope that if the people were to vote twenty years from now on the basis of what I have done during these twelve years that there might be some favorable response, but I don't know."

"But if you stay in the Army, you really won't have a choice between North Bend and Vincennes, will you?"

"No, not really. What do the rest of you think?"

Betsy spoke up first. "I would be content to stay right here."

"Yes, because you'll be closer to cousin John Short," young William Henry taunted.

"Well, Billy, where would you like to be?" his father asked.

"Oh, I don't know. It's all right here, I guess."

"They've got bigger boats on the Ohio River than on the Wabash," said Benjamin. "But I think I would like to go back to Vincennes someday."

The eldest son, John Cleaves Symmes, was more determined. "I *am* going back to Vincennes, and I'm going to live in Grouseland. May I, Father?"

"Of course, if that's what you want when you are old enough."

"What's old enough?" asked Cleaves.

"Oh, maybe when you have finished college."

"How soon can I go to college?"

"Maybe in another year or two."

"Why can't I just go back to Vincennes and go to the University there?"

"Well, I'm afraid it's not quite ready yet, not with the full course. I wish you could go there. But there's a good college over at Lexington that I think you'll like and it should provide a good education."

"What's that?"

"It's called Transylvania."

"Transylvania—'across the woods,' eh. Well, that sounds good to me if I can go back to Vincennes afterward."

John Scott said that he liked it in North Bend, but he was sure that someday he would like to go back to Indiana, at least for a while. Lucy said she would like to stay right here, she thought.

Meanwhile, Harrison said that everyone was going to stay right here until the war was over, so nobody had to decide anything right now.

By the end of the month, Harrison was growing uneasy about the situation at Fort Meigs. Mild weather had made Lake Erie navigable much earlier in the season than usual, and reports were coming in about Indian depredations all around the frontiers. He decided that he must get back as quickly as possible. On April 1, he set out from Cincinnati with Colonel John Miller and 120 regulars with the intention of reaching St. Marys in two days, and then taking boats down the Auglaize to arrive at Fort Meigs in three days. Companies of Kentucky militia were arriving at Newport, across the Ohio River from Cincinnati, and to expedite their march northward he assigned a packhorse to every two men in some of the companies. In addition, he sent orders for 150 of 180 militiamen who were then building boats at Fort Findlay, forty-four miles from the Rapids, to proceed at once to Fort Meigs.

When Harrison got back to Fort Meigs the first week of April, the Virginia and Pennsylvania militia already had left. He had there a force of 1,500 men, with a promise of as many more within a short time from Kentucky. He fervently hoped that the reinforcements would arrive before Procters's British and Tecumseh's Indians did.

2

From late December until March, Tecumseh and The Prophet, together with Main Poc for part of the way, travelled through northern Indiana and Illinois to impress upon the tribes the importance of collecting at Amherstburg in the spring, when they would join their British brothers in war against the Long Knives.

The Shawnee and other tribes were used to moving with the seasons. This year, Tecumseh urged them to leave their winter hunting camps for the upper Tippecanoe and then Canada where their British father would provide food and ammunition.

In late March, Tecumseh left The Prophet in charge of the assembly of the tribes on the upper Tippecanoe and went on back to Fort Malden where he reported to Procter that hundreds of warriors were on the way to join him, but they needed food. The British commander promised that he would send a pack train.

Tecumseh returned to Indiana to bring his followers on to Amherstburg. His sister, Tecumapease and her warrior husband, Wasabogoa, and their children as well as his son, Pachetha, came along, and The Prophet's wife accompanied him.

While the tribes were preparing to move, Tecumseh, in some excitement, told his brother what he had heard at Fort Malden about a great victory against the Long Knives on the River Raisin.

"Maybe the General Procter will fight," he said. "Sometimes he acts like yellow dog, sometimes like panther. He is not same as the General Brock."

"No, he is not same," The Prophet agreed. The younger

the "Grand Traverse," twelve feet high, twenty feet wide at the base, and nine hundred feet long. A second embankment, parallel to this, was seven hundred feet long. The trenches formed by digging the earth for the embankments provided protection for the men, and compartments angled at various places provided storage. The powder magazines were covered with mounds of earth several feet thick.

Rain hampered the digging of emplacements and the moving of guns, but on May 1 all was ready. Early that morning the British guns opened fire. The screams of the cannonballs and the bursting shells brought screams of delight from the Indians. While Harrison's men hustled into their trenches, Tecumseh's Indians surrounded the fort at a safe distance.

Thanks to the thick log walls and the traverses inside, four days of bombardment had little effect. Eighty men were killed and rather more wounded. Without the traverses, the losses would have been several times that. The wounded were taken to the hospital tent behind the rear embankment, and the dead were quietly buried each night.

This was a kind of fighting for which the Indians had no patience. Tecumseh sent a message to Harrison:

General Harrison:
I have with me 800 braves. You have an equal number in your hiding place. Come out and give me battle. You talked like a brave man when we met at Vincennes, and I respected you, but now you hide behind logs and in the earth like a groundhog.

Tecumseh

Procter had hopes that four days of almost incessant bombardment, and being surrounded by Indians, might move Harrison to an honorable surrender. After all, General Hull had given up Detroit without suffering long bombardment or being surrounded. But Harrison was not one to be unnerved either by the knowledge that he was surrounded nor by taking casualties. He had stood his ground at Tippecanoe without fortifications, and he would do as much here. He would not flinch. Harrison walked that narrow line between the heartlessness of insensitivity to the lives and injuries of his men and the total involvement in their feelings and their losses that would have rendered him altogether immobile and useless.

On the morning after the fourth day the British guns were silent. A sentinel reported the approach of someone with a white flag. Making sure that he was alone the guards admitted him.

It was a British officer who asked to see the General. A guard escorted him to where Harrison was standing near the fort's main battery. All the soldiers in the vicinity looked and listened with curiosity.

A certain smugness disappeared from the British officer's countenance as he looked about and saw no signs of what he had supposed would be hundreds of casualties resulting from the shelling. Approaching Harrison, he saluted and said, "Sir, I am Major Chambers. General Procter has directed me to demand the surrender of this post. He is anxious to avoid further bloodshed."

Harrison looked coolly at the Major and said, "This is a most extraordinary demand. Since General Procter did not demand surrender when he first arrived, I had thought that he had assumed I would do my duty. Now what does this indicate about his opinion of me?"

"Sir, General Procter meant no injury to the personal feelings of the General. General Harrison's character is well known and respected by him, but now he has effective artillery batteries in position, a considerable force of regulars, and the largest body of Indians ever assembled in this area. He considers it only a matter of time and is desirous of avoiding unnecessary suffering."

"I believe I have a correct assessment of General Procter's force," replied Harrison. "It is not such as to create the least apprehension about the outcome of the contest. You tell General Procter that he will never have this fort surrendered to him on any terms. If General Procter captures this fort, it will be under circumstances that will do him more honor than a thousand surrenders."

The soldiers sent up a tremendous cheer as the Major turned away and went out the gate.

Word that General Harrison was shut up in Fort Meigs spread consternation throughout northwestern Ohio. If the fort fell, the whole area would be open to attack. But cheers were coming from the southwest. Brig. Gen. Green Clay was on the way with his 1,200 men from Kentucky. At Chillicothe, Harrison's old friend, Thomas Worthington, was following the situation closely. Hearing that Clay's force was approaching the Maumee, Worthington thought it imperative to get word to Harrison both to forestall any premature surrender and to enable him to make the best use of the reinforcements to raise the siege.

Without a word to anyone else, Worthington slipped away from his great house, Adena, outside Chillicothe, and recruited

Major William Oliver of the Ohio militia and a friendly Delaware
Indian to accompany him on a special mission. Mounting fast
horses they rode rapidly northward. At Defiance, they found that
Clay's men already were floating down the river toward the
rapids. Worthington and Oliver disguised themselves as Indians,
and with their Delaware companion made their way up close to
the fort. There, Worthington wrote a message that Clay was only
two hours away, on the river, awaiting orders. Carefully, they
wrapped the message around an arrow and shot it into the fort. A
wave from the fort satisfied them that the message had been
found. Then, stealthily, they made their way back through the
Indian-infested woods, got their horses, and rode all the way back
to Chillicothe. Their report of what they had done set off wild
celebrations in Chillicothe and at Adena.

Pleased and heartened by the message, Harrison promptly sent
Captain Vernon Hamilton out to make his way through the
enemy lines with instructions for General Clay. The Kentuckians were to come on in their boats through the rapids until they
arrived close to the fort. Then a part of the force was to land on
the northwest bank, sweep up to the gun emplacements and
spike the guns on that side. A smaller force was to land on the
opposite bank. There, a sortie from the fort would join them to
spike the guns on the hill to the southeast. This done, all were to
move into the fort. To his message Harrison added a warning, "I
take occasion to warn you against that rash bravery which is so
characteristic of the Kentucky troops, and if persisted in, is as
fatal as cowardice."

Clay moved up as directed. He sent a detachment of eight
hundred men under Lt. Col. John Dudley for the mission on the
northwest bank, while he himself took the remaining four
hundred to the southeast bank.

Harrison glanced upward and saw a great eagle soaring
overhead. He took it as a good omen.

In spite of sharp musket and rifle fire from the British and
Indians, the Kentuckians carried out the plan well. Harrison sent
a sortie of 250 men under Colonel John Mills out of the fort to join
Clay's men in spiking the guns on the southeast. This they
accomplished with dispatch and got back into the fort. On the
northwest, Dudley's detachment as quickly overran the guns on
that side.

Seeing what was happening, Tecumseh instructed his front-
line warriors to run back through the woods while he positioned
others in the rear.

Lured on by their initial success, Dudley's detachment went too far. Instead of coming back quickly to the fort as instructed, they continued in pursuit. Watching from the main battery in the fort, Harrison cried out, "Zounds! They are lost! Damn it, can't I ever get them to obey orders?"

While Dudley's men chased the fleeing Indians for nearly two miles through woods and swamps, Tecumseh placed his thousand warriors around a big ravine to receive them. The result was disaster for the Kentuckians. Of the 800 under Dudley, only 150 made it back to Fort Meigs.

While the dead were scalped, the captured were rounded up, and Tecumseh sent them with about a third of his Indians back to the encampment at old Fort Miami. On the way back, the exultation of many of the Indians got the better of them, and they shot or tomahawked a number of the captives and then scalped them. The survivors were herded into an outdoor pen. Procter rode up and viewed the bag of prisoners with satisfaction. He told the Indians that each might choose a prisoner and dispose of him in any way he wished. This set off a massacre by tomahawk, knives, war clubs, and arrows.

Tecumseh now was riding back to the place, and attracted by the loud screams and whoops, he rode up at a fast gallop. He arrived just in time to see two Indians grab Colonel Dudley. While one held the colonel and jerked his head back by the hair, the other raised a knife to stab him. Tecumseh leaped from his horse, drew his war club, and pushed the Indian with the drawn knife. "Stop!" the chief shouted. The other assailant instead drew a knife from his belt and slashed Dudley's throat. Tecumseh felled the Indian with a mighty blow of his war club.

The other Indians fell silent and withdrew in amazement. Tecumseh spoke out, "Did we not direct in council that prisoners would not be slain. Did we not acknowledge that this kind of act is the act of cowards? Where is your bravery? What has become of my warriors?"

Then he turned to General Procter and pointing to him said, "Why have you allowed this?"

Procter replied simply, "Sir, your Indians cannot be commanded."

Tecumseh snarled, "Begone! You are unfit to command. I conquer to build; you to destroy. Go and put on petticoats!"

3

After the battle, many of the Indians found Dudley's boats filled with foodstuffs and other prizes. Many warriors picked up all the booty they could carry and drifted away. At the same time, the Canadian militia were growing restless. They wanted to get home in time to do their spring planting. On May 9, Procter gave up the siege and sailed back to Canada. Tecumseh and The Prophet who had watched the battle from a safe distance, returned to Amherstburg with only forty warriors. They established a village on the Huron River, south of Detroit, where they remained through June. But Tecumseh was not content to remain passively on the defensive. The British might be content merely to defend Canada, but that would not do for him. They must gain decisive victories over the Long Knives if the Indians were to win back their lost lands, or even hold those remaining in their hands, in Ohio, Indiana, and Illinois.

Harrison took advantage of the June lull to revisit Ohio towns in quest of more troops and to see about getting up supplies. He visited the various posts to inspect the troops and to urge continuous training and discipline. He found something of a morale problem in the civilian population as well as among the militiamen. Many of them blamed him for the losses of Dudley's detachment at Fort Meigs; and Ohio units, that were on the way to the fort when Procter withdrew his forces, thought that there should have been more of a pursuit of the British. They should have been destroyed as soon as they turned their backs to sail away to fight another day.

Harrison made his headquarters back at Franklinton during this time, where he was in a central location for visiting the various towns and posts and for overseeing the delivery of supplies. Somewhat to his chagrin, Harrison learned that the Secretary of War had cut back on supply support. The use of heavy trains of horses and oxen was to be curtailed. His special agents for the procurement of supplies were to limit their drafts on the War Department to $20,000 a month, and all supply officers were to forward their accounts to the War Department for settlement. The Secretary of War had entered into a contract with Benjamin Orr and Aaron Greely to supply rations for the Northwestern Army, and John C. Bartlett was appointed to serve as Quartermaster General for this army.

Harrison also learned, with much greater satisfaction, that Captain Thomas S. Jesup, who had been detailed a deputy quartermaster general and sent to Cleveland with instructions to build boats for support of the army on Lake Erie, now had three boat yards in operation at that place. The boats were referred to locally as "Schenectady boats." Each would be able to carry forty to fifty men with their arms, accoutrements, provisions, and baggage.

Harrison issued orders to ban the sale of liquor at the army posts, and he issued a strict proscription against duelling. Punishment by flogging had been banned in the U.S. Army just before the declaration of war, a step which had the recommendation of William Henry Harrison.

His leniency in exacting punishment for infractions of Army rules brought criticisms of tender-heartedness from regular Army officers. One said that he acted toward his troops more like a father than a military commander, and he possessed "too much of the milk of human kindness for an efficient Commander-in-Chief." But it won the love of the common soldier. One volunteer remarked that the Commander-in-Chief's disposition was such a mixture of sympathy, kindness, and humanity that "he was like my Uncle Toby, he would not hurt even a fly."

On one occasion, when a soldier was sentenced to be shot for falling asleep on his sentry post, Harrison arrived at the execution ground as the firing squad was forming up. The troops were formed in a hollow square. He watched as the culprit was blindfolded and tied to the stake. The drums rolled. Then as the corporal of the guard commanded, "Ready—aim—"

Harrison called out, "As you were!" He had the prisoner brought before him, and he read a pardon together with a lecture on the importance of keeping awake when on sentry duty.

On another occasion, a court martial at Franklinton sentenced to death four men for desertion. Harrison allowed the death sentence to be carried out on one of the men who had threatened to kill the arresting officer, but the others he pardoned with severe reprimands.

Generally Harrison was opposed to the death penalty on any account. Sometimes for desertions he approved the wooden-horse treatment. In this exercise the offender was made to sit astride the well-sharpened saddle of a single-bar wooden horse, with a ten-pound wooden clog tied to each leg, and a sign on his hat, "Deserter returning to camp on horseback." Afterward he was required to carry a bundle of straw on his back and beg his sergeant's pardon in front of the whole regiment. Most of the desertions were not desertions in face of the enemy, but what in a later generation would be labelled "absent without leave." These were activities which could not be countenanced, but Harrison thought about the difficulties of raising troops at all. Here were men who at least had volunteered while their friends remained safely at home. Harrison did not want to make it too difficult for them to enlist.

On another occasion, Harrison approved punishment of a militia private who had fallen asleep on his post. He was plunged in the Scioto River on two successive mornings and then required to clear brush for two hours a day for the next three days.

Anticipating again the expiration of short-term enlistments before a campaign could be launched, much less completed against Canada, Harrison appealed once more to Governor Shelby of Kentucky. But this time he added a new touch:

> To make this last effort, why not, dear sir, come in person—you would not object to a command that would be nominal only; I have such confidence in your wisdom, that you in fact should be the guiding head, and I the hand. The situation you would be placed in is not without parallel: Scipio, the conqueror of Carthage, did not disdain to act as the lieutenant of his younger and less experienced brother, Lucius.

Harrison opened himself to more criticism in his attempt to enlist the services of friendly Indians. Most White settlers did not trust any Indians. Those who purported to be friendly were looked upon as spies. Harrison considered friendly Indians as valuable, especially in serving as scouts and guides through the woods, and he was convinced that bands of friendly warriors could neutralize to some extent those who supported Tecumseh.

He arranged for a council with neutral Delaware, Seneca, Wyandot, and Shawnee chiefs on June 20. "I have heard from General Procter that he is willing to trade American prisoners now in his hands for Indians friendly to the United States. Apparently he thinks if we will allow you to join him you will fight for him. Your Father, the President wants no false friends. He must know now whether you fight for him or his enemies. If for neither, then you must move far away, beyond the Father of Waters."

After a brief consultation, Tarhe, the Crane, answered, "We have been waiting many moons for you to ask us to join you. We all agree."

Pleased, Harrison answered that he would let them know when they were needed. "But I must warn you, no one is to kill defenseless prisoners or old men or women or children." The chiefs nodded their understanding and agreement. Harrison went on with a smile, "General Procter has promised to deliver me into the hands of Tecumseh if I am captured. Now I tell you that if we capture General Procter, he shall be delivered to you as your prisoner, provided you will agree not to act as a coward and kill a defenseless prisoner, but only put petticoats on him and treat him as a squaw."

Again the chiefs nodded their understanding and assent, though now they added broad smiles and shook hands.

4

Early in July, six hundred Indians from Michillimackinac arrived at Amherstburg ready for action. Procter did not want to lose their services, and he thought perhaps the best use of them would be in an attack against American posts along the southern shore of Lake Erie, and then an attack against the American shipyards at Presque Isle on the shore of the Pennsylvania panhandle, where an American fleet was building to challenge the British on the lake.

Tecumseh, with the support of Roundhead, insisted on another try against Fort Meigs. Reluctantly Procter agreed to this as a first step.

This time Procter brought along little more than a token force of regulars and militia, but Tecumseh had a thousand Indians. In mid-July the whole force crossed Lake Erie in canoes and small gunboats.

Learning of the approach of the hostile force while he was at the little Fort Stephenson near the mouth of the Sandusky River, Harrison moved back to Fort Seneca, eleven miles up the Sandusky, where he could keep a better watch on Fort Defiance as well as Meigs, should they be threatened. He sent a message to Clay at Fort Meigs to advise him that he (Harrison) was applying to Governor Meigs for more troops, but no reinforcements should be expected soon.

On July 20, the British and Indians ascended the Maumee to Fort Meigs. At dawn the next day, they surrounded the fort. Procter had brought along several six-pounders, but he fired only a few rounds of artillery into the fort. Tecumseh had a different plan. He would try to entice the garrison to come out of the fort where his Indians could trap them outside their protective walls and earthworks. On the 23rd, Tecumseh led 800 mounted Indians away from the fort to the south. Clay reported this to Harrison. Clay thought that they might be on their way to attack Fort Winchester (Defiance). Harrison thought that they might be making a feint toward Defiance with the intention of turning back to the east to attack Fort Stephenson. Both were wrong. Tecumseh went down to an area just barely within sight of the fort. With exaggerated firing and moving about, he staged a sham battle. He wanted to create the impression that his Indians had fallen upon an American relief party in the hope that the garrison would rush out to the rescue.

It would have worked if left to the junior officers and private soldiers. They set up a great furor to go to the rescue of their compatriots and catch the Indians in between. But Clay held back. He remembered Harrison's message that no reinforcements should be expected soon. He would wait.

Guessing that the Indians and British might really be heading for Fort Stephenson, Harrison decided that the best part of wisdom would be to evacuate the place and destroy it before the enemy could get there. Harrison sent a message to that effect to Major George Croghan, twenty-two year old nephew of William and George Rogers Clark, who was in command of the 160-man garrison there. Two days later Harrison was surprised by a terse reply from the young major:

Sir: I have just received yours of yesterday, 10 o'clock, p.m., ordering me to destroy this place and make good my retreat, which was received too late to be carried into execution. We have determined to maintain this place, and by Heaven we will.

"Damn!" Harrison exploded. "Can't anybody carry out orders any more?"

In haste and fury, Harrison wrote out a message telling Croghan that he was relieved of his command. He called in Colonel Samuel Wells and told him to go with an escort of dragoons under Colonel Ball to deliver the message and take over the command. Within hours Croghan was back at Seneca to see Harrison.

"Sir," said the young major, "I had no intention of disobeying your orders, but your message was delayed twenty-four hours because the messenger got lost. When it reached me, we already had seen some Indians in the vicinity. Your earlier instructions were that we should not evacuate the fort if Indians invested the place."

"Well, yes, Major, you're right about that; better to stay inside a blockhouse if Indians are around."

"Yes, Sir. Well, I held a council with all the officers. All agreed that since Indians had been seen all around, we should not go outside. We remember what happened last year at Fort Dearborn."

"Yes," Harrison agreed with a grim smile. "We certainly don't want any more Dearborn massacres. But Major, weren't you a little insolent in your response?"

"I did not mean to be, Sir," Croghan protested. "No, Sir, I meant no discourtesy, but, you see, with Indians out there I was afraid the message might fall into their hands. If it did, I wanted them to be impressed with our determination."

Harrison took a slow walk around the room in deep thought. Suddenly he turned and said, "Croghan, we need more officers like you. Go back to your command." He extended his hand and Croghan took it.

The Major turned to depart. As he reached the door, Harrison called out, "Oh Croghan."

"Yes, Sir."

"Croghan, go back there and hold your fort. By heaven, you can!" Harrison smiled broadly.

Returning the smile, Croghan said simply, "Yes, Sir. Thank you, Sir." And he was away.

Giving up the attempt on Fort Meigs, Procter embarked his regulars and militia back on the boats and floated back down the Maumee to the lake. They coasted eastward along the lake shore until they came to Sandusky Bay. They turned into the bay and went on up the river toward Fort Stephenson. Tecumseh led his Indians eastward overland. They met just below the fort on August 1. Procter decided to give the fort a chance to surrender before opening fire. Major Chambers again had the honor of carrying the flag of truce. Matthew Elliott and Robert Dickson, Indian agents, accompanied him. Croghan would not even treat with them except through a subordinate. He sent Ensign Edmund Shipp to convey his refusal.

Major Chambers stated his mission, "I am instructed by General Procter to demand the surrender of this fort. The General is most anxious to avoid useless bloodshed."

Shipp replied, "And I, Sir, am instructed to advise you that the commandant and garrison of this fort are determined to defend it to the last extremity."

Dickson then said, "Sir, for God's sake, surrender and prevent the dreadful massacre that will be caused by your resistance. We will not be able to control the immense body of Indians out there."

Again speaking for Croghan, Shipp replied firmly, "Sir, if this fort is taken there will be no survivors for your savages to murder!"

The emissaries returned to their positions, and the British guns opened fire. The bombardment continued almost all night, but with little effect on the small but sturdily built stockade.

Procter decided to take the fort by storm. British regulars would lead the way with ladders and axes to cross the shallow, dry moat in front of the walls, and then chop an opening with their axes. Tecumseh would follow with his Indians to pour through the breach in the wall.

Croghan saw them coming. He had only one six-pounder cannon and 160 muskets for defense, but he determined to use them with best effect. He ordered the cannon loaded with grapeshot and set up to cover the moat. All men would load their muskets but hold their fire until given the signal.

In the absence of any defensive fire, the British moved recklessly into the moat. Then on Croghan's command the cannon and muskets raked the moat with devastating effect. The British who did not fall fled back. Tecumseh and the Indians did not even get into action, and they had no intention of assaulting the fort over open ground. The British suffered a hundred casualties, while the Americans had one man killed and seven wounded.

Procter did not have enough British survivors to man all the gun boats and had to leave one behind. Those who could took to the boats and sailed for Canada. The Indians, disheartened by successive failures, walked westward. Most of the Chippewas, Menominees, and Sacs and Foxes just kept walking, all the way to their homelands. Tecumseh was disgusted. He was becoming convinced that he could do better without the British, but he knew he needed their supplies.

Captain Charles Scott Todd, Harrison's most trusted aide,

brought the report to Harrison. The commander was elated. He sent off a commendation to Croghan and sent a further commendation for him in a letter to the Secretary of War.

Two days later Todd was in Harrison's headquarters office and said casually, "I hear that some of the men are circulating a report that the ladies of Chillicothe are presenting a petticoat to General Harrison and a silver sword to Major Croghan." He laughed, but Harrison showed no reaction either way.

Todd went on, "You know something, General, it seems that whenever there is some kind of defeat or set-back resulting from the foolishness of some subordinate, like Winchester on the River Raisin, or Dudley on the Maumee, it is always the fault of the top commander, but if there is some kind of success or victory, like Clay at Fort Meigs, or now Croghan at Fort Stephenson, and I suppose all the way back to Tippecanoe, it is attributable to subordinates."

Harrison smiled and said, "Yes, I guess that's just the way it is, but Todd, our job is to make it possible for those subordinates to win as many as they can."

5

That afternoon, as Harrison waited in his headquarters for further information on Procter's movements, Captain Todd came in to announce that a naval officer had arrived to see the General. It was Oliver Hazard Perry, a twenty-eight year old naval officer who had been busy all summer collecting and building a fleet at Presque Isle. Harrison greeted him cordially and showed him to a chair.

"Well, Commodore, I'm glad to see you. Can I call you 'Commodore' now?" By the single gold epaulette on the shoulder of his double-breasted blue coat, Perry might have been a lieutenant or a master commandant (commander), though Harrison knew him to be the latter. But as was customary, Harrison always used the courtesy title of the command when applicable. The commander of a vessel, whatever his formal rank, always was "captain." Similarly, the commander of a fleet or flotilla always was "commodore." The courtesy title of commodore carried with it the right to wear a silver star on the epaulette, but Perry had not added this insignia.

"Well, Sir, I have a fleet just about ready to go," answered Perry.

"Great, all at Presque Isle?"

"Yes, Sir, except our five smaller vessels have come out just today and have taken up positions outside the harbor. That's how I got here."

"Good, good," responded Harrison. "But tell me, Commodore, why did you choose Presque Isle to build your ships? That's about as far away from the enemy as you can get."

"Yes, Sir, that's just it. Actually the site was chosen before I arrived, but it was a good choice. You see it is far away from the main British ports, and it is as close as we could get to Pittsburgh. I have brought all my anchors, shot, cables, and galley stoves, and a lot of the gunpowder and other stores from Pittsburgh. And there is lots of timber good for shipbuilding in the area."

"Yes, I can see all those advantages."

"But there is yet another. There's a big sand bar all the way across the mouth of the harbor, so if the British tried to bring their brigs or larger vessels into the harbor to interfere with our work, they would run aground."

"Yes, but I thought you said you just brought your vessels out."

"Yes, Sir, the smaller ones. Our two brigs are still safe inside."

"Oh, I see." Harrison laughed and went on. "Yes, I see, Commodore, the sand bar keeps the British ships out. But tell me, just how in hell do you propose to get yours out? Sounds to me a little like the man who built a boat in his barn and then could not get it out through the door."

"Yes, I guess it does sound a little like that." Perry smiled and then asked, "How do the Arabs get across the sand?"

"Camels, I suppose, but what's that got to do—"

"Exactly! Camels. And that's what we are going to use."

"Well, I have heard camels called 'ships of the desert' but I didn't know we had any in Ohio or Pennsylvania or anywhere else on this side of the ocean."

"No? Well, actually what we call camels are really sealed scows. We fill these with water and pass beams through the portholes of the ship to rest on them, below the water line. Then we pump out the water and their buoyancy lifts the vessel."

"Sounds reasonable. Will they work?"

"They had better. We'll know in the next two or three days."

"How much lift do they have to provide?"

"The water is usually six feet deep at the sand bar, but now it's only four feet. The camels can lift two or three feet above the vessel's draft, so you can see it will be very difficult."

"I can see. Tell me, Commodore, doesn't this fresh water sailing seem a little strange to an old salt like you?" asked Harrison.

"Yes, I must confess it does. The vessels ride a little lower in the water, and the lake may be choppier than what we're used to, but the tactics will be the same."

"Where have you served previously?"

"Well, I went to sea when I was eleven. I have my kid brother, Alexander, who is thirteen, with me as cabin boy here. I served with my father in the West Indies during the naval war with France, and I was in the Mediterranean in the *Adams* in '02 -'03, and again in *Constellation* from 1802 - 1806, with some action against the Tripoli pirates."

"And lately?"

"At Newport, Rhode Island, with some gunboats."

"Aren't you from that part of the country?"

"Yes, Sir, Newport."

"Don't you have another brother in the Navy?"

"Yes, Sir, Matthew. He's nineteen now. When he was fifteen, he enlisted as a midshipman with me on the *Revenge*. The last two years he has been on the *President* with Commodore John Rodgers."

"Well, I can see you come from a nautical family. And you decided to leave the deep blue water for the lakes?"

"Yes, Sir, I thought there would be more action on the lakes, so I volunteered to come out here."

"And we're mighty glad you did. I dare say you'll see some action here, all right, especially if the British catch you trying to ride those camels across the sand."

"Oh, you're right about that. I hope we can get across before they come around. We even had to take all the guns off the brigs to make them lighter."

"Zounds! You are in a precarious position. For our sake as well as yours, I hope you make it."

"Yes, Sir, we'll make it, General. But I should mention one other problem."

"What's that?"

"Men. We're short of men."

"What kind of men?"

"We need ordinary seamen, and we need marines."

"What do you need marines for?" asked Harrison.

"To take the enemy's decks under musket fire when we come into close quarters—to keep officers and men away from their stations."

Harrison thought for awhile, reflecting on this. Then he sat up straight and said, "Commodore, our Kentucky riflemen can shoot the eyes out of any Marine musketeer."

"Hmm, maybe they could. Could you let me have some?"

"How many do you need?"

"Oh, a hundred or a hundred and fifty."

"All right, I'll tell you what I'll do. I'll give you a hundred Kentucky riflemen when you are ready to sail."

"Excellent! I'll be back when we are underway, within a week or two."

"Good! I'll be looking for you."

About midday on August 16, sentinels announced the approach of a fleet in Sandusky Bay. Harrison rode up to the shore for a look. He counted nine vessels—two brigs, larger than any of the others, a smaller brig, five schooners, and one sloop—all flying the American flag. He knew that this had to be Perry.

A few hours later, Perry came ashore.

"Well, Commodore, I see your camels made it!" Harrison shouted.

When he came closer, Perry explained, "But General it was a hell of a job. On the first try the *Lawrence* got stuck on the bar, and we had to try a second time. We had to work all night. We finally passed the bar at eight o'clock on the morning of the 5th, and just then the enemy came up."

"How did you escape him?"

"Our schooners, already outside, took them under fire. They exchanged a few shots and then retired, though I'm not sure why."

"Any more trouble?"

"No. Fortunately, they let us alone after that, and then the *Niagara* crossed without any trouble, and here we are, at full strength!"

"That is great," Harrison responded enthusiastically.

"General, we have several chores to do in getting our ships ready and especially the crews familiar with their duties, but how about coming aboard on Thursday. You can have supper with me, and we can talk about our plans."

"Oh, thank you, Commodore, I'll look forward to that, and it is essential that we coordinate plans. Meanwhile, I'll send up those Kentucky riflemen that I promised."

"Very good. I'll give you a signal by firing guns when I arrive at the bay."

On the morning of Wednesday, the 18th, Harrison, at Camp Seneca, heard Perry's signal guns as the commodore arrived at the point of the peninsula off Sandusky Bay. Harrison sent Colonel E. P. Gaines, with a small party of officers and a guard of Indians, to respond. They took a small boat out to the *Lawrence* and reported to Perry. Immediately Perry sent small boats to bring Harrison and his party.

Late the next evening, during a heavy rain, Harrison, together with McArthur and Cass and the members of his personal staff and twenty-six friendly Indian chiefs, went out to Perry's flagship and climbed aboard. Perry met Harrison on deck and showed him around the ship. Harrison noticed the special flag with the dying words of Captain Lawrence, "Don't Give Up the Ship."

Harrison remarked, "I have heard about Lawrence and the *Chesapeake*. In naming your ship and flying that flag, you pay a fine tribute to the memory of a gallant officer."

"Thank you, Sir," Perry said softly.

"And I suspect," Harrison went on, "you will be promoting a great tradition for the Navy."

Harrison admired the workmanship that had gone into the building of the ship. He examined with satisfaction her twenty guns—eighteen short 32-pounder carronades, capable of firing 32-pound projectiles, but at short range, and two long 12-pounders. He also was impressed by the high morale of the crew. He exchanged banter with some of the Kentucky riflemen who had just joined the ship's company the day before.

"This isn't too much different from an Ohio River flatboat, is it?" he asked.

"No, Sir," one of the men quickly came back, "just give us some five-hundred foot poles, and we'll push her right down the British throats!"

"Good. But most of all I want you to show these Navy boys how to shoot a rifle."

"Oh, we'll do that all right, 'cept we ain't seen many squirrels out here, and we got nothin' to shoot at 'cept seagulls."

After they had finished their tour of the ship, Harrison joined Perry in the Commodore's cabin. Over a supper of fried lake trout, fried potatoes, and white leavened bread they went into their informal planning conference.

"How soon will you be ready to move?" Perry asked.

"Major forces are now on the way from Kentucky. They probably cannot be here before another four weeks. Then we'll be ready to go."

"We may have to wait that long for the British to venture out from Malden," Perry said. "When they do, we'll be ready for them."

"What if they don't venture out?"

"Don't worry, they will. Just our presence here is going to interrupt their supply line on the lake. Sooner or later, and I think sooner, when they start running short of supplies, they'll have to come out to try to secure their supply lines."

"I'm sure you're right about that," agreed Harrison.

"What's your objective when you move?" inquired Perry.

"Malden and Amherstburg and Detroit, first of all," Harrison replied. "And in the process I hope we can eliminate the British and Indian army."

"Good! How do you propose to get there?"

"The traditional way has been to march around the end of the lake and on up to Detroit, then cross the Detroit River and come back down on the Canadian side against Amherstburg and Malden."

"Yes, I suppose so. Is that your preferred way?"

"Not necessarily. I'm thinking that if we had the boats we might go across the lake, straight to Amherstburg. That would be the way to do it, if we had the boats."

"And if there was no British fleet to interfere."

"Yes, of course, if there were no British fleet. What do you think? Could you get us across?"

"If we can eliminate the British fleet, we'll get you across."

"Great!"

"How many troops will you have?"

"About six thousand, I hope."

"Whew! It may take several trips."

"Well, the War Department has authorized a fleet of Schenectady boats to be built at Cleveland. If we can get enough of those, we should be able to make it."

"Yes. Let's get all the Schenectady boats we can find, and with those and the vessels of our fleet—"

"And those you capture from the British."

"And those we capture from the British, we ought to be able to do it. How many horses?"

"We'll have about 1,500 mounted troops, but my plan is to send them overland anyway. I'll send them overland to capture Detroit and then cross the river to meet us on the other side, while the main body of infantry crosses the lake to take Malden and Amherstburg."

"That sounds good to me."

"One more thing."

"What's that?"

"We'll need some craft of some kind to carry supplies across."

"Right. Anything else?"

"I was thinking it would be a good idea for us to establish a joint headquarters in the vicinity."

"Excellent. I suggest Put-in-Bay, out there in the Bass Islands. There I can keep a watch on Barclay."

"Barclay?"

"Yes, he's commander of the British naval force now at Amherstburg. Captain Robert Barclay. He lost an arm at Trafalgar, but he's still supposed to be a good sailor."

"Good. I'll have to spend a good deal of my time back at Seneca while our troops rendezvous, but, as soon as I can, I'll be out there."

"Good. Just be patient now for a few days, and I think we can catch our prize."

"Let me know of any developments."

While he awaited further word from Perry and the fate of the fleet against the British on Lake Erie, Harrison lost no time in preparing his army to advance. He received a message from Governor Shelby that 3,500 Kentuckians were swarming across the Ohio River. "Not a moment will be lost until I join you," wrote the Governor. He also reported that Colonel Richard Johnson, taking leave from Congress for this expedition, was on his way from Kentucky with one thousand horsemen. He would follow the route of the Auglaize to Fort Meigs.

Later reports, from observers in Ohio, indicated that Governor Shelby and his troops were being received as heroes in every town they passed. It had turned into a triumphal procession all the way. This gave Harrison a special thrill. When he had sent his invitation to Shelby to come in person with the troops,

Harrison held no real expectation that he would do so. But now he was on the way. There was probably no man in the country whom Harrison admired more than this old soldier-Governor. Here, at age sixty-three he was entering upon a campaign with all the fervor and enthusiasm of youth, but also with the wisdom and knowledge of long experience.

Harrison smiled to himself as he recalled how critical he had been of the earlier appointment of old veterans—the "silver-haired corps"—to positions of high command, men such as Hull, Winchester, Dearborn, and Wilkinson. Now, here he had urged another "old-timer" to join him. What was the difference? It was not their years, Harrison thought, but what they had done with those years, and what kind of attitude they had maintained. Look at the difference between Shelby and the others!

In addition, there were the Ohio and some Pennsylvania militiamen and a detachment of regulars of the 27th Regiment under Colonel George Paul, plus the troops already in garrison in the forts near the lake.

Harrison asked his commisary, Col. Benjamin G. Orr, to contract for 300,000 rations for delivery in Canada. He arranged for several hundred head of cattle to be started toward Detroit by way of Fort Meigs. He ordered his chief engineer, Major Wood, to move heavy ordnance to the Portage Peninsula to prepare for shipment across the lake. By September 8, he reported to Secretary of War Armstrong, "I am now in complete readiness to embark the troops the moment Gov. Shelby arrives." He also might have added, "And the moment Commodore Perry arrives with the watercraft."

Another source of reinforcement that Harrison welcomed, though they brought certain additional problems, were detachments of friendly Indians. He always had counted upon these to some extent, and he thought it especially important now to welcome Indians, whenever possible in order to weaken Tecumseh's dangerous coalition. Harrison knew that many tribesmen simply bent with the fortunes of war like a sapling in a high wind, bending in whatever direction the blow might be at the moment, even some, like Winamac, who had been most steadfast in earlier days, turned out to be opportunists. Walk-in-the-Water was at first on one side and then the other, but then there had been those, like Johnny Logan, who had remained faithful to the end and had died in his service.

Taking advantage of Indian defections after their failures

against Fort Meigs and Fort Stephenson, Harrison met with about two hundred Shawnees, Delawares, and Wyandots from Tarhe's town to try to elicit their support. They agreed to help him against his enemies. They were persuaded that, in the long run, the Americans could do more for them than the British could.

A little later, Harrison sent a message, by a party of friendly Wyandots and Senecas, to the Wyandots of Walk-in-the-Water at Brownstown, to urge them to make peace and to help the Americans.

At the same time, Tecumseh was working hard to stop the defections and hold on to his supporters. He, The Prophet, Roundhead, and Matthew Elliott all were at Brownstown when Harrison's message arrived for Walk-in-the-Water's Wyandots. The emissaries read their message before the whole assembled council. On behalf of the Long Knife chief, Harrison, they explained that the Americans now had a strong fleet on the lake that their supposed British friends were afraid to challenge. "Tecumseh and Procter have failed to capture any of the forts of the Long Knives on the other side of the lake," their chief spokesman said. "Soon the Long Knives will come here, and they will come to our villages across the river. Take pity on the women and children. Step forward and take the White Chief Harrison by the hand."

Immediately, Roundhead stepped forward to protest against this talk. "We are happy to learn that your Father, the coward Harrison, is coming out of his hole where he has been hiding like a groundhog. This will save us much trouble in going to meet him. Take the good advice of Tecumseh. If you will not help your Red brothers, stay at home and take no part in this war."

Matthew Elliott handed to the visitors copies of dispatches that reported British victories on Lake Champlain. He asked that these be delivered to Harrison with Elliott's compliments.

Satisfied that the council had shown a firm rejection of Harrison's proposals, Tecumseh and his party departed.

A few days later the emissaries returned to Harrison with a secret message from Walk-in-the-Water. The Wyandot chief at Brownstown had indicated that if the Americans invaded Canada his Wyandots would desert Tecumseh and come to the assistance of the Long Knives.

One matter especially worried Harrison now. A number of farmers in Ohio had been suffering losses of livestock, and their usual reaction was to blame such losses on Indians and then take revenge on the next Indians who happened by. Harrison knew that some of these losses might indeed be attributable to Indians. He also knew that some of the losses might be the result of unauthorized activities of some of the thousands of militiamen who were moving through the country, or even of unscrupulous government contractors who were trying to meet their quotas with the least possible effort and expense. And there always was the likelihood that some of the cattle and horses had simply strayed away. In any case, Harrison was worried that reprisals against unsuspecting Indians would turn friends and supporters into enemies and antagonists.

Harrison wanted to leave it up to the trusted chiefs to handle any complaints against their tribesmen. Especially concerned about the situation around Piqua where local settlers were accusing friendly Delawares of forays against their livestock, he wrote a long letter to Governor Meigs in which he said, "To attempt indiscriminately to murder these people, would inflict a blot upon the national honour that would never be effaced. Moreover, such an action would compromise the friendly attitude of that nation."

In early September, in northeastern Ohio, a band of Delawares who had remained loyal to the Americans were marching up to give their assistance to General Harrison. Before they reached Fort McArthur, a young Shawnee joined them. He went by the name of "Blue Jacket" because Blue Jacket the war chief had been his idol. He was determined to follow in the ways of the elder Blue Jacket and come to the aid of the great Tecumseh. The young Shawnee, gaining the confidence of one of the young Delawares whom he had befriended, confided in him and told his plan. Young Blue Jacket explained to his friend that he proposed to pose as a friendly Delaware to gain access to the White Chief Harrison, and then he would use his tomahawk to kill the leader of the Long Knives.

That night as they sat about the fire near Seneca, the young Delaware came up and challenged young Blue Jacket. "You will kill the White Chief Harrison?" he asked.

"I assure you," answered the young Shawnee, "how better to serve our people? I will kill him even if there is no escape for me. My reward will be with the Great Spirit."

"You will not kill our White Father!" the Delaware cried. And before there could be any other response, he plunged his own tomahawk into the skull of the young Blue Jacket.

The young Delaware was Beaver, the same one whom Harrison had taken to look after for a time following the execution of the boy's father. Beaver had rejoined his people several years ago, but he never had forgotten his White Father.

Another devoted protector of Harrison was a Shawnee war chief known as "Captain Tommy." He had been a big help in the battles at Fort Meigs, and when he asked permission thereafter to sleep at the door of the General's marquee every night, Harrison in a great demonstration of trust, readily agreed, and now everyone appreciated the arrangement.

When an American fleet appeared off the point at the mouth of the Detroit River, Tecumseh and a number of his followers launched their canoes and paddled out to Bois Blanc Island for a closer look. In awe, and even admiration, he looked out upon the ships. Never had he seen canoes so big or sails so high or so many big guns in one place. Then he looked back to the harbor of Amherstburg, where he could see the British ships. He knew that one of them, called *Detroit*, was the biggest of all, though he saw no sails unfurled. Often he had heard of the British mastery of the seas. Now he waited in anticipation, and with a certain excitement, for the British ships to come out and meet the American challenge. He waited all day. Nothing happened.

Disappointed and frustrated, Tecumseh paddled furiously back to Amherstburg and went straight to Procter. The Shawnee War Chief spoke sharply, "A few days ago you were boasting that you commanded the waters. Why do you not go out and meet the Americans? See, yonder they are waiting for you and daring for you to go out and meet them. Why do you wait?"

With something of a patronizing attitude, Procter replied, "I'm afraid you do not understand these things. We are not quite ready. The big ship *Detroit* is all finished, but has not yet received her guns. When all the guns are in place in a few days, our ships will go out and destroy the American fleet."

"Why were the Americans able to get their ships ready more quickly?"

"They had more men to work on then, but soon we shall destroy them."

Tecumseh felt all his frustrations of past weeks swelling up within him. "Why do you not attack the Long Knives in their forts? Why do you do nothing while they get ready to attack us?"

Procter said nothing.

Tecumseh went on, "Why do you treat your Red children like little papooses? Why do my Red Men get only horsemeat to eat, while your English have salt beef?"

Procter still seemed indifferent, until suddenly Tecumseh stopped short. He struck the General's sword with his open hand and stepping back, touched his own tomahawk and said, "You are Procter; I am Tecumseh."

Startled, the British commander promised equal treatment for the Indians from then on.

Whatever their wishes, Procter and Barclay were sure that the British fleet would have to go out to meet the Americans very soon, if for no other reason than to do something to alleviate the supply shortages. Tecumseh had been so successful in attracting Indians that now, Procter estimated with considerable exaggeration, fourteen thousand warriors, women, and children were encamped in villages around Amherstburg and depending upon the British for food. Barclay reported, "So perfectly destitute of provisions was the port that there was not a day's flour in store, and the crews of the squadron under my command were on half allowances of many things, and when this was done, there was no more."

Barclay and Procter were agreed that they had no choice but to adopt an attitude, "Here we come, ready or not."

On September 9, with the *Detroit*, roughly finished and fitted with a great variety of guns, including some from the batteries of Fort Malden, the British fleet sallied forth.

The next day Tecumseh and many of his warriors went up to the Point Pelee region to have a look. Shortly before noon they could hear a furious cannonading, and clouds of black gun smoke drifted northward across the lake. This continued for about three hours, but they had no idea of the result.

On the southern shore, the Americans could only guess that they were hearing the roar of distant guns rather than the thunder of a distant electrical storm. They could see nothing more than a haze in the distance. Harrison rode nervously up and down the shore on his horse. Then he retired back to his headquarters at Fort Seneca to await word. Two days later, it came.

Sentinels at Lower Sandusky saw a boat, with oarsmen rowing at a fast pace, coming up the river. Lieutenant Dulaney Forrest leaped from the boat and ran up to the fort shouting, "We've won! We've smashed the British fleet!"

At Fort Stephenson, "Good Bess," the iron six-pounder, went into action in firing a salute while the lieutenant jumped on a horse and raced up to Fort Seneca to find General Harrison. He rushed into the headquarters and handed the General a dirty piece of paper. Harrison took it. On the back of an old letter was a message scribbled in pencil:

Dear General: We have met the enemy and they are ours—two ships, two brigs, one schooner, and a sloop.

Yours with great respect and esteem,

Oliver Hazard Perry

CHAPTER XXIII

The End of the Trail

1

Tecumseh was kept waiting for several days for news of the outcome of the naval battle on Lake Erie, though by September 12, two days after the battle, he was suspecting the worst. Some of his warriors reported that Procter was going around in a sour mood and was ordering his aides to begin packing things in trunks and barrels and crates.

Tecumseh went to Procter for an explanation. What had happened to the fleet? Why had the ships not returned to the harbor after their great battle on the lake? The British commander put him off with an explanation that the British ships had been victorious, but they had suffered great damage and had to go to Put-in-Bay for repairs before they would be able to return.

The Chief was not satisfied. He was becoming fearful that Procter was preparing to leave without standing here to make a fight. He voiced his concerns to the Indian Agent, Matthew Elliott, whom he thought he could trust. Elliott gave vague explanations but could give no assurance that Procter would make a stand. Finally on the 17th, Elliott told Tecumseh that they were to arrange a council of all the chiefs and principal warriors for the next day, when the General would explain his plans.

They assembled in the great council chamber at Amherstburg. General Procter strode into the crowded room with no decline in his usual pompous manner. Tecumseh, no longer wearing the red coat or insignia of major general that the venerated General Brock had given him, stood near one end of the room with the other chiefs around him. He wore his neat deerskin suit. A single ostrich plume rose from the back of his head, and in his hands he held a big black wampum belt.

As Procter began to speak, the Indians became silent, but, with each sentence, their restlessness became more audible.

"My Red Children," he said, "the Long Knives brought many guns in their war canoes on the lake. Our ships have been damaged very much. It will be many moons before they can sail again to protect us here and to protect the food that comes for us on the lake."

"Now the Long Knife Chief Harrison has brought a very large army to the south shore of the lake, and he is preparing to invade Canada at any moment.

"The Long Knife Chief Harrison has many more warriors than we do. This is not a good place to defend. If we stay here, he will get behind us and cut off all our food and our means of escape. We cannot let that happen.

"Therefore I propose to move our forces eastward to the far end of the lake. There, near the Great Falls, are many British warriors and much food. We can join them and be strong again. There together we can defeat all the armies of the Long Knives.

"I invite all my Red Children to go with me. Bring your women and children to the Niagara. There we will give you plenty of food and gunpowder. There we will be successful."

Shouts of of "No! No!" greeted Procter's remarks.

Tecumseh stepped forward. He looked all around the room, holding his wampum belt high. Then, looking Procter directly in the eyes and speaking in firm, measured words, the Shawnee war chief spoke. The Indians fell silent. With each sentence their approval became more audible:

"In the name of the Indian chiefs and warriors, to major-general Procter, as the representative of their great Father, the King.

"Father, listen to your children! You have them now all before you. The war before this, our British father gave the hatchet to his Red Children, when our chiefs were alive. They are now dead. In that war, our Father was thrown on his back by the Americans, and our Father took them by the hand without our knowledge; and we are afraid that our Father will do so again at this time.

"Summer before last, when I came forward with my Red brethren, and was ready to take the hatchet in favor of our British Father, we were told not to be in a hurry, that he had not yet determined to fight the Americans.

"Listen! When war was declared, our Father stood up and gave us the tomahawk, and told us that he was then ready to strike the Americans; that he wanted our assistance, and that he would certainly get us our lands back, which the Americans had taken from us.

"Listen! You told us, at that time, to bring forward our families to this place, and we did so; and you promised to take care of them, and that they should want for nothing, while the men would go and fight the enemy, that we need not trouble ourselves about the enemy's garrison; that we knew nothing about them, and that our Father would attend to that part of the business. You also told your Red Children that you would take care of your garrison here, which made our hearts glad.

"Listen! When we were last to the Rapids, it is true we gave you little assistance. It is hard to fight people who live like groundhogs.

"Father, listen! Our fleet has gone out; we know they have fought; we have heard the great guns; but know nothing of what has happened to our father with one arm. Our ships have gone one way, and we are much astonished to see our Father tying up everything and preparing to run the other way, without letting his Red Children know what his intentions are. You always told us to remain here and take care of our lands; it made our hearts glad to hear that was your wish. Our great Father, the King, is our head, and you represent him. You always told us that you would never draw your foot off British ground; but now, Father we see you are drawing back, and we are sorry to see our Father doing so without seeing the enemy. We must compare our Father's conduct to a fat animal, that caries its tail upon its back, but when affrighted, drops it between his legs and runs off.

"Listen Father! The Americans have not yet defeated us by land; neither are we sure that they have done so by water. We, therefore, wish to remain here and fight our enemy if they should make their appearance. If they defeat us, we will then retreat with our Father.

"At the battle of the Rapids, last war, the Americans certainly defeated us; and when we retreated to our Father's fort at that place, the gates were shut against us. We were afraid that it would now be the case; but instead of that, we now see our British Father preparing to march out of his garrison.

"Father! You have got the arms and ammunition which our great Father sent for his Red Children. If you have an idea of going away, give them to us, and you may go. Our lives are in the hands of the Great Spirit. We are determined to defend our lands, and if it be his will we wish to leave our bones upon them."

Frenzied shouts of approval greeted the conclusion of Tecumseh's remarks. With loud war whoops, the warriors broke into impromptu war dances and brandished their weapons at the British. The vaulted ceiling echoed the cries in reverberation through the room.

Procter stood in a shocked stupor for several seconds, while Elliott intervened to restore order. Procter asked Tecumseh to meet again in three days to consider the matter further. To this, Tecumseh agreed.

The next three days were filled with private negotiations in which Elliott served as intermediary. Tecumseh told him to make it clear that if the British refused to make a stand all the Indians would cross over to Michigan and leave the British to deal with the Americans alone.

On the third day, September 21, Procter met privately with Tecumseh. The British commander spread maps out on the table and explained the vulnerability of their position. At least they must move back far enough to be out of range of the guns of the American fleet, and they must get back to a place where the Americans would not be able to surround them or cut off all their supplies. Such a place, said Procter, might be at Chatham on the Thames River. That was supposed to be beyond the head of navigation for the American ships, and the river and its tributaries would provide good barriers for defense. If the Indians would continue their assistance, Procter would offer this compromise instead of evacuating the whole area to Lake Ontario.

Tecumseh preferred to fight where they were. He disliked the idea of going farther and farther away from the homelands he was most interested in protecting, but he appreciated the vulnerability of their position, and he recognized that a successful stand at Chatham could result in a defeat of the Long Knives and in an opportunity to drive them back beyond the lakes. He agreed to take up the proposal with the other chiefs. After some discussion the others accepted Tecumseh's recommendation, and they prepared to move their families with them to escape the danger.

Tecumseh was aware that any retrograde movement is likely to stimulate fear, that withdrawal from danger often magnifies the danger in the minds of potential victims. He foresaw two major problems in preparing his people to move away. One was to prevent defections on the part of nervous warriors who saw withdrawal as a sign of defeat that ultimately might lead to disaster. The other was to prevent panic among women and children. Unchecked, panic could spread throughout the tribes, leaving the women incapable of doing their duties in preparing sustenance for their families and immobilizing warriors, and thus assuring the destruction that they feared.

Deliberately, without undue haste and with no sign of panic, Procter went about his preparations, though Tecumseh and the other Indians marveled at how the British commander requisitioned a dozen wagons and innumerable containers for his personal baggage.

For the last three days, Procter already had been sending supplies and baggage up to Sandwich on the Detroit River opposite Detroit. Indians and British soldiers moved up to that place between September 21 and 23. On the 22nd, the British commander burned the shipyards at Amherstburg to render them useless to the enemy, and the next day he burned Fort Malden and other private buildings. He then went to Sandwich to prepare for his next move.

2

Meanwhile on the south shore of Lake Erie, Harrison was concentrating his forces and preparing to invade Canada.

The very next day after receiving Perry's message of the naval victory on Lake Erie, Harrison moved up with a part of the troops from Fort Seneca to the mouth of the Portage River. There he established his headquarters on the lake, across the Portage Peninsula to the northwest, from Sandusky Bay. Major E. J. Wood already had arrived at that place with two companies and had sent a detachment of fifty men to handle the prisoners that Perry brought in. As Perry entered the harbor aboard his 112-ton schooner *Ariel*, tumultous shouting from the soldiers and the booming of cannon greeted him. As the Commodore landed, Harrison went up to greet him with hearty congratulations.

"And let me thank you, Sir, for those men, those Kentucky riflemen, you sent me," said Perry. "They behaved in a way as becomes good soldiers and good seamen. In fact, I would say that without their services we could not have achieved the victory."

Harrison smiled and said, "I'm glad to hear that. Now we are about ready to go after a bigger victory."

The next day, just as Perry was landing three hundred British prisoners, General Shelby arrived amidst great fanfare with his 3,500 Kentuckians. Here was what Harrison had been waiting for. Here was a force equal to the task. He greeted the Governor with all the enthusiasm that had been pent up in anticipation. As for Shelby, the long march had taken nothing either from his agility or his enthusiasm, and he greeted Harrison as a long-lost son, without any loss of respect or deference for him as the Commander-in-Chief.

Harrison noticed a big sow that was following the Governor's aides.

"Where did you get that porker?" he asked with a smile. "From some Ohio farmer who thinks he's been raided by Indians?"

"No, Sir, that sow has followed us all the way from Kentucky. She was some stray that just fell in with us as we marched toward the Ohio River. I decided I would bring her along as pork on the hoof for the General's table, but she has so endeared herself to everyone that no one can bear to shoot her. She has become the mascot of the whole army. The boys call her the 'Governor's pig.'"

"Well, I guess we'll have to try to find an extra boat for her," Harrison laughed.

"Either that or leave two or three of my loafers behind to make room for her," said Shelby.

The next day, the 15th, General Lewis Cass arrived with the remaining 800 regulars from Fort Seneca. Nearly two hundred friendly Indians—the Delawares, Wyandots, and Shawnees that Beaver accompanied—turned up. On the 16th, Colonel Johnson arrived with his one thousand mounted Kentuckians at Fort Meigs, where he would rest his horses and men, while awaiting further orders.

Harrison felt a certain exultation, a sense of fulfillment in seeing his command come together for what he hoped would be a decisive blow against the enemies of his country. It seemed that his whole life had been a preparation for this moment. No course he had ever taken, no book he had ever read, no experience he had ever had seemed irrelevant to the task before him.

Harrison was anxious to move for Canada as quickly as possible. His plan was to go by stages, first to Put-in-Bay on South Bass Island, then to the middle island of the Three Sisters, and thence to the Canadian shore near Amherstburg. Already he was embarking stores and artillery. He sent an urgent message to Brig. Gen. Duncan McArthur commanding the brigade of regulars at Fort Meigs, "Hurry on then, my friend, as soon as possible. If you do not come on immediately, I must leave you. Come on for God's sake as soon as possible."

McArthur left Fort Meigs on the 17th, the day after Johnson's arrival, for the three-day march through the tall prairie grass to the Portage area.

At the embarkation point, Major Wood led the way with six cannon mounted in six Mackinaw trading boats—heavy, flat-bottom row boats with pointed bow and square stern.

Harrison decided that it would not be practical to take the horses of Shelby's mounted troops; therefore, he had the Kentuckians leave one man in twenty as guard for the horses. They set to building a fence of timber and brush across a mile-and-a-half neck of the peninsula, so that the horses could be put out to pasture.

As the troops were embarking, a detachment of Pennsylvania militia, except for a hardy hundred, standing on their supposed legal grounds that militia could not be sent out of the country, refused to go. Harrison cried out to them, "Thank God I have enough Kentuckians to go on without you." He assigned them the duty of looking after the three hundred British prisoners.

For the others there was an air of excitement in embarking upon a great adventure. The whole area around Portage Bay, the mouth of the Portage River, was alive with activity. The relatively few regulars stood out in their uniforms of dark blue coats—cut at the waist in front, and to forked tails over the hips in back—light blue pantaloons, and black shakoes, or in some cases, the bigger "tar-bucket" caps. Some units of Ohio and Pennsylvania militia had uniforms cut similarly to those of the regulars, but gray in color. Some of the Kentucky militia officers wore uniforms similar to those of the regulars, but most of the Kentucky militiamen were wearing faded brown hunting shirts and pantaloons of linen or cotton, and soft slouch hats. Most wore a canteen, usually a small wooden drum filled with water from Lake Erie or adjacent streams, or corn whiskey from Kentucky or Pennsylvania, or spruce beer from Pennsylvania or Ohio, swung by a strap over one shoulder and a powder horn over the other. They carried knives and tomahawks in their belts, and most carried a light knapsack on their backs and had a blanket roll looped over one shoulder and tied at the opposite hip. The regulars still were carrying the standard U.S. musket, imposed upon them by unimaginative and inflexible bureau chiefs in Washington, while most of the militiamen clung to their trusty Kentucky rifles. Except for firearms and accoutrements, the dozens of civilian workers in the area, who were loading supplies, looked little different from the militiamen.

A loud cheer went up as the Governor's pig went on board one of the sailing vessels. Proudly, she wore on her head a shako, tied in place by one of the Kentuckians who had requisitioned it from a sleeping Pennsylvanian.

It took three trips for Perry's six available ships and scores of sail boats, Mackinaw boats, and Schenectady boats to transfer the nearly five thousand men to the island.

As they approached Put-in-Bay, officers and men of the ground troops were awed by the appearance of Perry's stricken flagship, *Lawrence* and the captured enemy ships that rode at anchor there. Hardly a foot of the *Lawrence* was unscathed; it looked beyond repair. The *Detroit*, largest of the British fleet, was only a naked hulk with not a spar left standing. The *Queen Charlotte* was heavily damaged but still usable. In fact, the British Commodore Barclay was still on board as a prisoner.

Harrison went on board to pay his respects to the British commander. He found that Barclay had suffered a painful wound to his remaining good arm. Harrison was pleased to learn from him that Perry had treated him with the utmost respect and consideration.

The troops, overrunning the whole island, enjoyed something of a holiday. Free from arduous cross-country marching or garrison drilling, and secure from the threat of enemy attack, they combed the island for wild berries and vegetables, explored caves for cool water, and made the acquaintance of soldiers and sailors from different parts of the country. Many of them, including some of the Indians, took delight in an opportunity to visit on board the *Queen Charlotte*.

A sour note came amidst these festivities in a court martial of a deserter. Harrison disliked death penalties and harsh treatment, but he found that the man was a three-time deserter, and mindful of the necessity of maintaining strict discipline as they approached the enemy, Harrison approved the verdict of the court, death by a firing squad, and he let the sentence be known throughout the camps.

Harrison went ahead with plans for the next stage of the move to Middle Sister Island. He sent orders to Colonel Johnson to proceed with his horsemen around the end of the lake to Detroit, and he ordered the commissary to follow Johnson with his herd of beef on the hoof.

Then a siege of hard rains and high winds set in—the "equinox storms," some of the old-timers explained. After several days' delay, the army was able to re-embark on the 25th, but this time the Governor's pig balked. She refused to board a vessel of any kind. "You see, she's a militia hog," Shelby explained. "She got too close to those damned Pennsylvanians, and now she is standing on her right not to be sent across the international line."

"Probably afraid she'll be made into Canadian bacon," Harrison mused.

All day long Perry's ships and the boats shuttled back and forth between Put-in-Bay and Middle Sister Island.

The next day, Harrison and his staff went with Perry in the *Ariel* for a reconnaissance of the Canadian shore to choose the best beach for a tactical landing. They could see the smouldering ruins of the navy facilities and storehouses at Malden, but saw no signs of enemy activity, yet Harrison was apprehensive lest Tecumseh and his Indians would be lying in wait. For the landing, Harrison and Perry agreed upon a broad extent of sandy beach around Point Hartly, about three miles below Amherstburg. They agreed that the landing should be made in full combat formation.

That done, they found a secluded spot on the American shore where Harrison put his faithful Shawnee guard, Captain Johnny, ashore with instructions to meet Colonel Johnson and guide him into Detroit. Johnson's troopers at that point were just approaching the River Raisin where they were startled to see the bleaching bones of fellow Kentuckians, victims of the massacre of the last year, now dug up by the Indians.

Harrison took advantage of the return trip to Middle Sister to prepare his orders for the next day's assault, but enroute another storm struck. They landed in heavy surf, and for a time they feared that high waves and heavy rain would engulf much of the island. The storm finally blew itself out about midnight, and September 27 dawned clear and cool. Harrison sent out word to all units to prepare to embark according to plan.

When all were ready, Harrison read out a proclamation to the troops: "The General entreats his brave troops to remember that they are the sons of sires whose fame is immortal; they are to fight for the rights of their insulted country, whilst their opponents combat for the unjust pretensions of a master. Kentuckians! Remember the River Raisin! But remember it only whilst the victory is suspended. The revenge of a soldier cannot be gratified upon a fallen enemy."

He looked over the assembled soldiers, catching as many eyes as he could. Then he raised his hat and shouted, "The goose honks high! Let's go!"

With excited shouts the troops scrambled into their assigned boats. Harrison and his staff went on board the *Ariel* with Perry. At nine o'clock Perry's fleet, now restored to nine ships, got underway escorting eighty boats filled with soldiers and including the six boats with Major Wood's artillery. Two thousand men in those boats would constitute the first assault wave. Another thousand, in the ships, would follow. The craft then would return to bring up the others as reinforcements. The landing beach was twelve miles away.

As they approached the mouth of the Detroit River, the boats formed a long column, in single file. They rounded the point just half a mile off to the right. Then each boat turned a hard right. This put them in a long line, all abreast, heading for the beach 800 yards away. Perry had his ships spread out and followed to provide protection. Gunners were standing by to open fire at any sign of hostile action.

Even Harrison and Perry, standing on the quarterdeck of the *Ariel*, looked out on the scene with a sense of excitement. Nobody here ever had seen anything like it. Harrison recalled accounts of Glover's and Hutchinson's amphibian regiments in the Revolution, but they had been used to ferry troops across rivers, not to storm hostile seashores. Harrison was also sure that cooperation between Army and Navy never had been closer.

"Ever see anything like this before, Hazard?" Harrison asked his companion.

"No, Sir, never have," Perry responded. "Even on the Barbary Coast we never tried such a thing."

"Well, Commodore, we may be opening up a new mode of warfare."

"That could be."

Reflecting on his historical reading, Harrison said, "Of course there are many examples of landings on hostile shores, dating at least from the Persians at Marathon, though I'm not sure they actually landed in battle formation."

"What about Hastings?"

"No, as in most cases, the army landed at a remote place and then moved up to fight an orthodox land battle."

"What about Quebec, when the English took it from the French?"

"That comes close to what we are talking about in a way, in the sense of close naval support, but again the battle was fought on the Plains of Abraham, not on the seashore or riverbank."

"Or Louisbourg?"

"Yes, that comes closer. At least Pepperrell's landing at Fresh-Water Cove in 1745, or whenever it was, and I guess even more of the sort of thing we're talking about was Amherst's landing there in 1758. I must admit, that was a great sea-land operation."

"No doubt about that."

"But I guess we might say that this is the first operation of this kind by the American Army and Navy."

"Ha, quite so, quite so"

"And look where we're heading! For *Amherstburg*! I wonder what the old boy would think about that."

Turning away, his hand shielding his eyes from the sun as he looked upward, Perry pointed overhead and said, "Look, see that eagle?"

"Ah, yes, I do."

"I'll tell you, General, that bird, or one just like him, soared overhead as though escorting me out when I met the British fleet. What was it, let's see, sixteen days ago. God, it seems a year now. Anyway, that eagle was right up there."

"And let me tell you something. On May 5—I guess that seems like two or three years ago now—when I was penned up in Fort Meigs, Green Clay had just arrived with his Kentuckians and we planned a foray out of the fort to meet his troops. Just before they went out, I looked up and saw that same eagle, or one just like it. We were successful, and four days later the British raised the siege."

"Hmm, interesting, very interesting."

"Yes, Sir, the good old American eagle. I tell you, Commodore, that is a good omen. It is an omen of victory."

They returned their attention to the boats now readying to make their run for the shore. By now it was midafternoon. Carefully the boats held their formation. Wood's artillerymen held lighted matches, ready to touch off their artillery at an instant's notice. Fifers and drummers in the boats and on the ships struck up "Yankee Doodle." Within just two or three minutes of each other, the boats all hit the sand. The men quickly leaped out and ran across the beach. Without opposition, they worked their way up the wooded embankment beyond and stopped to await orders.

The landing had gone unopposed, but not unobserved. Tecumseh and Matthew Elliott were watching from horseback from above Amherstburg. At sundown they went back up to Sandwich where the movement of the British and Indians had begun again.

Harrison and his aides went ashore and made their way to a farmhouse near the beach. A frightened woman opened the door to his knock. After being reassured of her own safety, she told them that the last of the British troops had left only the day before.

Harrison sent scouts out to scour the woods for lurking Indians or British snipers, and then gave word to have the troops form up and march into town. Returning to close order, they marched, flags flying and fifes and drums playing "Yankee Doodle," by parallel routes into Amherstburg and then past the ruins of Fort Malden while additional troops and supplies continued to land.

While most of the Canadian loyalists had fled northward ahead of Procter's forces and the Indians, a few civilians remained in the area. Women were frightened, especially when they saw Harrison's band of Indians. The commander told the Indians that if they offered the least violence to any of the inhabitants he would hang the perpetrator to the first tree he could find. He took quick steps to stop looting by vowing to apply "the utmost rigor of martial law" against those guilty of it.

Anticipating the American landings around Amherstburg on the 27th, Procter that morning prepared to resume his withdrawal eastward from Sandwich. This caused further resentment among the Indians even though Tecumseh earlier had explained the necessity of withdrawing to the Thames River. But many of the warriors, hearing that the Americans were coming, took the British withdrawal as a sign of defeat. Main Poc refused to go any farther. He led many of the Potawatomis, Ottawas, Chippewas, and Sacs and Foxes in the opposite direction. They crossed into Michigan where they plundered American property with immunity while they bided their time. They would take no part in the coming battle. If the Americans won, Main Poc's followers would simply flee to Lake Michigan and plea no contest. But if Tecumseh should win, then they would be in a position to fall upon the retreating Long Knives and help annihilate them.

While the remaining Indians moved out with Procter, Tecumseh and Elliott, returning from their observation of the American landings, stopped overnight at Sandwich and then went on the next morning to catch up with Procter.

Harrison on that day, the 28th, leaving a regiment of regulars to guard Malden, set out toward Sandwich. Four miles north of Amherstburg, scouts saved a bridge over Duck Creek that a rear detachment was in the process of burning, but all the other main bridges had been destroyed. It took two days to cover the eighteen miles to Sandwich.

In a day made gray by cold drizzle, Harrison set up his headquarters in what everyone came to refer to as the "Baby House", the home of Colonel James Baby of the Canadian militia. His first action was to go to the rescue of Detroit. The British had evacuated the town two days earlier, but not before setting fire to nearly two hundred buildings, and Indians had taken over many deserted houses and threatened general pillage. After writing a proclamation to announce the restoration of American rule, Harrison sent General McArthur with his brigade of 700 regulars to cross the river by boat and reoccupy the town.

As McArthur's troops approached in the boats, the daughter of Judge John May, in the manner of Alice in old Vincennes at the approach of George Rogers Clark's troops in 1779, raced to their attic to get a flag that she had hidden there and hoisted it over the house. Wild cheers greeted this gesture, and cries and tears of joy greeted the American soldiers as they marched up the street.

This was only the prelude. About noon the next day, on the 30th, under clearing skies Colonel Johnson arrived with his thousand Kentucky horsemen. With scouts out in front and to flanks and rear, the column emerged from the woods and marched up the road in column of twos. The column extended back for two miles. It took forty-five minutes for it to pass a given point in the street while spectators cheered all the while. Local citizens were almost overcome as they looked first at Johnson's lively horses and then at McArthur's regulars lining the streets, then gazed down at Perry's fleet on the river, and then looked across at more thousands of troops going into camp around Sandwich.

Harrison urged Johnson to cross the river with all his force at once so that there would be no further delay in taking up the pursuit of Procter and Tecumseh.

While Johnson's horses and men were being ferried across the river, Harrison was thinking about the best way to catch up with Procter. One was simply to follow him overland, around the southern edge of Lake St. Clair and up the Thames. But as he studied a British government map that he had found, the thought occurred to him of embarking his force in boats and going back through Lake Erie all the way to a site on the northern shore called Port Talbot. From there, he thought, it would be possible to march quickly overland to the Thames far in advance of where Procter could possibly be. He called in Perry and Shelby to test the idea. Both threw cold water on it.

"Damn the boats, Henry," Shelby said. "You know those Kentuckians are not good sailors, and I doubt they could last the trip in open boats."

"The Kentuckians were pretty good sailors for you, weren't they, Hazard?" rejoined Harrison.

"Yes, General, I'll have to grant that. But I'm afraid there are serious objections. We must not get carried away by the success of our last venture. Weather is pretty uncertain on the lake at this time of year. Strong winds might swamp the boats, and at best, make them almost unendurable for the men. Light winds might delay our naval vessels and hold up the whole expedition until we have lost all the advantage we might have gained."

"Well, damn it, all right," Harrison answered. "Maybe I am enamored with the sea-land approach. We'll have a council of war tomorrow morning, and I'll support your view."

Governor Shelby with all of his ten militia general officers, including his principal aide as well as his quartermaster general, met with Harrison and his aides, General Cass, and Commodore Perry to consider the proposed routes.

Introductory to getting to the main point Harrison said, "Gentlemen, first of all I want to congratulate you on that landing on Monday. That was the finest military operation I have seen. The lack of enemy opposition probably robbed it of the historical impact it deserves, but that cannot take away from the magnificence of the performance. Obviously your planning was done well, and your instructions to subordinates were good, and all went well even though there was no opportunity for rehearsal of what to us is a new art of warfare. I also want to commend the naval force under Commodore Perry for the finest Navy cooperation with the Army I know anything about. And, gentlemen, I should point out one more thing. From my reading of history, and it is fairly extensive, the surrender of the British fleet to Commodore Perry on September 10 last was the first time ever, the first time in history, that an entire British flotilla or squadron ever surrendered to anybody. Our congratulations as well as our thanks to Commodore Perry!"

There were cheers all around. Perry looked over to Shelby and winked as if to say, here comes the big push for the water route.

"Now," Harrison went on, "we've got to see to it that the British and Indian force ahead of us don't get away to come back and haunt us. One approach is simply to take out after them by the same route." Pointing to his map, he explained, "That would be to take this route generally eastward, south of Lake St. Clair to the mouth of the Thames and then up the Thames. Vessels could bring supplies up part of the way, but only to the head of navigation. The trouble with this route is that they have a three-day head start on us, and when Procter finds out he is being pursued he is likely to pick up reinforcements from Canadian militia. And another thing. Anyone who is pursuing Indians, and in this case several thousand of them, led by Chief Tecumseh, must exercise extreme caution."

"Now a possible alternative would be to take to our boats and go back on Lake Erie to this point here," as he pointed on the map, "where we could get way beyond Procter and hurry up to the Thames about here and cut him off. With good luck, that could be a lot faster. But the trouble with that is the uncertainty of the weather. Light winds might delay the naval ships, but high winds would make it difficult for the open boats."

"General," spoke up Kentucky Major General Joseph Desha, another (like Richard Johnson and Samuel Hopkins) who was a member of Congress.

"Yes, Desha."

"I'm thinking that if we take after Procter by the land route we might not be able to catch the general, but I'll betcha we can catch his waggons and make him drop his baggage."

"Yes, I think there might be a good chance of that. And well, the Governor and the Commodore, I understand, lean toward the land route, and after long consideration I am inclined to agree with that. Are there any objections? Any questions? All right then, so it shall be. We move at dawn tomorrow morning with Colonel Johnson's mounted force in the lead. General McArthur and his brigade will remain to protect Detroit. General Cass will leave his brigade here to protect Sandwich and our line of supply. General Cass will come along as aide on my staff."

Ater the council, Perry stayed back. After the others had gone he turned to Harrison and said, "General, how about letting me come along with you on this campaign?"

"Well, I thought it was all set that your vessels would come along on the river and Lake St. Clair to give us support and carry supplies. Aren't you ready to go?"

"Yes, yes, of course. We're all ready. But I meant personally; let me come along personally."

"Oh, that would be a good idea—give us close liason with the naval force."

"We'll maintain close liason all right, but I was hoping you would allow me to see some action. I'll put Lieutenant Fischer in command of the ships and boats, though I'll keep an eye on them. But I'll perform whatever personal service you may require."

Harrison smiled. "Can you ride a horse?" he asked.

"Of course I can ride a horse—when I have to, to get from one ship to another."

"Well, I guess anybody who can ride a camel on Lake Erie ought to be able to ride a horse on the Thames," Harrison said with a laugh. "All right. You asked for it. You are now an aide-de-camp on the staff of the Commander-in-Chief." He extended his hand in a cordial welcome and added, "Now I think it only fair for you to be recognized by everyone as commodore."

Harrison took one of his general's stars and pinned it to Perry's epaulette.

"Thank you, Sir. But, Sir, with this I'm afraid those Army men will think I'm a damned general."

"Not if you're up in front," Harrison laughed.

The remainder of Johnson's men and horses and the herd of beef cattle came across the river during the day. Complicating the preparatory activities, a problem of illness arose in the camps. A siege of ague and fevers threatened to decimate the whole command. Harrison suspected stagnant water in pools on the islands. He ordered all canteens and water containers emptied and refilled with water drawn from the deep channel of the Detroit River.

Determined to go with whatever he could muster, Harrison assembled late in the afternoon all the leaders and troops, who were not ill and could be spared from other tasks, to address them.

"Tomorrow at dawn we take out after Tecumseh and Procter and their Indian and British warriors. We must move fast and let nothing stop us. The camp will be closed tonight, and there will be no passes for anybody. Tomorrow will be a hard march, but nobody must grumble or complain." Harrison paused and looked out over the faces in front of him—some shaven, some bearded; some youthful, some lined. Then suddenly, totally, unaccountably, his thoughts turned to Anna. He remembered leaving her while expecting their eighth baby, Carter Bassett, just two years ago for the expedition to Tippecanoe. He thought of her at Grouseland and at Cincinnati and at Philadelphia. Then quickly he dragged his thoughts back to the present moment and he shouted, "Men, this is going to be a hard march, but no man must grumble or complain, or even *think* of his wife or sweetheart until Procter and his army are overtaken and defeated. And men, you must always be very careful about an Indian ambush. When Chief Tecumseh is leading the Indians we have to be very careful. But always push on, quickly, quickly."

3

Of the three thousand Indians, including many women and children, who had gone with Procter from Amherstburg, only about half remained when he reached the mouth of the Thames. Of those who did remain, most were intensely loyal and devoted to Tecumseh. Many of them, Kickapoos, Winnebagos, Potawatomis, Wyandots, and Shawnees, had been among his staunch followers since the days at Prophet's Town.

Arriving at the mouth of the Thames on October 1, Tecumseh was dismayed to learn that Procter had taken no steps for defense, but apparently was bent on continuing in headlong retreat. He also was dismayed that so many of his warriors, partly on account of Procter's attitude he was sure, had departed. For the first time, serious doubts overtook Tecumseh. All of his finely woven union of tribes seemed to be coming unravelled. All of his life's work; all of his training and service as a warrior; all of his long trips to the East, and the West, and the South to carry his message of unity; all of his effort to build a strong force to defend the Indian homelands, his buildup at Tippecanoe, his concentrations in Canada, all seemed to be coming to naught. All of his work of a lifetime was being threatened by the results of a few days. He wished desperately that he could rid himself of the British connection. It probably was a mistake to join one group of White men against another. It was like making a treaty with Matchemenetoo, the Evil Spirit. That never was good even when the purpose was good.

All White Men were bad for the Indian. Not that all White Men were bad. General Brock was a good man. John Galloway was a good man. Rebekah Galloway was a good woman. Most men were part bad and part good. Even Harrison. He was bad in making many treaties with Indians to take land from them without consent of all the tribes, and then not even keeping those treaties but always making new treaties to take more land. He was good in trying to keep firewater away from the Indians, in not murdering prisoners, and in not allowing harm to women and children.

But now was it possible to get along without the British? The Indians needed their food and ammunition. Why was this? Their fathers did not have to depend on any White groups, but now, having accepted food and other things from the White Men, the Red Men had become dependent upon them. White Men bearing presents could be just as devastating for the tribes as White Men bearing guns.

Now Tecumseh was wondering, what was he doing here so far away from his homeland in this strange country? It would have been better if he could have stayed at Tippecanoe and gathered all his warriors there. Then while the Long Knives were busy fighting the Red Coats in Canada, he might have threatened or even captured Fort Wayne. He could have captured Vincennes. Then perhaps the homelands would have been safe from White incursions. Maybe there was yet time. Maybe Main Poc was right. Maybe the thing to do now was to lead all the Indians back to Michigan, to unite with Main Poc, and then to urge all the tribes once more to converge at Tippecanoe.

Tecumseh voiced some of his doubts and even suggested to the other chiefs that perhaps they all should march west to Michigan and the big lake and then to Indiana, instead of marching eastward with the British to nowhere. But as soon as they heard of it, the Sioux and Chippewas made strong protests. They said that they could *not* withdraw, and there was no other leader in whom they had confidence. They reminded him that it was he who had induced them to join the British in the first place, and he ought not abandon them now, when they needed him most. If he could find a good defensive position, and, if he could persuade Procter to fight, they still were confident that he could lead them to victory. Tecumseh said that battle held no personal fear for him, and, if they insisted, he would remain with them.

He saw no way out. His people had to have food and warm clothing. Here the country was hostile in winter even when the people were not. No, he would have to fight, even though at a place not of his own choosing and under circumstances not of his own making.

The next day, October 2, Tecumseh caught up with Procter near Dalson's farm on the Thames. The Indian Chief still insisting on making a stand, Procter invited him to ride along in his gig, protected by mounted guards, to look for a suitable defensive position. They found it about four miles upstream at McGregor's Creek, where it emptied into the Thames, just below the little village of Chatham. As Procter pointed, Tecumseh nodded with satisfaction. It was an eminently defensible place. The creek, running almost at right angles to the Thames between steep banks, deep and unfordable, would offer a formidable barrier in front of the British and Indians. The Thames would protect their right flank and a swamp, their left.

"It is a good place," Tecumseh said. "When I look at the two streams they will remind me of the Wabash and the Tippecanoe."

Procter said, "On this spot we will defeat General Harrison or here will lay our bones."

With this assurance and with the choice of such an ideal place for defense, Tecumseh's spirits soared again. He was sure that here Harrison could be defeated.

Meanwhile on that October 2, Harrison had started his army moving at dawn. Perry's squadron of a brig and four schooners under the command of Lieutenant Commander Jesse D. Elliott, followed by a flotilla of boats that carried supplies and baggage for the army, already was underway. It was moving up the Detroit River to enter Lake St. Clair, and then follow the southern shore of that lake to the Thames.

Harrison left Cass's brigade of regulars and Lt. Col. James Ball's detachment at Sandwich to follow as soon as their knapsacks and blankets arrived from Middle Sister Island. The sick were left there in hospital tents. All these, together with the garrison of seven hundred regulars that had been left under McArthur at Detroit, left Harrison with a force of about 3,500, including 150 regulars and 200 friendly Indians for the march to the Thames. In the interest of rapid marching, they left their tents behind and carried no rations, other than the fresh beef that followed on the hoof.

With Johnson's horsemen leading the way and infantrymen often following at a run on the narrow road through country that was generally open prairie, the army covered twenty-five miles that first day. At sunset Harrison went into camp at the River Ruscomb, near Lake St. Clair about nine miles from the mouth of the Thames. Eight British deserters, brought in by mounted scouts, reported that Procter's main force was less than a day's march away. Finding the bridge over the River Ruscomb intact, Harrison concluded Procter was not aware of the approach of the Americans.

At sunrise, Harrison's army was on the move again. Reaching the mouth of the Thames, Harrison and Perry found that a sand bar, where the water had a depth of only six and one-half feet, blocked the entry of vessels of more than one-hundred tons. The brig *Caledonia* and the schooner *Ariel* anchored outside, but the schooners *Scorpion, Tigress,* and *Porcupine* were able to glide over the bar, and they continued with the boats up the Thames.

As the army continued eastward along the southern bank of the river, Johnson's advance guard encountered a detachment of a lieutenant and eleven privates of dragoons who were busy destroying the bridge over the first unfordable tributary of the Thames. All were taken prisoner. They indicated that the bridge over the next stream also had been partially destroyed, but that Procter had no idea of the nearness of his enemy. However, one of their riderless horses dashed away and got back to Procter with the warning.

It took less than an hour to repair the bridge, and Harrison's army resumed its march. A little later the advance guard broke up a small delaying force at the next bridge, and after short delay the army crossed over and went on to encamp at Drake's farm.

Harrison had no more than established himself when he noticed a belligerent woman striding across the yard toward him. She stopped an orderly and asked, "Where's your general?"

"Right there, ma'm," he said, waving his hand toward the commander.

As she approached, Harrison saluted, doffed his cap, and bowed. She was not to be put off by any such courtesies. "Sir, you are a rake and a rogue," she cried.

"My compliments to you, Madam," Harrison responded.

She went on without pause, "And your men are a bunch of thieves and robbers. Now they are robbing my bees. Not a single comb of honey will be left to me by morning."

"Madame," Harrison said politely, "I shall put a guard over the bees."

The guard was posted, all right, but he busied himself in looking for Indians while his comrades came by to help themselves to the honey. The woman was right. By morning not a comb was left. Harrison sent his quartermaster up to the house to extend his apologies and to make payment for the honey.

While Harrison was camping at Drake's farm, Tecumseh was fuming at Chatham. Bringing his warriors up and expecting to find the British preparing defensive positions along McGregor's Creek as agreed, Tecumseh found no defensive preparations. Instead, the British had crossed over to the north side of the Thames while Procter had gone on, they said, to search for another site. When the lieutenant's horse arrived from the detachment that was destroying the bridges, Procter had decided that there was not time to prepare positions and to clear out all the women and children before the enemy arrived. Furious, Tecumseh demanded that the British return across the river and take up the defensive positions they were supposed to. They remained unmoved. That afternoon (October 3), Tecumseh received a message from Procter advising that all forces should cross to the north side of the Thames and withdraw another eight miles to a site near Moravian Town where he had found a good defensive position, and where he promised to make a stand to defeat Harrison. Tecumseh might place a detachment of his warriors at McGregor's Creek to delay the enemy in order to protect the evacuation of the women and children. Tecumseh saw no alternative, though he hated having to govern himself by the whim of the weak British commander. He hid about three hundred warriors in positions where they could command the bridges while others began burning the bridges.

Dawn of October 4 brought a resumption of rapid marching by Harrison's army. By noon they had reached Dolson's farm. Above Dolson's, the river narrowed between steep banks though the water still was deep, and high trees appeared on either side. Harrison and Perry agreed that the schooners and the boats would be highly vulnerable to fire from Indians on the banks from here on. They decided it would be best to leave all the vessels here for the time being. Harrison detached a force of about 150 men to guard them. Continuing eastward up the river, the men of the army now were walking on streets paved with gold—dirt road and forest paths covered with autumn leaves of maple, oak, and beech, leaves of yellow and red and gold and russet.

About midafternoon, a report came back to Harrison that the advance guard had encountered sharp musket fire at McGregor's Creek. He hurried forward. The bridge to the immediate front was burning, and sporadic musket fire both here and at the bridge a mile to the right at McGregor's mills, indicated that the whole enemy force might be making a stand. The impulse of the troops was to rush out and put the fire out and press the attack, but Harrison cautioned against Indian ambush. He order two six-pounder cannon brought up. A few rounds of grapeshot dispersed the Indians from the far end of the burning bridge. Firing went on a little longer against Colonel Johnson's force on the right, but soon both bridges had been secured and the fire extinguished. Three men had been killed and six wounded. The flooring in the main bridge had been destroyed, but the timbers still were strong. It took about two hours to repair the bridges, and the troops passed across.

A group of fifty or sixty Indians walked up from the opposite direction. The Kentuckians were ready to open fire, but Harrison was there in time to see that the attitude of the Indians was completely friendly. It was Walk-on-the-Water and some of his Wyandots. He had decided to change sides again, and he was offering his assistance to the Americans. Harrison took this to be a good sign. He welcomed Walk-in-the-Water, but told him that no services would be required, that they should simply return to their villages and keep out of the war. This pleased the Wyandot chief and off he went. Harrison took the precaution of sending along a small detachment of Indians, known to be friendly, to make sure that these defectors stayed that way.

A house near the bridge was on fire. Some of the Kentucky infantry put out the fire and seized several hundred muskets that had been stored there. A little farther on, near the first farm beyond the bridge, a British vessel was burning on the river. It was impossible to put the fire out. They learned that the British and the main body of Indians had crossed over to the north side of the river and were continuing their retreat. Four miles above the bridge at Bowle's farm, Harrison's men found two more vessels burning. Then a shout went up from some Kentuckians.

"Look here, a still, a still, help, fire!"

Others went running over to a huge distillery that was in flames. Desperately they tried to put the fire out, but it had too much of a start. As soon as it could be approached with some degree of safety, they rushed in to save the contents. They were disappointed to find that the building was filled with vast quantities of ordnance and other stores. They did bring out two twenty-four pounder guns with carriages and an assortment of shot and shells, but that was something of a let-down for Kentuckians who were looking for whiskey.

There the army camped for the night.

On the other side, Tecumseh's warriors had not fought with their usual fervor. It was only a delaying action to be sure, but they had not delayed the Long Knives very long. After a few rounds of grapeshot from the cannon and several balls from musket and rifle fire had killed ten and wounded perhaps twice that number, including Tecumseh, who suffered a superficial wound on his left arm, many of the others had fled.

Tecumseh gathered his warriors as best he could, crossed the river, and filed on eastward to join the others near Moravian Town. Indeed they had not delayed long enough for the women and children to reach their destination yet. They had heard the exchange of fire across the river. They had seen some of their warriors fleeing. They knew that the Long Knives were drawing close, but fear overtook them before their enemies did.

Frightened Indian women searched the faces of their men for some sign of hope, some hint of reassurance that they would be safe. Finding none, many of them gave way to panic. Some were terrorized by stories that the Long Knives would brutally ravish them; others were horrified by unfounded reports that the Long Knives would butcher their babies.

Tecumseh rode up and stemmed the panic. As he rode on to join the other warriors, his despair caught a second wind. Seeing no way out, he simply resigned himself to his fate. His irritation and sense of frustration gave way to a calm serenity and even a depth of cheerfulness. While now he saw little real hope of imminent victory, and less yet of the ultimate triumph of his dream of Indian union and the recovery of lost lands, he was sustained by a feeling that somehow his work would be carried on, that his life would not have been for naught, and some day, in some way, surely it would please Manitou to rescue his people.

As he approached Moravian Town, Tecumseh was agreeably surprised to find that Procter was indeed preparing a defensive position. He saw that it lacked the barrier of an unfordable stream across the front and the open fields of fire of Chatham. Still, it had certain advantages: the Thames to protect the left flank, woods to give cover and concealment, a big swamp on the right to protect that flank and to provide good concealment from which to threaten the enemy's left flank, and a small swamp in between.

He voiced no protest to Procter, but simply would follow his instructions. The British would take position on the left in the beech woods, from the river to the small swamp. A cannon would be put in position on the road that ran along the British left flank. The Indians would take positions in the small swamp, through the woods between the swamps, and in the big swamp to threaten the enemy's left flank. Tecumseh took all the war chiefs to show them exactly where to place their warriors.

That evening in the center of the Indian encampment, to the rear and opposite the area between the two swamps, Tecumseh sat before the fire with several of his most trusted followers. Wasegobah, husband of his sister Tecumapease, sat on one side of him. Shabonee, his most trusted lieutenant and a chief of the Potawatomis, sat on the other side. A young Shawnee called Billy Caldwell, Chief Roundhead of the Wyandots, Black Hawk, a leader of the Sac and Foxes, and other chiefs and leading warriors sat near by. Calmly Tecumseh smoked his pipe and looked into the fire without speaking. All sat in silence, looking at the fire. All sensed a closeness of spirit in being together to face what all assumed would be an attack by the Long Knives.

Billy Caldwell broke the silence, eagerness on his face and in his voice. "Father, what are we to do? Are we to fight the Long Knives?"

"Yes, my Son," Tecumseh answered gravely. "Yes, my Son, the Long Knives are marching upon us. Before the sun sets tomorrow we will be in their smoke."

Silence settled over the group again for a few minutes. Then Tecumseh arose. He looked all around the group with a smile. "My Children!" he said. "Listen! Hear me well. My Father and two Brothers died in wars against the Long Knives. Now the time has come for Tecumseh to join them."

Murmurs and then cries of protest spread all around the group. Tecumseh raised his hand for silence and went on. "Yes, the time has come. I will leave my bones here as a sign of the life and death struggle in which all Red Men must share if they are to save their homelands. You have been devoted followers. You have been faithful when others gave up and turned to the White Men, our enemies. You have remained strong when others became weak. Now it will be for you to carry on the struggle for our People."

Then he removed all the symbols of rank and identification that he wore—medals, bracelets, necklaces, the two-feathered headband. He handed his knife to Roundhead, his tomahawk to Black Hawk. Then he took the sword that the British had given to him and handed it to Shabonee with a request, "When my son, Pachetha, becomes a great warrior, give this to him."

Tecumseh, wearing only his deerskin suit without distinctive decorations and retaining only the war club he had carried since the days he had fought beside his brother, Chiksika, and the rifle he would need to show the way in the fighting, he bade his comrades to rest well and to be ready to lead their warriors in the great battle that was coming.

4

October 5 dawned under a clear sky and cool breeze. Although the troops had marched over sixty miles, through broken country, in the preceding three days, they were ready for another forced march on this morning. They were ordered to draw strips of fresh beef for their ration and to leave all other provisions behind. Harrison's own baggage consisted of one valise and one blanket tied to his saddle. Again he sent the mounted troops out ahead. He mounted his white horse and moved with the horsemen. He asked Governor Shelby to follow with the foot soldiers as rapidly as possible.

There was an additional spark of excitement in the air as the troops moved out in anticipation of meeting the enemy's main force. Capturing two more gunboats and several batteaux loaded with provisions and ammunition, on the way, the whole army reached Arnold's Mills about nine o'clock in the morning. Harrison thought this the best site to cross the river. He sent scouts across the river for security and then looked for means to get the troops across. They found two boats and several Indian canoes which soon were plying back and forth across the river to land soldiers on the other bank, but it turned out that horses served as ferries for a greater number. Harrison asked each horseman to take a foot soldier on behind him. With these resources the entire command was across the river by noon.

Now Moravian Town was only four miles away on the same side of the river. Feeling certain that they were approaching close to the enemy, Harrison sent the advance party of Johnson's mounted regiment forward to see if it could make contact.

Less than two hours later an officer came galloping to Harrison to report that the British and Indians had formed a defensive line across the line of march less than three hundred yards to the front of Johnson's horsemen. The scouts had captured a British wagoner who had told of the British and Indian positions, and the scouts had ridden on up where they saw a six-pounder in the road and a swamp just where the wagoner had said. Accompanied by Perry, Cass, Major Wood, Captain Todd, and Lieutenant John O'Fallon, another aide, Harrison rode forward to meet Colonel Johnson.

Speaking loudly over the snorts of the horses, they held a conference in the saddle.

"General, let us make a mounted charge. We can go right through the British lines," Johnson said.

"Maybe so." Harrison answered. "Are your horses trained to gunfire? Will they shy at the rifle shots in their ears?"

"We had lots of practice coming through Ohio. We fired hundreds of cartridges mounted. The horses will be as steady as the men"

"We have to be careful about getting into one of Tecumseh's snares. He has done it before. He likes to let a force through somewhere and then ambush it."

Strictly speaking, Johnsons's regiment was mounted infantry, not cavalry. Ordinarily a cavalry unit fought mounted, with carbines and sabres and pistols. Mounted infantrymen, on the other hand, ordinarily rode their horses up close to the site of the battle and then behind a hill or in a woods they dismounted, and leaving their horses in the charge of orderly caretakers, they fought on foot with muskets or rifles just as other infantry. Now what Johnson was proposing actually was a cavalry charge.

"We have a special group of twenty volunteers that we call the 'Forlorn Hope,'" Johnson explained. "Their job is to ride out to draw the enemy's fire. Then before they can reload, the others overrun their positions."

Harrison sent Major Wood forward to have a look at the British line. Then General Shelby came up, and Harrison asked his opinion. Shelby was willing to do whatever Harrison wanted, but his own opinion was that a frontal infantry assault probably would be in order, with the mounted regiment to follow up for exploitation.

Harrison gave out his order for an infantry frontal attack on the right. As soon as this had broken through, Johnson's regiment was to attack the Indians on the left of the British. Cass, Perry, and the other aides rode out to get the troops in position.

Harrison rode back and forth across the front to supervise the formations. He looked in the distance through the woods on the left of the swamp, and he could see an Indian riding a chestnut horse across the front. It was Tecumseh.

Tecumseh, riding across the front to make sure the warriors were in their proper places looked through the thin woods and saw in the distance an officer on a white horse riding back and forth across the front. It was Harrison. Tecumseh, in an attitude of confidence rode across to reassure the British as well as his own warriors. Coming across Procter in the rear of the British lines, he called out, "Father, tell your men to be firm, and all will be well." Tecumseh then dismounted and took his place on the north side of the small swamp where he could watch the Indians in both swamps and the intervening woods. His instructions were for no one to fire until he gave the signal by firing his own rifle.

Tecumseh looked skyward. The sky was clear except for a great white cumulus cloud directly overhead. He watched it take the distinctive form of a buffalo. "My White Buffalo!" he thought. "This must be a good omen of triumph!" But as he watched, the cloud turned dark and then dissipated.

Major Wood came up to Harrison at a gallop to report the results of his reconnaissance. "General, the British occupy the right of the line, from the road to the swamp, and they are in extended order, very extended."

"Are you sure? That's impossible. They never form in open order, even when they're fighting Indians on open ground." Harrison said.

"Indeed they are," Wood persisted. "They are in extreme open order."

"Hmm," Harrison muttered, "that might very well make them very vulnerable to a cavalry charge." He reassessed the situation. The terrain was wooded, mostly beech trees, but they were not thick, and the underbrush was light. The Kentucky horsemen probably could manage that. If they could draw the enemy's fire at fairly long range and then ride with great speed to his positions before he could reload, the shock action of the horses might turn the trick. He would refuse his left flank by placing a division of the infantry troops *en potence*, at nearly right angles to the front, to guard against any Indian incursion from that quarter.

In a display of flexibility seldom seen in army commanders of that age, or of any age, Harrison changed his mind and countermanded his order. He rode over to Johnson who already was forming his regiment for a secondary attack on the left, and called out, "We have decided to change the mode of attack. You will now form your regiment to charge the enemy on the right by heads of columns."

This was a tactic not sanctioned by anything Harrison ever had seen or heard about, but he had convinced himself that it would succeed. Once more the aides went out with new instructions to get the units in order.

On the extreme right, in the narrow strip between the road and the river, the two companies of regulars, 120 men, under Colonel Paul, were to move up in column of sections of four to seize the artillery piece on the road while a dozen friendly Indians were to move along the bank of the river to the enemy rear to invite the defection of Indians. Johnson's mounted regiment was to form in close columns, its right about fifty yards from the road so that the trees might afford some protection from the six-pounder on the road, and its left near the small swamp.

Now in rear of the mounted regiment, Trotter's brigade of Kentucky volunteer militia infantry, 500 men, was to form the front line of infantry, with King's brigade on a second line 150 yards to the rear, and Chiles' brigade as a reserve in rear of Trotter's. These three brigades would form a division under Major General William Henry. At nearly right angles to this formation, Major General Joseph Deshai's division, comprising two brigades, guarded the flank from the direction of the large swamp.

By 2:30 in the afternoon, all were in order except that Colonel Johnson had taken it upon himself to divide his regiment in two battalions with the first, under his brother, Lieutenant Colonel James Johnson, to make the charge against the British lines, while Colonel Johnson would lead the second to attack the Indians on the other side of the small swamp.

General Shelby placed himself at the crotchet formed by the angle between his two divisions. Harrison placed himself in front of the infantry on the right where he could watch the cavalry charge and be in a position to move up the infantry when necessary.

Harrison rode up to a friendly Seneca chief and primed his pistols. He looked down the line and acknowledged signals that the infantry units were ready. James Johnson was going up and down his line of horsemen telling them, "Charge through the enemy's first fire and follow up close."

As the trumpet sounded, Harrison cried out, "Yo, the goose honks high! Charge them, my brave Kentuckians! Charge!"

With a tremendous yell the five hundred horsemen started forward. Harrison turned to Commodore Perry and said, "You may follow the horsemen and report back on the results."

Almost immediately a volley rang out from the British defenders. Nearly all of the horsemen leaped off their horses to seek cover. James Johnson rode furiously up and down shouting, "Remount! Remount!"

Commodore Perry came riding up at a gallop and shouting, "Back up on your horses!" he went on straight at the enemy.

Quickly the men remounted, to be greeted by a second British volley. But now they took off at a fast gallop with cries of

"Remember the Raisin! Remember the River Raisin!"

Now there was no time for the British to reload before the Kentucky riders were upon them. Firing from the saddle as defenders exposed themselves and then swinging their tomahawks as they continued their yelling, the Kentuckians rode right through both defensive lines and then wheeled right and left. The British surrendered wholesale. On the extreme right the detachment of U.S. regulars ran up the road and captured the single brass cannon in the way without difficulty since Procter had neglected to send up any ammunition to the position. Within ten minutes the battle was all over in the British sector, and Procter with forty dragoons was bolting for the rear.

When Commodore Perry returned with a report of the British rout, Harrison sent Major Wood with a detachment in pursuit of Procter, and with instructions to look out for the discipline of the troops as they raced through Moravian Town.

From his position on the other side of the small swamp, Tecumseh watched the approach of horsemen on his side. Some of them struggled with their horses through the thick underbrush. Others dismounted and continued their approach on foot. Tecumseh was dismayed at the collapse of the British on his left. But patiently he waited, waited until the attackers were within very close range. Then with a loud whoop he fired his rifle. Indians from both swamps and the thick parts of the woods in between opened fire with devastating effect. Fifteen members of Richard Johnson's "Forlorn Hope" fell dead and four others fell wounded. The whole battalion recoiled and fell back against the Infantry as the Indians, responding to shouts from Tecumseh, jumped into new positions to deliver further devastating fire.

Sensing trouble on his left, Harrison rode toward the firing. He called on General Shelby to send up the reserve infantry brigade to shore up the angle. But Shelby already had the brigade on the way. "A damned Captain Thomsen order," Harrison thought.

Richard Johnson, sustaining five wounds, already was getting his men back in order. As he rode his white horse, also bleeding from gunshot wounds, close to the Indian positions, a chief jumped out and came at him with a tomahawk. Johnson felled him with a pistol shot and then rode his weakening horse to the rear where both he and his horse collapsed.

For another half hour the battle raged in this sector.

Tecumseh's voice could be heard above it all, shouting encouragement, shouting new instructions. Tecumseh looked to his right and saw Roundhead fall. On his left Wasebagoh was hit. His last words were a feeble shout, "Look out!" Tecumseh turned to the front just in time to see a man coming at him with drawn rifle. Tecumseh lifted his own rifle and fired at the same time as his assailant. Both fell to the ground mortally wounded, Tecumseh with a gaping wound in the side, just above his right hip.

The voice of Tecumseh was stilled. And with that, the sounds of the Indian muskets and rifles were stilled. Indians who had been standing firm now gave way. Some more were killed and wounded, some as they stood there in a daze. A few were captured. Most of the others fled.

Only sporadic fire continued as Harrison rode up to look over the situation. A Kentucky lad who had been wounded the previous day at McGregor's Creek sprang up at the approach of Harrison and called out as he lifted his arm, "General, will you look at that, they have shot me again."

A little farther on another young militiaman came out holding a scalp. He shouted, "Look, General, look here. I've got it. My father was an old Indian fighter in Kentucky, and when I left he made me promise to bring him a scalp from an Indian I'd killed myself. This one is for him. Now I'm going to get one for myself."

Harrison frowned on scalp-taking, but he did not chastise the boy. He simply raised his hand in acknowledgement. "Now I'm going to get one for myself," the young Kentuckian repeated as he plunged back into the thicket.

Shelby's foot soldiers moved through the swamps to flush out any remaining Indians, and it was all over in that sector.

With the approach of Kentucky horsemen to Moravian Town, Indian maidens ran down and hurled themselves into the river to escape the ravishment they feared, and Indian mothers threw their babies into the river rather than suffer them to be butchered as they assumed they would be.

The horsemen overtook dozens of wagons filled with supplies and provisions. They captured the wagons carrying Procter's personal baggage and even his personal correspondence. But after a seven mile dash beyond the town, they gave up the pursuit of Procter himself.

Except for the escape of Procter the American victory was complete. The British regulars had twelve killed and twenty-two wounded while six hundred, including twenty-five officers, were captured. A company of Canadian militia in Moravian Town was captured. The Indians left thirty-three dead warriors on the battlefield, and as many dead and wounded were taken to the rear. The price for the Americans was twenty-five killed and about fifty wounded. Captured supplies and equipment had a value running to over a million dollars. These included the recovery of nearly five thousand muskets and rifles that had been lost by Hull at Detroit, by Winchester at the River Raisin, and by Dudley outside Fort Meigs. Most prized of all were three brass cannon that had been taken from Burgoyne at Saratoga in the Revolutionary War and then lost by Hull at Detroit.

That evening several Kentuckians returned to the battlefield in search of the body of Tecumseh. Mistaking that of Roundhead for Tecumseh's, they proceeded to scalp it and then completely flayed it in order, they said, to make razor strops and other souvenirs.

After dark, Black Hawk and a party of Indians crept back to look for the body of Tecumseh. They found it, undisturbed, where Black Hawk had seen him fall. Gently they carried back the body of their great leader. They took it back to a clump of trees where they dug a grave. With a short ritual they buried it. They spread the dirt and covered the grave with leaves so that it could never be found.

While this was going on, Harrison was receiving the captured British officers. He offered them strips of roast beef from his scanty mess. To a wounded officer, he gave his only blanket.

The next afternoon Harrison and his staff rode across the battlefield for a final look. Coming upon the mutilated body of Roundhead, Captain Todd said, "They say this is Tecumseh. General, is it truly he?"

"I cannot be sure. It is impossible to say with any certainty."

"In any case," Todd went on, "there seems to be no doubt that Tecumseh is dead. British and Indians both verify that. And this is supposed to be about where he fell."

Harrison gave a nod of satisfaction and a slight smile of approval. "This should end the Indian menace in the Northwest," he said. Then more soberly, with a twinge of sad respect, he added, "But wherever he is, there has fallen the noblest savage of them all."

CHAPTER XXIV

Epilogue

1

O Brave Warrior, leader of men,
   Whose dream of the union that might have been
   Dissolved with the clouds at the new River Thames
Knew the triumph of doubt when all hope ends,
Victim of good and bad in all men.

The sun had set at Tippecanoe. Night had fallen at the Thames. The Shooting Star had fallen to the earth.

What is a shooting star? It is a meteor, a mass of iron and rock ignited by the friction of the atmosphere as it falls toward the earth. Relative to the earth it is always falling. It only *appears* to be rising from certain perspectives. And so Tecumseh had appeared to be rising. He had been ignited by friction with the White man and appeared to be rising. Actually he, with all his civilization, had been falling earthward all the while. Yet his spirit continued to rise, and in the years to come his people would hold to a legend that one day he would return and lead them to a promised land, a great "town of towns" where they would be free of strife. The sign of his return would be a great shooting star across the southern sky.

611

As *The Indian* said, "When legends end, the dreams die, and when the dreams die there is no more greatness."

And as the British Prime Minister, William E. Gladstone, said in a later generation, "No greater calamity can happen to a people than to break utterly with its past."

Tecumapease, who had lost her husband as well as her brother in the Battle of the Thames, tried to hold out a hope of carrying on. She went with Pachetha, Tecumseh's son, as representatives of the Shawnees in a great Indian council in Quebec in March 1814. There she urged them to recognize Pachetha as their leader and to carry on Tecumseh's struggle. But the Indians had lost heart. They had no confidence in the twenty-year-old youth or in themselves.

The Prophet, who survived the Battle of the Thames and subsequent actions, continued to hope to retain ties with the past. He reasserted his position as leader of the Shawnees, and indeed claimed to be leader of all the western tribes, but with no lasting effects. He returned to northern Indiana and Ohio for a time after the war, but he encountered more hostility than welcome, and he fled back to Canada where he remained for over ten years. Later he moved to the upper Great Lakes and then joined bands of Shawnees in their removal beyond the Mississippi. He finally settled in the northeast corner of Kansas.

As for the Indian tribes, they went the course that Tecumseh had feared. In the Old Northwest a continuing succession of land cession treaties pushed the Indians westward. For a time there was a notion of a "permanent Indian frontier," roughly a line running from Green Bay diagonally across Wisconsin and Iowa to the northwest corner of Missouri, and thence southward along the western boundary of Missouri and Arkansas. Presumably the area to the west and northwest of that line would be closed to White settlement. But the idea gave way to plans for less expansive Indian reservations.

All the tribes of the Old Northwest—the Miamis, the Potawatomis, the Delawares, the Winnebagos, the Kickapoos, and all the others accepted their fate and moved beyond the Mississippi without any fuss except for a brief uprising of the Sacs and Foxes. Late in 1831, the last of those tribes were expelled from the area around Rock Island, Illinois, an area which Harrison had obtained in his treaty of 1804. With the loss of their corn crop, many faced starvation, and the following spring Black Hawk led about a thousand of them, including women and children, back across the river to plant corn in their old fields. The governor of Illinois raised a force of volunteer militia to root them out. Black Hawk and his warriors held out only briefly. Then they fled northward and then went down the Wisconsin River to the Mississippi. Their attempts to surrender were frustrated when they were caught between pursuing militia and an armed steamboat, and most of them were slaughtered. Only about 150 survived. Abraham Lincoln served about ninety days as captain and then as private in the militia during the Black Hawk War, though he never saw any fighting. When it was over, Black Hawk, taken prisoner, said simply, "I loved my villages; I loved my fields of corn; I loved my people. I was willing to fight for them."

The Shawnees moved out on a slow trek with The Prophet, still acknowledged as a leader for a time, first to Kansas and later to the Indian Territory (Oklahoma).

In the South only the Creeks and the Seminoles took the advice of Tecumseh to resist the White Americans by force. The Five Civilized Tribes had been fairly successful in adapting to farming, and they had lived at peace with the White settlers for years, but soon they too felt the pressure to reduce their land holdings. Controversy among the Creeks led to civil war within that tribe, but the belligerent "Red Sticks," adherents to the red sticks that Tecumseh had distributed in his appeal for war, got the upper hand. They did not join Tecumseh at Detroit, but under the Chief Red Eagle, who had been much impressed by Tecumseh's appeal, they carried on a fierce war in their own area in 1813-1814. It began when the Red Sticks pursued a band of their pro-American rivals into a White stockade, Fort Mimms, and then massacred most of the 400 Whites and Indians who had taken refuge there. It ended in the decisive battle at Horseshoe Bend, on the Tallapoosa River in northern Alabama. There Andrew Jackson won his great victory, with the assistance of a thousand Cherokees who had decided that it would be in their best interest to side with the United States.

Actually the defending Creeks repulsed the frontal assaults of Jackson's regulars and militia. It was only after his Cherokee allies had swum the river and taken the defenders from the rear that he was able to carry the day. The resistance of the Creek nation ended with the lives of nearly one thousand of their warriors there.

Jackson then opened peace negotiations. His terms: Give up 23 million acres of their lands in Georgia and Alabama. The Creeks protested.

Jackson replied, "Through this territory leads the path that Tecumseh trod. That path must be stopped. Until this is done, your nation cannot expect happiness, mine security."

The Creeks had no choice.

In the 1820's a big debate began in Congress on the question of Indian removals, of removing all the tribes east of the Mississippi River to areas west of the great river. In the House of Representatives William Lumpkin of Georgia presented the position of his state where many people were demanding removal of the Creeks and Cherokees, so that their lands could be had:

These distinguished individuals have arrived at the same results; that the only hope of saving the remnant tribes of Indians from ruin and extermination, was to remove them from their present abodes, and settle them in a permanent abode west of the Mississippi River.... I feel it my duty to warn this committee, and the nation, of the impending evils which must necessarily grow out of an imbecile course on the part of this Government.... The Cherokee Indians, who principally reside within the limits of Georgia, have, in the course of the past year, renewed their often-repeated declaration, that they will never—no, never—relinquish their present possessions.... They not only disregard Georgia, and the rights of Georgia, but they have actually enacted laws, and execute them, too, which are in direct violation of the laws of the United States.... This state of things cannot exist: something must be done, and the sooner it is done the better.... If we determine upon their emigration to the West, the sooner they know it the better, that they may send their Calebs and Joshuas to search out and view the promised land.

Oliver H. Smith of Indiana took a kind of half-hearted position in accepting the necessity of removal but warning against injustice to the Indians:

Sir, I consider the question...of momentous importance; it is of importance to the character of the United States, and of much greater importance to that most unfortunate and wretched people, that the future policy of the Government, in relation to them, should be marked with justice, humanity, and a magnanimity of purpose, that will atone, as far as possible, for the great injustice which we have done them. We cannot retrace our steps; we cannot affect the past; we cannot resuscitate or bring to life the thousands of this miserable people, who have wasted away and perished under the influence of our baneful policy. But, sir, we may, and I do most sincerely hope will, profit by the past experience of the nation, in the policy which has been pursued, and in our future legislation on this subject carefully avoid that course of policy which has produced such dire effects.... Then, sir, these people do stand in great need of the interposition of the strong arm of this Government to relieve them; and this Government is bound by every tie of humanity, justice, morality, and religion, to do all in her power to save the wreck of this people.

It was for John Woods of Ohio to come directly to the point of frank criticism of the policy:

> I am glad, Mr. Chairman, that this measure is thus brought forward, and that it stands before us in its proper form and nakedness, stripped of the pretence of disinterested humanity, which has been thrown around it. It is now presented in its true character, as a measure, not for the benefit of the Indians—not for their civilization and preservation—but for our interest, and only our interest. This appropriation is asked, as the means to effect measures for the removal of the Indians out of the limits of our States and Territories, that they may, by our aid, trail their bodies into the wilderness, and die where our delicacy and our senses may not be offended by their unburied carcasses. . . . We are told, sir, that this is a measure necessary for the happiness and preservation of the Indian—that we must adopt it, or they will perish, and become extinct as a people. I do not believe this is the only way in which we can save the Indians, or promote their happiness. In my opinion, this measure would effect more rapidly their extinction. Instead of being entitled "An act for the preservation and civilization of the Indian tribes within the United States," it should be called a scheme for their speedy extermination.

Samuel Vinton of Ohio opposed the removal of Indians to reservations in the West on what he took to be more immediately practical grounds:

> It proposes to take a whole people, nay, more, the remnant of forty nations, from their abodes, and place them down in the recesses of a distant and forbidding wilderness. . . . When the plan there marked out is understood by the people of the western country, it will fill them with alarm. . . . Such a disposition of the Indians greatly endangers the security of the whole western frontier, and renders the condition of Missouri, in particular, imminently perilous. . . . Place around Missouri on the north and west, in conjunction with the two hundred thousand that would be there besides, the sixty or seventy thousand Indians of the Southwest, and what have you done! You have executed, by a single movement, the great plan of Tecumseh, that carried terror and dismay to every cabin beyond the Alleghenies. . . . The policy we are now asked to adopt, of removing them without any previous governmental arrangement for their future regulation, will, if pursued, result in carrying them forward, at a single movement, almost half way to that ocean in which there is too much cause to fear they are destined, ultimately, to terminate their existence and their miseries together.

In the 1830's the Government granted to each of the Five Civilized Tribes a large tract of land in the eastern half of the Indian Territory (Oklahoma). But when orders came in 1836 for all the Creeks to leave their homelands in Georgia and Alabama for those new sites in the West, 1,500 of them refused to go and again went on the warpath. It took 11,000 troops (including 1,800 rival Creeks) to round them up and send them on. Still in the

1850's another 4,000 were rounded up and sent off. Many died of hunger and exposure enroute. It was estimated that no more than half of the nation of 25,000 survived the last years in Georgia and Alabama and the hardships of the trek to the Indian Territory.

The most fierce resistance of all was that of the Seminoles in Florida. After a seven-year war, 1835 to 1842, that cost the United States $20,000,000 and involved the use of over 30,000 soldiers, at least 1,500 of whom died, where a succession of ten different generals were in command, the Army finally dragged 3,000 Seminoles out of the swamps and sent them off to the Indian Territory. Others remained to resist, without ever giving up. The last peace treaty with them, signed in 1934, allowed them to stay.

The tribes who had opposed the advice of Tecumseh, those who sought security in cooperation with the United States, fared no better. The Choctaws and Chickasaws of Mississippi were uprooted in 1832 and 1834. They went peaceably and suffered less from White exploitation than the others, but they suffered nearly as much from the hardships, though a number of them went by steamboat up the Mississippi and then up the Arkansas.

Alexis de Tocqueville, eminent French traveller in America, on observing a group of Choctaws crossing the Mississippi, wrote,

> Never will that solemn spectacle fade from my remembrance. No cry, no sob, was heard among the assembled crowd; all was silent. Their calamities were of ancient date, and they knew them to be irremediable.

Most ironic of all was the situation of the Cherokees in northern Georgia and Alabama, southeastern Tennessee, and western North Carolina. They had succeeded best of all in learning the farming skills of the White Man, including even the holding of black slaves; in building substantial houses; and in governing themselves. They even developed a written alphabet for their language in the 1820's, and adopted a written constitution. They had been most successful in avoiding conflict with the White settlers and most zealous in fighting for the United States. But their turn for removal came just the same.

A sizeable part of the Cherokee nation had moved earlier, and they became known as the Cherokee West. It remained for the Cherokee East to suffer the greatest hardships. During the hot summer of 1838, some 13,000 were brought by steamboat, by a new railroad, or by overland walking to concentration camps. Their procession westward began on October 1. Just a few went by steamboat down the Tennessee River to the Ohio, then to the Mississippi, and finally up the Arkansas. All the rest, in detachments of about a thousand, went slowly overland across Tennessee and Kentucky, crossed the Ohio River into southern Illinois, crossed the Mississippi above St. Louis, and then west and southwest to their new homeland. Ever after they remembered this as the "Trail of Tears." All through a bitterly cold winter, they trudged on. The first groups arrived at their destination in early January. Others kept straggling in until late March. Hunger, disease, exposure, and fatigue overtook large numbers. It was estimated that no less than 4,000 Cherokees perished in the concentration camps or on the 800-mile march to the West. A rather substantial group was able to evade the roundup and to remain behind in the mountains of North Carolina.

In the Indian Territory, the Five Civilized Tribes were fairly successful in getting a new start. Then other tribes, from the Old Northwest and from the Western Plains were brought in. And again the demands of White settlers for more land set in. These Indian nations allied themselves with the South in the Civil War, and this cost them a good part of their land. The western half of the Indian Territory was opened to White settlement in 1889, and this became Oklahoma Territory. This, together with the Indian Territory, formed the state of Oklahoma which was admitted into the Union in 1907. The Indian nations lost their identity as separate entities, and though their descendants carried on some of the old tribal traditions, they mostly became assimilated into the new state as citizens.

Tocqueville had observed in the 1830's:

It is impossible to destroy men with more respect for humanity.

Settling into a mode of retirement, The Prophet frequently was the object of curious journalists, painters, and other visitors. On one occasion, in the summer of 1836, he received a group of visitors who informed him that the former White Chief of the Indiana Territory was a candidate for President of the United States that year.

"So Harrison wants to be the Great Chief of the Twenty-four Fires?"

"This year it is twenty-five fires," one of the visitors explained.

"Twenty-five, yes? Well Harrison always wanted to keep growing and adding territory, didn't he?" The aging holy man, looking more aged than his years—gave a brief, cynical smile, and then assumed a bitter attitude as he said, "Well, Harrison will not win this year to become Great Chief. But he may win next time. Yes, I think he may win next time. But it will be no good. I tell you, if Harrison becomes Great Chief, he will not finish his term. He will die in his office."

"No President has ever died in office," a visitor protested.

"But Harrison will die," The Prophet went on. And when he dies you will remember the death of the great Tecumseh, my Brother. You think that I have lost my powers, I who caused the sun to darken and caused Red Men to give up firewater. But I tell you that Harrison will die. And after him, every Great Chief who is chosen in each twentieth year thereafter will also die in the office. And when each one dies, let the world remember the death of our people."

The visitors stirred with some uneasiness at what they called, "The Curse of The Prophet."

The Prophet concluded, "Who is the Great Chief? Maybe Harrison will become Chief of the Twenty-four or Twenty-five fires, maybe he will be your President, Chief of a great and powerful nation, but a hundred years from now, and a hundred and fifty years from now, Tecumseh will be better remembered and more honored by his enemies than Harrison will be by his friends."

In November of that year, The Prophet died. He died with the satisfaction of knowing that Harrison had not been elected President.

His wife recalled to friends that of all those turbulent years through which she had lived, the best had been those few at Tippecanoe.

Tecumseh's son survived a number of years more, but he never rose to any position of leadership or prominence.

Tecumseh lived on in story and tradition. When a new capital city was created for Indiana, Marston Clark, who had been aide to Harrison at Tippecanoe, was a member of the committee to name it (1821). He proposed to name it "Tecumseh." He held out until he almost succeeded, but finally gave in to a compromise, "Indianapolis." Towns or cities were named "Tecumseh" in Kansas, Michigan, Nebraska, Oklahoma, and Ontario.

One of the most notable generals in the Civil War was William Tecumseh Sherman of Ohio (the name William being added by his foster mother when the boy was nine years old in the belief that a heathen name would not do for Christian baptism).

And Tecumseh became known to every midshipman at the U.S. Naval Academy at Annapolis, Maryland, after 1866. In that year the Academy received a wooden figurehead that had decorated an old ship of the line, the U.S.S. Delaware, and it was set up on the grounds. Actually the figure was supposed to be that of Tamanend, chief of the *Delaware* tribe in Pennsylvania at the time of William Penn. Quickly the midshipmen corrupted the name to one more familiar to them—Tecumseh—and so it remained ever after. The statue of "Tecumseh" became the "god of 'C'," the passing grade at the Academy, and the idol to whom prayers and offerings of pennies were directed in appeals for success in examinations and in athletic contests, in particular before the annual football game against Army. Special honor on occasions of appeals for help in examinations and athletics came to be rendered in the form of the left-handed salute, as well as in tossing pennies to the statue.

A nuclear submarine of the United States Fleet, at first carrying Polaris missiles and later Poseidan, was named U.S.S. *Tecumseh*.

Tecumseh even became something of an American folk hero in Europe, where children of Austria and Germany eagerly read books of his story.

2

Just as The Prophet realized that the effective end of Tecumseh's and his dream of preserving Indian civilization in American was the Thames, not Tippecanoe, William Henry Harrison knew that the effective termination of the Indian threat in the Old Northwest was not Tippecanoe, but the Thames.

After the Battle of the Thames, most of the militiamen that constituted the bulk of Harrison's Northwestern army returned to their homes. Harrison hoped to reconstitute his army with the regulars that Secretary of War Armstrong had been promising for the last year, and then move eastward along Lake Erie to join in the fighting in the Niagara sector. Instead Armstrong assigned him to an administrative post in Cincinnati. Then the Secretary proceeded to issue orders to one of Harrison's subordinates without even going through the General. Harrison abruptly resigned his commission in May 1814. Govenor Shelby and others rushed letters to President Madison to urge him not to accept Harrison's resignation. But the letters arrived while Madison was away vacationing at his Montpelier estate. In the President's absence, Armstrong promptly accepted the resignation.

Harrison still was interested in politics, but sensing that his political goose was cooked in Indiana Territory where Jonathan Jennings had gained the upper hand during his absence, he returned to North Bend. There he extended his modest log and clapboard house to a twenty-two room mansion to rival that of his father-in-law. Two more children, Anna Tuthill and James Findlay, rounded the number to ten, though the last, little James Findlay, died in infancy.

In 1816 Harrison was elected to the U.S. House of Representatives from Ohio, where he served two terms. Also in 1816, the House voted a gold medal for him and Governor Shelby of Kentucky, who had commanded the Kentucky militia, for their contributions in the victory at the Thames. But the Senate, where Harrison's political opponents insisted that the pursuit of Procter had been only by the influence of Shelby, struck Harrison's name. After a long and laudatory letter from Shelby, the Senate reversed its action in 1818, and agreed to award Harrison the medal.

Harrison had collected the $4,000 in land from William McIntosh as a result of the suit for slander. But he returned two-thirds of that to McIntosh as an indication that the suit had not been filed in the interest of money, and now he set aside the other one-third for the benefit of the orphan children of several distinguished citizens who were killed in the War of 1812.

Indiana was admitted to the Union in 1816. Jonathan Jennings became the first Governor of the State.

Harrison was elected to the Ohio State Senate in 1819, and then did not run for reelection to the U.S. House in 1820. He failed in a bid for Congress in 1822, but in 1824 he was elected to the U.S. Senate. During this time he was instrumental in obtaining an appointment to the U.S. Military Academy, West Point, for the son of Spier Spencer, the boy who had accompanied his father and had seen him die at the Battle of Tippecanoe.

In 1828 he was appointed minister to Colombia by John Quincy Adams, but he hardly had arrived in Bogota when Andrew Jackson recalled him to make way for a Jacksonian Democrat.

Back on his Ohio farm in the 1830's, he served as clerk of the local court. Then leaders of the newly forming Whig party began mentioning him for the presidency. He was one of five Whig candidates nominated for the election of 1836, when he ran second to Democrat Martin Van Buren. This put him in a strong position for 1840. The successful candidate for Vice President with Van Buren in 1836 was Col. Richard M. Johnson of Kentucky, the man who some claimed had shot Tecumseh. Political supporters pushed Johnson as the hero of the Thames who had killed Tecumseh, and they urged him to question publicly Harrison's military leadership in that campaign. This Johnson steadfastly refused to do.

The electoral campaign of 1840 was quite a different matter. For this effort the Whigs held their first national convention in December 1839, at Harrisburg, Pennsylvania. Harrison won the presidential nomination and for Vice President chose his old neighbor from Virginia, John Tyler.

The Whig campaign got off to an unprecedented start with a gigantic rally at the Tippecanoe battleground in Indiana. By wagon, by carriage or cart, by horseback, by boats, by walking, a throng of 30,000 people gathered there to sing the praises of "Old Tippecanoe" Harrison and to denounce Martin Van Buren. The crowd and the enthusiasm were beyond anything anyone had seen for this kind of event. It was a kind of political "Cane Ridge" revival, with a torrent of speeches, songfests, and feasting. To the tune of "The Old Oaken Bucket" they sang:

> The iron-armed soldier,
> The true-hearted soldier,
> The gallant old soldier,
> of Tippecanoe."

And others would shout:

> Van, Van,
> You're not our man
> To guide the ship,
> We'll try Old Tip.

And someone shouted, "Tippecanoe and Tyler too!" And the whole crowd took it up as a battle cry.

Hawkers moved through the crowd selling souvenirs including pencil cases and razor strops purported to have been made from the skin of Tecumseh.

Other rallies across the country followed the pattern of the one at Tippecanoe. Scores of campaign songs poured forth, and colorful handbills, kerchiefs with drawings to represent Harrison's career, special newspapers, and campaign biographies. Out of a quip by an opponent that, if given a pension and a barrel of hard cider, Harrison would be content to retire to a log cabin came the theme *motif* for the campaign. Now in a campaign featuring coonskin caps, cider barrels, and log cabins, Harrison, the man of Berkeley Plantation, Grouseland, and North Bend, became the candidate of the common man. Local bands, torchlight parades, and speeches of little substance swept a tide of popular opinion. The result was an overwhelming electoral victory for the hero of Tippecanoe—and Tyler too.

About the only Harrison partisan who failed to reflect all the emotional enthusiasm of the party was Anna Harrison. Now content at North Bend near her children and grandchildren, but frail in health, she almost dreaded a successful outcome in the election. The glamour of Washington held no appeal for her. Still, she did rejoice in William Henry's success and in the recognition he had received, and she always wanted to be at his side and give all the help and support that she could.

By 1840 Harrison had lost something of the glint and cheerfulness of his earlier years. He still maintained a cheerful attitude and a confident lilt in his walk, but they were labored. His hair now was gray and a little thin. Sometimes his stance was unsteady, though he remained unbent.

The years and ten children and multiple bereavements had taken their toll on Anna Harrison. To others, she appeared frail and pale, with drawn face and old lace, though her hair remained dark. To William Henry, she still appeared the most beautiful girl in the world.

They had been deeply saddened by the loss of three children in three successive years—William Henry, junior, in 1838, Carter Bassett in 1839, and Benjamin in 1840. In addition to James Findlay who had died in infancy in 1817, two others had died earlier—Lucy in 1826 and John Cleves Symmes in 1830.

Still they had had the satisfaction of seeing notable achievements on the part of all of their children, and they had had the real enjoyment of numerous grandchildren about them.

Betsy married John Cleves Short, son of Peyton Short and Maria, sister of Anna Harrison. Her husband was a lawyer, though he never practiced, and he read the classics in the original

Greek and Latin. They lived in a great mansion on an estate adjacent to that of her parents' at North Bend. Their only child died in infancy.

The eldest son, John Cleves Symmes, had been educated at Transylvania University in Kentucky. He had married Clarissa Pike, a daughter of General Zebulon Pike. They had five children. They had lived for some years in his father's old mansion, Grouseland, at Vincennes, and later had moved to Boone County Kentucky, across the Ohio River from North Bend.

Lucy Singleton had married Judge David K. Este of Cincinnati who became one of the wealthiest men in the West and built a great stone mansion in Cincinnati. They had one child, a daughter.

William Henry, junior, had graduated from Transylvania University and became a lawyer in Cincinnati. He had married Jane Irwin, and they had two sons, one of whom died in infancy. In addition to their city residence they had built a home on his father's farm at North Bend, across the valley of Indian Creek from the elder Harrison's big house.

John Scott was educated at Miami University of Ohio, and he lived on a six-hundred acre farm that his father had given him on the Ohio River where the Big Miami joined it at the boundary of Indiana. He served as a member of Congress from the Cincinnati district. He was married twice. His first wife was Lucretia Knapp Johnson of Boone County, Kentucky. They had one son who died in infancy, and two daughters. His second wife was Elizabeth Irwin, sister of Jane Irwin who had married his brother, William Henry. They had five sons, two of whom died in infancy, and three daughters. Their second son was Benjamin who resided in Indianapolis and became the twenty-third President of the United States.

Benjamin had graduated from Cincinnati College and then studied medicine in Baltimore. He had practiced medicine in Vincennes and Cincinnati. He was married first to Louise Bonner of Vincennes with whom he had two sons and a daughter. Later he had married Mary Rainy of Cincinnati.

Mary Symmes married John Henry Fitzhugh Thornton who became a prominent physician in Cincinnati. They had three sons and two daughters. The youngest son, Fitzhugh, married Eliza Morgan who was a great granddaughter of Dr. Stephen Wood, who had performed the wedding ceremony for Mary's parents, William Henry and Anna.

Carter Bassett had graduated from Miami University and became a lawyer in Hamilton, Ohio. He had married Mary Sutherland, and they had one daughter.

The youngest daughter, Anna Tuthill, married a second cousin, William Henry Harrison Taylor of Richmond, Virginia. They lived at Cincinnati where he was a local official for a time. They had three sons and seven daughters, one of whom died in infancy. On the death of President William Henry Harrison, Anna Tuthill and her husband moved to North Bend where they took over the management of the farm and Anna Harrison's business affairs. Later they moved to St. Paul, Minnesota, where Taylor served a number of years as state librarian.

As the time approached for the President-elect to leave for Washington, the doctors confirmed Harrison's own judgment that Anna should not risk the trip in the dead of winter.

On a cold January morning (1841), Harrison prepared to take his leave. Anna helped supervise the loading of baggage onto the wagon, and she helped the two girls, their daughter, Anna Tuthill Taylor, and their daughter-in-law, Jane Findlay Harrison, (who indeed was Mrs. William Henry Harrison, but the widow of William Henry, junior) who would serve as White House hostesses and thus would accompany him, get ready. Harrison sent the others out to tell the drivers that he was ready, and then alone, he turned to Anna.

"Well, my dearest Anna, I must go. The only thing that robs this day of excitement is that you cannot go along."

"No, I'm not overly anxious to go to Washington, but I am anxious about sending you off there without me."

"The only thing that makes it bearable for me is the thought that you will be with me in spring, and with you there it will be ever so much more beautiful."

"It will be beautiful wherever and whenever we can be together again."

"Yes, and we don't want to take any chances on delaying that, so I'm giving you a General Harrison order."

"What's that?"

"An order to be carried out straightaway and without question, and that order now is that you take very good care of yourself so that you will be strong enough for the trip in May."

"Oh, don't worry about me; I'll be all right. And Henry, you do be careful. Sometimes those politicians can be more dangerous than the Indians."

"Yes, I know, but I've had lots of practice. Now, I want you to be as strong as Zenobia of Palmyra, and Joan of Arc, and Catherine of Russia."

"And Red-headed Nance?" she laughed. "Oh, Henry, I am proud of you. Remember how we used to look at our little sons and say, 'Who knows, someday he may be President of the United States'? And now look, their father himself—President of the United States!"

"But the President will be only as great as the lady who shares it with him. Now I must go, but I just want you to know that I love you more now than that day over forty-five years ago when we had that secret wedding in front of all those people in your father's house!" And softly he whispered, "I do, you know. I'll see you in May."

"And Henry, I love you more too. See you in May."

He took her in his arms for a long embrace and kissed her tenderly. With no indication that he noticed a tear coursing down her cheek, he turned away with a smile. At the porch he turned back for a waive.

"The goose honks high!" he called. "Until May!"

Harrison's trip to Washington was like a triumphal procession all the way. There had been nothing like it since Washington's journey from Mount Vernon to New York to be inaugurated as the first President.

At the Cincinnati wharf, Harrison and his party boarded the steamboat *Benjamin Franklin* to the roar of cannon and the playing of bands. Alerted by a preceding boat, crowds gathered at every town along the way and often crowded the banks in between. There was a banquet in Pittsburgh and then the further boat ride up the Monongohela to Brownsville where a shiny new coach, decorated with scenes depicting Harrison's career, awaited.

And then there were more crowds and cheering all along the National Road through Cumberland and Hagerstown to Baltimore. At Baltimore he took a railway train to Washington and arrived in the capital city in a snowstorm on his sixty-eighth birthday, February 9, 1841.

He took quarters at Gadsby's Hotel where he conferred with Senators Daniel Webster, Henry Clay, John Crittendon, and other Whig leaders on the make-up of the new cabinet. He called on President Van Buren at the White House with such cordial results that the President and his entire cabinet paid a return call to Harrison at Gadsby's, and then invited the President-elect to dinner at the White House.

A few days later, Harrison returned to his old Virginia home, Berkeley, to write his inaugural address. Allowing only a couple of days for resting and visiting, he went to his mother's old bedroom, the room in which he was born. He pushed a desk to a south window where he could look out to the gardens and the James River. He had some of his favorite books of Greek and Roman classics at his side. Taking up a quill pen, he started to write:

* * * * *

It was the remark of a Roman consul in an early period of that celebrated Republic that a most striking contrast was observable in the conduct of candidates for offices of power and trust before and after obtaining them, they seldom carrying out in the latter case the pledges and promises made in the former.... The outline of principles to govern and measures to be adopted by an Administration not yet begun will soon be exchanged for immutable history, and I shall stand either exonerated by my countrymen or classed with the mass of those who promised that they might deceive and flatter with the intention to betray.

* * * * *

Those who are called upon to administer.... must recognize as its leading principle the duty of shaping their measures so as to produce the greatest good to the greatest number.

* * * * *

It is the part of wisdom for a republic to limit the service of that officer at least to whom she has intrusted the management of her foreign relations, the execution of her laws, and the command of her armies and navies to a period so short as to prevent his forgetting that he is the accountable agent, not the principal; the servant, not the master. Until an amendment of the Constitution can be effected public opinion may secure the desired object. I give my aid to it by renewing the pledge heretofore given that under no circumstances will I consent to serve a second term.

* * * * *

It is in this District only where American citizens are to be found who under a settled policy are deprived of many important political privileges without any inspiring hope as to the future.... The people of the district of Columbia are not the subjects of the people of the States, but are free American citizens.

* * * * *

The liberties of a people depend on their own constant attention to its preservation. The danger is.... the old trick of those who would usurp the government of their country. In the name of democracy they speak, warning the people against the influence of wealth and the danger of aristocracy. History, ancient and modern, is full of such examples. Caesar became the master of the Roman people and senate under the pretense of supporting the democratic claims of the former against the aristocracy of the latter; Cromwell, in the character of protector of the liberties of the people, became the dictator of England, and Bolivar possessed himself of unlimited power with the title of his country's liberator.

At one point Harrison rose from his desk and walked about. He looked out over the James and thought about the Wabash and the Tippecanoe. He thought about The Prophet and Tecumseh. He returned to his desk and resumed his writing:

In our intercourse with our aboriginal neighbors the same liberality and justice which marked the course prescribed to me by two of my illustrious predecessors when acting under their direction in the discharge of the duties of superintendent and commissioner shall be strictly observed. I can conceive of no more sublime spectacle, none more likely to propitiate an impartial and common Creator, than a rigid adherence to the principles of justice on the part of a powerful nation in its transactions with a weaker and uncivilized people whom circumstances have placed at its disposal.

* * * * *

If parties in a republic are necessary to secure a degree of vigilance sufficient to keep the public functionaries within the bounds of law and duty, at that point their usefulness ends. . . . It was the beautiful remark of a distinguished English writer that "in the Roman senate Octavius had a party and Antony had a party, but the Commonwealth had none." Yet the senate continued to meet in the temple of liberty to talk of the sacredness and beauty of the Commonwealth, and the people assembled in the forum, not, as in the days of Camillus and the Scipios, to cast their free votes for annual magistrates, or pass upon the acts of the senate, but to receive from the hands of the leaders of the respective parties their share of the spoils and to shout for one or the other. The spirit of liberty had fled, and, avoiding the abodes of civilized man, had sought protection in the wilds of Cythia or Scandinavia; and so under the operation of the same causes and influences it will fly from our capitol and our forums. . . . It becomes my duty to say to [my countrymen]. . . that there exists in the land a spirit hostile to their best interests—hostile to liberty itself. It is a spirit contracted in its views, selfish in its objects. It looks to the aggrandizement of a few even to the destruction of the interests of the whole. The entire remedy is with the people. . . .

I deem the present occasion sufficiently important and solemn to justify me in expressing to my fellow citizens a profound reverence for the Christian religion and a thorough conviction that sound morals, religious liberty, and a just sense of religious responsibility are essentially connected with all true and lasting happiness. . . .

After three days and forty-eight manuscript pages, Harrison emerged with the draft of his "Inaugural." In the company of Vice President-elect John Tyler who had been at his Virginia home, George Badger of North Carolina who was slated to be Secretary of the Navy, and Henry Harrison of Berkeley, a grand nephew who was to serve as presidential secretary, Harrison returned to Washington.

He showed the draft of his address to Daniel Webster who confided to a friend that he (Webster) had "killed seventeen Roman proconsuls as dead as smelts," then to Henry Clay. Harrison then made a few changes.

As usually was the case, Inauguration Day, March 4, was gray and cold. Harrison rode a white horse up Pennsylvania Avenue at the head of a two-mile-long procession of soldiers, floats, students, political clubs, and veterans groups. At the Capitol, he witnessed John Tyler take the oath as Vice President, in the Senate chamber, and then stepped outside in the cold to face a crowd of 50,000 people for his address. Standing bareheaded and without overcoat or gloves, Harrison spoke for an hour and forty minutes, concluding, "Fellow citizens, being fully invested with that high office to which the partiality of my countrymen has called me, I now take an affectionate leave of you."

Beside him was his son, John Scott Harrison, who one day would be a member of Congress. John's son, Benjamin, would one day also become President of the United States so that John Scott Harrison would be the only man in the history of the United States to be the son of a President and the father of a President.

After the exposure to the cold weather, Harrison developed a lingering cold. On March 27, he was seized with a chill and fever. The next day, it was diagnosed as pneumonia with congestion of the stomach and intestines. The physicians determined that his age and condition made blood-letting inadvisable. He died a few minutes before one o'clock on the morning of April 4. His last words were, "Sir, I wish you to understand the true principles of the Government. I wish them carried out. I ask nothing more."

For the first time, a President of the United States had died in office.

Anna Harrison was preparing to leave for Washington—to be there "in May"—when word reached her of her husband's death. She was so grief-stricken that she remained almost in a stupor for months. Then she finally recovered and lived on for another twenty years at North Bend. In her memories she often relived all the years of her life, but she always came to the conclusion that the best of all had been the years at Vincennes. She died on February 25, 1864, at the age of eighty-eight.

William Henry Harrison, elected in 1840, was the first President of the United States to die in office. And "The Curse of The Prophet" persisted. Of his successors elected every twentieth year thereafter:

1860, Abraham Lincoln, was assassinated
1880, James A. Garfield, was assassinated
1900, William McKinley, was assassinated
1920, Warren G. Harding, died in office
1940, Franklin D. Roosevelt, died in office
1960, John F. Kennedy, was assassinated

The sun had set at Tippecanoe. Darkness had fallen on the Thames. The Shooting Star had fallen to the earth. For the American nation, sunrise tomorrow would usher in a bright new day full of hope and promise. For the Shawnee there would be no sunrise. There would be no tomorrow.

But a tribute to old Chief Meshingomesia, last tribal chief of the Miamis in Indiana, inscribed on the entry hall of a country club house at Marion, Indiana, on the banks of the Mississinewa, was in tribute to all the Red nations that passed this way:

> Ye say that all have passed away
> That noble race and brave,
> That their light canoes have vanished
> From off the crested wave.
>
> That mid the forest where they roamed
> There rings no hunter's shout,
> But their name is on your waters,
> Ye may not wash it out!

> (Frank Butterworth, Sr., 1886)

To order additional copies of this book, please use coupon below.

Mail to:

Brunswick Publishing Company
ROUTE 1, BOX 1-A-1
LAWRENCEVILLE, VIRGINIA 23868

Order Form

Please send me ___ copy(s) of *Counterpoint* by James Huston, ISBN 1-556-18024-1 (hardcover), at $27.95 — ISBN 1-556-18025-X (paperback), at 17.95 per copy plus $2.00 mailing and handling. Virginia residents add 4.5% sales tax. Payment of $_____ enclosed.

☐ Check Enclosed

CHARGE TO MY:
(Check One)

MasterCard **MASTERCARD** ☐   VISA **VISA** ☐

ACCOUNT NO. ☐☐☐☐☐☐☐☐☐☐☐☐☐☐☐☐

Card Expires | MO. | YR.

SIGNATURE _____

Name _____

Address _____

City _____ State _____ Zip_____

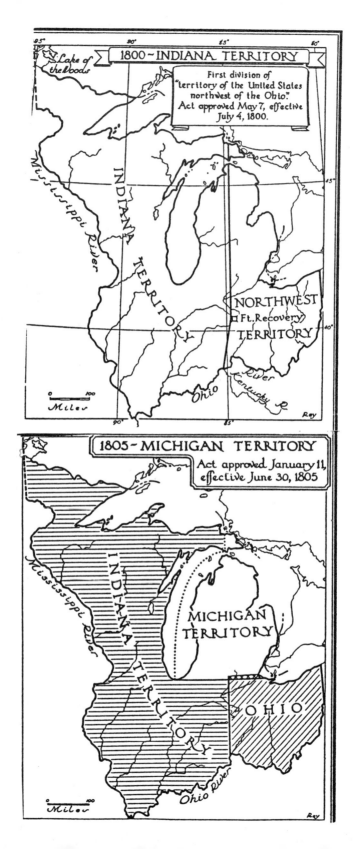

≡ 1803~OHIO ADMITTED ≡
Enabling act approved
April 30, 1802

INDIANA

TERRITORY

OHIO

Claimed by Ohio Constitution which was approved February 19, 1803 without mention of change in boundary.

Mississippi

Ohio R.

0   100 Miles

Ray

1809 ~ ILLINOIS TERRITORY
By act approved February 3,
effective March 1, 1809.

ILLINOIS TERRITORY

MICHIGAN
TERRITORY

INDIANA
TERRITORY

OHIO

Mississippi River

Ohio River

0   100
Miles

Ray